T0311796

ROUTLEDGE HANDBOOK OF ECOLOGICAL ECONOMICS

Since becoming formally established with an international academic society in the late 1980s, ecological economics has advanced understanding of the interactions between social and biophysical reality. It initially combined questioning of the basis of mainstream economics with a concern for environmental degradation and limits to growth, but has now advanced well beyond critique into theoretical, analytical and policy alternatives. Social ecological economics and transformation to an alternative future now form core ideas in an interdisciplinary approach combining insights from a range of disciplines including heterodox economics, political ecology, sociology, political science, social psychology, applied philosophy, environmental ethics and a range of natural sciences.

This handbook, edited by a leading figure in the field, demonstrates the dynamism of ecological economics in a wide-ranging collection of state-of-the-art essays. Containing contributions from an array of international researchers who are pushing the boundaries of the field, the *Routledge Handbook of Ecological Economics* showcases the diversity of the field and points the way forward. A critical analytical perspective is combined with realism about how economic systems operate and their essential connection to the natural world and society. This provides a rich understanding of how biophysical reality relates to and integrates with social reality. Chapters provide succinct overviews of the literature covering a range of subject areas including: heterodox thought on the environment; society, power and politics, markets and consumption; value and ethics; science and society; methods for evaluation and policy analysis; policy challenges; and the future post-growth society. The rich contents dispel the myth of there being no alternatives to current economic thought and the political economy it supports.

The *Routledge Handbook of Ecological Economics* provides a guide to the literature on ecological economics in an informative and easily accessible form. It is essential reading for those interested in exploring and understanding the interactions between the social, ecological and economic and is an important resource for those interested in fields such as: human ecology, political ecology, environmental politics, human geography, environmental management, environmental evaluation, future and transition studies, environmental policy, development studies and heterodox economics.

Clive L. Spash is an economist with extensive international experience who has specialised in environmental research for over three decades. He currently holds the Chair of Public Policy and Governance at WU, Vienna University of Economics and Business, Austria.

ROUTLEDGE HANDBOOK OF ECOLOGICAL ECONOMICS

Nature and Society

Edited by Clive L. Spash

Routledge
Taylor & Francis Group

LONDON AND NEW YORK

First published 2017
by Routledge

2 Park Square, Milton Park, Abingdon, Oxfordshire OX14 4RN
52 Vanderbilt Avenue, New York, NY 10017

Routledge is an imprint of the Taylor & Francis Group, an informa business

First issued in paperback 2018

British Library Cataloguing in Publication Data
A catalogue record for this book is available from the British Library

Library of Congress Cataloging in Publication Data
Names: Spash, Clive L., editor.
Title: Routledge handbook of ecological economics : nature and society / edited by Clive L. Spash.
Description: Abingdon, Oxon ; New York, NY : Routledge, 2017. | Includes index.
Identifiers: LCCN 2016046308| ISBN 9781138931510 (hardback) | ISBN 9781315679747 (ebook)Subjects: LCSH: Environmental economics. | Environmental policy--Economic aspects. | Ecology--Economic aspects.
Classification: LCC HC79.E5 R6747 2017 | DDC 333.7--dc23
LC record available at https://lccn.loc.gov/2016046308

ISBN: 978-1-138-93151-0 (hbk)
ISBN: 978-0-367-03114-5 (pbk)

Typeset in Bembo
by Saxon Graphics Ltd, Derby

CONTENTS

Contents

FIGURES

TABLES

PREFACE

The *Routledge Handbook of Ecological Economics: Nature and Society* brings together an international and diverse group of people to reveal how there is an extensive body of theoretically well-grounded thought about problems with and alternatives to the current political economy. This is a book that substitutes for the missing alternative economics textbook that, if it existed, would combine economics with social and ecological understanding (not use economic concepts to dominate others); a book that would not fall back into some comfort zone of half-hearted reproduction of mainstream formal economics supplemented by apologetic qualifications. Such radically alternative textbooks need to be written and will come, but for now pulling together the diverse community of concerned thinkers addressing the combined social ecological economic crises of our times is a task on its own. Before going further, I would therefore like to thank my secretary, Ursula Grafeneder, for helping me in the considerable job of bringing this volume together, including carefully checking references, reformatting text, compiling the prelims and herding the academic cats.

The authors are a mixture of young and old with more on the younger side. There are a few long-time active ecological economic campaigners, such as Dick Norgaard and Joan Martinez-Alier, followed by a solid group of the not yet retired and then the majority of up and coming. One concern in terms of representation in a patriarchal society is the female voice, and here an active effort achieved a third of authors; women who must typically show more dedication to their work to achieve the same as their male counterparts. This is not then a volume collecting together the good and the great, grey haired, alpha males of ecological economics, and neither are the contributors all card carrying members of the ecological economics community. Rather, this is a work driven by topics and subjects with chapters written by those who have something to contribute to the structure and content of an evolving body of knowledge.

The overall structure of the *Handbook* is built around core ideas in ecological economics combined with political economy and my own preliminary vision for an integrated interdisciplinary social theory. My perspectives are influenced by what I read and those with whom I come into contact and discuss. As a result they are always evolving, but the central focus remains on my objects of study, namely the social economy, the development of human societies and their relationships with Nature. I have also aimed to create a coherent whole that maintains a certain consistency throughout the various topics covered and brings together a substantive body of work that reveals the common developing alternative agenda and the insights gained from ecological economics over the last 25 years.

As with any handbook, or edited volume, the contributors reflect the editors' own networks. There is a large minority representation from Austria (a fifth by residency), although that is also indicative of the vibrant alternative intellectual community that Vienna has attracted in recent years, including the English, Italian, German and Norwegian nationals contributing to the *Handbook*. In addition, the *Handbook* is largely European (three-quarters by residency) but that should not be taken as implying a narrow internationally uninformed perspective. Most of the authors have worked and lived elsewhere and many are actively engaged internationally in non-European countries and on other continents. This is reflected in both theoretical contributions (e.g. environmentalism of the poor, imperial mode of living, needs, power, resistance, social movements, unequal exchange) and topic coverage (e.g. commons, eco-social development, mining conflicts). Social ecological economics [Chapter 1] is an approach that I identify as a strong theoretical undercurrent in such work and that I believe has the potential to unify it, as well as providing critical analysis of the 'growth' and 'development' agendas. Indeed my personal preference was for a volume entitled *Social Ecological Economics*, but the publishers felt the time was not yet ripe for such a handbook and therefore the subtitle 'Nature and Society' was agreed upon.

Authors were requested to follow some standard elements in formatting and structuring their chapters. This involved requirements for an introduction, main text, future directions concluding remarks, three to five recommended follow-up readings that had been cited in the text and a restricted list of references cited. The structure for the main section was left flexible, with general guidance to authors to cover the definition of their subject area, explain relevant research and key topics, and assess the current challenges. Chapters were restricted to 5,000 words, or less, in order to achieve breadth of coverage in the *Handbook* as a whole. This has also kept each entry succinct but substantial enough to inform the reader. The aim was for authors to provide an overview of their assigned topic area with enough detail to create informed debate and discussion. Within the bounds set there is considerable variety in terms of the length devoted by different authors to different sections and in how far they deviated from the main section guidance to explore topics in their own way. The overall common structure provides consistency across diverse literatures and should aid readers whether pursuing personal or directed study. The chapters were also structured with assignment for teaching purposes in mind. Extensive cross-referencing of the *Handbook* chapters has also been undertaken to aid linking across topics, and such references are given in square brackets enclosing the chapter number [Chapter 1]. The chapters have also been edited for consistency in use of terminology.

The 50 chapters are organised into 10 major parts of unequal length. The volume starts with the shortest section, Part I: Foundations, consisting of two chapters that aim to lay out some background and theory. The first is my own perspective on the need for an integrated knowledge that, as mentioned, I term social ecological economics. This presents a critical analysis of current economic thought and the operations of the modern economy, while highlighting future directions that are linked to other chapters in the *Handbook*. The second is a chapter explaining the philosophy of science that is required to advance interdisciplinary understanding and achieve integration of knowledge, namely a combination of critical social science and realism. This is not such a popular position in postmodern times, where every opinion is supposedly equally valid and the world is constructed in one's own image with an 'anything goes' attitude. The foundations of ecological economics in both natural and social sciences require integration that cannot indulge in such denialism of reality as postmodernism entertains. The value of postmodernism has been to deconstruct some aspects of modernist thought that created denial of the role played by social influences in the construction of knowledge. That, however, does not equate to accepting total relativism. A realist stance is present throughout the *Handbook*, but a critical one.

The foundational positions put forward clearly make ecological economics an heterodox approach in terms of economics. In Part II: Heterodox thought on the environment, a selection of authors were asked to write pieces representative of certain fields of knowledge that offer the potential (not yet realised) for a new combined and coherent alternative economics that addresses environmental issues. The mixture presented involves a critical institutional perspective, political ecology, ecofeminism, eco-Marxism, post-Keynesianism and evolutionary economics. The aim here is not to offer an already coherent set of thought but rather reflections upon what each of these various approaches have to offer and how they address environmental issues, or have failed to do so. While ecological economics can be criticised for inadequate coverage of the social and political, a considerable part of the heterodoxy in economics (e.g., post-Keynesians, traditional Marxists, neo-Austrians) has fared no better, and generally much worse, in terms of addressing biophysical reality and the environment. Not least among the challenges for many heterodox economists is the impossibility of sustaining the fossil fuel, capital accumulating, growth economy, recognising the limits to price-making markets. Yet, the chapters in this section also reveal the potential for mutual reflection in search of synthesis and areas where mutual benefits could arise (e.g. eco-Marxism). The section also offers a broader perspective on what economics is and the fields of knowledge that have important contributions to make to its redefinition (e.g. political ecology, ecofeminism). Critical institutional economics has already engaged with ecological economics, and the importance of institutional analysis is key, but there is more to be done in developing a unifying theory.

Part III: Biophysical reality and its implications turns to a primary aspect of the ecological economics approach, namely relating to the natural sciences. That the natural world is a foundation for all human activity might seem rather obvious but typically receives little attention from economists. This section provides an overview of the role of energy and materials in the reproduction of economic activity and social structure. A core understanding of ecological economics is how thermodynamics, especially entropy, materials use and the social metabolism of human systems combine to provide new realisations about the potential and limitations for social and economic activity. In addition, the biological interaction with the physical is the subject of ecosystems, their structure and functioning, with further implications. Chapters are provided covering the understanding of ecosystems, and how human and natural systems change together or coevolve.

From the biophysical world we move to the human in Part IV: Society, power and politics. Here is where ecological economics in Europe has differed from other regions but especially North America. The superficial understanding attributed to the social, as nothing more than a collection of individuals (methodological individualism), is rejected as totally inadequate. The social also cannot be understood without addressing power relationships. That in turn means concern for the poorest is more than the promise of crumbs from an ever bigger monetary cake (trickle down theory) or reducible to the provision of $1.25 per day. Mainstream economics is a failure in all aspects related to power, politics, distribution, justice, social inequity and the meaning of society. It long ago chose to ignore all these topics in the hopes of becoming a value-free form of science. Social reality includes economic relationships which are inherently constituted of power relationships that raise a series of questions. Who gets to consume what resources and use which aspects of the environment as a waste sink? How is redistribution of resources and wealth institutionalised and why is this accepted? What is the moral basis for relationships of extraction, production and consumption? The chapters in Part IV bring together insights into the relevance of power and social struggles for understanding the geo-political situation in which resource wars and the environmental crises are being played out. So here we have coverage of social theories of power, the imperial mode of living, environmental justice movements including environmentalism of the poor, and the role of social movements and resistance.

While ignoring these aspects, mainstream neoclassical economics is supposedly meant to have a core understanding that can explain markets, theory of the firm, consumption and work. However, in Part V: Markets, production and consumption this claim is deconstructed. The chapters reveal how far removed orthodox economics has become from the objects it claims to study and how it misconceptualises all of the above. Each topic is shown to involve a much richer meaning that has little to do with commonly held economic beliefs. When markets are placed in historical context they are easily seen to involve more than price-making arrangements. The real economy involves a rich set of social practices and institutions. Actual firms, not theoretical ones, can be understood using behavioural psychology and critical institutional analysis. In this way, for example, the politically domineering multinational corporation can be brought into focus. The role of consumption as a simple act of utility maximisation bears no relationship to reality. Consumption is redefined as an institutionally framed and psychologically self-defining practice that is pushed by both corporations and government but also bought into by citizens for social and psychological reasons. Work as nothing more than wage slavery ignores its social importance but redefining it raises questions of how we relate to money, time, leisure and the need for playfulness. This section probes some of the most common economic concepts and offers insights for the creation of a new economic theory that relates to social reality.

Part VI: Value and ethics addresses itself to core concerns of social ecological economics that have developed over the last two decades. These include value pluralism and the implications of incommensurability, the meaning of the concept of intrinsic value (exposing failures of environmental economics), the importance of needs and their association with satisfiers, and the moral considerability of future generations. Central to these chapters is the richness of environmental values, the existence of multiple values and the benefits of grounding our understanding of value in philosophy. How needs are to be understood and met remains debated. However, the reality of objective needs, not subject to social redefinition, does not exclude meeting them in many different ways and that is what creates cultural diversity. The means of their fulfilment through culturally specific institutional arrangements refocuses the aims of economic processes and places price-making markets in context as only one institutional arrangement through which a limited range of needs might be satisfied.

Part VII: Science and society: uncertainty and precaution addresses the response required in recognition of limits to human knowledge. The distinction between weak and strong uncertainty is explored; the former leading to risk management and the latter to precaution and safe minimum standards. More fundamentally, the limits to scientific knowledge raise questions as to the ability of normal science practice to inform policy, and here the post-normal science approach is introduced. This is also followed up in the first chapter of the methods section with a chapter on the practical investigation of public policy from a post-normal science perspective.

The largest section of this book is Part VIII: Methods. This is an indication of the availability of alternatives for evaluation and policy analysis, and is not even an attempt to be comprehensive. Here we have nine chapters exploring a range of ways in which ecological economists can scientifically investigate and critically analyse the world. They show ample room for analytical work to be undertaken to address values, institutions and public policy. The methods covered are: multiple criteria analysis and value mapping, Q-sorts, participatory approaches and modelling, deliberative monetary valuation, input–output analysis, and sustainability indicators. The reviews of these methods aim to explain their main features and how they are conducted, provide critical reflection on their current use, expose problems in application and indicate possibilities for development. They give a sampler of the methods and provide guidance as to further sources for those interested in pursuing their application.

Part IX: Policy challenges introduces a set of specific application areas. These provide critical reflections on a set of topical public policy challenges. They cover the commons, development policy (specifically in South Africa), mining, Peak-Oil, human-induced climate change and ecosystem services. How each issue has been framed is explained along with the problems with ongoing public policy. Authors also make recommendations for changes in how issues are being addressed. The chapters survey institutional policy developments (e.g., extending markets, privatisation, corporatisation) and power relationships, and reveal the conflicts between State, corporations and the public.

The *Handbook* closes with Part X: Future post-growth society. The subtitle reflects the needed end of the growth paradigm, but also that it will end regardless of what we do because it is unsustainable. The question is how do we reorganise the social economy before it collapses? The section starts with three chapters reflecting on three theories aiming to offer alternatives to the growth society: namely degrowth, steady state and post-growth. The degrowth chapter raises issues around the link of democracy to the growth economy and what this implies once that economy is no more. The steady state and post-growth chapters advocate specific approaches that have been popularised in the USA and Germany respectively. The former is heavily associated with Herman Daly and is primarily concerned to restrict the scale of the economy, while leaving its operation as a capitalist system untouched. The latter is a more fundamental challenge to the whole structure, calling upon individual action in a bottom-up radical reform of Western lifestyles. Then we turn to more specific ideas relating to potential future societal organisation with coverage of bioregionalism, sustainable cities and eco-social enterprises. The first two are discussed in theoretical terms, while the last combines theory with analysis of international case studies. The book closes with a discussion of the potential for a democratic, participatory society that accepts the need for social planning. Planning is, in reality, involved in all economies in different ways and undertaken by different institutions, e.g. the centrally planned multinational corporation. The chapters in this section are indicative of the work needed to formulate scientific utopian visions for the future and begin the necessary reflection on their implications and the gap between where we are and where we might like to go.

The *Routledge Handbook of Ecological Economics* achieves several things. It provides a guide to the literature in an informative and easily accessible form. It is a valuable source of information for those interested in exploring and understanding the interactions between the social, ecological and economic. This includes guidance as to the state of the art and further readings across a diverse set of interdisciplinary knowledge. It is a key for reference, an aid for teaching and a means of self-education.

The *Handbook* also fulfils its own social aim. There are many people working across the social, ecological and economic crises that modernity creates, but who do not unite or even know about one another. They go to different conferences, have different colleagues, live in different countries, read different literatures, speak different languages and so on. As a result there is a failure of unity amongst the deep Green, socially concerned and politically active, who seek a radical social ecological transformation, which is where this book lies. So one aim is achieved merely by bringing a diverse range of authors together.

The book also signifies a change in academic and political thought away from the separation of the social, ecological and economic. This is a synthesis that requires much more work, but the *Handbook* indicates the potential and key areas for debate. The failures of current economic theory relates to the entire body of orthodox economics, but also elements of the heterodoxy (e.g. post-Keynesians, traditional Marxists). Particular concerns are ignoring biophysical reality, dismissing plural and incommensurable values and maintaining a narrow view of human institutional arrangements. These are not matters for specialist sub-disciplinary fields, but fundamental to our understanding of real economic systems.

A key concern of this handbook is to explain how the economy exists within the context of the social and ecological. Ecological economics must therefore address the social to make a meaningful contribution. The content makes clear that the interdisciplinarity of ecological economics must consistently and seriously include the social sciences and social issues. This volume is more than a step in that direction; it is a challenge to those who would prefer ecological economics to be a sterile subject area that had no political or emancipatory message. It is also a statement of commitment by a diverse group of authors to a common project of social ecological transformation away from the current system and towards a better future for humans and non-humans alike.

This is also an exercise in empowerment. Maintaining academic communities that dare to expresses a critical voice against those in power is always subject to the threat of discrimination, censorship and political oppression. Encouraging an atmosphere of fear over lost promotion and potential dismissal has long been employed as a means for enforcing conformity and self-censorship. International solidarity is required, especially in times when the politics of hate and fear is on the rise. We should not forget the period still just within living memory. The Austro-fascist Nazi era that destroyed Austria from within during the 1920s and 1930s, removed the progressive and socially inclusive red Vienna government in a coup, and drove critical intellectuals into exile, before uniting with German Nazis to conduct the Holocaust and start a world war. Austria today is something of a political backwater and just one amongst many in the throes of a resurgent extreme right nationalism. Other supposed democracies have already advanced the political suppression of academic free voice and radical ideas using as means and excuses managerialism, financial control, austerity measures and securitisation. We live in dangerous times.

Last but not least, the *Handbook* addresses the simple task of destroying a dominant rhetorical claim made when mainstream economists, neoliberals and apologists for orthodox growth and consumerism lose an argument. That is, that there are no alternatives to the existing structures and system. This is extended to claims that there are no alternative theories as rigorous as mainstream macro and neoclassical micro economics. Going even further, the assertion is made that there are no alternative methods for social science research than quantification, the econometrics of orthodox economics and government statistical agencies. Then we are told there is no other future than a growth society, the ultimate utopian dream. The *Routledge Handbook of Ecological Economics* shows there are alternatives to everything. So read on, find out and join in.

Clive L. Spash
Vienna, Austria
September, 2016

To all social and environmental activists who dedicate their lives to the struggle for a better world in which both humans and non-humans can flourish.

PART I

Foundations

1

SOCIAL ECOLOGICAL ECONOMICS

Clive L. Spash

Introduction

Social ecological economists have been present since the creation of the International Society for Ecological Economics (ISEE) and provide the main approach in the European Society for Ecological Economics (ESEE) (Røpke, 2005; Spash, 1999). They recognise the importance of political economy, social ecology and the role of institutions for understanding the economic system and its interactions with Nature. They practice serious interdisciplinary knowledge integration across social and natural sciences (Spash, 2012a). They realise the need for a radical social ecological transformation based on their (natural and social) scientific knowledge. Social ecological economics is for many the core understanding of ecological economics (Spash, 2013; Spash and Ryan, 2012).

Ecological economics was founded upon the importance of placing the economy within its biophysical limits, while recognising the need for the conduct of human society to respect others both present and future, human and non-human. Key concerns included the failures of economic policy to address environmental impacts and the existing economic structure and its institutions to meet minimal standards of ethical conduct. However, different forces have shaped how the field of knowledge has combined topics and addressed (or not) these various issues. In particular, the gradual but persistent neoliberalisation of society since the 1980s has pushed an ecologically informed environmental policy discourse into the language of economics and finance (Spash and Aslaksen, 2015). The result has been a mainstreaming of environmentalism in general and ecological economics in particular (Spash, 2013). Economics has become identified with what Polanyi (1957) termed 'formal economics', where a narrow market exchange model dominates, a model that misconstrues the historical meaning of markets, trade and money, and so is blind to the potential alternative forms of social integration and organisation. Many have lost their way due to the supposed necessity of being pragmatic in terms of adopting formal economic concepts, converting Nature into capital, ecosystem functions into goods and services, and pollution into a traded commodity. Explicit ethical judgement is replaced by the dogma of saving money to meet an ill-defined goal of economic efficiency, as if this had no ethical implications.

If the journal of the name *Ecological Economics* is taken as an indicator, then the field is disunited, conflicted and internally self-contradictory. This situation occurs because the journal was allowed to become a commercial project of Elsevier, expanding rapidly beyond the ability of meaningful content to be provided by the fledgling ecological economics community of the early 1990s, with its anti-establishment concerns for limits to material and energy throughput and restricting the scale of the economy. Success measured by publishers' citation metrics, growth and returns are ironically what has determined the content, while quality in production has declined and academic direction is lacking. In the process, the journal has become a contested space in which mainstream environmental and resource economists fight to obtain kudos through formal models and monetary valuation studies, while new environmental pragmatists compete to find the easiest formulae for supplying palatable messages in the hope of courting unconcerned corporations and unconscious consumers (Spash, 2013). The foundational social ecological ideas are lost in the mix. A good example is coverage of climate change in the journal, a discussion that largely ignores key contributions from the field and instead conducts a formal mainstream economic discourse (Anderson and M'Gonigle, 2012). The editors seem oblivious to the need for getting contributors to actually read or address the relevant ecological economics literature. Thus, core papers, arguments and critiques run in parallel with a mass of totally separate formal economic, and other, content that ignores the essence of ecological economics, its concepts and their meaning.

One result of the neoliberalisation of environmentalism, and the adoption of concepts from formal economics, is the increasing prevalence of pseudoscience, especially in the form of numbers. This is evident in natural scientists adopting whatever aspects of social science appear to them to be convenient. A typical approach is creating money numbers from thin air in the vain hope of impressing the mythical decision-maker and general public that the environment matters (Spash, 2013; Spash and Vatn, 2006). Along the way the importance of social science is downplayed, and often treated as some simple add-on to the 'objective' natural science information that is believed to supply all we really need to know. Inevitably the division between environmental and social concerns has grown as the expression of plural values and complexity are replaced by monistic measures and simple messages. Perversely, the politically naïve use of formal economic language, concepts and methods by ecologists and conservation biologists has undercut their own message, disempowered their policy relevance and damaged the environmental movement in the process (e.g., in the area of biodiversity, see Spash, 2015a). Rather than progress in uniting an understanding of the biophysical, social and economic, what we have seen is the domination of the social and biophysical by a narrow discourse that reduces everything to exchange in price-making markets.

Social ecological economics is then a call for the interdisciplinary reunification of different bodies of knowledge in a way that reflects their competencies in relation to the objects they study (Spash, 2012a). The social, in social ecological economics, emphasises the necessity of understanding the reality of how humans and their societies operate if we are to gain any insight concerning the multiple crises into which the current system is plunging the world. Historical and descriptive analysis of the past and its institutions is essential to understanding the future and its potentiality (Spash, 2011).

Ecological economics lacks a coherent social theory and connection with other social scientists working on the same topics in other fields (e.g. political science, political ecology, sociology, social psychology, social anthropology). Some have felt threatened by the social and have downplayed if not derided its relevance. In the USA the social is quickly connected to socialism, which since McCarthyism has been associated with communism and branded as un-American. There have even been attempts to suppress those following the social ecological economics agenda within ecological economics itself, while promoting mainstream economists in their stead (Røpke, 2005; Spash, 2011). This suppression failed, not least because social and environmental problems are inseparable and formal economics is no substitute. Polanyi (1957) thought formal economics was valid in a restricted field of knowledge relating to nineteenth- and twentieth-century market economies. In contrast, I argue that it fails as either a description, explanation or predictor of the modern market economy, and as a result is dangerously misleading as a guide to social and environmental policy.

In this brief overview I will start by substantiating this last point, not least because there are too many apologists for mainstream thinking and the extent of economic inadequacies is not well or widely understood. This leads to the need for alternatives to current formal economic theories, but also to the current economic system it advocates with its pricing, capital accumulation, competition, growth and social and environmental exploitation. After dismissing the dominant economists' defensive stance – that there are no alternatives – I explore in turn why the economy must be understood as a social ecology economy in biophysical and social terms. This is carried out by overviewing the environmental and social implications of the current economic system, its problematic elements and the biophysical and social implications of its operations. That sets the agenda for new directions and the needed research to achieve the necessary social ecological transformation.

Modern economics as a distraction from reality

Economics as a discipline has become a narrow prescriptive field which defines itself by its methodology rather than its content or object of study, namely the social economic system. To be an economist today means being able to abstract from reality using mathematical symbols to represent loosely defined concepts such as goods, services, labour, land, capital, prices, money, markets, trade, employment and utility. The approach employs deduction, which means the foundational axioms, and inferences drawn from them, have no requirement for realism at all. The inferences need only be logically drawn from the axioms and the derived equations and models internally consistent. On this basis the discipline has created a deductive dogma that is divorced from actual and empirical economic systems and their operations. This is something that is only disturbed by the invasion of reality into the economists' closed world.

Reality comes in the form of economic collapse, misdirected policy and publicly visible ignorance. A financial disaster, such as the 1929 or 2008 crashes, brings home to many (otherwise generally unconcerned) citizens of industrially modernised economies how economics has become detached from the reality it is supposed to explain and the future it promises to predict. Yet, the economics profession seems to remain amazingly untouched by the irrelevance of their own theories. Like the neoliberals, who created the 2008 crash and ongoing world economic crisis through deregulation and financial greed, the majority of economists continue to recommend price-making market mechanisms on the basis of arguments that have no relationship to real markets and their operation. They justify passing power to the least trustworthy without even realising this because their models have no concept of power. If they did, their dogmatic commitment to mathematical formalism would make it merely another symbol in an equation of little practical consequence. They make recommendations for society on the basis of a discipline that has no theory of society, nor indeed any conception of social structure, but rather merely regards society as an aggregation of individual agents, each pursuing their own self-interest (i.e. methodological individualism).

Microeconomics, based on preference utilitarianism, regards humans as optimising machines whose decisions leave no room for emotion, psychology or social embeddedness. *Homo œconomicus* is an automaton, maximising utility on the basis of a preordained set of preferences. If such individuals existed, they would have no freedom to choose because all their choices would be preprogrammed; they would merely execute the optimising rule. This machine-like human is matched by a similar model of the business enterprise or firm. Firms are assumed to merely execute a rule of profit maximisation. They have no structure, no people, and no institutions within which they operate and of which they are constructed. They are involved in no struggles over ownership of the means of production nor concerns over exploitation, no lobbying of politicians nor regulatory capture of government agencies. There is nothing like a multinational corporation in the microeconomic literature, let alone the aggressive mining industry, fossil fuel sector, petrochemical and agro-industries, loggers, aerospace/telecommunications/computing/robotics industrial–military complex, soft drinks and fast food franchises, supermarket chains, property developers, building contractors, speculators, stock traders, bankers and financiers. Accordingly, there is no theory of cost-shifting enterprises that deliberately harm others in order to profit themselves (see Kapp, 1978), but instead the dominant characterisation of firms is as neutral agents of production at the service of the sovereign consumer (Fellner and Spash, 2015). Economic theory explains systemic failures as externally caused and so absolves economic agents of responsibility. Thus, pollution is termed an 'externality' that is only problematic because it lies outside the pricing system of which firms are mere functionaries. The historical development of the modern economy, dominated by corporations and the financial sector, is as inexplicable for the economist trained in modern theory as is the necessity of a biophysical reality.

Macroeconomics is just as unreal and ontologically flawed. The basic economic model that underlies all macro-theory assumes a totally isolated economic system with no inputs and no outputs of either materials or energy. There is only a flow of goods and services between firms and households. Households supply labour to firms and get paid; they in turn demand goods and services for which they pay. Physical flows in one direction are matched by monetary flows in the other. Economic growth is merely how fast the flows occur. In this ontology the presumption is that economic reality consists only of the firm and household and their exchanges, and economic growth can go on forever as an exchange between the two. Nothing could be more utopian. Sophisticated models may add a government sector, although the major concern has increasingly become that such a sector is problematic for an efficient economy and its role should be minimised. Treasury models have no banking or finance sector and cannot then say anything about the need for their regulation. Instead government must take the blame for financial crises and be cut back through austerity measures. The focus, whether orthodox or heterodox macroeconomics, is upon a utopian economy of production, growth and capital accumulation. All else is secondary or treated as of no consequence.

Paradoxically, the very irrelevance of modern economics as a means for understanding the functioning of the economy is why it can exist. It is harmless for key power interests, namely a political elite, the rich and multinational corporations. They can use its models and concepts as rhetorical devices when convenient and ignore them just as easily. Yet, the paucity of economic analysis has real implications because it supports claims such as: all is well with the world, there is such a thing as an efficient competitive economy, the rich deserve their wealth, corporations are a valid and good institution, markets supply freedom and economic growth will eradicate poverty. The world is defined as a market economy that is the highest form of human evolution. This results in the propaganda slogan that "there is no alternative" to the capital accumulating market economy driven by competition, innovation, technology and the desire for ever more material affluence.

If you spend time engaging with the economics profession, and the related defenders of faith in the current economic system, there will repeatedly be points at which they are forced to admit the validity of criticisms of both their own economic understanding and the current political economy. In fact they will admit so many criticisms as to leave no doubt that an alternative to both should be adopted. However, their last line of defence is that there is nothing better to replace the existing approach, that alternatives have been tried and failed, and while things are bad, the alternatives are much worse. In terms of supporting the current economic system their arguments will cite the failures of the Soviet Union, the bureaucracy of planning systems, the inefficiency of barter, and so on. Defence through this means of rhetoric aims to divert attention from the actual economic system and claim all its flaws must be accepted because nothing else can be done.

Can you imagine a bridge built with poor materials and structural flaws and yet being defended on such a logic? Who would trust an engineer who admitted their bridge was clearly defective, and also prone to collapse, but argued you should still use it because there is nothing better available, or we tried boats in the past but they were less efficient. Following economists, the engineer could respond to those exposing the dangers of the bridge by saying: 'you are not experts so what do you know?' and 'you have no right to criticise my structure before building your own and showing it is better'.

The logic of these arguments, as commonly employed by economists, is as flawed as the theory and system they try to defend. There is no onus on somebody pointing out the failings of either the economics profession or the management of the economy to keep quiet because they have not written an alternative textbook or constructed their own economic theory. At the same time these defensive arguments are unscientific and aim to divert attention away from seeking legitimate alternatives. They paint the attempts to pursue alternative economic systems in the worst possible light, without actually taking any time to research them. They attribute to all alternatives the word 'utopian', as a derogatory expression, while ironically placing their own faith in a totally romantic utopia of modernist techno-optimism and ever expanding materialism. A scientific approach would explore potentialities, analyse alternative structures and question the necessity and usefulness of existing approaches. Most importantly it would relate to biophysical and social reality.

The social ecological economy

What is the aim of an economy? The typical answer to such a question revolves around resource allocation. Real economic systems move goods and services through a process of extraction, transportation, transformation and on to 'final use' by a range of social actors before returning all energy and materials to the environment. The complexity of the system of resource use is misleadingly simplified by reduction down to 'production' by a 'firm'. Similarly, the range of social actors is not reducible to 'consumers', let alone sovereign ones (Fellner and Spash, 2015), but involves the government at multiple levels, the military, firms, corporations and social groups, as well as individuals. This social complexity requires institutions (i.e. conventions, norms, rules) for coordination and social integration. The institutions humans employ also create, preserve and destroy values in society; they promote some and demote others (e.g. competition vs. cooperation). What is permitted and restricted in this social process of material and energy use determines how the economy interacts with the environment.

The biophysical economy

Traditionally human society has consisted of a mostly rural population and agriculturally based activities. Supply chains, the modern term for getting resources from origin to production and on to consumption, for most of human history were generally short and localised. Goods that could be traded were restricted and the use of money exchange limited to specific types of trade, while money was not simply (or even principally) a means of exchange but performed a variety of roles (Hodges, 1989; Polanyi, 1957). Some items of trade did already travel over long distances by the late medieval period and early Renaissance (e.g. in Europe, spices from Asia, herring from Norway, wine from the Mediterranean, silk from China, gold and silver from South America, slaves from Africa), but daily life for the vast majority involved much self-sufficiency and only local trade, which was not limited to price-making markets.[1] The difficulties of long-distance transportation, most conveniently undertaken by sea, meant highly valued commodities were the main trade items for most of human history. This meant self-sufficiency, kinship, cooperative and non-market exchange and bioregional economies [Chapter 47] were the historical norm for most people. Material flows were largely kept within regional ecosystems and the primary source of energy was solar transformed via agriculture, forestry and fisheries.

A major transformation began with the Industrial Revolution and the increasing use of coal via steam engines leading to the development of steam trains and ships in the nineteenth century, and an associated increasing use of iron and steel. Yet, most economies and the majority of people, even in the industrialising world, did not engage in this revolution but remained within the social metabolism of the traditional economy, working and living close to food and resources for local and regional use and employing animals, not machines, to supplement labour. Vast technological leaps, driven by State investment in the military, substantively changed the world economic system. Two world wars accelerated the role of oil, gas and petrochemicals as the foundation for new modes of processing and transporting resources and transforming them into new products. Traditional social organisation of the economic process, that was already being removed by the drive for capital accumulation aided by the Industrial Revolution, now became explicitly targeted for eradication.[2]

The arrival of this latest phase of modernity would change all social ecological interactions. Farming would use artificial fertilizers from the Haber-Bosch process, developed to supply explosives and based on natural gas. Commodities would be shipped by metal boats powered by oil engines and flown around the world by metal aeroplanes using jet engines and high octane fuel. People would live at ever greater distances from their places of work and commute back and forth daily in metal cars driven by petrol engines. The biomass- and solar-driven local/regional economy was being replaced by a petrochemical national/international economy with dependence upon the use of concentrated minerals and fossil fuel energy. This was a major shift in the social metabolism of human systems and their requirements for reproduction.

The concept of a social metabolism is used in ecological economics and industrial ecology to capture the need of any human society for materials and energy, in the same way as any biological organism has a metabolism [see Chapter 11]. Order is created on the basis of using low entropy (Georgescu-Roegen, 1971), and the sources upon which humans are most dependent are stocks of concentrated minerals and the solar flow of radiant energy [Chapters 9 and 10]. Traditional societies relied on direct and indirect means of using the latter, with minimal use of the former. Modernity is built upon massive exploitation of the former.

A simple truth that ecological economics has been at pains to state and restate is that by definition a given stock is finite. A society built and dependent upon depletion of a non-renewable resource will collapse. Only if the resource stock can be replenished or substituted can this be avoided. Modernity's stock dependence in terms of materials and fossil fuel energy therefore leads directly to the drive for new technologies and innovative ways of substituting resources. That means creating an ever-changing society without any stability because the economic process must continuously seek new ways of doing things and social practice must change accordingly. The fundamental requirement is to maintain the exploitation of low entropy at a rate that renews the economic structure.

The growth of the economy in material and energy results in always needing more for the reproductive process to continue. In addition, the fact that energy and matter are never destroyed, but merely transformed, means all that goes into the economy comes out in equal amount but qualitatively different—high entropy, unconcentrated—form at the other end. This matter and energy, that humans call waste, must go into either the land, air or water. Pollution 'control' shifts the waste of the human system from one medium to another, in search of a way to neutralise the worst impacts, often with unintended feedbacks for humans and non-humans alike. Pollution is an inevitable part of the economic process, not an avoidable externality that disappears if the prices are 'right', and it inevitably increases with economic growth because that growth is dependent upon material and energy throughput. In addition, the drive for new innovative products and substitutes for materials and energy means creating novel artificial substances that change and destabilise existing structures and their functions with unknown consequences; for example, chlorofluorocarbons changing the atmospheric chemical balance of the stratosphere and destroying the ozone layer, or pesticides and insecticides changing the balance of species and the functioning of agricultural ecosystems.

Scenarios combined with systems analysis were famously used in the 1970s to illustrate how exponential growth on a finite planet hits limits (Meadows *et al.*, 1972). A basic storyline was that the continuous expansion of industrial output and human population can lead to a range of possible crisis in terms of competition for resources and food supplies and environmental impacts from pollution. Contrary to critics' remarks, scenarios are not meant to be historical or empirical explanations nor predictions, but are thought experiments about plausible futures. They may aid identifying causal mechanisms leading to what would otherwise be surprise events and stimulate actions to avoid them.

This raises a foundational issue in the conduct of science policy. The empirical dominates scientific discourse, which requires that phenomena must be both actualised and observed. Hence, for example, awaiting empirical evidence of substantive harm due to human induced climate change will prevent action to avoid substantive harm. This is the reason for precaution [Chapter 26] and safe minimum standards [Chapter 27]. Humans may well maintain exploitative relationships with Nature that empirically appear unproblematic for a long time. This was a central argument made in the 1970s explanation of how exponential growth patterns in human society could lead to collapse without being recognised by traditional scientific empiricism (Meadows et al., 1972). The structure of our material and energy throughput economy is incompatible with maintaining the structure and functioning of ecological systems, but empiricism is backward-looking and will reveal the full scale of the disaster only after the event, when action is too late.

The capital accumulating growth economy is a system in a continuous battle against the instability it creates through the destruction of that upon which it depends. It is also socially divisive and empirically selective. Environmental impacts affecting the poor, indigenous, disenfranchised and non-human are easily ignored in a system obsessed by financial flows. At the same time social and economic systems mediate how environmental crises actually materialise and there is a legitimate criticism that these aspects have been poorly theorised in ecological economics. Beyond the biophysical reality of an economic system, there is the social reality.

The social economy

If we qualify economic with social, what does this mean? Can an economy exist without a society? Clearly the answer is 'No'. Can an economy be understood without the social context? Here there is division, with the mainstream economist answering 'Yes' and many heterodox economists and other social scientists generally answering 'No'. On what basis could the mainstream justify their position? The argument is an engineering one. For example, studying a car engine and its operation can make sense without the context of a road system or even knowing the exact design of the car into which the engine might be placed. The efficient running of the mechanical device alone is an object of study. This mechanistic epistemology has been incorporated at the heart of mainstream economics (Georgescu-Roegen, 2009 [1979]: 107).

Rejecting the engineering approach to economics quickly leads to the necessity of placing the economy in its social context, which involves knowing the specifics of institutions and politics. The economic engine is meaningless outside of this context and cannot be understood as an independent object of study. Engineering economics could only then be justified for a small field of specialists who would be embedded in a larger team bringing together the necessary social sciences. In contrast, economic practice today regards the engineering economist as the only legitimate members of the team and treats the need for others as superfluous. The result is that economic engines are being designed without any idea of whether they would be of any practical use for humanity and ignoring their social and political implications. There is no conceptualisation of the vehicle they are supposed to drive or what is required in terms of the social system that would make such vehicles operative. That the mechanistic epistemology dominates economics also explains why economists are obsessed with efficiency.

Yet, even engineering efficiency is not a primary concern for transportation, let alone economies. For example, cars today can have very efficient engines in terms of fuel consumption, compared to the past, but can be embedded in massive vehicles used by single occupants burning more fuel per passenger mile than in a system of less efficient smaller vehicles that are shared. The institutional design and social structure of the system, and resulting human behaviour within that system, are far more important than technical and engineering design (e.g., aerodynamic vehicles or low-fuel-consumption engines). The American idealisation of the car created a cultural icon connected with freedom, the idea of roaming freely across the open plain. The construction of desires for a fast car or motorbike has targeted male egos and connected the powerful engine to sexual attractiveness, e.g., advertising using bikini-clad female models. This macho car culture need bear no relationship to social reality. That reality is the hum drum daily commute, stuck in traffic and polluting the air that the occupants pump into their luxury metal boxes to fill their lungs, while the road infrastructure has cut up the open planes and created motorway, autobahn and highway systems that act as barriers to non-humans and non-motorised humans alike. The removal of peace and quiet and the contamination of air, soils and water are absent from the iconic image of the car, as is the discrimination entailed against the freedom of others (an implicit power relationship).

The configuration of and requirements for transport, like all human activities, are socially and politically conditional. That means that what are taken as essential requirements under one social structure are unnecessary under another. Indeed, why do we organise society in cities structured to require millions of people to go back and forth everyday from home to work? Towns and cities were redesigned in the twentieth century to serve the car, creating extensive physical infrastructure and a social structural lock-in. State and public funds have massively subsidised this mode of transport. The same is true for flying and airports. These are major State-planned investments including extensive supporting infrastructure. Yet, only directly State-owned railways are generally recognised as planned and subsidised.

The role of the State is indeed a major issue in social and political economy. Neoliberalism as actualised has made the State a support for corporate, rather than public, interest, but at the same time the hope of many is that the State will be an environmental protector and enforcer of justice. The State's role in promoting technology and infrastructure then becomes crucial, e.g. transport, aerospace and telecommunications. For example, industrial-military technology developed the rockets that allowed construction of a military satellite infrastructure that led to use of weapons targeting global positioning systems that are now common in vehicles and mobile phones. Such technologies change human expectations and behaviour in unpredictable ways but are also potentially invasive (e.g. security and military monitoring). Innovation and technology are heavily supported by States as the hope for avoiding the otherwise inevitable end of the growth economy through finding substitutes for disappearing energy sources and concentrated minerals, as well as finding miracle cures for the consequences of environmental pollution (from bugs that eat waste to geoengineering the planetary climate). The State and corporations have a vested interest in promoting all technological developments as inherently good, underfunding and suppressing research into problems and overriding public concerns (e.g. over nanotechnology, biotechnology, genetic modification, nuclear power, microwave transmitters, radiofrequency electromagnetic fields, household chemicals, plastics).

An interesting aspect of new products with innovative technologies is how readily they are actually accepted, along with the major changes in social relations they entail. This is in stark contrast to direct social planning to which people strongly object. Indeed social acceptance in the market economy is defined by owning the 'right' technological device, and having the most up-to-date version, which changes at least every year. The ownership of products has become an expression of identity. The corporate marketers know the importance of linking into society and making their products part of daily practices. Those who resist technological advance are regarded as Neanderthals who should be ostracised, and over time the construction of physical and social infrastructure makes resistance harder and results in social exclusion. The lie of (neo) liberal political philosophy is that agents always have a free choice. Why do people have mobile phones? Because other people have mobile phones and now you are expected to have one to be 'normal'. In fact, technology is designing our social systems and not the other way around.

Regaining social practices from the corporations and their products is a major task as they use the internet and mobile phone technologies to reconceptualise friendship through 'social media', and redefine social standing via new metrics (e.g. 'likes', 'hits' and 'followers'). This capture and redefinition of social interaction happens almost imperceptibly, as does technologically driven behavioural change (e.g., adults habitually checking their phone, ignoring each other in preference for their phones, giving children a mobile phone or computer rather than interacting with them). The type of technology incorporated into an economy has social implications and hi-tech, not appropriate technology, is demanded by the growth economy. Corporate self-interest and government commitment to hi-tech, innovation and growth mean positive social, economic and environmental aspects are always highlighted and the new is always promoted as better than the old.

That there are other forms of social economy is both an historical fact and present reality. Yet these alternatives are dismissed by equating economic growth with development and technology with progress. Under this paradigm the rural is derided in favour of the urban. Urbanisation is a policy of the growth economy that targets the destruction of rural livelihoods in the drive for mechanised industrial agriculture and the creation of an urban underclass to work in the unskilled jobs of factories and to carry out undesirable reproductive tasks. On a measure of poverty based on a dollar metric (e.g. the World Bank's $1.25 per day) the process might appear to successfully reduce poverty, because the metric does not account for anything non-monetary. In India and China, for example, there is a high rate of suicide amongst subsistence farmers who lose their livelihoods due to ongoing 'modernisation' that replaces unpaid subsistence work and familial exchange with wage labour in factories and industrial agriculture. Meaningful lives are made, quite literally, meaningless.

Adoption of formal economics, price-making markets, and equating money trade and exchange, all narrow down the richness of human relationships and their potential. Reciprocity and redistribution as forms of social integration and coordination are far older than market exchange. Market exchange is also possible in different forms than suggested by the economists' equilibrating supply-demand models (Polanyi, 1957). Yet such alternative institutional arrangements are again derided as backward and not progressive, because the presumption is that price-making market exchange has achieved freedom from such social requirements. In contrast, a substantive economic understanding reveals markets, as institutions, depend upon a whole range of ancient institutional arrangements including centralised rules, norms and conventions built around creating trust.

Ecofeminism has also emphasised another black hole in the formal economic understanding: that is the failure to address the role of care giving and social reproduction because this is 'women's work'. There are then serious issues in the failure of modern economics to address the social reality of how the economy operates on the basis of the role traditionally played by women, their exploitation by men and the conceptualisation of what constitutes work [see Chapter 5].

Social relationships to others also extend to the way in which resources are obtained and the rules for their use or non-use. The productivist growth economy requires land, minerals, energy and cheap labour on an ever increasing scale. These requirements must come from somewhere and that somewhere is ever more distant from the final users (aiding ignorance and dismissal of social and environmental exploitation). Resource appropriation means intervening in the lives of others and removing resources from their use. Formal economics reduces this relationship down to free trade and comparative advantage. In contrast, land-grabbing, for example, is one aspect of the 'development' project ongoing internationally and has been a tradition of the Western 'development' model enforced via imperialism. Real resource control is based on military-backed political power and the use of that power to force allegiances that allow resource exploitation and trade. For example, the USA has repeatedly destabilised other countries using 'intelligence services' leading to the overthrow of governments and the establishment of regimes that will 'trade' and support their corporate interests. This has nothing to do with promoting democracy; for example, the removal of a democratic left wing government in Chile replaced by a bloody military dictator in the form of Pinochet who was actively supported by the USA, or consider their training of paramilitary groups around the world or the trade with oil-rich, undemocratic, totalitarian nations. Industrialised economies did not get rich through fair trade but unequal exchange [Chapter 4], and modern economies persist in the exploitation of others in order to maintain their populations in an imperial mode of living [Chapter 15], or at least enough of the population to keep the lid on social unrest.

The remaining missing 'other' being exploited is the non-human world. Some living in the industrially developed economic systems have even postulated that there is only society. The likes of Bruno Latour appear to vacillate between regarding Nature as a social construct, existing only in our minds, to having to admit there must be something existing in an external reality (Pollini, 2013). Perhaps living in cities has made such postmodern theorists unable to look at the sky and see the Milky Way every night to get a daily reminder of how insignificant humanity is in the universe. That such positions can be seriously advocated and considered as valid is an indicator of how far modern humanity has become divorced from the natural world on which it depends and in which it is embedded. There is a certain arrogance in considering humanity as so dominant in the universe that there is nothing else but that which humans create. It is also disturbing in terms of the implications for the ethical treatment of non-humans.

In economics the non-human is merely a resource to be exploited subject to individual preferences. If nobody has a strong preference for, say, species preservation or the species fails to provide a good rate of return (e.g. reproducing too slowly) they can be eradicated on efficiency grounds. The ethics of preference utilitarianism leaves no room for anything but that which humans deem useful and it must be useful enough to outweigh its maintenance 'costs', measured as opportunity costs, i.e. doing something else with the resources (Spash, 2015a). Leaving space for other species to flourish, for no other reason than that they should be allowed to do so, is beyond the comprehension of such economics. The idea that non-human social organisation (as revealed by socioecology) might have value in itself also has no place. Environmental ethics has questioned the ability of any of the dominant anthropocentric ethical systems to adequately value the non-human world, so raising the need for new ethical approaches. What is clear is that the current economic system is wiping out species at an unprecedented rate (Spash, 2015b). In summary, the structure of the social economy not defines only personal identity and the relationships between humans, but also humanity's relationships to the non-human world.

Future directions

Social ecological economists have strong associations with communities and movements seeking serious social ecological transformation and see activism as an essential part of being a committed ecological economist. Social practice should link to self awareness. As research opens the eyes of the researcher to what is wrong and needs to change they have a duty of responsibility to act on that information. As recognised in philosophy of science by the logical empiricism of the left wing of the Vienna Circle, articulating and defending a scientific worldview is then both an academic position and a political act aimed at social reform and emancipation (Spash, 2012b: 38); a position shared by critical realism (ibid.: 44) [see also Chapter 2].

A core aspect of social ecological economics is a foundation in philosophy of science: ontology, epistemology and methodology (Spash, 2012b). The synthesis needed must combine critical social science with a realist perspective, but one that recognises the role of social construction in the creation of knowledge through conceptualisation. This approach builds on both logical empiricism and weak social constructivism in placing science within the context of social learning while not denying the reality and independence of biophysical entities, systems, structure and their mechanisms of operation. The epistemological limits of human ability to understand the consequences of any given action are no more self-evident than in environmental policy. Yet, that humans are fallible is denied by claims that more scientific research is needed to remove uncertainty before action can be taken, and/or that scientific claims, such as humans are inducing climate change, have not been 'proven'. Public policy is rife with the failure to understand the meaning and content of uncertainty, and its different forms [see Chapters 26–28], as well as ignorance as to what makes a claim valid. A critical realist position can help provide the required philosophy of science [Chapter 2], but that still leaves the need for a social theory.

The social here is taken to include the cultural and political, without which no economy can be run or understood (as argued above). A critical institutional economics is essential to analyse the conventions, norms, practices, rules and regulations that humanity employs to coordinate social interaction, including those that are economic [see Chapter 3]. Social ecological economics is then an appeal to return to the roots of concern for how society is structured and the direction it takes as a result – as expressed in the political economy writings of the likes of Kapp (1978), Georgescu-Roegen (2009 [1975]) and Polanyi (1944). The open assertion of social ecological economics is a wake-up call to those drifting into unthinking economic conformity, as well as to those social scientists (including heterodox economists) who ignore environmental and biophysical reality.

This chapter has outlined the importance of combining the social, ecological and economic. The future direction required is one that builds alternatives that are better than the capital accumulating growth economy of today, that is built on exploitation and which is driving humanity towards ever more serious resource wars and inequity under the guise of free trade and competition. I have not attempted to describe the constituents of an alternative social ecological economy; that is work for the future. However, I have touched upon some of the key elements that have been, and are, central to a meaningful radical and deep ecological economics in performing that much needed work. Here I mean radical in its original sense of going to the very root of an issue (*radicalis* from *radix* or root; *Oxford English Dictionary on Historical Principles*). Radical social ecological transformation from the present economy requires identification of the fundamental things and principles that matter.

Progress has been made in recognising the radical elements of a social ecological economy and the needed transformation. The monism of economics is replaced by value pluralism and acceptance of incommensurability [Chapter 22]. A return to political economy means explicitly addressing power and structure in society [Chapter 14]. Efficiency is relegated to a secondary, or even lesser, goal while the primary goals are meeting basic needs [Chapter 24] in a society that is ethical, respects the moral standing of others (both human and non-human animals), seeks equality and upholds justice. The meaning of economic activity including work and leisure is redefined once the productivist logic of modernity is removed [Chapter 21]. Rather than being focussed on production, the emphasis is on the reproduction and reproducibility of society in ways that do not transgress social and ecological constraints. Biophysical reality and the role of energy and materials is then central [Chapters 4, 9–11], but also the role of women and the real division of labour in social reproduction [Chapter 5].

The growth economy is leading to an inevitable series of ongoing crises, creating harm, death and destruction. However, total collapse of the social and economic system is not as inevitable as Marx thought, and major crises have been repeatedly overcome by capitalism. The current trajectory is one of further divisions within society both nationally and globally, so that the 'successful' capital accumulating economies can persist much longer through securitisation, militarisation and an increasingly authoritarian system of governance. Instability has been used to play on the fear of others and an atmosphere of hatred means representative democracies have become susceptible to governance by the extreme right, as a united minority oppresses a disunited majority. As the growth economy stumbles and falls into recession and stagnation, more desperate means of seeking growth are pursued. New means for the financialisation of Nature, more speculation, new derivatives markets, more novel hi-tech, faster innovation, more resource extraction with ever greater environmental and social harm pushed on to 'others'. The category of others expands as the system must create more social division in an economy built on an ever diminishing set of resources essential to reproduce the system. The privileged will maintain that system as long as possible in a process of self-preservation that sacrifices the many for the few.

That the resources required by the modern capital accumulating economy are becoming scarcer is a basic fact, as is the diminishing capacity of the Earth to handle human pollution. This is no more self-evident than with the limited capacity for further releases of human-generated greenhouse gases, and especially carbon, if further climate forcing is to be prevented; indeed, the much touted 2°C target has already been passed (Spash, 2016). Yet, human induced climate change is also being used as a distraction from the broad range of systemic issues and is only one of the many environmental problems existing today – soil erosion, deforestation, water salinisation, insecticides and pesticides, particulates in the air, tropospheric ozone pollution, stratospheric ozone loss, acidic deposition, toxic chemical waste, heavy metals, asbestos, nuclear waste, biodiversity loss, acidification of the oceans, hormone discharges into the water supply, pollution from plastics, light, noise and so on. The material and energy throughput of the economy cannot continue to grow without destructive effects socially and ecologically. As I have argued elsewhere (Spash, 2007), humanity would do better to create an economic system that is smaller by design, not disaster. A social economy that reproduces itself in harmony with Nature rather than through domination over it. That is the job ahead.

Conclusions

Humanity can no more afford to continue giving credence to a redundant economics profession than it can persist with a destructive and divisive economic system. Social ecological economics explains how and why the modern mode of production and consumption is socially unjust and ecologically unsustainable. The next step is to develop the theoretical basis for alternative structures, a scientific utopian vision and a radical social ecological transformation. The motto of social ecological economics is: 'There are only alternatives.'

Notes

1 The Roman Empire achieved widespread maritime trade, including routes from North Africa to Northern Europe. According to Polanyi (1957: 256), 'trade' in the late Roman Empire was for redistribution, not sale in markets. Roman 'trade' included large quantities of grains. For example, boats brought 175,200 tons of Egyptian grain to Constantinople as late as the sixth century (Hodges, 1989: 94). Such large-scale transfers (and trade in basic commodities) disappeared as the Empire collapsed first in Northern and Western Europe and then more slowly in the East within the surviving Byzantine Empire. Similar levels of trade only reappeared in the late medieval period circa the eleventh century.
2 A process that continues today and in recent times has been most dramatically enforced in the modernisation drives of China and India.

Key further readings cited

Georgescu-Roegen, N. (2009 [1975]). Energy and Economic Myths. In: Spash, C.L. (ed.). *Ecological Economics: Critical Concepts in the Environment*, 4 Volumes. London: Routledge, 328–373.
Kapp, K.W. (1978). *The Social Costs of Business Enterprise*. Nottingham: Spokesman.
Polanyi, K. (1957). The Market as Instituted Process. In: Polanyi, K., Arensberg, C.M. and Pearson, H.W. (eds). *Trade and Market in the Early Empires*. Chicago: Henry Regnery Company, 243–270.
Spash, C.L. (2011). Social ecological economics: Understanding the past to see the future. *American Journal of Economics and Sociology*, 70 (2): 340–375.
Spash, C.L. (2013). The shallow or the deep ecological economics movement? *Ecological Economics*, 93 (September): 351–362.

Other literature cited

Anderson, B. and M'Gonigle, M. (2012). Does ecological economics have a future? Contradiction and reinvention in the age of climate change. *Ecological Economics*, 84 (December): 37–48.
Fellner, W. and Spash, C.L. (2015). The Role of Consumer Sovereignty in Sustaining the Market Economy. In: Reisch, L.A. and Thørgersen, J. (eds). *Handbook of Research on Sustainable Consumption*. Cheltenham: Edward Elgar, 394–409.
Georgescu-Roegen, N. (1971). *The Entropy Law and the Economic Process*. Cambridge, Massachusetts: Harvard University Press.

Georgescu-Roegen, N. (2009 [1979]). Methods in economic science. In: Spash, C.L. (ed.). *Ecological Economics: Critical Concepts in the Environment*, 4 Volumes. London: Routledge, 105–115.

Hodges, R. (1989). *Dark Age Economics: The Origins of Towns and Trade AD 600–1000*. London: Duckworth.

Meadows, D.H., Meadows, D.L., Randers, J. and Behrens III, W.W. (1972). *The Limits to Growth*. London: Pan.

Polanyi, K. (1944). *The Great Transformation*. New York/Toronto: Rinehart & Company Inc.

Pollini, J. (2013). Bruno Latour and the ontological dissolution of nature in the social sciences: A critical review. *Environmental Values*, 22(1): 25–42.

Røpke, I. (2005). Trends in the development of ecological economics from the late 1980s to the early 2000s. *Ecological Economics*, 55(2): 262–290.

Spash, C.L. (1999). The development of environmental thinking in economics. *Environmental Values*, 8(4): 413–435.

Spash, C.L. (2007). The economics of climate change impacts à la Stern: Novel and nuanced or rhetorically restricted? *Ecological Economics*, 63(4): 706–713.

Spash, C.L. (2012a). Towards the integration of social, economic and ecological knowledge. In: Gerber, J.-F. and Steppacher, R. (eds). *Towards an Integrated Paradigm in Heterodox Economics*. Basingstoke: Palgrave Macmillan, 26–46.

Spash, C.L. (2012b). New foundations for ecological economics. *Ecological Economics*, 77 (May): 36–47.

Spash, C.L. (2015a). Bulldozing biodiversity: The economics of offsets and trading-in Nature. *Biological Conservation*, 192 (December): 541–551.

Spash, C.L. (2015b). The dying planet index: Life, death and man's domination of Nature. *Environmental Values*, 24(1): 1–7.

Spash, C.L. (2016). This changes nothing: The Paris Agreement to ignore reality. *Globalizations*, 13(6): 928–933.

Spash, C.L. and Aslaksen, I. (2015). Re-establishing an ecological discourse in the policy debate over how to value ecosystems and biodiversity. *Journal of Environmental Management*, 159 (August): 245–253.

Spash, C.L. and Ryan, A. (2012). Economic schools of thought on the environment: Investigating unity and division. *Cambridge Journal of Economics*, 36(5): 1091–1121.

Spash, C.L. and Vatn, A. (2006). Transferring environmental value estimates: Issues and alternatives. *Ecological Economics*, 60(2): 379–388.

2

A CRITICAL AND REALIST APPROACH TO ECOLOGICAL ECONOMICS

Armin Puller and Tone Smith

Introduction

Ecological economics is based on preanalytic assumptions informing scientific practices,[1] guiding the theoretical construction of objects of knowledge, as well as instructing the process of researching particular phenomena or events. The task of reflecting these, mostly implicit, assumptions is the domain of philosophy of science—covering issues such as:

1   the nature of reality and the basic categories and principles of being (ontology), e.g., the relations between structure and agency [see Chapter 14] or the causal role of discourses;
2   the nature, certainty and objectivity of scientific knowledge about this reality [see Chapters 26 and 28], and the necessary conditions for and modes of acquiring it (epistemology); and
3   the properties and conditions of appropriate analytical strategies and research designs (methodology).

Assumptions about reality, knowledge and knowledge production have major impacts on the perspectives of a discipline, how it perceives its subject matter and how it examines phenomena. As an interdisciplinary field emphasising and investigating the dynamic interrelations between biophysical systems, societies and their economies, ecological economics research necessitates well-elaborated reflections on the combination of different scientific objects and bodies of knowledge.

This chapter argues for a critical and realist approach as the best way forward. Critical realism aids conceptualising the complex relations between society and nature beyond reductionist accounts. It directs research designs towards the generation of depth-explanations on efficacious tendencies, causes and reasons responsible for events to occur and phenomena to exist. In addition, it combines different methods of empirical investigation to appropriately assess reality's manifold aspects.

Realism of a critical type is a viable alternative to naïve objectivism and strong (social) constructivism. It is anchored in the "basic realist principle" (Sayer, 2000: 33) of understanding the natural and social objects studied by science as existing independently of scientific discourses in which researchers engage. Contrary to (empirical) realisms of a shallow type that conflate the real with observations and experiences of it, the realism proposed here rejects idealist or relativist accounts of the natural and social world on grounds of a realist depth-ontology. Furthermore, a realism taking seriously the challenges posed by post-structuralisms and postmodernism, but rejecting the relativist view of knowledge, must be committed to understanding science as a developmental and always incomplete process-in-motion, producing results destined to be revised as investigations proceed (epistemic fallibilism contra dogmatism). It must also be committed to the historicity and sociality of knowledge and knowledge production (epistemological relativity contra absolutism), as well as to the possibility of distinguishing between competing forms of knowledge and rationally deciding between them (judgemental rationality contra relativism).

Criticality refers to the emancipatory potential of social science to demystify systems, practices and beliefs that reproduce existing unsustainable and unjust social relations. Critical realism realises this potential by identifying underlying structures and mechanisms as well as assessing the causes for the dominance and persistency of phenomena (explanatory critique). Contrary to the belief in value-neutrality, a critical scientific approach needs to engage in developing explicit and well-reasoned (hence debatable) concepts of the human good and environmental sustainability. This position rejects hiding normative standpoints or restricting critique to mere attitudes of enhanced self-reflection.

The state of theory in ecological economics

The very starting point of ecological economics was a break with mainstream economics, because of the latter's failure to relate to the complexity of reality, in particular biophysical reality [Chapters 9–13]. This core claim expresses a belief in a reality independent of our perception or knowledge of it. Such independent reality has been most clearly formulated in the Laws of Thermodynamics [Chapter 9], central to the conceptualisation of ecological economics and one of its foundational building blocks.

From its formal establishment in the late 1980s, ecological economics sought to be open and inclusive of critical voices. Still, early statements by key persons expressed the need to clarify "what is ontologically different about ecological economics" (Spash, 2012: 36). However, this was never followed through, and the newly established field instead quickly moved into doing 'policy-relevant science' and simply taking an open-minded and pluralist position on methodology. Norgaard (1989) promoted 'methodological pluralism' in the first issue of the journal *Ecological Economics*, based on an uneasy balance between criticising the positivism of mainstream economics,[2] while at the same time not rejecting it because of its dominance in economics. However, it seems illogical that a new field trying to break with mainstream economics should refrain from rejecting mainstream core assumptions and methodology after having identified them as being naïve and flawed.

Since this initial opening phase, few attempts have been made to sort good theory and practice from bad, or synthesise the field based on solid philosophical grounds that would have avoided internal theoretical contradictions. Instead, ecological economics has developed with many streams of theory and no clear meta-theory. The kind of articles accepted in the journal indicates a lasting mainstream economics dominance, as, for example, shown by Anderson and M'Gonigle (2012) with respect to the topic of climate change.

At the same time, there is a grouping of constructivists or relativists in the community. Post-normal science has had a strong position in ecological economics from the beginning, and claims about strong uncertainty, interest-ladenness and value-pluralism have correspondences with post-normal science [Chapter 28]. However, while post-normal science leaves its philosophical foundations implicit, it makes use of constructivist arguments, and has clear links to the constructivist field of Science and Technology Studies (STS).

Tacconi (1998) has suggested a constructivist approach in a rare attempt to develop an ontology and epistemology suited to ecological economics. He ends up suggesting strong constructivism, while at the same time accepting the existence of a reality independent of human cognition. What he really needs is a different philosophy of science avoiding the traps and dilemmas of eclecticism.

Appeals for pluralism within ecological economics seem to be made on democratic criteria rather than on philosophical grounds. For example, Söderbaum (2008) suggests a pluralist approach where there should be room for both positivist economics and 'more recent developments' of hermeneutics and social constructivism. However, his presentation of neoclassical economics as one narrative amongst many is a constructivist interpretation that does not respect the essence of positivism. His call for attention to theory of science, as just a broadening of perspectives beyond positivism (Söderbaum, 2011), is also difficult to interpret. It may indicate an American Pragmatist position, but he makes no such claim. Others have made explicit reference to American Pragmatism (e.g., Kallis and Norgaard, 2010; Zografos and Howarth, 2008), but without promoting it as a foundational theory of science for ecological economics (perhaps an exception here is Bromley, 2008).

The lack of engagement with methodological issues, and the confusion and lack of clarity as to what should form the basis of the field, has left ecological economics in a situation of ambivalences and contradictions. Røpke (2005), in her study of the history of ecological economics, concludes that the identity of the field is weak and that the knowledge base is neither well-structured nor systematically organised. Anderson and M'Gonigle (2012: 37) claim that the field's formal embrace of methodological pluralism renders ecological economics theoretically incoherent, a situation that "undermines the field's historical promise as an alternative economic paradigm". They therefore call for a critical treatment of methodology. Spash (2012) has gone even further and called for "new foundations for ecological economics".

However, what should constitute these new foundations? How shall we critically address methodology and develop a more structured and integrated knowledge base? Ecological economists seem to be searching for a way to combine a perception of the world as independent of our knowledge, while at the same time admitting the social construction of knowledge and the role of meaning-making in the social realm. This probably reflects an understanding that social constructivism appears to help us comprehend some kinds of reality, while admitting that there is also a world independent of our beliefs and knowledge, or independent of human intentionality. Hence, positivism is left in because it fills this gap. However, this does not do justice to either of the philosophies, as they are both meant to be all-encompassing.

The approach, which ecological economists seem to be searching for, but of which—apart from a few researchers (e.g., Røpke, 1998; Spash, 2012; Tacconi, 2000; Vatn, 2005)—the field seems to be ignorant, can be found in critical realism. As pointed out by Spash (2012), ecological economists (despite their many divergences) agree on some fundamentally important propositions about reality, such as the independence of our perception and reality; the inseparability of social facts and values; the nature of reality as characterised by complexity and emergence; and the irreducibility of complex (biophysical and social) systems to its component parts. Similarly, ecological economists may agree on certain claims about knowledge, such as the uncertainty and fallibility of knowledge; the existence of manifold forms of knowledge (such as scientific expert knowledge, lay knowledge, indigenous knowledge); and the situatedness of knowledge and researchers as being temporally, geographically, culturally and socially embedded. The combination of these claims does not fit into research approaches committed to either positivist or constructivist positions within philosophy of science, but thoroughly correspond to critical realist ontology and epistemology.

Core positions of a critical and realist approach

The critical realist position within philosophy of science emerged with Roy Bhaskar's critique of the reduction of assumptions on being to assumptions on knowledge about it (epistemic fallacy), thereby highlighting the importance of reflecting the often neglected ontological issues implicitly present in all scientific research (Bhaskar, 2008). The main intention of critical realism is to 'underlabour' science by investigating the conditions, practices and implications of the production of scientific knowledge. By transcendentally analysing the necessary conditions of reality for science to be possible, critical realism asserts that the world is characterised by the phenomena of stratification and emergence (contrary to flatness), as well as openness and complex multicausal structuration (contrary to closedness), and proposes an ontology embracing both a relational and a realist aspect. The relational aspect emphasises that the subject matter of the human sciences comprises contextual relationships and neither easily isolatable objects nor regularities in patterns of events or in sets of meanings. The realist aspect warns against conflating reality with appearances. Reality is more than a set of events to be observed (as flat ontologies claim). It also encompasses an underlying domain consisting of structures and powers (natural and social), that exist independently of our observations and (in)adequate understanding of the world in which we live.

Critical realism's depth-ontology understands the real as not only embracing exercised and actualised powers of objects, but also unactualised and even unexercised potentials (Bhaskar, 1998, 2008; Sayer, 2000: 11–13). It distinguishes between the real as the domain of whatever *exists* and the actual as the domain of whatever *happens* (i.e., particular actualised powers and events). Experiences of these events belong to the domain of the empirical. This layering of reality explains the gaps between empirical experiences, actual events and real powers, and exposes the necessity for science to examine them at the correct level. Furthermore, reality is conceived as stratified, consisting of multiple strata—e.g., physical, chemical, biological, psychological, social or economic—formed by mechanisms that are taxonomically and causally irreducible to, despite being unilaterally dependent upon, one another. The strata of reality are characterised by the phenomenon of emergence: Natural and social processes arise from the complex interaction of multiple aspects resulting in new emergent properties and powers that cannot be reduced to its constituting component parts. Emergence explains why social relations or institutions cannot be reduced to individuals (contra methodological individualism) or why humans cannot be reduced to biological or chemical processes.

Critical realism, like empirical realism, conceives the natural and social world as characterised by causalities (Bhaskar, 2008; Sayer, 2010). However, it advocates a concept of causation differing in complexity by rejecting the view of causal laws as constant conjunctions of events and in favour of analysing reality as an interplay of manifold generative mechanisms of a variety of natural and social structures as well as social actors. Structures have certain properties, powers and liabilities (passive powers), and are responsible for phenomena existing and events happening (under specific conditions) on the level of the actual, thereby creating potentially observable effects.

In the social world, the term structure refers to relations between social positions (such as those found in capitalist production, gender arrangements or political institutions). These positions are necessarily internally related, e.g., the positions of landlord and tenant, and their connection to the systems of private property, rent and economic surplus production (see Sayer, 2010: 63–64). They are associated with specific roles to be populated by human actors. As the properties and causal powers of social structures are qualitatively different from those of actors, they are irreducible to them, even though they depend on agency to be reproduced. As structures cause real effects (such as affecting actors' practices or conditioning outcomes), they should not be understood as entities constructed within the thought process. Mechanisms are essential (albeit space-time-specific) aspects of structures and are analysed as tendencies existing regardless of their exertion, actualisation or observation and producing specific effects according to different contexts. Examples are the tendencies of capitalist economies to accumulate capital, fuelling the growth dynamic and increasing the throughput of resources; the tendency of post-democratic competition states to selectively relate to and integrate neoliberal political projects and policies; or the tendency of industrial agriculture to degrade the soil and pollute the environment, and hence reduce biodiversity. Critical realism agrees with constructivists that social reality is concept-dependent and experienced through language and systems of meanings, but opposes the view that structures could be reduced to them or conceived as virtual rather than existing.

On the level of social ontology, this concept of causation is combined with a critical version of naturalism that defends the existence of real structures and mechanisms not only in the natural, but also in the social realm. Thereby, it defines as specificities of social structures their dependence on social activities, on agents' conceptions of what they are doing in these activities and on space-time (Bhaskar, 1998, 2009: 130–132). Emphasising the interpretive dimension of social reality, critical realism regards social phenomena as intrinsically meaningful, entailing the view that also reasons (and the process of producing meaning in general) can be causes as they inform practices and motivate people to act in certain ways (Bhaskar, 1998: 88–99). It combines this insight with the insistence on the complex relationship between meanings and the non-discursive dimension of social life (Sayer, 2000).

Another important feature of critical naturalism is the distinction between social structures and human agents, as well as the analysis of their interdependencies. As solution to the innumerable fights in the human sciences between structuralism, intentionalism and structuration theory (compacting structure and agency together as inseparable), an analytical dualism is proposed for the connection between social agents and society (Bhaskar, 1998). Neither do agents (individual and collective) exist outside society, nor does society exist without agents. The common dichotomy between determinism and voluntarism is shifted towards dialectical duality. Social structures are understood as both necessary and ever-present, constraining and enabling conditions of human activity, as well as its continually reproduced outcome (duality of structure). At the same time, (ongoing) human agency is conceived as conscious and intentional interaction, as well as the (generally unconscious and unintended) reproduction or transformation of society (duality of praxis). For example, the capitalist economy is a necessary condition for activities of wage-labour, yet its reproduction depends upon them. At the same time, people do not work to reproduce the capitalist economy, but it is the unintended necessary consequence of their activities.

Epistemologically, critical realism links the fallibility of knowledge to the necessity to distinguish between two dimensions of science (Bhaskar, 2008). First, the intransitive dimension of the being of real objects of knowledge, referring to natural and social entities and relations (such as physical processes or social phenomena including material and ideational aspects).[3] Second, the transitive dimension of the thought objects of knowledge belonging to the (transient, incomplete and open) epistemological process and formed by the competing scientific theories and models about the world. Critical realism understands knowledge as produced within a social process by means of knowledge under specific settings (e.g., historical, social economic, cultural). As we can only know the world by means of particular historically transient descriptions, and within perspectival epistemic frameworks, knowledge is neither absolute nor timeless (Bhaskar, 2009: 66). Hence, contrary to the belief in knowledge as the discovery of facts (the position of naïve objectivism), critical realists emphasise that observations or experiences are only ever interpreted through cognitive, epistemic and theoretical filters by socially positioned researchers.

However, the emphasis on production must not be conflated with understanding knowledge as construction of intersubjectively shared interpretations by researchers or social actors in general. In such strong constructivist accounts, the situatedness of knowledge and researchers is overemphasised and articulated with a flat or even idealist ontology that conflates real and thought objects. The result is a reduction of knowledge production to an effect of epistemic frameworks and discourses, thereby neglecting its referential relations to extra-discursive properties of the world.

Due to its commitment to ontological realism, and contrary to strong constructivism, critical realism has no difficulties in accepting epistemic relativity and combining it with judgemental rationality to provide a (limited) sense of truth. The social character and the epistemic or theoretical non-neutrality of knowledge production is not necessarily an obstacle to the development of objective, or practically adequate, knowledge, nor does it imply indecisiveness between the adequacy of different theories. If reality is mind-independent, the status of knowledge cannot depend upon agreement, but essentially on its adequacy to access the world's properties and ways of functioning. In this regard, Sayer (2000: 90–92) has stressed the importance of disambiguating strong constructivism with its claim that the social world is constituted by discourse and meaning-giving practices of human beings, and weak constructivism embracing the idea of the concept-dependency (rather than the concept-determinacy) of social phenomena. Only the latter is compatible with ontological realism.

Within critical realist epistemology, knowledge takes the form of descriptions of structures and mechanisms causally generating observable phenomena, and of explanations about the causes of its existence. The task of science is to improve our understanding of reality and produce explanations that reflect its ontological depth. Furthermore, critical realism is committed to the idea that scientific knowledge supports the enlightenment project of human emancipation in the sense of informing the transformation of social structures connected to the "unwanted and unneeded" in favour of "wanted and needed" sources of determination (Bhaskar, 2009: 171), and to realising potentialities grounded in actual conditions for more just and sustainable societies. It accentuates human sciences' critical aspects implied by their general non-neutrality towards competing scientific, as well as ideological, accounts and their connection to prevailing asymmetrical social relations.

As explanatory critique, it goes beyond mere criticism by trying to identify not only the immanent errors and absences within a specific problematic system, practice or belief, but also the causes being responsible for their existence and reproduction. By showing that human sciences necessarily evaluate their subject matter (be it positive or negative), the common positivist dichotomies between facts and values or between analysis and critique are rejected in favour of uncovering and reflecting their implicit complex dynamics, as well as ethical standpoints (Bhaskar, 2009: 169–211; Collier, 1994: 169–204). In an emerging normative turn, critical realists engage in examining the intransitive dimension of ethics (ethical naturalism) based on human beings' (objective and pluralist rather than relativist) capacities for flourishing and suffering. This allows the inclusion of reasoning on ethical life within scientific enquiry.

Methodology and application

Methodology covers reflections on research strategies, methods and research designs including their specific combination of theories, models and empirical investigation. In line with its epistemology, critical realism's methodology is not restricted to certain methods or methodical schools, but rather is compatible with a wide range of research methods. In the prevalent hostilities between quantitative and qualitative methodologists, it advocates a position of critical or structured plurality highlighting the link between methodology and ontology. First and foremost, methodological reflection needs to be adequate to the real object under study. Thus, Tony Lawson (1997) has argued for an "ontological turn" in economics to overcome the implausible assumptions of mainstream economics constituted by its closed-system methods, mathematical formalism and econometric modelling.

Regarding research purposes, critical realism is primarily concerned with explanation of a phenomenon's underlying structures and mechanisms (necessitating as starting point the availability or production of descriptions about them) for which it has directly elaborated specific methods. Explanation should not be conflated with the research purpose of (strong) prediction, which is restricted to closed systems—a feature applying neither to social nor to biophysical systems, and only equated with explanation in epistemologies corresponding to naïve objectivism. According to its ontological assumptions, critical realism emphasises the interdependence of structural, causal and interpretive analysis as well as the importance of identifying deep structures and causal mechanisms as the basis for choosing methods.

The research strategy advocated by critical realism requires inference using 'retroduction' to establish explanatory models about the interplay of structures, mechanisms and their conditions that produces specific effects (Danermark et al., 2002). As structures and mechanisms are not directly observable, retroduction is a (non-formalised) mode of inference from traceable, or observable, effects to the underlying explanatory structures. Retroduction employs transfactual argumentation (contrary to generalisation) for examining the properties and the contingent circumstances that make something what it is and prompt it to act in specific ways. At the level of methods, retroduction relates to structural and causal analysis (Sayer, 2010: 58–103). Structural analysis investigates substantive internal relations and properties of objects or practices in order to identify their emergent powers. Causal analysis deals with explanations about why particular events happen in terms of conjunctures of various interacting structures and mechanisms. To grasp the interpretive dimension of social reality, retroduction needs to be supplemented by interpretive research strategies that are concerned with understanding social actors' discourses, motives and beliefs.

Research based on retroduction usually involves the following stages (Danermark et al., 2002: 41–70; cf. Bhaskar, 2009: 68, 107–108):

1   the description of a complex event;
2   the decompository analysis of aspects involved;
3   its redescription in theoretical terms;
4   retroductive reasoning on what makes these components exist and its interplay possible, involving also analogies with existing phenomena;
5   the elaboration of explanations in comparison with different theories and abstractions; and
6   the concretisation and contextualisation of the hypothesised mechanisms.

As a mechanism cannot be 'demonstrated', the link between theories, models and empirical investigation depends upon documenting the effects of a retroduced mechanism and upon ongoing theoretical reflection on conceptualisations and empirical findings in light of explanatory models. Sayer (2010: 162–169) refers to such research designs as "intensive research", producing explanations by combining theoretical research, on substantial relations, properties and powers of social objects, with empirical research on actual events and processes as results of multiple determinations in a specific context. It is distinguished from "extensive research", which is occupied with inference by generalising from empirical findings, exploring merely formal relations of similarity and producing taxonomic descriptions of variables in order to analyse the statistical representativeness of cases.

Future directions

A central contribution of critical realism to ecological economics can be found in the area of interdisciplinarity. On a theoretical level, Bhaskar (2010) has emphasised the concept of "laminated explanations" as a way to combine different academic fields in interdisciplinary studies to integrate mechanisms at several levels and to handle complexity or joint determination. Thereby, practicing both methodological specificity and plurality depends on meta-theoretical unity. Regarding society–nature relationships, critical realism emphasises that biophysical and social processes exist as complex irreducible orders that cannot be fully incorporated into one another, but rather need to be analysed in terms of their specific dependencies and mutual effects on each other (Bhaskar, 2009). In this vein, Ted Benton (1992) has analysed the idea of limits to growth through an in-depth examination of the interplay of biophysical and social limits.

Examples of the application of critical realism in fields related to ecological economics can be found (amongst others) in planning studies and heterodox economics. Petter Næss has applied critical realism to several areas of relevance to ecological economics. From an ontological perspective, he undertakes the deconstruction of cost-benefit analysis as a planning tool in order to show its unrealistic model assumptions and how it legitimises market-based policies (Næss, 2006a). In a study on the unsustainability of capitalism, Næss (2006b) examines the deep causes of the growth dynamic and the limitations of the decoupling strategy [see Chapter 11]. Another example is Jin Xue's (2012) case study comparing Hangzhou, China and Copenhagen, Denmark that reveals the impossibility of decoupling environmental impacts from housing sector growth and economic growth.

In the field of heterodox economics, Jamie Morgan has applied critical realism to topics as diverse as finance, monetary policy and labour (e.g. Morgan and Sheehan, 2015). Reflection on the use of different methods in economics have been undertaken by Fred Lee (2012) who suggested how critical realism can be combined with grounded theory to develop new economic theory. Another example of a critical realist inspired study on methodology is Downward and Mearman's (2007) suggestion to combine retroduction and triangulation as a form of interdisciplinarity in methodology.

Concluding remarks

Ecological economics is a field of research requiring interdisciplinarity and non-deterministic openness to the various academic disciplines that cover biophysical, social and economic subject matters. Based on the combination of epistemological relativity and ontological realism, critical realism has much to offer ecological economics, in particular a (currently missing) meta-theoretical scheme, solutions for prevailing philosophical contradictions, and a structured methodological plurality. As an 'underlabourer' for ecological economics, critical realism does not replace empirical investigation or distract attention from it. Rather, it restricts itself to the role of providing philosophical reflection for scientific practices, informing theoretical frameworks to explain particular phenomena and structuring research designs.

Moreover, critical realism goes beyond analysing problems in actualised social systems by identifying the yet unactualised potentials, which allow transformation towards an alternative society. Ecological economics has aimed from the beginning to influence policy, 'manage sustainability', and help create a better, sustainable and just world. Critical realism shows that changing the world necessitates a comprehensive understanding of the deeper structures of social, economic and biophysical reality, including a stronger focus on the underlying causes of prevailing problems, such as environmental degradation and inequality. Ecological economics has tended to neglect issues of structure in favour of analysing norms and behaviour, making it ill-prepared and unable to address the necessary social ecological economic transformations ahead. Reversing that failure can be facilitated by critical realism. It offers an in-depth conceptualisation of the natural and social aspects of the world, as well as of the dependencies and interactions between them. Ecological economics needs an approach that unites scientific realism with critical social science.

Notes

1 Science and scientific endeavours are taken to cover both the natural and the social sciences unless otherwise specified.
2 Positivism comes in many versions from naïve objectivism to logical empiricism (Spash, 2012).
3 Intransitivity is a necessary condition of all scientific enquiries and does not relate to the distinction between the material and the ideational.

Key further readings cited

Bhaskar, R. (1998). *The Possibility of Naturalism. A Philosophical Critique of the Contemporary Human Sciences.* 3rd edition. London: Routledge.
Collier, A. (1994). *Critical Realism.* London: Verso.
Danermark, B., Ekström, M., Jakobsen, L., and Karlsson, J.C. (2002). *Explaining Society. Critical Realism in the Social Sciences.* London: Routledge.
Sayer, A. (2010). *Method in Social Science.* 2nd edition. London: Routledge.
Spash, C.L. (2012). New foundations for ecological economics. *Ecological Economics* 77(May), 36–47.

Other literature cited

Anderson, B., and M'Gonigle, M. (2012). Does ecological economics have a future? *Ecological Economics* 84, 37–48.
Benton, T. (1992). Ecology, Socialism and the Mastery of Nature: A Reply to Reiner Grundmann. *New Left Review* 194(Jul-Aug), 55–74.
Bhaskar, R. (2008). *A Realist Theory of Science.* London: Routledge.
Bhaskar, R. (2009). *Scientific Realism and Human Emancipation.* London: Routledge.
Bhaskar, R. (2010). Contexts of interdisciplinarity: interdisciplinarity and climate change. In R. Bhaskar, C. Frank, K.G. Høyer, P. Næss, and J. Parker (eds.), *Interdisciplinarity and Climate Change* (pp. 1–24). London: Routledge.
Bromley, D.W. (2008). Volitional pragmatism. *Ecological Economics* 68(1–2), 1–13.
Downward, P., and Mearman, A. (2007). Retroduction as mixed-methods triangulation in economic research: reorienting economics into social science. *Cambridge Journal of Economics* 31(1), 77–99.
Kallis, G., and Norgaard, R.B. (2010). Coevolutionary ecological economics. *Ecological Economics* 69(1), 690–699.
Lawson, T. (1997). *Economics and Reality.* London: Routledge.
Lee, F. (2012). *Critical realism, grounded theory, and theory construction in heterodox economics.* MPRA Paper No. 40341, July 2012.
Morgan, J., and Sheehan, B. (2015). The concept of trust and the political economy of John Maynard Keynes. *Review of Social Economy* 73(1), 113–137.
Næss, P. (2006a). Cost-benefit analyses of transportation investments: neither critical nor realistic. *Journal of Critical Realism* 5(1), 32–60.
Næss, P. (2006b). Unsustainable growth, unsustainable capitalism. *Journal of Critical Realism* 5(2), 197–227.
Norgaard, R.B. (1989). The case for methodological pluralism. *Ecological Economics* 1(1), 37–57.

Røpke, I. (1998). Sustainability and structural change. In S. Faucheux, M. O'Connor and J. Van Der Straaten (eds.), *Sustainable Development: Concepts, Rationalities and Strategies* (pp. 141–155). The Hague: Kluwer.

Røpke, I. (2005). Trends in the development of ecological economics from the late 1980s to the early 2000s. *Ecological Economics 55*(2), 262–290.

Sayer, A. (2000). *Realism and Social Science*. London: Sage.

Söderbaum, P. (2008). *Understanding Sustainability Economics. Towards Pluralism in Economics*. London: Earthscan.

Söderbaum, P. (2011). Sustainability economics as a contested concept. *Ecological Economics 70*(6), 1019–1020.

Tacconi, L. (1998). Scientific methodology for ecological economics. *Ecological Economics 27*(1), 91–105.

Tacconi, L. (2000). *Biodiversity and Ecological Economics: Participation, Values and Resource Management*. London: Earthscan.

Vatn, A. (2005). *Institutions and the Environment*. Cheltenham: Edward Elgar.

Xue, J. (2012). A critical realist perspective on decoupling negative environmental impacts from housing sector growth and economic growth. *Journal of Critical Realism 11*(4), 438–461.

Zografos, C., and Howarth, R.B. (eds.). (2008). *Deliberative Ecological Economics*. Oxford: OUP.

PART II

Heterodox thought on the environment

3

CRITICAL INSTITUTIONAL ECONOMICS

Arild Vatn

Introduction

Many ecological economists question the 'rational choice' basis of mainstream economics. We acknowledge the existence of plural values. We question individual preferences as the ultimate judge of decisions regarding environmental issues as we observe the interdependencies involved between people given common environments. We also emphasise the importance of ignorance. Nevertheless, a fleshed out and coherent alternative 'economics' of ecological economics is lacking.

The aim of this chapter is to show that institutional economics could help fill this gap. While the tradition is itself rather heterodox, I concentrate here on the direction in institutional economics developed from a critical stand towards its neoclassical counterpart. The chapter is structured as follows: First, I offer a brief overview of two main strands of institutional economics—the 'new' or neoclassically inspired position and the 'classical' and more critical one. I link the latter to the wider realm of institutional analysis as found in fields like political science and sociology. Second, I present key focal areas of institutional analysis grounded in its specific ontology and epistemology. Third, I discuss how classical institutional theory responds to three basic issues in ecological economics, namely: (i), the systems perspective, (ii) valuation of Nature and (iii) environmental governance. Fourth, I follow up with a short section on future directions, before I conclude.

Positions in institutional economics

Institutional economics developed as a reaction to the neoclassical tradition more than 100 years ago. Thorstein Veblen may be considered its 'father'.[1] He criticised the idea, or assumption, of the 'isolated' individual so fundamental to the expanding neoclassical paradigm. He saw institutions not only as formed by, but also forming individuals. In clarifying the different perspectives and theories in this field, a brief presentation of neoclassical economics is necessary.

Neoclassical economics

Neoclassical economics has dominated the profession since, at least, the 1950s. Following Becker (1976) and Eggertsson (1990), we may define the following *core* of the neoclassical model:

- rational choice as maximising individual utility;
- stable preferences; and
- equilibrium outcomes.

Utility is derived from preference satisfaction and the preferences of individuals are typically seen as stable. At least they are seen as strictly individual; uninfluenced by societal or cultural factors. This is the essence of the individualist perspective underlying standard rational choice. Rational agents will exchange goods until a point is reached where no more gains appear and an equilibrium state is produced. Agents cannot get all they want, as they have limited access to resources (income). Hence, they have to prioritise and find the way (means) that increases their preference satisfaction (ends) the most.

Any model of the economy also needs to make assumptions about the context within which economic agents operate. Following Eggertsson (1990), the *standard context or application area* of neoclassical economics can be defined as:

- no information costs;
- no transaction costs; and
- private property rights for all goods that are exchanged in competitive markets.

The only institutional element appearing here is property rights. While the task of the State is to form and guard these rights, the analysis of how this comes about is regarded as outside the scope of economics. Given the kind of rationality involved, the only form of interaction implied by the model is the trading of goods and resources. Interaction will, moreover, appear 'by itself' as long as utility can be increased through such exchanges. In a model based on individualism and zero transaction costs, the market is taken to be a cost free and 'natural order of things'.

While the above represents the standard version of the model, much research among neoclassical economists includes studies of decision-making under risk and uncertainty. We also observe that the issue of transaction costs is being more and more included in economic textbooks. These developments imply, among other things, dispensing with the assumption that information is cost-free. This has, however, created problems, because accepting that there are positive information costs is inconsistent with the assumption of maximisation (e.g., see Knudsen, 1993).

New institutional economics

While institutional issues are largely ignored by the neoclassical position, some mainstream economists nevertheless started to ask questions, such as: If transacting, or coordinating, is costly, are markets always the best way to allocate resources? Firms may be better (Coase, 1937; Williamson, 1985). Even State allocations could sometimes be more efficient (Coase, 1960; Williamson, 2000).

Douglas North has taken the above perspectives further in some seminal publications forming the basis for the tradition of 'new institutional economics'. He has defined institutions as "the *rules of the game* in a society or, more formally [...] the humanly devised constraints that shape human interaction" (North, 1990: 3, emphasis added). Institutions are seen as rules and operate as constraints. New institutional economics builds largely on the core of the neoclassical economics model. Humans act to maximise individual utility and preferences are unaffected by the institutional context. Under such an understanding of humans and human action, the only way institutions can operate is as constraints.

The most important 'rules of the game' are those defining the rights each individual holds, for example, the rules concerning ownership of resources. Given these rules and the existing distribution of endowments, individuals transact to get what, in the end, is considered best for them. Transacting is, however, costly and uncertain. According to this position, institutions are invented to reduce transaction costs and uncertainty. They are instruments that make production and exchange more predictable and efficient. Property rights, the institution of money, contracts and various measurement scales are all understood as invented to simplify transactions.

While institutions are human or social constructs, the individual agents are not seen as such according to this position. The 'mature' North (2005) moved somewhat away from utility maximisation as being a good description of human choice. Nevertheless, he did not grant any role to institutions in forming preferences. In that sense, the individualist tenets of rational choice institutionalism was kept intact.

Classical institutional economics

What is here termed classical institutional economics (CIE) was developed as a critique of neoclassical economics that emerged from the 1870s onwards. Veblen (1899) emphasised the influence of society and its institutions on human preferences themselves. While this tradition had a strong position especially in the USA until the 1940s, it lost influence and did not really revive before the late 1980s (Hodgson, 1988; Bromley, 1989).

CIE defines institutions in a similar way to new institutional economics, but attributes them a very different role and does not limit them to operating only as constraints. Institutions are primarily understood as formative of the individual and as creating different contexts of meaning. Synthesising the position, I have formulated the following definition:

> Institutions are the conventions, norms and formally sanctioned rules of a society. They provide expectations, stability and meaning essential to human existence and coordination. Institutions support certain values, and produce and protect interests.
>
> (Vatn, 2005: 60)

Contrasting CIE to the neoclassical position, we observe that the latter see the human as *multi-rational* (Hodgson, 1988, 2007; Sjöstrand, 1995). The idea of maximising individual utility as the only form of rationality finds little support. Rather there can be different types of rationality, and the institutional context defines which is expected to operate. In some contexts, like a market, institutions seem formed to support choices that ensure what is best for the individual, e.g., 'individual rationality'. In the family context, care is the formative logic, constituting a type of 'social rationality'. Hence, considering what is right and wrong is an alternative form of rationality compared to the calculus of individual gain. What is right or wrong depends, moreover, on the kind of situation in which one finds oneself. Preferences and values are also seen as social constructs. Focus among representatives of this school is therefore not on equilibrium, but on change and the evolution of institutions, perceptions, preferences and values (Hodgson, 1996).

Concerning the *application area*, CIE and new institutional economics overlap somewhat. Hence, CIE emphasises the importance of information and transaction costs for understanding human action and the functioning of institutionalised systems like markets, firms, political and civil organisations. They differ, however, regarding why such structures exist and change. While reducing transaction costs may be important, CIE emphasises the role of power and interest protection as important when explaining the development of economic structures like markets and firms (Schmid, 1987; Hodgson, 1988; Bromley, 2006). CIE is finally interested in studying a wide variety of institutional structures (e.g., forms of property rights) and these again are discussed not only in relation to efficiency, but also with regard to the issue of power and interest protection (Schmid, 1987; Bromley, 2006). Thus, CIE challenges all the fundamental assumptions of the neoclassical model with important consequences for the evaluation of public policy.

Institutionalism in other social sciences

Regarding institutionalism in other social sciences, I simplify by distinguishing between historical and sociological institutionalism. There is a lot of common ground between these and CIE. Historical institutionalism is dominated by political scientists and sociologists and focuses less on economic issues. It puts strong emphasis on the normative role of institutions and the importance of power [see also Chapter 14]. Regarding the normative, the focus is to a large extent on what is the appropriate or the right thing to do (March and Olsen, 1995). In this respect, the historical school represents a further development of the ideas of early sociologists— Durkheim, through Parsons to Selznick—emphasising the normative dimension of institutions (Scott, 2014). Like CIE, prominence is given to how institutional structures facilitate or obstruct the access that various interest groups have to arenas of decision-making. Historical institutionalists also strongly emphasise the role of path dependence in understanding the development of institutions, which means that existing institutions influence the kind of changes that will/can happen.

The development within mainstream sociology itself has taken a somewhat different direction regarding institutional analysis (Scott, 2014). Again, any distinction, or grouping, must be treated with care. Nevertheless, in recent decades there has been an observable turn away from emphasising the normative importance, and more towards the cognitive significance of institutions. Institutions are not only formal rules and norms, but also symbolic systems, cognitive scripts and categorisations that make action possible and offer meaning to a situation. Hall and Taylor (1996: 948) note: "Institutions influence behaviour not simply by specifying what one should do but also by specifying what one can imagine oneself doing in a given context." This implies an emphasis on what I term conventions, not just as practical rules to organise interaction, but also as symbolic systems influencing perception. 'Facts' do not present themselves to us in a straight forward way as assumed by rational choice. What we observe, and how we understand what we observe, depends upon the concepts we have learned to use [see also Chapter 2].

Doing institutional analysis

Institutional analysis focuses predominantly on understanding the relationships between human action and institutions. It therefore looks at the relationships between actors and structures, both to understand societal dynamics and to develop ideas about how alternative institutional structures may facilitate behavioural change. This is of great importance in the field of environmental action.

Studies in institutional economics concentrating on environmental issues have been undertaken by a wide number of researchers (e.g., Arun Agrawal, Daniel Bromley and Elinor Ostrom). Synthesising this kind of work, I note four key aspects (Vatn, 2015a):

1   Rights and responsibilities
2   Transaction costs
3   Perceptions
4   Preferences and motivations.

There are certainly variations across authors regarding both emphasis and understanding of these issues. Nevertheless, I find it possible to formulate an overview that is consistent and captures the main features of CIE.

Rights and responsibilities

Rights and responsibilities may be formal or informal. Rights to resources (e.g., property or use rights) are crucial for people's ability to sustain their lives. The literature typically distinguishes between private, common, State (public) property and open access (e.g., Bromley, 2006). While there is some distinctiveness to each type, these are wide categories, and internal variation is also very important. Understanding rights and the dynamics behind their formation is crucial to understanding distribution of resources and the various forms of (unequal) economic and political power [see Chapters 4, 14 and 15].

Due to social and environmental interdependencies, the actions of one person typically influence the opportunities of others. In this regard, the concept of responsibility is also key. The institutional structure may be such that the actor is free to do whatever she or he wants. She or he can 'shift costs' on to others (Kapp, 1971). Alternatively, a responsibility may be defined that makes such an action unacceptable. The interests of 'the other' are institutionally protected.

Transaction costs

Transaction costs are the costs of interaction. We may interact via trade, command or community arrangements. These formats are all defined by institutions. In answering his question "why we have firms rather than just markets", Coase (1937) concluded that command is sometimes more efficient, less costly, than trade. While CIE emphasises the importance of power and interest protection—e.g., the control of labour—to understand the existence of firms, it acknowledges that transaction costs are important for the functioning of organisational solutions. One example regards common property, as an alternative to private property. It may facilitate coordinated use of a resource like a forest, a pasture or water body. 'Cost shifting' as following from individual uses of common-pool resources is regulated through common rules. This is often an efficient and flexible alternative to regulations by States or through individual contracting. Another example is the present emphasis on turning to trade to solve environmental problems, like biodiversity loss and climate change. A key notion is payments for ecosystem services (PES). Vatn (2015b) shows that these transactions mainly involve public resources as raised by taxes and fees. While some of these resources are distributed through auctions and other 'trade-like' systems, command and not trade dominates in PES. The cost of operating markets for ecosystem services is a key explanation for this fact [for more on ecosystem services, see Chapter 43].

Perceptions

Acting happens based on beliefs about what needs to be acted upon and the effects of action. These beliefs depend upon our perceptions about what the issues are and how the physical and social worlds 'work'. Due to great complexity and the subsequent high levels of ignorance and uncertainty, "fixing beliefs" is not in any way straightforward (Bromley, 2006).

Language is itself an institutionalised structure and crucial for our understanding. It offers predefined concepts through which we learn to understand the world around us. Understanding is founded on (subjective) experiences that are objectified through language-based 'models of mind'. While there is a reality, perceptions of it may differ. Moreover, not all reality can be observed. What we know of the world around us depends on how we conceptualise it. Hence, changes in conceptualisations may result in new insights and, all the time, we have to be 'critical' of our conceptualisations [hence the importance of critical realism; see also Chapter 2].

We learn through a social process of standardising beliefs. In relation to this, we may talk of primary and secondary socialisation. Primary socialisation includes learning about the concepts and norms of the culture in which we are raised. Secondary socialisation refers to specialised (professional) competence. We learn to become a farmer, a plumber, a teacher, an engineer, and so on. Specialised knowledge implies specialised vocabulary. This is a necessary element in modern societies, while it implies that people develop particular capacities to perceive. This makes possible the development of skills and insights that would be impossible in a less specialised society, but specialisation may also create conflicts, as we tend to see and value different things as well as value things differently (Trainor, 2006).

Preferences and motivations

While acting rests on beliefs, it also depends on preferences and motivations. As observed from a CIE perspective, the following aspects seem central:

- There is a distinct social component to the formation of preferences. Hence, different cultures are characterised by different conventions and norms regarding what, for example, are normal consumption patterns. Being socialised implies—learning these conventions and norms.
- Our interests are strongly influenced by the rights we have, respectively, the type of role within which we operate. This shows up in our actions as different preferences. While roles are not straightjackets, they define what is seen as normal and appropriate.
- Hence, people hold different sets of preferences and have the capacity to act in accordance with different types of rationalities. They may be motivated by what is best for themselves. They may, however, also be motivated to act in ways that are best for the group they belong to or for others.
- While people are characterised by multiple sets of preferences and a plurality of motivations, it is the institutional context that defines which type of motivation, and hence what set of preferences is expected.

So human preferences can change through processes of socialisation. Deliberation over what preferences are best to hold then becomes both possible and necessary. This is important in a world of interconnectedness. Certainly, keeping such deliberations open and reflective is very demanding. When establishing or changing institutional structures, when introducing policy instruments like laws and payments into a given resource regime, one needs to notice that this does not only change what seems 'best to do'. It may change the very logic by which actors perceive the problems faced, as in the theory of 'crowding out' (Rode et al., 2015).

So we observe that rights, transaction costs, perceptions and motivations are interdependent. Hence, basing human interactions on private property and trade creates different outcomes—

protect different values and interests—compared to, for example, common property and community rules. Understanding the relationships and dynamics here is crucial for societies to handle environmental problems. There is, however, high complexity, and outcomes are typically emergent. While we are able to create knowledge describing key characteristics of various combinations of property rights and interaction formats, results in the form of behavioural patterns are often contextual in profound ways. Hence, a certain institutional change that may offer good outcomes in one societal context may fail to do so in another. This is a challenge of which institutional analysis makes us aware and helps us study.

Relations to ecological economics

As already emphasised, institutional theory offers a good platform for analysing key issues raised by ecological economists. I will illustrate this by looking at the systems orientation of ecological economics, its emphasis on plural values and engagement with environmental policy and governance.

Systems thinking

Ecological economics is systems oriented. It emphasises interdependencies between ecological and economic systems, or, even more broadly, between the non-human and human world. Accentuating systems thinking implies embracing complexity and hence emergence. CIE tries to understand human action in a systems perspective and emphasises relations. While its neoclassical counterpart is reductionist, which means that explanations to social phenomena should be found by reducing the analysis to the level of the 'smallest part' (i.e., the individual), CIE emphasises the interplay between individuals and institutional structures. The latter is seen as generating social constructs fundamental both to the creation of the individuals and the forms of interaction.

Institutions do not determine action. They offer expectations and must be interpreted. Different institutional contexts (e.g., the market, the firm, the family, the community) favour different types of interaction, and hence different rationalities. However, individuals interpret and evaluate the contexts. While much action is automatic, humans are also reflexive. We have the capacity to reflect on the process of our development and on the reasonableness of the social environments within which we act. Evolution of institutions is different from pure biological evolution. It is subject to reasoned choice, while dependent on history as embedded in perceptions, interests and power relations.

Valuation

Turning to more concrete areas of ecological economics, institutional theory offers a distinct approach to the issue of environmental valuation. It defines valuation methods like cost-benefit analysis, multiple criteria analysis and mapping [Chapters 30 and 31] and deliberative methods [Chapter 33–34] as value articulating institutions (VAIs). As such, these methods are distinct in the way they define who participates and in what capacity, e.g., consumers or citizens. They define what is considered relevant data and the form they should take, e.g., prices or arguments. They finally define how data should be used and conclusions formed, e.g., price aggregation vs. communicative judgements.

The VAIs therefore influence what values can be expressed and in what form, what way knowledge is produced, communicated and evaluated (perceptions), and finally which logic underlies the process of analysis (type of motivation). Hence, the various methods may result in different recommendations. CIE theory may help explain why this is so, as well as offering a basis for choosing between methods dependent on the values/issues involved.

Ecological economists emphasise the existence of plural values and of strong uncertainty [see Chapters 26–28]. From the perspective of CIE, a key aspect regards the distinction between individual/egocentric vs. social preferences. CIE offers a frame for understanding this distinction as well as discussing which type of preferences should be emphasised in cases where we evaluate common goods, specifically those influencing future generations. In a monist perspective like that of neoclassical economics, such issues are made invisible. In a world of interdependent actions, claiming that one's preferences should not be reasoned over and challenged is problematic. CIE emphasises the role of deliberative methods as a way to reason over the meaning and implications of the preferences an individual holds, whether egocentric or social.

Environmental policy and governance

While valuation emphasises issues regarding perceptions and motivations, studies of environmental policy and governance will have to engage with all four aspects mentioned in the preceding section on 'Doing institutional analysis'. The fundamental policy issues are what values and whose interests to protect, and whose side to take in a conflict. These issues concern rights and responsibilities. Moreover, governance implies interaction, communication and coordination. One aspect here regards the costs of interaction (transaction costs). These vary between different institutional structures affecting both how access to resources can be organised (property and use rights) and how owners/managers of resources can interact. These costs influence the capacity to handle various forms of cost shifting so fundamental to environmental governance—note the above discussion regarding treatment of cost shifting in a context of private property/markets as opposed to common property.

Finally, institutions influence both perceptions and motivations. One aspect is the way institutions protect but also create interests. Decisions by firms are directed by their ability to create an economic surplus. In a world of global competition in commodities, the need to protect these interests creates tremendous constraints on environmental policies, so evident both in general and in areas like climate policy more specifically. Another aspect regards the way policy instruments themselves influence the way environmental issues are perceived and how they influence the logic of action. In a situation where the 'logic of money' already dominates, using economic instruments may work according to standard expectations. In other contexts, this may not be the case (Vatn, 2015a).

So environmental policy is not about getting prices right. They are artefacts of existing institutional structures and have little meaning beyond these. Policy and governance demands comparative analyses of institutional structures, being reflexive on perceptions and taking a stand on rights and evaluating transaction costs and motivational implications. These are complex issues. Therefore, CIE does not claim that the issue is to get the institutions 'right' either, but rather the creation of institutional structures that can ensure workable and legitimate solutions to identified problems.

According to CIE, environmental problems are not accidental effects of production and consumption. They are systemic effects of the existing dominant institutions (Kapp, 1971). These institutions have been established over the last centuries to strengthen independent choices, e.g., firms/corporations as operating in markets. This is, however, done in a physical environment of interdependencies. This development has facilitated economic growth, which has—despite vast and even deepened inequalities—taken many out of poverty. Economic growth has, however, also created heavy pressures on the environment and threatens the basis for future well-being. Environmental policies have been established to reduce negative impacts when they have been acknowledged and become politically accepted. We nevertheless observe a conflict between an economic system with institutions demanding growth to work well and an environment that cannot manage the intensifying pressures. Based on perspectives from CIE, one may ask if present environmental policy programmes can handle this conflict.

Future directions

While CIE already delivers a series of important insights useful for ecological economics, further developments are needed. I emphasise three issues that require focus.

First, there is a need for engaging ecological economists in a systematic discussion about the 'economics' of ecological economics. I think insights from CIE should inform that discussion, while a better conceptualisation of human–Nature and society–Nature relationships is then necessary. Here is an area where ecological economists could inform the future development of CIE.

Second, while there is increased understanding of the relationships between institutions, motivations and action, we have just started to scratch the surface. CIE offers a good basis for the development of hypotheses and for interpretation of existing findings. Much more research in this field is necessary to support the future development both of ecological economics as well as of environmental policies. Certainly, success within this area may also have the capacity to influence the mainstream.

Third, the existing institutions for economic activity do not form a good basis for fostering sustainable futures. They create interests and motivations that are largely irresponsible and insensitive regarding environmental limits. The future seems to demand a fundamental restructuring of the economy making it much less dependent on growth and the interests protected by growth. It demands policies and economic actors that are socially and ecologically responsible. We must admit that we are far behind on developing ideas regarding what kind of institutions should be created to foster sustainability. CIE seems to offer important building blocks for the necessary conceptualisations. However, tremendous future effort is needed regarding both theory development and empirical research.

Concluding remarks

Institutional theory—not least as developed within CIE—offers a very good basis for conceptualising and understanding the relationships between humans, their societies and their physical environments. The concept of institutions helps clarify how interests are formed and protected, how the 'world around us' is perceived, and how human action is motivated and interaction is facilitated. Its specific understanding of actor–structure relationships seems productive for the topical research areas of ecological economics. There are substantial challenges ahead, though. These concern the need for developing ideas regarding (economic) institutions that could foster sustainable futures. A key area is better understanding and reflection about how institutional structures influence human motivation and action, including our willingness and ability to take the interests of 'the other' (e.g., future generations) into account.

Note

1   Editor's Note: Veblen was also responsible for creating the term neoclassical economics.

Key further readings cited

Kapp, K.W. (1971). *The Social Costs of Private Enterprise*. New York: Schoken Books.

Scott, W.R. (2014). *Institutions and Organizations: Ideas, Interests and Identities*. Los Angeles: Sage Publications, 4th edition.

Vatn, A. (2005). *Institutions and the Environment*. Cheltenham: Edward Elgar.

Other literature cited

Becker, G. (1976). *The Economic Approach to Human Behavior*. Chicago: University of Chicago Press.

Bromley, D.W. (1989). *Economic Interests and Institutions. The Conceptual Foundations of Public Policy*. Oxford: Basil Blackwell.

Bromley, D.W. (2006). *Sufficient Reason: Volitional Pragmatism and the Meaning of Economic Institutions*. Princeton: Princeton University Press.

Coase, R.H. (1937). The Nature of the Firm. *Economica*, 4(16), 386–405.

Coase, R.H. (1960). The Problem of Social Cost. *The Journal of Law and Economics*, 3(October), 1–44.

Eggertsson, T. (1990). *Economic Behaviour and Institutions*. Cambridge: Cambridge University Press.

Hall, P.A. and Taylor, R.C.R. (1996). Political Science and the Three New Institutionalisms. *Political Studies*, 44(December), 936–957.

Hodgson, G.M. (1988). *Economics and Institutions: A Manifesto for a Modern Institutional Economics*. Cambridge: Cambridge Polity Press.

Hodgson, G.M. (1996). *Economics and Evolution. Bringing Life Back into Economics*. Ann Arbor, MI: The University of Michigan Press.

Hodgson, G.M. (2007). The Revival of Veblenian Institutional Economics. *Journal of Economic Issues*, 41(2), 325–340.

Knudsen, C. (1993). Equilibrium, Perfect Rationality and the Problem of Self-Reference in Economics. In Mäki, U., B. Gustafsson and C. Knudsen (Eds.), *Rationality, Institutions and "Economic Methodology"* (pp. 133–170). London: Routledge.

March, J.G. and Olsen, J.P. (1995). *Democratic Governance*. New York: Free Press.

North, D.C. (1990). *Institutions, Institutional Change and Economic Performance*. Cambridge: Cambridge University Press.

North, D.C. (2005). *Understanding the Process of Economic Change*. Princeton, NJ: Princeton University Press.

Rode, J., Gómez-Baggethun, E. and Krause, M. (2015). Motivation Crowding by Economic Payments in Conservation Policy: A Review of the Empirical Evidence. *Ecological Economics*, 117(September), 270–282.

Schmid, A.A., 1987. *Property, Power, and Public Choice. An inquiry into law and economics*. New York: Praeger.

Sjöstrand, S.E. (1995). Towards a Theory of Institutional Change. In Groenewegen, J., C. Pitelis and S.-E. Sjöstrand (Eds.), *On Economic Institutions. Theory and Application* (pp. 19–44). Aldershot: Edward Elgar.

Trainor, S.F. (2006). Realms of value: Conflicting natural resource values and incommensurability. *Environmental Values*, 15(1), 3–29.

Vatn, A. (2015a). *Environmental Governance. Institutions, Policies and Action*. Cheltenham: Edward Elgar.

Vatn, A. (2015b). Markets in Environmental Governance. From Theory to Practice. *Ecological Economics*, 117(September), 225–233.

Veblen, T. (1899). *The Theory of the Leisure Class: An Economic Study of Institutions*. New York: MacMillan.

Williamson, O.E. (1985). *The Economic Institutions of Capitalism*. New York: Free Press.

Williamson, O.E. (2000). The new institutional economics: Taking stock/looking ahead. *Journal of Economic Literature*, 38(3), 595–613.

4

POLITICAL ECOLOGY AND UNEQUAL EXCHANGE

Alf Hornborg

Introduction[1]

Political ecology comprises a wide range of research across the social sciences, but a shared foundational conviction is that obstacles to sustainable human–environmental relations arise from societal power structures. It takes the interfusion of natural and social science perspectives for granted. Political ecology frequently applies transdisciplinary approaches to empirical case studies of human ecology investigating the politics and local details of human–environmental relations in a particular geographical area.[2] As will be shown in this chapter, the approach also helps clarify the currently mystified relations between economies, energy flows and technological progress. The emphasis here, true to the heterodox concerns of political ecology, is on the function of these mystifications as components of a discourse on sustainability that ultimately obscures capitalist power relations.

In the next section I sketch the origins of political ecology, its relations to cultural ecology and their common roots in Marxist thought. This raises issues over the relative importance attributed to biophysical versus social factors in human affairs. I then turn to an historical analysis of trade and exchange that highlights the material and moral aspects missing from modern economic thought. The role of money in facilitating unequal exchange is explained and the need to fundamentally redesign the operation of money is highlighted.

Cultural versus political ecology

Political ecology refers to a genre of research on human–environmental relations that is permeated by a critical, basically Marxian, perspective on the relation between social and ecological systems [see also Chapter 15]. It emerged in the 1970s and 1980s amongst anthropologists and geographers who were dissatisfied with the functionalist assumptions of cultural ecology, which in the 1960s focused on case studies of traditional subsistence practices in local communities as adaptations to the non-human environment. Pioneers of political ecology, such as Eric Wolf and Piers Blaikie, rejected functionalism and instead emphasised the role of power inequalities and global political economy in shaping human–environmental relations, demonstrating how the local resource flows studied by cultural ecology were connected to the asymmetric metabolic flows of the world-system. The focus on power, inequalities, and conflict, rather than adaptation and consensus, defines political ecology as clearly heterodox in relation to mainstream economic approaches. There is thus significant overlap between the concerns of political ecology and ecological economics, not only in terms of the transdisciplinary nature of their concerns, but generally also in terms of their critical outlook on the rationale and prospects of global development (M'Gonigle, 1999) and their commitment to social justice (Martinez-Alier, 2002).

The aspiration to integrate social and ecological phenomena within a common theoretical framework appears to involve a choice between a primarily consensus- versus conflict-based approach. This polarity strongly echoes the perspectives and arguments present in the tension between cultural and political ecology in the 1970s. The division has recently been revived in the opposition between political ecology and resilience theory (Hornborg, 2013a; Watts, 2015). The two central keywords in this polarity continue to be power versus adaptation. Although the explanatory potential of power relations overwhelmingly surpasses that of adaptation (cf. Hornborg et al., 2012), resilience theorists bluntly ignore the contributions of political ecology even when professing to consider them (Peterson, 2000).

The recurrent pitfall of transdisciplinary approaches attempting to integrate the social and ecological—or the cultural and material—is to assume that the latter is somehow causally primary. Perhaps because ecology and the laws of thermodynamics predate human society and culture by billions of years, the physical conditions of human existence are often understood (by cultural ecologists and resilience theorists alike) to exert a directly formative influence on the organisation of human societies. In view of the fact that political ecology is explicitly Marxian in orientation (McCarthy et al., 2015: 621), it is ironic that the cultural ecology of anthropologists like Julian Steward and Leslie White, and even more conspicuously the cultural materialism of Marvin Harris, was inspired by Karl Marx's propositions regarding the determination of society's superstructure by its material infrastructure. Much of the debate between adaptationists and political ecologists thus seems to be conducted within a binary field ultimately defined by the analytical framework outlined by Marx.

The adaptationists, who tend to lean towards natural sciences like systems ecology, seem unable to perceive social systems as sources of autonomous structural incentives that are detrimental to sustainability and need to be confronted. Much classical Marxian thought, on the other hand, has dismissed the causal power of ecological constraints and instead asserted the freedom of social structures and productive forces to develop according to their own trajectories. This Nature–Society dualism continues to generate misleading propositions which both political ecology and ecological economics struggle to transcend. The challenge for a post-dualist study of human ecology is to grant material aspects due significance without attributing a general causal priority to them.

The fact that both cultural and political ecology are able to refer to passages from Marx clearly illustrates the difficulties that he must have had in dealing with the dualist matrix which was so prevalent in his time. The primary objection of political to cultural ecology concerns the latter's contention that specific social and cultural forms have been shaped, or even determined, by a given ecological setting. To be sure, the physical environment has constrained various aspects of culture in traditional societies (e.g., pre-modern Inuit were unlikely to be vegetarians!), but sociopolitical processes leading to highly stratified, complex polities engaged in long-distance trade have emerged in a variety of ecological habitats, from the desert coast of Peru to the tropical rainforest of the Mexican Gulf Coast (just to mention some New World examples). Social processes may obviously be propelled by structural forces which cannot be reduced to ecological circumstances. Political ecologists, who tend to lean towards social sciences like anthropology, geography and sociology, are inclined to look towards social structures rather than environmental conditions for explanations of particular forms of human–environmental relations.

This does not mean, however, that political ecologists are unaware of the various ways in which the non-human, material environment constrains and impinges on social processes. They view the biophysical environment not simply as either a determinant or material outcome of such processes, but as inextricably intertwined with, and implicated in, them. Transcending the binary of Nature versus Society cannot mean completely dissolving the analytical boundary between these categories, but ought rather to mean acknowledging how economic and political processes are necessarily and simultaneously also ecological. For instance, the emergence of modern industrial society was contingent on global economic and political as well as ecological circumstances, and its present and future transformations similarly depend on ecology as well as economics and politics. The environmental history of the Industrial Revolution thus deserves to be reconceived as historical political ecology (Hornborg, 2007, 2013b; Davis, 2015; Barca and Bridge, 2015). The Industrial Revolution illustrates that the relationship between social and ecological processes is recursive or, as Marxists would say, dialectical [see also Chapter 2]. Economic and political structures are contingent on, transform, and are transformed by particular constellations of ecological circumstances.

In addition to the irony of their common roots in Marxian materialism, the tension between cultural and political ecology is paradoxical with regard to their different approaches to energy. Whereas the cultural ecology of the 1960s had viewed energy flows as central to its understanding of local human–environmental relations, political ecology in the 1980s reduced energy to merely one of several kinds of resources prone to conflict between different social interests (Huber, 2015). This abandonment of the centrality of energy is unfortunate, because the organisation and implications of energy flows should be central to political ecology (Hornborg, 2013b; Huber, 2015). Once again, in confronting cultural ecology, political ecology's references to Marx seem to illuminate an ambiguity in the Marxian framework. Although Marx and Engels were not persuaded by Sergei Podolinsky's proposal in 1880 that the theory of surplus value could be phrased in terms of energy (Martinez-Alier, 1987), and although the eco-Marxists John Bellamy Foster and Paul Burkett (2008) have consistently defended Engels's dismissal of Podolinsky as an energy reductionist, there are reasons to believe that what Marx actually had in mind, in his deliberations on the exploitation of labour, was actually something akin to energy. Even Foster and Burkett attribute a thermodynamic foundation to Marx's theory of surplus value, and Foster has recently endorsed the 'embodied energy' framework of Podolinsky's intellectual heir Howard Odum (Foster and Holleman, 2014). What Podolinsky recognised was that Marx's notion that economic value derives from the material agency of labour suggests an intuitive understanding of the role of thermodynamics in economic processes. I argue that energy is the common denominator of the various kinds of unequal exchange and asymmetric resource transfers that have been prerequisite to successive modes of capital accumulation throughout history. Conceived as material infrastructure, the accumulation, maintenance and reproduction of capital is as contingent on a net appropriation of energy as any biological system.

The history of unequal exchange: materiality and morality

Capitalism is a term generally applied to a particular economic system inaugurated in Europe no earlier than the sixteenth century, but some theorists have dismissed such an historical discontinuity and instead attempted to trace processes of global capital accumulation several millennia back in time. In this latter view, the crucial modern discontinuity was the shift to fossil fuels in late eighteenth-century Britain (e.g., Pomeranz, 2000). From this perspective, the deliberations of classical political economists, such as David Ricardo and Marx, can be understood as reflections not on a completely new mode of production, but on the new kind of society generated by steam power. Capital accumulation had been pervasive in stratified societies for millennia preceding the Industrial Revolution, but steam-driven technologies were the particular form of capital analysed by Marx. Preindustrial forms of capital included farmland, livestock, roads, canals, armies, ships, and architecture. They, too, were material infrastructures that could be accumulated through the appropriation of labour-power and natural resources, and whose expansion in turn contributed to further such appropriation.

The dependence of technology on asymmetric resource flows can be illustrated by considering the emergence of steam power in late eighteenth-century Britain. The material metabolism of steam-driven textile factories in early industrial Britain hinged on the inexpensive labour employed in the American cotton fields and British coal mines, and the inexpensive land available for the American cotton plantations. The world market prices of raw cotton versus cotton textiles in 1850 ensured that a British factory owner, who sold cotton cloth and bought raw cotton for the same sum of money, made a net gain in terms of invested labour time and, more dramatically, in terms of utilised space. Technological progress can be reconceptualised as the saving or liberation of human time and natural space in core regions of the world-system, at the expense of time and space lost in the periphery. I have called this time-space appropriation (Hornborg, 2013b).

A conventional economic analysis would only discern the flows of money, but by considering biophysical metrics such as embodied labour and land, we can identify asymmetric flows of resources obscured by the apparent reciprocity of market prices. Asymmetric flows of embodied labour time in modern economies have been revealed by economists working in the Marxian tradition (e.g., Emmanuel, 1972; cf. Simas et al., 2015), whereas the asymmetric flows of embodied land indicate that there is also an ecologically unequal exchange. Recent research has shown that core regions of the modern world-system—the United States of America, the European Union, and Japan—are all net importers of embodied energy and materials (Lenzen et al., 2012, 2013) as well as embodied space (Yu et al., 2013).

The rise of modern economic thought

The net gains in embodied labour and land, which for the past two centuries have been the prerequisite for core expansion, have implied a net loss of such resources for other parts of the world-system. Economics has obscured such material asymmetries and their moral implications by simultaneously excluding concerns with the material substance of traded commodities and concerns with morality. This view of world trade as neither material nor moral was promoted through the nineteenth-century marginalist revolution that established neoclassical economics. It dismissed earlier concerns of political economy with embodied labour and land, and continues to dominate the discipline and support economic policy prescriptions today. Considering how its preoccupation with market equilibrium systematically obscures the sources and mechanisms of global power and inequalities, it is a paradigmatic illustration of an ideology.

The simultaneous detachment of economics from concerns with materiality and morality is epitomised by the meaninglessness, in the eyes of neoclassical economists, of the notion of unequal exchange. Although the concept is sometimes used to denote market power, such as monopoly, the theoretical framework of mainstream economics does not conceive of the occurrence of unequal exchange as defined here; that is, as an asymmetric flow of energy and other material resources contributing to growing inequalities. Neoclassical economic theory is exclusively concerned with market prices and monetary metrics. Unless market actors are deemed to have exerted (monopoly or oligopoly) power in setting market prices, market transactions are by definition fair or, at least, morally neutral. The mutual agreement signified by a given exchange rate obviates any additional concerns with reciprocity.

This premise of modern economics is at odds with the outlook of earlier schools of economic thought that had emphasised material aspects of commodity trade. These included the mercantilists' focus on precious metals, the Physiocrats' preoccupation with embodied land, and the classical economists' concern with embodied labour. These schools all based their moral evaluations of trade on the material substance of the commodities exchanged. Neoclassical economics abandoned such concerns in favour of an exclusive focus on market equilibrium, and was left with no other criterion for morally evaluating trade than the extent to which it gave market mechanisms free reign. Thus, the incontrovertibly asymmetric global flows of embodied labour, land, energy, and materials remain outside the mainstream economists' field of vision.

Political ecology shows how economics must necessarily deal with morality. There can be no pretence that the rates at which humans exchange their labour and other resources on the market are automatically liberated from concerns for justice. The economists' preoccupation with money has entailed an illusory delegation of moral regulation to the mindless cybernetics of the market. Countering this requires analysis of the very idea of money.

The role of money

The capacity to use money tokens to represent exchange relations, and to anchor expanding social structures to such extra-somatic artefacts, is uniquely human. For millennia, different kinds of money tokens have been used to concretise and regulate various transmutations of social reciprocity and indebtedness. Like other sign systems, however, the management of money tokens has tended to become a game of its own, with rules continuously rewritten. The human makers of money have become subservient to the logic of their artefacts. This reification of interpersonal relations, and the concomitant inversion of power between human subjects and their money objects, has been deplored for two and a half millennia. Aristotle called it 'chrematistics'. St. Paul asserted that the love of money was the root of all evil. Thomas Aquinas proclaimed that greed was a cardinal sin. Marx aptly coined the concept of money fetishism. Meanwhile, another strain of thought progressively embraced the reification of human exchange. In the seventeenth and eighteenth centuries, philosophers such as Mandeville asserted that commerce was preferable to passions, paving the way for Adam Smith's *The Wealth of Nations*. Stripped of its concern with labour value, Smith's celebration of unconstrained market exchange remains foundational for modern economics.

This growing appreciation of commerce and accumulation since the early modern period reflects the increasing significance of money in the European merchant states of the time. In contrast to the largely agrarian societies of medieval Europe, the Genoese, Dutch and British trading empires thrived primarily through the accumulation of money profits. Whereas agrarian societies were predominantly focused on harvesting solar energy through crops, livestock and the labour of humans and draft animals, mercantile societies shifted focus to the management of money. Although modern concepts of energy did not appear until the mid-nineteenth century, humans have no doubt always been intuitively aware of the vital significance of the Sun and what we know as photosynthesis. The growing preoccupation with money did not represent a liberation from these vital flows of energy, but a new strategy for gaining access to them through purchasing power. The money accumulating in Europe provided access to vast solar derived resources on other continents, including farmland, forests, livestock, game, fish and, not least, human labour. Money can be viewed as a kind of fictive energy, in the sense that it is imagined as a vital flow that nourishes society.

The modern trade system

During the period of late eighteenth-century merchant capitalism, textile manufacturers in Britain adopted steam power. Engineering was a necessary condition for this development, but not a sufficient one. The technological breakthrough represented by James Watt's steam engine would neither have occurred nor have proven useful if there had not been great global demand for inexpensive cotton cloth among West African slave traders and American slave owners. Slavery, slave plantations and the triangular trade between Europe, Africa and America were the foundation for the Industrial Revolution—creating demand for products, providing cheap labour for harvesting raw materials and offering the plantation as a template for the organisation of industrial production. Industrial technology was contingent on processes in the eighteenth-century world-system.

As the resource flows provisioning a machine are contingent on market exchange rates, we must conclude that the existence of a given technological infrastructure is contingent on the relative market prices of labour and other resources. To locally replace the expenditure of labour time with technologies requiring inputs of imported resources and labour time expended somewhere else, is feasible only when wage differences between the two areas make it economically rational to do so. Globalised technologies are products of arbitrage. This is the logic behind contemporary exports to Europe and North America of various kinds of electrical equipment manufactured in China. Similar ratios between differently priced resources apply to the utilisation of space.

After Britain repealed its protectionist Corn Laws in 1846, the increasing imports of grain to England reflected lower production costs, including land rents and wages, in Prussia and North America, compared to those of England. To assert that the relatively low wages and land rents of nineteenth-century Prussia and twenty-first-century China offer these countries a comparative advantage in world trade, as would any follower of Ricardo, is a euphemism for other countries taking advantage of their poverty and relatively lax environmental legislation. Since the days of Ricardo, the language of free trade has promoted the displacement of both work and environmental loads to less affluent sectors of the world-system. It continues to justify increasing polarisation and deepening inequalities. The mainstream denunciation of protectionism implies a dismissal of any policy to encourage self-sufficiency, reduce vulnerability, and restrain global transports. Given its implicit endorsement of asymmetric resource flows and economic polarisation, the concept of globalisation ultimately represents a less offensive way of talking about imperialism. In the context of current concerns with climate change [see Chapter 42], we should add that this same neoliberal worldview simultaneously promotes some of the most important sources of greenhouse gas emissions, such as industrial agriculture, deforestation, and global transports of bulk goods.

The nineteenth-century British shift to fossil fuels as a source of mechanical energy fundamentally transformed the conditions of economic rationality. It relaxed the ancient imperative to extract energy—firewood and fodder for draft animals—from the surface of the landscape and generally reduced the significance attributed to land as a factor of production. Ricardo concluded that the three factors of production (land, labour and capital) were substitutable, so that, for example, a British shortage of land could be compensated for by an abundance of capital. This observation was based on the experience of the Industrial Revolution, but it did not raise any concerns regarding the global implications of locally substituting capital for land. As the repeal of the Corn Laws illustrated, the appropriation, through trade, of the products of other nations' land, is tantamount to environmental load displacement. The ecological relief which fossil fuels and imports of grain, timber, cotton, sugar, and other colonial produce granted to Britain represented a geographical space several times the total land area of Great Britain (Pomeranz, 2000). Industrialisation can thus be seen as a strategy for appropriating eco-productive space elsewhere in the world-system, and modern calculations of ecological footprints confirm that the same strategy has continued to be fundamental to economic growth and technological progress in core countries for over two hundred years.

Neoclassical economics abandoned all considerations of the substance of trade in favour of an exclusive concern with abstract exchange value, or utility. Although the concept of utility in late nineteenth-century economics may have been inspired by the concept of energy in physics (Mirowski, 1989), it paradoxically represents a definitive dismissal of material factors in the determination of market prices. This mainstream detachment from material considerations is precisely what heterodox approaches, such as ecological and Marxian economics, tend to criticise. Both schools have proposed that the exchange values which preoccupy neoclassical economists do injustice to the intrinsic values of commodities exchanged on the market. Marxian economists phrase this discrepancy in terms of the difference between exchange value and use value, where the former is the market price of goods and services and the latter is conceived as their real material properties, such as the underpaid productive potential of labour power. Many ecological economists similarly refer to underpaid natural values conceived, for instance, as ecosystem services or embodied energy. This convergence has generated similar approaches to the issue of unequal exchange, which in both schools has been theorised in terms of underpayment of real material values (Lonergan, 1988; Foster and Holleman, 2014).

At first sight, such a definition of unequal exchange may seem indistinguishable from the identification of asymmetric resource flows outlined above, but the difference is important. Positing the existence of material 'values' that are unrecognised by market actors is theoretically untenable. Economic values are determined by humans based on their preferences and assets. The material resources that are asymmetrically exchanged on the market should be conceptualised precisely as material resources, rather than as values. Regardless of whether it derives from human labour, draft animals or fossil fuels, energy is not a value. Notions of underpaid material use values and natural values confuse the physical and the economic. The inclination of some ecological economists to equate energy and value has been as misleading as the Marxian distinction between them has been ambiguous and contradictory. The struggles of Marxian and ecological economics to conceptualise how market exchange orchestrates asymmetric material transfers is based on a valid intuition about the interaction of money and energy, but the assertion that labour power and other forms of energy represent underpaid values is analytically flawed. The significance of asymmetric transfers of material resources is not that they represent underpaid values, but that they contribute to the physical expansion of productive infrastructure at the receiving end. The accumulation of such technological infrastructure may yield an expanding output of economic value, but this is not equivalent to saying that the resources that are embodied in infrastructure have an objective value in excess of their price. This objection to the ambiguous conceptualisation of unequal exchange in Marxian and ecological economics is necessary in order to encourage an analytically rigorous, transdisciplinary argument with a solid grounding in both physics and economics.

Future directions

A central challenge for future research in political ecology, and in ecological economics, is to establish an analytically precise definition, grounded in thermodynamics, of concepts such as unequal exchange, appropriation and exploitation. This simultaneously implies reconceptualising technological progress as a process of capital accumulation that is contingent on such unequal exchange. An implication of this understanding of technology as contingent on ecologically unequal exchange is that we have reasons to be sceptical towards proposals for solving problems of sustainability that are founded on expectations of technological progress. Technological utopianism is an integral part of the modern worldview that accompanied the Industrial Revolution. To address the root of sustainability problems, a political ecology approach must instead acknowledge the destructive consequences of modern money.

Concluding remarks

Money is what has made unequal market exchange, impoverishment and technological overdevelopment possible. In making everything that humans desire commensurable and interchangeable, money automatically encourages the exchange of industrial commodities for increasing quantities of the natural resources that were used to produce them. The world market rewards an accelerating dissipation of resources by providing access to ever more resources to dissipate. The conundrum we need to address is what policy implications can be drawn from Nicholas Georgescu-Roegen's (1971) recognition that economic processes simultaneously increase utility and entropy, i.e. monetary profits and material disorder.

Once we grasp the systematic discrepancy between the accumulation of money and the dissipation of matter and energy, the immediate response tends to be to propose some way of counteracting the transdisciplinary logic of Georgescu-Roegen's observation by better aligning money and energy. Such intuitively justifiable proposals have challenged neoclassical economics since its inception (Martinez-Alier, 1987). However, to tie tokens of human exchange relations to energy would be as futile as to peg them to a gold standard. Human sign systems and thermodynamics follow completely different trajectories. Economics cannot be reduced to physics. Rather than try to make money reflect material reality, we should aspire to make it safeguard everybody's material needs. A complementary currency could theoretically be designed so as to insulate localised flows of necessities, and the integrity and resilience of communities as well as ecosystems, from the globalised arenas of financial speculation. Whether our priority is to avoid global financial crises or catastrophic climate change, we shall have to fundamentally redesign the operation of money.

Notes

1   This chapter contains some previously published material from "Conclusions: Money, Technology, and Magic", in Hornborg (2016).
2   Editor's Note: Social ecological economics [Chapter 1] is an interdisciplinary approach which overlaps with concerns of political ecology and a strong (as opposed to weak) transdisciplinary approach involving public engagement in knowledge creation (Spash, 2013), something which is also found in post-normal science [Chapter 28].

Key further readings cited

Hornborg, A. (2007). Environmental History as Political Ecology. In A. Hornborg, J. R. McNeill and J. Martinez-Alier (Eds.), *Rethinking Environmental History: World-System History and Global Environmental Change* (pp. 1–24). Lanham: AltaMira Press.
Hornborg, A. (2013a). Revelations of resilience: From the ideological disarmament of disaster to the revolutionary implications of (P)anarchy. *Resilience: International Policies, Practices and Discourses* 1(2): 116–129.

Hornborg, A. (2013b). *Global Ecology and Unequal Exchange: Fetishism in a Zero-Sum World*. Revised paperback edition. London: Routledge.

Hornborg, A., Clark, B. and Hermele, K. (2012). *Ecology and Power: Struggles over Land and Material Resources in the Past, Present, and Future*. London: Routledge.

Other literature cited

Barca, S. and Bridge, G. (2015). Industrialization and environmental change. In T. Perreault, G. Bridge and J. McCarthy (Eds.), *The Routledge Handbook of Political Ecology* (pp. 366–377). London: Routledge.

Davis, D. K. (2015). Historical approaches to political ecology. In T. Perreault, G. Bridge and J. McCarthy (Eds.), *The Routledge Handbook of Political Ecology* (pp. 263–275). London: Routledge.

Emmanuel, A. (1972). *Unequal Exchange: A Study of the Imperialism of Trade*. New York: Monthly Review Press.

Foster, J.B. and Burkett, P. (2008). Classical Marxism and the second law of thermodynamics: Marx/Engels, the heat death of the universe hypothesis, and the origins of ecological economics. *Organization & Environment* 21(1), 3–37.

Foster, J. B. and Holleman, H. (2014). The theory of unequal ecological exchange: A Marx-Odum dialectic. *The Journal of Peasant Studies* 41(2), 199–233.

Georgescu-Roegen, N. (1971). *The Entropy Law and the Economic Process*. Cambridge, Mass.: Harvard University Press.

Hornborg, A. (2016). *Global Magic: Technologies of Appropriation from Ancient Rome to Wall Street*. Basingstoke: Palgrave Macmillan.

Huber, M. (2015). Energy and social power: From political ecology to the ecology of politics in T. Perreault, G. Bridge and J. McCarthy (Eds.), *The Routledge Handbook of Political Ecology* (pp. 481–492). London: Routledge.

Lenzen, M., K. Kanemoto, D. Moran and A. Geschke (2012). Mapping the structure of the world economy. *Environmental Science & Technology* 46(15), 8374–8381.

Lenzen, M., D. Moran, K. Kanemoto and A. Geschke (2013). Building Eora: A global multi-regional input-output database at high country and sector resolution. *Economic Systems Research* 25(1), 20–49.

Lonergan, S.C. (1988). Theory and measurement of unequal exchange: A comparison between a Marxist approach and an energy theory of value. *Ecological Modeling* 41, 127–145.

Martinez-Alier, J. (1987). *Ecological Economics: Energy, Environment and Society*. Oxford: Blackwell.

Martinez-Alier, J. (2002). *The Environmentalism of the Poor: A Study of Ecological Conflicts and Evaluation*. Cheltenham: Edward Elgar.

McCarthy, J., T. Perreault and G. Bridge (2015). Editors' conclusion. In T. Perreault, G. Bridge and J. McCarthy (Eds.), *The Routledge Handbook of Political Ecology* (pp. 620–629). London: Routledge.

M'Gonigle, R.M. (1999). Ecological economics and political ecology: Towards a necessary synthesis. *Ecological Economics* 28, 11–26.

Mirowski, P. (1989). *More Heat than Light: Economics as Social Physics, Physics as Nature's Economics*. New York: Cambridge University Press.

Peterson, G. (2000). Political ecology and ecological resilience: An integration of human and ecological dynamics. *Ecological Economics* 35, 323–336.

Pomeranz, K. (2000). *The Great Divergence: China, Europe, and the Making of the Modern World Economy*. Princeton: Princeton University Press.

Simas, M., R. Wood and E. Hertwich (2015). Labor embodied in trade: The role of labor and energy productivity and implications for greenhouse gas emissions. *Journal of Industrial Ecology* 19(3), 343–356.

Spash, C.L. (2013). The shallow or the deep ecological economics movement? *Ecological Economics*, 93 (September), 351–362.

Watts, M.J. (2015). Now and then: The origins of political ecology and the rebirth of adaptation as a form of thought, in T. Perreault, G. Bridge and J. McCarthy (Eds.), *The Routledge Handbook of Political Ecology* (pp. 19–50). London: Routledge.

Yu, Y., K. Feng, and K. Hubacek (2013). Tele-connecting local consumption to global land use. *Global Environmental Change* 23(5), 1178–1186.

5

ECOFEMINISM

Ariel Salleh

Introduction

Ecological feminism is sometimes understood as a subset of social ecology. This is true in as much as ecofeminism addresses the interaction of social and natural processes. However, it would be false to suggest that ecofeminism derives from social ecology, or from deep ecology, or eco-Marxism [Chapter 6]. Ecological feminism is *sui generis*; its first premise being that society–nature relations in the dominant global economy are fundamentally sex-gendered in both material and ideological senses. In this respect, ecofeminism takes a methodological quantum leap beyond other political frameworks. Ecofeminism is also distinct from liberal and socialist feminisms, since these perspectives focus rather uncritically on the pursuit of equality. Ecofeminists are not looking for an equal slice of a toxic pie. Attention to the positive and negative implications of sex-gender difference is prioritised by ecofeminists, before attending to an equality that simply reinforces Eurocentric masculinist values as the universal norm. Likewise, respect for the principle of difference as cultural autonomy joins ecofeminism and postcolonial concerns. Further, the framing of liberal and socialist feminisms has been anthropocentric, whereas ecofeminism is oriented towards *oikos* and the interconnection of all life on Earth.

Historically and geopolitically, men's control of women's embodied fertility has been an economic imperative. Accordingly ecofeminism reflects women's experiences of everyday care-giving labour. More generally, however, when work involves the reproduction of living cycles, whether in the metabolism of nature-at-large or in human bodies-as-nature, people—men or women—readily learn how sustainability and justice fit together. Care-giving means facilitating living metabolic transfers using complex skills and a precautionary ethic. For those exposed to this empirical vantage point, social and ecological crises are clearly linked to competitive sex-gendered attitudes, embedded in and reinforced by the political economy of international institutions. While patriarchal domination has a ten-thousand-year history, capitalist modernisation does little to rectify it.

Past research issues and methods

Ideological dualism

Ecofeminism emerged as both a political movement and a critical discourse about four decades ago, but the literature is now so vast that only a small selection can be sampled here. While ecofeminist insights are shared by women across the globe, there have been regional differences in formulation. In Germany, for example, Mies (1986) offered a materialist analysis and even anticipated the imperial mode of living construct now emergent in social ecological economics [Chapter 15]. By contrast, ecofeminism in the United States of America (USA) has tended to rely on the tools of cultural analysis. As Griffin (1978) noted, since ancient times the identification of one sex-gender with public citizenship, and the other sex-gender with nature, diminished women. Conventionally, the patriarchal 'othering' hierarchy extended from women downwards to children, and on to animals, plants, air, water, rocks and indigenes, each being objectified as a resource by this practice. Powerfully energised by the Eurocentric masculine consciousness, sex-gender domination has served as the linchpin for a complex of political oppressions. This is why ecofeminism is simultaneously a feminist and an ecological politics. Charkiewicz (2009) has traced the genealogy of women's juridico-political subjection from classical Greece to Chicago School economics. Federici (2004) has observed how under mercantilism the multiple regenerative labours of women and black slaves were indispensable to capital accumulation. Meanwhile, the use of witch-hunts to force the enclosure of women's food growing lands is still rife in parts of Africa.

In the history of European colonial expansion, sexual and racialised metaphors were used interchangeably by ruling elites: just as women were described as closer to nature and unclean, so were natives; and the exotic oriental man was said to be feminine. Over the centuries, the naturalising dualism of sex-gender ideology has justified the social marginality and economic resourcing of so-called lesser others at serious cost to all life on Earth. In challenging this naturalisation as a crude rationale for domination and exploitation, ecofeminists have deconstructed patriarchal fundamentalisms from Islam to neoliberalism. Merchant (1980) teased out the masculinist character of European Enlightenment science and mechanistic medicine. In studies of Indian subsistence models, Shiva (1989) has contrasted sustainable local indigenous provisioning with the devastation wrought by agricultural technology in the name of the Green Revolution.

Today women across ethnicities supply about two-thirds of global gross domestic product (GDP) without remuneration. They make up three-quarters of the world's poor and own 1 per cent of the world's property. Table 5.1 (from Mellor, 2009: 253) reveals this sex-gendered structuration operating as two parallel paradigms, an individualistic monetised economy (ME), and a non-monetised relational economy (WE). The latter materially maintains the former, yet is regarded as a sphere of natural activity, not economic activity. The same category mistake can be observed in Marx's economic thinking and contemporary eco-socialist models [Chapter 6]. While liberal and socialist feminists read the above discrepancy quantitatively as a failure of the principle of equality, ecofeminists attend to both its distributive justice aspect and its qualitative potential for a future society-wide transvaluation and adoption of WE values. The respective logics of productivist ME versus regenerative or reproductive WE thought styles are amplified in the following discussion.

Table 5.1 The ME and WE dichotomy

ME high value	WE low value
Economic 'Man'	Women's work
Market value	Subsistence
Personal wealth	Social reciprocity
Labour/intellect	Body, emotions
Skills/tradeable knowledge	Feelings, wisdom
Able-bodied workers	Sick, needy, old, young
Exploitable resources	Eco-systems, wild nature
Unlimited consumption	Sufficiency

Source: adapted from Mellor (2009: 253)

Relations of reproduction

Understanding how the intimately embodied masculinist psychology of othering and dualism is sublimated, displaced, enacted, and institutionalised, is integral to explaining social relations in the mainstream productivist economy. The fact that society–nature relations are historically sex-gendered necessitates a critical reassessment of all disciplinary terms. Burkett (2006), an eco-Marxist theorist, is quite right to point out that too many economists treat the market as a black box, failing to unpack the core relations of production that turn nature into exchange value. However, Marxists have their own black box regarding how core relations of production are reliant on a labour surplus generated by sex-gender exploitation in the care-giving domestic sphere. In counterpoint to the critique of relations of production, ecofeminists emphasise living organic relations of reproduction and demand a thorough-going embodied materialism (Salleh, 1997).

The material process by which human bodies take matter–energy from nature, digest, and give back in return is known as the humanity–nature metabolism. Foster (2000), following Marx, argues that the global environmental crisis issues from the fact that capitalist industrialisation and the rise of cities created a metabolic rift in this thermodynamic reciprocity. That said, most Marxist accounts fall short of an integrated social ecology. Their interest is limited to the waged industrial worker generating a surplus for the entrepreneur but not receiving back in wages a monetary value equal to the time he or she puts into making the commodity. Contained by the classic dualism of humanity versus nature, this focus on surplus value emphasises a social debt owed by one class to another. An ecofeminist embodied materialist lens, on the other hand, makes clear that there is also a thermodynamic extraction from the body of the worker. The labour theory of value downplays that reproductive dimension, just as it under-theorises the theft of value from nature-at-large.

An embodied materialist ecofeminism argues that in addition to use values, generation of a metabolic value form (Salleh, 2010; Odih, 2014) should be acknowledged by Marxist and other economists. The generation of a surplus, capitalist exchange value, implicitly relies on the creation of use values in a conventionally sex-gendered domestic reproductive sector. In the global North, this labour of domestic care-givers is also attuned to protection of natural metabolic cycles, embodied ones. Likewise, the labour of peasants or gatherers in the Global South demonstrates a good interactive fit between human needs and biological growth (Via Campesina, 2007). These culturally diverse workers share a distinct set of economic skills in a society–nature co-evolution that is simultaneously material, epistemological, and ethical. The non-monetised regenerative activities of this hitherto nameless meta-industrial class—

care-givers, peasants, indigenes—are entirely necessary for everyday life and for the global economy to function (Salleh, 1997). However, the unique rationality of this labour is a capacity for provisioning in eco-sufficiency, without the entropy of social, embodied or ecological debt.

Embodied debt

This analysis of relations of reproduction is a reminder of why both the biological sexuality and the cultural gendering of people's bodies remains structurally relevant to economics, even as men begin to share housework, and even as lesbian, gay, bisexual and transgender emancipation becomes a reality for many others. For the greater majority of women in the global system of accumulation, sex-gender violence, bodily intimidation and psychological harassment are variously applied to ensure their labour compliance. Materially speaking, a further extraction or embodied debt occurs as women reproduce the capitalist labour force without compensation for their own lost opportunity costs. For instance, Spitzner (2009), reporting on climate research for the European Parliament, shows most cars are owned by men whose daily usage is a simple trip between home and work. By contrast, most women as society's unpaid child-caring multi-taskers are found scrambling from here to there on public transport. The net effect is that while women save ecosystem energies by this enforced, albeit sound, choice, it adds to their own energetic exhaustion and time poverty. Embodied debt takes multiple forms. It is registered each time a Brazilian woman carries water uphill to the favela, and so-called 'development' does not necessarily put an end to it. Thus, as mechanisation of fisheries in Kerala profits village men, women lose access to customary food supplies.

Consumption economies risk poverty far more than does locally autonomous prosumption.[1] Moreover, modernising programmes for land registration, bank loans and structural adjustment bring serious sociological disruption to sex-gender relations. Even in Australia, now facing neoliberal austerity measures, alcoholism and domestic violence result in a statistical average of two wife murders per week. Other sources of embodied debt are the collateral health impacts of technologies like atmospheric electromagnetic radiation or glyphosate pesticide in water. These typical productivist cost-shifting exercises (Kapp, 1978) are routinely left for unwaged care-givers to manage. Recall the isolation and stress of native Marshall Islander grandmothers nursing children through cancers, after the USA tested its nuclear arsenal on their community lands. The sex-gender blindness of capitalist patriarchal policy makers knows no bounds. Consider how the conservation zones established in Costa Rica under the United Nations Framework Convention on Climate Change (UNFCCC) displace forest dwelling families, driving women into urban prostitution for economic survival (Isla, 2015).

While both ecological economic and Marxist notions of exploitation may discuss an unequal exchange in monetary or energetic terms, the ecofeminist reference to embodied debt emphasises a direct physiological appropriation of human energy and well-being. Some ecological economists may object to this as a moral reading of an analysis that is the proper purview of physics and economics [Chapter 4]. An ecofeminist response will suggest that such a judgement lacks critical reflexivity on the tacit masculinist and Eurocentric interests that frame the conceptual development of disciplines like physics and economics.

Meta-industrial labour

In relation to the unequal exchange of humanly embodied debt, ecofeminists describe women's domestic labour contribution to the economy as an input of biological time. Under existing conditions, liberal feminists emphasise that women are personally disadvantaged and marginalised by the fact that the timing of reproductive labour tasks is slower than the speed of capitalist time. This is because the cyclic logic of regenerative care-giving work is about preserving, not interrupting, the flow of natural cycles. Ecofeminists observe that this is precisely the epistemological basis for shifting gears from immanent economic concerns to transcendent political critique. So too, whether in traditional subsistence farming or postmodern permaculture communes, life-regenerative, reproductive meta-industrial labour standing outside of productivism may appear to be achieving little, while in fact, it realises the highest goal of balancing economic provisioning with ecological sustainability.

In the time-consuming daily negotiation of material livelihood, reproductive workers already apply what economists abstract as complexity, multi-criteria valuation, and intergenerational modelling. The labour of mothers especially, replaces risk by precaution, uses a synergistic approach to balancing livelihood resources with needs and redefines development by health and sustainability. This embodied materialism speaks to an epistemology fully grounded in society–nature interactions, but its status as a meta-industrial economy remains subliminal—unrecognised in theory and policy alike. Instead, governments and multilateral agencies introduce aberrations, such as mainstreaming, which save them from having to deal with the specific needs of biologically and socially reproductive labour. Waring's (1987) global analysis of the wageless domestic sector entails a thorough critique of the sex-gender relationships that causes incoherencies in standard accounting practices. Her cost-benefit analysis of mother's milk poses a major challenge to a capitalist patriarchal economics based on the categorical dissociation of humanity from nature.

Current assessment of major issues

Commodification

The above attention to relations of reproduction tests conventional approaches to valuation. From a sex-gendered perspective, there appears to be an unconscious slippage in the discussion of value between abstract symbolic monetised exchange value, that leaves environmental effects ultimately unknown, and the grounded thermodynamic process of enhancing metabolic value (Salleh, 2010). The former dictates international decision-making, but the unitary abstraction of money is incommensurable with ecosystem flows [Chapter 12]. Thus, ecofeminists reject the commodification of nature as an object of sale and speculation. However, the global establishment of governments, business, and UN agencies, newly aware of the purifying action of sun, soil bacteria, streams and plants, now gives living organic processes a market price under the term 'payment for ecosystem services' (PES) [Chapter 43]. The trend to commodification escalated after the 1992 UN Earth Summit, and the corporate promise of a Green bio-economy would become central to the 2012 Rio+20 agenda. Likewise, negotiations of the UNFCCC have been tailored to monetised market solutions like carbon emissions trading.

A related capitalist innovation is the Clean Development Mechanism, wherein the world's affluent polluters induce indebted countries to offer up their forests as carbon sinks (Spash, 2010). However, women activists in Ecuador have turned the physicist's ideology of Earth as an equilibrium system into an historical diagnosis of a social system in disequilibrium. A 500-year long appropriation of minerals, timber and seed has left the global North far more in debt to the South than vice versa. If a notional monetary value is imputed for extractivism and consequent metabolic degradation of the landscape, the ecological debt to former colonies far exceeds unpaid World Bank loans (Bravo and Donoso, 2003). Pharmaceutical patents on indigenous genetic knowledge are described as another facet of ecological debt owed to the geopolitical periphery. Beyond this, once mined and priced by capital, an emptied-out notional nature enters the digital circuits of financial speculation and hedging.

Techno-policy

The political interests of ecofeminist thinkers and activists range across neoliberal capital, militarism, corporate science, worker alienation, reproductive technologies, sex tourism, child molestation, neo-colonialism, mining, nuclear weapons, land and water grabs, deforestation, animal liberation, genetic engineering, climate change and the mythology of progress. Growth is intrinsic to the linear crash-through logic of capitalist accumulation; but the escalation of false needs through advertising or optimistic ecological modernist emphasis on efficiency in manufacture fails to address that dynamic. SERI (2006) cite differential rates of consumption between global North and South as 10 to 1, respectively. So there is no doubt that an eco-sufficiency policy would require very sharp reductions in industrial resource use, or degrowth, in the words of D'Alisa et al. (2014) [see also Chapter 44]. However then, a sociological problem occurs in that even a cautious sustainability science will threaten factory workers and professionals whose livelihoods are reliant on productivism. Similarly, if politicians identify with the rhetoric of international trade, academics identify with the dissociated methodologies of instrumental reason. The tools of that top-down managerialism are mathematical formulae based on: input–output models, material flow analysis, complex systems, probability distributions, decision theory, ecological services, Green accounting, millennium assessments, risk monitoring and uncertainty reduction. Malthusian population arguments persist in some quarters as well, serving as a surrogate for unexamined sex-gender or race bias.

When materially embodied, libidinally charged, sex-gendered attitudes go unexamined, they lead philosophers, political theorists and economists into essentialised thinking. Discussing differences with respect to regional consumption, and communicating that through the ecological footprint indicator (Wackernagel and Rees, 1996), seems easy. However, if the measure is applied in a sex-gender-literate way, it will demonstrate the markedly lower ecological footprint of women compared to men. In the context of global warming, the climate crisis is sex-gendered in causes, effects, solutions and policies. Yet governments, multilateral agencies and mainstream environmentalists, treat women as equally culpable for climate change. On the contrary, as the majority of world poor, they may live without electricity, with few acquisitions and no money for energy expensive cars and pastimes. Even in the global North, women's spending goes mostly into shared necessities and weekly perishables.

The nature accounting of Hawken et al. (1999) exemplifies an economics unconscious of the materially embodied social relations that make it possible. In a related vein, Costanza (2007), assuming that governments can be trusted to be independent of the corporate sector, selects politically appointed trusts to manage resources as a commons. His managed commons would include what he calls "assets", such as the atmosphere, water, airwaves, social networks and cultures. This commodifying technocratic vision collides headlong with the emancipatory meaning of autonomous people's commoning [Chapter 38], as exemplified in the Global South, where earth, air, fire, water, plant and animal life are still freely shared (Esteva and Prakash, 1998; De Angelis, 2003). The natural capital school does not acknowledge that valuation by linear indices is epistemologically reductive of biocomplexity, and so readily imposes violence on fragile web-like matter-energy transfers in nature. Conversely, the economic practices of meta-industrial labour—care-givers, peasants, indigenes—are hands-on and precautionary, empirically grounded and honed by consequential feedback loops.

Future directions

The preferred masculinist response to the global environmental crisis employs high-tech innovation, claiming to be both environmentally dematerialising and economically efficient. However, the productivist optimisation of material and energy throughput rarely factors in all relevant operations—mining, smelting, transport, waste disposal—let alone the costs of humanly embodied and ecosystemic debt. When these moments are fully researched, ecological modernist expectations of sustainability are shown to be unrealisable (York and Rosa, 2003). At this point, ecofeminists call for professional capacity building, North and South. That said, a number of ecological economists have remarked on the social contradictions of globalisation, and, indeed, Norgaard's (1994) assessment of modernity is that it is in shambles. Others whose thinking draws economics closer to a social ecology in the generic sense include: Max-Neef et al. (1991), Latouche (1993), Martinez-Alier and Gha (1997) and Gowdy (1998). Marxist economists like Altvater (1998) have also helped historicise a relatively unreflexive discipline.

So can humans satisfy material and cultural needs without the ravages of ecological and humanly embodied debt? Under existing capitalist patriarchal relations of production, the answer is surely "No!", because the commodification and quantification of living habitat is intrinsically destructive. Ecofeminists who identify the capitalist system as an expression of competitive masculinity refuse the scientific reductionism of high-tech problem solving in favour of synergistic and prefigurative solutions. In prioritising relations of reproduction, ecofeminists try to put economics back on its feet, offering a transcendent critique, as opposed to the immanent critique that simply band-aids failures within the existing system. Against academic convention, an embodied materialist lens bridges the dualism of economy and ecology by highlighting the unspoken contribution of meta-industrial labour. Table 5.2 (adapted from Salleh, 2010: 210–12) sets out features of: (i) the ecological economy, (ii) the productivist economy, and (iii) the subliminal reproductive or meta-industrial economy that mediates the other two.

This real life triangulation exposes the false ideological dualism of valued ME and non-valued WE economies. The consequence of blindness to the meta-industrial labour class is externalisation—downwardly cost-shifting entropy and debt to care-giving women, peasants, indigenous peoples; in short, squandering the living metabolic value. Will a new generation of textbooks now make this unique subliminal paradigm visible?

Table 5.2 The subliminal economy

	Mode of regeneration	*Mode of production*	*Mode of reproduction*
Actors	soils, water, plants, animals	entrepreneurs, wage labour	meta-industrials, domestic, peasant, indigenous
Aims	thermodynamic continuity	accumulation, power, structural reform	well-being, sufficiency, cultural autonomy
Logic	relational, cyclic energy flows, biocomplexity	reductionist, linear, stock focus	relational, cyclic energy flows, biocomplexity
Benefit	metabolic value	exchange value	use value, metabolic value
Cost	nil	entropy × 3 • exploitation of workers' surplus • exhaustion of domestic/peasant labour • degradation of natural metabolism	nil

Source: adapted from Salleh (2010: 210–212)

Concluding remarks

Ecofeminists reject the linear logic of consumerism and energy wasting free trade, favouring a cyclic economy, locally engaged in permanent regeneration of the humanity–nature metabolism. However, if simplicity and eco-sufficiency is second nature to meta-industrial provisioning, it is rarely found in the master discourse. Yet, there is a precedent for deep structural critique, judging from the 2007 International Society for Ecological Economics (ISEE) conference in New Delhi. As Chiesura (2007) reported the event: McNeill was asking colleagues to draw on history, so as to think in a more concrete and grounded way. Vatn talked about sociopolitical embeddedness of the economy and the need for more inclusive, integrative institutions [Chapter 3]. Chopra recommended the focus on technological efficiency be replaced by an entirely new development paradigm. Haberl was demanding radical qualitative change, and McGlade challenged the profession to speak to people's everyday lives. However, no ISEE plenary speaker conceded the fundamentally sex-gendered character of their disciplinary constructs, methods and problems.

Ecofeminist arguments are based on materialist claims, not on an identity politics. On the one hand, they are about socially constructed institutions, discourses, norms and practices and, on the other, an epistemology grounded experientially in meta-industrial labour. Individuals who benefit from the present social ecological status quo are often reluctant to accept the veracity of this new class analysis. Although, certainly, politically aware men have supported ecofeminist standpoints in journals like *Environmental Ethics* or *Capitalism Nature Socialism*. These advocates of change already have fluency in techniques of ideology critique, sex-gender literacy and personal reflexivity.

The global majority of women as care-givers have been historically positioned as labour, right at the ontological point where humanity and nature interact; so, too, are men and women nominally outside of capital, such as small farmers and forest dwellers in postcolonial regions. Unlike factory or clerical workers, these culturally diverse groupings oversee biological flows and sustain matter–energy exchanges in nature. The entire thermodynamic machinery of global capital rests on material transactions mediated by the labour of this unspoken meta-industrial class. An embodied debt is accrued when their sex-gendered and racialised efforts are ignored. Conversely, the unique rationality of meta-industrial labour is a capacity for economic provisioning without the entropy of social, embodied or ecological debt.

Moreover, these life-affirming agents of co-evolving complexity model alternatives to capitalism. Researchers, political leaders and movement activists—including social ecologists—need to learn from women, peasants and indigenes to see how sustainability and justice can fit together. This is not an argument for regenerative labour to be waged, nor for monetising nature's metabolic functions as services. Commodifying moves, such as these, give false validation to a failing international system. If life on Earth has a future, it inheres in the commitment of affluent nations to degrowth, debt cancellation and redirection of military spending into the social reproduction of life. Along with post-development scholars, ecofeminists seek bioregional autonomy, common land rights and people's sovereignty over land, food, water and energy. The interlinked notions of embodied debt, meta-industrial labour and regenerative eco-sufficiency, will be strategic categories in transitioning away from modernist patriarchal illusions of control.

Note

1   Editor's Note: Prosumption is a term for the simultaneous act of production and consumption by the final user. It is used variously by ecofeminists to cover anything from non-capitalist livelihood economies in the Global South to do-it-yourself eco-sufficiency in the global North.

Key further readings cited

Mellor, M. (2009). Ecofeminist Political Economy and the Politics of Money. In A. Salleh (ed.), *Eco-Sufficiency & Global Justice: Women Write Political Ecology* (pp. 251–267). London: Pluto Press.

Mies, M. (1986). *Patriarchy and Accumulation on a World Scale*. London: Zed Books.

Salleh, A. (1997). *Ecofeminism as Politics: Nature, Marx, and the Postmodern*. London: Zed.

Salleh, A. (2010). From Metabolic Rift to "Metabolic Value": Reflections on Environmental Sociology and the Alternative Globalization Movement. *Organization & Environment*, 23(2), 205–219.

Shiva, V. (1989). *Staying Alive: Women, Ecology, and Development*. London: Zed Books.

Other literature cited

Altvater, E. (1998). Global Order and Nature. In R. Keil et al. (eds.), *Political Ecology: Global and Local* (pp. 19–44). London: Routledge.

Bravo, E. and Donoso, A. (2003). Ecological Debt. *Accion Ecologia*. Ecuador.

Burkett, P. (2006). *Marxism and Ecological Economics*. Leiden: Brill.

Charkiewicz, E. (2009). Who is the He, of He Who Decides in Economic Discourse? In A. Salleh (ed.), *Eco-Sufficiency & Global Justice: Women Write Political Ecology* (pp. 66–86). London: Pluto Press.

Chiesura, A. (2007). Ecological Economics for What? *International Society of Ecological Economics Newsletter*, January.

Costanza, R. (2007) Review of Peter Barnes' Capitalism 3.0. *Nature*, 446, 613–614.

D'Alisa, G., Demaria, F. and Kallis, G. (eds.) (2014). *Degrowth: A Vocabulary for a New Era*. London: Routledge.

De Angelis, M. (2003). Neoliberal Governance, Reproduction and Accumulation. *The Commoner*, 7, 1–26.

Esteva, G. and Prakash, M. S. (1998). *Grassroots Postmodernism*. London: Zed Books.

Federici, S. (2004). *Caliban and the Witch: Women, the Body, and Primitive Accumulation*. New York: Autonomedia.

Foster, J.B. (2000) *Marx's Ecology*. New York: Monthly Review.

Gowdy, J. (ed.). (1998). *Limited Wants, Unlimited Needs*. Washington, DC: Island Press.

Griffin, S. (1978). *Woman and Nature: The Roaring Inside Her*. New York: Harper.

Hawken, P., Lovins, A. and Lovins, H. (1999). *Natural Capitalism: Creating the Next Industrial Revolution*. London: Little Brown.

Isla, A. (2015). *The Greening of Costa Rica*. Toronto: University of Toronto Press.

Kapp, K.W. (1978). *The Social Costs of Business Enterprise* (3rd edition). Nottingham: Spokesman.

Latouche, S. (1993). *In the Wake of the Affluent Society*. London: Zed Books.

Martinez-Alier, J. and Guha, R. (1997). *Varieties of Environmentalism*. London: Earthscan.

Max-Neef, M., Elizalde, A. and Hopenhayn, M. (1991). *Human Scale Development*. New York: Apex.

Merchant, C. (1980). *The Death of Nature: Women, Ecology, and the Scientific Revolution*. New York: Harper.

Norgaard, R. (1994). *Development Betrayed*. New York: Routledge.

Odih, P. (2014). *Watersheds in Marxist Ecofeminism*. Cambridge: Cambridge Scholars Publishing.

SERI (2006). *Environment and Innovation*. Report by the Sustainable Europe Research Institute, UN University, and Finland Futures Research Centre, Vienna.

Spash, C.L. (2010). The Brave New World of Carbon Trading, *New Political Economy*, 15(2): 169–195.

Spitzner, M. (2009). How Global Warming is Gendered: A View from the EU. In A. Salleh (ed.), *Eco-Sufficiency & Global Justice: Women Write Political Ecology* (pp. 218–229). London: Pluto Press.

Via Campesina. (2007). Small Scale Sustainable Farmers are Cooling Down the Earth. 5 November.

Wackernagel, M. and Rees, W. (1996). *Our Ecological Footprint: Reducing Human Impact on the Earth*. Gabriola Island, BC: New Society.

Waring, M. (1987). *Counting for Nothing*. Sydney: Allen & Unwin.

York, R. and Rosa, E. (2003). Key Challenges to Ecological Modernization Theory, *Organization & Environment*, 16(2), 273–288.

6

ECOLOGICAL MARXISM AND ECOLOGICAL ECONOMICS

From misunderstanding to meaningful dialogue

Ali Douai

Introduction

Ecological dimensions of Karl Marx's thought have recently generated vigorous debates about their meaning, adequacy and relevance. The nexus between ecological Marxism (EM) and ecological economics (EE) has largely fuelled these debates. Since the late 1980s, both schools have developed as diverse and fragmented movements. Undoubtedly, their respective evolution has been influenced by the gradual changes in their relations. Although dealing with the same general object of study—human relations with Nature—EM–EE's relationships have shifted from antagonism to a growing recognition of the need for a meaningful dialogue. Burkett (2006: 6), for example, wants to demonstrate that "Marxist class analysis can help answer many of the questions raised by ecological economists, [and] at the same time that the substantive agenda of ecological economics can enrich the materialist dimension of Marxism". Spash and Ryan (2012: 1097–8) stress that "there certainly seems more to unite than divide those concerned about the impacts […] from the current economic system" and that "[s]ynthesising neo-Marxism and ecological economics can be seen as following up with theory the call for a Red-Green alliance".

This chapter has two main purposes. First, to provide an overview of past controversies and debates about Marx's ecological thought in the context of EE's development, as well as of current topics that stimulate the discussion between EM and EE. Second, to argue for a balanced assessment of Marx's legacy. This assessment should depart from, on the one hand, the typical 'Green view' that accuses Marxism of productivism and affirms that Marx had no conception either of Nature or of the finite character of resources (Tanuro, 2010), and on the other, the claim that there is a ready-to-use "Marx's ecology" or that ecology is at the heart of Marxism (see Foster and Burkett, 2004). What is not to be missed in such an evaluation is "the concept of societal relations of human to nature" founded on the basic categories of Marx's critique of political economy, and which "can be used for a better understanding of contemporary ecological problems" (Altvater, 2004: 2). Equally central is the idea that "the radical [Marxist] critique of commodity production is indispensable for understanding the environmental crisis as a crisis of the relationship between humanity and nature, and thus as a social crisis" (Tanuro, 2010: 92). This would allow overcoming "a sterile opposition between a traditional Marxist critique of social relations severed from human relations with nature and a simplistic ecological critique of human relations with nature that makes no reference to the social relations within which humanity pursues its project of domesticating nature" (Harribey, 2008: 191).

In chapter I of *Capital*, Marx (1976: 133–4) stated:

> Labour […], as the creator of use-values […] is a condition of human existence which is independent of all forms of society; it is an eternal necessity which mediates the metabolism between man and nature, and therefore human life itself.
>
> Use-values like coat, linen, etc., in short, the bodies of commodities, are combinations of two elements, the material provided by nature, and labour. […] When man engages in production, he can only proceed as nature does herself, i.e. he can only change the form of the materials. Furthermore, even in this work of modification he is constantly helped by natural forces. Labour is therefore not the only source of material wealth, i.e. of the use-values he produces. As William Petty says, labour is the father of material wealth, the earth is its mother.

This quotation encapsulates the key issues that have framed debates about Marx's and Marxists' conception of Nature (Schmidt, 1971). Soddy (the 1921 Nobel Prize winner in chemistry and an important forerunner of EE) "was an admirer of Marx—arguing that it was a common error to think that Marx saw the source of all wealth as human labour" (Foster and Clark, 2009: 12). He also followed Marx (and Aristotle) in distinguishing between "oikonomia (dealing with the use values delivered by the material provisioning of the human economy) and chrematistics (as the study of market prices)" (Martinez-Alier, 2007: 228). However, proto and modern ecological economists have argued that Marx and Engels did not consider the relationships between their conceptual framework and a biophysical approach to the economy, as they could have done in their work after the 1850s. Moreover, Soddy commented that Marx's "disciples […] forgot all about the mother" (quoted in Martinez-Alier and Schlupmann, 1987: 134), and, as a result, "the development of a Marxist ecological economics was delayed for well over a century" (Harriss-White, 2012: 102).

From an EM's perspective, Marx's concept of "social metabolism" lays the foundations for the formulation of a "naturalistic materialism" (Harribey, 2008), and allows us to "penetrate the economy-nature relation much more thoroughly than most of even the more critical approaches to ecological economics" (Altvater, 2007: 61). *Man–Nature metabolism*, on the one hand, follows quasi-eternal laws of Nature and, on the other hand, is ruled by the dynamics of the capitalist social formation. From this conceptualisation arises the relevance of the Marxian category of *the double character of labour and production*, namely: (i) the labour process in general that leads to the production of use-values; (ii) the labour process particular to capitalism that leads to the production of economic value for the sake of capital accumulation. According to Benton (1989), the principle of an ecological critique of capitalism is already, at least implicitly, contained in this distinction. It underpins a *structural contradiction* between capital and Nature that adds to the contradiction between capital and labour. This is termed "a metabolic rift" between society and Nature.

The three points in italics will be elaborated in the next section. This is followed by coverage of controversial issues in EE—(in)commensurability of values [Chapter 22] and wealth measurement in monetary terms—in relation to Marx's theory of value, and the underlying concepts of wealth, commodity, economic value and money. Finally, the state of the art in EM will be shown to have created the conditions for a meaningful EE–EM dialogue on at least three issues: environmental governance in a neoliberal era; capitalism and degrowth; the theory of unequal ecological exchange.

Metabolism, labour and the ecological contradiction of capitalism

Metabolism: society in Nature

As early as the 1840s Marx's writing shows that he understood the "metabolic character" of natural transformations performed by human labour. Labour is the universal condition for "metabolic interaction", or the process of "material exchanges" between humanity and Nature, in which Nature is used as a resource and a sink for the satisfaction of human needs that are socially produced. Altvater (2007) emphasises that this metabolism is central to the making of human history; transformations of Nature are transformations of society and of man. Furthermore, the natural conditions of the labour process are transformed by labour as it simultaneously causes productive and destructive effects. Inspired by the work of the agro-chemist Liebig (amongst others), Marx understood that capitalist social relations in agriculture and urbanisation interrupt nutrient cycling and result in fertility loss. Part Four of Volume I of *Capital* ends with these words (Marx, 1976: 638):

> all progress in capitalist agriculture is a progress in the art, not only of robbing the worker, but of robbing the soil. [...] Capitalist production, therefore, only develops the techniques and the degree of combination of the social process of production by simultaneously undermining the original sources of all wealth—the soil and the worker.

The substitution, in agriculture, of natural cycles and their time-space regimes by industrial cycles and their time-space regimes, along with the separation of town and country, provoked an "irreparable rift" in social metabolism (Altvater, 2004).

Martinez-Alier (2007: 224) claims that, though Marx/Engels were interested in energy, "in his published work Marx did not refer to the flow of energy as metabolism". A break of Marx/Engels from accepting the second law of thermodynamics (namely entropy [Chapter 9]) is illustrated by Engels's negative comments on Podolinsky's work of 1880 on agricultural energetics, which was, according to Martinez-Alier and Schlupmann (1987: xviii), "a missed chance for an ecological Marxism". Foster and Burkett (2004, 2008) radically challenge this view. They argue that Engels did not criticise the entropy law itself but its extrapolation into a "heat death theory of the universe". The authors also affirm that Marx/Engels did not abruptly reject Podolinsky's attempt to combine a labour theory of value with an energy theory of value. Their critique was directed against his "energy reductionism", though others argue that there is far more to Podolinsky's work than this (Harribey, 2008). Burkett (2006: 183) asserts that "Marx applies metabolic-energy categories quite literally to human production, not as a mere analogy", while Hornborg (2015: 190–1) responds that "it is counter-productive to try to cover up for [Marx's] analytical shortcomings through selective exegesis". Yet, Tanuro (2010: 93) insists that Marx/Engels did not grasp, at a global level, the economic and ecological consequences of the shift from a renewable (wood) to a non-renewable (coal) fuel. For him, if Marx/Engels had done so, "[their] brilliant concept of 'human metabolism' would have led [them] to foresee the energy impasse into which capitalism was to drag humanity".

The double character of labour

At the start of *Capital*, Marx distinguished between the labour process in general, as an anthropological dimension of social life, and the process of capitalist production, as an historical phenomenon that produces economic value for capital. This distinction is related to the double character of the commodity (which is conceived as "the cell-form" of the capitalist society): use-value and exchange-value. As objects with use-value, commodities are incommensurable [see Chapter 22]. As objects with exchange-value, two commodities are necessarily made commensurable by reducing them to something they have in common, namely the labour used to produce them. However, these concrete or private labours are qualitatively different. What commodities have in common, and what will count in the exchange relation, is the "expenditure of human labour-power" (Marx, 1976: 134):

> the useful character of the kinds of labour embodied in them [...] disappears; this in turn entails the disappearance of the different concrete forms of labour. They can no longer be distinguished, but are all together reduced to the same kind of labour, human labour in the abstract.
>
> (Marx, 1976: 128)

Abstract labour is what is common to all commodities, and is the substance of a purely social phenomenon—economic value—exchange-value being only its form of appearance. Contrary to the physical objectivity of commodities as use-values, the being of commodities as economic value is a purely social and immaterial objectivity that commodities only acquire insofar as they are crystallizations of the same social substance, i.e., abstract labour.

In the latter case, the production of use-values ceases to be an end in itself and is merely a means for economic value as the end. Therefore, the possibility exists that real social needs will not be satisfied and that social "counter-utilities" will be generated by a mode of production focused on profit (Harribey, 2008). The use-value produced by concrete labour is the result of the transformation of matter and energy. It is an integral part of the human–Nature metabolism. The economic value produced by abstract labour is nothing else than an immaterial social relation in capitalism, although the production and exchange of commodities has a material and energetic quality. For Altvater (2007: 58), "the category of the double character of labour, production, and the commodity [...] is of utmost importance (Marx called it the 'Springpunkt'), because it bridges the rift between society and Nature, between the openness of social practice and hard natural laws".

The ecological contradiction of capitalism

James O'Connor (1988) has proposed the foundation of an "ecological Marxism" by grafting onto the traditional Marxist crisis theory a "second contradiction of capitalism" based on a Polanyian analysis of the conditions of production. He locates this contradiction in the antagonistic relationship between the forces and relations of production and the conditions of production (particularly external Nature). The contradiction lies in capital's tendency to destroy, rather than reproduce, its own conditions of production, thus leading to a crisis of underproduction, which threatens profits and the reproduction of capital. Interestingly, O'Connor (1988: 37) emphasises that social conflicts about these conditions "are more than class issues" and links to Martinez-Alier's concept of the environmentalism of the poor [see Chapter 16].

Altvater (2004), Burkett (2006) and Harribey (2008), among others, have criticised this approach on two grounds. The first relates to the category of underproduction. This category is functionalist and requires the possibility of reproducibility of the natural/external conditions of production, whereas, in Nature, all processes are characterised by irreversibility. The second sees this framework as less powerful than the basic Marxian categories because it tends to artificially separate both kinds of exploitation that characterises capitalism. As Harribey (2008: 195) states, the characterisation of the ecological contradiction as external is "a retreat from the materialist postulate of the necessary integration of capitalist production into the natural environment". Since "without the exploitation of nature, exploitation of labour would have no material support; and without the exploitation of labour, exploitation of nature could not have been extended and generalised", both contradictions are to be considered as internal to capitalism and from this the conclusion follows that the social and ecological crisis cannot be separated.

In contrast, Altvater (2004) draws on the laws of thermodynamics to locate an ecological contradiction of capitalism in the double character of the capitalist labour process, i.e., that commodity production is simultaneously the quantitative transformation of economic value and the qualitative transformation of materials and energy. As a result, there is an inherent tension between the expansionary requirements of capitalist growth and the necessary increase in entropy. For Burkett (2006: 171–172), capitalism experiences two types of intertwined crises. First is the crises of capital accumulation. Second is "the crisis in the quality of natural wealth as a condition of human development" because, in Marx's dialectical view, ecological and social costs of economic value accumulation are endogenous to the metabolic process of human–nature reproduction in its specifically capitalist form.

Wealth and economic value: Marxian insights for (social) ecological economics

Since the late 1990s, social ecological economics (SEE) [Chapter 1] (Spash, 2011) has devoted much effort to developing a pluralist theory of environmental values and governance as an alternative to monetary valuation and to the market logic invoked by standard economic analysis. Harribey (2013), Douai (2009), Burkett (2006) and Nelson (2001) have tried to show how Marx's theory of value and the related conception of wealth can contribute to the SEE perspective. SEE has been successful in making most environmentalists suspicious about the monetary valuation of Nature and in making them sensitive to value incommensurability. This has been achieved by: (i) critically assessing the philosophical assumptions of the neoclassical theory of choice; (ii) highlighting the ethical limits of commodification [Chapter 22]; and (iii) stressing the need for discursive institutions [Chapters 3, 33, 34]. Yet, SEE has neglected to provide an alternative understanding of the concepts of commodity, economic value, money and wealth. This leads to two issues. The first is a *de facto* acceptance of neoclassical value theory, except when dealing with natural resources. The second is a weakened capacity to connect environmental conflicts with socio-historical conditions that account for both the global ecological crisis and the domination of monetary values.

In these respects, Martinez-Alier et al.'s (1998) position on neoclassical value theory is worth discussing. They state:

> We are not against giving economic value to natural resources. [...] A location may be valuable for its biodiversity [...], and have also economic value (measured by differential rent, and also by the travel cost method or contingent valuation). These are different types of value [...]. We understand and share their efforts to value environmental amenities, life-support systems, biodiversity, human lives by contingent valuation or other similar methods [...] our contention is that the environment, as also human lives or non-human species, has other values which are not commensurable in money terms.
>
> (Martinez-Alier et al., 1998: 283)

This position is logically inconsistent (unless the critique only relates to intrinsic value) and detrimental to SEE. The neoclassical concept of economic value does not aim at taking into account *just some* values or modes of valuation. Its *raison d'être* lies in its alleged ability to capture the essence of all human–Nature interactions. As Marx and Engels (1975: 410) stated in their critique of Bentham, the underlying philosophical presupposition is that "money … represents the value of all things, people and social relations", whatever the institutional context and nature of human motivations. In this perspective, Turner et al.'s (2003: 496) attempt to separate "historical, cultural, symbolic values" from the concept of total economic value is also logically inconsistent. They claim that the former may relate to a "different moral 'plane' within which there is no acceptable substitute". Yet, there are two scenarios. First, if the concept of economic value is adopted then so must be its claim of ethical neutrality because human–Nature relationships are treated as independent of cultural context. Second, if total economic value is related to a specific moral plane, then the claims for objectivity and universality must be left aside and concepts of economic value, price and money must be (re)considered as socio-historical categories, whose meaning rests on specific social relations, as Marx insisted.

The economic valuation approach is based on the rejection of the old Aristotelian distinction between use-value and exchange-value, while, as Marx argued, use-value is a necessary but not sufficient condition for exchange-value. The arbitrary identification of these two notions conveys the idea that maximum well-being can only be achieved through maximising economic value, i.e., through the commodification of the world. On the contrary, the distinction between use-value and exchange-value leads to the irreducibility of wealth to economic value and market categories. Wealth always consists of use-values and

> a thing can be a use-value without being a[n economic] value. This is the case whenever its utility to man is not mediated through labour. Air, virgin soil, natural meadows, unplanted forests, etc. fall into this category. A thing can be useful, and a product of human labour, without being a commodity. He who satisfies his own need with the product of his own labour admittedly creates use-values, but not commodities […].
>
> (Marx, 1976: 131)

Three comments are in order. First, Marx established the indifference of economic value to wealth, i.e., to natural, material and social conditions of its production. The "auto-movement" of economic value means that the concrete character, as well as the social and environmental consequences of production, are not part of the social nature of commodities. Second, Marx did not neglect the "value of Nature". Nature (considered here as the condition of production) is not producing economic value, but it has a use-value. Third, following from this argument, Nature has no intrinsic economic value (Harribey, 2013). Economic value (like its monetary form) is an expression of social relations that are exclusively specific to capitalism. These are socio-historical categories "designed to ensure [the] reproduction and expanding accumulation of a particular social power" (Nelson, 2001: 504). Hence, non-market ecological resources have no intrinsic economic value. The scope of economic value is a socio-historical matter and depends on the state of power relationships within society [see Chapter 14]. Any resource can become the "material substratum" or the "carriers" of economic value. In all other cases, the incommensurability of natural elements and ordinary commodities precludes applying the labour theory of value to natural elements. The value of Nature differs in kind from economic value and refers to ethical values. However, this does not discredit the labour theory of value, which has always had, and can only have, a scope limited to the commodity.

Future directions

Neoliberal conservation

An interdisciplinary Marxist-based approach to environmental governance focuses on neoliberal (biodiversity) conservation as "an amalgamation of *ideology* and *techniques* informed by the premise that natures can only be 'saved' through their submission to capital and its subsequent revaluation in capitalist terms" (Büscher et al., 2012: 4). It critically analyses the extent to which Nature is "conserved" in and through the expansion of capitalism, a movement driven by a "political ideology that aims to subject political, social, and ecological affairs to capitalist market dynamics" (Büscher et al., 2012: 5). This literature refers to EE as a divided field between those embracing the natural capital concept and those disapproving of instruments like PES or biodiversity offsets (see Muradian et al., 2010). It criticises the former stance on the grounds that it would conflate economic terminology with the ideology and practices of neoliberal capitalism. The SEE critical strand tends to consider neoliberal conservation as a broad and abstract category that does not pay enough attention to the wide diversity and complexity of instruments in practice. A fruitful area of dialogue and common understanding could be found by analysing neoliberal conservation practices as embedded in social, material and epistemological realms, i.e., cultural and institutional contexts that affect the political-economic architecture of individual schemes/instruments and that explain the actual deviation from the rhetoric surrounding them (Muradian et al., 2010; Büscher et al., 2012). Moreover, the conceptual research on the characteristics of economic valuation and neoliberal conservation and their social ecological implications is also a fertile ground for achieving a unified description and thus for delivering a stronger normative stance to citizens and decision-makers (Kosoy and Corbera, 2010; Burkett, 2006).

Capitalism and degrowth

Some ecological economists advocate *sustainable degrowth*—rooted in the French *décroissance* movement [see Chapter 44]. Martinez-Alier et al. (2010: 1741–3) describe this as "an equitable and democratic transition to a smaller economy with less production and consumption". Rather than an exact opposition to economic growth, it advocates a fundamental change of collective imagination against the "growth fetish". Sustainable degrowth is conceived of as potentially complementary to a steady state economy [see Chapter 45], which might be achieved after a "post-degrowth transition" (Martinez-Alier et al., 2010: 1744). Uncertainty surrounds whether the purpose is economic or physical degrowth—downsizing throughput as measured by material and energy flows. Martinez-Alier et al. (2010: 1743) claim that sustainable degrowth is centred on "the development of physical indicators and measuring well-being and sustainability", while also claiming that "by reducing the physical indicators of throughput, the magnitude of macro-level chrematistic indicators such as GDP would also be reduced".

Foster (2011: 29) argues that this concept gives rise to two questions: "Is degrowth feasible in a capitalist grow-or-die society and [...] what does this say about the transition to a new society?" Harribey (2013) and Foster (2011) both argue that this gets rid of capital accumulation as the main governing principle of our societies and introduces, instead, the concept of economic growth. Martinez-Alier et al. (2010: 1742) confusedly refer to capitalism as an ideology. EM authors reject the idea that everything at stake concerns collective imagination and stress the lack of attention given to social relations, social structures and the organisation of society. A point for discussion with EM authors is the possibility of "delink[ing] citizens' revenue from wage unemployment" (Martinez-Alier et al., 2010: 1746), since any created and distributable monetary value originates from social abstract labour. Another issue is to understand how substantial changes in energetic, transport and other systems, and thus massive investments, could be realised in a context of degrowth. Put differently, degrowth appears to be a finality rather than a transition.

Unequal ecological exchange

Hornborg [Chapter 4], Brand and Wissen [Chapter 15] and Martinez-Alier [Chapter 16] provide SEE with a significant body of work relating to exchange relations between the core and periphery of the capitalist world economy. Studies of unequal exchange seek to measure, in biophysical terms, the ecological disadvantages that have been systematically imposed on the periphery. In short, in the same way as unequal economic exchange theory postulated the exchange of more labour for less, unequal ecological exchange theory is based on the exchange of more ecological "units" for less.

A crucial theoretical and conceptual debate is ongoing on the topic. Hornborg (2014: 11) aims at conceptually grounding "'ecologically unequal exchange' without fully subscribing to the conceptual framework of Marxist economic theory". Interestingly, he endorses Georgescu-Roegen's approach to economic value—that "accepts the mainstream perception among neoclassical economists of consumer utility as equivalent to economic value" (ibid.: 13)—to support an analytical distinction between "cultural" and "material" aspects of economic processes. This distinction is seen as "more to the point" than the one between use-value and exchange-value, based on the mistaken idea that Marx's concept of use-value neglects its "cultural dimension". Foster and Holleman (2014) argue in the opposite direction. They try to show how a Marxian world-system analysis—that draws on Howard Odum's energy systems approach (termed "emergy")—can be aligned with Marx's metabolic rift analysis. Hornborg (2015: 191) insists that "unequal exchange should be identified and discussed in terms of asymmetric flows of biophysical resources, rather than in terms of asymmetric flows of 'values'", as an implication of Georgescu-Roegen's conceptualisation of the relation between economics and thermodynamics [Chapter 9]. Both contributions are worth reading because, besides the unequal ecological exchange issue, they outline key theoretical and philosophical debates that remain to be addressed between EM and EE.[1]

Concluding remarks

Marx was ambivalent with regard to the conception of Nature in his critique of political economy. He followed the signals of rational enlightenment and the related myth of progress that marked the nineteenth century. Although conscious of the ecological consequences of capitalist development, he still partially neglected them. However, there is much more in Marx than ecological intuitions. The conditions exist for a meaningful dialogue between Marxist critique of capitalism and EE's critique of productivism. Yet, two pitfalls must be avoided: (i) the naturalisation of social conditions creating an ecological approach that would deny the structural role of capital accumulation and its consequences for human–Nature relationships; (ii) the idea that traditional Marxism exhausts challenges raised by the development of modern societies.

Note

1   Editor's Note: See also the critical perspective of Salleh [Chapter 5] on the failure of EM to address sex-gender issues and her rejection of energy theories of value (a position also held by Georgescu-Roegen with specific reference to Howard Odum's ideas).

Key further readings cited

Altvater, E. (2007). A Marxist Ecological Economics. *Monthly Review*, 58(8), 54–64.

Burkett, P. (2006). *Marxism and Ecological Economics: Towards a Red and Green Political Economy*. Boston: Brill.

Harribey, J.M. (2008). Ecological Marxism or Marxian Political Ecology? In J. Bidet and S. Kouvelakis (eds.), *Critical Companion to Contemporary Marxism* (pp. 189–207). Leiden: Brill.

Tanuro, D. (2010). Marxism, Energy, and Ecology: The Moment of Truth. *Capitalism Nature Socialism*, 21(4), 89–101.

Other literature cited

Altvater, E. (2004). Is there an Ecological Marxism? In J.D. Schmidt (Ed.), *Development Studies and Political Ecology in a North-South Perspective* (pp. 2–25). Aalborg: DIR & Institute for History, International and Social Studies, Aalborg University.

Benton, T. (1989). Marxism and natural limits: An ecological critique and reconstruction, *New Left Review*, 178 (November–December), 51–86.

Büscher, B., Sullivan, S., Neves, K., Igoe, J., Brockington, D. (2012). Towards a synthesized critique of neoliberal biodiversity conservation. *Capitalism Nature Socialism*, 23(2), 4–30.

Douai, A. (2009). Value theory in ecological economics: The contribution of a political economy of wealth. *Environmental Values*, 18(3), 257–284.

Foster, J.B. (2011). Capitalism and degrowth: An impossibility theorem. *Monthly Review*, 62(8), 26–33.

Foster, J.B., Burkett, P. (2004). Ecological economics and classical Marxism: The "Podolinsky Business" reconsidered. *Organization & Environment*, 17(1), 32–60.

Foster, J.B., Burkett, P. (2008). Classical Marxism and the second law of thermodynamics: Marx/Engels, the heat death of the universe hypothesis, and the origins of ecological economics. *Organization & Environment*, 21(1), 3–37.

Foster, J.B., Clark, B. (2009). The paradox of wealth: Capitalism and ecological destruction. *Monthly Review*, 61(6): 1–19.

Foster, J.B., Holleman, H. (2014). The theory of unequal ecological exchange: A Marx-Odum dialectic. *The Journal of Peasant Studies*, 41(2), 199–233.

Harribey, J.M. (2013). *La richesse, la valeur et l'inestimable : fondements d'une critique socio-écologique de l'économie capitaliste*. Paris: LLL.

Harriss-White, B. (2012). Ecology and the environment. In B. Fine and A. Saad-Filho (Eds.), *The Elgar Companion to Marxist Economics* (pp. 102–110). Cheltenham: Edward Elgar.

Hornborg, A. (2014). Ecological economics, Marxism, and technological progress: Some explorations of the conceptual foundations of theories of ecologically unequal exchange. *Ecological Economics*, 105(September), 11–18.

Hornborg, A. (2015). Why economics needs to be distinguished from physics, and why economists need to talk to physicists: a response to Foster and Holleman. *Journal of Peasant Studies*, 42(1), 187–192.

Kosoy, N., Corbera, E. (2010). Payments for ecosystem services as commodity fetishism. *Ecological Economics*, 69(6), 1228–1236.

Martinez-Alier, J. (2007). Marxism, social metabolism, and international trade. In A. Hornborg, J. R. McNeill and J. Martinez-Alier (eds.), *Rethinking Environmental History: World-System History and Global Environmental Change* (pp. 221–238). Lanham: AltaMira Press.

Martinez-Alier, J. (with K. Schlupmann) (1987). *Ecological Economics: Energy, Environment and Society*. Oxford: Blackwell.

Martinez-Alier, J., Munda, G., O'Neill, J. (1998). Weak comparability of values as a foundation for ecological economics. *Ecological Economics*, 26(3), 277–286.

Martinez-Alier, J., Pascual, U., Vivien, F.D., Zaccai, E. (2010). Sustainable de-growth: Mapping the context, criticisms and future prospects of an emergent paradigm. *Ecological Economics*, 69(9), 1741–1747.

Marx, K. (1976). *Capital*, vol. I. London: Penguin Books.

Marx, K., and Engels F. (1975). *Collected Works*, vol. V. Moscow: Progress Publishers.

Muradian, R., Corbera, E., Pascual, U., Kosoy, N., May, P. (2010). Reconciling theory and practice: An alternative conceptual framework for understanding payments for ecosystem services. *Ecological Economics*, 69(6), 1202–1208.

Nelson, A. (2001). The poverty of money: Marxian insights for ecological economists. *Ecological Economics*, 36(3), 499–511.

O'Connor, J. (1988). The second contradiction of capitalism. *Capitalism Nature Socialism*, 1(1), 1–38.

Schmidt, A. (1971). *The Concept of Nature in Marx*. London: NLB.

Spash, C.L. (2011). Social ecological economics: Understanding the past to see the future. *American Journal of Economics and Sociology*, 70 (2): 340–375.

Spash, C.L., Ryan, A. (2012), Economic schools of thought on the environment: investigating unity and division. *Cambridge Journal of Economics*, 36(5), 1901-1121.

Turner, R.K., Paavola, J., Cooper, P., Farber, S., Jessamy, V., Georgiou, S. (2003). Valuing nature: lessons learned and future research directions. *Ecological Economics*, 46(3), 493–510.

7

POST KEYNESIAN ECONOMICS AND SUSTAINABLE DEVELOPMENT

Eric Berr

Introduction

Post Keynesian economics (PKE), as part of heterodox economics, holds presuppositions that emphasise realism, holism, reasonable rationality, production and instability instead of instrumentalism, atomism, absolute rationality, scarcity and market equilibrium. It extends and generalises the seminal ideas that were developed by John Maynard Keynes, Michal Kalecki and their heirs, notably Nicholas Kaldor and Joan Robinson. However, during the early 1970s several American economists—in particular Alfred Eichner, Edward Nell and Paul Davidson—contributed in their own way to this tradition and helped to institutionalise PKE, which can be viewed as a comprehensive alternative to the prevailing neoclassical paradigm.

Post Keynesian economists share some specificities held within the heterodox tradition that are discussed next. I then investigate why they have not focused on the environmental and sustainability until recently. I follow this by arguing that they have the tools to construct an heterodox political economy of sustainable development together with ecological economists. Although I note some divergences still need to be addressed.

What is PKE about?

PKE is distinguished by its focus on some core interrelated ideas: the principle of effective demand, causality running from investment to saving, an environment of strong uncertainty, the insistence that time is historical and irreversible and the study of a monetised production economy (Lavoie, 2014). Each of these is discussed in turn.

The principle of effective demand represents the crux of Keynes's theory of employment. That theory explains aggregate demand as the main force that determines output and employment, whether in the short or the long run. Aggregate demand is linked to one of the key elements of the "Keynesian revolution" and thus a key feature of Post Keynesianism, i.e. that investment determines savings. Neoclassical economists consider that savings drive investment. Hence, they favour policies aiming at increasing income and wealth of those that have more savings, i.e. the richest, thus fostering the financialisation of the economy. If savings govern investment, the trickle-down effect (whereby the poor benefit from general economic growth that favours the rich), which is at the basis of the Kuznets curve, is assumed to operate, and so creating economic growth is argued to result in decreasing inequality in the long run. Neoclassical economists also promote fiscal austerity policies, and a balanced budget, because they regard government deficits as being negative government savings, and this reduces the pool of national savings available for investment, thereby reducing the level of investment. By showing that investment determines savings, and by considering savings as residual, Keynes allows us to reject neoliberal policies and the social justification of great inequality of wealth.

The principle of effective demand derives from the notion of strong uncertainty that underlies all of Keynes's economic philosophy and is a forerunner of the precautionary principle (Section 4). According to Keynes, we can never be sure of the results of our actions nor even of their desirable nature. Consequently, we live in a largely non-probabilistic world where neoclassical mechanics cannot function any more. Therefore, we must reason in terms of strong uncertainty, i.e. in a world where there is no scientific basis on which to form or calculate probabilities. However, action is required and decisions may then be undertaken on the basis of expectations by allowing an agent to determine what is conventional behaviour, guided to a considerable degree by those facts about which they feel somewhat confident. This is the case argued by Keynes, even though such facts may be less decisively relevant to the issue than other facts about which our knowledge is vague and scanty (Keynes, 1936a, p. 148). Needless to say, the foundations of such a model based on conventional behaviour are not very solid and may lead rather to situations where rumour, fear, disillusion or hope—which are non-probabilistic elements—can involve a brutal and sudden revision of these expectations.

Post Keynesians consider historical time, or chronological time, which is irreversible, in contrast to the logical or abstract concept of time used by neoclassical economists, who study equilibrium while excluding the processes involved in reaching it. On the contrary, Post Keynesians underline the need to consider and describe the transition from one position to another, recognising that the conditions under which this transition occurs may affect the final position of equilibrium. Thus, history matters in the sense that the past influences subsequent outcomes.

Post Keynesian economics evolves in a monetised economy. As such, it questions relative prices and substitution effects—where consumers' and producers' choices depend on such relative prices—and favours nominal values and income effects where aggregates are more influenced by income fluctuations and technical change. As Holt and Spash (2009, p. 15) point out:

> One consequence of the primacy of income effects is that we cannot rely on the price system to get things right or lead to optimal outcomes. In the real world, prices reflect market power and current short-term perspectives only. They are also affected by speculation. Because prices do not reflect scarcity, we cannot count on prices to deal with current overutilization of resources or to protect the planet from the enhanced greenhouse effect.

If markets are not self-adjusting mechanisms, then institutions [Chapter 3] are important.

Why have Post Keynesians paid limited attention to the environment?

Post Keynesians have faced some difficulties with involving themselves in sustainable development and including environmental issues in their analysis. Davidson (2002) reminds us that ecological concern, or the economic implications of the depletion of resources, has been significantly ignored and should be included in the analysis. This failure is evident in the lack of any specific entry on sustainable development in the first edition of John King's *Elgar Companion to Post Keynesian Economics* (published in 2003) where there is only an environmental economics entry referring to a microeconomic approach. The second edition (King, 2012) rectified this omission and may indicate an overdue interest of Post Keynesians in sustainability issues.

Mearman (2005, 2007) argues that there are many reasons why Post Keynesians have said little on the environment. However, he stresses three of them. First, Post Keynesians were engaged in a struggle with the mainstream by developing a critique of neoclassical economics and by constructing their own theoretical positions. As such, the "pioneers" of Post Keynesian economics—Keynes, Kalecki, Robinson, Kaldor, and so on—worked on the main social issues of the day such as employment, growth, income distribution or money and neglected environmental issues. Second, Post Keynesians used static tools ill-equipped for analysing the environment. Davidson (1979), who is a rare example of a Post Keynesian who has engaged in environmental issues, thinks that the orthodoxy needs to be attacked on its own ground. As such, his approach to the environment—particularly his earliest works—appears to be more Marshallian than Post Keynesian as he uses a microeconomic approach and marginalist terminology. Following Davidson, most Post Keynesian economists view environmental issues as microeconomic, while the focus of their work has been on macroeconomics. According to Mearman (2005, 2007), this could explain their lack of interest in the environment. One notable exception is Lavoie (2006) who considers that environmental questions could also be studied from a macroeconomic perspective. Third, the preoccupation with growth and employment by the Post Keynesians may have made them reluctant to focus on the environment given the obvious ecological implications (Chester and Paton, 2013). Moreover, the rejection of the concept of scarcity and the emphasis put on demand and short-term analysis may lead to the denial of any ecological constraint.

Does all this mean that Post Keynesians have nothing to say and that they have no tools to tackle environment issues? Of course not, and we can find some interesting reflections from early Post Keynesian economists. For Robinson (1972), the environment is a "critical question". She adds that "the consumption of resources, including air to breathe, has evidently impoverished the world" (Robinson, 1977, p. 1336), leading her to wonder, what is growth for? As Mearman (2007) reminds us, Galbraith (1958) addresses the effects of economic activity on the environment, particularly pollution, while Georgescu-Roegen could be linked with Post Keynesian economics, as Lavoie (2006) suggests. This leads Berr (2009, 2015), Fontana and Sawyer (2013), Jespersen (2004), Holt (2005, 2009) and Mearman (2005, 2007) to claim that there are foundations. However, the task of current Post Keynesian economists is to tackle this issue and build an ecologically sustainable and socially just economy.

The potential for a Post Keynesian sustainable development

The foundations of a Post Keynesian approach on environmental and sustainability issues can be found in Keynes's own works, which give us many elements to build on. His search for beauty makes him concerned with ecological issues. Strong uncertainty leads to the precautionary principle. More generally, Post Keynesian economics seems to be compatible with eco-development and strong sustainability.

The search for beauty

Keynes was not only a famous economist, he was a lover of the Arts. As such, his social economic philosophy is marked with the search for beauty (Berr, 2009). Keynes feels that the purpose of life is to enjoy beauty, knowledge, friendship, and love, all concepts that are not primarily concerned with economics. He rejects the "classical" vision, based on Benthamite utilitarianism, which he considers to be a catastrophic change for civilisation. In his opinion, the Arts, like Nature, must be disconnected from economic considerations because "the exploitation and incidental destruction of the divine gift of the public entertainer by prostituting it to the purposes of financial gain is one of the worst crimes of present-day capitalism" (Keynes, 1936b, p. 344).

Keynes continues by denouncing the fact that the same rule of self-destructive financial calculation governs every walk of life.

> We destroy the beauty of the countryside because the unappropriated splendours of nature have no economic value. We are capable of shutting off the sun and the stars because they do not pay a dividend.... Or again, we have until recently conceived it a moral duty to ruin the tillers of the soil and destroy the age-long human traditions attendant on husbandry if we could get a loaf of bread thereby a tenth of a penny cheaper.
>
> (Keynes, 1933, p. 242)

Keynes realises that economic and financial logic are in opposition to ecological and social reasoning. He condemns environmental destructions and reacts to the disfigurement of the planet, which led him to minimise the role of economics (Keynes, 1930).

Uncertainty and the precautionary principle

Keynes's conceptualisation of uncertainty encourages a convention of behaviour based on a precautionary attitude, which allows a better understanding of how behaviour should be conducted concerning environmental questions. Indeed, numerous studies show the unsustainability of the Western model of development, of which human induced climate change is currently just the most prominent. However, if we are unsure future changes will occur in terms of being unaware of the form that they will take, then, according to Keynes, we have weak confidence. This weak confidence can prevent us from fully taking into account the associated problem. This implies that what is most important for action is not to know that changes will happen, but to believe in their eventual manifestation.

However, because ecological matters become an increasingly important component of expectations as environmental risks become more visible, we should adopt a more precautionary attitude. If we consider that we live in a world where strong uncertainty prevails, we must promote a necessary precautionary principle (Berr, 2015). This principle, which appeared for the first time in Germany at the end of the 1960s, is now widely accepted. For instance, the Rio Declaration on Environment and Development (1992), gives in its Principle No. 15 the following definition:

> In order to protect the environment, the precautionary approach shall be widely applied by States according to their capabilities. Where there are threats of serious or irreversible damage, lack of full scientific certainty shall not be used as a reason for postponing cost-effective measures to prevent environmental degradation.

This principle gave place to two antagonistic conceptions. First, a weak precautionary principle is based on cost-benefit analysis expressed as risk management. In that case, the burden of proof of the danger falls onto the opponents of a decision. Thus, this approach recognises the primacy of economic values on the basis that highlighting economic benefits is easier than calculating human and ecological costs. Second, a strong precautionary principle requires that the promoters of a potentially dangerous decision have to show the absence of serious risk. This approach states that environmental issues—and one could add social issues—prevail over economic questions. It is a vision that does not undermine the Keynesian notion of the primacy of investment but does ask questions about the investments' substance. This intimates a greater role for the State, which—notably using its law-making capabilities—can try to motivate firms to adopt an ethical stance and commit to "clean" investments. Kalecki (1964) went further by considering that the State must be both the planner and promoter of development, and, if need be, even the producer. In this view, the State has a responsibility for indicating development priorities and ensuring that needed investments take place. In turn, this implies the use of certain forms of planning.

Eco-development and strong sustainability

If we must acknowledge that a unified Post Keynesian approach that deals with a global sustainable development does not exist yet, then we can see that sustainable development, when viewed through the prism of a Post Keynesian paradigm, is comparable with eco-development. The latter has been theorized by Ignacy Sachs (1980)—once a close colleague of Kalecki at the Warsaw School of Planning and Statistics—who recognises his Kaleckian affiliation. In short, eco-development relies on three pillars (Sachs, 1980, p. 32): (i) self-reliance, which encourages autonomous decisions and the emergence of modes of alternative development encompassing the historical, cultural, and ecological contexts that are specific to each country; (ii) a fair assessment of everyone's essential material and immaterial needs, especially people's need to realise themselves through a meaningful life; and (iii) ecological prudence, or the search for a kind of development that is in harmony with Nature.

By asking that the fight against underdevelopment include limits on wealthy countries' overdevelopment and encouraging developing countries to rely on their own strengths, trust themselves, and no longer depend on rich countries, eco-development provoked great enthusiasm in the developing world. It also provoked the ire of the administration in the USA, whose reaction was to progressively marginalise eco-development and replace it with sustainable development as defined in the Brundtland report (Berr, 2015). However, two visions of sustainable development continued to vie with one another. The first was neoclassical in inspiration and served as the basis for weak sustainability. It tried, at the microeconomic level, to give monetary value to natural elements so that they could be integrated into a cost–benefit analysis. At the macroeconomic level, it extended the Solow model and tried to build theoretical models justifying an empirical argument rooted in an allegedly virtuous relationship between economic growth and environmental quality—encapsulated in the environmental Kuznets curve. It also tried to formulate a "sustainability rule", whereby the per capita value of the total stock of capital in a given society could only be maintained if one postulated perfect substitutability between the different forms of capital—physical, social, human, natural.

The second approach, which has come to form the basis of what might be called strong sustainability, is less focused on economic aspects alone and offers a more radical vision. Here, ecological sustainability postulates the preservation of a stock of critical natural capital, rejecting the principle of the substitutability of production factors and emphasising their complementarity instead. It disagrees with the monetary valuation of natural elements and tries to construct a new economy of well-being based on non-utilitarian "ethical" values and the search for new measurements of wealth. Social sustainability is grounded in the implementation of a development process that combines an acceptable level of social homogeneity, a fair distribution of incomes, and full employment with fair access to social services. Economic sustainability depends not only on a more efficient distribution and management of resources, but also on a constant flow of both public and private investments destined to modernise the productive apparatus in an attempt to save on natural resources and alleviate human distress.

Clearly, the presence of post Keynesians in the field of sustainable development, if deserved at all, can only happen in a framework of strong sustainability, which is the only one that explicitly breaks with neoclassical theory and is in phase with eco-development and what is now called social ecological economics, i.e. an heterodox interdisciplinary movement in political economy focusing on the interconnection of power with environmental and institutional arrangements (Spash, 2011; Holt and Spash, 2009).

Future directions

However, to be fully relevant on environmental and sustainability issues, Post Keynesianism has to be clear on its position as regards growth and its emphasis on demand. Indeed, the Post Keynesian focus on growth seems incompatible with social ecological economics which views growth as a potential cause of the current environmental crisis (Spash and Schandl, 2009; Spash, 2011). Likewise, the emphasis on the demand side seems to say that scarcity of resources does not exist. On both issues, the problems are not insuperable and future reconciliation can be viewed optimistically by promoting a political economy approach that is common to Post Keynesian economics and social ecological economics.

How growth may be compatible with sustainable development

The final chapter of Keynes's *General Theory* gives us the core elements of what Keynes himself calls his social philosophy. According to him, "the outstanding faults of the economic society in which we live are its failure to provide for full employment and its arbitrary and inequitable distribution of wealth and incomes" (Keynes, 1936a, pp. 372). Thus, fighting against unemployment and inequality appears to be the root of Keynes's social economic philosophy. As Spash and Schandl (2009) acknowledge, growth, for Keynes, only appears to be a means to an end, or even a result, while neoclassical economists view it as a goal in itself. Keynes and the post Keynesians would also reject degrowth as an objective *per se* because they stick to a neoclassical-based approach which claims that we cannot do anything favouring social and environmental aspects if there is no growth. What is the most important is to implement policies that improve the social conditions of the population and promote investment that avoids environmental degradation and favours full employment. In other words, the main objective is a better distribution and use of wealth, but in this case whether the result is growth or degrowth remains an open question.

If Post Keynesians do not reject growth, two questions must be answered if we want to ensure that growth does not lead to unsustainable development: (i) What is supposed to grow? (ii) How can we ensure that the wealth produced benefits the whole population fairly without damaging the environment? Thus, the question of the distribution of wealth cannot be dissociated from that of growth.

When claiming that full employment could be achieved through an increase in public expenditure in order to favour investment, regardless of what those investments are, Keynes seems to allow unsustainable paths of development. This is true even if he considers "the vital importance of establishing certain central controls in matters which are now left in the main to individual initiative" (Keynes, 1936a, pp. 377-378). After all, if full employment requires more investment and/or consumption, we must acknowledge that we are now living in a world where the ecological constraint prevails. Thus, in order to achieve sustainable paths there is an indispensable role for the State in orienting consumption and investment—even when implementing investment in Kalecki's view.

More recently, Courvisanos (2012) developed an "eco-sustainable framework"; that is, an innovation and investment policy framework for sustainable development. This framework, borrowing from Lowe and Kalecki, has three main elements that drive innovation and investment (Courvisanos, 2012, pp. 207):

1   Agreed ecological sustainable rules (or conventions), including capital investment that is resource-saving within long-term sustainable carrying capacities—a precautionary principle under strong uncertainty;
2   Perspective planning with flexible risk-adverse investment strategy—a satisficing principle under iterative strategic planning of innovation and investment;
3   Cumulative effective demand with a strong local niche market share for environmental-based goods and services—a demand-oriented stimulus and support.

In conclusion, the argument is that growth will not be the enemy of sustainable development as long as it is accompanied by a redistribution of wealth favourable to the least advantaged social classes, and also by prudent management of natural resources.

Aggregate demand in a sustainability perspective

For Holt (2009), a tension exists between Post Keynesians and sustainable development according to the role that effective demand plays in maintaining full employment in a modern, money-using, entrepreneurial economy. Indeed, the principle of effective demand highlights the fact that modern capitalist economies are marked by the coexistence of an underemployed workforce and excessive production capacities. By excluding any notion of scarcity, Keynes—and Post Keynesians in his wake—considers that both short- and long-term demand should be highlighted. An approach of this kind would appear to contradict sustainable development because, by refusing to distinguish between physical and natural capital, it intimates that the latter is also overabundant insofar as it has not been used in its entirety.

Current Post Keynesians are very aware of environmental problems. They stress intergenerational solidarity as well as the insurmountable nature of the ecological constraint. This causes Post Keynesians to reject the principle of the substitutability of production factors and to highlight a kind of complementarity that meshes well with the notion of a reasonable management of natural resources. For Post Keynesians, any actions undertaken today have effects tomorrow, not only on people but also on the biosphere.

They also observe that, with increasing living standards in developed countries, populations are less and less inclined to question a system that fights unemployment by wasting resources. Hence the need for the State, but also civil society, to get involved in redirecting the economy toward a more sustainable development path. Post Keynesians agree on the need to resort to a certain form of planning, because they want to correct market imperfections. Their approach to the environment includes targets that can be achieved via planning while focusing more closely on the social consequences of the distribution of wealth associated with this process. Consequently, Post Keynesians could follow eco-development, and social ecological economics, in seeking to modify the relationships between State, market, and civil society to the benefit of the latter. The purpose is not to abandon the market or overemphasise the role of the State. This is a framework where the planner's role is to negotiate with different parties and devise an acceptable common position. However, to be effective, planners must pay attention to the diversity of situations encountered and compile maximum information, something that assumes the largest possible participation of local populations so that their problems and needs can be identified, along with the potential of the local natural environment.

Toward a political economy of sustainable development

The possible unsustainable nature of growth and an emphasis on demand leading to the denial of any scarcity of natural resources can be easily overcome if we adopt an approach in terms of political economy. Such an approach is common to Post Keynesian economics and to any heterodox sustainable development movement, in particular eco-development and social ecological economics. This leads to the incorporation of ethical judgements, following Keynes who considers economics as a moral science.

Kalecki (1943) stresses the role of vested interest when he emphasises that the influence of economic ideas in shaping policy is severely constrained by the prevailing social and political institutions. Along these lines, an analytical grid highlighting power relationships, as formulated by Galbraith (1984) or Boulding (1989), would be very useful and help to highlight the institutional obstacles that must be overcome. The application of new ideas is far too often constrained by the fact that they may not serve the interests of those who have the power to change things. Perhaps the missing links between Post Keynesian and social ecological economics lie somewhere between Galbraith and Kapp (Spash and Schandl, 2009), and maybe something of Boulding could be added (Scott, 2009).

Undoubtedly, Post Keynesian economists provide many concepts which they perceive to be extremely relevant for "grasping the environment", such as uncertainty, institutions, path dependency, irreversibility, historical time, cumulative causation or procedural rationality (Chester and Paton, 2013, p.109). However, the synthesis of these concepts into a broadly coherent economic–environment framework has yet to be realised. By adopting a political economy approach which includes power relationships, ethical values and ideology, convergences between Post Keynesian and social ecological economics can be viewed optimistically. Vatn (2009) sees a potential for cooperation between these two traditions as ecological economics is engaged in understanding what characterises resilient systems, but mainly at the local level, while Post Keynesians tackle such issues at a macro level. The consumer choice theory of Lavoie (2009) is an outcome of such a cooperation.

Concluding remarks

Today there is no doubt that Post Keynesians have solid arguments qualifying them to enter the field of sustainable development and to participate in the preparation of models that offer an alternative to the orthodoxy. While acknowledging that a unified Post Keynesian approach on the environment does not exist yet, this chapter has shown that there is the potential for Post Keynesian economics to contribute to the advent of a heterodox political economy of sustainable development. Indeed, the interlinkage between the social and ecological dimensions of sustainable development requires radical institutional change to ensure greater fairness, whether on an intra- or intergenerational basis. Breaking with the orthodoxy is the first step. The second step is how to enter economic sustainability or, as Holt (2005, pp. 174) put it, "how you deal with unemployment and poverty today without damaging and depleting the natural resources and ecological systems needed for economic opportunities for future generations". In both regards, there is no doubt that Post Keynesian economics and social ecological economics are travelling on the same boat.

Key further readings cited

Berr, E. (2015). Sustainable development in a post Keynesian perspective: why eco-development is relevant to post Keynesian economics. *Journal of Post Keynesian Economics*, *37*(3), 459-480.
Holt, R.P.F., Pressman, S., Spash C.L. (Eds). (2009). *Post Keynesian and Ecological Economics: Confronting Environmental Issues*. Cheltenham: Edward Elgar.
Lavoie, M. (2014). *Post-Keynesian Economics: New Foundations*. Cheltenham: Edward Elgar.

Other literature cited

Berr, E. (2009). Keynes and sustainable development. *International Journal of Political Economy*, *38*(3), 22–38.
Boulding, K.E. (1989). *Three Faces of Power*. London: Sage.
Chester, L., Paton, J. (2013). The economic–environment relation: can post-Keynesians, Régulationists and Polanyians offer insights? *European Journal of Economics and Economic Policies: Intervention*, *10*(1), 106–121.
Courvisanos, J.A. (2012). *Cycles, Crises and Innovation: Path to Sustainable Development — A Kaleckian-Schumpeterian Synthesis*. Cheltenham: Edward Elgar.
Davidson, P. (1979). Natural resources. In A. S. Eichner (ed.), *A Guide to Post-Keynesian Economics* (pp. 151–164). London: Macmillan.
Davidson, P. (2002). Restating the purpose of the JPKE after 25 years. *Journal of Post Keynesian Economics*, *25*(1), 3–7.
Fontana, G., Sawyer, M. (2013). Post-Keynesian and Kaleckian thoughts on ecological macroeconomics. *European Journal of Economics and Economic Policies: Intervention*, *10*(2), 256–267.
Galbraith, J.K. (1958). *The Affluent Society*. Boston: Houghton Mifflin, 1969.
Galbraith, J.K. (1984). *The Anatomy of Power*. London: Hamish Hamilton.
Holt, R.P.F. (2005). Post-Keynesian economics and sustainable development. *International Journal of Environment, Workplace and Employment*, *1*(2), 174–186.
Holt, R.P.F. (2009). The relevance of Post-Keynesian economics to sustainable development. In P. Lawn (ed.), *Environment and Employment: A Reconciliation* (pp. 146–160). London: Routledge.
Holt, R.P.F., Spash, C.L. (2009). Post Keynesian and ecological economics: alternative perspectives on sustainability and environmental economics. In R.P.F Holt, S. Pressman & and C.L. Spash (eds.), *Post Keynesian and Ecological Economics: Confronting Environmental Issues* (pp. 3–24). Cheltenham: Edward Elgar.
Jespersen, J. (2004). Macroeconomic stability: Sustainable development and full employment. In L. A. Reisch & I. Røpke (eds.), *The Ecological Economics of Consumption* (pp. 233–249). Cheltenham: Edward Elgar.
Kalecki, M. (1943). Political aspects of full employment. In M. Kalecki (ed.) *Selected Essays on the Dynamics of the Capitalist Economy 1933–1970* (pp. 138–145). Cambridge: Cambridge University Press.
Kalecki, M. (1964). Observations on social and economic aspects of 'Intermediate Regimes'. In J. Osiatynski (ed.), (1993), *Collected Works of Michal Kalecki*, vol. 5: Developing Economies (pp. 6–12). Oxford: Clarendon Press.
Keynes, J.M. (1930). Economic possibilities for our grandchildren. In *The Collected Writings of John Maynard Keynes*, vol. 9 (pp. 321–332). London: Macmillan.
Keynes, J.M. (1933). National self-sufficiency. In *The Collected Writings of John Maynard Keynes*, vol. 21 (pp. 233–246). London: Macmillan, 1982.
Keynes, J.M. (1936a). *The General Theory of Employment, Interest and Money*. London: Macmillan. In *The Collected Writings of John Maynard Keynes*, vol. 7. London: Macmillan, 1973.
Keynes, J.M. (1936b). Art and the State. In *The Collected Writings of John Maynard Keynes*, vol. 28 (pp. 341–349). London: Macmillan.
King, J. (ed.) (2012). *The Elgar Companion to Post Keynesian Economics*, 2nd ed. Cheltenham: Edward Elgar.
Lavoie, M. (2006). *Introduction to Post-Keynesian Economics*. Basingstoke: Palgrave Macmillan.

Lavoie, M. (2009). Post Keynesian consumer choice theory and ecological economics. In R. P. F. Holt, S. Pressman & and C. L. Spash (eds.), *Post Keynesian and Ecological Economics: Confronting Environmental Issues* (pp. 141–157). Cheltenham: Edward Elgar.

Mearman, A. (2005). Why Have Post-Keynesians Had (Relatively) Little to Say on the Economics of the Environment? *International Journal of Environment, Workplace and Employment*, *1*(2), 131–154.

Mearman, A. (2007). Post Keynesian economics and the environment: waking up and smelling the coffee burning? *International Journal of Green Economics*, *1*(3/4), 374 –380.

Robinson, J. (1972). The second crisis of economic theory. *American Economic Review*, *62*(1/2), 1–10.

Robinson, J. (1977). What Are the Questions? *Journal of Economic Literature*, *15*(4), 1318–1339.

Sachs, I. (1980). *Stratégies de l'écodéveloppement*. Paris: Editions économie et humanisme, Les éditions ouvrières.

Scott, R.H. (2009). The Post Keynesian/ecological economics of Kenneth Boulding. In R. P. F. Holt, S. Pressman & and C. L. Spash (eds.), *Post Keynesian and Ecological Economics: Confronting Environmental Issues* (pp. 99–113). Cheltenham: Edward Elgar.

Spash, C.L. (2011). Social ecological economics: Understanding the past to see the future. *American Journal of Economics and Sociology*, *70*(2), 340–375.

Spash, C.L., Schandl, H. (2009). Challenges for post Keynesian growth theory: utopia meets environmental and social reality. In R.P.F Holt, S. Pressman & and C.L. Spash (eds.), *Post Keynesian and Ecological Economics: Confronting Environmental Issues* (pp. 47–76). Cheltenham: Edward Elgar.

Vatn, A. (2009). Combining Post Keynesian, ecological and institutional economics perspectives. In R. P. F. Holt, S. Pressman & and C.L. Spash (eds.), *Post Keynesian and Ecological Economics: Confronting Environmental Issues* (pp. 114–138). Cheltenham: Edward Elgar.

8
EVOLUTIONARY ECONOMICS

Karolina Safarzynska

Introduction

This chapter argues that evolutionary theorising and modelling can provide insights into debates in ecological economics. In fact, evolutionary thinking and ecological economics have ontological [Chapter 2] presuppositions in common. Both acknowledge that an economy is an open adaptive system, where complex interactions create emergent properties. In both, interactions occur at multiple timescales and across multiple levels, while the social structure cannot be inferred from the aggregation of individuals.

Guiding the economy towards sustainability requires an understanding of how behaviours, technologies and institutions coevolve together over time [see Chapter 13]. Coevolution is one of the pillars of evolutionary economics. A coevolutionary approach has also been recognised as a key framework for studying changes in complex social ecological systems, institutions and behaviours, production and consumption patterns, and sustainability transitions (Norgaard, 1984; Kallis and Norgaard, 2009). For instance, Kallis and Norgaard (2009) identify four emerging research fields of coevolutionary studies in ecological economics, namely: (i) environmental degradation and development failure in peripheral regions; (ii) the lock-in of unsustainable production/consumption patterns; (iii) the vicious cycle between human efforts to control organisms and the evolution of these organisms; and (iv) the adaptive advantages of other-regarding, cooperative behaviours and institutions.

Core evolutionary elements and mechanisms are diversity, innovations and selection. Additional building blocks include path dependence and lock-in, coevolution and bounded rationality. In evolutionary systems, changes result from progressive adaptations through selection that works at multiple levels. Competition, regulations and institutions are the main drivers of selection reducing diversity of practices and technologies. Innovation is a mechanism of variety-generation. Although innovations are intrinsically uncertain, and, for this reason, in most evolutionary economic models treated as stochastic, thinking of the process of innovation as totally random would be incorrect. Typically, innovations are preceded by the accumulation of relevant technical advances, which has been referred to in the literature as technological paradigms (Dosi et al., 1988).

Evolutionary economics offers formal tools and frameworks for the analysis of policies aimed at inducing behavioural, technological and institutional change. It provides theories that explicitly deal with novelty, social interactions, evolving preferences and habit formation on the consumer side. Individuals in evolutionary economics are socially embedded; their preferences change as a result of social interactions. They follow rules instead of optimising their choices, i.e. they are subject to bounded rationality. The notion of bounded rationality originated in the 1950s from Herbert Simon's critique of 'economic man'. Simon (1955) questioned human computational capacities and, thus, an individual's potential to make optimal choices in complex situations.

Evolutionary economic theorising and modelling allow studying possible pathways of change, as well as feedback mechanisms underlying coevolutionary dynamics. This is because evolutionary economic models account for social learning and interactions to explain the evolution of institutions and the role of endogenous innovations in economic growth and technological change. As a result, evolutionary economic models are equipped to examine possible secondary effects of implemented policies, such as behavioural and technological adjustments to policies. However, a coherent framework for policy analysis from the evolutionary economic perspective is missing. This relates to the fact that evolutionary economics is a very diverse field. There is no agreement on the canonical model of individual behaviour. As a result, how to assess wellbeing and welfare from the evolutionary economic perspective remains unclear.

This chapter is organised into the following sections: Next is a brief introduction to the field of evolutionary economics. This is followed by a discussion of models in evolutionary economics relevant to environmental policy. That leads into reflections on major issues in evolutionary economic theorising. The penultimate section discusses policy evaluation and evolution, indicating directions for future research, and the final section makes some concluding remarks.

"Why is economics not an evolutionary science?"

This was Veblen's (1898) question in laying the foundations for both critical institutional [Chapter 3] and evolutionary economics. Evolutionary economics is a very diverse field. There is no consensus regarding assumptions made about economic reality, or how to use concepts from evolutionary biology in economic theorising (Witt, 2008). In particular, evolutionary theories diverge on the basis of whether changes in nature and in economics belong to the same or different spheres of reality. A naturalistic perspective takes as a starting point that humans are an animal species. It suggests the ontological continuity between the two spheres: economy (human behaviour) and biology (human genetic endowments). Accordingly, mechanisms, under which species evolved, influence the process of the cultural evolution. This idea is rejected by a dualistic ontology. The latter ignores, or treats as irrelevant, the influences of the human genetic endowment on economic behaviour. This approach prevails, for instance, in neo-Schumpeterian models of technological change (Witt, 2008).

According to the naturalistic approach the evolutionary origins of human capabilities are important to understand modern organisations (Stoelhorst and Richerson, 2013). For instance, large-scale cooperation—essential to functioning of modern organisations and firms—has evolved as a result of cultural transmission of norms and institutions that favoured cooperation (understood as a genetic disposition). On the other hand, neo-Schumpeterian models explain economic and organisational change as a result of evolutionary forces acting on the population of firms: innovations introducing new varieties to the population and selection causing differential growth of firms. As a result, neo-Schumpeterian theories try to explain decision-making within firms without acknowledging explicitly the role of genetic endowments on functioning and the evolution of organisations.

In evolutionary economics, the economy is perceived as a complex, hierarchical structure compromising various levels and subsystems, which are linked together through strong feedback mechanisms. Variation and selection processes occurring in any of these subsystems create changes in the total environment. Evolutionary economics recognises that the economy operates far from optimum (a global attractor) and that directions of economic changes depend on the interactions of many elements that can act in parallel. The global economy as an adaptive non-linear network is a difficult subject for traditional formal modelling. Traditional economic tools are insufficient, or incapable, of dealing with the complexity of economic systems, path dependency, diversity and novelty.

Coevolutionary dynamics underlie many social economic processes. Formally, the term 'coevolution' refers to a situation in which two or more evolutionary systems or populations are linked together in such a way that each influences the evolutionary trajectory of the other(s). It is achieved through reciprocal selective pressures among the evolving populations. So far, two types of coevolutionary models have received a lot of attention in evolutionary economics: the coevolution of behaviour and social norms; and demand and supply coevolution. In the first type of models, individuals follow various heuristics or imitate others through networks. Over time, social interactions may induce a shift in preferences of individuals or cause the emergence of specific patterns of behaviours. The emergent patterns feedback onto individual behaviour, giving rise to coevolutionary dynamics between behaviours and institutions. In models of the coevolution between demand and supply, the direction of technological change depends on changing preferences of consumers, which evolve over time because of consumers' interactions (due to various network effects) and novel technologies appearing in the marketplace.

The diversity of behavioural assumptions made in evolutionary theorising is vast, and, as a result, an integrated, systematic approach to understanding individual behaviour is lacking. In fact, the concept of the individual builds loosely on stylised facts from other disciplines. Individuals are often seen as rule or habit followers. Although everyone has some intuitive understanding of the notion of habit, its precise definition varies between different disciplines. For instance, Becker (1992) defines habits as displaying a positive relation between past and current behaviour, which subsequently can be measured by the past frequency of different behaviours. He claims that habits can act as metafunctions, according to which individuals rationally choose to follow habits or to optimise their utilities. However, in light of the evidence from social psychology, habits cannot be reduced to past behavioural frequency, but are a psychological construct capturing predispositions and capacity to perform certain behaviours. Along these lines, habits in evolutionary economics can be understood as dispositions to behave.

Alternatively, individuals in evolutionary economic models can be conceptualised with utility functions, as in neoclassical economics. However, in contrast to neoclassical economics, here agents change their preferences as the result of social interactions and individual learning. The distinction is made between needs [Chapter 24], which are inherent, and thus difficult to influence, and socially constructed desires. Agents can acquire new wants by searching for opportunities to experience new consumption possibilities after the satiation of existing wants. Alternatively, the search for new consumption possibilities may be motivated by status competition. A distinction can be also made between socially constructed desires and wants formed due to deliberation. Preferences, which change under the influence of advertising or cultural norms, i.e. forces of which an agent herself is unaware, would constitute an example of socially constructed desires. Alternatively, preferences can be formed in the process of deliberation and adaptive learning over which wants individuals pursue.

Individual and social learning are important mechanisms behind changes in both habits and wants. However, functionality of habits (performance) underlies learning of new habits, while the acquisition of new wants often relies on the process of searching for pleasurable experiences. Imitation is the simplest form of learning. It can take the form of either copying 'the most successful' or 'the majority' strategy. Copying 'the most successful' is also known as prestigious bias transmission; it occurs when individuals seek to copy the most influential, knowledgeable or skilful behaviour (Henrich et al., 2001). Copying the majority strategy has been termed by Boyd and Richardson (1985) as conformist transmission. It refers to a propensity of an individual to adopt cultural traits that appear most frequently in the population.

Evolutionary economists' contributions differ with respect to formal methods, which can be classified as: evolutionary game theory, evolutionary computation and agent-based models (Safarzynska and van den Bergh, 2010). In evolutionary game theory and evolutionary computation, individuals do not change over time but a population evolves due to selective replication and variation processes. Here, individuals are carriers of simple strategies. Payoffs, associated with these strategies, determine the number of 'offspring' in the next population. Evolutionary game theory and evolutionary economics are sometimes considered as two distinct fields in the literature (Witt, 2008; Hodgson and Huang, 2012). Nelson (2001) claims this is due to evolutionary game theory being less empirically oriented than evolutionary economics and mainly serving to study the adjustment dynamics towards different equilibrium configurations.

Evolutionary economists tend to favour agent-based modelling (Hodgson and Huang, 2012). The technique allows conceptualisation of non-linear interactions among different types of heterogeneous agents. It has become increasingly popular in social science over the last 20 years. Formally, agents are defined as computational entities, characterised by some form of bounded rationality (myopia, local search). They are capable of exhibiting goal-oriented behaviour, and of interacting with other agents. Agents' interactions as well as feedback from aggregate (macro) to disaggregate (micro) phenomena can generate non-linear dynamics. Behavioural assumptions in such models are not determined by what is mathematically convenient, but are typically designed in line with insights from psychology. As a result, such models constitute great laboratories to examine macroeconomic consequences of alternative behavioural assumptions, as well as different 'what if' scenarios.

Past research and main issues

This section reviews evolutionary economic models that can offer insights into environmental policy making. This involves coverage of models in the areas of the evolution of consumer behaviour, coevolutionary demand and supply, evolution of growth and resource dynamics. The aim is not to be exhaustive but rather illustrative of models that explicitly acknowledge environmental problems.

A theory of consumer behaviour from the evolutionary economic perspective needs to deal realistically with how individuals respond to novelty (Nelson and Consoli, 2010), and account for how the evolution of wants and socially constructed desires evolve over time. Along these lines, Nelson and Consoli (2010) propose a general theory of consumer behaviour, where each household has a set of wants it intends to satisfy through purchasing specific goods and services. Wants are shaped by the cultural environment, in which a household is embedded. Following Maslow (1943), wants are hierarchical in nature, i.e. some wants must be fulfilled before others can be addressed. People learn with time and experience how to satisfy their desires, leading to the coevolution of wants and household competencies over time. The framework can be employed to study the escalation of wants beyond sustainable levels. Alternatively, Marechal (2010) argues that the notion of habits provides a good starting point for building a model of consumer behaviour to study sustainability policies. He considers habits as a form of behavioural lock-in, which drives energy consumption, and suggests specific policies to break unsustainable habits.

In coevolutionary models of demand and supply, the substitution of an incumbent by a new technology relies on the pace of technological change and evolving consumer preferences. For instance, Windrum and Birchenhall (1998) propose a formal model of demand and supply coevolution to examine determinants of technological succession. In their framework, firms offer products to satisfy clients in consumer classes, to which they are randomly assigned. In addition, firms engage in product innovations to attract new consumers. Consumers move between consumer classes depending on the relative attractiveness of products offered by incumbent firms. Evolving preferences determine which firms are successful, and thus the direction of product innovations. Windrum et al. (2009) applied this approach to study the substitution of more polluting firms by those that pollute relatively less.

Important questions that arise are how to facilitate the diffusion of environmental innovations, but also how to induce producers to innovate in the environmental direction. In this context, Safarzynska and van den Bergh (2011) propose a model to study selection and innovation in a population of boundedly rational investors, who decide each period on the allocation of investment capital among different technological options. Investors tend to choose the most cost-competitive technologies. The authors derive the optimal diversity of technologies in terms of minimising the total cost of investments in the short and long run. Diversifying a research portfolio turns out to be an important source of innovation due to novel combinations of incumbent technologies (recombinant innovation), which in the long run may also ensure the lowest cost. The authors apply their framework to model stylised energy transitions, and they derive the optimal rate of investments in renewable energy technologies.

Energy has been rarely acknowledged in evolutionary economic models. Recently, Foster (2014) proposes a coevolutionary model placing energy at the centre of economic growth. In his framework, energy use coevolves with the applications of new knowledge to energy use. In particular, energy-driven capital stock constitutes the repository of embedded knowledge, which drives economic growth. He tested his model against two centuries of British data. The results show that movements in energy prices play a significant role in the economic growth. As another exception, Safarzynska (2012) introduces energy as an input in production to the coevolutionary demand and supply model. She shows that a network effect on the consumer side prevents the entrance of new firms with energy efficient technologies and so creates a rebound effect. The rebound effect refers to the phenomena whereby policy measures implemented with the aim of encouraging energy savings in production and consumption generate the opposite result, i.e. more energy and resource use.

Economic theories of managing renewable resources, such as fisheries and forestry, traditionally rely on perfectly rational agents, who are capable of computing the optimal harvest. Evolutionary economists challenge this view and examine how the bounded rationality of harvesters affects resource dynamics. For instance, Noailly et al. (2003) present an evolutionary economic model, where fishers face a choice between a low and high effort harvesting strategy. The distribution of strategies in the population is governed by a replicator dynamics equation, according to which strategies yielding above average profits are more demanded than strategies yielding below average profits. In this context, the authors derive conditions (environmental policies) under which both strategies coexist in the long run, and can prevent overharvesting of resources.

Current assessment of major issues

The main message from the coevolutionary models of demand and supply is that consumers are key drivers of sustainability. In particular, environmentally conscious consumers, who attach high weight to environmental features (service characteristics) of products, may initiate their wider adoption and induce a shift in innovative activities of firms towards improving the environmental dimension of their products. However, without deeper changes in values and beliefs, even if consumers temporarily adopt popular environmental innovations, they will be tempted to buy new products in the future, regardless of their environmental impacts. Alternatively, they may re-spend extra income due to energy savings on other energy intensive products. This relates to the fact that the growth of material production and consumption is deeply embedded in the current social ecological regime. In this context, a regime shift cannot occur without changing the integrated system of worldviews, institutions and technologies (Beddoe et al., 2008). So far, changes in values and beliefs have been overlooked in evolutionary economic theory.

In particular, individuals are often conceived in evolutionary economics as following social laws (e.g. of imitation) without any reflection. However, people are more likely to imitate specific behaviours or adopt certain technologies based on their experiences, individual predispositions and social circumstances. They are also capable of 'higher level' reasoning over beliefs and values underlying the process of deliberation. Reflecting upon whether one's objectives are justified, is referred to in the literature as theoretical reasoning, and may lead to preference change. On the other hand, evaluations through exploring the meaning of the good, i.e. moral reasoning, may lead to attaching different weight to principles upon which individuals act. The role of deliberation and reflexivity in changing preferences is overlooked in evolutionary theory. Yet, without deeper understanding of this process, it is impossible to study radical changes in social economic systems required to achieve sustainability.

Evolutionary economic models in policy analysis use baseline model simulations to compare with results from model simulation under a specific policy. However, steering the economy towards sustainability requires constantly adjusting policy goals and visions of future developments. Evolutionary economics offers tools and formal frameworks to study learning by policy makers. Yet, adaptive policy making requires further scrutiny.

Finally, the role of power [see Chapter 14] within and between groups in the process of institutional change has been neglected in evolutionary economic theory. Cultural group selection might be applicable to the study of the coevolution of institutions and power relations (van den Bergh and Gowdy, 2009). Individuals alone may be incapable of inducing changes in the desired direction of, for example, sustainability. Only by acting together may they be able to create a momentum to make institutional change possible. The process involves interactions within and between groups. This may take various forms, such as: competition for scarce (financial) resources; hidden or explicit conflict negotiation in political voting processes; growth of group size; takeover or fusion; and mutual influence. These processes can be conceptualised within a group selection framework. Accordingly, selection would be operative at the levels of both individuals and groups. During interactions within groups, individuals can use their power to influence social interactions to their advantage. From this perspective, power can be seen as a mechanism of social transmission within groups. Due to interactions between groups, certain behaviours are enforced and institutionalised. Future research along these lines could enhance our understanding of the process of institutional change, and also of environmental policies.

Future directions

Recent transformations in mainstream economics offer opportunities for evolutionary and institutional [Chapter 3] economics (Hodgson, 2007). This is because evolutionary economics provides formal tools and theoretical approaches, which rely on the notions of dynamics, disequilibrium and bounded rationality. However, so far, a coherent approach to policy making from the evolutionary perspective is missing. This relates to the fact that policy criteria for evaluating evolutionary outcomes and processes are ambiguous. In particular, there is a lack of clarity as to which ethical theories match well with evolutionary dynamics and how to evaluate individual and social welfare from the evolutionary perspective. Yet, these questions are important if evolutionary economics is to deliver policy insight.

The theoretical foundations of evolutionary economics could encourage the adoption of alternative ethical theories to the utilitarianism of mainstream economics and enrich policy evaluation. This could include sensory utilitarianism and deontological or virtue ethics. In particular, the inducement of new preferences by innovations, social influences or advertising in evolutionary economics creates difficulty in interpreting growing standards of living through the traditional preference satisfaction view (Blinder and Witt, 2011). Witt and Schubert (2010) argue that sensory utilitarianism better matches evolutionary theories of preference change than classical utilitarianism. Sensory utilitarianism specifies sources of utility as the enjoyment of pleasures and avoidance of pains. The evolutionary perspective complements these insights by the theory of conditional and reinforcement learning of needs [Chapter 24] and wants. In this context, Witt and Schubert (2010) suggest that the distinction between different consumers' motivations, namely between consumption aimed at reducing deprivations of needs and at satisfying cognitively constructed motives, justifies assigning unequal normative weights to them in welfare analysis.

The deontological perspective requires that individuals comply with universal moral norms. It justifies institutions and norms constraining opportunistic behaviours, where individuals do not follow norms voluntarily. Employing deontological ethics in evolutionary economic policy analysis could justify regulations aimed at curbing status seeking and conformist behaviours and changing unsustainable habits and routines. Yet, the assumption of bounded rationality in evolutionary economics questions the capacity of individuals to judge the degree to which their actions conform to abstract principles, which deontological approaches entail. This view neglects also the variety of motives, the complexity of moral situations and the evolution of values over time.

The ontological presuppositions of evolutionary economics would also provide space for adopting virtue ethics as a foundation. In virtue ethics, the assessment of responsibility does not depend upon universal rules, as in deontological theories, but entails evaluating the combination of motivations and reasons in specific contexts (van Staveren, 2007). Virtue ethics is personal ethics, which creates difficulty in employing it for welfare analysis.

One possibility to overcome this problem is to focus on economic practices [see also Chapter 20]. Economic practices can be defined as a set of economic activities, during which external value is realised to sustain the practice over time (MacIntyre, 1987). Accordingly, individual behaviour is driven by motivations and reasons inherent to, or associated with, specific practices, and should not be made too instrumental towards the pursuit of ends outside the practice (van Staveren, 2007). An evolutionary perspective can shed light on how practices in different domains (e.g. food, transport, energy use) evolve, and which human tendencies drive specific wants and habits associated with different practices. Along these lines, Safarzynska (2013) suggests applying virtue ethics to evaluate consumption practices in different domains. This work identifies five categories of consumer rules related to food consumption and suggests evaluating them with rules of good conduct that have evolved within the practice.

Concluding remarks

This chapter has argued that the theory and models of evolutionary economics can offer insights to environmental policies. In particular, core mechanisms and evolutionary economic building blocks allow the study of complex interactions in social ecological systems and the examination of emergent properties as a result of these interactions. For instance, an important class of coevolutionary frameworks has shown that evolving preferences of consumers can influence producers to innovate in the direction of improved environmental performance. In addition, evolutionary economics allows policy analysis beyond existing mainstream models through the exploration of the secondary effects of policies, such as behavioural and technological adjustments. Social interactions, in particular network effects on the consumer side, can be a source of the rebound effect, causing policies aimed at promoting energy savings to use more energy. Similarly, evolutionary economic models of resource use start from the premise that resource users and harvesters suffer from bounded rationality. Alternative policy prescriptions (from those of mainstream economics) then arise with regard to preventing resource exhaustion.

Yet, so far, evolutionary economics has not offered a unified policy framework. This relates to the fact that there is no coherent model of individual behaviour. Adaptive policy making and the evolution of power relations are neglected in evolutionary economic theory, while how to evaluate progress from the evolutionary economic perspective remains unclear. More work is necessary on how the policy criteria vary with different ethical standpoints in order for evolutionary economics to offer a better basis for advice on future environmental policy.

Key further readings cited

Boyd, R., Richardson, P. (1985). *Culture and the Evolutionary Process*. Chicago: University of Chicago Press.

Dosi, G., Freeman, C., Nelson, R., Silverberg, G. and L. Soete (1988) (eds.). *Technical Change and Economic Theory*, London: Pinter Publishers.

Hodgson, G. (2007). Evolutionary and institutional economics as the new mainstream. *Evolutionary and Institutional Economics Review* 4(1), 7–25.

Kallis, G., Norgaard, R. (2009). Special Section: Coevolutionary ecological economics: theory and application. *Ecological Economics* 69, 675–930.

Witt, U. (2008). What is specific about evolutionary economics? *Journal of Evolutionary Economics* 15, 547–575.

Other literature cited

Becker, G. (1992). Habits, additions, and tradition. *Kyklos*, 45, 327–345.

Beddoe, R., Constanza, R., Farley, J., Garza, E., Kent, J., Kubiszewski, I., Martinez, L., McCowen, T., Murphy, K., Myers, N., Ogden, Z., Stapleton, K. and Woodward, J. (2008). Overcoming system roadblocks to sustainability: the evolutionary redesign of worldviews, institutions, and Technologies. *PNAS* 106, 2483–2489.

Blinder, M., Witt, U. (2011). As innovations drive economic growth, do they also raise well-being. Max Planck Discussion Paper 1105.

Foster, J. (2014). Energy, knowledge and economic growth. *Journal of Evolutionary Economics* 24(2), 209–238.

Henrich, J., Albers, W., Boyd, R., McCabe, K., Gigerenzer, G., Young, H. P. and Ockenfels, A. (2001). What Is the role of culture in bounded rationality? In G. Gigerenzer and R. Selten (Ed.), *Bounded Rationality: The Adaptive Toolbox* (pp. 343–359). Cambridge, MA, MIT Press.

Hodgson, G.M., Huang, K. (2012). Evolutionary game theory and evolutionary economics: are they different species? *Journal of Evolutionary Economics* 22(2), 345–366.

MacIntyre, A. (1987). *After Virtue: A Study in Moral Theory*. London: Duckworth.

Marechal, K. (2010). Not irrational but habitual: the importance of behavioural lock-in in energy consumption. *Ecological Economics* 69(5), 1104–1114.

Maslow, A. (1943). A theory of human motivation. *Psychological Review* 50, 370–396.

Nelson, R. (2001). Evolutionary theories of economic change. In A. Nicita, U. Pagano, (Eds.) *The Evolution of Economic Diversity* (pp. 199–215). London: Routledge.

Nelson, R., Consoli, D. (2010). An evolutionary theory of household consumption behaviour. *Journal of Evolutionary Economics* 20, 665–687.

Noailly, J., van den Bergh, J., Cees, A.W. (2003). Evolution of harvesting strategies: replicator and resource dynamics. *Journal of Evolutionary Economics* 13(2), 183–200.

Norgaard, R.B. (1984). Coevolutionary development potential, *Land Economics*, 60, 160–173.

Safarzynska, K. (2012). Modelling the rebound effect in two manufacturing industries. *Technological Forecasting and Social Change* 79(6), 1135–1154.

Safarzynska, K. (2013). Evolutionary economic policies for sustainable consumption. *Ecological Economic.* 90, 187–195.

Safarzynska, K., van den Bergh, J. (2010). Evolutionary modelling in economics: a survey of methods and building blocks. *Journal of Evolutionary Economics* 20, 329–373.

Safarzynska, K., van den Bergh, J. (2011). Beyond replicator dynamics: selection-innovation dynamics and optimal diversity. *Journal of Economic Behaviour and Organisation* 78, 229–245.

Simon, H. (1955). A behavioural model of rational choice. *The Quarterly Journal of Economics* 69(1), 99–118.

Stoelhorst, J.W., Richerson, P.J., (2013). A naturalistic theory of economic organisation. *Journal of Economic Behaviour and Organisation* 90S, S45–S56.

van den Bergh, J.C., Gowdy, J. M. (2009). A group selection perspective on economic behaviour, institutions and organisations. *Journal of Economic Behaviour and Organisation* 72(1), 1–20.

van Staveren, I. (2007). Beyond utilitarianism and deontology: ethics in economics. *Review of Political Economy* 19, 21–35.

Veblen, T.B. (1898). Why economics is not an evolutionary science? *The Quarterly Journal of Economics* 12(July), 373–397.

Windrum, P., Birchenhall, C. (1998). Is life cycle theory a special case? Dominant designs and emergence of market niches through coevolutionary learning. *Structural Change and Economic Dynamics* 9(1), 109–134.

Windrum, P., Carli, T., Birchenhall, C. (2009). Environmental impact, quality, and price: consumer trade-offs and the development of environmentally friendly technologies. *Technological Forecasting and Structural Change* 76(4), 533–551.

Witt, U., Schubert, C. (2010). Extending the informational basis of welfare economics: the case of preference dynamics. Max Planck Discussion Paper 1005. Jena: Max Planck Institute of Economics.

PART III

Biophysical reality and its implications

9

THERMODYNAMICS

Relevance, implications, misuse and ways forward

Kozo Torasan Mayumi

Introduction

Despite the partial reorientation of neoclassical economists toward resource and environmental issues they still cling to the dogma of mechanistic epistemology. William Stanley Jevons, a founder of neoclassical economic thought, expressed this as building an economic science in terms of "the mechanics of self-interest and utility". Since mechanics distinguishes only mass, position and speed, energy and matter entering into any process must leave that process in exactly the same quantity and quality (Georgescu-Roegen, 2009 [1975]). Strictly applying the mechanistic analogy in economics leads to the logical conclusion that the economic process is an eternal circular one that can never affect the quantity or quality of energy and matter in any way at all. Thus, there is no essential need for energy or matter to be included in the analytical picture of economic analysis. Furthermore, this logical conclusion entails an implicit and fallacious mechanistic epistemology, namely, energy and material flows are forthcoming from an immutable eternal source. This parallels David Ricardo's idea of land, in the classical school of economics, as being "the original and indestructible powers of soil". The common economic myth is that a stationary social economic system with zero-growth of both endosomatic population (human body) and exosomatic population (detachable material structures outside of the human body) can be completely freed from energy and material constraints. This is why mainstream economists talk as if humans need never worry about the scarcity of natural resources or environmental constraints.

Yet, in contrast to neoclassical economics' use of a mechanistic dogma, the laws of thermodynamics do have a central importance for social and economic systems, as recognised by ecological economics (Baumgärtner, 1996; Spash, 2012). Thermodynamics is a branch of physics that directly deals with qualitative transformation of energy and matter. The irreversible nature of thermodynamics can provide a suitable natural science foundation for sustainability, providing one of the most important theoretical and practical pillars for understanding the economic process (Georgescu-Roegen, 1971).

Some brief explanation relating to thermodynamic concepts and laws is necessary before going further. Energy is the capacity of a system to do mechanical work, and heat is the transfer of energy caused by a difference in temperature. The first law of thermodynamics stipulates that energy is always conserved in an isolated system—defined as having no exchange of either energy or matter across the system boundary. The second law of thermodynamics has two equivalent formulations: (i) no cyclic process is possible where heat is taken from a hot source and converted completely into work with no other change (William Thomson, Baron Kelvin, 1824–1907) or (ii) heat cannot by itself pass from a colder to a warmer body without an accompanying change elsewhere (Rudolph Clausius 1822–1888).[1] Lambert (2002) provides an instructive definition that grasps the essence of the second law: energy of any type disperses from a high localisation and spreads out, if it is not constrained. In summary, entropy is a measure of how dispersed energy is at any point in a process. Energy cannot be recycled because it becomes dispersed, and so it can only be used once to do mechanical work.

The remaining four sections of the chapter cover in turn: the relevance of thermodynamics to ecological economics; five important implications; and a mechanism for entropy disposal on Earth; several misuses of thermodynamic concepts; and caveats and ways forward on the use of a thermodynamic approach for ecological economics.

Relevance of thermodynamics to ecological economics

There are four principal influential contributions that lay some foundations for ecological economics from the thermodynamic perspective, namely those of Soddy, Boulding, Ayres and Georgescu-Roegen. Frederick Soddy (1877–1956) was a Nobel laureate in chemistry who emphasised the importance of energy for social progress based on real wealth formation, as distinct from virtual wealth and a debt accumulation process: "From the energetic standpoint progress may be regarded as a successive mastery and control over sources of energy" (Soddy, 1926: 48). Interestingly Soddy also paid attention to the role of money emphasising the endogenous supply of liquidity through debt finance. In more recent times, Kenneth Boulding (1966) employed a metaphor of Spaceship Earth to explain the fundamental resource limitations faced by humanity, a topic previously addressed by Henry Georges's *Progress and Poverty* in 1879. Furthermore, perhaps Boulding was the first modern economist to recognise the importance of waste management. In fact, he clearly stated: "Oddly enough, it seems to be in pollution rather than in exhaustion that the problem is first becoming salient" (1966: 12). Following Boulding's concern, Robert Ayres argued that a common failure in economics is to treat the disposal of residuals as at variance with the first law of conservation of energy and mass (Ayres and Kneese, 1969). While Ayres' approach was still confined within the general equilibrium framework, nonetheless his work paved the way for the new field of industrial ecology based on the materials balance approach. Finally, Nicholas Georgescu-Roegen (1971) developed a more comprehensive, systematic and in-depth approach that invoked the second law to emphasise the irreversible character of the economic process and created an alternative production theory, the flow-fund scheme. Georgescu-Roegen (1977) also stressed the importance of mineral resources in ecological economic interactions and proposed the fourth law of thermodynamics.[2] There are four overall lessons to be learnt from this and related literature for understanding the relevance of thermodynamics to ecological economics.

First, thermodynamics can capture the biophysical dimension of energy and material transformation in the economic process. Controlling energy and material flows is vital for the progress of the civilisation. Being the branch of physics that deals with transformations of energy and matter, thermodynamics gives an appropriate natural science foundation for a description of what goes on when human societies interact with the environment. Thus, thermodynamics is a necessary complement and prerequisite for ecological economic assessment. Furthermore, thermodynamics provides a theoretical foundation and bio-geophysical basis for technology assessment informing sustainability.

Second, thermodynamics can furnish a unifying framework and perspective for ecological economics. As all transformation processes are, at bottom, processes of energy and material transformation, the concepts and laws of thermodynamics can be applied to all such processes. This unites the analysis of economic systems and ecosystems. This interdisciplinarity allows ecological economists to ask questions that would otherwise be left unexamined by a mono-disciplinary approach.

Third, thermodynamics helps ecological economists to understand the characteristics of the ultimate bio-geophysical constraints on the scale of economic activities. Bio-geophysical constraints include not only the scarcity of energy and material flows for the economy, but also the waste assimilating capacity of the environment. Thermodynamic concepts allow physical driving forces and constraints to be incorporated into our understanding of the interplay between the economy and the environment. They are essential to our comprehension of resource and energy scarcity, Nature's capacity to assimilate wastes and pollutants, the irreversibility of transformation processes and the overall constraints on economic activities. Thermodynamic concepts thus allow ecological economists to relate to the bio-geophysical basis of economics, and gain insight into the relationships which are unavailable for economists focusing on monetary evaluations alone. There is one caution: including the second law explicitly in economics is inadequate for understanding *all constraints* created by environmental degradation, because it tells us nothing about the specific *chemical and biological impacts* that waste streams have on specific ecosystems and the biosphere as a whole.

Fourth, thermodynamics is useful for schematically describing economic and environmental interactions. Economics is typically concerned with consumption and production, while the laws of thermodynamics place constraints on any transformation of energy and material flows. These constraints may be applied at two levels, corresponding to two different schemes. The first is the descriptive scheme, which relies on words and diagrammatic tools to convey a simplified version of reality that is the prerequisite before doing a quantitative analysis. This scheme is necessarily qualitative and may be thought of as the "preanalytic cognitive act". The descriptive scheme places ecological economic theory in the context of physical reality by incorporating the first and second laws of thermodynamics. Second is the quantification of thermodynamic limits to the output generated by economic processes, which has been most extensively undertaken at the level of individual processes, in particular thermal or chemical process.

Economic implications of thermodynamics

Conventional economic policy has been directed towards simple material growth, so more consumption and production is glamourised. In contrast, ecological economics aims at establishing a harmony between economic activities and resource and environmental constraints. In this respect the laws of thermodynamics have important economic implications for sustainability. In this section, I will consider five key economic implications (Glucina and Mayumi, 2010), two from each of the first and second laws and one from a combination of the laws.

First, the only stocks of natural resources on Earth are those that already exist. From the first law, matter-energy cannot be created, so stock deposits, such as fossil fuels and minerals, can be exhausted. Stock exhaustion implies losing any unique characteristics of the material involved and being unable to conduct economic processes reliant upon that resource and its characteristics. So, the weak sustainability concept in environmental economics loses any operational meaning [see also Chapters 10 and 25].

Second, what has already been produced cannot be removed from existence. The first law states that matter-energy cannot be destroyed, so any unwanted waste flows will end up residing somewhere in the environment. Any such waste flow then inevitably becomes a waste management issue. For example, radioactive wastes have proven a particularly problematic menace to all the biological existence on Earth.

Third, the second law implies that all real processes are irreversible. In practice, this means that humanity can use available energy only once. There cannot be perpetual motion machines, and neither can energy be recycled. Therefore energy coming from a stock, like fossil fuels, is only available once. For energy coming as a flow, like solar or geothermal energy, the energy used per unit of time cannot exceed the energy flow per unit time. Solar energy cannot be concentrated to allow its use at a higher rate than the incoming solar energy flow. However, because of the first law of thermodynamics, additional energy use creates waste heat that must be discarded into the environment and becomes a source of global thermal energy warming adding to warming due to the humanly enhanced greenhouse effect.

Fourth, energy transformation technology has limits. The maximum amount of mechanical work that can be achieved by a system depends only on the temperature difference between the system and its surroundings. Improving the technology used to transform heat into work can only ever get closer to the thermodynamic maximum, and can never surpass it. Thus there is a theoretical limit to all energy efficiency improvements. Furthermore, such improvements are a necessary but not sufficient condition for reducing overall energy consumption, *ceteris paribus*. An increase in energy efficiency of a resource used in a process can actually increase energy use due to the stimulus given to individuals to increase their general resource consumption. This is the phenomenon called the Jevons paradox (or rebound effect), and is extremely important in relation to sustainability, because it challenges the conventional wisdom of energy policy based on using technology to improve energy efficiency on the basis that this will reduce resource consumption.

Fifth, economic growth has ultimate limits, if it requires energy. Some available energy comes from finite stocks. Some energy also comes from a quasi-fund with a finite flow-rate. Technology for harnessing renewable energy sources is very unlikely to completely substitute for non-renewable fuel stocks at current consumption rates, because energy cannot be created or recycled. All production "uses up" available energy. Infinite growth in the use of energy stocks is impossible. Renewable energy flows may not be exhaustible through human use, but cannot be used at a faster rate than their incoming flow-rate. This means growth in energy use beyond the rate of incoming energy flows is impossible, and continuous growth in energy use is also impossible.

However, this logical argument alone is insufficient to conclude that growth in energy use is constrained *in practice*. Determining if this is the case requires knowing the magnitude of the energy requirement for a given social metabolism [Chapter 11] of an economy in relation to the magnitude of energy flows and funds. Fossil fuel stocks—principally oil—are now widely acknowledged as peaking in production given the current social metabolism [see Chapter 41]. In contrast, our primary energy flow, solar energy, does seem, at least at first glance, to be enormous in comparison to the requirements of the existing societal metabolism. Smil (2003) estimates that solar radiation is received by the Earth at ground level at an approximate rate of 2×10^{16} Watts. This number is three orders of magnitude higher than our rate of energy use, e.g., about 1.6×10^{13} Watts in 2006. This difference may be construed as evidence that growth in energy use is 'not practically constrained'. However, while the incoming solar energy is indeed a very large number, this needs to be considered relative to the power of exponential growth. Using a yearly growth rate in world energy consumption of 2 per cent (the average rate during the period 1980–2006), a simple calculation shows that our total energy consumption rate would equal the total solar energy influx in less than 400 years (Glucina and Mayumi,

2010). Besides the obvious absurdities of appropriating all incoming solar energy, this would reduce 'sustainable growth' to a fairly unambitious time frame. On this basis I would conclude that growth in the social metabolism of the economy *is* practically constrained by the energy required.

Let me now turn, briefly, to understanding the mechanism by which the Earth avoids entropic degradation, i.e. how come the system does not collapse. The Earth is an open system which means energy flows across the system boundaries, but it is in effect closed; i.e., there is no material flow, only flows of energy. Tsuchida has shown—using Schrödinger's (1967) idea of entropy disposal—that the Earth can be regarded as a Carnot engine powered by the temperature difference between the Sun and outer space (Tsuchida and Murota, 1987). Air convection and the water cycle constitute an atmospheric heat engine, which guarantees the existence of life on Earth by continually discarding entropy into outer space. Within this heat engine, water and air circulate between the surface area of the Earth (15°C on average) and the air at high altitudes (−18°C). Thermal entropy generated after various activities on Earth is discarded annually, roughly at a rate of 34.6 cal/°C/cm^2.

The low temperature of the upper atmosphere (−18°C), created by the adiabatic expansion of the air, disposes of thermal entropy, and more of the same heat quantity is removed at a lower rather than a higher temperature. At about −18°C, since the vapour pressure is sufficiently low and the air is so dry, sunlight can pass easily through the atmosphere. Water cycles emerge due to the fact that the molecular weight of water vapour is 18 g/mol, while the average molecular weight of air is 29 g/mol. This difference in molecular weight creates a kind of air pump that lifts water vapour into the upper atmosphere. Through the operation of water cycles created by the Earth's atmosphere, living things on the Earth can effectively dispose of heat entropy.

Misuse of thermodynamics

Thermodynamics is relevant for building a descriptive scheme, or preanalytic vision, of economics (Baumgärtner, 2004). Trying to apply the descriptive scheme of thermodynamic analysis to the economic domain presupposes the existence of an analogy. However, difficulties arise in ascertaining whether, or not, thermodynamic concepts can be transferred into a particular domain of economic analysis through the use of analogies and to what extent analogies can be safely adopted. If economic phenomena can be seen in a new light and give rise to new questions and hypotheses, the analogy has heuristic value in bridging the gap between thermodynamics and economics (Baumgärtner, 2004). In fact, such a formal analogy was once successfully utilized by Samuelson (1947). He established the comparative statics method based on the Le Chatelier Principle from chemical thermodynamic equilibrium theory. This has provided a very powerful tool and found widespread use in modern economics.

Unfortunately, rather than identifying analogies properly, the adopted analogies are often responsible for much of the confusion concerning the role of thermodynamics in economics due to their arbitrary and unjustified application. For example, while there is a formal similarity between classical thermodynamics and neoclassical consumer choice theory (Sousa and Domingos, 2006), there arise a number of crucial differences and problems when an equilibrium thermodynamic analogy is used for such economic phenomena. First, there are a number of thermodynamic variables with physical dimensions (temperature, pressure, entropy and so on) that do not have counterparts in economics. The existence of a purely formal relationship does not justify the misuse of analogies. Second, the economic process is inevitably dominated by continuous qualitative changes due to innovation and novelty [Chapter 8]. Therefore, the economic process will never reach an equilibrium state and no formal system of equations can describe its evolutionary nature. Third, there is an important difference between flow and fund elements in the economic process. Theorists in physics need not include fund elements in their description of thermodynamic systems, but the omission of fund elements is a fatal analytical error for a realistic description of the thermodynamic systems within the economic process.

Some people have equated entropy with disorder. The concept of order is a state of affairs where all elements in a system are so related to each other that we may learn from our acquaintance with some spatial and temporal configurations of a part of the system to form exact expectations concerning the rest of the system, or at least expectations that have a good chance of predicting the spatial and temporal configurations of the rest. Thermodynamic entropy describes only the general tendency of a heat diffusion process and cannot predict precise spatial and temporal configurations of elements belonging to a particular system. Furthermore, the thermodynamic entropy of a solid body can change due to heat-flow creating variation in the energy levels of the body's constituent atoms which, being in a solid body, have limited freedom to change spatial position. Thus, the entropy of a system is in no way related to the extent to which it appears orderly.

There is another type of misuse of thermodynamic entropy in relation to Shannon's measure of information (Shannon, 1948). In fact, Shannon is responsible for the serious confusion shared with some distinguished scientists who mistakenly equate thermodynamic entropy with information entropy (e.g., Szilard, 1929; Jaynes, 1957; Brillouin, 1951). Three points should be emphasised: (i) quantity plays a central role in information theory as a measure of information where a communication source produces independent signal elements with probability. However, the concept of information and the capacity of a communication source transmission were treated as separate concepts within Shannon's framework; (ii) accidentally Shannon reaches the function H through two different routes, an axiomatic treatment of information and a method of typical sequences; and (iii) Shannon misidentifies a source of vernacular language with an ergodic stochastic Markov chain. In summary, Shannon's measure of information has nothing to do with thermodynamic entropy except mathematical formalism. As already cited, there is yet another formalist nonsense, the alleged equivalence between negative entropy and information, suggested implicitly or explicitly by Szilard (1929), Jaynes (1957) and Brillouin (1951).[3] The thermodynamic entropy concept cannot apply to a system with a small number of molecules, and these suggested models violate the physical dimensional consistency as well.

Finally the implication of thermodynamics analysis cannot offer an alternative principle of evaluation, let alone normative insights. There has been in the past a claim by some, including Costanza (1980), that an energy theory of value can be created. This is a theoretical absurdity. The non-substitution theorem implies that under very strict assumptions the value of a good or service is given by the total amount of a non-producible production factor (such as labour) in its production. There are four crucial and narrow assumptions: (i) there is only one primary non-producible production factor; (ii) this one primary factor is used in the production of every intermediate and all final goods and services; (iii) all production processes are subject to constant returns to scale; and (iv) there is no joint production. If we apply the non-substitution theorem to energy as primary non-producible production factor, it is clear that the energy theory of value is totally unrealistic and unrealisable.

Future directions

As Soddy correctly remarked, "life works according to, not against, the principles of the physical sciences" (Soddy, 1926: 24). Economic life cannot escape the limitations set by physical laws. Thus, no one can propose repealing the laws of thermodynamics. Yet, "Physics Envy" seems to prevent some social scientists from squarely examining if (and to what extent) thermodynamic analysis is directly applicable to the issues of societal and ecosystem metabolism and from creating a much more useful methodology that effectively deals with these issues.

Lotka pointed out inherent limitations of approaches that rely only on strict thermodynamic considerations:

> the austere virtue of this impartiality with respect to substance and form, becomes something of a vice when information is sought regarding certain systems in which mechanism plays, not an incidental, but the leading role. Here thermodynamics may be found powerless to assist us greatly, and the need for new methods may be felt.
>
> (1956: 327)

As Lotka indicates, the standard representations of thermodynamic transformations are too generic to be applied to the analysis of metabolic systems. Lotka (1956) developed his own framework to investigate how distributed and localised sources of energy in Nature are accumulated and dissipated through anabolism and catabolism. He identified three factors in energy transformations: (i) depictors, consisting of receptors and elaborators, that can perceive and recognise the external world; (ii) adjustors that determine particular reactions based on the information coming from depictors; and (iii) effectors that take certain actions for energy transformation based on adjusters' judgement. Lotka's deep understanding of thermodynamics seems to demand us to search for an alternative method beyond purely thermodynamic analysis that is more useful for the societal and ecosystem metabolism issues.

Elaborating on Lotka's brilliant ideas, Georgescu-Roegen (1971) introduced the flow-fund scheme to analyse the economic process. Flows act as elements that enter but do not come out of the production process (like onion for curry soup), or elements that come out of the production process without having entered (like products). On the other hand, funds are agents of production that enter and leave the process unchanged such as Ricardian land, capital and labour. Within the flow-fund representation of a given social economic system, the set of flow-fund elements does have a specific identity depending on the history of that particular system. Thus we can easily identify what is an "energy input flow" (a specific flow transformed by a specific fund element), what is "efficiency" (a ratio between two flows getting in and out of the same fund element) and what is "useful work" (a task making it possible to reproduce the fund structure). The representation given by thermodynamics is insufficient when studying metabolic systems. For example, hay is an energy input for horses whereas gasoline is an energy input for cars. Since the relation between these two types of flows and funds is system specific, they cannot be easily switched! Each transformation mechanism of a metabolic system is special and defines what should be considered as an energy input or a waste on its own. In order to ascertain whether or not a certain source of energy would be an appropriate input for a system, one must first carefully observe the characteristics of the energy and material transformation system. Humans cannot be fed gasoline, nor can they power a refrigerator with pizzas. This is the reason why indicators based on strict thermodynamic concepts, defined without specifying the identity of flow elements associated with the identity of the fund elements, such as entropy or exergy,[4] are often meaningless.

There is another important problem with the classical thermodynamic framework when applied to the analysis of metabolic systems. The metabolic rate associated with the various fund elements—the pace of energy conversions—is a crucial characteristic when studying metabolic systems. However, this characteristic is completely ignored by classical thermodynamics due to the difficulty of dealing with the transient behaviour of thermodynamic systems. Equilibrium thermodynamics cannot be extended to non-equilibrium thermodynamics since we do not have a proper definition of temperature in non-equilibrium thermodynamics. Thus, Prigogine had to acknowledge formidable limitation in using Gibbs equilibrium thermodynamics formula for non-equilibrium conditions as he stated:

> The Gibbs formula (3.17) was originally proved for the equilibrium conditions, and *its use for the non-equilibrium conditions is a new postulate on which the whole of the thermodynamics of irreversible processes is based.* The physical interpretation of this basic formula is that, even without equilibrium, entropy depends only on the same independent variables as for equilibrium processes. *This is certainly not true very far from equilibrium.*
>
> (Italics added, Prigogine, 1961: 93)

Prigogine acknowledged the inherent contradiction introduced into his non-equilibrium thermodynamics. We do not have any powerful scientific framework that can deal with the transient behaviour of metabolic systems. We have to go beyond the thermodynamic framework (both equilibrium and non-equilibrium) to deal with the behaviour of these systems.

Furthermore, as Georgescu-Roegen (1977) explained, the substantial dissipation of matter, particularly of mineral elements, cannot be properly treated in a thermodynamic framework. While Georgescu-Roegen's fourth law of thermodynamics is incompatible with the other laws of thermodynamics, the general concern for the dissipation of matter cannot be ignored. As physical capital stock is increased (as in the capitalist system), the mineral resources required to maintain and expand the fund structure must be dramatically increased. Indeed, as far back as 1867, Clausius tried to find a quantitative measure for the dissipation of matter—"the disgregation".

A final research question is whether or not there are ways to overcome thermodynamic limits in economic and environmental interactions. For example, what are the 'energy' inputs of our societal metabolism? Three main *different* energy forms can be distinguished in industrialised economies: fuels, process heat and electricity. These are termed energy carriers. These three energy forms are used in different proportions in different economies, depending on what types of primary energy sources are available. Energy carriers are created from primary energy sources. Certain types of energy carriers can also be created from another energy carrier, e.g. electricity generated from natural gas. These interactions have implications for the reproduction and reproducibility of systems. Research has also been ongoing to establish a flow-fund representation of the interactions and interdependencies of societal and ecosystem metabolisms (Giampietro et al., 2013).

Concluding remarks

The generic nature of thermodynamics limits its role in creating a robust framework that can be used to study societal and ecosystem metabolism. Thermodynamics can say nothing about the associated political barriers, monetary costs or toxicological impacts. Thermodynamics is also of very limited use for mathematical models in economics. On the other hand, thermodynamics plays a vital role in the critique of mainstream economics, its lack of realism and the related framing of the obstacles to sustainability. At the policy level, thermodynamics can inform us about the opportunities for energy transformation improvements that can be used for overall energy policy, and it raises some basic issues about the unsustainability of current societal practices both in terms of energy and materials use.

Notes

1 In Kelvin's definition, the phrase "with no other change" is essential, since a well-known toy, a drinking bird, can continue a cyclic movement as long as water is supplied. Furthermore, a heat source at one temperature can be transformed completely into work—the isothermal expansion phase in the Carnot cycle. Practically, an infinite length of a piston expanding beyond any limit is never available to humans. So "the cyclic process" is indispensable for Kelvin's statement.

2 Editor's Note: This proved theoretically problematic, as mentioned later in the chapter, and so of no use. However, the role of materials [see Chapter 10] is too easily forgotten in an over emphasis on energy and this was really the point and the importance of his contribution here.

3 Editor's Note: also found in Boulding (1966).

4 Exergy is the maximum amount of mechanical work obtainable from a system as it reversibly approaches thermodynamic equilibrium with its environment.

Key further readings cited

Baumgärtner, S. (1996). Use of the entropy concept in ecological economics. In: Faber, M., Manstetten, R. and Proops, J. (Eds.). *Ecological Economics: Concepts and Methods*. Cheltenham, England: Edward Elgar, 115–135.

Georgescu-Roegen, N. (1971). *The Entropy Law and the Economic Process*. Cambridge, MA: Harvard University Press.

Georgescu-Roegen, N. (2009 [1975]). Energy and economic myths. In: Spash, C.L. (ed). *Ecological Economics: Critical Concepts in the Environment, 4 Volumes*. London: Routledge, 328–373.

Giampietro, M., Mayumi, K.T. and Sorman, A. (2013). *Energy Analysis for a Sustainable Future: Multi-Scale Integrated Analysis of Societal and Ecosystem Metabolism*. London: Routledge.

Other literature cited

Ayres, R.U. and Kneese, A.V. (1969). Production, consumption, and externalities, *American Economic Review* 59(3), 282–297.

Baumgärtner, S. (2004). Modelling in ecological economics. In J. Proops and P. Safanov (Eds.), *Modelling in Ecological Economics* (pp. 102–129). London: Edward Elgar.

Boulding, K.E. (1966). The economics of the coming spaceship earth. In H. Jarrett (ed.), *Environmental Quality in a Growing Economy* (pp. 3–14). Baltimore: Johns Hopkins University Press.

Brillouin, L. (1951). Maxwell's demon cannot operate: information and entropy I. *Journal of Applied Physics* 22(3), 334–337.

Costanza, R. (1980). Embodied energy and economic valuation. *Science* 210(4475), 1219–1224.

Georgescu-Roegen, N. (1977). The steady state and ecological salvation: A thermodynamic analysis, *BioScience* 27 (4), 266–270.

Glucina, M.D. and Mayumi, K.T. (2010). Connecting thermodynamics and economics: Well-lit roads and burned bridges, *Annals of the New York Academy of Sciences*, 1185: Issue: *Ecological Economics Reviews* 11–29.

Jaynes, E.T. (1957). Information theory and statistical mechanics. *Physical Review* 106, 620–630.

Lambert, F.L. (2002). Entropy is simple, qualitatively. *Journal of Chemical Education* 79(10), 1241–1246.

Lotka, A.J. (1956). *Elements of Mathematical Biology*. New York: Dover Publications.

Prigogine, I. (1961). *Introduction to Thermodynamics of Irreversible Processes*. Second, Revised Edition. New York: Interscience Publishers.

Samuelson, P.A. (1947). *Foundations of Economic Analysis*. Cambridge, MA: Harvard University Press.

Schrödinger, E. (1967). *What is Life & Mind and Matter*. London: Cambridge University Press.

Shannon, C.E. (1948). A mathematical theory of communication. *The Bell System Technical Journal* 27 (3), 379–423) and 27 (4), 623–656.

Smil, V. (2003). *Energy at the Crossroads: Global Perspectives and Uncertainties*. Cambridge, MA: MIT Press.

Soddy, F. (1926). *Wealth, Virtual Wealth and Debt: The Solution of the Economic Paradox*. London: George Allen & Unwin Ltd.

Sousa, T. and Domingos, T. (2006). Is neoclassical microeconomics formally valid? An approach based on an analogy with equilibrium thermodynamics. *Ecological Economics* 58(1), 160–169.

Spash, C.L. (2012). New foundations for ecological economics. *Ecological Economics* 77, 36–47.

Szilard, L. (1929). Über die Entropieverminderung in einem thermodynamischen System bei Eingriffen intelligenter Wesen. *Zeitschrift für Physik* 53, 840–856.

Tsuchida, A. and Murota, T. (1987). Fundamentals in the entropy theory of ecocycle and human economy. In G. Pillet and T. Murota (eds.), *Environmental Economics: The Analysis of A Major Interface* (pp. 11–35). Geneva: R. Leimgruber.

10

GEOPHYSICAL LIMITS, RAW MATERIAL USE AND THEIR POLICY IMPLICATIONS

Armin Dieter

Introduction

Raw materials are the physical basis of the economy. Global extraction and consumption of raw materials has increased significantly in both industrialised and emerging economies driven by economic growth and increasing material wealth. Primary sources of non-energy raw materials and specialty raw materials are rare within the European Union (EU) and its economy is highly dependent on imports. High import dependence and supply restrictions, as well as limited mining activities in Europe, have raised concerns amongst European industrial leaders, governments and the European Commission (EC) over the sufficiency of the supply of raw materials (CEO, 2011).

In 2008, the EC published *The Raw Materials Initiative: Meeting our critical need for jobs and growth in Europe* (EC, 2008), hereafter RMI. The strategy is based on three pillars:

1   Securing access to raw materials via international markets;
2   Improving the framework conditions for raw materials extraction in Europe; and
3   Reducing the EU's consumption of primary raw materials and increasing resource efficiency.

From a physical point of view, this strategy consists of assuring the constant and increasing supply of raw materials from primary and secondary sources. Recycling, substitution through less scarce raw materials, or renewable resources, and increasing resource efficiency are part of the third pillar of the strategy. However, the strategy is aimed primarily at addressing the problem of a geopolitical supply shortage, while ignoring the geophysical basis of raw materials supply. Research makes clear that there are mineralogical and geological limitations to the minable deposits of mineral and metal ores on Earth (Skinner, 1979; Singer and Menzie, 2010). Moreover, there is an increasing concern over the looming peaks of resource extraction [Chapter 41] and the threat of resource depletion (Bardi, 2014). Both make the growth and input driven raw materials strategy of the EU look poorly founded in physical reality.

This chapter reviews the geophysical basis of the economy. This offers a perspective that deconstructs the position of the RMI. The chapter primarily focuses on the availability of raw materials from primary sources: extraction and substitution. This reveals the interdependences of technological progress, increasing resource efficiency and recycling. The following sections cover: (i) the geological basis of the economy; (ii) the physical limits to substitution, increasing efficiency, technological progress and recycling; and (iii) an outline of an option for an alternative approach to dealing with physical limits. The chapter closes with some concluding remarks that reflect back on the strategy of the RMI.

Understanding virgin material supply

Geophysical basis

Minerals and ores as well as solid, liquid and gaseous fossil fuels are extracted from the Earth's crust and form part of the physical basis of the economy. Both the oceanic and the continental crust contain traces of all naturally existing elements of the periodic table. More than 99 per cent of the continental crust is composed of the oxides of just ten elements: Si, Ti, Al, Fe, Mn, Mg, Ca, Na, K and P. All others are less abundant, occurring in traces of less than 0.1 per cent by weight of the crust. These are defined as "geochemically scarce elements" (Skinner, 1979), or scarce elements for short.

The crustal abundance of elements allows no general statement about their quality, concentration or existence in (economically) exploitable deposits or whether mining is feasible let alone politically desired (Singer and Menzie, 2010). The physical origins of ore and mineral deposits are complex processes of rock-formation occurring over long geological time periods. This means the deposits are for all practical purposes non-renewable as far as humans are concerned. In a physical sense the stocks of primary sources are fixed regardless of whether they are explored and exploited or not.

The mineralogical barrier: geophysical scarcity

Skinner (1979) developed a theory about the probable distribution of geochemically scarce elements in the Earth's crust. He introduced the concept of the 'mineralogical barrier'. This distinguishes the large amount of geochemically scarce elements from the relatively small amount (0.001 per cent to 0.01 per cent) of ores (sulphides and oxides) available for mining. The scarce elements are trapped as substitutes to other elements in the atomic structure of common rock (silicate minerals). Figure 10.1 displays the bimodal curve of the probable distribution of geochemical scarce elements on Earth and the mineralogical barrier. The large peak, to the left of the mineralogical barrier represents the amount of geochemical scarce elements trapped as atomic substitutes for abundant metals in common rocks. The small peak, to the right of the mineralogical barrier represents the small amount of geochemical scarce elements in mineable deposits resulting from ore forming geological processes. Those are the sources of geologically scarce elements from current mining activities.

For extraction from common rock, the energy input increases by two to three orders of magnitude (Skinner, 1979). Considering that energy for mining originates mainly from fossil fuel sources (Norgate and Haque, 2010) and that 5 per cent to 10 per cent of global carbon emissions are attached to the mining industry (Bardi, 2013), this would imply a large but currently unknown increase in carbon emissions. Moreover, mining beyond the mineralogical barrier would imply extracting huge additional amounts of more abundant elements proportionally to their crustal abundance and so generating vast amounts of waste rock (Skinner, 1979).

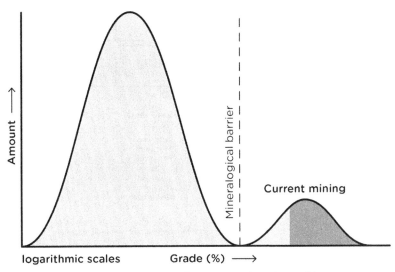

Figure 10.1   Probable distribution of geochemically scarce metals in the Earth's crust.
Source: adapted from Skinner (1979).

Reserves and resources

There is limited knowledge on the detailed spatial distribution of ore bodies assumed to be within the Earth's crust. This leaves considerable room for different estimates and speculation over the available deposits of geochemically scarce elements (Singer and Menzie, 2010). These uncertainties are reflected in the McKevley diagram, which is shown in Figure 10.2. The diagram divides the amount of minerals that are assumed to be currently, or potentially, feasible for mining into three major categories based on their geological certainty, or assurance, and their economic viability: (i) resources, (ii) reserve base, and (iii) reserves (USGS, 2014). Resources are defined as the total amount of a mineral occurring in a concentration at which extraction is currently or potentially feasible. Resources include all undiscovered deposits feasible for mining, even with strong uncertainty of their existence, and so enter into a highly speculative range of subjective probability. The reserve base is the share of the identified resources that meets the chemical and physical requirements for mining given the present state of technology. The reserves are the part of the reserve base that could be mined economically, at the present state (Gordon et al., 2007). The division is based on the economics of extraction, depending on costs and prices as well as factors such as the applied technology, efficiency of production and processing losses, including uncertainties in the estimate of grades, missing data and poor reporting (Gordon et al., 2007; Singer and Menzie, 2010). Therefore, all data of available resources of an element in the Earth's crust, and especially reserve data, are subject to strong uncertainty [see Chapters 26 and 27] and estimates continually change. There are calls for precaution because, even accepting a deposit does actually exist, this tells nothing about its usability (Georgescu-Roegen, 1975). For practical reasons, the inability to quantify materials that no one has even searched for would suggest they be excluded from counting as a resource (Singer, 1995). Therefore, statements about the future availability of raw materials based on the estimates of their reserves have to be read and interpreted with extreme caution.

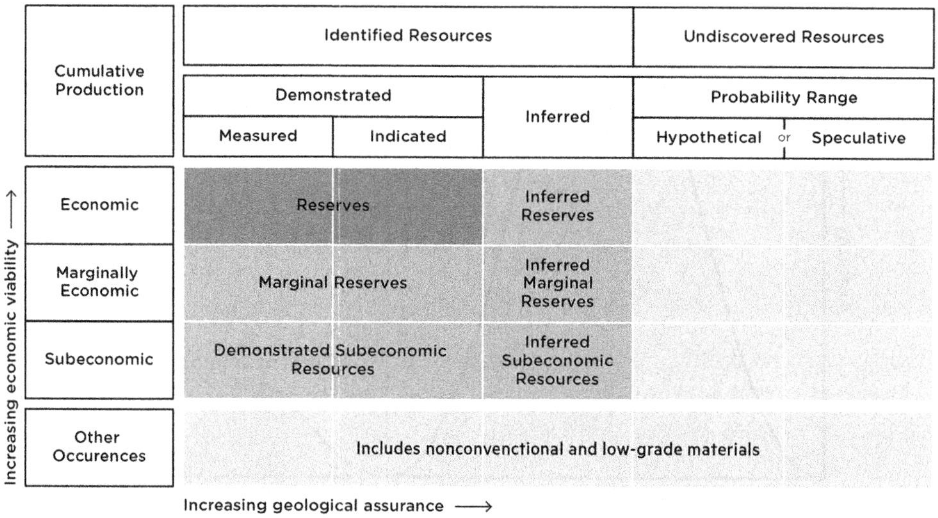

Cumulative Production		Identified Resources			Undiscovered Resources	
		Demonstrated		Inferred	Probability Range	
		Measured	Indicated		Hypothetical or Speculative	
Economic		Reserves		Inferred Reserves		
Marginally Economic		Marginal Reserves		Inferred Marginal Reserves		
Subeconomic		Demonstrated Subeconomic Resources		Inferred Subeconomic Resources		
Other Occurences		Includes nonconventional and low-grade materials				

↑ Increasing economic viability

Increasing geological assurance ⟶

Figure 10.2   McKevley diagram: resource reserves.
Source: adapted from McKevley (1972) and Gordon et al. (2007).

Economic scarcity

Economists tend to discuss issues of resource depletion as part of economic scarcity from the perspective of production costs. The basic logic is that, if a resource becomes physically scarce, unit costs (i.e., labour and capital costs) will rise. Barnett and Morse (1963) produced an historical study that claimed labour and capital costs per unit of mineral resources output in the USA had declined in the period between the US civil war and 1957. This heavily cited work has been updated and revised with similar results (Barnett, 1979; Krautkraemer, 2005). The authors justified their findings and the claim that material prices would continue to decline on the basis of technological progress. However, they did not consider the necessity of an increasing energy input per unit. Labour-capital costs declined and labour-capital efficiency increased because of the availability of cheap fossil fuels (Cleveland, 1991).

The opportunity cost paradigm, new deposits and technological progress

The opportunity cost paradigm is another approach that invokes market prices and costs for assessing resources scarcity (Tilton, 1996). Here, market prices are not as the indicator of supply shortage. Market prices are meant to drive technological progress emerging out of human creativity and generate incentives for new exploration activities. Increasing prices are meant to increase resources efficiency along the supply chain and favour recycling or substitution. Long before the extraction of the last unit of a resource the price is expected to have increased sending a signal that slows the rate of depletion and stimulates human ingenuity to discover (near perfect) substitutes. By strongly focusing on the unlimited potential of technological progress for overcoming resource depletion, this paradigm rejects the idea of fixed stocks. This technological optimism leads to the presumption that there are always more minerals to find and/or extraction can go beyond the mineralogical barrier (Wellmer and Dalheimer, 2012).[1]

The current knowledge on the location of deposits is limited and many undiscovered deposits are expected to lie under the cover of sediments. Additionally, private and public funds for exploration have decreased constantly within the last decades and education in mining and exploration techniques has reduced because mining has limited social acceptance. This has raised concerns over how new deposits will be found in order to overcome supply shortages expected to emerge due to economic growth in developing countries and for wealth creation in rich nations (Menzie et al., 2005).

Technological progress and innovation are expected to counteract the cost-increasing effect of resource depletion (Wellmer and Dalheimer, 2012). However, technological progress has been strongly dependent on the availability of fossil fuels (Cleveland, 1991). That is, technological progress has been highly correlated with the availability of a specific energy carrier (Bardi, 2014). Mining and processing of ores are still dependent on massive and even increasing fossil fuel inputs, especially at decreasing ore grades (Norgate and Haque, 2010). On the other hand, the reserves of fossil fuels are limited and production is estimated to have already peaked or to peak in the near future [see Chapter 41]. Even optimistic projections tend to assume the unlimited availability of renewable energy when projecting technological progress as a solution to overcoming geological scarcity of non-renewable resources (e.g., Steinbach and Wellmer, 2010).

Substitution of materials

Practical limits to substitution

The economic discussion on supply shortage and substitution is price-driven. Ecological economics has pointed out that this discussion leaves aside the physical basis. Prices are assumed to rise in a close to linear fashion and act as a signal of scarcity and so provide an economic price incentive for developing substitutes (Tilton, 1996). However, there are practical limits to finding and developing substitutes for scarce or expensive materials that are determined by physical, social and economic factors. The substitutability of scarce materials for more abundant or less expensive ones is determined by the existence of suitable materials, elements or compounds, their 'unlimited' availability as well as unrestricted access and sufficient development time (Graedel, 2001). Additionally, the substitutability of one material for another is determined by long-lasting business relationships, the threat of loss in performance and subsequent potential economic losses, costs of transition (capital costs, development costs, risk of loss in knowledge relating to existing processes) and even the risk of fluctuating material prices (Messner, 2002). The desire to maximise profits greatly constrains the idea of developing substitutes as long as no supply shortage can be foreseen.

The interdependence between the desired properties of a product and the unique physio-chemical properties of an element, as part of a chemical compound, substantially reduce the possibilities for substitution. In some cases, just a single chemical element determines these unique physio-chemical properties. There are then no substitutes available for the specific chemical compound that provides the desired properties that are required to supply a specific end-product (Graedel et al., 2015). In other cases, substitution may cause a loss in performance or the supply of the substitute may itself be susceptible to disruption by geological or geopolitical factors. Moreover, the countries of origin of some of these raw materials are politically unstable. Reflecting the core concerns of the RMI, supply shortage could emerge from political issues. Thus, the availability of a single element can determine the availability of a technology (Graedel et al., 2015). In the worst case, this could result in abandoning what are meant to be sustainable technologies, e.g., photovoltaics.

Efficiency, technology and the rebound effect

Increasing resource efficiency is a major target of the EU's raw materials policy and by itself a tool of the strategy. Gains in efficiency emerge either from exploiting unused potentials or from technological progress. Both result in cost savings and lower prices, which in turn can result in higher consumption that exceeds original levels. This is termed the rebound effect. Rebound effects can occur on both the consumer and the producer side. The rebound effect is assumed to be stronger for producers, especially in the case of energy-intensive sectors, core process technologies and general purpose technologies (Sorrell, 2009).

Research on the rebound effect primarily focuses on energy efficiency (e.g., Sorrell and Dimitropoulos, 2008). However, energy savings through technological progress tend not just to imply a rebound effect on energy consumption but also to increase the consumption of other resources. Thus, energy savings emerging from technological progress have been identified as drivers of economic growth that is built on increased resource consumption (Holm and Englund, 2009). Focusing policy primarily on increasing resource efficiency is then inadequate and policies will have to be introduced that reduce material affluence and channel potential increases in energy and resource efficiency towards non-consumptive activities.

Recycling of materials

Practical limits to recycling

Metals are not lost when they are used to make products, and theoretically they can be reused infinitely (Graedel and Reck, 2014).[2] Metals are integrated into the compounds that form consumer goods. The spatial distribution of end-of-life products and their low material content mean there is a high dissipation of matter (Reller et al., 2009). The low monetary value of the metal resulting from the low content of metals in a product leads to low recycling rates, so that recovery requires considerable technological effort (hydrometallurgy) and huge energy input (Hagelüken, 2014). At the same time, the ore grades, especially of precious metals contained in products, often exceed naturally occurring ore grades by orders of magnitude. However, the metal 'deposits' contained in products are often chemically far more complex than when naturally occurring. Purer elements (i.e., not occurring in compounds in Nature) are combined with the purpose of creating unique properties in a final product (Wellmer and Dalheimer, 2012). The physical properties of these artificial compounds limit the recyclability of all the metals involved. Metals for recycling are selected on the basis of their highest monetary value according to their overall content in a product and this determines the extent of recycling (Hagelüken, 2014). If other metals are economically valueless they will not be recovered. Metals may also have negative impacts on processing steps for recovery of other metals. Some metals will then get lost either in the recycled metals or as atomic substitutes in side streams, tailings and slag (Hagelüken and Meskers, 2010). The traces of non-recycled metals can negatively impact on the properties of the recovered metals. In addition, during recycling such metals get dissipated to the extent that they become practically irretrievable (Reller et al., 2009).

Recycling and virgin materials supply

Replacing material losses and increasing the purity of the recycled metals by diluting the traces of the contained non-recycled metals calls for a constant supply of virgin metals. Recycling contributes to reducing the extraction of virgin metals, but recycling rates of most metals are low (UNEP, 2011). There is therefore increasing virgin metal extraction due to increasing demand for speciality metals for new products and for replacing dissipative losses due to the production of short-lived consumer goods. Simultaneously, metals are stored in huge stocks of investment goods in the technosphere (Reller et al., 2009) [see also Chapter 11]. The long useful life of these products makes the raw materials unavailable for recycling over decades (Graedel et al., 2011, Menzie et al., 2005). Consequently, regardless of reducing their demand for raw materials from virgin supply, recycling does not work without a constant share of virgin supply.

Future directions

The functioning of technologies is not dependent on raw materials themselves but on the functionalities provided by their physio-chemical properties. Focusing on the functionalities along with further research on the applicability of more abundant minerals and metal ores could serve as a first step for substituting speciality metals. This could represent an alternative for overcoming situations of supply shortage and serve to develop a raw materials policy that addresses the geophysical boundaries. For example, the photovoltaic industry that is regarded as part of a transition to a sustainable society is subject to key material constraints. Technologically feasible alternatives with more abundant materials have been discussed and feasible solutions have been proposed (Wadia et al., 2009). These approaches could complement proposals to focus on more abundant metals for avoiding potential impacts emerging from geological scarcity (Skinner, 1979). Moreover, focusing on functionalities broadens the perspective on raw materials from the supply side to looking at the entire life cycle. Additionally, multiple and qualitative criteria can be assessed. Reframing the perspective serves to identify raw materials that are not just more abundant but even less harmful at all stages of the life cycle and particularly when being dissipated at the end of life phase.

Concluding remarks

In terms of geological supply, there is scientific evidence both showing that the known minable resources of raw materials are limited and indicating the existence of a threshold, the mineralogical barrier. The idea of claiming undiscovered deposits as feasible for mining should be treated with extreme caution. These resources cannot be quantified and estimating their existence neither implies their availability nor their accessibility. The mineralogical barrier signifies a threshold where humanity would be mining metals from common rock. This is impractical and impossible with known technologies, and would, in addition, require amounts of low entropy energy that are simply absent.

Even the solutions aimed at reducing the consumption of primary raw materials require virgin material input. Substitution shifts the demand from one material to another. Technological progress depends on increasing energy inputs. Efficiency gains can be overcompensated by increasing the total demand for other goods and services. Complete recycling is practically impossible, because at least a part of the worn-out materials, if not all, have to be replaced by virgin material supply. Replacing all worn-out material by virgin supply is the case for many specialty metals and counteracts the original intention of the European raw materials strategy.

The European RMI was initiated by industry, driven by experts and industry representatives, and focused on political concerns over jobs and growth, under economic pressure of recession. Uncertainties tend to have been treated through a narrow focus on risk management. Alternative approaches and potential solutions might have arisen from a conceptualisation of strong uncertainty and precaution [Chapters 26 and 27], complexity and the need for knowledge to be founded on a broader scientific and democratic basis [Chapter 28]. The proposed 'strategy' that resulted is—similar to those of other industrialised nations—primarily focused on safeguarding the supply chain of particular raw materials. This chapter has raised a series of issues that reveal the inadequacies of such polices. An alternative focus on the functionalities provided by raw materials might have opened up the opportunity to identify raw materials that are more abundant and at the same time less harmful, especially with regard to end of use disposal into the environment.

Where no substitutes are available for specific elements and geological resources are limited to politically unstable countries, a combination of technological limitation and geopolitical constraints arise. Moreover, recycling rates of speciality metals are often low. If, at the same time, their economic importance is high, a situation of criticality arises. Therein lies a problem exacerbated by lack of foresight and planning in a world driven by markets and profiteering and locked into a growth economy that promotes conspicuous, high-tech, throwaway, fashion conscious consumption.

Notes

1　Editor's Note: This has formed a central part of the mainstream economists rejection of limits to growth since the 1970s e.g., Beckerman (1974).
2　Editor's Note: This is indeed the hope of the currently popular idea of a circular economy; the technical qualifications being the necessity for both low entropy energy and knowledge of how to extract the metals.

Key further readings cited

Bardi, U. (2014). *Extracted: How the quest for mineral wealth is plundering the planet. A report to the Club of Rome*. White River Junction, Vermont: Chelsea Green Publishers.

Corporate European Observatory (CEO) (2011). Europe's Resource Grab: Vested interests at work in the European Parliament. *Corporate Europe Observatory*. http://corporateeurope.org/sites/default/files/publications/europes_resource_grab.pdf. Accessed 14 June 2013.

Georgescu-Roegen, N. (1975). Energy and economic myths. *Southern Economic Journal* 41 (3), 347–381.

Menzie, W.D., Singer, D.A., DeYoung, J.H., (2005). Mineral Resources and Consumption in the Twenty-First Century. In: Simpson, R. D., Toman, M. A., Ayres, R. U. (Eds.), Scarcity and growth revisited. *Natural resources and the environment in the new millennium*. Resources for the Future (pp. 33–53). Washington, DC: Resources for the Future.

Sorrell, S. (2009). Jevons' Paradox revisited: The evidence for backfire from improved energy efficiency. *Energy Policy* 37 (4), 1456–1469.

Other literature cited

Bardi, U. (2013). The mineral question: How energy and technology will determine the future of mining. *Front. Energy Res.* 1 (9): 1–11.

Barnett, H. J. (1979). Scarcity and growth revisited. In Smith, K.V. (ed.), *Scarcity and growth reconsidered* (pp. 163–217). The Johns Hopkins University Press, Resources for the future.

Barnett, H. J., Morse, C. (1963). *Scarcity and growth: The economics of natural resources availability*. Baltimore, MD: The Johns Hopkins Press.

Beckerman, W. (1974). *In Defence of Economic Growth*. London: Jonathan Cape.

Cleveland, C. (1991). Natural resource scarcity and economic growth revisited: Economic and biophysical perspectives. In Constanza, R. (ed.), *Ecological Economics*: The science and management of sustainability (pp. 289–317). New York: Columbia University Press.

EC, European Commission (2008). The Raw Materials Initiative: Meeting Our Critical Needs for Growth and Jobs in Europe, COM (2008) 699, SEC 2741 Brussels: European Commission, pp. 1–14.

Gordon, R.B., Bertram, M., Graedel, T.E. (2007). On the sustainability of metal supplies: A response to Tilton and Lagos. *Resources Policy* 32 (1–2), 24–28.

Graedel, T.E. (2001). Material substitution: A resource supply perspective. *Resources Conservation and Recycling* 34 (2), 107–115.

Graedel, T.E., Allwood, J., Birat, J.P., Buchert, M., Hagelüken, C., Reck, B.K., Sibley, S.F., Sonnemann, G. (2011). What do we know about metal recycling rates? *Journal of Industrial Ecology* 15 (3), 355–366.

Graedel, T.E., Harper, E.M., Nassar, N.T., Reck, B.K. (2015). On the materials basis of modern society. *Proceedings of the National Academy of Sciences.* 112 (20): 6295–6300.

Graedel, T.E., Reck, B.K (2014). Recycling in context. In: Worrell, E., Reuter, M.A. (Eds.), *A handbook of recycling. State-of-the-art for practitioners, analysts, and scientists.* Amsterdam: Elsevier, 17–26.

Hagelüken, C. (2014). Technologiemetalle – Systemische Voraussetzungen entlang der Recyclingkette. In Kausch, P., Bertau, M., Gutzmer, J., Matschullat, J. (eds.), *Strategische Rohstoffe - Risikovorsorge.* (pp. 161–172) Imprint: Springer Spektrum, Berlin, Heidelberg.

Hagelüken, C., Meskers, C.E.M. (2010). Complex life cycles of precious and special metals. In Graedel, T.E., van der Voet, E. (eds.), *Linkages of sustainability.* Cambridge, MA: MIT Press, 163–197.

Holm, S.O., Englund, G. (2009). Increased ecoefficiency and gross rebound effect: Evidence from USA and six European countries 1960–2002. *Ecological Economics* 68 (3), 879–887.

Krautkraemer, J.A. (2005). Economics of scarcity: The state of the debate. In Simpson, R.D., Toman, M.A., Ayres, R.U. (eds.), *Scarcity and growth revisited. Natural resources and the environment in the new millennium.* (pp. 54–77) Washington, DC: Resources for the Future.

McKelvey, V.E. (1972). Mineral resource estimates and public policy. *American Scientist* 60 (1), 32–40.

Messner, F. (2002). Material substitution and path dependence: empirical evidence on the substitution of copper for aluminium. *Ecological Economics* 42 (1–2), 259–271.

Norgate, T., Haque, N. (2010). Energy and greenhouse gas impacts of mining and mineral processing operations. *Journal of Cleaner Production* 18 (3), 266–274.

Reller, A., Bublies, T., Staudinger, T., Oswald, I., Meißner, S., Allen, M., (2009). The Mobile Phone: Powerful Communicator and Potential Metal Dissipator. *GAIA* (2), 127–135.

Singer, D.A. (1995). World class base and precious metal deposits: A quantitative analysis. *Economic Geology* 90 (1), 88–104.

Singer, D.A., Menzie, W.D. (2010). *Quantitative mineral resource assessments: An integrated approach.* New York: Oxford University Press.

Skinner, B.J. (1979). A second iron age ahead. In Trudinger, P.A., Swaine, D.J. (eds.), *Biogeochemical cycling of mineral-forming elements* (pp. 556–575). Elsevier Scientific Pub. Co., Amsterdam, New York.

Sorrell, S., Dimitropoulos, J. (2008). The rebound effect: Microeconomic definitions, limitations and extensions. *Ecological Economics* 65 (3), 636–649.

Steinbach, V., Wellmer, F.W. (2010). Consumption and Use of Non-Renewable Mineral and Energy Raw Materials from an Economic Geology Point of View. *Sustainability* 2 (5), 1408–1430.

Tilton, J.E. (1996). Exhaustible resources and sustainable development. *Resources Policy* 22 (1–2), 91–97.

U.S. Geological Survey (USGS) (2014). Mineral commodity summaries 2014. Washington, DC: U.S. Geological Survey, US Government Printing Office.

UNEP (2011). *Recycling rates of metals: A status report.* United Nations Environment Programme, Nairobi, Kenya.

Wadia, C., Alivisatos, A.P., Kammen, D.M. (2009). Materials Availability Expands the Opportunity for Large-Scale Photovoltaics Deployment. *Environ. Sci. Technol.* 43 (6), 2072–2077.

Wellmer, F.W., Dalheimer, M. (2012). The feedback control cycle as regulator of past and future mineral supply. *Miner Deposita* 47 (7), 713–729.

11

SOCIAL METABOLISM

Fridolin Krausmann

Introduction

In the last century the global consumption of materials, energy and water and associated pollution has increased by several orders of magnitude. Many of the most pressing global sustainability problems are caused by the extraction and processing of resources and their discharge after use. The increase in atmospheric carbon dioxide (CO_2) concentration contributing to global climate change is but one of the many consequences of human resource use. Humanity appropriates roughly 25 per cent of the biomass produced annually by green plants to provide food, feed and fibre. Human activities have doubled the amount of reactive nitrogen in the biosphere. Meanwhile, the amount of some metals accumulating in landfills and in-use stocks (e.g. buildings, infrastructure or machinery) has reached a size similar to that of known reserves.

Social metabolism is a concept that addresses these biophysical exchange processes, between society and Nature, and the related sustainability problems. It studies the biophysical basis of the economy and provides a framework to investigate patterns and dynamics of social economic material and energy flows and their drivers; knowledge crucial to manage resource flows in a more sustainable way. This chapter introduces the concept of social metabolism and the corresponding methodology of material flow accounting and provides an overview of metabolism research of the last two decades.

Social metabolism and material flow analysis

The social metabolism concept

Robert Ayres coined the term industrial metabolism which he defined as "the whole integrated collection of physical processes that convert raw materials and energy, plus labour, into finished products and wastes" (Ayres, 1994: 16). More broadly, the concept has also been termed social or social economic metabolism. It is used in analogy to the metabolism of biological organisms.

Human beings, like all other organisms, depend on a continuous throughput of materials: water and food being the most essential. Food, a specific mix of digestible biomass, provides humans with nutritional energy and the organic and mineral components necessary to build up and maintain the body and its functioning. After being used or stored in the human metabolic system, all intakes leave the body in the form of excrements or through the respiratory system.

The same applies to society. Social metabolism refers to social economic systems as thermodynamically open, hybrid systems, comprising both a cultural system (a system of recurrent self-referential communication) and material components, the biophysical structures of society (Fischer-Kowalski and Weisz, 1999)—including physical infrastructure such as buildings, machines, artefacts. For the production and reproduction of its biophysical structures society mobilises flows of materials and energy. In addition to food and water, society needs fuel to provide for heat, work, light, and mobility, and metals, minerals and other raw materials to build and maintain dwellings, supply and discharge networks, transport and communication infrastructures, machinery and consumer goods.

Humans extract the necessary materials from the natural environment. Some of the materials, like fuel and food, are used within a short period of time after extraction, while others are stored for decades or even centuries in buildings or infrastructures. However, everything that society extracts from the environment is transformed and sooner or later returned to the environment in the form of waste and emissions. The metabolism of society is the major driver of global environmental change and exerts pressures on the environment both on the input side, when resources are extracted, during the use phase and finally on the output side when wastes and emissions are discharged. In addition to environmental pressures, scarcity and overuse have increasingly become issues of concern [see also Chapters 10 and 41]. Several of the key resources for industrial development have become increasingly scarce which means they become more costly to produce and eventually systems dependent upon them cannot be sustained.

History of the concept

Social metabolism is not a new concept. The idea can be traced back to the nineteenth century, when it was still common sense for economists to treat the economy as inherently biophysical, and acknowledge that flows of energy and materials are the basis of all economic activity. The concept today can be traced to the works of Karl Marx in the 1850s. It was reintroduced a century later by Wolman (1965) and Ayres and Kneese (1969), and its emergence as a core concept in ecological economics and industrial ecology is well documented (Fischer-Kowalski and Hüttler, 1998; Gonzales de Molina and Toledo, 2014). While the analysis of social economic energy flows has a long tradition, material flow analysis (MFA) was advanced only in the 1990s. A seminal study by Adriaanse and colleagues (1997) provided aggregate information on material use in industrial economies. Since then, a variety of tools for studying material flows at different temporal and spatial scales, and for different applications, have been developed (Baccini and Brunner, 2012). At the regional scale urban metabolism studies emerged as an important field of application (Barles, 2010). At the national level, economy-wide MFA is now an agreed-upon and standardised tool for investigating the size and structure of social economic material flows (Fischer-Kowalski et al., 2011). Statistical offices around the globe have begun to compile material flow data and publish headline indicators derived from MFA (e.g. OECD, 2008; Eurostat, 2012). The International Resource Panel of the United Nations (http://www.unep.org/resourcepanel) publishes a series of reports on core issues of social metabolism (e.g. decoupling, recycling).

Principles of material flow analysis

MFA provides reliable and comparable data and aggregate material flow indicators. Full-scale economy wide material flow accounts are consistent compilations of the overall material inputs (except for water and air) into national economies, the changes of material stock within the economic system and the material outputs to other economies or the environment. These flows are illustrated in Figure 11.1.

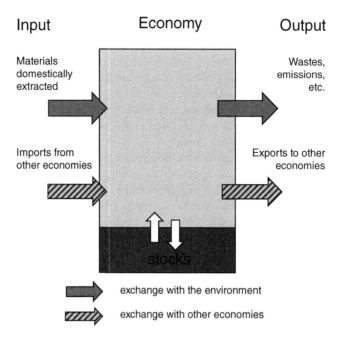

Figure 11.1 Material flow accounting scheme.
Source: adapted from Eurostat (2012).

Domestic material consumption (DMC) is an important indicator of material use. DMC is calculated as the sum total of all materials extracted from the domestic environment of an observed economy—domestic extraction (DE)—and all materials imported from other social economic systems minus all exports. DMC is a measure of apparent consumption and designed in a way that is consistent with gross domestic product (GDP). It measures the physical size of the economy and also indicates its waste and emissions potential. DMC per capita is often termed metabolic rate. DMC per unit of GDP measures material intensity (MI), and its inverse is called material productivity.

The variety of materials society uses is huge. Some, such as the platinum group of metals, are used in only small quantities, while others, such as limestone, are extracted in vast amounts. Material flow accounts distinguish several hundred different materials. For presentation these are usually aggregated to only a few groups with similar properties. Most commonly these are biomass (crops, used crop residues, grazed biomass, wood, fish), fossil energy carriers (coal, petroleum, natural gas, peat), and minerals. Minerals are further separated into the broad groups of metallic ores, non-metallic minerals for industrial use and the much larger flow of bulk minerals used for construction (sand, gravel, crushed stone).

A drawback of these types of MFA studies is that they typically treat the economy as a black box and are unable to analyse how exactly materials flow through the economic system. In order to achieve this, analysis can be undertaken at the level of individual substances. Such substance flow analysis is a variant of MFA that follows the same accounting principles but tracks the flow of substances—such as carbon, phosphorus or copper—through social economic systems (Brunner and Rechberger, 2004; Chen and Graedel, 2012). This chapter focuses on aggregate material flows and discusses patterns and trends of global material flows.

The metabolic transition

Material flows in human history

Human induced flows of materials and energy have greatly increased throughout human history. During the period of hunter-gatherers, DMC is assumed to have generally grown in parallel with population and is estimated to have reached some 7 million tons of biomass per year by the advent of the Neolithic revolution. During the approximately 10,000 years from the emergence of agriculture to the onset of the Industrial Revolution, the size of the global metabolism further multiplied and had climbed to roughly 2 gigatonnes per year (Gt/yr) by the mid-seventeenth century. At this time biomass still accounted for more than 90 per cent of all materials used. Two factors contributed to the growth of material use in that period: the adoption of agriculture facilitated unprecedented population growth, and the mode of subsistence of agriculturalists was much more resource intensive than that of foraging societies, particularly because of livestock husbandry and a growing stock of built structures. By 1850, when most European countries had joined the British path of coal-based industrialisation, global material use had doubled to approximately 4 Gt/yr (Krausmann et al., 2016).

While these figures all have to be considered rough estimates, better data exist for the last two centuries. Based on early statistical records and modelling, a number of studies have compiled evidence for the long-term historical development of material flows in industrial countries, exploring what has been termed the 'metabolic transition' from the agrarian to the industrial metabolic pattern (Krausmann et al., 2008). Figure 11.2 illustrates the transition in Japan. While Japan was one of the latecomers to the Industrial Revolution, the patterns in material use show characteristic features of the associated metabolic transition. In all observed cases aggregate material use increased by one to two orders of magnitude. During the coal phase material use rises but high population growth rates cause per capita material use to grow at only moderate rates. In the twentieth century the transition towards mass production and mass consumption accelerated growth of material use. In this phase material use grew much faster than population and metabolic rates surged. This is impressively shown in Figure 11.2a for Japan, where material use per capita multiplied within only two decades after World War II. Similarly, growth in most industrial economies slowed down or even came to a halt in the 1970s, coinciding with the oil price shocks of 1973 and 1979.

Figure 11.2a also shows that during the metabolic transition the composition of material use changes fundamentally. The share of renewable biomass which dominated material use through most of human history declines from above 95 per cent to typically around 20 per cent in industrial economies. The material basis of the industrial economy consists of a mix of non-metallic minerals (used mostly for construction), fossil energy carriers and ores. These materials become dominant, although they do not replace biomass but rather add on top of a still growing input of biomass.

As society rapidly builds up large stocks of infrastructure, buildings and machinery, the share of materials that accumulate in long-lasting stocks of artefacts increases from less than 20 per cent to above 50 per cent of total material inputs. Quantitative assessments of material stock development are still rare (e.g. Tanikawa et al., 2015). The few existing estimates show that during the twentieth century social economic stocks of materials increased from around 10 tonnes per capita (t/cap) to several hundred t/cap and that stocks—in contrast to flows—continued to grow after the 1970s. This is illustrated for Japan in Figure 11.2b. Due to their long lifetime, large and growing stocks constitute a major legacy creating societal lock-in for future resource use and emissions. The role of stocks in linking service provision to energy and material throughput is a key issue which

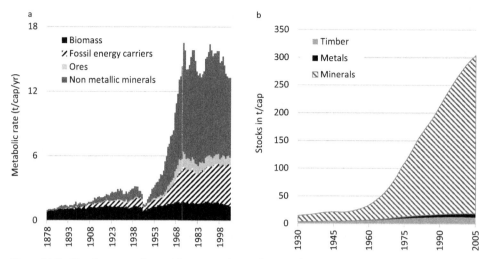

Figure 11.2 Development of material consumption and material stocks in Japan.
Notes: Metabolic rate in t/cap/yr (2a) and material stocks in t/cap (2b).
Source: adapted from Krausmann et al. (2011) and Fishman et al. (2014).

metabolism research only begins to address (Pauliuk and Müller, 2014). Stock dynamics are also of high significance for advancing the circularity of the economy. Materials stored in stocks are not immediately available for recycling and limit the potential contribution of recycling to close material loops in present times. However, the stored materials may become important resources for future urban mining (Krook and Baas, 2013).

Global patterns and trends in material use

At the global scale population growth and the growth in metabolic rates in industrial and emerging economies have driven a tenfold increase in material extraction from 7 Gt/yr in 1900 to 73 Gt/yr in 2009; simultaneously the average global metabolic rate has roughly doubled from 4.5 to 10 t/cap/yr (Krausmann et al., 2009). Material use patterns differ strongly across countries and world regions. In an evaluation of global MFA data, Giljum et al. (2014) have shown that growth in material use in the emerging economies of the so-called BRICS+ countries—Brazil, Russia, India, China, South Africa (BRICS); plus South Korea, Singapore and Mexico—has accelerated in the last decade. As illustrated in Figure 11.3, these fast growing economies have now displaced the Organisation for Economics Cooperation and Development (OECD) countries in their long dominance of global material flows. The share of the BRICS+ countries in global material use has increased from 31 per cent to 46 per cent since 1980. On the one hand, as illustrated in Figure 11.3a, the global financial crisis of 2008 severely impacted the physical economy and caused a considerable reduction in material use in the OECD countries, and on the other hand metabolic rates in the BRICS+ countries have risen considerably, especially in the last decade. In particular China has emerged as a driver for the growth of the global physical economy (Schandl and West, 2012). In the last ten years alone, China has doubled its per capita material use to around 18 t/cap/yr. Economic growth driven by urbanisation, large-scale infrastructure projects and the expansion of production capacities for both domestic and foreign markets have changed China's metabolic profile towards convergence with that of industrial economies. In contrast, growth in the large group of other non-OECD countries is still only moderate. In the least developed countries hardly any growth in material

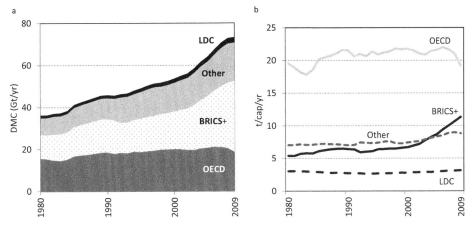

Figure 11.3 Global material use by world regions 1980–2009.
Notes: OECD members of 1980; BRICS+: Brazil, Russian Federation, India, China, South Africa, Korea, Singapore, Mexico; LDC (Least Developed Countries) according to UN.
Source: adapted from Giljum et al. 2014.

use occurred in the last 30 years. These countries consume only 3 per cent of global resources— average DMC of only 3 t/cap/yr—but are inhabited by 12 per cent of the global human population.

Besides material consumption, trade flows are also an important issue in global metabolism research. Global exports have risen from 7 per cent of global extraction in 1950 to 15 per cent in 2010, when more than 10 Gt of materials were shipped internationally. The volume of physical exports is growing even faster than global GDP. While most industrial countries are net importers of materials, the main exporting regions are: Australia, the Russian Federation, some Latin American countries, and the oil producing countries of the Middle East. Asia has only recently become a net importing region, but imports are rising fast. An important theme in metabolism research is ecologically unequal exchange (Vallejo, 2010), where countries of the Global South export natural resources and high impact commodities to high income economies, allowing them to shift their environmental burden onto those countries [see Chapters 4 and 15].

Drivers of material use

The differences in metabolic rates across country groups, illustrated in Figure 11.3b, indicate that economic development is an important factor driving material use. Figure 11.4a, in which metabolic rates of 167 countries are plotted against per capita GDP, shows that indeed differences in GDP can explain much of the differences in metabolic rates. In general, countries with high GDP also consume a higher amount of materials. Note that the graph is in logarithmic form and obscures the relation between GDP and metabolic rate, which is much steeper at lower GDP levels but levels off at higher GDP.

This also holds for the development of individual countries, as illustrated for Japan in Figure 11.4b. DMC rose fast during early periods of economic growth but saturated at high GDP levels. Figure 11.4a also clearly shows that GDP does not explain all the observed differences. There are many exceptions to the rule and countries on a similar GDP level can use a substantially different amount of materials. Within the high GDP member states of the European Union, for example, DMC ranges between 9 t/cap/yr in the UK to 32 t/cap/yr in Finland, although the GDP of the two economies is almost the same.

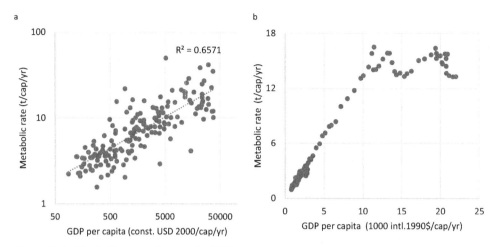

Figure 11.4 Metabolic rates and per capita GDP.
Notes: 167 countries in the year 2000 (11.4a); Japan 1878–2005 (11.4b).
Source: UNEP (2011) and Krausmann et al. (2011).

Next to GDP a range of other factors have an influence on the size of per capita material use (Steinberger et al., 2010; Weisz et al., 2006) The significance of resource intensive industries plays a role. Countries with high resource endowments and large extractive sectors are typically raw material exporters and have higher DMC per capita than import dependent countries. Also low population density and extreme climatic conditions can contribute to above average metabolic rates.

Dematerialisation

The big question is: Can economic growth be decoupled from material consumption and an effective dematerialisation of the economy be achieved? A number of studies have investigated the relationship between material use and economic development in the search for evidence of decoupling (Bringezu et al., 2004; Steinberger et al., 2013). Empirical evidence shows, that in the past, considerable improvements in material productivity (GDP per unit of DMC) have been achieved. In industrial countries material productivity has been growing at rates between 1 per cent and 2 per cent per year. As a consequence, today 40–80 per cent less materials are required to produce one unit of GDP than a century ago. Gains in material productivity were highest for biomass, as biomass consumption typically does not grow with GDP but rather with population. Figure 11.5 shows that for Japan less and less biomass was used per unit of GDP. Improvements in material productivity were less significant for the group of fossil and mineral materials, the key resources for industrial development. For these, material intensity increased during early periods of industrialisation and improvements only set in at later stages of development. In Japan the turning point of material intensity for fossil and mineral materials occurred only in the 1970s, but since then considerable improvements have been achieved as illustrated in Figure 11.5.

The observed improvements in material productivity have been attributed to technological progress, which allows the same service to be provided with less material input, and to structural change in the economy from industry to less resource intensive service sectors. However, in spite of continuous and considerable improvements, evidence of absolute dematerialisation is rare. Most countries show 'relative decoupling'. In this case gains in material productivity keep

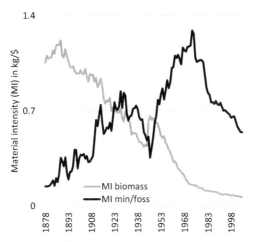

Figure 11.5 Development of material intensity in Japan.
Notes: Material intensity is DMC/GDP for biomass and fossil and mineral materials.
Source: based on Krausmann et al. (2011).

the growth of material use relative to GDP low, but do not yield any effective decline of material use. Empirical evidence indicates that a reduction in material use typically occurs when economic growth is very low (Steinberger et al., 2013). Periods of recession or low growth are often related to a reduction in material use, but with economic recovery resource use rises again. Only very few countries show absolute dematerialisation for prolonged periods, among them the UK, Germany and also Japan. Japan was the first country to incorporate goals for a sound material cycle society based on the 3R principle (reduce, reuse and recycle) in the 1990s and it has effectively reduced its DMC by 17 per cent since then (see Figure 11.2a). However, Japan's economy has also been growing at very low rates during that period which likely helped to keep material use low. In addition, the location shifting of resource intensive processes is a factor contributing to the reduction in domestic material use. The reductions of material use in the UK and Germany are mainly related to deindustrialisation and the closure of material intensive coal and steel industries.

Material footprints

An issue that has received considerable attention in recent research is the shifting of material use through trade and its consequences for resource productivity and decoupling. Traditional MFA only measures the amount of resources directly used in a national economy, and ignores upstream resource flows of imported commodities. This means that net importing countries like Japan or the UK may have a lower DMC than net exporting countries, simply because large amounts of materials used in producing the imported products are accounted for in the exporting countries, driving up their DMC. This has triggered the development of MFA methods that quantify the indirect resource flows of trade and final consumption. This is, for example, possible on the basis of environmentally extended global input–output analysis [Chapter 36] that can be used to derive multipliers representing all upstream global material requirements associated with one unit of product. This allows the calculation of material footprints, which measure the actual material demand related to final consumption in a country. This approach has also been termed consumption based material flow accounting, vis-à-vis production based conventional MFA. In a global study, Wiedmann et al. (2015) have shown that the inclusion of upstream flows can significantly alter the picture. For the case of Japan these calculations show that, while Japan has succeeded in decoupling DMC from economic growth, the material footprint has actually been growing with GDP.

Future directions

Social metabolism research is still a young field. In the last two decades MFA has become a standard tool in ecological economics and environmental accounting. While conventional MFA has meanwhile been largely standardised, the relatively new material footprint methodologies still require harmonisation of data and methods in order to provide robust consumption based indicators (Schaffartzik et al., 2014). Also, better linkages between MFA and waste and recycling flows have to be established to support waste management and recycling policy. Metabolism research has achieved a basic knowledge about global patterns and trends of material flows, and the underlying drivers. In the next step gaining a deeper understanding of the mechanisms behind the observed patterns and trends in material flows will be important. This requires opening up the black box of the economy in order to analyse the interrelation of different flows and material groups and biophysical stocks and flows of materials and energy. So far little is known about the size and dynamics of social economic stocks of materials, how stocks drive the flow of resources and legacies of stocks with long lifetimes (Pauliuk and Müller, 2014). Similarly, a better understanding of the coupling of material flows and economic development, as well as quality of life, and the significance of rebound effects [see Chapter 46] is required to analyse the limitations and potentials of conventional (e.g. decoupling) but also alternative (e.g. degrowth [Chapter 44]) economic strategies to dematerialise the economy. A major research agenda is the development of models of social economic metabolism which take biophysical interrelations into account and of scenarios of future resource use under different economic and biophysical conditions. This will be essential to improve the usefulness of MFA for the design and assessment of resource policies and the definition of targets of sustainable resource use (Bringezu, 2015).

Concluding remarks

Metabolism research has shown that industrialisation drives growth in material use and that what emerges is a typical pattern of high metabolic rates, low share of renewable biomass and a large amount of materials stored in stocks of built structure. The collected evidence does not give rise to optimism that reducing resource use is possible while the economy keeps growing. The high income countries seem to have stabilised their resource use at a high level and it remains to be seen if the reductions in material use observed in many OECD countries after the financial crisis of 2008 are a sign of lasting change. Globally, there are indications that economic growth in the Global South will drive resource use for some time. A global convergence in metabolic rates at the current metabolic profile of industrial countries paired with the expected growth in global population would lead to a doubling or tripling of global resource use. These additional resources are unlikely to be available, and we cannot expect the global ecosystem to have the capacity to absorb the corresponding wastes and emissions.

The obvious conclusion is that the scale of social economic metabolism cannot continue to grow as in the past, and humanity must find ways to return to a safe operating space for material use within planetary boundaries. This will require a significant reduction of resource use in the industrial world and ways to obtain wealth and quality of life in the emerging economies without emulating the metabolic profile of the old industrial core. Achieving this will be unlikely through gradual changes or technological fixes alone. A sustainability transformation may well require fundamental changes in society similar to the historical agrarian–industrial transformation. Completing this on a global scale may be physically impossible due to resource constraints; however, in all cases, failing to make this transformation would wreak havoc with the Earth's biotic and climatic systems. Metabolism research can help identify potentials and limitations for sustainable resource use strategies and provides information and headline indicators required for the formulation of targets, and development and evaluation of policy.

Key further readings cited

Adriaanse, A., Bringezu, S., Hammond, A., Moriguchi, Y., Rodenburg, E., Rogich, D. and Schütz, H. (1997). *Resource flows: the material basis of industrial economies*. Washington, DC: World Resources Institute.

Baccini, P. and Brunner, P.H. (2012). *Metabolism of the Anthroposphere: analysis, evaluation, design*. Cambridge, Mass: Mit Pr.

Fischer-Kowalski, M., Krausmann, F. Giljum, S., Lutter, S., Mayer, A., Bringezu, S., Moriguchi, Y., Schütz, H., Schandl, H. and Weisz, H. (2011). Methodology and indicators of economy wide material flow accounting: state of the art and reliablity across sources. *Journal of Industrial Ecology* 15(6): 855–876.

Gonzales de Molina, M. and Toledo, V. (2014). *The social metabolism: a socio-ecological theory of historical change*. Vol. 3. Environmental History. New York, Heidelberg: Springer.

Krausmann, F., Gingrich, S., Eisenmenger, N., Erb, K.H., Haberl, H. and Fischer-Kowalski, M. (2009). Growth in global materials use, GDP and population during the 20th century. *Ecological Economics* 68(10): 2696–2705.

Other literature cited

Ayres, R.U. (1994). Industrial metabolism: Theory and policy. In *Industrial metabolism: restructuring for sustainable development*. Tokyo: United Nations University Press.

Ayres, R.U. and Kneese, A. V. (1969). Production, consumption, and externalities. *The American Economic Review* 59(3): 282–297.

Barles, S. (2010). Society, energy and materials: the contribution of urban metabolism studies to sustainable urban development issues. *Journal of Environmental Planning and Management* 53(4): 439–455.

Bringezu, S. (2015). Possible target corridor for sustainable use of global material. *Resources* 4(1): 25–54.

Bringezu, S., Schütz, H., Steger, S. and Baudisch, J. (2004). International comparison of resource use and its relation to economic growth: The development of total material requirement, direct material inputs and hidden flows and the structure of TMR. *Ecological Economics* 51(1–2): 97–124.

Brunner, P.H. and Rechberger, H. (2004). *Practical handbook of material flow analysis*. Boca Raton, FL: CRC Press.

Chen, W.Q. and Graedel, T.E. (2012). Anthropogenic cycles of the elements: a critical review. *Environmental Science & Technology* 46(16): 8574–8586.

Eurostat (2012). *Economy-wide Material Flow Accounts (EW-MFA). Compilation Guide 2012*. Luxembourg: European Statistical Office.

Fischer-Kowalski, M. and Hüttler, W. (1998). Society's metabolism. *Journal of Industrial Ecology* 2(4): 107–136.

Fischer-Kowalski, M. and Weisz, H. (1999). Society as a hybrid between material and symbolic realms. Toward a theoretical framework of society-nature interaction. Ed. by Lee Freese. *Advances in Human Ecology* 8: 215–251. Bingley, UK: Emerald Group Publishing Limited.

Fishman, T., Schandl, H., Tanikawa, H., Walker, P. and Krausmann, F. (2014). Accounting for the material stock of nations. *Journal of Industrial Ecology* 18(3): 407–420.

Giljum, S., Dittrich, M., Lieber, M. and Lutter, S. (2014). Global patterns of material flows and their socio-economic and environmental implications: a MFA study on all countries world-wide from 1980 to 2009. *Resources* 3(1): 319–339.

Krausmann, F., Fischer-Kowalski, M., Schandl, H. and Eisenmenger, N. (2008). The global sociometabolic transition. *Journal of Industrial Ecology* 12(5–6): 637–656.

Krausmann, F., Gingrich, S. and Nourbakhch-Sabet, R. (2011). The metabolic transition in Japan. *Journal of Industrial Ecology* 15(6): 877–892.

Krausmann, F., Weisz, H., Eisenmenger, N. 2016. Transitions in socio-metabolic regimes through human history. In: *Social ecology: society-nature relations across time and space*. Haberl, H., Fischer-Kowalski, M., Krausmann, F., Winiwarter, V. New York, Heidelberg: Springer.

Krook, J. and Baas, L. (2013). Getting serious about mining the technosphere: a review of recent landfill mining and urban mining research. *Journal of Cleaner Production* 55: 1–9.

OECD (2008). *Measuring material flows and resource productivity. Volume I. The OECD Guide*. Paris: OECD.

Pauliuk, S. and Müller, D.B. (2014). The role of in-use stocks in the social metabolism and in climate change mitigation. *Global Environmental Change* 24: 132–142.

Schaffartzik, A., Eisenmenger, N., Krausmann, F. and Weisz, H. (2014). Consumption-based material flow accounting. *Journal of Industrial Ecology* 18(1): 102–112.

Schandl, H., West, J. (2012). Material flows and material productivity in China, Australia, and Japan. *Journal of Industrial Ecology* 16, 352–364.

Steinberger, J.K., Krausmann, F. and Eisenmenger, N. (2010). Global patterns of materials use: A socioeconomic and geophysical analysis. *Ecological Economics* 69(5): 1148–1158.

Steinberger, J. K., Krausmann, F., Getzner, M., Schandl, H. and West, J. (2013). Development and dematerialization: an international study. *PLoS ONE* 8(10): e70385.

Tanikawa, H., Fishman, T., Okuoka, K., Sugimoto, K. (2015). The weight of society over time and space: a comprehensive account of the construction material stock of Japan, 1945–2010. *Journal of Industrial Ecology* 19(5), 778–791.

UNEP (2011). Decoupling Natural Resource Use and Environmental Impacts from Economic Growth, A Report of the Working Group on Decoupling to the International Resource Panel. Nairobi: UNEP.

Vallejo, M.C. (2010). Biophysical structure of the Ecuadorian economy, foreign trade, and policy implications. *Ecological Economics* 70(2): 159–169.

Weisz, H., Krausmann, F., Amann, C., Eisenmenger, N., Erb, K.H., Hubacek, K. and Fischer-Kowalski, M. (2006). The physical economy of the European Union: Cross-country comparison and determinants of material consumption. *Ecological Economics* 58(4): 676–698.

Wiedmann, T.O., Schandl, H., Lenzen, M., Moran, D., Suh, S., West, J. and Kanemoto, K. (2015). The material footprint of nations. *Proceedings of the National Academy of Sciences* 112(20): 6271–6276.

Wolman, A. (1965). The metabolism of cities. *Scientific American* 213(3): 179–190.

12

THE BIOPHYSICAL REALITIES OF ECOSYSTEMS

Vincent Devictor

Introduction

Although policy makers and managers are keen on scientific measures of ecosystem health, stability, resilience, resistance, productivity and other properties representing positive values, ecosystems are, by nature, open, dynamic and constantly changing. Contemporary ecology and social ecological economics are faced with the dilemma of delineating ecosystems and simplifying their complexity to make them intelligible in order to address their mismanagement while accounting for the reality of their biophysical structure and functioning. This dilemma produces two extreme postures depending on how ecosystems are conceived. At one extreme, when considered as irreducible and fundamentally complex systems, ecosystems risk becoming excessively abstract and arbitrary conventions with vague, or no, scientific grounding. At the other, when reduced to some mechanical aggregation of physicochemical phenomenon, ecosystems risk losing their specificity as biological phenomena. Any ecological system is best viewed as a subsystem of a wider environment. Therefore, a practical approach to ecosystem understanding lies in the identification of the limits of the subsystems and of the wider environment (their distinctiveness) as well as in the recognition of their mutual limitations (their reciprocal influence).

Ecosystem ecology tries to anticipate ecosystem structure, process and dynamics. Several approaches have been proposed; for example, studying ecosystem energy flows and cycling of materials, leading to description of the distribution of key elements (e.g., carbon, phosphorus, or nitrogenous) within and between living and non-living forms, and the balance between energy entrance and dissipation. Another alternative is to focus on how the diversity and composition of living forms contribute to ecosystem functioning defined through specific variables such as biomass production or specific properties such as resilience or resistance. Changes in approach have involved redefinitions and critiques of the ecosystem concept that have forged the history of ecology (Golley, 1993).

However, two elements can be considered as stable focal points of interest in any ecological perspective. First, ecologists recognise ecosystems as designating the interactions between living and non-living forms. An ecosystem is therefore neither an organism nor a collection of organisms but a combination of biotic and abiotic entities. Second, ecologists adopt a criterion to delineate specific spatial and temporal extents in which these interactions occur. The spatial and temporal scales of ecosystems are not specified *a priori* but rather depend on the organisms and processes of interest. In other words, defining ecosystems corresponds to the delineation of specific interactions which can vary from a few centimetres to hundreds of kilometres.

A general definition of ecosystems is therefore: the ensemble of conditions allowing the interactions between biotic and abiotic elements in a given space and time. As such, any ecosystem is an open system linked to other ecosystems. Once delineated, a given ecosystem is characterised by its structure (describing how the different living and non-living forms interact) and its processes (the consequences of these interactions on the properties of the system). By definition, living forms are dynamic and interactions between biotic and abiotic components produce modifications of their own state and fate. Ecosystems are therefore also dynamic.

These basic understandings inform this chapter. Ecosystems are then univocally biological units, although as will be explained, they are too often not interpreted as such. An important aspect of ecosystems is how they represent boundaries around specific biophysical realities as is explored in the next section. Three concepts are highlighted with respect to ecosystems: horizontal structure that conditions the extent and dynamics of each of the biological components of an ecosystem; vertical structure that corresponds to the interactions between components; and ecosystem dynamics. Over the next three sections I critically review carrying capacity in relation to horizontal limits, emergent properties in relation to vertical limits, and ecological complexity in relation dynamism. This reveals how the concept of ecosystems has been highly contested with repeated attempts to convert ecology into a reductionist management tool while making biological knowledge conform to anthropomorphic reinterpretations suited to economic and political interests.

Biophysical realism in ecosystem understanding

Understanding ecosystems requires acknowledging the existence of fundamental limits and this is a major intuition of early ecologists. The study of the growth of human population is a good example. The population of the United States of American (USA) has grown exponentially as shown by the model best-fitted to the data (official Census Bureau), with no sign of any deceleration. Surprisingly, an exponential model would even provide you with very high accuracy, suggesting that there is no reason to believe that population growth can be any different. One of the earliest ecologists, Raymond Pearl (1879–1940), had a strong feeling that something was necessarily missing in this reasoning. According to him, because simple exponential growth cannot become asymptotic, this endless growth model must be wrong (Pearl and Reed, 1920). This led Pearl to rediscover one of the major biophysical realities of the natural world: the growth of a population is intrinsically bounded. This applies to any ecological phenomena, from individuals' growth to ecosystems, and this forms a central pillar of ecological science. No matter whether American population is still following the exponential phase, growth is necessarily intrinsically limited; the deceleration is not yet visible, but it is inevitable.

If one describes biophysical realities in a hierarchical manner, we might move from abiotic elements to communities up to the biosphere; but each given ecological entity (a population, a species assemblage or an ecosystem) is finite in time and constrained in space. This leads to the first type of limit that I refer to as being "horizontal" because it corresponds to the spatio-temporal boundary of one specific level.

Understanding ecosystem processes requires acknowledging other types of limits. In fact, even with only two interacting species another emergent biophysical reality is added: one species can limit or favour the existence of the other through positive or negative interactions. More generally, in any network of interacting species and abiotic components, only some specific trajectories are possible because of the mutual dependencies within and among ecosystem components. I refer to these limits as being "vertical" because they emerge from the interactions within and among ecological levels.

The recognition of vertical limits was a key step in the emergence of ecology and relates to one of the first observations of ecosystem collapse in the USA. When farmers there produced record crops in 1931, this appeared to be the successful realisation of the domination of Nature through application of knowledge and technology to increase economic productivity. However, things went unexpectedly wrong because this overproduction led to: severely reduced market prices, massive replacement of natural drought-resistant grasses by wheat, drastic change in soil ecosystems and formation of a rapid, large-scale erosion. This was the "Dust Bowl" phenomena, whereby eroded cultivated lands were reduced to dust which blew away with the wind. When the wheat died, its roots no longer held the soil in place. Soil was revealed to be a living, not dead, substrate with which plants interact.

The Dust Bowl played a central role in the consolidation of ecological science and in the progressive recognition of major vertical limits in biophysical realities. It offered a large-scale ecological experiment. At that time, Frederic Clements (1874–1945) was arguably the most influential ecologist, and he considered that each region of the world, which he called a "biome", had stable climate and a corresponding optimal "formation" of plants. These formations reached a mature stage called the "climax", after a deterministic succession of species. The Dust Bowl could be seen as an obvious disturbance along this trajectory. Humans were fundamentally disrupting the "balance of nature".

However, the Dust Bowl also weakened this very view because it suggested to other ecologists that plant associations resulted from succeeding disturbances involving plants and soil and their interactions. Humans were fundamentally witnessing, as well as being part of, an interacting "ecosystem". There was no need for any harmony or ideal trajectory of natural communities to understand what happened. Describing the modification of species interactions and abiotic factors was sufficient. Following the Dust Bowl, The concept of "ecosystem" was proposed in 1935 by Arthur Tansley (1871–1955) to challenge the teleological idea of equilibrium in plant formations.

Ecology learnt from the emergence of ecosystem concepts that not only are growth paths intrinsically bounded, but also that multiple potential growth paths interact, leading to the complex dynamics of living and non-living forms. Some "vertical limits" resulting from the interactions between ecological levels must be considered in addition to the horizontal limits of each level.

However, these two types of biophysical structural realities do not cover all aspects of ecosystems. A new contemporary ecology has emphasised the intrinsic difficulty of studying complex systems with standard equations (Schneider and Kay, 1994). In discovering that complex dynamic systems were often chaotic—i.e. that small interactions between their components have important consequences on the trajectory of the whole system—ecologists have challenged the possibility of making precise, mechanistic and accurate predictions about the future of ecosystems. Understanding ecosystems is compromised by non-linear interactions between components, emergence of new structures and functions, and unpredictable events. Obviously, some of this lack of predictability can be attributed to our lack of knowledge. However, ecologists have progressively shown there is always partial ignorance of ecosystems (i.e. strong uncertainty, see Spash, 2002). This third type of phenomena is the dynamic reality of ecosystems.

The three aspects of ecosystems identified above (the horizontal and vertical limits as well as their dynamic nature) have been central to key developments in the economic treatment of the environment and the discipline of ecology. In the following three sections, I will clarify these three dimensions of ecosystem understanding in a critical overview of central concepts, namely carrying capacity, emergent properties and ecological complexity.

Horizontal limits and carrying capacity

In Nature, no population can grow indefinitely. Growth is always bounded. This very basic phenomenon can be considered as a central pillar of ecology. Take N_t individuals at time t (you can always observe a new number of individuals, N_{t+1}, at time t+1); the growth rate of the population is given by $r = N_{t+1}/N_t$. This simply means that from one step to another the population size is multiplied by its growth rate and this is true for any time step $dN/dt = rN$.

However, obviously, this cannot be the case in a limited world. That is what Pearl added to this basic equation to make it compatible with the simple truth that there must be a maximum number of individuals that any environment can support—as also previously noticed by the mathematician Pierre-François Verhulst (1804–1849). This limit represents the maximum population size and is traditionally called "carrying capacity" (K) in ecological science. The modified equation is given by $dN/dt = rN(1-N/K)$. We immediately see with this new equation that when N is very small, growth is nearly exponential $dN/dt \approx rN$, but when N is approaching the value of K, growth is null $dN/dt \approx 0$. The shape of this equation is composed of an exponential phase, a transition and a limit. Here is the first fundamental biophysical reality that ecology brings up: any ecological system is necessarily constrained by some horizontal limits.

Beyond this very simple equation, the huge influence of the notion of "carrying capacity", however, must be critically examined. The term was most likely transferred from shipping and engineering to livestock and grazing management and then to wildlife management. It was originally used to refer to the amount of things another thing was designed to "carry" (Sayre, 2008). However, it was progressively redefined and made increasingly abstract. It was applied to humans and non-humans, and from petri dishes to the globe. However, the same general idea prevailed, that a "domain of restriction" for each ecological state must exist even if the range of this domain is not fixed.

This simple equation and famous limit are far from being neutral when applied to Nature protection. Indeed, carrying capacity is hard to identify in Nature. Some species might reach a saturation point but others have fluctuating dynamics that are almost impossible to stabilise. The limit may then be viewed as a property of the environment itself, not of the process of growth. However, this means a given species can be treated as a crop and the environment as something humans can supply from the outside. According to this view, the carrying capacity can easily be interpreted as a flexible and manageable characteristic.

Carrying capacity has thus been used to rationalise wildlife management in almost all conservation projects. This is probably what made the concept attractive to administrations keen on stable and numerical, but also revocable, limits. For instance, this had (and still has) a huge influence in fisheries, where scientists are regularly called upon to discuss the "carrying capacity" of fish stocks (Bell et al. 2006). Fishing effort is adjusted to a limit estimated by ecologists. This limit, however, is always revised and treated as a flexible property rather than a definitive ecological constraint.

This first kind of biophysical limit was also appealing to ecological economists claiming that a stationary state economy was desirable and necessary to align with the saturated shape of any growth process in a finite world (e.g. Daly, 1977) [see also Chapter 45]. However, when applied to global scales and to human populations, carrying capacity has also played a controversial role. It first served the claim that the world was overpopulated. Neo-Malthusian ecologists such as Garret Hardin, Paul Ehrlich or Gretchen Daily used this argument to suggest that an area is overpopulated as soon as its long-term carrying capacity is degraded (Daily and Ehrlich, 1992). These authors conceive of human impact as the product of population size, per capita consumption, and environmental damage generated by technologies. According to this view, the rapid depletion of essential resources coupled with the degradation of land and atmospheric quality indicates that the carrying capacities of the world (either social or biophysical) have been reached because this essential 'natural capital' has been exploited too fast. Others have tried to convert consumption and production to land area to estimate the carrying capacity using the metaphor of an "ecological footprint" for human population (Rees, 1992).

However, again, describing a carrying capacity for the Earth, and emphasising human impacts, also leads to strong normative conclusions. The fundamental recognition of biophysical limits and interdependencies between the social and natural world has unfortunately paved the road to a "new environmental pragmatism", keen on mainstreaming a utilitarian approach to ecological problems (Spash, 2009). An example is setting goals to maximise efficiency in resource consumption in translating ecosystem processes to "ecosystem services" [Chapter 43], defined as the benefits that humans can take from Nature (Daily, 1997). Economists and ecologist, in a joint effort, have proposed that human demand is kept within the amount of what Nature can supply and have called for the best use of technology to optimise this trade-off (Wackernagel et al., 2002). The rhetoric of applying instrumental values to Nature, often using the tools of cost-benefit analysis, has thus flourished and was rapidly endorsed by economists, ecologists and institutions.

Over time the recognition that there exist limits to ecosystem exploitation was reframed to allow new forms of environmental exploitation. This economic turn should not be used to undermine the existence of effective limits due to biophysical realities, but should draw attention to how ecology can be twisted from systems preservation to items use or transformation (Vatn, 2000). The same movement can be shown with respect to vertical limits and emergent properties of ecosystems to which I turn next.

Vertical limits and emergent properties

The Dust Bowl catastrophe suggested that rapid and massive soil erosion could result from the modifications in the interactions between soil, plants and atmosphere. This problem stimulated Tansley to consider "ecosystems" as the fundamental unit in Nature. The existence of vertical limits in ecosystems is, at first sight, very simple to understand: emergence appears when the structure and dynamics of the whole cannot be explained using the component parts alone, or in other words when "more is different" (Anderson, 1972). However, ecology and conservation sciences are haunted by this problem. This scaling-up issue has even been identified as "the" central problem of ecology and conservation (Levin, 1992).

Of course, an emerging structure, or dynamics, at a given hierarchical level (population, species, community or ecosystem) can simply result from our partial knowledge of the individual entities of this level. A "weak" emergence is then simply a matter of how errors are spreading through levels of organisation or scales. Such weak emergence may be difficult to overcome simply because of uncertainty about how numerous uncontrolled variables change between levels or scales. Weak emergence, however, is not a theoretical obstacle to the understanding of ecosystems. In contrast, "strong" emergence results from the formal impossibility of reducing the property of the whole to its individual elements. Strong emergence is not a limit of knowledge but rather lies in the autonomy and self-organisation of each level (Rooney et al., 2007). In this case, the combination of individual species has new and unpredictable dynamics that cannot be derived from the knowledge of the dynamics of each species.

However, even when vertical limits are recognised, ecosystems can still be described as simplistic hierarchies structured by energy flux and production. Besides, soon after ecologists admitted that ecosystems were fundamental units in Nature, they grouped organisms within ecosystems into a series of discrete trophic levels according to their "role" as "producers", "primary consumers", "secondary consumers", and so on (Lindeman, 1942). They aligned dependencies between biotic and abiotic sub-components to production–consumption relationships. In this respect, ecologists have immediately interpreted vertical limits in a simplified and manageable manner with strong normative consequences.

For instance, Eugene Odum added a new holism to the concept proposed by Tansley and transferred physiological concepts such as homeostasis, metabolism and stability to the level of whole ecosystems. This approach was popularised by Eugene's brother, Howard Odum, who referred to ecosystems as systems under energy control and management by man. According to Howard, a "new enterprise", called "ecological engineering" must be developed to "fashion synthetic systems" with well-planned energy budgets (Odum, 1962, 57). The influence of the Odum brothers was huge. Ecological engineering and restoration ecology are deeply influenced by this legacy (Mitsch, 2012). Adopting this viewpoint, Howard Odum stated that money saving and natural seeds are analogous, because in his world they both become forms of capital.

Therefore, a new tension emerged from the recognition of the vertical limits of biophysical realities. Once ecosystems were described again as self-organising units they were equated to productive machines to be protected but also replaced, restored or exploited. The ecological crisis was reduced again to a management problem. Recognising the importance of vertical limits has not constituted a barrier to the commodification of Nature in orthodox economics. Again the concept of ecosystem as 'services' has been applied to ecosystem processes such as regulation, recycling and storage. Biodiversity has been reconceptualised as a storehouse of commodities that can be managed as if produced by industrial machines. The mechanisms of mainstream economics and ecological engineering have encouraged this approach while some (but far from all) ecological economists and conservation biologist have questioned this tendency to ignore the biological dimensions of ecosystems.

Dynamic realism and ecological complexity

As noted earlier, the concept of an ecosystem removed the separation between the organic and the inorganic. Then, systems thinking, feedback loop mechanisms, energy flows, and cybernetics blurred the boundaries between natural phenomenon and techno-industrial objects. This way of thinking inherited from a new mode of knowledge production after World War II in which the government, private, civil and military interests converged towards the management and control of the world (Bocking, 2013). Ecosystem thinking was thus installed in a new regime of machine vision. The planet and biodiversity conceived as a unified biosphere was thought of as a collection of ecosystems responsive to management (Elichirigoity, 1999). Horizontal and vertical limits were easy to integrate into the managing vision of ecological problems, because concepts such as carrying capacity, stability or productivity could support them.

The idea of equilibrium reinstalled by Odumian ecology, however, was challenged once again. Ecologists have moved from trying to understand structured producer/consumer relationships to the study of chaotic dynamics, hazards and sudden transitions. A post-Odumian ecology emerged in the 1980s from the study of disturbance, non-linearity and instability (Worster, 1990). From this new perspective, ecosystems are not described as a vertical hierarchy from producers to consumers but as complex interactive networks. According to this 'new ecology,' ecological systems should be viewed as non-equilibrating, fluctuating processes that exhibit short-lived properties that are distributed unevenly across space and time.

New aspects of biophysical reality are thus revealed: non-linearity, chaos and surprise, a few of the many restrictions to our domination of Nature. Things are not only limited, non-renewable or fragile; they also have abrupt and unpredictable trajectories (Scheffer et al., 2001). Ecologists also casted some doubts on important theoretical and empirical results produced by equilibrium ecology. For instance, ecologists have shown that some patterns long attributed to species interactions could be reproduced using null models and random simulations. Probabilistic processes could replace most deterministic ones. Ecosystems and communities were eventually viewed as descriptive conventions with unclear spatial limits (Ricklefs, 2008). Therefore, this third characteristic of biophysical reality is neither related to horizontal nor vertical properties but relates to the very possibility of defining any coherent ecological "level" such as an ecosystem with predictable dynamics.

These limits to our knowledge of ecosystem dynamics have had strong consequences in ecological science, but also on the environmental movement. For instance, some authors came to view ecology as a case-study discipline with no fixed rules and proposed to revise the normative ground of ecology accordingly (Shrader-Frechette and McCoy, 1993). Indeed, environmentalists could not rest any more on the canonical, albeit vague, ideas of harmony, equilibrium and ecosystems. If there is no equilibrium in Nature, no coherent ecological units, and very few robust predictions, how can conservation be justified without anthropocentric and instrumental arguments?

In fact, acknowledging that some ecosystem processes escape from our predictions neither requires discarding horizontal and vertical realities nor the ethical foundations for Nature protection. Acknowledging major sources of uncertainty in Nature does not mean that for a given population within a specific domain of space and time growth is unlimited and interactions unimportant. Ecosystems can still be sized to specific temporal and spatial scales compatible with some degree of predictability. Moreover, ever changing communities can still be sufficiently homogeneous within a given spatial and temporal scale to generate moral obligations (Callicott, 1996). What needs to be endorsed is precisely that ecosystems are not, by nature, reducible to machines under control at all spatial and time scales.[1]

Future directions

Recent advances in ecology have emphasised that horizontal limits are still central issues. Populations of thousands species of including the most common ones are declining, and many biodiversity indicators are in bad shape (Butchart et al., 2010). Climate change will make the situation of ecological systems deteriorate further and faster in the next decades. Vertical limits are also central: human impacts are responsible for the trophic downgrading of ecosystems (Estes et al., 2011). The loss of even a few species can have cascading effects in terrestrial, marine and freshwater ecosystems worldwide. The still valid rule of thumb set by ecosystem ecology states that everything is both bounded and connected.

However, the fundamental mainstream economic ethos pretends to overcome the horizontal and vertical limits introduced by biophysical realities. This claim assumes that ecosystems can be treated as mechanical objects provided that clever concepts such as "externalities", "ecosystem services", or "biodiversity offset" are proposed. A first agenda for ecology and ecological economic is to critically assess the pervasive modifications of horizontal and vertical limits that reduces them to commodities.

However, even more critical perhaps is the need to question the tendency to always ignore the biological specificities of ecosystems and change the concepts of ecology into those of economics (Spash and Aslaksen, 2015). The preceding sections have explained how a series of real advances in ecology have suffered a similar countermovement from managerialism: the set of ecological constraints is always modified to make it flexible and governable. This reduction promotes the systematic domestication of Nature. The rationale for such motivations must be challenged.

How and for what ends Nature should be exploited or protected must be made explicit. Recognising that ecosystems are, by their very nature, driven by unpredictable dynamics should encourage the respect of their external, and non-internalisable, distinctiveness. New ecological economics cannot integrate old-fashioned ecology anchored in a reductionist view of Nature whereby the teleological and metaphorical idea of equilibrium is defended to control Nature as a productive machine. Interestingly, this avenue is compatible with the critical realism [Chapter 2] endorsed by social ecological economics (Spash, 2012): we must acknowledge the realistic side of horizontal and vertical limits of ecosystems while knowing that knowledge about what ecological systems are is necessarily contingent, value-laden, scale dependent and fallible.

Concluding remarks

In the Great Plains, farmers and ranchers have reduced erosion. Apparently, 70 years after the Dust Bowl, the USA has managed to 'repair' this great environmental disaster. However, this is only an appearance: this highly productive system now relies on heavy irrigation and ground-water aquifers are drying up. Technology is good at displacing limits and transferring problems from place to place but lessons from the Dust Bowl have not really been learnt. Land conversion by intensive monoculture is expanding globally and similar dust bowls are expected to increase under climate change (Field et al., 2010). Overall, this chapter emphasises that some ecologists have erroneously adopted the same tendency to handle the world as a machine—a trait common amongst many economists—thereby minimising and avoiding the fundamental challenges implied by the existence of the biophysical realities of ecosystems. Acknowledging the limits as well as the spontaneity and unpredictability of Nature challenges the drive for the domestication and management of everything.

Knowing that ecosystems are limited and interacting does not provide us with simple laws to predict ecosystem dynamics. Describing bounded and interacting growth in natural systems would still be compatible with a Newtonian worldview, whereby all states of the system can be explained by linear connections. Contemporary ecology shows that understanding ecosystems requires the adoption of a dynamic realism in which a prediction problem is added to the issue of delineating horizontal and vertical boundaries.

Ecological science has revealed fundamental properties of the natural world. Industrialised societies, however, think and behave as if resources were infinite, and if not infinite then renewable, and if not renewable then still replaceable by something else. Ecology is, first and foremost, a call for more realistic thinking and offers essential arguments in support of ecological economics. Yet ecology is strongly normative and structured by hidden ideological premises affecting its outcomes. Human ecosystems are not simple matters of food chains or predators but include objectives, techniques and normative choices. Recognising horizontal and vertical limits of ecosystems and their low predictability should lead us to welcome the autonomous existence of natural phenomenon, and critically assess our blind, endless and careless development.

Note

1   Editor's Note: The concerns here would also justify precautionary approaches and going beyond risk management and the reductionist methodologies of normal science, as discussed in Chapter 26–28. A core issue is the creation and meaning of knowledge in open dynamic systems, which is a central concern of critical realism [Chapter 2].

Key further readings cited

Bocking, S. (2013). The ecosystem: research and practice in North America. *Web Ecology*, 13(1), 43–47.

Estes, J.A., Terborgh, J., Brashares, J.S., Power, M.E., Berger, J., Bond, W.J., Wardle, D.A. (2011). Trophic downgrading of planet Earth. *Science*, 333(6040), 301–306.

Golley, F.B. (1993). *A History of the Ecosystem Concept in Ecology: More Than the Sum of the Parts*. New Haven: Yale University Press.

Other literature cited

Anderson, P.W. (1972). More is different. *Science*, 177(4047), 393–396.

Bell, J.D., Bartley, D.M., Lorenzen, K., and Loneragan, N.R. (2006). Restocking and stock enhancement of coastal fisheries: Potential, problems and progress. *Fisheries Research*, 80(1), 1–8.

Butchart, S.H.M., Walpole, M., Collen, B., van Strien, A., Scharlemann, J.P.W., Almond, R.E.A., Watson, R. (2010). Global biodiversity: indicators of recent declines. *Science*, 328(5982), 1164–1168.

Callicott, J.B. (1996). Do deconstructive ecology and sociobiology undermine Leopold's land ethic? *Environmental Ethics*, 18(4), 353–372.

Daily, G.C. (Ed.) (1997). Nature's Services. *Societal Dependence on Natural Ecosystems*. Washington, D.C.: Island Press.

Daily, G.C., and Ehrlich, P.R. (1992). Population, sustainability, and Earth's carrying capacity. *BioScience*, 42, 761–771.

Daly, H.E. (1977). *Steady-State Economics*. San Francisco: W.H. Freeman.

Elichirigoity, F. (1999). *Planet Management: Limits to Growth, Computer Simulation, and the Emergence of Global Spaces*. Evanston, Illinois: Northwestern University Press.

Field, J.P., Belnap, J., Breshears, D.D., Neff, J.C., Okin, G.S., Whicker, J.J., Reynolds, R.L. (2010). The ecology of dust. *Frontiers in Ecology and the Environment*, 8(8), 423–430.

Levin, S.A. (1992). The problem of pattern and scale in ecology: The Robert H. MacArthur Award Lecture. *Ecology*, 73(6), 1943.

Lindeman, R.L. (1942). The trophic-dynamic aspect of ecology. *Ecology*, 23(4), 399–417.

Mitsch, W.J. (2012). What is ecological engineering? *Ecological Engineering*, 45(October), 5–12.

Odum, H. T. (1962). Ecological tools and their use: Man and the ecosystem. *Proceedings of the Lockwood Conference on the Suburban Forest and Ecology*, 652, 57–75.

Pearl, R., and Reed, L.J. (1920). On the rate of growth of the population of the United States since 1790 and its mathematical representation. *Proceedings of the National Academy of Sciences*, 6(6), 275–288.

Rees, W.E. (1992). Ecological footprints and appropriated carrying capacity: What urban economics leaves out. *Environment and Urbanization*, 4(2), 121–130.

Ricklefs, R.E. (2008). Disintegration of the ecological community. *American Naturalist*, 172, 741–750.

Rooney, N., McCann, K.S. and Noakes, D.L.G. (2007). *From Energetics to Ecosystems: The Dynamics and Structure of Ecological Systems*. Springer: Dordrecht, The Netherlands.

Sayre, N.F. (2008). The genesis, history and limits of carrying capacity. *Annals of the Association of American Geographers*, 98(December 2006), 120–134.

Scheffer, M., Carpenter, S., Foley, J., Folke, C. and Walker, B. (2001). Catastrophic shifts in ecosystems. *Nature*, 413(6856), 591–596.

Schneider, E.D. and Kay, J. (1994). Complexity and thermodynamics: Towards a new ecology. *Futures*, 26(6), 626–647.

Shrader-Frechette, K.S. and McCoy, E.D. (1993). *Method in Ecology: Strategies for Conservation*. Cambridge: Cambridge University Press.

Spash, C. L. (2002). Strong uncertainty: Ignorance and indeterminacy. In C.L. Spash (Ed.), *Greenhouse Economics: Value and Ethics* (pp. 120–152). London: Routledge.

Spash, C.L. (2009). The new environmental pragmatists, pluralism and sustainability. *Environmental Values*, 18(3), 253–256.

Spash, C.L. (2012). New foundations for ecological economics. *Ecological Economics*, 77(May), 36–47.

Spash, C.L., Aslaksen, I. (2015). Re-establishing an ecological discourse in the policy debate over how to value ecosystems and biodiversity. *Journal of Environmental Management* 159(August), 245–253.

Vatn, A. (2000). The environment as a commodity. *Environmental Values*, 9, 493–509.

Wackernagel, M., Schulz, N.B., Deumling, D., Linares, A. C., Jenkins, M., Kapos, V., Randers, J. (2002). Tracking the ecological overshoot of the human economy. Proceedings of the National Academy of Sciences of the United States of America, 99(14), 9266–9271.

Worster, D. (1990). The ecology of order and chaos. *Environmental History Review*, 14(1), 1–18.

13

COEVOLUTIONARY SOCIAL ECOLOGICAL ECONOMICS

Richard B. Norgaard

Introduction

Can scientists really predict the future, understand the forces that influence it, guide engineers and resource managers to correctly alter those forces, and plan for better times? This has been the dream of natural scientists since Francis Bacon nearly half a millennia ago. In economics, policy, and planning this mode of thinking has not simply been a dream; it has been a presumption. History, of course, has only occasionally turned out as economists have expected. Continual policy adjustments to manage new causal mechanisms affecting the economic system, most of them unforeseen, are required to offset completely unexpected phenomena. Frequently, natural scientists, as well as economists, argue that the systems and their dynamics simply need to be better understood, as if economies, or natural systems, had knowable fixed properties and dynamics. Natural scientists and economists just need to understand their respective systems better. Biological scientists, of course, know that species evolve, that whole new properties can emerge. Few biologists keep this at the forefront of their thinking, typically presuming that evolutionary process occur over longer time periods than those relevant for human planning. Insects and bacteria have proven difficult to manage precisely because generations are short and evolution happens quickly. Evolutionary and coevolutionary thinking directly yet constructively juxtaposes the dominant perspective of a world that is ultimately knowable. Partly for this reason, the coevolutionary perspective can be especially important for understanding the implications of being in a world dominated by human activity (Gowdy, 1994; Kallis and Norgaard, 2010; Norgaard, 1981; 1984; 1994; 2009).

Defining the topic

Biological systems change in ways that cannot be effectively derived in a Newtonian mechanical framework. The distribution of characteristics within a species can shift through selection and through the introduction of individuals with new characteristics from other ecosystems [Chapter 12]. Wholly new properties can emerge in a species through mutations. The characteristics that prove fit are retained. Evolution is usually described with a story. For example, tortoises were able to move into drier and drier environments because those individuals with the characteristics that allowed them to do so had higher survival rates and were more successful at reproducing themselves. Fitness, however, is not simply a matter of fitting the physical environment. An individual's environment is made up of other individuals and species. Selective pressures are brought to bear by each of the other species with which each species interacts. This process of mutual selection between interacting species is called coevolution.

Of course, Charles Darwin (1809–1882) knew that a species' environment consisted largely of other species. The theory of evolution, however, was most easily explained and remembered in the context of a fixed physical environment to which a species became more and more fit. Furthermore, this process of becoming more fit meshed with the idea of progress, which reigned even more strongly in Darwin's time than now and helped spread Darwin's thinking. Darwinian evolution had been around for a century before Paul Ehrlich and Peter Raven provided a clear, empirical example of coevolution, coined the term, and instigated a steady stream of theoretical and empirical research on the concept (Ehrlich and Raven, 1964).

Once a scholar fully realises that each species evolves in the context of other species, he or she is drawn into a coevolutionary framework and its significance blossoms.

> Overall, the coevolutionary process permeates the history of life on Earth, the continued development of biodiversity, the maintenance of genetic diversity, and the organisation of biological communities. The more we learn about how species have adapted to their environments and to other species, the more it seems that much of evolution is actually about coevolution.
>
> *(Thompson, 2002: 183)*

Like the idea of evolution after Darwin, the coevolutionary way of thinking leapt the boundaries of biology into anthropology and psychology in the 1970s and on to economics in the 1980s.

Thinking in a coevolutionary framework can be disturbing for scholars who are firmly in the grip of the idea of progress. Unlike evolution in response to the selective pressures of a fixed environment, when species are coevolving with respect to each other, there is no fixed direction, no progress. Indeed, a coevolving system could go in circles without necessarily circling upward. Two species, for example, can coevolve together so tightly that they become so specialised with respect to the existence of the other as to become increasingly vulnerable to extinction. Similarly, in a coevolving system of species, those species that do not evolve fast enough with respect to each other can be driven to extinction. In a coevolving system, optimal, efficient solutions, even if dynamic, can be quickly passé. The mechanistic thinking of economics has desperately needed such a counter-perspective. At the same time, coevolution sheds light on how systems might acquire resilience and can be sustainable even while changing.

Past research

Coevolutionary thinking is recognised within the field of ecological economics, but is by no means widely practiced. Two presidents of the International Society for Ecological Economics have undertaken seminal work (Gowdy, 1994; Norgaard, 1994). Spash (1999) includes it in his review of the origins of ecological economics but then critiques it in a later paper (Spash, 2013). Several ecological economics texts elaborate the coevolutionary framework (Daly and Farley, 2011; Costanza et al., 2015). Giorgos Kallis and Richard Norgaard (2010) provide a thorough review of the coevolutionary literature pertinent to ecological economics in an opening article to a special issue of *Ecological Economics* consisting of multiple articles using coevolutionary frameworks. A shorter review of the literature can be found in an earlier special issue on coevolution (Rammel et al., 2007).

Kallis and Norgaard (2010) developed a taxonomy that divides the literature related to coevolution in ecological economics into five categories:

1 coevolution in biology;
2 evolutionary and institutional economics literature, gene–culture coevolution;
3 coevolution between genes and cultures;
4 bio-social coevolution consisting of specific case studies such as the coevolution of pests, pesticides, and pest management practices and institutions; and
5 diffuse coevolution between multiple social categories and the environment.

First is the literature on coevolution in biology. This inspires and informs ecological economists working in the field. People have affected the habitats and relative abundance of species' characteristics through hunting and agriculture and thereby affected the coevolution of other species in nearby environments. These biological evolutionary changes have, in turn, 'selected on' the biological and cultural characteristics that prove fit for people. These mutually selective pressures and systemic evolution in hunter-gatherer and later agricultural societies provide early parallels to the processes underway today and have attracted the attention of ecological economists thinking about the resilience and sustainability of human–Nature systems in the industrial age (for example: Gowdy, 1994; Rammel and van den Bergh, 2003).

New understandings in biological coevolution have transferred quickly into coevolution of ecological economic systems. For example, Gould and Eldredge (1977) argued that coevolution in biological systems can happen quickly in punctuations that are followed by the more common portrayal of evolution as being slower or at a standstill. Gowdy (1994) explored the significance of punctuated equilibrium for understanding the rapid economic changes that have occurred with the arrival of agriculture, industry, and, more recently, information technology. Punctuated equilibrium answers the criticism of many social scientists who see biological evolution as slow and social change as fast. At the same time it offsets the strong tendency in economics to portray change as small steps at the margin and steady growth on a broad canvass of human progress.

Second, within the evolutionary economics [Chapter 8] and institutional economics [Chapter 3] literature, economists have written on the coevolution between social categories such as technology and institutions (Nelson, 2002), or more specific examples such as universities and industries. While this category of the literature does not include coevolution with the natural environment, it can be easily extended to the environment and key journals in these fields have provided audiences for ecological economics' coevolutionary arguments (Swaney, 1986; van den Bergh, 2007; Noailly, 2008).

The third category in the Kallis and Norgaard (2010) taxonomy is gene-culture coevolution. The literature in this area originates in biology (Lumsden and Wilson, 1981) and its interactions with anthropology (Durham, 1976; 1991). Work here both informs and lends credence to research in ecological economics.

The fourth category consists of studies that have used the coevolutionary framework to describe particular dynamics between people and Nature. Norgaard (1984) and Noailly (2008), for example argue that pests, pesticides, the human and environmental effects of pesticides, and pesticide laws and regulations have coevolved together. This is a clear case where the particulars of the evolution of pesticide resistance and the surprises of new environmental problems arising from the decisions to use a different selection of pesticides drive the selection of new pesticide control legislation.

Fifth is diffuse coevolution. I developed a particular, but very broad, framework of coevolutionary reasoning that is unusually inclusive yet also abstract and diffuse. In the late

1970s, while working on an Amazon planning team in Brazil, I grew extremely frustrated with the idea that, with enough science and good planning, Brazil could colonise the Amazon in an ideal way. I argued that no civilisation in the history of humankind had developed through excellent knowledge and planning. Rather, humans succeeded by trial and error and learning from their efforts. Only a few efforts were successful, and sometimes they had disastrous outcomes, but failure contributed to later success, at least for some people. Natural science can now help planners better understand how human experiments have gone wrong and continue to go wrong. However, I could not convince the Brazilian scientists and planners to visit the existing settlements that were struggling in order to learn from them. Nor could I convince them to design multiple experiments based on existing experience and a programme of learning between the experiments. This led to an article on social and ecological coevolution in the Amazon (Norgaard, 1981), followed by another decade of expanding on the idea that resulted in a broad critique of Western deterministic thinking and a portrayal of insights on the possibilities for sustainability that come from a coevolutionary framing (Norgaard, 1994).

Personally I perceive coevolution occurring all around us. Some forms of social organisation make some types of technologies more fit, and vice versa; some ways of knowing fit with some types of values, and vice versa. Everything is selecting on everything else in one massive coevolutionary collective of changing things. However, key categories need to be identified to describe the process. The outstanding nature of people is that they are social, smart, use tools, and develop moral frameworks to guide their behaviour. Other species have some of these characteristics, but not all. These categories suggest the coevolutionary framework shown in Figure 13.1. It stresses people's organisational, knowledge, technological and value systems. This is deliberately a framework that is more detailed on the social side than the environmental. When we have environmental problems, we need ways of re-examining ourselves, for we humans, not the environment, are typically the problem. Environmental conditions, of course, also change and coevolve in the absence of people, but the framework shown in Figure 13.1 does not bring this out because the changing physical and biological categories are separated. These categories are so broad that pretty much everything can be conceived of as fitting within one of the five, although sometimes not exclusively in one of them. Figure 13.1 is a theory of everything, but only in the most abstract, aggregated sense of "thing". The framework, nonetheless, helps order the details of history and elicit some insights into the future.

Starting from the top and going clockwise, the value category includes all the ways we define, redefine, and communicate values through parent–child relations, religion, storytelling and song, art, and, later, in human history through law, literature, and moral philosophy. Social organisation includes families and tribes, unions between tribes all the way to nations and the hierarchy and authority of modern corporations and government bureaucracy. Social organisation includes both democracy and concentrated power. It also includes the institutions of public, common and private property. Markets are also in the social organisational category. This seems so inclusive as to be useless, yet insights arise.

The technological category includes the technologies of farming, harnessing energy, manufacturing, transporting, communicating, as well as technologies that help us find and store knowledge, from rock art to books and libraries all the way to our modern day computers. The environmental category includes stocks of minerals, the flows of physical systems, and life in all of its forms and interactions including those with physical systems resulting, for example, in soils. The knowledge category includes stocks of knowledge created in the past that are accessible to different people, the patterns of thinking different people have for understanding the world, and a society's ability to bring knowledge to bear in public decision-making.

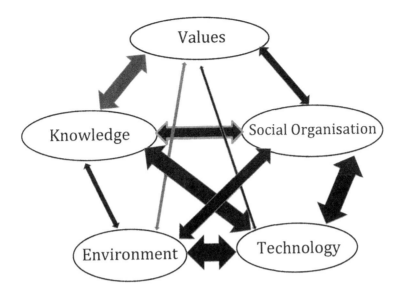

Figure 13.1 Coevolutionary change.
Notes: The arrows represent both "mechanical" relationships and evolutionary selective pressures. The wider arrows suggest stronger relationships.

To see things coevolve, imagine there are a variety of ways of knowing, ways of organising, types of technologies and sets of values. Environments are also different in different places, as are the societies who live there. These different types all interact directly with each other and with characteristics in the other categories. Some tools within the technology category combined with knowledge, values and social organisation, for example, result in environmental changes, good and bad. These are direct interactions. The relative dominance of characteristics in each of the categories also 'select on' each other across categories. Through the selection process different properties become dominant.

Like genes, the characteristics of each of the categories must be able to reproduce themselves. However, like genes, characteristics do not always reproduce themselves perfectly. Beliefs and knowledge, for example, are passed on from one generation to the next, supported and reproduced through stories, music and other forms of communication. The reproduction of beliefs and knowledge is imperfect. They can drift with time. People, furthermore, occasionally experiment, imagining and implementing new characteristics in the process. The primary concern in social ecological economic interactions is typically for the operation of open systems into which new characteristics can arrive from other systems. Because characteristics do not replicate perfectly and because, in open coevolving systems, new characteristics can come from systems outside the one research and policy focus upon, systems and the categories within them keep changing. Without imperfect replication and introduction of characteristics, the coevolving categories could come to equilibrium, but change is to be expected.

The coevolutionary framework helps explicate how factors both interact in a mechanical way and how they evolve in coevolutionary ways: selecting on each other such that they fit together with respect to each other, or lock-in with each other. Yet, at the same time, coevolution entails changing together as new innovations arise, random trials or experiments appear, new species invade, or features of other societies are tried or are imposed upon them.

The analyst using this approach should also remember that the distribution of access across people to knowledge, technology, and the environment, affects power [see Chapter 14]; power affects how direct changes occur; and which direct changes occur affects the coevolution of the system as a whole. When power is unevenly distributed, the distribution of who accepts which values will affect the course of history. Marxists' [Chapter 6] emphasis on power is compatible with the coevolutionary framework. However, thinking in a coevolutionary framework suggests why exercising power can also be a disconcerting process where success is not guaranteed.

Many people, especially physical scientists, think the distinguishing feature of science, as opposed to non-scientific thinking, is the ability to predict. Uncertainty is merely the absence of complete knowledge and can be reduced by learning more (i.e., what Spash, 2002 terms weak uncertainty). Thinking in evolutionary terms, rather than mechanical cause and effect terms, leads us to realise otherwise. Our understanding always lags behind an evolving system. Knowledge becomes obsolete and new knowledge is needed.

The coevolutionary framework reminds us that the imperfect replication of characteristics, the introduction of new characteristics from other systems, and the discovery of new knowledge, technologies and forms of social organisation lead to change and make prediction eventually impossible. In this sense, the scientists' desire to learn more to reduce uncertainty and improve the predictability of science can become a new source of unpredictability in the system as a whole. The coevolutionary framework helps us understand why the exercise of power to achieve particular ends, even when power is relatively evenly distributed and exercised democratically, may not be very effective in the long run due to both the difficulty of trying to understand complexity and unforeseeable imperfect replication or introductions to each of the categories in Figure 13.1. This coevolutionary framework, as put forward by Norgaard (1994), has inspired adaptations and applications; for example, by Dove (1993), Kallis (2010) and Rios-Nunez et al. (2013).

The coevolutionary framework shown here has natural and social categories, but it can immediately be seen that both mechanical relations and coevolutionary processes mean they are interlinked, blurring the Nature–society divide. The natural is co-created by the social over time and vice versa, such that the distinctions between natural and social become increasingly less meaningful. Blurring the natural and the social contrasts with the environmental limits literature (Meadows et al., 1972; Rockström et al., 2009) and Daly's (1973, 2014) long-standing argument that the economy must fit within the environmental system and so cannot possibly keep growing. This does not mean that these ways of understanding how people are destroying their environment are incorrect, but a coevolutionary way of thinking does give us another perspective.

The coevolutionary framework that I have developed in the context of ecological economics provides an interesting representation of the situation where people have become a major factor in the behaviour of Nature. Anthropogenic climate change, for example, provides social reasons to reduce our production of greenhouse gases and other materials affecting the balance of climate [Chapter 42]; it impels humans to adapt to ongoing change, such as increased forest fires, and provides reasons to invest so that adaptation is easier in the future. Anthropogenic climate change shows the importance of acquiring new knowledge, switching technologies, adapting our organisational structures and seriously questioning our values; each of these things being interactive and selecting on the other.

Main issues and brief assessment

There are four issues that are frequently seen as critically important. First is the difficulty, or impossibility, of proving that coevolution, rather than some other process of change, is happening; and, thus, why would anyone argue that the coevolutionary framework could possibly be important? This revolves around the problem of what is the equivalent of a gene in the coevolution between two species when we speak of the coevolution between technology and social organisation, or the other categories of Figure 13.1. Dawkins (1976) introduced the term "meme" as the cultural equivalent of gene, and biologists and cultural anthropologists have invoked the term since, as if it had equivalent standing to gene. Of course, it does not. However, the accepted meaning of the term gene has dramatically changed over time. The field of genetics meanwhile was successfully applied even as its underlying component was rapidly changing. The term "atom" was used for millennia and very successfully used as the basis for chemistry for nearly two centuries before an atom was identified in an electron microscope. Nevertheless, the concept of coevolution beyond genetics has been sharply criticised for its lack of specificity as to what is actually coevolving with what (Winder et al., 2005).

The second issue is that the coevolutionary framework provides a broad way to order the past and suggests why the future is so unpredictable, but it is not typically seen to be very constructive for formulating policy. This issue is also one of perception and reality. If the world is indeed a giant mechanical system and is understood correctly as such, then the effects of applying different policies on the system can be predicted and policy makers can choose between them. If the world, however, is a giant coevolving collective but it is understood as being atomistic and mechanical, then false predictions and policies will follow. If reality is coevolving and perceived to be so, some policy recommendations do follow: diversity is good, considerable effort is needed to keep monitoring the ever changing conditions, and nimble responsiveness to changing conditions is beneficial. Nevertheless, the coevolutionary framing is so broad, that these policy recommendations are consistent across seemingly more specific problems.

The first and second issues lead directly to the third. Is the coevolutionary framework limited to the big picture using broad, vague categories like those in Figure 13.1? If the policy recommendations follow directly from the pattern of thinking, why waste much time using the framework to investigate a specific problem? Does it ever cast new light? One response is: "Does the theory of market failure, or externalities, ever lead to a policy other than a tax, subsidy, or cap and trade?" Policy recommendations are inherent to the framework through which the problem is perceived.

Lastly, the fourth issue is related to scale, largely geographical. In biology, coevolution is a process within an ecosystem [Chapter 12]. Ecosystem boundaries, however, are human constructs that change depending upon whether the researcher is focusing on microbes or elephants. Yet, winds blow microbes and elephants transport them too. The geographical dimensions of species interactions become even more nebulous for species that migrate over long distances, from Monarch butterflies to Blue whales (Thomson, 2005). Hunter-gatherer societies were geographically confined relative to capitalist societies today. Note also that time is not well specified in the coevolutionary framework. Just as microbes and elephants evolve at different rates in ecological systems, social organisation may evolve at a different rate than knowledge or technology.

Before becoming too bogged down in these issues and concluding that they are so great as to make the coevolutionary framework useless, recall that each of them has parallels in market theory. Marginal costs, supply, marginal utility and demand are all abstractions. While the coevolutionary framework may do little more than remind analysts that diversity is good, this is useful because the market framework does little more than highlight that efficiency is good. Economists rarely include space, time or transactions costs formally in their analyses of problems and solutions, even though these factors are critically important in reality. One of the great advantages of considering a new framework is that it can take us back to our undergraduate efforts to grapple with now familiar frameworks and question their underlying conceptualisations.

Future directions

There is certainly the possibility that coevolutionary social ecological economic thinking will become more sophisticated in the future. Computer models of coevolution in a geographical mosaic and coevolution in hierarchical systems have been developed in other fields, but their usefulness has been limited by lack of clear definitions of the actual unit that reproduces and on which selection occurs. In my judgement, however, the coevolutionary framework will continue to inspire grandiose abstract arguments that are plausible and insightful and that suggest wholly new approaches to thinking about sustainability, albeit in a generalised and vague way.

Concluding remarks

As humanity rushes headlong into the future, with the practitioners of natural and social sciences divorced from the critical need for collective understanding, my thoughts keep returning to my experience with Amazon development planners. For the vast majority of human history, people coevolved with their environment in relatively small and only occasionally connected groups. Today, given the state of human knowledge, multiple experiments make more sense than a single global systemic approach.

Key further readings cited

Gowdy, J. (1994). *Coevolutionary Economics: The Economy, Society and the Environment*. Norwell, MA: Kluwer.

Kallis, G. and Norgaard, R.B. (2010). Coevolutionary economics. *Ecological Economics* 69(4): 690–699.

Norgaard, R.B. (1994). *Development Betrayed: The End of Progress and a Coevolutionary Reinterpretation of the Future*. London: Routledge.

Norgaard, R.B. (2009 [1984]) Coevolutionary Development Potential. In: Spash, C.L. (Ed.), *Ecological Economics: Critical Concepts in the Environment, 4 Volumes*. London, Routledge: pp. 61–79.

Other literature cited

Costanza, R. Cumberland, J., Daly, H., Goodland, R., Norgaard, R. (2015). *An Introduction to Ecological Economics*. Boca Raton, Fl.: CRC Press.

Daly, H.E. (1973). *Toward a Steady-State Economy*. W. H. Freeman: San Francisco.

Daly, H.E. (2014). *From Uneconomic Growth to a Steady-State Economy*. Cheltenham, UK: Edward Elgar.

Daly, H.E. and Farley, J. (2011). *Ecological Economics: Principles and Applications*. 2nd edition. Washington D.C.: Island Press.

Dawkins, R. (1976). *The Selfish Gene*. Oxford: Oxford University Press.

Dove, M.R. (1993). The coevolution of population and environment: the ecology and ideology of feedback relations in Pakistan. *Population and Environment* 15 (2), 89–111.

Durham, W.H. (1976). The adaptive significance of cultural behavior, *Human Ecology* 4, 89–121.

Durham, W.H. 1991. *Coevolution: Genes, Culture, and Human Diversity*. Stanford: Stanford University Press.

Ehrlich, P.R. and Raven, P. (1964). Butterflies and plants: A study in coevolution. *Evolution* 18, 586–608.

Gould, S.J. and Eldredge, N. (1977). Punctuated equilibria: the tempo and mode of evolution reconsidered. *Paleobiology* 3 (2), 115–151.

Kallis, G. (2010). Coevolution in water resource development. The vicious cycle of water supply and demand in Athens, Greece. *Ecological Economics* 69, 796–809.

Lumsden, C.J. and Wilson, E.O. (1981). *Genes, Mind, and Culture: The Coevolutionary Process*. Cambridge, MA: Harvard University Press.

Meadows, D.H., Meadows, D.L. Randers, J., Behrens, W.W. (1972). *The Limits to Growth*. New York: Universe Books.

Nelson, R.R. (2002). Bringing institutions into evolutionary growth theory. *Journal of Evolutionary Economics* 12 (1), 17–28.

Noailly, J. (2008). Coevolution of economic and ecological systems. An application to agricultural pesticide resistance. *Journal of Evolutionary Economics* 18 (1), 1–29.

Norgaard, R.B. (1981) Sociosystem and ecosystem coevolution in the Amazon. *Journal of Environmental Economics and Management* 8 (3), 238–254.

Norgaard, R.B. (1984) Coevolutionary agricultural development. *Economic Development and Cultural Change* 32(3), 525–546.

Rammel, C. and van den Bergh, Jeroen C.JM (2003). Evolutionary policies for sustainable development: adaptive flexibility and risk minimising. *Ecological Economics* 47 (2–3), 121–133.

Rammel, C., McIntosh, B.S., Jeffrey, P. (2007). (Co)evolutionary approaches to sustainable development. *International Journal of Sustainable Development & Global Change* 14, 1–3.

Rios-Nunez, S., Coq-Huelva, D. and Garcia-Trujillo, R. (2013). The Spanish livestock model: A coevolutionary analysis. *Ecological Economics* 93, 342–350.

Rockström, J., Steffen, W., Noone, K., Persson, Å., Chapin, F.St. III, Lambin, E.F., Lenton, T.M., Scheffer, M., Folke, C., Schellnhuber, H.J., Nykvist, B., de Wit, C.A., Hughes, T., van der Leeuw, S., Rodhe, H., Sörlin, S., Snyder, P.K., Costanza, R., Svedin, U., Falkenmark, M., Karlberg, L., Corell, R.W., Fabry, V.J., Hansen, J., Walker, B., Liverman, D., Richardson, K., Crutzen, P., Foley, J.A. (2009). A safe operating space for humanity. *Nature* 461 (7263), 72–75.

Spash, C.L. (1999). The development of environmental thinking in economics. *Environmental Values* 8 (4), 413–435.

Spash, C.L. (2002). Weak uncertainty: Risk and imperfect information. In C.L. Spash (ed.), *Greenhouse Economics: Value and Ethics* (pp. 97–119). London: Routledge.

Spash, C.L. (2013). The shallow or the deep ecological economics movement. *Ecological Economics* 93 (September), 351–362.

Swaney, James A. (1986). A coevolutionary model of structural change. *Journal of Economic Issues* 20 (2), 393–401.

Thompson, J.N. (2002). Coevolution. In: M. Pagel (ed.), *Encyclopedia of Evolution*. Oxford: Oxford University Press.

Thomson, J.N. (2005). *The Geographic Mosaic of Coevolution*. Chicago: University of Chicago Press.

van den Bergh, J. (2007). Evolutionary thinking in environmental economics. *Journal of Evolutionary Economics* 17 (5), 521–549.

Winder, N., McIntosh, B.S., Jeffrey, P. (2005). The origin, diagnostic attributes and practical application of co-evolutionary theory. Ecological Economics 54 (4), 347–361.

PART IV

Society, power and politics

14

THEORIES OF POWER

Lorenz Stör

Introduction

Power is a core element of society and its analysis deeply characterises social science. As Hay (2002: 168) states: "power is to political analysis what economy is to economics". While many theorists of political economy might reject this view for seemingly renouncing power's significance as a core concept in economics, this simple phrase shows the extraordinary relevance that power's discussion plays in understanding society. However, the question of what constitutes power is a matter of ongoing contestation, deeply rooted in the historical circumstances and ontological considerations of scientific inquiry [see Chapter 2].

Neoclassical economics hardly considers aspects of power despite their extraordinary relevance for social science research (Gale, 1998). Its methodological individualist epistemology ostensibly only allows for an agential perspective per definition. However, agents under rational choice assumptions do not allow for contingency, as their characteristics are predefined (e.g. rational, utility maximising, egoistic, complete preformed preferences). As Hay (2002: 53) criticises, "a rational actor in a given context will always choose precisely the same course of action". Paradoxically, structure is then conceptualised through determined agents, which allows for a deductive methodological approach. The tools of such mainstream economic analysis reduce rational 'choice' to one rational 'option' and therefore defeat their own logic (Hay, 2002: 104). The will to make a difference turns out to be quite the opposite of the neoclassical calculus and the rational choice assumptions are mistakenly considered agential or episodic.

The philosophical roots defining what power is, or what it ought to be, and how it functions can be traced back to ancient Greek philosophy, such as Aristotle's six-fold classification of governments. The analytical discussion on power only began with modernist reasoning. In particular, Niccolò Machiavelli (1469–1527) and Thomas Hobbes (1588–1679) laid the foundations for contemporary conceptualisations of power. The discussion was revived in the twentieth century, including prominent thinkers such as: the 'faces of power' debate over a three-dimensional view of power involving Dahl, Bachrach, Baratz and Lukes; Gramsci's concept of hegemony, Giddens' structuration theory, Foucault's post-structuralist notions and a critical realist account by Hay and Jessop. This chapter will review all these ideas.

Different conceptualisations often have fundamentally different views on the characteristics of power and its qualities, including whether it is analytical or normative; relational or possessive;

negative or positive; repressive or productive; constraining ('power over') or enabling ('power to'); intentional or not; or constituted through social structures or human agency. Such oppositional positions support the notion that power is an "essentially contested concept" (Lukes, 2005: 105). However, this chapter's theoretical overview and analysis of a selection of existing power theories will show that the understanding of power is less contested than Lukes suggests, and that the structure–agency debate can serve as a framework around which to organise the different conceptualisations. The chapter proceeds by explaining the conceptualisation of structure and agency and their relation to power. This is followed by an historical overview of the power theories mentioned above, their contextualisation, future directions, and concluding remarks.

Power, structure and agency

Power is at the heart of social and political phenomena, which are expressed through social relations. Social science has a long tradition in distinguishing between structural and agential explanations of such phenomena. Hay (2002) provides a useful source for helping define the meaning of this structure and agency dichotomy based upon a critical realist philosophy of science [see Chapter 2].

He gives structure two meanings. First, *context*, which "refers to the setting within which social, political and economic events occur and acquire meaning" (Hay, 2002: 94). While the setting may include biophysical or social structures and exist irrespectively of observation, the 'acquisition of meaning' incorporates an interpretive element. Second, *regularity* over time, which is exhibited by political and social institutions, practices, routines and conventions [see Chapter 3]. This assumes that political, social or economic phenomena bear an element of order, making them theoretically more predictable. In a critical realist approach, structures consist of relations between social positions comprising active and passive powers that are set in motion as tendencies. This means that the actualisation of such structures is contingent upon specific factors. If the structures are not actualised, they remain latent, albeit existent (Sayer, 2000). Pure structuralism would imply full determinacy and disable every individual or social unit from the ability to make autonomous decisions or influence any process, i.e. depriving all agents of the power to make a difference. Structural realism and world systems theory are examples of such theories (Hay, 2002).

Agency means action or conduct. It is the "ability or capacity of an actor to act consciously and, in so doing, to attempt to realise his or her intentions" (Hay, 2002: 94). Agential factors are characterised by a sense of free will, choice, autonomy and conscious deliberation and have been highly important throughout the history of philosophy. When René Descartes (1596–1650) heralded the age of enlightenment with his famous statement '*cogito ergo sum*' (I am thinking therefore I exist), elements of reasoning and rationality laid the basis for a whole liberal political and economic tradition that put the actor at the centre of its considerations. However, agency is not restricted to individual humans but extends to organised or collective actors who realise their capacity to act, e.g. trade unions calling for strikes or corporations setting prices. Agency is the capacity to make a difference—the element that distinguishes the natural from the social world and constitutes the social science struggle to explain, let alone predict, social phenomena. However, agency is also the key to understanding why positivist approaches in social science, transferred directly from natural science, are subject to failure.

If structuralism is one extreme, then the other is pure voluntarism where actors are able to fully realise their intentions; also called intentionalism. However, even in agent centred approaches this is mostly regarded as a tendency, since pure intentionalism would remove all historical contexts and institutions that constrain and influence the opportunities of an actor. This concentration on the present moment "can say nothing about the process of social and political change over time" (Hay, 2002: 112) and therefore, again, deprives the analysis of any explanatory power. The following review explains how structure and agency are in actuality intertwined and why some theoretical conceptualisations reject an ontological divide altogether. However, this framework serves as a useful reference point to put diverse theories into perspective.

Historical overview of power theories

The existing literature on power theories is extensive and the following subsections can only discuss a selection of relevant approaches. Placing them within the structure–agency context provides a pathway to conceptualise the approaches and put them in context vis-à-vis the others. For that purpose, the chapter follows neither a strict chronological nor taxonomic presentation but, rather, aims to explain the development of power theories via key conceptualisations.

Hobbes & Machiavelli: The godfathers of power

Niccolò Machiavelli (1469–1527) was a diplomat during the reign of the Medici in Florence and the military turmoil as France and Spain fought for the control of Italy. In his famous treatise *The Prince*, first published in Rome as *De Principatibus*, Machiavelli (1998 [1532]) describes power as a set of strategies to achieve certain outcomes. For him the important question was "what does power do?" (Clegg, 1989: 5). He characterised power as decentralised, strategic and contingent. Power cannot be possessed, does not belong to a certain place or sovereign, but is rather evaluated upon the effectiveness of strategies that are deployed to achieve a greater scope for action (Clegg, 1989). Some scholars regard Machiavelli's writings on power to be 'postmodern' (despite his works having preceded modernity), which helps explain the renewed appreciation for his ideas that arose in the 1970s.

Thomas Hobbes (1588–1679) wrote the *Leviathan* in 1651 while living in France and employed as tutor by the then exiled future King Charles II of England. He was essentially concerned with sovereignty and the question: what is power? Based on his impressions of the English Civil War, Hobbes (2010 [1651]) regards humans as competitive, egoistic and rational beings, who can only escape from a condition of devastating rivalry if they use their reason and agree to subordinate to an absolute sovereign State, the Leviathan. The argument undermined the religious justification for sovereignty and instead condoned either a monarchy or a commonwealth; the result was his expulsion from the royal court and his subsequent return to England where he lived under Cromwell's Commonwealth. Hobbes's mechanical perceptions of power are based on an actor centred, causal and episodic understanding of human nature. Power consists of the abilities to acquire a certain good and is therefore itself instrumental. These characteristics fit within the emerging modernist age of reason because they entailed an element of observability and measurability. According to Clegg (1989: 4), this meant, "Hobbes' conception was to be the intellectual victor" over Machiavelli's notion of power. Hobbes's ideas have informed theorists such as sociologist Max Weber and political scientists in more recent times. However, the two foundational traditions of Machiavelli and Hobbes have become increasingly intertwined in recent times.

Lukes and the three-dimensional view of power

The Hobbesian mechanistic and causal understanding was challenged in the 'faces of power' debate outlined by Lukes's (2005 [1974]) 'three-dimensional view' on power. Lukes thereby contributed to an increasing acknowledgement of the complexity of power.

The writings of behavioural political scientist Robert Dahl in the 1960s represent a first dimension of power, which is a clear continuation of the Hobbesian tradition, as he uses an intentional and active interpretation of power. Dahl (1957: 202–203) defines power in this way: "A has power over B to the extent that he can get B to do something that B would not otherwise do". The method of Dahl's studies puts a focus on the visibility and empirical measurability of power, resulting in a perception of a 'plurality' of equally powerful actors. Power is exercised in concrete situations and understood as decision making in the political arena. This accessible, classical understanding remains influential as a common perception of what constitutes power today.

Peter Bachrach and Morton Baratz (1962) regarded this conception of power as too narrow, and added a second dimension where decision making is intentionally limited to relatively non-controversial matters. They drew on the idea that "all forms of political organisation have a bias in favour of the exploitation of some kinds of conflict and the suppression of others because organisation is the mobilisation of bias" (Schattschneider, 1960: 71). Power is then also a matter of non-decision making and agenda setting. Bachrach and Baratz are interested not only in agenda issues that are actualised, but also potential issues. Both these dimensions still stress the existence of observable conflict, overt or covert. If there is no conflict then consensus on the prevailing allocation of values is assumed (Lukes, 2005: 23).

This view is challenged by Lukes's third dimension of power. He criticises the first and second dimensions' behaviourist and methodological individualist viewpoints and the limited focus on observable conflicts. Lukes acknowledges that "A may exercise power over B by getting him to do what he does not want to do, but he also exercises power over him by influencing, shaping or determining his very wants" (Lukes, 2005: 27). This adds the element of preference shaping to the powers of decision making and agenda setting, which reveals Lukes's concern about the latent and hidden aspects of power. The existence of latent conflicts allows for a very subtle form of domination in which 'perceived interests' obscure the 'real interests' of the dominated, and acquiescence is fulfilled without their awareness. What exactly constitutes those real interests is essentially a normative, evaluative matter which has provoked considerable critique of Lukes's position (Clegg, 1989; Hay, 2002).

The reason why Lukes speaks of a three-dimensional view is that he regards these views as a subset of a specific concept of power. The three views are not mutually exclusive but rather gain depth by complementing each other, as the dimension metaphor already suggests. They all build upon one concept "according to which A exercises power over B when A affects B in a manner contrary to B's interests" (Lukes, 2005: 30). This is a clear actor centred conception of power, although Lukes's own third dimension, paralleling hegemony, suggests that structural factors also play a role in obscuring real interests.

Gramsci and hegemony

During his imprisonment by Mussolini's fascist Italian regime in the 1920s and 1930s, Antonio Gramsci developed an extensive analysis of the political economy, published posthumously as *Prison Notebooks* (Gramsci, 1971). He prominently elaborated on the idea of hegemony, "which constitutes a system of dominant ideas that receive consent from the relatively powerless or subaltern groups" (Haugaard, 2009: 239) in a society.[1] Hegemonic power is perceived as an asymmetrical acceptance of mutual interdependence of the dominant and the dominated. It consists of material and ideological consensus, which leads to compliance with this domination, a self-subjugation. However, these asymmetrical social power relations go largely unrecognised by the dominated. Their consciousness, emotions and actions are shaped by the ideology of the dominant, which is hegemonic when it connects to the 'common sense' of the people and thereby allows integrating subaltern classes into (the asymmetrically structured) civil society. Brand and Wissen (2013) explicitly draw on the role of hegemony in their explanation of modern society as imposing an 'imperial mode of living' [Chapter 15].

The concept of hegemony is particularly noteworthy in the structure–agency context. On the one hand, hegemony is a source of domination, which recalls the three-dimensional view of 'power over' an actor. On the other hand, it is based upon the consent of the dominated, which acknowledges an empowering 'power to' element. Hegemony therefore carried the dualism between 'power to' and 'power over' long before it was discovered as a useful conceptual distinction in the 1970s (Haugaard, 2006: 50). Gramsci is directly referring to the strategic character of power in Machiavelli's writings when employing this "dyadic opposition [of] force and consent, violence and persuasion" (Fontana, 2006: 28). However, this dualism carries a theoretical tension, as conflictual and consensual understandings of power seem to be in opposition to each other. Revealing this dualism lays the ground for potential synergies in the structure–agency debate. Gramsci's considerations acknowledge that "transformations in the social group or social structure are contingent upon the nature and degree of integration and disintegration, mobilization and fragmentation" (Fontana, 2006: 31). This contingency leaves extensive room for political agents as historical subjects in the formation of hegemony, with hegemony itself constituting a social structure. Gramsci's writings were later used in an unorthodox attempt to rescue Marxism from its structural and deterministic interpretations.

Giddens' structuration theory

The aim of 'structuration theory', as developed by Anthony Giddens (1984) in *The Constitution of Society*, is to transcend the dualism of structure and agency through what he calls the duality of structure. This regards both as complementary and therefore rejects a divide. As Dowding (2008: 29) argues, "structure is both the medium through which action is made possible and structure is reproduced through social practice itself". In other words, structure and social action (i.e. human agency) create and reproduce each other in the course of structuration—a structure shaping, continuing process of action. Structure is therefore enabling and constraining at the same time (Giddens, 1984). Giddens defines power as the capacity to achieve outcomes. Rather than impeding freedom or emancipation power is "their very medium" (Giddens, 1984: 257). Language, for example, is a structure that constrains the possibilities of what can be said through a given set of grammar and meaningful sentences, but it only exists through the active speaking and writing of subjects that enable their communication. The structure is thereby simultaneously being reproduced and gradually transformed. Giddens demonstrated that neither structure nor agency alone explains how social relations are formed, and his considerations appear to be an appealing conceptualisation of our day-to-day reality. However, Clegg (1989) argues, that despite all efforts, the structure–agency duality "remains tightly coupled to the individualist and voluntarist side of dualism" (Clegg, 1989: 140). It follows that in structuration theory, power is essentially defined in terms of agency that does not acknowledge a reality of structures external to social action, but rather claims its virtual existence.

Foucault and the post-structuralist response

The post-structuralist contributions by Michel Foucault in the 1970s challenged hitherto established theories and went beyond the scope of structure–agency conceptualisations of power. His approach, which focused on discursive practices, "admits of no rational, unified human being, nor class nor gendered subject, which is the locus or source of the expression of identity" (Clegg, 1989: 151). Structure and agency themselves are "constructed through power strategies that are operating at the level of discourse" (Torfing, 2009: 112). Identities are therefore not given with regard to mechanistic agency conceptualisations, but are produced by discourses and are part of discourse formations and dispositives. Such identities are always seen as historically specific, contingent and relational with respect to dominant forms of power and to dominant power techniques. This evokes the Machiavellian notion of power where it is therefore neither identified as 'power over' nor as 'power to' but rather as a set of 'power strategies' that form and regulate relational identities of social actors. If actors do not have the capacity to act freely and take part in such identity shaping (e.g. because of State repression), Foucault considers this as domination, not as power. Power thus is a productive, but also a regulative and disciplinary, force that "is everywhere; not because it embraces everything but because it comes from everywhere" (Foucault, 1978: 93).

In his seminal work *Discipline and Punish* (1995 [1977]), Foucault depicts how, with the transition to a modern liberal society, the sovereign power of the feudal State made room for disciplinary techniques and normalising practices. This enabled "subtle attempts to mobilise and shape the freedom of individual actors and target groups on the basis of institutionalised goals, standards and norms" (Torfing, 2009: 113). Such practices act as a form of internalised knowledge and are disseminated and institutionalised through schools, the army, prisons, hospitals, psychiatric institutions or factories. Foucault regards knowledge and power to be internally related in power/knowledge complexes and states that knowledge and its production relate to specific forms and techniques of power. Jeremy Bentham's concept of the 'Panopticon' exemplifies the emergence of such disciplinary practices. The Panopticon is a building with an architectural shape that allows a watchman to observe inmates of an institution without them knowing whether they are being watched or not. However, the mere chance of being observed has a normalising effect on the individual. "The surveillance is permanent in its effects, even if it is discontinuous in its action [so] that the perfection of power should tend to render its actual exercise unnecessary" (Foucault, 1995: 201). While prisons indeed exist that imitate the architecture of the Panopticon, Foucault extends it conceptually to the 'ideal type' of all modern disciplinary institutions, illustrating the functioning of modern power relations.

As a post-structuralist, Foucault evades being placed in the structure–agency context. Still, there is a strong urge in the literature to make sense of such new insights by putting them in context with their theoretical and historical surroundings. In this attempt, Foucault's conceptualisation of power is also discussed as a fourth dimension of power (Haugaard, 2012), adding to Lukes' three-dimensional view. This is misleading because it does not properly credit the novel thinking that accompanied post-structural thinking on an ontological level. While the three-dimensional view shares the conceptual agency perspective, post-structuralism plays on its own conceptual level and cannot be regarded as a mere additional view. This opened up a new era of possibilities for sociological and political thinking in general and for reconceptualising power in particular.

Hay and Jessop and the critical realist approach

Colin Hay's critical realist approach to the structure–agency debate addresses Lukes' failure to differentiate between the normative critique and the analytical identification of power. Power is not only about conduct-shaping but also about context-shaping. That is, the "consequences of A's choices for the actions of B [vs.] the capacity of actors to redefine the parameters of what is socially, politically and economically possible for others" (Hay, 2002: 185). The agential element of conduct and the structural element of context are thereby direct and indirect forms of exercising power, but are equally relevant for an analytical approach to associate structure and agency. This is further developed in the strategic-relational approach outlined by critical realist Bob Jessop (2005, 2008). A new conceptual language draws the distinction between 'strategic action' and 'strategically selective context'. It leads from the abstract conceptual dualism of structure vs. agency to the concrete conceptual duality of strategic action and selective context by examining "structure in relation to action, action in relation to structure, rather than bracketing one of them" (Jessop, 2005: 48). Sum and Jessop (2013) further divide those selectivities into four modes: structural, discursive, technological and agential. Structural selectivity, or structurally inscribed strategic selectivity, refers to the asymmetrical configuration of social forces that is reproduced through social practices over time. Discursive selectivity refers to the constraints and opportunities expressed through discourses. It goes beyond linguistic aspects and includes sense-making, or semiotic resources, constraining what can be imagined. Discursive selectivity is also asymmetrical, as it defines who enunciates which message. Technological selectivity addresses specific technologies of governmentality, with which social relations of production or the transformation of Nature occur, and therefore implies material effects. Agential selectivities refer to the capabilities of agents to make a difference. Those capabilities are influenced by the other selectivities, as all of them need to be seen in combination with each other. These four modes of strategic selectivity allow for sense and meaning making to conceptualise the underlying real structures acknowledged by critical realists. The selectivities thereby aim to reduce complexity without being reductionist.

Many of the theories outlined above can be seen in the context of one of the four modes developed by Sum and Jessop. Structural selectivity builds a bridge to Gramsci's thoughts on hegemony, while discursive and technological selectivities are relevant with regard to the writings of Foucault and agential selectivity is prominent in all other conceptualisations.

Future directions

All theories outlined bear specific historical characteristics and are manifestations of constantly changing societal circumstances. Figure 14.1 depicts an overview of the theories presented in this chapter. The figure attempts to order the theories along structure–agency lines as far as possible. Such simplifications always suffer from a certain degree of reductionism and should only be regarded as an approximation that helps to make sense of structure and agency conceptualisations of power. Approaches that transcend this categorisation—such as structuration theory and post-structuralist approaches—are depicted with dotted lines.

Once a vibrant and prominent element of social science research, the discussion and theorising about power has waned recently. However, ongoing social ecological economic challenges, such as climate change, can serve as an incentive to consider power issues as a highly relevant topic for ecological economics. Reviewing the power literature shows that simple conceptualisations of understanding social power relations do not adequately reflect the social complexity of phenomenon. Therefore, a multifaceted, multi-theoretical approach to power

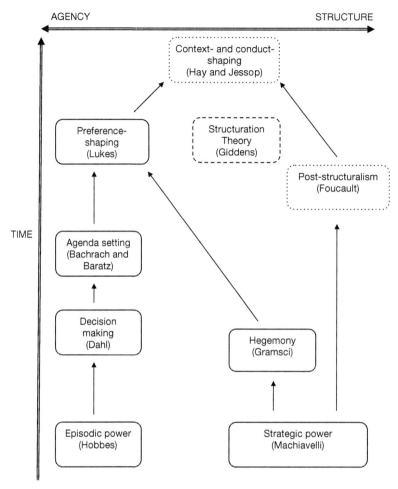

Figure 14.1 Power theories in the structure–agency context.

Note: Theoretical variety in adoption of structure-agency conceptualisation is depicted by different borders: (i) solid signifying acceptance; (ii) dashed signifying rejection by structuration theory; (iii) dotted signifying reconceptualisation by post-structuralism and critical realism.

is necessary to match reality. In order to aid the development of future research in social ecological economics, Table 14.1 provides an overview of the main aspects of each power theory discussed and summarises their essential characteristics.

The ability to conceptualise the complexity of structure and agency lies in the ontological and epistemological foundations of an approach. Rationalism fails to recognise those foundations and more broadly positivist approaches are unable to make sense of the relationship between structure, agency and power. Dynamic and disruptive occasions of change and transformation are not explicable within such frameworks. Critical social science, and more specifically the philosophy of critical realism [Chapter 2], can be a post-positivist way forward to integrate the relationship between structure and agency, and between context and conduct. Incorporating power into social ecological economics research on the basis of such ontological considerations would not only remediate the mainstream economic failure to include power relations but also enhance the scientific inquiry towards a political economy of a social ecological economics [Chapter 1].

Table 14.1 Key elements of the power theories discussed

	Concept	*View*	*Characteristics*	*Statement/Main concern*
Machiavelli	Agency	Strategic view	Decentralized, contingent	What does power do?
Hobbes	Agency	Episodic view	Mechanical, causal, absolute	What is power?
Dahl	Agency	1st dimension: Decision-making	Pluralistic, overt	A has power over B to the extent that he can get B to do something that B would not otherwise do
Bachrach and Baratz	Agency	2nd dimension: Agenda-setting	Exclude unwanted interests, covert	Power is about the mobilisation of bias
Lukes	Agency	3rd dimension: Preference-shaping	Obscuring 'real interest', latent	A exercises power by influencing, shaping or determining B's very wants
Gramsci	Structure and agency	Hegemony	Domination and consensus	Domination of one social class over others, consent and integration of civil society
Giddens	Structuration	Duality of structure	Rejecting the structure-agency dualism, reproducing, enabling and constraining	Power as recursive and reciprocal process
Foucault	Post-structural	Power is productive and regulative	Discursive practices and dispositivs, power/ knowledge, discipline and bio-power	Power analysed in terms of strategies, its specific techniques and functioning
Hay and Jessop	Critical realist approach	Duality of structure, duality of practice	Power as context-shaping and conduct-shaping	Examining the interplay of structural and agential aspects of power

Power issues connected to social ecological economics research are manifold. Struggles of actors against environmental degradation such as mining conflicts [Chapter 40] are visible manifestations of classic episodic power relations and reveal the role of corporate power and State authority in contestation with civil society. Such manifestations of power as force often provoke the mobilisation of resistance through social movements [Chapter 17] such as degrowth initiatives [Chapter 44] or bioregionalism [Chapter 47], which are often concerned about local struggles embedded in a larger context of structurally inscribed global injustices [Chapter 16]. Movements mobilise actors to formulate counter hegemonic strategies to the status quo, often accompanied by a shift in discursive strategies towards participatory and empowering methods of interaction [Chapter 33]. Social and environmental movements point at the discrepancy between the biophysical realities [Chapters 9–13] and societies' inability to handle them adequately in the context of globalised consumption patterns [Chapter 20] and the role of markets to allocate goods and resources [Chapter 18]. Wherever such structural powers are challenged (e.g. through other forms of goods provision and allocation [Chapters 38 and 50]) the interconnection of structural and agential powers becomes visible for empirical research in social ecological economics.

Concluding remarks

The way to conceptualise power presented in this chapter aims for a broad variety of approaches without losing itself in eclecticism. The review of concepts shows how theories have built on each other and the structure–agency debate serves as a framework to contextualise the changing themes. This debate touches upon the very foundations of what the respective approaches presume exists and can be known. Those ontological and epistemological dimensions show that research addressing the distinction between structural and agential accounts of power cannot merely define this as a 'problem' that can be solved empirically on positivist accounts. Meaningfully grasping the multiplicity of the debate requires the consideration of post-positivist philosophies of social science. Accepting this sheds light on the blind spot of power, as observed in mainstream economics, and enables a more realistic understanding of economic research as we head towards a social ecological economics.

Note

1 Editor's Note: The term "subaltern" refers to a person of inferior rank or status to another, a subordinate. It derives from Latin, *sub* "below" plus *alternus* "every other". In the current context, a class below all others in society.

Key further readings cited

Hay, C. (2002). *Political Analysis: A Critical Introduction*. Hampshire: Palgrave Macmillan.
Lukes, S. (2005 [1974]). *Power: A Radical View*. 2nd Edition. Hampshire: Palgrave Macmillan

Other literature cited

Bachrach, P., Baratz, M.S. (1962). Two Faces of Power. *American Political Science Review*, 56 (4), 947–952.
Brand, U., Wissen, M. (2013). Crisis and Continuity of Capitalist Societal Nature Relations: The Imperial Mode of Living and the Limits to Environmental Governance. *Review of International Political Economy*, 20 (4), 687–711.
Clegg, S.R. (1989). *Frameworks of Power*. London: Sage Publications.
Dahl, R.A. (1957). The Concept of Power. *Behavioural Science*, 2 (3), 201–215.
Dowding, K. (2008). Agency and Structure: Interpreting Power Relationships. *Journal of Power*, 1 (1), 21–36.
Fontana, B. (2006). State and Society: The Concept of Hegemony in Gramsci. In M. Haugaard and H. Lentner (Eds.), *Hegemony and Power: Consensus and Coercion in Contemporary Politics* (pp. 23–44). Lanham: Lexington Books.
Foucault, M. (1978). *The History of Sexuality, Vol. 1*. New York: Pantheon Books.
Foucault, M. (1995 [1977]). *Discipline and Punish. The Birth of the Prison*. 2nd Edition. New York: Vintage Books.
Gale, F.P. (1998). Theorizing Power in Ecological Economics. *Ecological Economics*, 27 (2), 131–138.
Giddens, A. (1984). *The Constitution of Society: Outline of the Theory of Structuration*. Cambridge: Polity Press.
Gramsci, A. (1971). *Selections from the Prison Notebooks*. London: Lawrence and Wishart.
Haugaard, M. (2006). Power and Hegemony in Social Theory. In M. Haugaard and H. Lentner (Eds.), *Hegemony and Power: Consensus and Coercion in Contemporary Politics* (pp. 45–63). Lanham: Lexington Books.
Haugaard, M. (2009). Power and Hegemony. In S.R. Clegg and M. Haugaard (Eds.), *The SAGE Handbook of Power* (pp. 239–255). London: Sage Publications.
Haugaard, M. (2012). Rethinking the Four Dimensions of Power: Domination and Empowerment. *Journal of Political Power*, 5 (1), 33–54.
Hobbes, T. (2010 [1651]). *Leviathan: Or the Matter, Forme, and Power of a Common-Wealth Ecclesiasticall and Civill*. Yale: Yale University Press.

Jessop, B. (2005). Critical Realism and the Strategic-Relational Approach. *New Formations: A Journal of Culture, Theory and Politics*, 56, 40–53.

Jessop, B. (2008). *State Power: A Strategic-Relational Approach*. Cambridge: Polity Press.

Machiavelli, N. (1998 [1532]). *The Prince*. Chicago: University of Chicago Press.

Sayer, A. (2000). *Realism and Social Science*. London: Sage Publications.

Schattschneider, E.E. (1960). *The Semi-Sovereign People: A Realist's View of Democracy in America*. New York: Holt, Rhinehart & Winston.

Sum, N., Jessop, B. (2013). *Towards a Cultural Political Economy: Putting Culture in its Place in Political Economy*. Cheltenham: Edward Elgar.

Torfing, J. (2009). Power and Discourse: Towards an Anti-Foundationalist Concept of Power. In S.R. Clegg and M. Haugaard (Eds.), *The SAGE Handbook of Power* (pp. 108–124). London: Sage Publications.

15

THE IMPERIAL MODE OF LIVING

Ulrich Brand and Markus Wissen

Introduction

Despite increasing geopolitical and geo-economic rivalry, a strong global compromise seems to exist which, on the one hand, nurtures those rivalries and deepens the ecological crisis and, on the other, constitutes a stabilising moment in the crisis of capitalism. We refer to a broad consensus in political and (social) scientific debates. The further exploitation of natural resources and the use of global sinks are considered as the basis of global capitalist development and the overcoming of its various crises. Behind this stands a global consensus about the attractiveness of modern capitalist everyday practices, what we call the "imperial mode of living" (hereafter IML).[1]

The concept of an IML has been recently introduced by the authors of this chapter. Here we will explain the concept and its importance. This reveals the relevance of the IML to the broad and developing agenda of social ecological economics ([Chapter 1]; Spash, 2011). The next section provides the background to how we define and use the concept of an IML and show the links to other literature. We then place the IML in historical context before presenting future directions for the IML and drawing some conclusions.

What does the IML mean?

The concept of the IML highlights the fact that capitalism both implies uneven development in time and space as well as a constant and accelerating universalisation of a Western production model. The logic of liberal markets since the nineteenth century, and especially since World War II, has been inscribed into everyday practices that are normalised and usually unconsciously reproduced [Chapter 5]. They are a main driver of the ecological crisis.

The IML concept implies that people's everyday practices, including individual and societal orientations, as well as identities, rely heavily on: (i) the unlimited appropriation of resources; (ii) a disproportionate claim to global and local ecosystems and sinks; and (iii) cheap labour from elsewhere. This availability of commodities is organised through the world market, backed by military force and/or the asymmetric relations of forces as they have been inscribed in international institutions. The concrete production conditions of the consumed commodities, which are essential to particular modes of living, are usually invisible. For example, as far as agricultural products are concerned, McMichael (2010: 612) speaks of "food from nowhere".

In recent years, the globally attractive IML has been unevenly globalised. A large group of "new consumers" (Myers and Kent, 2004; UNEP, 2010) has emerged in countries like China, India, and Brazil, i.e. consumers who integrate the consumption of meat, automobility and electronic apparatuses into their everyday lives. The IML contributes to safeguarding social stability in the global North and provides a hegemonic orientation in many societies of the Global South. The social relations—like those of production and consumption—underlying the IML, and possible ways to transform them, are insufficiently reflected in current political debates, official reports and research.

The IML is not socially neutral. People with relatively high levels of education, incomes and environmental consciousness also have some of the highest per capita resource use, while classes with lower environmental consciousness use fewer resources because of their lower incomes. Moreover, the concept goes beyond lifestyles of different social milieus and aims to recognise the dominant patterns of production, distribution and consumption. This then relates to discourses concerning the meaning and content of "a good life".

How the IML combines theoretical ideas

As an interdisciplinary conceptualisation, the IML links to and can be used in various fields of research. Simultaneously the concept benefits from and builds upon various theoretical traditions and concepts, including eco-Marxism [Chapter 6]. The starting point is that the capitalist mode of production is expansive and geared towards increasing surplus value, production and consumption. This goes hand-in-hand with an extension of the capitalist (world) market and a capitalist valorisation of ever more areas of life. Brand and Wissen (2013, 2015) refer especially to political ecology [Chapter 4], regulation theory and the Gramscian concept of hegemony [Chapters 14 and 17]. In addition, there are several other influences that are correspondences to literatures and ideas that are specified in this section. Each of these areas is discussed next in turn.

Political ecology

The IML concept regards the ecological crisis as more than simply an overuse of resources and sinks, and emphasises the unequal appropriation of Nature. It provides a critique of concepts like planetary boundaries [see also Chapter 12] that neglect social relations in favour of an abstract notion of "humankind". Instead it draws on the insights of political ecology (Robbins, 2004; Peet et al., 2011, Perreault et al., 2015; Bryant, 2015). The ecological crisis is then understood as a medium and a result of an unequal distribution of power along the lines of class, gender and ethnicity. The "environment" from a political ecology perspective is always "politicised" (Bryant and Bailey, 1997). Consequently, the key to overcoming the ecological crisis is neither the market nor technological innovation but the struggle against social power and domination. Democratising "societal relations with nature" (Görg, 2011) and rejecting exclusive property rights—in support of, say, extractivist practices or privatisation of genetic resources—is not only an aim in itself but also a means of ecological sustainability. An important component of such a transformation would be to overcome the destructive patterns of production and consumption which are at the heart of the IML.

Regulation theory

One central category of regulation theory—a French school of thought on capitalism and its mechanism of reproduction in spite of its inherent contradictions—is that of the "mode of development". This refers to the temporary coherence between the historical development of a mode of production and distribution, and a mode of consumption (the regime of accumulation), which is safeguarded by a range of institutional forms that together constitute a mode of regulation. Capitalist social relations include capital itself, the wage relation, money, the State, and modes of distribution, but also social relations indirectly linked to capitalism, such as gender relations [Chapter 5]. These are better reproduced if a "stable" regime of accumulation emerges in the sense of more or less calculable and incremental changes. Under regulation theory, the various segments of the production process—production and consumer goods industries—and the prevailing standards in these processes must be more or less compatible with the conditions of final consumption. Aglietta argues that after World War II the emergence of a working class mode of consumption, centred around standardised housing and automobile transport, became "an essential condition of capitalist accumulation" (1979: 154). This is an important factor for the generalisation of wage labour in Fordism (Huber, 2013, links fossilist capitalism and the wage relation). IML adds to regulation theory by assigning greater weight to the micro-level of everyday practice and everyday knowledge.

Hegemony theory

Hegemony theory originated in the writings of Antonio Gramsci [see also Chapters 14 & 17]. A hegemonic (i.e. broadly accepted and institutionally secured) mode of living can emerge that is deeply rooted in the everyday practices of people and safeguarded by the State. This is argued to happen in certain historical phases building on coherence between norms of production and consumption. This highlights aspects of domination (along class, gender, race, international and postcolonial lines) that the dominated largely accept. Hegemony can exist along with different modes of living. However, alternatives remain at the margins and may gain strength mainly in situations of crisis.

Modes of production and consumption that become hegemonic in certain regions or countries can be generalised globally through a "capillary" process, meaning in a broken manner and with considerable gaps in time and space. That process is associated with concrete corporate strategies and interests in capital valorisation, trade, investment, and geopolitics; with purchasing power; and with dispositives of an attractive mode of living that predominates in the societies into which these modes diffuse by way of the world market. Generalisation does not mean that all people live alike, but rather that certain, deeply rooted concepts of the "good life" and societal development are generated and reflected in the everyday life of a growing number of people, not only symbolically but also materially.

Other connections to IML

Feminist economics, ecofeminism and other feminist social sciences, make important contributions to a broader understanding of economies and societies [Chapter 5]. Beyond the formal economy, capital investment, financial markets and wage labour, there are other structures and processes that are the precondition for the functioning of the formal and money mediated economy. Predominantly, people are raised and the elderly are cared for outside the formal market economy. Biesecker and Hofmeister (2010) argue that the capitalist economy is structured as one of separation and externalisation, i.e. hiding the forms of activities upon which it depends. Ecofeminism highlights the role of unpaid reproduction and its many environmental dimensions. This is highly relevant for the IML where modes of living and formal production impact on a society's reproductive ability and create manifold forms of gendered domination.

The notion of the IML is very close to what Foster and Clark have termed "ecological imperialism". They describe this as:

> the pillage of the resources of some countries by others and the transformation of whole ecosystems upon which states and nations depend; massive movements of population and labour that are interconnected with the extraction and transfer of resources; the exploitation of ecological vulnerabilities of societies to promote imperialist control; the dumping of ecological wastes in ways that widen the chasm between centre and periphery; and overall, the creation of a global 'metabolic rift' that characterises the relation of capitalism to the environment, and at the same time limits capitalist development.
>
> *(Foster and Clark, 2003: 187)*

IML adds to this perspective by asking: "How is ecological imperialism rooted in everyday practices and supported by State institutions?" "How is this normalised in a way that hides the imperialism it entails?"

Practice theories are a cornerstone for the concept of IML. They argue that social practices are shared behavioural routines that are constituted by sets of interconnected elements [see Chapter 20]. The elements include: social and political institutions, socio-technical configurations, such as the physical infrastructures, available knowledge and prevailing symbolic orientations and forms of power (Spaargaren, 2011). Environmentally detrimental social practices, such as driving a car, are hard to steer intentionally and to manage or influence via consciousness raising campaigns.

Social ecology helps us to understand the longue durée of society's colonisation of Nature and the specificity of the industrial socio-metabolic regime and its particular energy sources [Chapter 11]. The prevailing patterns of production and consumption in the global North were enabled by replacing self-renewing biomass with non-renewable fossil fuels. Currently, two-thirds of the world's population are in transition from the agrarian to the industrial regime (Haberl et al., 2011). This highlights the material implications of fossilist patterns of production and consumption that are currently spreading to the middle and upper classes of the Global South.

The IML in historical perspective

The concept enables a particular understanding of history and current developments. In principle, the IML started with the colonisation of the world. Minerals like copper and agricultural commodities like coffee, tea or bananas were extracted and grown by slave or wage labour and brought to Europe. For centuries, these products were luxury goods for the upper classes, inputs for production processes and means of exchange or to stores of value, e.g. gold and silver. Liberal capitalism in the nineteenth century extended the IML towards the evolving middle classes in Europe and the upper classes in regions like Latin America, where the colonies became independent and national bourgeoisies emerged. Historical imperialism between 1875 and 1914 reveals the nation state's economy attempting to extend and deepen the IML. For example, Kloppenburg (1988) shows how plant genetic resources played a major role in creating an imperial world order at the level of everyday practices.

Mitchell (2011) reminds us that the struggle for and enactment of political and social rights in modern societies are closely linked to fossil fuels. He argues that since the nineteenth century workers achieved political and social inclusion, especially through their power in the extraction, distribution and use of coal. He calls this "carbon democracy". The widespread use of coal gave rise to new worker power. Labour intensive production made the new coal economy susceptible to strikes. Mitchell (2011: 236) argues that this led to appeasement and political reform (e.g., democracy, workers' rights, health and safety regulation). However, the modes of living were not deeply affected, and many workers remained within a subsistence economy and not part of the IML.

The Fordist mode of development after World War II brought an enormous extension of the IML. Fordism is a mode of social and economic development whereby the workers have high enough wages to purchase products they themselves produce, e.g. a car factory worker being able to buy a Ford Model-T. This congruence of the norm of production and consumption is ensured by welfare State institutions and labour rights, which themselves are a result of social struggles (e.g., labour conflicts following the Great Depression and Roosevelt's New Deal). Fordism implies a model of well-being that includes the masses of the global North in hitherto unknown forms of political participation, high annual growth and profit rates and the use of resources and sinks. This involves a predominant and intensive regime of accumulation in which the reproduction of the wage earners becomes a sphere of capital valorisation. Semi-subsistent forms of reproduction are replaced by commodity-based forms, and wages are linked to productivity. In the semi-periphery, parts of the urban middle-classes join this attractive mode of living. This resource intensive model is a central causal mechanism of the ecological crisis (Altvater, 1993).

The conceptualisation of what constitutes an attractive form of living developed around the male bread-winner model, automobility, processed and cheap food, meat consumption and use of electronic equipment. The capitalistically produced commodities, and associated social relations, needed to be accepted and practically lived by the people who reproduce themselves materially and symbolically through these commodities. The Fordist mode of development generated a high level of social consensus and also shaped subjectivities and gender relations, i.e. a consolidation of patriarchal gender relations occurred [Chapter 5]. The State has played a major role in constituting and stabilising the IML by not only externally securing access to strategic resources but also internally guaranteeing a certain living standard for the masses through social insurance systems and labour market regulations. This provides the material basis of the IML and it turns the State into an "educator" that aims to "make certain habits and practices disappear, while seeking to spread others" (Gramsci, 1996 [1932–1934]: 1548, our translation).

Unlike in the nineteenth century, Mitchell (2011) argues, workers were less powerful in the post-war period given the more decentralised (pipelines) and internationalised production of oil (especially through the role of authoritarian governments in the Arab world). On the other hand, industrialism based on oil (and gas) shaped the modes of living of workers and ordinary people in a profound way. Clothes, plastics, food and mobility became readily available and products became increasingly fossil fuel based (Huber, 2013). Concerning the relationship of the national and the international scales, national economies were cushioned through an "embedded liberalism" (Ruggie, 1982); that is, open markets with certain regulations. The financial sector, in particular, was strongly regulated, especially because of the financial crisis of 1929, and subordinated to the interests of industrial capital.

In the 1970s, a crisis hit Fordist accumulation strategies and the related institutional arrangements. Profit rates declined and class conflicts intensified in many parts of the world. The ecological destructiveness of the Fordist mode of development was politicised by scientists, environmental movements and, in some cases, by concerned bureaucrats. In the capitalist centres, the Fordist class compromise was dismissed from above, while in many peripheral countries (particularly in Latin America) military dictatorships took over State power. Reorientation towards world markets was one strategy to overcome the crisis, albeit with limited success. Despite various changes—new technologies, gains in productivity, rationalisation, reshaping societal power relations towards private investors and asset holders and transnationalisation—the contradictions of globalised capitalism impeded the emergence of a more or less coherent new "post-Fordist" mode of development.

The politicisation of the ecological crisis failed to prevent intensification of the appropriation of Nature. In the capitalist centres profit rates did indeed rise again. However, since the 1990s the interests of private investors gained influence and a partial shift towards patterns of financialisation has played an increasing role in the reproduction of the IML. This goes hand in hand with the financialisation of Nature and mechanisms like carbon trading (Spash, 2010).

Since the financial collapse of 2008 the IML has constituted an important element of societal consensus. In the capitalist centres of the world system, funding the costs of the reproduction of wage-earners has been challenged by neoliberalism. However, the cost can be reduced through enhanced access to globally produced commodities traded in liberalised markets that exploit labour elsewhere i.e., increasing relative surplus value. This process occurs along structural lines of class, gender and ethnicity, but it is broadly accepted and its deepening is a crucial crisis management strategy.

Furthermore, the IML is unevenly universalised in many countries of the Global South. Development there is defined as capitalist modernisation with a more or less selective world market integration, and this is broadly accepted by elites and urban middle classes. Some regions of the Global South have been brought into the IML through rapid economic growth due to industrialisation and proletarisation, as in China, and the development of a globally oriented service economy, as in India.

Ecological crisis phenomena—biodiversity loss, climate change—have been caused by the spread of industrial production and consumption patterns. These create resource and land-use conflicts, geopolitical tensions and intense capitalist competition. Exclusive access to resources, guaranteed by contracts or through open violence, and the shifting on to others of the social ecological costs that using these resources entails (Kapp, 1978), are the *conditio sine qua non* of the global North's mode of production and living, which therefore can be called "imperial".

Future directions

The IML enables us to understand better both historical and current developments. The future use of the IML for concrete research and within different conceptual frameworks will show its analytical usefulness. It sheds light on how the unsustainable mode of production and living can persist, despite the highly politicised ecological crisis. This helps expose the related strategies of various actors. Using the concept of the IML gives a broad perspective of the economic, political and cultural foundations of the ecological crisis and its links to the structural problems of the economy. The concept contributes to a better understanding of the limitations of existing global environmental politics as well as politics at national and local scales. This reveals how the highly conflictive character of international economic and resource politics happens against the background of maintaining the IML. More specifically, there are several areas for future research.

Green-grabbing, financialisation of Nature and "Landnahme"

The universalisation of the IML turns mineral and agricultural resources as well as sinks into increasingly scarce goods. Valorisation means, for example, enhancing mining activities under capitalist conditions and turning commons or supposedly uncultivated land into capitalist commodities [see Chapters 38 and 40]. The process of valorising such activities is one that makes them increasingly attractive to business. In the tradition of Rosa Luxemburg (1951 [1913]) this can be called a further *land-grabbing* or "Landnahme" (Dörre, 2015). It applies not only to mining and agricultural capital but also financial capital in search of new investment opportunities in a crisis of over-accumulation. If land-grabbing takes place for alleged environmental ends—biodiversity offsetting or forest CO_2 sequestration—it is called *green-grabbing* (Fairhead et al., 2012). Such investments in Nature may not provide for the highest rates of return on capital, but they may be regarded as more durable and secure than other options.

The State and the international political system

A critical theorising of the State that understands it as a social relation is important. The State is a terrain of contest that is asymmetrically structured and has biases towards certain interests such as powerful groups and dynamics of the growth imperative. Jessop (2007) calls this "strategic selectivities" [see also Chapter 14]. In that sense, the State cannot be understood without considering social forces and their interests (which at the same time are shaped by the State), and the economic and cultural constellations of a society, i.e. the modes of production and living as well as the material and symbolic discursive relations. Moreover, the State should not be equated with the nation state but seen as a multi-scalar set of social relations operating at the local, regional and international levels (Brand et al., 2011). Future research should also analyse the ways in which the State at various levels stabilises or shapes the IML.

Limitations of a Green Economy

The current efforts to 'green' the economy mean that the resource dependence of the prevailing patterns of production and consumption shift from fossils to other minerals, as well as to agricultural resources (e.g., biomass for fuels, copper for renewable energy; cf. Spash, 2012). The greening of the economy is nothing else than the perpetuation of the IML through its ecological modernisation. It will strengthen the demand for natural resources, a demand that has already been rising due to the spread of "Northern" production and consumption patterns to the Global South, as well as forms of land-grabbing and green-grabbing.

Green Capitalism

A further field of inquiry is whether the current drive for ecological modernisation of the economy might lead some countries to a new, more or less coherent, mode of capitalist development. This could be called Green Capitalism (Brand and Wissen, 2015; Koch, 2012). At the level of political strategies and legitimisation, such a project might be framed as a Green Economy. A driving force of such a Green Capitalist project would be the further valorisation of Nature as an important constituent of crisis management, for the very reason that it is located at the interface of various crisis phenomena. These phenomena operate by offsetting one dimension of crisis i.e., energy and resources, including food) against another (i.e., economic crisis). This occurs through signalling a scarcity of important goods and natural resources which could be converted into commodities. Such a project will evolve unevenly in space and time. In the medium term, it could be successful in countries like Germany and Austria, provided that a range of social forces gather to support it. Such forces comprise, amongst others, the Green factions of capital, sections of trade unions and environmental and consumer associations, all of which are articulated through political parties and are, for the moment, present in certain State apparatuses.

Alternatives and social ecological transformation

The IML is an analytical concept to show how unsustainable patterns of production and consumption are reproduced, not only through capital and State strategies but also through everyday practices. In that sense, politics and social contestations to really overcome the ecological crisis—or, better said: the social ecological crisis as part of a multiple crises of capitalism—need to consider this deep rootedness of unsustainability. There are promising debates such as those concerning on degrowth [Chapter 44], the good life, commons [Chapter 38], environmentalism of the poor [Chapter 16] or social ecological transformation [Chapter 17] (Brand, 2016). A reflection on the IML enables the discussions and practices around the concepts to avoid reducing perspectives of change to questions of adequate State control, management strategies or political voluntarism. Social change in an emancipatory direction cannot overlook the ambiguous experiences of people related to fossilist capitalism such as forms of well-being and social inclusion. The degrowth debate insists, rightly, that the link between growth and well-being is broken (Muraca, 2013). However, it still exists not only through the desperate "growth strategies" of capital and governments but also as a powerful imaginary and through everyday practices. Alternative thinking and practices need to take this into account.

Concluding remarks

The dominant forms of the appropriation of Nature lead to a deepening and spatial expansion of the fossilist capitalist mode of development and its expression as the imperial mode of production and living. The ecological crisis is thus also a crisis of the global North's mode of living, which is currently spreading across the globe regardless of the fact that it cannot be generalised without enhancing the ecological crisis. Despite the crises of capitalism and ecology this entails, universalising the IML remains a dominant position.

In summary, the IML concept helps understanding in several ways:

1   Despite the crisis of neoliberal imperial globalisation resource and energy intensive everyday practices persist and continue to have severe social ecological consequences;
2   The hegemonic (i.e., largely accepted) forms of living are closely linked to the dominant mode of production and capital's valorisation strategies, politics and structures of the State, and prevailing orientations and dispositives of action;
3   Environmental politics, especially at the global scale but also at national and local ones, is largely ineffective and we experience a severe "crisis of crisis management" because the IML core of the crisis is ignored. The very structure of national and international politics is deeply linked to the dominant mode of production and living;
4   Despite all talk to the contrary, there is a fostering of (neo-)imperialist strategies with respect to natural resources—like the Raw Materials Initiative of the EU [see Chapter 10]—and sinks in order to maintain existing power relations and interests, but also the IML;
5   In the current economic crisis, the difficult challenge is the development and strengthening of resistance and alternatives to dominant crisis politics and the promotion of a social ecological transformation;
6   Countering the hegemonic IML by transforming modes of living is a starting point. In addition, counter hegemonic struggles require blocking unsustainable capital and State

strategies. An entry point for alternatives is to create more solidarity through alternative social ecological modes of production and living that might become universalised.

Note

1   We would like to thank Melanie Pichler and Clive Spash for extremely useful comments.

Key further readings cited

Biesecker, A., Hofmeister, S. (2010). (Re)productivity: Sustainable relations both between society and nature and between the genders. *Ecological Economics* 69(8), 1703–1711.

Brand, U. (2016). How to get out of the multiple crisis? Towards a critical theory of social ecological transformation. *Environmental Values* 25(5), 503–525.

Brand, U., Wissen, M. (2013). Crisis and continuity of capitalist societal nature relations. The imperial mode of living and the limits to environmental governance. *Review of International Political Economy* 20(4), 687–711.

Kloppenburg, J.R. (1988). *First the Seed. The Political Economy of Plant Technology, 1492–2000*. Cambridge: Cambridge University Press.

Mitchell, T. (2011). *Carbon Democracy. Political Power in the Age of Oil*. London: Verso.

Other literature cited

Aglietta, M. (1979). *A Theory of Capitalist Regulation. The US Experience*. London: Verso.

Altvater, E. (1993). *The Future of Market*. London: Verso.

Brand, U., Wissen, M. (2015). Strategies of a green economy, contours of a green capitalism. In K. van der Pijl (Ed.). *The International Political Economy of Production* (pp. 508–523). Cheltenham: Edward Elgar.

Brand, U., Görg, C., Wissen, M. (2011). Second-order condensations of societal power relations. Environmental politics and the internationalization of the state from a Neo-poulantzian perspective. *Antipode* 43(1), 149–175.

Bryant, R.L. (Ed.) (2015): *The International Handbook of Political Ecology*. Cheltenham: Edward Elgar.

Bryant, R.L., Bailey, S. (1997): *Third World Political Ecology*. London: Routledge.

Dörre, K. (2015). Social capitalism and crisis: From the internal to the external landnahme. In Dörre, K., Lessenich, S., Rosa, H. (Eds.). *Sociology, Capitalism, Critique* (pp. 247–279). London: Verso.

Fairhead, J., Leach, M., Scoones, I. (2012). Green grabbing: a new appropriation of nature? *The Journal of Peasant Studies* 39(2), 237–261.

Foster, J.B., Clark, B. (2003). Ecological imperialism: The curse of capitalism. *Socialist Register 2004*. London: Merlin, pp. 186–201.

Görg, C. (2011). Societal relationships with nature: A dialectical approach to environmental politics. In A. Biro (Ed.). *Critical Ecologies. The Frankfurt School and Contemporary Environmental Crises* (pp. 43–72). Toronto: University of Toronto Press.

Gramsci, A. (1996). *Prison Notebook*, vol. 7. Quoted from the German edition. Hamburg: Argument.

Haberl, H., Fischer-Kowalski, M., Krausmann, F., Martinez-Alier, J., Winiwarter, V. (2011). A Socio-metabolic transition towards sustainability? Challenges for another great transformation. *Sustainable Development* 19(1), 1–14.

Huber, M. (2013). Fueling capitalism: Oil, the regulation approach, and the ecology of capital. *Economic Geography* 89(2), 171–194.

Jessop, B. (2007). *State Power: A Strategic-Relational Approach*. Cambridge: Polity.

Kapp, K.W. (1978). *The Social Costs of Business Enterprise* (3rd ed.). Nottingham: Spokesman.

Koch, M. 2012. *Capitalism and Climate Change*. London: Palgrave/MacMillan.

Luxemburg, R. (1913/1951). *The Accumulation of Capital*. London: Routledge.

McMichael, P. (2010). Agrofuels in the food regime. *The Journal of Peasant Studies* 37(4), 609–629.

Muraca, B. (2012). Towards a fair degrowth-society: Justice and the right to a 'good life' beyond growth. *Futures* 44(6): 535–545.

Myers, N., Kent, J. (2004). *The New Consumers: The Influence of Affluence on the Environment*. Washington: Island Press.

Peet, R., Robbins, P., Watts, M. (Eds.) (2011). *Global Political Ecology*. London: Routledge.

Perreault, T., Bridge, G., McCarthy, J. (Eds.) (2015): *The Routledge Handbook of Political Ecology*. London: Routledge.

Robbins, P. (2004). *Political Ecology. A Critical Introduction*. Malden MA: Blackwell.

Ruggie, J.G. (1982). International regimes, transactions, and change: embedded liberalism in the postwar economic order. *International Organization* 36(2), 379–415.

Spaargaren, G. (2011). Theories of practices: Agency, technology, and culture Exploring the relevance of practice theories for the governance of sustainable consumption practices in the new world-order. *Global Environmental Change* 21(3), 813–822.

Spash, C.L. (2010). The brave new world of carbon trading. *New Political Economy* 15(2), 169–195.

Spash, C.L. (2011). Social ecological economics: Understanding the past to see the future, *American Journal of Economics and Sociology*, 70(2), 340–375.

Spash, C.L. (2012). Green Economy, Red Herring. *Environmental Values* 21(2), 95–99.

UNEP (2010). *Assessing the Environmental Impacts of Consumption and Production: Priority Products and Materials*. Nairobi: UNEP.

16

A GUIDE TO ENVIRONMENTAL JUSTICE MOVEMENTS AND THE LANGUAGE OF ECOLOGICAL DISTRIBUTION CONFLICTS

Joan Martinez-Alier

Introduction

A global movement for environmental justice (EJ)—overlapping with gender, class, caste, ethnic and national struggles—is asserting itself to address the environmental crisis. The world social metabolism, the flows of energy and materials, is increasing [Chapter 11]. The economy uses more inputs and it produces more waste. The inputs often come from the "commodity extraction frontiers", and the waste is dumped locally or internationally. Fossil fuel combustion releases carbon dioxide (CO_2) which is deposited in the atmosphere increasing the greenhouse effect or finds its way to acidify the oceans. The economy is not circular; it is entropic (Haas et al., 2015) [see also Chapter 9]. Even renewable resources such as water from aquifers, timber, and fisheries are overexploited, the fertility of the soil is jeopardised and biodiversity is depleted. The growing and changing metabolism of industrial economies gives rise to ecological distribution conflicts [Chapters 4 and 15].

Ecological distribution conflicts are different from economic distribution conflicts over salaries, prices, profits, taxes and rents. They are conflicts over the distribution of the burdens of pollution, access to natural resources and conditions of livelihood. These conflicts are expressed as struggles over valuation, in two senses. First, which are the values deemed relevant for decision making in particular projects (e.g., market values including fictitious money values elicited through contingent valuation; livelihood values; sacredness; indigenous territorial rights; ecological values in their own units of account)? Second, and more importantly, who has the power to include or exclude relevant values, and to allow or prevent trade-offs [see Chapter 14 on power]? For instance, does sacredness imply a veto power (Martinez-Alier et al., 1998; Martinez-Alier, 2002; Temper and Martinez-Alier, 2013)?

This chapter opens with an explanation of ecological distribution conflicts and the origins of EJ. A broad categorisation is presented. The main section then reviews a series of environmental and resource conflicts and reveals how a range of resistance movements have developed their own terminology, concepts and language [see also Chapter 17]. This is a new language of resistance. The chapter provides a guide to the breadth of terms employed by EJ organisations (EJOs) in the political struggle, the types of conflict in which they are engaged and the associated non-governmental organisations and activists.

Ecological distribution conflicts and the rise of EJ

Social mobilisations over resource extraction, environmental degradation and waste disposal are not only about the distribution of environmental benefits and costs (expressed in monetary or non-monetary valuation languages), but also about participation in decision making and recognition of group identities. EJ research encompasses issues of exclusion (Agarwal, 2001) and the potential for new leadership by different social actors, e.g. in the environmentalism of the poor and indigenous the contribution of women is important to recognise in both rural and urban communities. Since the 1980s, EJOs and their networks have provided definitions and analyses of a wide array of concepts and slogans related to environmental inequities, and explored the connections between them. Thus, demands for food sovereignty from the Via Campesina fit in with complaints against biopiracy, land-grabbing and tree plantations, and also with climate change issues, as in the slogan "traditional peasant agriculture cools down the Earth". EJ has spread through organisations like Friends of the Earth, which, while born in California as a white conservationist movement, brought in EJOs that had existed since the 1980s like CENSAT in Colombia and WALHI in Indonesia. These activist and social movement provided the concepts of EJ that were then taken up in academic research on Southern countries by political ecology [Chapter 4]. Going beyond case studies, researchers now generate statistics on ecological distribution conflicts (Özkaynak et al., 2015; Temper et al., 2015) as encapsulated by the EJAtlas (www.ejatlas.org).

There are many conflicts relating to resource extraction, transport and waste disposal as shown in the EJAtlas and other inventories produced by EJOs. There are also many successful examples of stopping projects and developing alternatives, testifying to the existence of a rural and urban global movement for EJ. Moreover, since the 1980s and 1990s this movement developed a set of concepts and campaign slogans to intervene in such conflicts (Martinez-Alier et al., 2014).

Ecological distribution conflicts (Martinez-Alier, 1995; Martinez-Alier and O'Connor, 1996) is a term which has its origin in ecological economics. For instance, a factory may be polluting the river that belongs to nobody or belongs to a community that manages the river. This is not a damage valued in the market. The same happens with climate change, causing perhaps sea level rise impacting small island States. These are more than market failures, a terminology that implies that such 'externalities' could be valued in money terms and internalised into the price system. These are "cost-shifting" successes for the polluters (Kapp, 1950), that have increasingly led to complaints from those bearing the costs.

Such ecological distribution conflicts were perceived in terms of persistent injustices towards "people of colour" in the United States of America (USA) giving rise to a social movement in the 1980s when the EJ concept began to be used in struggles against the disproportionate dumping of toxic waste in periurban African American residential areas. As early as 1991, at the Washington, D.C., 'People of Colour Environmental Leadership Summit', ties were forged so as "to build a national and international movement of all peoples of colour to fight the destruction and taking of our lands and communities".

Another concept related to EJ is the "environmentalism of the poor" applied to rural and indigenous populations in India and Latin America by academics and activists in the late 1980s. Since the mid-1990s the explicit connection between the EJ movement in the USA and the environmentalism of the poor in Latin America, Africa, and Asia, was established (Guha and Martinez-Alier, 1997). This followed the deaths of Chico Mendes in 1988 fighting deforestation in Brazil, and of Ken Saro-Wiwa and his Ogoni comrades in the Niger Delta in 1995 fighting against oil extraction and gas flaring by Shell. Classic books analysing movements against dams

Table 16.1 A classification and some examples of ecological distribution conflicts

	Geographic scope		
	Local	*National and regional*	*Global*
Extraction	Resource conflicts in tribal areas: bauxite (Odisha), coal or uranium (Jharkhand), oil (Amazon, Ecuador, Peru, Niger Delta).	Mangrove uprooting. Tree plantations for wood or paper pulp. Collapses of fisheries.	Plunder of minerals and fossil fuels at the "commodity" frontiers. Bio-piracy. Corporate accountability.
Transport and trade	Motorways or railways creating noise, pollution, landscape loss, human mortality and morbidity.	Inter-basin water transport. Oil/gas pipelines (Burma to Thailand and China). No TAV (no high speed train Turin-Lyon) movement (Italy). Isiboro Sécure National Park and Indigenous Territory (TIPNIS) anti-roads (Bolivia).	Oil spills at sea. Resource grabbing. Ecologically unequal exchange, South to North.
Waste and pollution	Conflicts on incinerators (dioxins) or volatile organic compounds, nitrous oxides, ozone, particulate matter.	Acid rain from sulphur dioxide. Nuclear waste disposal (Yucca Mt., USA). Ship dismantling (Alang-Sosiya, Chittagong).	Greenhouse gases (climate change). Ocean acidification. Chloroflurocarbons (ozone holes). Persistent organic pollutants in remote pristine areas. Ecological debt. Climate justice

(McCully, 1996) and tree plantations (Carrere and Lohmann, 1996) were published by activists at that time. There are several types of ecological distribution conflicts that can be a classified along the commodity chains, and occur at different geographical scales, as shown in Table 16.1. These include conflicts over resource extraction, transportation and waste disposal.

A new vocabulary of environmental justice

Critical to the development of global EJ networks has been the conceptual language that has arisen from particular conflicts. Short definitions and the dates of origin of such concepts are provided in Table 16.2. Information was acquired through the EJOLT project (2011–2015), the compilation of the EJAtlas and via collaborative research with activists over many years (Martinez-Alier, 2002; Healy et al., 2012). This has been part of building a combination ecological economics and political ecology from the ground up. There are also concepts of academic origin (such as ecologically unequal trade [Chapter 4] and ecological footprint) that are used, or could be used, by the global EJ movement. However, my primary concern here is to focus on concepts of non-academic origin.

The first concept in the list is EJ born in the USA in struggles against waste dumping in North Carolina in 1982. Activist authors such as sociologist Robert Bullard, but also civil rights activists with no academic affiliation and members of Christian Churches, saw themselves as militants of EJ (Bullard, 1993; Agyeman et al., 2003; Pellow and Brulle, 2005). The fight against the disproportionate incidence of pollution was also seen as a fight against "environmental racism", a concept that, in the language of EJO, means to treat other people badly by subjecting

Table 16.2 Vocabulary of the global environmental justice movement

	Responsible EJ Organisations (EJOs)	Short description
Environmental Justice (EJ)	USA Civil Rights Movement, North Carolina 1982 (Bullard 1993).	"People of colour" and low-income populations suffer harm from waste sites, refineries and incinerators, transport infrastructures.
Environmental racism	Reverend Chavis, c. 1982	The fight for EJ, against pollution in Black, Hispanic, Indigenous areas, was seen as a fight against *environmental racism*.
Ecological debt	Instituto Ecologia Política, Chile, 1992, Acción Ecológica 1997	Rich countries' liability from resource plunder and disproportionate use of space for dumping greenhouse gases and other waste.
Popular epidemiology	Brown (1997)	"Lay" local knowledge of illnesses from pollution may be more valid than official knowledge (sometimes absent).
Environmentalism of the poor	Agarwal and Narain (CSE, Delhi), 1989	Struggles by poor/indigenous peoples against deforestation, dams, mining; Collective projects for water harvesting, forest conservation.
Food sovereignty	Via Campesina, 1996	People's right to healthy, culturally appropriate, sustainably produced food. Right to define own food and agriculture systems.
Biopiracy	RAFI (Pat Mooney) 1993, Vandana Shiva	Appropriation of genetic resources without recognition of knowledge and property rights of indigenous peoples.
Climate justice	CES (Delhi), 1991, Durban Alliance, CorpWatch 1999–2002	Radically reduce excessive per capita emissions of greenhouse gases. "Subsistence emissions vs. luxury emissions".
Water justice, hydric justice	Rutgerd Boelens, EJOs in Latin America (e.g. CENSAT). 2011.	Water should not run towards money, or towards power. It should go to those needing it for livelihood.
Water as human right	P. Solon (Bolivian envoy to UN), M. Barlow (Council of Canadians), 2001	Human right to water recognised at UN level in 2011, as an independent human right.
"Green deserts"	Brazil, network *Rede Alerta contra o Deserto Verde*, 1999	Brazilian local term for eucalyptus plantations, used by EJOs, communities, researchers and activists for any tree plantation.
Tree plantations are not forests	Carrere and Lohmann (1996), World Rainforest Movement (WRM)	WRM informs on plantation conflicts; wants to change FAO forest definition to exclude monocultures.
Land-grabbing	GRAIN (pro-peasant EJO) 2008	Land acquisitions Global South; plantations for exports; compiles statistics.
(Continued overleaf)		

Table 16.2 (continued)

	Responsible EJ Organisations (EJOs)	Short description
Resource caps	Resource Cap Coalition, Europe, 2010	Reduce global resource use and poverty. European energy quota scheme and ratification of the Rimini Protocol.
To Ogonize/Yasunize	ERA Nigeria, Acción Ecológica, Oilwatch, 1997–2007	Leave oil in the soil to prevent damage to human rights and biodiversity, and against climate change. Adopted also by anti shale gas fracking, tar sands and coal mining movements.
Rights of Nature	Ecuador, Constitutional Assembly, 2008	In Constitution of Ecuador 2008, art 71, pushed by Acción Ecológica and Alberto Acosta. Actionable in court.
Corporate accountability	Friends of the Earth International, 1992–2002	UN Johannesburg summit, FoE proposed the adoption of a Corporate Accountability Convention, stronger than corporate social responsibility.
"Critical mass", cyclists rights	San Francisco 1992 (Chris Carlsson)	International movement reclaiming the streets; cyclists marching to impose cyclists rights.
Urban waste recyclers movements	2005, GAIA against incineration and "energy valorization" of urban waste	Unions or cooperatives of urban waste gatherers, with their positive environmental impact (movements in Delhi, Pune, Bogota).
Urban "guerrilla food gardening"	2000, started by "food justice" networks	Vacant lot food growing, permaculture, community gardening movements in cities around the world.
Toxic colonialism, toxic imperialism	BAN, Basel Action Network, 2000	Fighting the long-distance export of waste from rich to poor countries, forbidden by the Basel Treaty, e.g. ship-breaking in India or Bangladesh, chemical residues or nuclear waste, electronic waste.
Post-extractivism	Latin America 2007 Gudynas (CLAES), Alberto Acosta, Maristella Svampa	Against the reprimarization of L.A. economies. Transition to a sustainable economy based on solar energy and renewable materials. Impose quotas and taxes on raw materials exports.
Buen Vivir, Sumak Kawsay	Ecuador and Bolivia 2008	Adopted in Constitutions of both countries, inspired by indigenous traditions and by the "post-development" approach.
Indigenous rights	Convention 169 of ILO, 1989; adivasi forest rights, India	Conflicts on mining, oil exploitation, dams. Communities ask for applying legislation defending indigenous rights.
"Sand mafias"	2005 India, term adopted by media	The illegal "mining" of sand and gravel in India in many rivers, driven by the growing building and public works industry.
"Cancer villages"	China, term adopted by academics, officials (Lora-Wainright, 2013)	Industrially polluted rural villages (e.g. heavy metals). Lay knowledge of illness; subdued protests.

them to pollution or resource extraction injustices on the grounds of their membership of particular ethnic groups, social class or caste. In EJ conflicts, evidence of the disproportionate incidence of morbidity and mortality sometimes cannot be proven from official statistics because of the lack of doctors or hospitals in the areas concerned. Hence the rise of what is termed popular epidemiology (Brown, 1997). This is a relevant concept in many struggles inside and outside the USA. It implies that lay knowledge of pollution illnesses is no less valid than official knowledge (fitting into the post-normal science theory, Funtowicz and Ravetz, 1993; [Chapter 28]).

Environmentalism of the poor

Reflecting the specific environmental challenges and distributional inequities of the Global South, some EJOs adopted the term environmentalism of the poor, which is very close to the notion of EJ, but applies more to rural peoples in the Global South. Academics started to use this term around 1988. Similar words had been used by Anil Agarwal, the founder of the Centre for Science and Environment (CSE) in Delhi, and editor of the first citizens' reports on the state of India's environment. His successor, Sunita Narain, often uses the term environmentalism of the poor to refer to the struggles in India against dams, deforestation, mining projects, and nuclear power stations (Narain, 2008). In many ecological distribution conflicts, the poor are often on the side of preservation of Nature against business firms and the State. This behaviour by poor and/or indigenous peoples is consistent with their interests and their values. Those affected will be motivated to act provided they are not suffocated by fear or violently repressed, as is often the case. In the EJAtlas for about 12 per cent of the conflicts, one of the outcomes is death for those trying to defend the environment.

Unequal exchange

A primary environmental challenge faced by populations of the Global South stems from an economic system that produces ecologically unequal trade, an academic concept (Hornborg et al., 2007). One aspect of such unequal trade was given the name of biopiracy by Pat Mooney of RAFI in 1993 (Shiva, 1997). Biopiracy denotes the appropriation of genetic resources in medicinal or agricultural plants without any recognition of the original knowledge and property rights of indigenous peoples. The word biopiracy is used by EJOs and State authorities in Brazil, India and other countries, and also by academics and doctoral students (Robinson, 2010).

There are a number of other EJO concepts and policies that stem from conflicts over biomass. The many complaints against tree plantations grown for wood or paper pulp, depriving local people of land and water, gave rise 20 years ago to the slogan and movement "Plantations are not forests". In Brazil, "green deserts" was the spontaneous, bottom-up name for eucalyptus plantations in Espiritu Santo and other regions, opposed by local peasants and indigenous peoples. This was certainly a form of enclosure of forest commons. The driving force was the export of paper pulp and cellulose. The EJAtlas highlights a number of such cases, and identifies the firms involved (such as Smurfit), their networks and the outcomes of such conflicts.

A related concept is food sovereignty. This term was introduced in the early 1990s by Via Campesina, meaning the right of rural people (including women in particular) to grow their own food for themselves and for local markets, against corporate agriculture, particularly against agrofuel and tree plantations (GRAIN, 2005). In 2008, a small organisation called GRAIN introduced the first land-grabbing statistics for the wave of land acquisitions being forced through in the Global South.

Ecological debt

A term that has been very successful in the fights against ecologically unequal trade and climate change is ecological debt. There was an alternative treaty in Rio de Janeiro in 1992 on the ecological debt from North to South, and Acción Ecológica of Ecuador took up the term and the struggle in 1997, with several publications which included a definition and many examples (www.accionecologica.org/deuda-ecologica). Ecological debt arises from the plunder of resources and the occupation of disproportionate environmental space by rich countries. Some governments from countries of the South have deployed the concept of ecological debt (or one part of it, the climate debt) in international negotiations (Bond, 2013). The origins of the concept are mainly due to Latin American EJOs. Academics, who joined in later, have produced calculations attempting to show the unequal international distribution of environmental costs and the burden placed upon the poor (Srinivasan et al., 2008; Warlenius et al., 2015). Pope Francis' encyclical *Laudato si* of June 2015 devotes two paragraphs (51 and 52) to the ecological debt from North to South.

Climate justice

EJOs are also responsible for introducing and developing the concept of climate justice. An influential role in its dissemination was played by the CSE booklet, *Global Warming in an Unequal World: A Case of Environmental Colonialism* (Agarwal and Narain, 1991). This pointed out that there were subsistence CO_2 emissions that could be contrasted with luxury CO_2 emissions. Then in the late 1990s came the Jubilee campaign comparing the ecological debt from North to South with the financial debt from South to North (Simms, 2005).

In 2000 in The Hague, the first conference on climate justice was held, sponsored by the New York group CorpWatch (Bond, 2013). Before the meeting, in November 1999, CorpWatch stated that:

> Climate Justice means, first of all, removing the causes of global warming and allowing the Earth to continue to nourish our lives and those of all living beings. This entails radically reducing emissions of carbon dioxide and other greenhouse gases. Climate Justice means opposing destruction wreaked by the Greenhouse Gangsters at every step of the production and distribution process—from a moratorium on new oil exploration, to stopping the poisoning of communities by refinery emissions—from drastic domestic reductions in auto emissions, to the promotion of efficient and effective public transportation.
>
> *(Bruno et al., 1999)*

Four years later, the Durban Group for Climate Justice was launched with a strong campaign against fake carbon offsetting projects (being promoted under the United Nations clean development mechanism; see Spash, 2010).

Water justice

The concept of water justice is associated with a university professor, Rutgerd Boelens (Wageningen University), who has been working closely with activists for many years (Boelens et al., 2011). Their favourite slogans are "water runs towards power" and "water runs towards money", unless stopped by civil society movements. Anti-dam movements continue to denounce water enclosures along with forced acquisition of land, diversion of rivers, and dispossession and displacement of rural and indigenous communities inhabiting territories rich in biodiversity and water sources. They include the Brazilian Movement of People Affected by Dams (MAB) and the MAPDER network in Mexico. The EJAtlas provides many cases of conflicts on water in which contrasting valuation languages are deployed. In municipal water management, paradigmatic movements against privatisation of urban water services as in Cochabamba, Bolivia, are sources of inspiration for the defence of the commons in general (including access to information) and the human right to water.

Resource extractivism and energy policy

Proposals to "leave oil in the soil", also in defence of the commons, were first put forward in 1997 by Acción Ecológica Ecuador (ERA) of Nigeria, and the Oilwatch network founded in 1995. These Yasunizing or Ogonising proposals apply also to tar sands, coal ("leave coal in the hole") and shale gas. The associated campaigns add to local reasons for stopping resource extraction with concerns over protecting biodiversity value, preventing threats to human rights and reducing greenhouse gas emissions. The last highlights that there are now "unburnable fuels" (Temper et al., 2013). In her book on climate justice, Naomi Klein (2014) introduced the word "Blockadia" which she learnt in the blockades against oil and gas pipelines in Canada and the USA. Regional resistance against extractivism can take many forms. For example, in India conflicts on sand and gravel mining from rivers and beaches are particularly acute, and the new label "sand mafias" has been given to this phenomenon.

The anti-growth movements

In the field of energy policy, civil society movements have opposed nuclear energy since the 1960s and have contributed a range of concepts. One of them, in Germany, was *Energiewende* (born in Wheyl, circa 1980), now used as the term for official public policy. Germans sometimes use a parallel term, *Wachstumwende* (growth turnaround), to translate the French *décroissance*, which builds on alternative urban or rural movements that disengage mentally and practically from the growth economy. In Germany, *post-Wachstum* is also used. The degrowth movement might support EJ (Healy et al., 2012) by asking for resource caps on extraction of materials (Spangenberg, 1995) and in terms of calculating fair shares in the use of limited resources. The degrowth movement has different sources (D'Alisa et al., 2014; Muraca, 2013), including ecological economics and also the post-development movement of the 1980s. An alliance between the degrowth movement in the North and the global EJ movement would be desirable, and could parallel the South American calls for a post-extractivist economy leading to *Buen Vivir* instead of economic growth.

Pollution and toxic waste

There is a movement in Southern Italy campaigning against waste dumping. They complain about "biocide". In China, in the complaints against pollution not only in urban areas but also in rural areas, the term "cancer villages" arose over the last ten years or so. Researchers investigating such complaints in China appeal to the aforementioned notion of popular epidemiology. In Argentina there is a movement against glyphosate (used for transgenic soy cultivation introduced by Monsanto), under the name *paremos de fumigar* (stop fumigating). This links up with EJ campaigns by the Pesticide Action Network.

Concerns about pollution impacts extend to the transportation of materials. In Brazil one term from local transport conflicts is *justiça nos trilhos*, "justice in the railways" against loss of life in accidents caused by massive iron ore transport to the export harbours. The EJ movement in the USA maps trajectories of so-called "bomb trains", claiming that risks from hazardous transport are disproportionately felt in Black or Hispanic areas (http://midwestenergynews. com/2015/04/09/in-chicago-bomb-trains-hidden-in-plain-sight).

Urban environmental justice

The urban-based People of Color Environmental Leadership in the USA defined a good environment as a safe, non-polluted place for living and making a living—environment is where we live, work, and play. Inside cities, there are inter-connected movements introducing new concepts for a less unsustainable economy, such as food justice, transit justice, pedestrian rights, cyclists' critical mass movements (Carlsson, 2008), struggles for the pacification of transit (a term originating in The Netherlands from the movements of provos and kabouters) and fights against gentrification. Such urban movements give a political meaning to squatting (Cattaneo, 2011). They remake places for groups in danger of being displaced, reassert traditional or new practices of land use, urban food production and water harvesting, and try to protect territory from pollution, land-grabbing and real estate speculation (Gottlieb, 2009; Gottlieb and Joshi, 2010; Anguelovski and Martinez-Alier, 2014).

Future directions

Legal and rights-based approaches are potential areas where new EJ concepts are arising. Ideas growing among the EJOs are energy sovereignty, sacrifice zones (Lerner, 2010), ecocide and the call for an international environmental crimes tribunal. The EJOs have asked for corporate accountability (Clapp and Utting, 2008) instead of corporate social responsibility. The new provision on the Rights of Nature (introduced in Ecuador's Constitution 2008, article 71) is also popular among the EJOs. Resistance to social environmental injustice has given birth to local and international EJOs pushing for alternative social transformations in what could be called a global movement for EJ (Martinez-Alier et al., 2016).

Concluding remarks

The world economy is still growing. Even a non-growing industrial economy would need fresh supplies of fossil fuels, because energy is not recyclable [Chapter 9], and also new supplies of materials which are only recyclable in part [Chapter 10]. The gains and losses of the use of the environment are often unjustly distributed not only as regards other species or future generations of humans but also among humans living today. There are therefore many local movements expressing their grievances over such environmental injustices. Several groups have been producing inventories of ecological distribution conflicts (by country or by theme), such as OCMAL in Latin America on mining conflicts, or in Brazil, Fiocruz (Porto de Souza, 2012).

The global movement for EJ is formed not only by many local foci of resistance in the South and the North, but also by intermediary rural- and urban-based organisations that have developed their own vocabulary and slogans and put forward interlinked claims at several scales. All this testifies to the existence of a global movement for EJ born from ecological distribution conflicts.

Key further readings cited

Martinez-Alier, J. (2002). *The environmentalism of the poor: A study of ecological conflicts and valuation.* Cheltenham: Edward Elgar.

Martinez-Alier, J., Anguelovski, I., Bond, P., et al. (2014). Between activism and science: Grassroots concepts for sustainability coined by environmental justice organizations. *Journal of Political Ecology,* 21, 19–60.

Martinez-Alier J., O'Connor, M. (1996). Economic and ecological distribution conflicts, in R. Costanza, O. Segura and J. Martinez-Alier (eds,), *Getting down to Earth: Practical applications of ecological economics,* Washington, D.C.: Island Press.

Martinez-Alier J., Temper, L., Del Bene, D., Scheidel, A. (2016). Is there a Global Environmental Justice Movement? *Jounal of Peasant Studies,* 43(3), 731–755.

Temper L., Del Bene, D., Martinez-Alier, J. (2015). Mapping the frontiers and front lines of global environmental justice: the EJAtlas. *Journal of Political Ecology* 22, 255–278.

Other literature cited

Agarwal A. and Narain, S. (1991). *Global warming in an unequal world: a case of environmental colonialism.* Delhi: Centre for Science and Environment.

Agarwal, B. (2001). Participatory exclusions, community forests and gender: An analysis for South Asia and a conceptual framework. *World Development* 29 (10), 1623–1648.

Agyeman, J., Bullard, R., Evans, B. (eds.) (2003). *Just sustainabilities: Development in an unequal world.* Cambridge, MA: MIT Press.

Anguelovski, I., Martinez-Alier, J. (2014). The 'Environmentalism of the Poor' revisited: Territory and place in disconnected global struggles. *Ecological Economics* 102, 167–176.

Boelens, R., Cremers, L., Zwarteveen, M., (eds.) (2011), *Justicia Hídrica. Acumulación, conflicto y acción social,* Lima: Instituto de Estudios Peruanos.

Bond, P. (2013). Climate justice. In C. Death (ed.). *Critical environmental politics,* (pp. 133–145). London: Routledge.

Brown, P. (1997). Popular rpidemiology revisited. *Current Sociology* 45, 137–156.

Bruno, K., Karliner, J., Brotsky, C. (1999). Greenhouse Gangsters vs. Climate Justice. CorpWatch: http://www.corpwatch.org/article.php?id=1048. Accessed 24 November 2016.

Bullard, R. D. (1993). *Confronting environmental racism: Voices from the grassroots.* Boston: South End Press.

Carlsson, C. (2008). *Nowtopia: How pirate programmers, outlaw bicyclists and vacant-lot gardeners are inventing the future today.* Oakland, CA: AK Press.

Carrere, R., Lohmann, L. (1996). *Pulping the South. Industrial tree plantation and the world paper economy.* London: Zed Books.

Cattaneo, C. (2011). The money-free life of Spanish squatters, in A. Nelson (ed.). *Life without money.* London: Pluto Press.

Clapp, J., Utting, P. (eds.) (2008). *Corporate accountability and sustainable development.* Delhi: Oxford University Press.

D'Alisa, G., Demaria, F., Kallis, G. (eds.) (2014). *Degrowth: a vocabulary for a new era,* London: Routledge.

Funtowicz, S.O., Ravetz, J.R. (1993). Science for the post-normal age. *Futures* 25, 735–755.

Gottlieb, R. (2009). Where we live, work, play . . . and eat: Expanding the environmental justice agenda. *Environmental Justice* 2, 7–8.

Gottlieb, R. Joshi, A. (2010). *Food justice.* Cambridge, MA: MIT Press.

GRAIN (2005). Food sovereignty: Turning the global food system upside down. *Seedling.* https://www.grain.org/article/entries/491-food-sovereignty-turning-the-global-food-system-upside-down (accessed 28 March 2013).

Guha, R., Martinez-Alier, J. (1997). *Varieties of environmentalism. Essays North and South.* London: Earthscan.

Haas, W., Krausmann, F., Wiedenhofer, D., Heinz, M. (2015). How circular is the global economy? An assessment of material flows, waste production, and recycling in the European Union and the world in 2005. *Journal of Industrial Ecology* 19 (5), pp. 765–777.

Healy, H., Martinez-Alier, J., Temper, L., Walter, M., Gerber, J.F. (eds.) (2012). *Ecological economics from the ground up.* London: Routledge.

Hornborg, A., McNeill, J.R., Martinez-Alier, J., (eds.) (2007). *Rethinking environmental history, world-system history and global environmental change.* Lanham, MD: Atamira Press.

Kapp, K.W. (1950). *Social costs of business enterprise.* London: Asia Publishing House.

Klein, N. (2014). *This changes everything, Capitalism vs. the climate.* London: Allen Lane.

Lerner, S. (2010) *Sacrifice zones. The front lines of toxic chemical exposure in the United States,* Cambridge, MA: MIT Press.

Lora-Wainwright, A. (2013). Fighting for breath: cancer, healing and social change in a Sichuan village. Honolulu: University of Hawaii Press.

Martinez-Alier, J. (1995). Distributional issues in ecological economics. *Review of Social Economy,* 53(4): 511–528.

Martinez-Alier, J., Munda, G., O'Neill, J. (1998). Weak comparability of values as a foundation for ecological economics, *Ecological Economics* 26(3), 277–286.

McCully, P. (1996). *Silenced rivers: The ecology and politics of large dams.* London: Zed Books.

Muraca, B. (2013). Décroissance: A project for a radical transformation of society. *Environmental Values,* 22 (2): 147–169.

Narain, S. (2008). Learn to walk lightly. *Business Standard* (August 1, 2008).

Özkaynak, B., Rodriguez-Labajos, B., Aydın, C.İ., Yanez, I., Garibay, C. (2015). *Towards environmental justice success in mining conflicts: An empirical investigation,* EJOLT Report No.14.

Pellow, D.N., Brulle, R.J. (2005). *Power, justice, and the environment: A critical appraisal of the environmental justice movement.* Cambridge, MA: MIT Press.

Porto de Souza, M.F. (2012). Movements and the network of environmental justice in Brazil. *Environmental Justice* 5 (2), 100–104.

Robinson, D.F. (2010). *Confronting biopiracy. Challenges, cases and international debates.* (191) London: Earthscan.

Shiva, V. (1997). *Biopiracy: The plunder of nature and knowledge.* Boston: South End.

Simms, A. (2005). *Ecological debt. The health of the planet and the wealth of nations.* London: Pluto Press.

Spangenberg, J. (ed.) (1995). *Towards sustainable Europe. A study from the Wuppertal Institute for Friends of the Earth Europe.* Luton/Brussels: FoE Publications Ltd.

Spash, C.L. (2010). The brave new world of carbon trading. *New Political Economy,* 15(2), 169–195.

Srinivasan, U. T., S.P. Carey, E. Hallstein, P.A.T. Higgins, A.C. Kerr, L.E. Koteen, A.B. Smith, R. Watson, J. Harte, and R.B. Norgaard (2008). The debt of nations and the distribution of ecological impacts from human activities. *PNAS* 5, 1768–1773.

Temper, L. and Martinez-Alier, J. (2013). The god of the mountain and Godavarman: Net Present Value, indigenous territorial rights and sacredness in a bauxite mining conflict in India. *Ecological Economics* 96, 79–87.

Temper, L., Yánez, I., K. Sharife, O. Godwin and J. Martinez-Alier (2013). *Towards a post-oil civilization: Yasunization and other initiatives to leave fossil fuels in the soil.* EJOLT Report No.6.

Warlenius, R., Pierce, G., Ramasar, V. (2015). Reversing the arrow of arrears: The concept of "ecological debt" and its value for environmental justice. *Global Environmental Change* 30, 21–30.

17

SOCIAL MOVEMENTS AND RESISTANCE

Viviana Asara[1]

Introduction

Definitions of the term social movement are varied, displaying different shades of emphasis and focus depending on the author's perspective. In this chapter I rely on the inclusive definition provided by Snow (2004: 11), which defines social movements as:

> collective challenges to systems or structures of authority or, more concretely, as collectivities acting with some degree of organisation (could be formal, hierarchical, networked, etc.) and continuity (more continuous than crowd or protest events but not institutionalised or routinized [sic] in the sense of being institutionally or organisationally calendarized [sic]) primarily outside of institutional or organisational channels for the purpose of challenging extant systems of authority, or resisting change in such systems, in the organisation, society, culture or world order of which they are part.

The way the term social movement is defined has some implication for the term resistance and vice versa; in this respect they can be thought of as co-implicated. I will argue that all social movements are about resistance. Indeed, both the concepts of social movements and resistance hold a core essence centring around some notion of conflict, some perpetrated challenges and/ or claims (e.g., see definitions by Melucci, 1989; Della Porta and Diani, 2006; Snow, 2004; McAdam et al., 2001).

Resistance understood as challenges to systems or structures of authority can be thought of as the central gist that constitutes social movements. Additional conditions that can turn resistance (or 'resistant individuals') into social movements are:

1   some sort of 'collectivity' holding some coordination or organisation between individuals, and a collective identity (Melucci, 1989; Della Porta and Diani, 2006);
2   some temporal continuity of the challenge being confronted;
3   their primarily non-institutional level (different from other 'institutionalised' social political groups such as political parties and trade unions).

Although social movements are concerned with resistance, there has been surprisingly little effort towards conceptualising and problematising resistance within social movement studies

(Hollander and Einwohner, 2004; Trom and Cefai, 2013). One result is a relative lack of theoretical clarity on the relationship between the two concepts. Hence this chapter aims to address this gap. In the next section the field of social movement studies is overviewed and scrutinised in terms of how various ideas and definitions have appeared relating to resistance. The legacies and limitations of the work of five authors is then reviewed to provide insight into the role of resistance, namely: Antonio Gramsci, Karl Polanyi, James Scott, Michel Foucault, Michel de Certeau. The new conceptual framework that I draw is able to tackle diverse 'environmental movements', grossly conceived, that cannot be fully comprehended through the tools of conventional social movement studies, such as political consumerism or the transition and sustainable community movements.

Social movement studies

Social movement studies have addressed different sets of main questions (Della Porta and Diani, 2006). In the following, I will focus on the research undertaken since the 1960s, which I will group into three main clusters of questions: how they mobilise, why they emerge and how they frame problems and their self-understanding.

The first set of questions concerns how a certain context or set of interests affect mobilisation (Melucci, 1989). This has been investigated using two paradigms: Resource Mobilisation and Political Process Theory. Resource Mobilisation was based on rational choice perspectives, and conceived of participation as the result of an individual cost-benefit weighting of the implications stemming from such participation, following Mancur Olson's demonstration of the paradox of the free rider (McCarthy and Zald, 1977). Resource Mobilisation scholars tended to take resistance for granted in order to conceptualise how movement actors are mobilised effectively, i.e. in relation to formally organised and professional social movement organisations, resource availability and access. Its political variant, the Political Process Theory, focuses instead on how the expansion of political opportunities affects a movement's probability of achieving mobilisation, the form it takes and the relationships between institutionalised politics and social movements (McAdam et al., 2001).

Resource Mobilisation and Political Process Theory have been criticised for oversimplifying the role of grievances, and downplaying the role of values and cultural elements. Political Process Theory has been charged with over reliance on a structuralist perspective, while the progressive expansion of the political opportunities concept, as a way to include cultural and agency factors, has contributed to washing away its analytical meaning (Goodwin and Jasper, 1999). Further, understanding social movements as solely targeting the State is reductionist, because many contemporary movements struggle against more abstract targets (such as racism, patriarchy or environmental degradation) and attempt to initiate social change by means of self-change (Snow, 2004).

These criticisms can be thought of as having brought about the 'cultural turn' of the 1980s. New social movement theories are one of the two big threads within the cultural turn, and they have been contributing to the second set of questions analysed here. These involve the links between structural change and social economic transformations, and patterns of conflicts and social movements (Della Porta and Diani, 2006). In essence, this second set of questions asks "Why does a movement emerge?" (Melucci, 1989). The analysis takes a historically specific social formation differently referred to as post-industrial society, late modernity, information society or advanced capitalism. Such a historical base provides the structural determining factor for the emergence of 'new movements', which are perceived to differ from the more traditional, or 'old', working class movements. Some central elements of these new social movements include the politicisation of everyday life, the rejection of instrumental rationality, decentralised forms of organisation and the importance of symbolic action and the cultural sphere, along with political goals. Another central element of difference from old social movements is referred to as the development of post-materialist values (e.g. Inglehart, 1977). These are less centred on material satisfaction and redistributional issues and more on the quality of life and search for autonomy and democracy. In general, the logic of resistance to a systemic logic of commodification and bureaucracy and an increasingly homogeneous social life is a dominant theme in the new social movement literature (Buechler, 1995).

New social movement theory has often been criticised for failing to scrutinise the mechanisms leading from structural determinants to mobilisation; that is, the analysis of the intermediate levels connecting individual grievances with macro-structural change (Melucci, 1989). Inglehart's (1977) post-materialist interpretation was questioned by ecological economists, political ecologists and environmental sociologists because it failed to consider the environmentalism of the poor [Chapter 16] and treadmill of production theories (Martinez-Alier, 1995; Dunlap and York, 2008; Givens and Jorgenson, 2011; Asara, 2016). In addition, new social movements were perceived to have emerged as a reaction to the expanding control of the (welfare) state into everyday life, linked to the Fordist welfare state compromise, and to be the expression of conflicts in the realm of cultural reproduction (as opposed to material reproduction). Nevertheless, in the 1990s, neoliberal globalisation and the emergence of the social justice movement followed by the global economic crisis in 2008 and the Occupy/ Indignados and anti-austerity movements, placed redistributional issues centre stage, and led to calls for bringing back the problematic of capitalism into social movement studies (Della Porta, 2015). Others have called for a renewed approach that goes beyond the dichotomies of materialistic and post-materialistic, symbolic and material values, reflecting the movements' metapolitical critique (Asara, 2016).

Indeed, the relationship between structural change and social movements has occupied a central role in the neo-Marxist World System Theory as developed by Wallerstein (2004). Theorising the history of global capitalism, it sees an important role for (anti-systemic) social movements in the resistance to global capitalism, offering a structuralist account of collective action. This approach has been particularly used in research on social movements against developmentalism, neoliberalism, and dispossessions in the Global South since the 1980s (Motta and Gunvald Nilsen, 2011). In the literature at the crossroads between political ecology and ecological economics, the growth in global social metabolism is one main cause of global and local environmental injustices and therefore of resistance (Muradian et al., 2012). Political ecology [Chapter 4] is combined with the tool of social metabolism [Chapter 11] to analyse the connections between energy and materials use by some social actors and the environmental impacts on others, which can lead to resistance patterns. In environmental justice literature [Chapter 16], urban conflicts stem from environmental inequalities in exposure to dumping and contamination but also in access to environmental goods and services, i.e. ecological distribution conflicts.

The other strand within the cultural turn, which constitutes the third broad set of questions, is the perspective adopted on framing and collective identity. This has been concerned with the collective, interactive processes through which social movements attribute meaning and significance to events and behaviours, facilitating mobilisation (Della Porta and Diani, 2006). That is, how do movements identify social problems as potential objects of collective action? How do they develop a collective identity? Originally inspired by the work of Goffman (1974), the idea of a frame as an interpretative script was developed by Snow and Benford (1988) to explain collective action. There are three core framing tasks, namely: diagnostic, prognostic and motivational. These serve to identify a problem, advance partial solutions (including tactics and strategies), and provide a rationale for action (e.g. a sense of urgency and emotional motives). A core element for igniting resistance is related to the identification of an injustice; that is, the transformation from an indignity of daily life into a shared grievance with a focused target.

The concept of master frames was forged to mean the broad interpretation of reality during a period of concentrated social movements, often associated with the practice of cross-movement activism and networking. A distinctive environmental justice master frame has, for example, been retrieved and crafted from an injustice frame linking environment, labour and social justice, i.e., frame bridging (Taylor, 2000). Opposition to neoliberal globalisation has been found to operate as a master frame in the global justice movement.

However, the framing perspective has been criticised for its descriptive and static bents, and its tendency to fall into reification. Also, frames have at times been treated as another type of resource, subject to strategic use by leaders of social movements, while setting aside the role of non-cognitive elements, such as emotions, in mobilisation. Finally, such a social constructivist perspective is by itself incapable of grasping the structural patterns of inequalities and domination that are linked to the emergence of broad interpretative processes of attributing blame and causality.

In summary, the most important conceptual and methodological tools of social movement studies are not always able to conceptualise and explain resistance by combining micro to meso and macro levels of mobilisation, or linking structure with agency. For these reasons, many authors have often resorted to intellectual sources outside the mainstream field of social movement studies to better explain and understand resistance mechanisms. I turn to these sources next.

Resistance: genealogies and conceptualisations

There is little consensus on the definition of resistance. Based on a systematic literature review, Hollander and Einwohner (2004) argue that while there is agreement that resistance includes a sense of action and a sense of opposition, lines of disagreements revolve around the concepts of recognition (whether an oppositional action must be readily apparent to others and recognised as resistance) and intentionality (whether an actor must be conscious that she/he is resisting). Nevertheless, only the recognition line of disagreement would be relevant for social movements, because they imply some sort of intentionality. Snow (2004) makes a more useful and meaningful distinction, relating to understanding resistance by social movements, between challenges that are direct (straightforward, overt appeals and demands) and indirect (covert or ambiguous challenges, or that seek to divest themselves of the authority by escaping from it). This is able to address the recognition cleavage identified by Hollander and Einwohner (2004), while offering a sounder basis for an inclusive definition because 'indirect challenges' can also be thought of as comprising post-structuralist understandings of resistance.

In this section I will delve into conceptualisations of resistance crafted by Gramsci, Polanyi, Scott, Foucault and de Certeau, giving examples of how social movement scholars have employed their ideas. While the first two authors are more easily associated with the category of direct resistance, the latter three offer useful perspectives for understanding indirect resistance. Such an overview aids reflection about the implications of an inclusive definition of resistance for environmental movements in general.

Resistance as counter hegemony

Gramsci [see also Chapters 14 and 15] understood resistance as the struggle to counter hegemony. Hegemony is the power exercised and the consent gained by a ruling class (or group) over subordinate classes and other social forces. This power is exercised through coercion and persuasion by means of political and ideological struggle. A hegemonic class exercises power at three levels: (i) relations of production, (ii) coercive relations that characterise the State, and (iii) all other social relations that constitute civil society. The last is the sphere where the struggle for hegemony between the working and the capitalist classes, and popular democratic struggles, take place in advanced capitalist societies. The type of counter-hegemony Gramsci imagined in advanced capitalist societies was a war of position, a revolutionary process of expansion of the working class hegemony by building alliances with other social forces. This would create a new historic bloc unified by a common conception of the world. Hegemony can only be achieved if a class does not confine itself to class interests but involves other popular and democratic struggles to constitute a national popular collective will, in a process of intellectual and moral reform that involves the consciousness of the individuals who are part of those social groups. Indeed, common sense, the largely unconscious and uncritical realm where individuals perceive the world, is the locus of ideology construction, but also of resistance to that ideology. For Gramsci the new ideological system would emerge gradually in the course of political and economic struggles, and organic intellectuals and the Communist Party would have a predominant role in such a process.

Gramsci is often cited in studies on resistance and social movements and some examples follow. Goodman and Salleh (2013) analysed the World Social Forum mediated People's Summit against the United Nations Rio+20 summit as a counter hegemonic force, where a vision for an ecologically sensitive and socially just bio-civilisation countered the hegemonic 'Green Economy' formulation of corporations, multilateral agencies, unions and big non-governmental organisations. Routledge (1994) coined the term 'terrain of resistance' to refer to the sites of contestation between hegemonic and counter hegemonic powers and discourses. A neo-Gramscian perspective has been also applied to explain the failure or unsuccessful results of movements, explained as the incapacity to articulate a counter hegemonic discourse or force (Bieler, 2010) or a genuine collective will (Chodor, 2014).

Resistance as counter movement

While for Gramsci civil society is a terrain of struggle, for Polanyi (1944) society can represent the locus of spontaneous resistance against the annihilating effects of the market economy. Resistance is understood as a counter movement involving protective measures taken by various groups to reassert social control over a self-regulating market and to counteract the process of turning land, labour and money into fictitious commodities. He described the social history of the nineteenth century as the result of a double movement: (i) the extension of the market, and (ii) its restriction with respect to spreading fictitious commodities. The extension was embodied in the principle of economic liberalism, supported by the trading classes, the capitalists and bourgeoisie, while the restriction aimed at the conservation of humanity and Nature and was incarnated in the principle of social protection, put forward by the working and landed classes. The countermovement against economic liberalism represented a defensive spontaneous reaction, as the utopia of a self-regulating market threatened the demolition of society, and led to protectionism in the second half of the nineteenth century.

Neoliberal globalisation has been seen through the lens of a Polanyian second great transformation (Altvater and Mahnkopf, 1997) and contemporary countermovements have been identified in the global justice, anti-austerity and indigenous movements of the Global South (Tarrow, 2005; Juris, 2004: 356). Nevertheless in the Polanyian framework, collectivity as assumed in a movement or society is an almost homogeneous category, while a degraded and lethargic working class is perceived to spontaneously spring to life for its self-defence (Burawoy, 2003). In contrast, Thompson (1971) argues that resistance in the form of food riots and other direct action materialises because of a pre-existing moral economy of the poor, that is a consistent traditional view of social norms and obligations that can potentially turn deprivation into outrage. In political ecology, Thompson's work has been important for deciphering the ways in which norms and customs impinge on struggles over access to resources and the environment.

Resistance as infrapolitics

The missing link between outright defiance and submerged popular resistance strategies is investigated by Scott (1985; 1990), who conceptualises resistance as indirect challenges. The main thrust of Scott's work is to critique the Gramscian concept of hegemony, and to argue that, instead, in exploitative relations, behind the façade of complicity and quiescence of the underclass (or subaltern) can lie a demystification of the prevailing ideology and dissimulation. Focusing his analysis on peasant rebellions in Southeast Asia, he scrutinises what he calls 'infrapolitics'; that is, the low profile, strategic, disguised resistance of subjects in contexts in which open or institutionalised political action is not viable because of oppressive domination. Infrapolitics can be depicted as the ground that lies between what he calls hidden transcripts and public transcripts. Public transcripts are the "self-portrait of dominant elites as they would have themselves seen" (Scott, 1990: 18), a partial and partisan narrative aimed at the naturalisation of power relations. Hidden transcripts are the offstage responses to public transcripts, springing out of the experience of indignities. It is the field of non-hegemonic dissident discourse, occurring in sequestered social sites where a resistant culture can be nurtured. The hidden transcript can hence give rise to infrapolitics, where a politics of disguise and anonymity takes place in public view but is designed to have a double meaning or to shield the identity of the messenger.

Infrapolitics also includes low profile stratagems aimed at minimising or thwarting appropriation such as everyday forms of peasant resistance (Scott, 1985), that is the peasants' constant struggle against power holders seeking to extract labour, food, taxes and rents. These can be individual self-help activities but are often coordinated by dense informal networks. Scott stresses how infrapolitics is equally political as outright defiance. His understanding of resistance is class based, and his work inspired the rise of subaltern studies in the 1980s, as a project to rethink history from below, and studies addressing land-grabbing (Sivaramakrishnan, 2005; Johansson and Vinthagen, 2014). In environmental justice and political ecology, everyday forms of environmental resistance are connected to grassroots movements struggling against environmental degradation and natural resource exploitation (Sikor and Newell, 2014). His approach has also been used as an analytical tool for deciphering urban movements and subcultures such as hip hop, graffiti, skateboarding, and urban gardening.

Resistance as counter conduct, tactic and counter-space

Although Foucault has been criticised for failing to theorise collective resistance (Raby, 2005), a few studies have used his work to analyse indirect resistance by social movements. A Foucauldian framework conceives power as relational and diffuse [Chapter 14]. This goes beyond conceptualising social movements and protest as the act of resistance opposing power/domination, that is especially characteristic of Political Process Theory, or of literature positing global social movements as the vanguard of resistance. Indeed, post-structuralist understandings of power observe that resistance does not come from outside of power, but is imbricated within it, as power is intertwined with resistance (Raby, 2005). Power is not something to be overthrown but to be used and transformed (Cresswell, 2000), while the assumed oppositional nature of groups and movements neglects their complicity in sustaining those power relationships (Raby, 2005).

The concept of counter-conduct is a "struggle against the processes implemented for conducting others" (Foucault, 2007a: 201), and embodies the will "not to be governed like that, by that, in the name of those principles" (Foucault, 2007b: 44). This has been used to examine how power and resistance are mutually constitutive. For example, Rosol (2014) argues that neither co-optation nor rebellion can capture urban movements against rezoning in Vancouver, as their protest was not set against city development policies *per se* but targeted the implementation of specific city policies.

Within post-structuralism, de Certeau (1984/2011) makes a distinction between strategies of power and tactics of resistance.

> [Tactics of resistance] cannot count on a proper (spatial or institutional) localisation, nor thus on a borderline distinguishing the other as a visible totality. The place of a tactic belongs to the other. A tactic insinuates into the other's place.
>
> *(de Certeau, 1984 [2011]: xix)*

They display "other interests and desires that are neither determined nor captured by the systems in which they develop" (ibid.: xviii). On similar lines, Lefebvre's (1991) concept of counter-space is "an initially utopian alternative to actually existing 'real' space" (ibid.: 349). Hence we can think of resistance as not just being about opposition and challenges for their own sake, but always presupposing other values, desires and utopias (the imagination of a different future).

Reconceptualising resistance and social movements

The dividing line that some authors, such as Tilly (1978) and Castells (1983), have drawn between resistance (reactive movements) and alternatives (proactive movements) is at best blurred. All social movements are about resistance. Resistance could be thought to contain within itself the seeds of an alternative vision and its enactment, in different shades of intensity, in a continuum. Similarly, movements focusing on the implementation or prefiguration of some alternatives do not avoid conflict but see struggle as the incremental modification of the underlying structures of a system and its mechanisms of social reproduction that cumulatively transform the system (Wright, 2010: 228). Hence they can be intended as a form of resistance.

The concept of resistance as indirect challenges—Scott, Foucault and de Certeau—allows the inclusion of diverse phenomena and movements. This might cover submerged networks linked to political consumerism and communal movements as well as collective escapes or exits (Hirschman, 1970) that do not typically fall within the conceptualisation of resistance as contentious politics (Snow, 2004).

Future directions

Resistance as conceived above offers a possible avenue for understanding everyday (indirect) resistance to mass consumerism, neoliberal globalisation and the imperial mode of living [Chapter 15] in the form of what has been variously labelled, with broadly overlapping terms, political consumerism (Micheletti, 2003), sustainable community movements (Forno and Graziano, 2014), transition movements (Sage, 2014), and autonomous geographies (Chatterton, 2005). These terms include disparate phenomena such as solidarity purchasing groups and food cooperatives, community supported agriculture, eco-villages, voluntary simplicity, slow food and food cooperatives. Some of the features characterising these movements are, in a Polanyian bent, the identification of the market as a fundamental space of political struggle, considering both the consumption and production side, and the use of new social economic practices going beyond the politics of protest, focusing on the creation of alternatives. These movements and forms of action display a more expansive understanding of what counts as resistance, they articulate economic concerns with calls for alternative ways of life and systems, while recognising the economy, culture and Nature as focal points for crisis and struggle (Masquelier, 2013; Asara, 2016).

Still, work on these issues remains largely based on case studies, with limited theoretical treatment and little ability to combine the different topics. Research on political consumerism, (environmental) social movements, environmental justice, urban political ecology and environmental political thought constitutes more or less isolated bodies of work. Conventional tools and frameworks to analyse these phenomena are still inadequate and new tools and cross-fertilisation between disciplines are needed.

Concluding remarks

The articulation and interweaving of the different conceptualisations of resistance can offer an analytical lens for understanding different types of movements. Resistance can also be indirect—disguised (Scott) and not pure (Foucault)—contrary to the dichotomous conceptualisation of power versus resistance, and could contain within itself alternative visions (de Certeau). If resistance can encapsulate the seed of enacting alternatives, then we can reconceptualise the distinction that has been drawn between reactive movements (resistance) and proactive movements (alternative creating). All social movements should be concerned with resistance, and the dividing line between resistance and alternatives should be reconsidered. Applying this reasoning to environmental movements in general means going beyond environmental justice groups protesting against inequalities in the distribution of environmental amenities or, as in political ecology, against the destruction of resources linked to their livelihoods. Movements are also constituted when collective action is organised around an alternative system of needs satisfaction, politicising consumption and production and targeting the market as a site of political struggle. Ecological economics as a discipline has offered important tools such as social metabolism for understanding everyday forms of environmental resistance, in a way that complements the fields of political ecology and environmental justice. But it still has to grapple with other types of environmental movements such as sustainable community movements, which require an expansive understanding of resistance.

Note

1   I acknowledge the financial support of the Spanish government through the project CSO2014-54513-R SINALECO. I thank Joan Martinez-Alier and Clive Spash for their comments.

Key further readings cited

Della Porta, D., Diani, M. (2006). *Social movements: An introduction.* Second edition. Oxford, UK: Blackwell Publishing.
Hollander, J. A., Einwohner, R. L. (2004). Conceptualising resistance. *Sociological Forum*, 19(4): 533–554.
Snow, D.A. (2004). Social movements as challenges to authority: Resistance to an emerging conceptual hegemony. *Research in Social Movements, Conflicts and Change*, 25, 3–25.

Other literature cited

Altvater, E. and Mahnkopf, B. (1997). The world market unbound. *Review of International Political Economy* 4 (3), 448–471.

Asara, V. (2016). The Indignados as a socio-environmental movement. Framing the crisis and democracy. *Environmental Policy and Governance*. Available at http://onlinelibrary.wiley.com/wol1/doi/10.1002/eet.1721/abstract. Accessed 25 November 2016.

Bieler, A. (2010). Labor, New Social Movements and the resistance to neoliberal restructuring in Europe. *New Political Economy*, 16(2), 163–183.

Buechler, S.M. (1995). New social movements theories. *Sociological Quarterly*, 36(3), 441–464.

Burawoy, M. (2003). For a sociological Marxism: The complementary convergence of Antonio Gramsci and Karl Polanyi. *Politics & Society*, 31(2), 193–261.

Castells, M. (1983). *The city and the grassroots. A cross-cultural theory of urban social movements.* London: Edward Arnold.

Chatterton, P. 2005. Making autonomous geographies: Argentina's popular uprising and the "Movimiento de Trabajadores Desocupados". *Geoforum*, 36(5), 545–561.

Chodor, T. (2014). Not throwing the baby out with the bathwater: a Gramscian response to post-hegemony. *Contemporary Politics*, 20(4), 489–502.

Cresswell, T. (2000). Falling down: Resistance as diagnostic. In J. Sharp, P. Routledge, C. Philo, and R. Paddison (eds.), *Entanglements of power: Geographies of domination/resistance* (pp. 256–258). London: Routledge.

De Certeau, M. (1984[2011]). *The practice of everyday life.* Berkeley: University of California Press.

Della Porta, D. (2015). *Social movements in times of austerity: Bringing back capitalism into protest analysis.* Cambridge: Polity Press.

Dunlap, R.E. and York, R. (2008). The globalization of environmental concern and the limits of the postmaterialist values explanation: Evidence from four multinational surveys. *The Sociological Quarterly*, 49, 529–563.

Forno, F. and Graziano, P. (2014). Sustainable community movement organisations. *Journal of Consumer Culture*, 14(2), 139–157.

Foucault, M. (2007a). *Security, Territory, Population: Lectures at the Collège de France 1977–1978.* Basingstoke: Palgrave MacMillan.

Foucault, M. (2007b). *The Politics of Truth.* Los Angeles: Semiotext(e).

Givens, J., Jorgenson, A. (2011). The effects of affluence, economic development, and environmental degradation on environmental concern: a multilevel analysis. *Organization Environment* 24(1), 74–91.

Goffman, E. (1974). *Frame analysis: An essay on the organization of experience.* Garden City: Anchor Books.

Goodman, J., Salleh, A. (2013). The 'Green Economy': class hegemony and counter-hegemony. *Globalizations*, 10(3), 411–424.

Goodwin, J. and Jasper, J. (1999). Caught in a winding, snarling vine: The structural bias of Political Process Theory. *Sociological Forum*, 14(1), 27–54.

Hirschman, A. (1970). *Exit, voice and loyalty: Responses to decline in firms, organizations, and states.* The President and Fellows of Harvard College.

Inglehart, R. (1977). *The silent revolution: Changing values and political styles among Western publics.* Princeton: Princeton University Press.

Johansson, A., Vinthagen, S. (2014). Dimensions of everyday resistance: An analytical framework. *Critical Sociology*, 40(3), 1–19.

Juris, J. (2004). Networked social movements: Global movements for global justice. In M. Castells (ed.), *The network society: A cross-cultural perspective.* Cheltenham (UK): Edward Elgar.

Lefebvre, H. (1991). *The production of space.* Oxford: Blackwell Publishing.

Martinez-Alier, J. (1995). The environment as a luxury good or "too poor to be green"? *Ecological Economics,* 13(1), 1–10.

Masquelier, C. (2013). Critical theory and contemporary social movements: Conceptualising resistance in the neoliberal age. *European Journal of Social Theory*, 16(4), 395–412.

McAdam, D., Tarrow, S., Tilly, C. (2001). *Dynamics of contention.* Cambridge, UK: Cambridge University Press.

McCarthy, J., Zald, M. N. (1977). Resource mobilisation by local social movement organisations: Agency, strategy and organisation in the movement against drunk driving. *American Sociological Review,* 61(6), 1070–1088.

Melucci, A. (1989). *Nomads of the present. Social movements and individual needs in contemporary society.* Philadelphia: Temple University Press..

Micheletti, M. (2003). *Political Virtue and Shopping: Individuals, Consumerism and Collective Action.* London: Palgrave Macmillan.

Motta, S. and Gunvald Nilsen, A. (2011). *Social movements in the Global South.* New York: Palgrave Macmillan.

Muradian, R., Walter, M., Martinez-Alier, J. (2012). Hegemonic transitions and global shifts in social metabolism. *Global Environmental Change*, 22(3), 559–567.

Polanyi, K. (1944). *The great transformation.* Boston: Beacon Press Books.

Raby, R. (2005). What is resistance? *Journal of Youth Studies*, b(2), 151–171.

Rosol, M. (2014). On resistance in the post-political city: conduct and counter-conduct in Vancouver. *Space and Polity*, 18(1), 70–84.

Routledge, P. (1994). Backstreet, barricades, and blackouts: Urban terrains of resistance in Nepal. *Environment and Planning D: Society and Space*, 12, 559–578.

Sage, C. (2014). The transition movement and food sovereignty: From local resilience to global engagement in good system transformation. *Journal of Consumer Culture*, 14(2), 254–275.

Scott, J.C. (1985). *Weapons of the weak: Everyday forms of peasant resistance.* New Haven: Yale University Press.

Scott, J.C. (1990). *Domination and the arts of resistance: Hidden transcripts.* New Haven: Yale University Press.

Sikor, T. and Newell, P. (2014). Globalizing environmental justice? *Geoforum* 54, 151–157.

Sivaramakrishnan, K. (2005). Some intellectual genealogies for the concept of everyday resistance. *American Anthropologist*, 107(3), 346–355.

Snow, D.A., Benford, R.D. (1988). Ideology, frame resonance, and participant mobilization. *International Social Movement Research,* 1(1), 197–218.

Tarrow, S. (2005). *The new transnational activism.* Cambridge (UK): Cambridge University Press.

Taylor, D.E. (2000). The rise of the environmental justice paradigm: Injustice framing and the social construction of environmental discourses. *American Behavioral Scientist*, 43(3), 508–580

Thompson, E.P. (1971). The moral economy of the English crowd in the Eighteenth Century. *Past & Present*, 50, 76–136.

Tilly, C. (1978). *From mobilisation to revolution.* Reading, MA: Addison-Wesley .

Trom, D., Cefai, D. (2013). Resistance. In D. Snow, D. Della Porta, B. Klandermans, and D. McAdams (eds.), *Wiley-Blackwell Encyclopedia of Social and Political movements.* Malden: Wiley-Blackwell.

Wallerstein, I. (2004). *World Systems Analysis: An Introduction.* Durham, NC: Duke University Press.

Wright, E.O. (2010). *Envisioning real utopias.* London: Verso Books.

PART V

Markets, production and consumption

18

UNREGULATED MARKETS AND THE TRANSFORMATION OF SOCIETY

Asad Zaman

Introduction

As industrialised human society barrels down the fast track to ecological suicide, there is a well-funded campaign to spread stories that create confusion about problems such as climate change, because environmental protection interferes with corporate profits. Species of plants and animals which evolved over billions of years, and cannot be replaced, are becoming extinct at a rapidly increasing rate. Precious environmental treasures like coral reefs and rainforests are being destroyed. The cost of what has already been destroyed cannot be calculated. In addition, industrialised society is using up planetary resources at a rate which is much higher than the ability of the planet to replenish or renew. The wastes being produced by human beings are changing the composition of the atmosphere, oceans, lakes and rivers, and affecting all forms of life. How can some elite groups act as "Merchants of Doubt" (Oreskes and Conway, 2011) prepared to destroy the planet to make a profit?

Experiments show that humans have radically different sets of internalised norms for market and social behaviour. On appeal to social norms, many will gladly volunteer to donate blood, but will refuse to give the same donation for payment. The conflict between the norms of markets and society means that the two cannot coexist peacefully. Throughout history markets have been subordinate to society. Modern society is unique in having sought to reverse this relationship, subordinating social relations to market norms. This chapter follows the framework of Polanyi (1944), who describes the bloody battles between markets and society as the "Great Transformation". The operation of a market society required the conversion of human beings and their habitat into marketable commodities, leading to the dissolution of society and environmental destruction. Current efforts to 'solve' environmental problems within the market framework fail to either recognise these fundamental conflicts or to go far enough to address the structural causal mechanisms. In line with social ecological economics [Chapter 1], I will argue that radical remedies are required to address the root causes of the problems. In particular, the great transformation needs to be reversed and the subordinate role of markets to society recognised.

One of the key theses of Polanyi (1944) is that unregulated markets are so extremely harmful to society, that society must take steps to protect itself. In order to understand the history of market societies Polanyi introduces the concept of the 'double movement'—on the one hand the expansion of markets and, on the other, the efforts to protect humans and Nature against harms caused by commodification. The second movement means that society always blocks complete freedom for markets, but this also means that free market ideologues can argue that any failure of capitalism was due to the failure to fully follow policies of *laissez faire*.

In this chapter the struggle between market societies and traditional societies is explained as occurring simultaneously on two fronts. One is the front of practice—the replacement of traditional institutions and customs by market institutions. The other is the ideological front—the practice of capitalism that requires faith in the accompanying ideology, which is often strongly opposed to natural instincts and traditional social norms.

Pre-market societies

In market societies, production and consumption are the main objectives of life. In contrast, traditional societies nurture and develop human capabilities in diverse dimensions. For example, humans can learn to break bricks with their bare hands, walk over burning coals, acquire excellence in sports, create extraordinary beauty in literary or artistic forms, or travel on spiritual pathways to destinations unimagined. In the transformation of the 1800s the romantic poets recognised the loss of traditional values. Wordsworth expressed his sense of loss in the words: "getting and spending, we lay waste our powers."

Traditional communities are self-sufficient and produce most necessities. Distribution employs social mechanisms that ensure the provision of necessities to everyone by transfer without markets. Polanyi (1944: 47) writes that reciprocity and redistribution were the main mechanisms for production and the distribution of goods. This means that markets were peripheral to society, and were used for trading of luxuries, like silk, spices, silver, sugar and fine textiles. Furthermore, there was general awareness that market activities are harmful to society, and markets were regulated and contained so as to limit their influence. Whereas self-sufficiency is considered a virtue in traditional societies, market societies require the creation of dependencies that create the basis for trade. The economic theory of comparative advantage is a mythical argument that counters traditional beliefs with the idea that specialisation and mutual trade is superior to self-sufficiency. (See Daly and Cobb, 1994, on the conflict between free trade and community values.)

Whereas market societies are characterised by massive excess production, an important corollary of self-sufficiency is that there is minimal excess production. Again this is reflected in the opposition between market values and social values. Frugality, avoiding waste, making do with what you have, are all virtues in traditional societies. A significant cause of environmental degradation is that market societies encourage waste, luxury and ostentatious consumption.

In pre-market societies, social status was not determined by consumption standards, and life was not focused around production and consumption. In conformity with Biblical doctrines, ostentation and wealth were regarded with disfavour. Emergence of capitalism requires a reversal of this norm. The change in attitude can be illustrated by the contrast between the miser Scrooge in Dickens and his latter-day counterpart Scrooge McDuck in Disney. Whereas the Dickensian Scrooge must repent and learn generosity to be saved from an early death and hell-fire, Scrooge McDuck is portrayed as a lovable character. His wealth derives from his cleverness, and his love of money is a charming quirk.

Traditional societies were characterised by social cooperation and harmony with Nature. This is not a romantic idealisation; rather these characteristics were required for survival. That no human is an island remains true—human lives depend to a large extent on the efforts of others. In communities characterising traditional society, this dependence was acknowledged via social norms of cooperation. Awareness of this dependence was clear and immediate—if any team of hunters succeeded, the whole village would eat. Human lives were embedded within social networks, and derived meaning and purpose from their communities. The same dependence exists in market societies, but is concealed via the market mechanisms, creating and encouraging an illusion of independence.

Similarly, living in harmony with Nature was a requirement of survival. Human beings are embedded within natural ecosystems [Chapter 12]. For example, humans breathe oxygen and exhale carbon dioxide, while trees and plants do the reverse, creating an ecological balance. Throughout the world, human societies created an amazing variety of ways of living in harmony with their varied biophysical environments. Think of the Eskimos, the Australian Aborigines, nomads of the Sahara desert, the tribes of the steppes, the Amazon River tribes, European peasants, African jungle dwellers, and so on. Human beings are dependent upon natural ecosystems, taking their needs from them and contributing to the preservation and enhancement of their habitat and home. Geography and seasons impacted heavily on societies, leading to migrations, variations in types of available foods, practices of planting and harvesting. Thus patterns of life harmonised with the environment, and created awareness of our dependence upon it.[1]

The emergence of market societies

The transition from a traditional society to a market society requires a large number of changes along a number of different dimensions. In a nutshell, the transition to market societies is about how the biblical maxim of 'Love of money is the root of all evil' was replaced by the Shavian maxim that 'Lack of money is the root of all evil'. A historical account of this transition from the sixteenth century to the eighteenth century is given by Tawney (1998 [1926]).

Capitalism is a system where some people have wealth, while others have only their lives, which they must sell to survive in a market economy. How did this division occur initially? The capitalist myth, invented by Adam Smith, suggests that hard working people accumulated wealth, while the lazy ones did not. Marx, in contrast, wrote that "capital comes dripping from head to toe, from every pore, with blood and dirt" (Marx, 1977: 926). Workers were "tortured by grotesquely terroristic laws into accepting the discipline necessary for the system of wage-labour" (ibid.: 899). Marx also stresses the ideological component of this process, by which the labourer comes to believe in the necessity of his own enslavement to work. Wealth concentrates in the hands of a minority, while the masses must sell their labour to survive. "The advance of capitalist production develops a working class which by education, tradition and habit looks upon the requirements of that mode of production as self-evident natural laws" (Marx, 1977: 899–900).

Ultimately, Nature is the source of all human wealth, which is a tautological truth once human beings are recognised as being part of Nature. Accumulation of wealth requires creation of walls which separate humans from Nature and which appropriate the commons, shared resources, for private use. Sevilla-Buitrago (2015) has identified the general process of creating 'enclosures' as one of the core strategies of capitalism. Specifically, enclosures in England achieved two goals simultaneously. First was the acquisition of large areas of land as private property by a few. Second was the separation of the peasantry from non-market access to land: arable and grazing land, forests, wetlands and all the rest. The creation of enclosures was accompanied by the creation of a theory of property radically different from the dominant conceptions of traditional societies. Tawney (1998 [1926]: 79) states the traditional theory of limited rights to property as follows:

> The owner is a trustee. [...] the peasant may not cultivate his land in the way which he may think most profitable to himself, but is bound by the law of the village to grow

the crops which the village needs [...] so the lord is required both by custom and by statute to forego anti-social profits [...] which injure his neighbours.

This concept of property as a trust was replaced by the modern version of private property: "the individual is absolute master and may exploit it purely for profit, unrestrained by any social obligations."

When people have access to commons, they cannot be turned into commodities and forced into producing excess for the benefit of others. Thus, a first step required for creation of surplus production is separation of men and women from their habitat. Rapid political changes in England created conditions which allowed the aristocracy to make a major land-grab, privatising a huge amount of common land. This dispossessed a large population from access to the commons, leaving them no option but to sell themselves as labour, to acquire basic needs. Agricultural innovations created the surplus food necessary to feed a labour force engaged in industrial production. Coincident innovations enabled production of surplus goods, principally textiles, using cheaply available labour. Thus, historical accidents created the possibility of production of vast amounts of surplus, which is a distinguishing feature of market economies.

Market societies face a central problem: "what is to be done with surplus production?" Imperialism is one part of the answer. By destroying self-sufficient communities all over the world, imperialism creates consumers for the excess production. In addition, destruction of communities frees land and makes available labour that can be harnessed in mechanised mass production. While the idea that imperialism is a necessary accompaniment of capitalism is widely accepted among left-wing writers, it is hotly contested by capitalist ideologues. Such a conflict is natural since each mode of production creates ideologies to justify itself.

Early capitalism was characterised by disembedding men and women from Nature and traditional society, stripping them bare of all attachments and thereby turning them into homogenous and identical factors of production. The same strategy was adopted with respect to Nature. The market eye turned amazingly diverse flora and fauna and other wonders of the world into commodities (timber, leather) and counted the result as profit. This was undertaken on a global basis, destroying local ways of living and turning everything into raw materials to be fed to the industrial machine. Massive destruction and exploitation went unaccounted for, e.g., the genocide of the Native Americans was not to count as a cost, while the gold and silver taken from their lands could count as a benefit.

The irrational pursuit of wealth for its own sake leads to production for profit as the central activity, the *raison d'être*, of market economies (Weber, 1958). In contrast, production is undertaken for a purpose in traditional societies including fulfilling personal needs and as a service to society. However, production is not for profits and accumulation (Zaman, 2015).

The creation of fictitious commodities

Turning human beings into commodities for hire on the market, and turning living forests into furniture or firewood, is central to the process of creating wealth at the heart of capitalism. Commodification of humans and Nature requires the dissolution of the bonds of humanity which tie us to each other, as well as the bonds between human beings and Nature. Tawney (1998 [1926]: 20) writes that: "From the twelfth century to the sixteenth, ... the [fundamental and commonplace] analogy by which society is described ... is that of the human body. Each member has its own function, prayer, or defence, or merchandise, or tilling the soil."

From this organistic ideal, there was a transition to a legalistic view of people living together with agreement to follow a common set of rules, but not united in any common purpose or endeavour. One of the crucial elements in this ideological shift was the accommodation of religion. Tawney (1998 [1926]) and Weber (1958) have identified elements of the theological configuration which created the possibility of capitalism. The cold and callous process of commodification required by the capitalist economy could be started only in a secular society, where business was driven purely by laws of profit, and not by consideration and compassion as required by religion. Tawney (1926: Chapter 4) writes that only after a violent struggle on many dimensions did ethics and justice disappear as constraints on business.

If market based production is to become the central mechanism for distribution of goods, then a regular and stable supply of the 'factors of production' is essential. A key argument of Polanyi (1944) is that this requires the creation of three artificial (or fictitious) commodities: land, labour, and money. These are artificial in the sense that they are not produced, although they are treated as if they were produced. Treating human beings and Nature as commodities degrades and devalues them. This exploitation is one of the keys as to how capitalism generates wealth. Polanyi prophesied that treating human beings and natural resources as commodities would lead to widespread destruction of society and environment. Since free markets would destroy human beings and their planet, Polanyi argued that, paradoxically, the survival of the capitalist system depended on the effectiveness of the measures taken by society to protect itself from these harmful effects.

For accumulation of wealth, we need a process for excess production, and a financial market to allow the conversion of this wealth to a widely acceptable symbol of purchasing power; that is, money. The ability to convert excess production to purchasing power over a wide range of commodities as well as over time and space is crucial to the creation of a market society. The mythology of capitalism holds that money came into being naturally as a way to simplify barter. History provides a much grimmer picture. Graeber (2014) has highlighted an extremely important and neglected dimension of transformation in the concept of debt, and how it affects social relations. In traditional humane economies, debt creates cooperation, bonding and community. All people acknowledge their debt to their society and Nature, and recognise the impossibility of repaying this debt. Cooperation, sacrifice, generosity and social responsibility for the weak are all a partial acknowledgement and repayment of our debt to society. A major argument of Graeber (2014) is that when the imprecise, informal, community-building indebtedness of humane economies is replaced by mathematically precise, firmly enforced debts, widespread impoverishment and violence are common results. Whereas providing someone in need with aid leads to a warm feeling in humane societies, conversion of this into quantifiable debt has led to the eventual confiscation of property and humans living as slaves in repayment for this debt.

The conversion of human debts into quantitative money debts which are transferable is an ideological shift which creates the possibility of financial markets. One of the key insights of Graeber (2014) is that money came into being as a means of quantifying debts. Hodgson (2015: 162) quotes neglected British economist Henry Dunning MacLeod:

> If we were asked—Who made the discovery which has most deeply affected the fortunes of the human race? We think, after full consideration, we might safely answer—The man who first discovered that a Debt is a Saleable Commodity.

As Brown (2007) has argued, the power of money creation and leveraging allows an elite to amass wealth at the expense of the masses. Empirical evidence regarding the concentration of wealth and power and its harmful social effects is well known (e.g. Stiglitz, 2011; Piketty, 2014).

Polanyi (1944: 127) writes that the failure of attempts to provide poor relief in England led economists to conclude incorrectly that: "The principle of gravitation is not more certain than the tendency of (Poor) laws to change wealth and vigour into misery and weakness [...] [leading to] universal poverty." Belief in these ironclad laws removed compassion from the hearts and steeled human beings to renounce solidarity and perform an act of vivisection on the body of society. A strong faith in the laws of a capitalist free market is required to contemplate without distress the billions living in extreme poverty, even though current defence budgets would comfortably provide food, clothing, housing, health care and education for all people on the planet.

Economic laws are created by human beings, by our choice of the institutional arrangements for production, consumption and distribution. The capitalist myth, perpetuated with all seriousness in current university economics textbooks, is that these economic laws are "positive"—factual, objective and empirically valid. Even though this is manifestly false, students are trained to believe that the laws of supply and demand are on par with the law of gravity. Zaman (2012) makes explicit numerous normative assumptions embedded within the framework of economic theory without acknowledgement or awareness.

The next great transformation

The capital accumulating economy portrays itself as creating wealth for all and equates this with well-being. Wealth becomes the sole marker of status, and wealth and power concentrate in the hands of a small group to create plutocracies. The mythology of capitalism celebrates this accumulation of wealth, while completely ignoring the costs of this accumulation; see Stiglitz (2011) and Zaman (2014). However, wealth is not created out of nowhere. Rather all wealth is created by destroying something else. That which is destroyed is often irreplaceable. Polanyi (1944) notes that wealth is created by the conversion of priceless and irreplaceable natural resources (including humans) into marketable commodities. Schumacher (2011 [1973]) explains that what is called growth and wealth creation is actually destruction and dimunition of wealth because there is no full accounting for the environmental costs. Growth is celebrated while the costs are hidden in the accounting.

Appropriation and exploitation of Nature and humans transforms these into resources available to those with power, which is the link between capitalism and global conquest via imperialism [Chapter 15]. This creates a frontier between that which has been appropriated and that which remains. If some resource is exhausted, the frontier disappears together with further opportunities for appropriation or exploitation. Moore (2015) convincingly argues that the growth of capitalism has depended on the availability and appropriation of cheap labour, food, energy, and raw materials. The dynamic nature of capitalism with its rapid growth imperatives, leads to the exhaustion of the raw material. However creative energies have always found new frontiers to exploit, when old ones have become exhausted. Now however, the situation appears different. Evidence from numerous sources points to the impending exhaustion of planetary ecological resources, the final frontier. While true believers in capitalism continue to maintain faith in the opening up of a new frontier, as in the past, those with open eyes ask "where will we find a new planet?". Amongst many works on the subject, Kolbert (2014) provides excellent documentation of the magnitude and urgency of the impending ecological catastrophe as planetary resources are destroyed beyond the possibility of redemption.

The Polanyian double movement is today revealed in the search for solutions to environmental problems within the framework of a market economy. The attempt is being made to retain markets and growth, but ensure that production processes respect ecological imperatives— Green Capitalism. The proponents of sustainable development argue that we can tinker with the economic system by introducing market mechanisms like emission permits, biodiversity offsets, and other similar proposals to reduce ecological damage (for critiques of both see Spash, 2010, 2015). However, many ecological economists long ago realised growth itself is incompatible with saving the planet from ecological destruction. They have therefore come up with proposals for zero-growth (e.g. Daly, 1977), although they have not explicitly explored the relationship this has to the continuity of capitalism.

The organisation of market economies is such that growth is required for the economic system to perform. Smith (2015) argues that pursuing zero-growth without addressing the structure of capitalism would lead to heavy unemployment, and capitalism deliberately limits support for the unemployed so as to avoid interfering with the labour market. Modern market economies are based on acquisition, exploitation, and appropriation and these features are incompatible with zero-growth. The inevitable conclusion is that zero-growth means a radical system change rather than minor modifications and reforms. Smith (2015) argues that the highest priority for ecological economists today is to develop a post-capitalist ecological economy.

Future directions

Capitalism has survived numerous severe crises and confident prophecies of its demise. Nonetheless, exhaustion of planetary resources suggests that humanity may indeed be facing the final crisis of capitalism. Many are thinking about ways to save the planet from the ravages of exploitation and appropriation necessary for the capitalist economic system. For the moment, these responses seem weak and incoherent, and completely inadequate in face of the magnitude of the multiple crises. Growing awareness and apparent moves towards solutions, as in the Paris Agreement, might engender optimism. This must be tempered by the realisation that corporations are firmly in control of political processes, have a virtual monopoly on the media, and have enough savvy to make placatory moves for public consumption while continuing with business as usual. Some therefore argue that Paris changes nothing (Spash, 2016).

Combating the excesses of the capitalist system is difficult for many reasons. Perhaps the most important is the ideological component which glorifies capitalism and conceals its defects. Hollywood movies celebrating capitalist values have infiltrated the hearts and minds of many on the planet. As Nelson (2012) perceptively remarks, market ideologies have poisoned the well from which social scientists get their ideas about economics. To craft a campaign for radical change, researchers need a common vision around which they can create consensus, and build new non-capitalist institutions to spearhead a revolution. Despite repeated crises, capitalism is alive and well, and actively engaged in combat on the ideological front. This means that all campaigns will take place on heavily contested grounds, where a massive amount of resources are in the hands of the controlling elite who benefit from the current system. Those oppressed by the current system have the strength of numbers on their side, but perhaps too little else.

The future social ecological transformation requires understanding forms of resistance [Chapter 17] and the role and forms of power [Chapter 14]. Possibilities for opposition may lie in local organisation, small gatherings and person-to-person, and each-one-reach-one campaigns to persuade groups of the problems and empower them to act. In my own opinion, since the top is firmly in the hands of the elite, their sympathisers and beneficiaries, only a bottom-up campaign appears feasible. The means to an ethically just overthrow of hegemonic power, and the social ecological transformation of society, remain contested within both social movements and research, but the problems are urgently in need of redress.

A second step should be to build resilient self-sufficient communities that are low-tech, low footprint, which live close to the ground in ecological harmony. There are large numbers of alienated workers, living on the dregs (i.e., 'trickle down') from the capitalist dream, who might form the nucleus of new communities.. Some communities still remain on the planet that have survived the onslaught of modernity, but many are under direct attack (e.g. conversion of rural India and China). Research is required that studies working models like the Amish community and Jewish communes and identifies the conditions for replicating their success on a large scale across the globe. However, small communities are fragile and easily destroyed. Therefore building global linkages which connect these into a global community appears a necessary part of transformation.

Nation-states came into being by an act of imagination. A powerful vision is now needed to repair our connections with communities and Nature, rejecting the isolationist philosophy of individualism. The military-industrial complex at the heart of modern capitalism feeds on wars, conflicts and hatred, which today is evident in the manufacture of mythical monsters of religious terrorism. The reality is that most wars, weapons, deaths and terrorism are caused by the inexorable workings of capital seeking profits. This means transformation away from capitalism is also transformation towards the pursuit of peace and the promotion of the common bonds of humanity that are far stronger than the superficial differences of language, culture, religion and race that separate us.

Concluding remarks

This chapter has provided a critical overview reflecting on the role of markets in modern society and highlighted the problems they have created since the Industrial Revolution. In terms of the double movement of Polanyi, not just humanity, but the planet itself is now creating a counter movement to protect itself from the ravages of capitalism. Human induced climate change is often highlighted and headlined but is merely one of the many crises created in the complex of social ecological and economic interactions. Reversing the great transformation to a capitalist market system means transformation to simpler lifestyles based on social cooperation and harmony with Nature. Therein lies the challenge for the social ecological economist.

Note

1   Editor's Note: This corresponds with the explanation of mutual dependency in coevolutionary development applied to social ecological economic systems, although there is no inevitable harmonisation in coevolution in terms of avoiding negative outcomes such as species extinction [see Chapter 13].

Key further readings cited

Kolbert, E. (2014). *The Sixth Extinction: An Unnatural History.* New York: Henry Holt & Co.

Moore, J. (2015). *Capitalism in the Web of Life: Ecology and the Accumulation of Capital.* London: Verso.

Polanyi, K. (1944). *The Great Transformation: The Political And Economic Origins Of Our Time.* New York/Toronto: Rinehart & Company Inc.

Smith, R. (2015). *Green Capitalism: The God that Failed.* Bristol: World Economic Association Books.

Zaman, A. (2014). Evaluating the Costs of Growth. *Real World Economics Review* 67(May), 41–51.

Other literature cited

Brown, E.H. (2007). *Web of Debt: The Shocking Truth about Our Money System.* Baton Rouge: Third Millennium Press.

Daly, H.E. (1977). *Steady-State Economics.* San Francisco: W.H. Freeman.

Daly, H.E., Cobb, J.B., Cobb, C.W. (1994). *For the Common Good: Redirecting the Economy Toward Community, the Environment, and a Sustainable Future*. Boston: Beacon Press.

Graeber, D. (2014). *Debt-Updated and Expanded: The First 5,000 Years*. New York: Melville House Books.

Hodgson, G.M. (2015). *Conceptualising Capitalism: Institutions, Evolution, Future*. Chicago: University of Chicago Press.

Marx, K. (1977). *Capital: A Critique of Political Economy* (Volume 1). New York: Vintage Books

Nelson, J. (2012). *Poisoning the Well, or How Economic Theory Damages Moral Imagination*. Global Development and Environment Institute Working Paper No.12-07 Tufts University.

Oreskes, N., Conway, E.M. (2011). *Merchants of Doubt: How a Handful of Scientists Obscured the Truth on Issues from Tobacco Smoke to Global Warming*. New York: Bloomsbury Press.

Piketty, T. (2014). *Capitalism in the Twenty-First Century*. Cambridge, MA: Belknap Press.

Schumacher, E.F. (2011 [1973]). *Small is Beautiful: A Study of Economics as if People Mattered*. New York: Random House.

Sevilla-Buitrago, A. (2015) Capitalist Formations of Enclosure: Space and the Extinction of the Commons. *Antipode*, 47(4), 999–1020.

Spash, C.L. (2010). The Brave New World of Carbon Trading. *New Political Economy* 15(2): 169–195.

Spash, C.L. (2015). Bulldozing Biodiversity: The Economics of Offsets and Trading-in Nature. *Biological Conservation* 192(December): 541–551.

Spash, C.L. (2016). This Changes Nothing: The Paris Agreement to Ignore Reality. *Globalizations* 13 (6): 928–933.

Stiglitz, J. (2011). Of the 1%, by the 1%, for the 1%. *Vanity Fair*, 31 March.

Tawney, R.H. (1998[1926]). *Religion and the Rise of Capitalism*. New Brunswick, N.J.: Transaction Publishers.

Weber, M. (1958). *The Protestant Ethic and the Spirit of Capitalism*. Translation by Talcott Parsons. New York: Charles Scribner's Sons.

Zaman, A. (2012). The Normative Foundations of Scarcity, *Real World Economics Review*, 61(September), 22–39.

Zaman, A. (2015). Islam Versus Economics. In K. Hassan and M. Lewis (eds.) *Handbook on Islam and Economic Life*. Cheltenham: Edward Elgar Press.

19

THEORY OF THE FIRM

Peter E. Earl

Introduction

Ecological economists need to have knowledge of the theory of the firm because damage to ecosystems is largely the result of production processes of firms or due to the consumption of the products that firms choose to supply to their customers. Policies aimed at limiting or overcoming ecosystem damage may fail if firms do not respond to incentives in the ways the policy designers expect. For example, firms may fail to change their behaviour in response to economic incentives (e.g., tax or subsidy) contrary to mainstream economic expectations. If the theory correctly predicts such behaviour it will inspire the search for alternative policies such as direct regulation. A contention of this chapter is that a more realistic understanding of the firm is indeed necessary.

Unfortunately, the 'theory of the firm' covers a wide range of perspectives on firms, which address different areas and, depending on context, may offer different predictions—for a heterodox pluralistic survey see Earl (1995, chapters 6–11); for an excellent comprehensive textbook see Ricketts (2003); and for a very useful handbook see Dietrich and Krafft (2012). Some theorists see firms 'as if' they are 'black boxes' that purchase inputs and transform them into outputs with the aid of the optimal technology chosen from a 'given' set of blueprints that fully specify how the inputs are to be used. They typically proceed 'as if all the firms in the industry are identical in the information they possess and how they interpret it, and in the technology set they face. Others view firms as complex organisations that may be actively involved in generating new technologies and whose set of capabilities and perceptions are affected by their unique histories. Whereas the former see policy as a matter of incentive design, the latter are more likely to be concerned that changes towards eco-friendly strategies may be impeded by difficulties in changing prevalent attitudes within firms about how they go about their business. In this chapter I will cover in turn: the ecological significance of firms being coalitions of diverse stakeholders with different goals; how firms combat changing business conditions; why firms can survive despite not attaining 'best practice' levels of productivity; and multinational corporations.

The firm as an organisational coalition

Mainstream economics textbooks portray firms as if they are on a mission to maximise profits for shareholders come what may. The firm will only eschew a 'race to the bottom' strategy— locating production in jurisdictions with the most lax environmental and workforce protection laws—if this could harm profits. Such harm could arise if target customers care about the social and environmental conditions of production. Alternatively, cheaper conditions might have offsetting adverse effects on productivity and quality. Workers and their managers are viewed as united in doing whatever they can to help maximise profits, because they fear being replaced by others who are willing to work harder or for lower hourly remuneration towards that end. This unity of purpose, coupled with an assumption that everyone actually, or potentially, involved in the firm's production processes knows the technology set available to the firm, removes the theorist's perceived need to view firms as organisations.

This view contrasts sharply with the behavioural theory of the firm proposed by Cyert and March (1963), who follow Simon (1959) in rejecting the idea that the firm is able to maximise anything. Uncertainty and complexity make the identification of optimal choices problematic, especially when managers are grappling with open-ended decision problems and face pressing deadlines; all that they can do is 'satisfice', that is, set targets ('aspiration levels') and keep searching until they come across potential solutions that seem 'good enough'. Goals can thus end up proving to be unduly modest or wildly overambitious. If attainments repeatedly differ from aspiration levels, they will adjust the latter to align with the former. However, in deciding how bold to be, decision-makers may use the performance levels achieved by rivals, rather than their own past performances, as indicators of what they can realistically hope to achieve. Sometimes, firms will need to review which businesses they use as their external reference standards and change their views about the competitive league of which they can realistically presume to be a member.

Cyert and March go further in their rejection of profit maximisation: they characterise the firm as a coalition of stakeholders with very different interests and aspirations. Despite their differences, they are willing to be members of such a coalition because it provides a means to benefit from pooling diverse but complementary inputs. On this view, the boundaries of the firm are fuzzy, for the group of stakeholders can be seen as including not merely the shareholders, managers and workers but also other parties with whom the organisation has ongoing relationships, such as its bankers, supply chain members and loyal customers. The firm may have some publicly espoused goals—in order to keep external stakeholders happy, to frighten off potential rivals, and in the hope of providing some cohesion to its actions—but ultimately the members of the coalition are all trying to pursue their personal sub-goals. They will stay with the firm so long as they feel they have a good enough chance of meeting these goals.

Scope for actions that go against shareholder interests comes from the division of knowledge and/or information between members of the coalition that comprises the firm. In any relationship that is at arm's length, or based on differences in expertise, an agent who is acting on behalf of a principal is potentially able to operate in a self-serving way: the principal cannot monitor the agent's actions without incurring the cost of doing so (or the risk entailed in delegating the monitoring task to another agent) and may in any case lack the expertise to know to what extent the agent is exploiting the situation. For the division of labour to take place, principals must trust agents and leave them to get on with their jobs. With luck, moral codes and socio-cultural pressures will ensure that the agents generally do the right thing on their behalf. Contracts that precisely specify what an agent is to deliver obviate the need to monitor the actions of the agent if the output can readily be observed, but where this is impossible the buyer ultimately has to trust the supplier. However, there can be payoffs to leaving expected outputs somewhat vague, for this could result in agents doing a better job than when they know precisely what they can get away with.

The pursuit of sub-goals could have diverse ecological consequences. For example, shareholders who are interested in more than purely financial returns, and wish to have their money invested in firms that operate in a socially and ecologically responsible manner, may discover too late what the firm *really* has been doing (as with the 2015 diesel emissions scandal at Volkswagen).[1] Managers may have much shorter time horizons than shareholders if managerial remuneration packages include major bonus incentives based on recent profit performance (providing stepping stones for promotion or moves from one firm to another). Such managers may thus sanction policies that help the firm's current earnings but have disastrous long-term consequences. Engineers may conceal from their bosses the means they have used to (seem to) meet performance standards. On the other hand, a firm's scientists and engineers might use the firm's resources on pet projects that sacrifice current profits in pursuit of their own environmental goals, having guilefully argued their case for the resources in a manner that promised profits would increase. While lazy workers might operate in a slipshod manner and waste inputs, others, with pride in their work, might deliberately flout corporate procedures that were designed to be cost efficient by saving time at the expense of avoidable use of other inputs.

Where differences among stakeholders in access to information and knowledge open up the possibility of pursuing sub-goals, a strong corporate culture—in the form of a particular shared sense of 'how we do business here'—can play a major role in preventing different areas of the firm from pulling in different directions and creating coordination failures. It may also affect the extent to which the firm operates in an eco-friendly manner. However, a corporate culture may have dysfunctional blinkering effects, especially when 'how we do business' is anchored firmly to a particular view of 'what business we are in'. For example, a firm that views itself as in the business of providing cheap power to its customers might resist renewable energy technologies and concentrate on making better use of easily accessible supplies of brown coal and feeding electricity into a national grid, whereas a firm that views itself as in the business of serving its customers' energy needs in a sustainable way might become a provider of decentralised solar/battery systems. The ease with which firms can change their espoused goals will depend on their internal politics, i.e., on the formation and disintegration of sub-coalitions that determine the internal balance of power. Variations in a firm's fortunes can create internal political shifts that change its strategic and operational focus, e.g., from the pursuit of bold 'grand designs' to 'bean-counting' austerity, or vice versa.

The firm's capacity to survive shocks

If a firm faces unexpectedly tougher external business conditions it may maintain its previous rate of output even if it can no longer cover the full (private) costs of production. This is possible because the latter include outlays made in past periods (sunk costs), such as investments in buildings, plant and machinery, marketing and training. If continued production is to be viable, the average revenue the firm receives for its output only needs to cover the expenses that it incurs in the period in question that it could have avoided by producing less or ceasing production altogether. These costs include managerial overheads, payments to line workers and suppliers of raw materials and components, rent and local authority taxes. The sunk costs only affect current net revenues insofar as the past investments constrain the productivity of the firm's operations (the current costs it incurs to produce its output) and leave a legacy of debt-servicing charges that must be honoured if the firm is to avoid bankruptcy. This means that at any time an industry can consist of firms that are operating with very different cost structures and ages of equipment (with some firms themselves operating with a mix of vintages of technologies in different locations), earning very different rates of return on an historic cost basis (Salter, 1964).

This is very significant in ecological terms. It means that, for example, energy-hungry production methods may continue in operation for many years after the discovery of much more frugal technologies. This is because managers will only introduce the latter if there is the prospect of recovering the full (private) costs of production within their target time horizon. In traditional theories of the firm, such horizons would extend as far into the future as the investment would be able to generate revenues, with costs and revenues all being discounted into present values. In contrast, behavioural theories acknowledge that uncertainty about the future results in guesses about costs and revenues being made and assessed only for relatively short target 'payback periods' (Neild, 1964). Old technologies, whose capital costs have already been incurred, may continue in operation for many years, with new, more eco-friendly, technologies only replacing them as they become economically unviable to repair or operate. Even if new technologies rapidly lead to the abandonment of older vintages in high-wage economies, because the average total costs of the new are less than the operating costs of the old, the older technologies may remain in use elsewhere. For example, they may be shipped to economies where lower wages offset the higher costs in terms of energy and/or other inputs relative to those of the new technology.

The neoclassical analysis of the firm that dominates the conventional textbook wisdom presents a very mechanistic view of how firms deal with external shocks—including new environmental policies of governments. Firms are portrayed as adapting to surprises—considered as impacts on marginal revenue and marginal cost functions—by changing their output levels in the short run and/or changing their production technology in the long run when, by definition, fixed factors can be adjusted. This is a very different view of adjustment from that offered earlier by Marshall (1890), who did not see firms 'as if' they face a comprehensive set of rival technologies encompassing all manner of different combinations of labour and capital. In Marshall's analysis, the existing set of available technologies is limited and reflects past attempts to devise solutions to production challenges in the context of relative factor prices that prevailed at the time. Hence in the Marshallian theory of the firm, the long-run adjustment process is portrayed as one in which firms have had enough time to adapt to changed conditions by generating or accessing new knowledge that restores their abilities to earn at least normal profits. It helps to be close to other firms in a similar line of business (in a 'Marshallian business district'), as this facilitates the spread of newly discovered techniques; for example, via local switches of workers between firms, with the workers taking new knowledge with them.

Firms may thus be wasting resources if they are out of touch with the latest techniques, quite apart from having failed so far to have the creative vision necessary to push the production possibility frontier into new territory. This view of inefficiency is absent from the neoclassical theory of the firm because it assumes the production function is fully known. Production can then only be 'inefficient' if the mix of factors is suboptimal (the firm is on a socially inefficient point on the production possibility frontier due, say, to relative factor price distortions induced by trade unions exercising their bargaining power), or because firms use monopoly power to push up prices and thus deliberately produce less from their production systems than they would if they were in a more competitive market situation. In recognition of this oddly limited dominant view of inefficiency, Leibenstein (1966) coined the phrase X-inefficiency to characterise situations in which firms are operating inside the production possibility frontier. As well as taking account of the possibility that firms might be ignorant of best-practice technologies,

Leibenstein recognised that productivity could be lower than possible, even if the firm had the best-practice technology and corresponding staffing levels, because: (i) workers were taking advantage of vague employment contracts and not working as hard as they could, and (ii) imperfections in the market for managers had caused a suboptimal distribution of management expertise between firms.

Whereas ignorance of best-practice production methods might result in natural resources being wasted, the other sources of X-inefficiency seem to concern time and expertise being wasted due to workers enjoying a quiet life and managers failing, for example, to make good matches between workers and tasks. In ecological terms, productivity losses of the latter kinds may actually be a good thing, so long as poor management does not also result in avoidable pollution and waste of material inputs. The reason is that instead of achieving higher real income levels (in terms of traditional measures) and engaging in more consumption, workers get to enjoy 'on the job leisure' [see Chapter 21]. For some, however, wellbeing might be reduced by feelings of frustration and exasperation associated with seeing the quality of decisions their bosses are making!

The loosely specified nature of employment contracts and the vagueness of other ties that bind together members of the firm into a coalition help to make the firm more robust in the face of shocks coming from its external business conditions, or arising internally (e.g., an explosion or fire). Although vague contracts may permit slack behaviour, production systems depend on people being prepared to exercise a degree of 'give and take' in order to deal with disturbances; attempts to stick rigidly to contractual stipulations can cause production to grind to a halt, as when members of a trade union 'work to rule'. Moreover, as Coase (1937) was the first to realise, coordination costs can be reduced, despite the costs of paying for managers, by leaving contracts vague and building them around a hierarchy of authority relationships. Central to Coase's view of the firm is the employment of managers to decide what needs to be done, and to get subordinates to do it, as events unfold. To deal with change without incurring the costs of hiring managers involves significant transaction costs, as fresh contracts will need to be negotiated to deal with every unforeseen event as it arises. This process might also disastrously delay responses. Attempts to insure against possible contingencies would create highly detailed contracts that stretch far into the future, have many redundant clauses and still fail to cover some events that have not been anticipated, not least due to strong uncertainty [Chapter 26].

The firm's robustness is enhanced by its capacity: (i) to innovate (Downie, 1958; Nelson and Winter, 1982), (ii) to reduce X-inefficiency by hiring consultants or new mangers, and (iii) to take up 'organisational slack' that has accumulated in good times (Cyert and March, 1963). All three possibilities are absent in the neoclassical theory of the firm 'as if' it is an omniscient profit maximiser. The first two involve creating new knowledge or making better use of existing knowledge, whereas the third entails changing the distribution of returns among the firm's stakeholder. Organisational slack arises because, when the going is easy, attainments of members of the corporate coalition will tend to exceed 'transfer fee' (minimum acceptable) levels. Potentially, one group could extract more at the expense of another without causing the latter to exit, but if the latter's minimum requirements are not known, this could misfire. Stakeholders will therefore be reluctant to 'push their luck' if things are going 'OK'. In challenging times, when their attainments start falling short of their aspirations, they will be more willing to get assertive and may find that others are prepared to make concessions because their own returns are still more than adequate. Thus, for example, managers may find they can get workers to be more productive, get banks to reschedule loan repayments or get away with cutting dividends to shareholders.

This understanding of the firm is very significant for ecological economists. It means that firms could operate in a more eco-friendly manner than they currently claim or believe themselves to be capable of doing. Indeed, if environmental regulations put them under pressure, they may be able to find ways of conforming to the regulations that actually improve returns for their shareholders. For example, if consumer durables have eventually to be dismantled and recycled by their manufacturers, there is pressure on firms to design products that are easy to disassemble, but this may result in them being cheaper to assemble in the first place.

The view that environmental regulation will promote innovation that may even enable compliance to be achieved in a profit enhancing way is known as the 'Porter Hypothesis', after the work of Porter and van der Linde (1995). However, en route to their hypothesis they made no use of the seminal contributions referred to here. Rather, they based it on the signals that regulations send to managers about the case for trying to invent more eco-friendly ways of operating; these signals may result in reduced uncertainty about whether improving performance is worthwhile in the area in question and may decrease fears that attempts to do so could result in the firm losing relative competitiveness due to its rivals not bothering to make similar investments. While there is much evidence that tighter environmental regulation does promote innovation, it has so far proved difficult to determine the robustness of the strong 'no trade-offs' version of the Porter Hypothesis. This is partly because the full payoffs to eco-friendly innovations may take many years and partly because of the challenges involved in making international comparisons of different regulatory regimes (for a survey, see Ambec et al., 2013).

The theory of the multinational/transnational firm

Multinational enterprises (MNEs), or transnational corporations (TNCs), commonly arouse hostility among ecological activists because the scale of their operations affords them considerable bargaining power. If not granted the kind of environmental permits that they seek, some can credibly threaten to locate in other nations, with consequent losses of job opportunities and export sales for nations that try to protect their ecosystems. Although threats to move elsewhere may be hollow in the case of MNEs involved in the extraction of natural resources that are concentrated in only a few areas, these concerns certainly warrant serious consideration in sectors whose operations are genuinely footloose.

However, the literature on the theory of the multinational firm has focussed on why firms bother to set-up offshore subsidiaries given the challenges of running operations at arm's length and in unfamiliar cultural, legal and institutional settings. To avoid such challenges, firms should prefer to produce domestically on a large scale and export to overseas markets. Where exporting is problematic due to tariffs or transportation issues, the need for an overseas subsidiary may be avoided by having the product manufactured under license in offshore markets (as Coca-Cola does). Firms based in high-wage economies may be able to enjoy the benefits of low offshore wage costs by outsourcing the manufacture of their products to firms in developing countries (as Nike does). Even if a major corporation organises its global operations by these latter means, without setting up subsidiaries offshore, it can still exert its bargaining power by threatening to award contracts to suppliers in other nations if it does not like the environmental terms associated with deals it is being offered. Of course, if MNEs wish to garner reputations for operating in an eco-friendly manner (or with high health and safety standards and without using child labour), they may be able to do this in developing countries without setting up offshore subsidiaries: they can require that suppliers in economies with lax official standards meet higher standards, with the threat that contracts will be terminated if breaches are discovered.

Given the market contract–based alternatives open to MNEs, the focus of the theory of the multinational firm—beginning with Hymer (1976), originally his 1960 doctoral dissertation—has been on why such alternatives might be rejected. Key points of focus have been on the possibility of contractual failures associated with the other party not meeting the firm's standards or pirating its intellectual property, with the result that the firm may end up earning less than it would have done had it set up its own subsidiaries and thereby been better able to protect its reputation and prevent/delay seepage of its technologies. This perspective has significant ecological implications. A multinational subsidiary could be a better ecological agent than a local corporation supplying for an offshore corporation, since the MNE's head office may be better able and better motivated to ensure environmental standards are met if it operates offshore via subsidiaries rather than relying on offshore contractors: a well-publicised lapse by a contractor in one country could have disastrous impacts on its global reputation. Moreover, if a key role of foreign direct investment strategies is to limit the speed at which technological expertise escapes from firms, then this is likely to delay economic development in host nations, with mixed potential consequences: on the one hand, slower development may limit resource depletion, but on the other hand, it may delay moves towards higher environmental standards achieved in richer countries.

Future directions

So far, innovation has been mentioned as a reactive means by which firms may raise their game when the going gets tough or new regulations are imposed. However, innovation is, as Nelson and Winter (1982) emphasise, a pro-active aspect of the typical modern firm's operations, undertaken to try to keep the firm out of trouble and avoid nasty surprises at the hands of innovative competitors and regulators. This is absent from the neoclassical theory of the firm, whose static methodology condemns it to analysing competition between firms primarily in terms of price strategies in contexts in which firms can operate as price-makers rather than price-takers and may need to try to anticipate the behaviour of their rivals. Clearly, such an approach can be applicable for understanding how firms might respond in the short run if presented with unexpected environmental regulations or a new rival that has emerged without warning. Yet, even seemingly short-run puzzles may be impossible to resolve without taking a more dynamic view. For example, from a static perspective, the emergence of Tesla, the pioneering manufacturer of high-performance long-range electric vehicles, invites mainly the question of whether it would be possible to drive Tesla out of business by predatory pricing. The theory proves inadequate because the competitive threat posed by Tesla raises bigger questions, such as: Will improvements in fuel economy of gasoline-powered vehicles be enough to keep Tesla limited to a small market in the long run? Should established carmakers try to beat Tesla at its own game by developing their own electric vehicles even if this cannibalises sales of their conventional vehicles?

In order to address these kinds of questions, the theory of the firm will have to change in several ways. Concentration on the significance of static economies of large-scale production (e.g., analysis of 'natural monopolies') needs to be replaced by attention to economies of scope (the sharing of investment elements between several products) and learning curves (whereby unit costs fall with cumulative experience in production), for these will shape the speed at which eco-friendly technologies become viable. The typical focus on a single product, and the 'representative consumer's' demand for it, simply will not do if the viability of products for users depends upon them being able to build, or hook into, entire systems of products whose viability is, in turn, driven by network externalities (i.e., by how many other consumers have adopted the product). Traditional theorising about the demand for the firm's products is misleading because it treats choice 'as if' the consumer will always be prepared to substitute to a rival kind of product if 'the price is right': buyers, like firms and individuals in firms, may select aspiration levels and reject products that conflict with their checklists of requirements; for example, only being willing to buy an electric car with a range of at least 300 miles and a price of under $50,000—which would rule out a 2015 Tesla, but perhaps not 2020 ones. To the extent that many consumers set similar targets, the patterns of sales that firms experience may shift sharply as some players learn how to offer products that are acceptable in terms of popular checklists (see Earl and Wakeley, 2010). The mainstream theory of the firm offers a means to analyse competition in terms of marginal revenues and costs as they currently stand for rival firms, or in terms of a game with a given set of rules. It is of limited use for analysing the upcoming prospective world of disruptive, game-changing, more eco-friendly products that may result in dramatic changes in the relative fortunes of major corporations.

Concluding remarks

When applied to environmental issues, the neoclassical theory of the firm reduces policy designs to a matter of changing incentives or adding regulatory constraints in order to divert behaviour along desired lines. Its underlying message is that, if a firm is damaging the ecosystem, it is doing so because this serves the interests of its shareholders. However, pulling on the levers of the price mechanism may be rather ineffectual if firms operate with various forms of slack and can for long periods continue operating production systems that do not cover their full costs. Yet, under pressure, firms may be able to come up with innovations that then result in rapid but unforeseen changes, for good or bad. The organisational complexity of modern corporations may result in changed incentives not registering with top-level decision makers. It may also lead to ignorance of activities of the firm that are damaging ecosystems and potentially threaten shareholder interests, but which have appeared to some employees as acceptable ways of dealing with environmental regulations. This is why, despite the lack of coverage in today's textbooks, so much attention has been given here to a behavioural/evolutionary view of the firm.

Note

1   Volkswagen has admitted that 11 million of its vehicles were equipped with software that was used to cheat on emissions tests. The software sensed when the car was being tested and then activated equipment that reduced emissions, but readjusted during regular driving, increasing emissions far above legal limits. A US$14.7 billion settlement was made in 2016 covering only cars in the USA.

Key further readings cited

Dietrich, M., and Krafft, J. (eds.) (2012). *Handbook of the Economics and Theory of the Firm*. Cheltenham: Edward Elgar.

Earl, P.E. (1995). *Microeconomics for Business and Marketing*. Aldershot: Edward Elgar.

Ricketts, M. (2003). *The Economics of Business Enterprise: An Introduction to Economic Organisation and the Theory of the Firm* (3rd edition). Cheltenham: Edward Elgar.

Other literature cited

Ambec, S., Cohen, M.A., Elgie, S., and Lanoie, P. (2013). The Porter hypothesis at 20: Can environmental regulation enhance innovation and competitiveness? *Review of Environmental Economics and Policy*, 7(1, winter), 2–22.

Coase, R.H. (1937). The nature of the firm. *Economica, 4*(16) (November), 386–405.

Cyert, R.M., and March, J.G. (1963). *A Behavioral Theory of the Firm.* Englewood Cliffs, NJ: Prentice-Hall.

Downie, J. (1958). *The Competitive Process.* London: Duckworth.

Earl, P.E., and Wakeley, T. (2010). Economic perspectives on the development of complex products for increasingly demanding customers. *Research Policy, 39*(8), 1122–1132.

Hymer, S.H. (1976). *The International Operations of National Firms: A Study of Direct Foreign Investment.* Cambridge, MA: MIT Press.

Leibenstein, H. (1966). Allocative efficiency vs. "X-efficiency". *American Economic Review, 56*(3, June), 392–414.

Marshall, A. (1890). *Principles of Economics* (1st ed.). London: Macmillan.

Neild, R.R. (1964). Replacement policy. *National Institute Economic Review, 30*(November), 30–43.

Nelson, R.R., and Winter, S.G. (1982). *An Evolutionary Theory of Economic Change.* Cambridge, MA: Belknap Press of Harvard University Press.

Porter, M.E., and van der Linde, C. (1995). Towards a new conception of the environment-competitiveness relationship. *Journal of Economic Perspectives, 9*(4, Fall), 97–118.

Salter, W.E.G. (1964). *Productivity and Technical Change.* Cambridge: Cambridge University Press.

Simon, H.A. (1959). Theories of decision-making in economics and behavioral science. *American Economic Review, 49*(3, June), 253–283.

20

THEORIES OF (UN)SUSTAINABLE CONSUMPTION

Clive L. Spash and Karin Dobernig

Introduction

This chapter explores different theories of consumption and explains alternative disciplinary perspectives on the determinants of (un)sustainable behaviours and practices. Consumption is a major concern for social ecological economics because of the recognised need for societal transformation away from material and energy intensive economies and lifestyles in order to avoid environmental impacts [see Chapter 11]. Policy interest in the field has also increased due to the mounting pressure to decarbonise the economy to prevent human induced climate change.

A core policy objective is to achieve higher rates of economic growth decoupled from energy and material use. Reducing the material intensity of consumer lifestyles is meant to allow the continuation of 'business as usual'. This weak sustainable consumption approach is linked to ecological modernisation, adjusting prices via market-based policies and using voluntary instruments (e.g. eco-labelling). Businesses via innovation and consumers via purchasing are assumed to act as key agents of change mediated through the market as an institution of efficient resource allocation. Paradoxically, technologies that are meant to increase resource efficiency have actually led to increased total resource consumption; something called the "rebound effect" [Chapter 10] or the Jevons paradox (Polimeni et al., 2008).

In contrast, notions of downshifting, voluntary simplicity, degrowth [Chapter 44] and post growth [Chapter 46] call for both a change in consumption patterns and a decrease in absolute consumption levels of material and energy resources. Such strong sustainable consumption claims a double dividend—degrowth of consumption lessens environmental impacts while reduced work time increases well-being. The consumer economy is criticised for creating temporary hedonic pleasures and failing to deliver the 'good life' for anybody, let alone for all. The emphasis of economic growth on material affluence ignores, and indeed denigrates, the non-pecuniary aspects of life (Easterlin, 2003), such as social relationships, health and playfulness [see Chapter 21]. Consumption as a means for providing status is a continually self-defeating exercise that prevents economic growth from making everyone socially 'better-off' (Hirsch, 1977). Such critiques pose the questions: what is the meaning of consumption and what is it for?

Understanding consumption requires accepting there are some fundamental social, psychological and biophysical realities that underlie, and act as co-determinants of, all consumption behaviour, but also multiple causal mechanisms that combine to create actual behaviour in dynamic and multifaceted ways. This chapter starts by reviewing some standard approaches to consumption from different disciplines (e.g. economics, psychology, sociology, anthropology). We highlight the dichotomy of agency versus structure and attempts by theories of practice to move beyond this, while also noting the continuing prevalence of individualistic approaches. We then outline some of the long-standing structural explanations for consumption practices. This presentation reveals that the field of consumption research has an ongoing tendency to draw divisive dichotomies—structure vs. agency, determinism vs. voluntarism, social vs. individual—that compete to provide 'the' single dominant explanation for consumer behaviour. An alternative would be to take a dialectical approach consistent with critical realism [Chapter 2]. In noting future directions, and consistent with these suggestions, we highlight the importance of connecting understanding of individuals as social agents with the institutions and social structures within which they operate.

Alternative conceptual models of consumption

Different disciplinary biases are important for understanding how researchers conceptualise consumer practices, the role of consumption and the causal mechanisms attributed to consumer behaviour. Mainstream economics is devoted to the rational individual actor model of *homo œconomicus*. Social psychology focuses on values, attitudes, and norms as causes of sustainable behaviours. Sociology emphasises the symbolic values of products in a consumer society and stresses that people do not consume products *per se* but the meanings attached to them. Social anthropologists place the individual in a social context of rituals and shared practices. Evolutionary economists attribute consumer practices to predetermined dispositions that are claimed to have formerly aided survival. These approaches appear to offer considerable variety as to how consumption might be understood.

However, a common underlying and restrictive methodological individualism tends to prevail. For example, in critically reviewing a core anthropological position, Røpke (1999: 409) states that "human beings are conceived of as social, but they are just as unpleasant pursuers of their own interests as they are in economics". Theories of practice have promised a more comprehensive approach. However, practitioners of this newer perspective have also tended to ignore, trivialise and/or downplay structure, power, and biophysical aspects in their empirical case studies. In this section, we critically review and contrast the dominant individualistic theories with theories of social practice, before turning to a third, much older, set of currently neglected arguments relating to power and structure as determinants of consumption.

Theories emphasising the individual agent

The conventional microeconomic view on human behaviour conceptualises the individual as an utility maximiser who calculates how to allocate a fixed income across consumption choices on the basis of relative prices and preferences. This individualistic account of consumer behaviour rests upon the assumptions that the consumer is sovereign and has fixed endogenous preferences and perfect information. Despite being a purely deductive model, the account still dominates conventional consumer policies. It is employed to promote the use of price signals to correct 'market failures' by 'internalising' social and environmental costs, and to support information provision (e.g. labelling, advertising) as a means of raising awareness and altering attitudes, with the ultimate aim of behavioural change (Southerton et al., 2011). Implicitly, motivators (e.g. attitudes, norms) are claimed to determine behaviour, although economists have no such explanatory relationship in their model.

What lies behind the promotion of this approach appears to be a political ideology that encapsulates an idealised liberal political economy. This reflects a form of governance that regards consumers as citizens free to choose and responsible for making the right choices. Government is then deemed to have a legitimate role in achieving market perfectionism and correcting market failures. Hence, citizens are mainly "addressed as autonomous shoppers whose choices, in the aggregate, determine the fate and future of the planet" (Shove, 2004: 113). Their choices only go wrong due to a lack of information and incorrect pricing (i.e. an information deficit model).

In parallel with this microeconomic view, environmental and social psychologists describe an attitude-behaviour gap. They argue that information based measures might influence attitudes but fail to translate into actual behavioural change (e.g. Vermeir and Verbeke, 2008). Social psychologists further distinguish between intended and actual behaviour, and show how these can also be divorced from one another. Indeed, attitudes may play no role in mediating actual behaviour. For example, increasing awareness of environmental consequences, such as climate change, and pro-environmental attitudes, fail to change consumer behaviour that remains locked-in to environmentally destructive acts, such as fossil fuel consumption.

More generally, environmental and social psychologists conceptualise sustainable consumption as a conglomerate of different pro-environmental behaviours (e.g. recycling, eating less meat, using public transportation) and use empirical methods to study the causal factors hypothesised to be responsible for these behaviours. They then employ scales to measure broadly defined concepts such as values, worldviews and norms. They aim to understand the reasons behind individual actions and develop strategies that encourage pro-environmental behaviour. Their perspective often regards sustainable consumption as involving a conflict between individual and collective interests, e.g. travelling by public transportation is better for the environment but less convenient for the individual.

In such approaches, the extent to which individuals consciously deliberate over and control their actions is highly questionable. Contrary to the information deficit model, many everyday decisions and behaviours appear to be motivated by subconscious routines. The attitude–behaviour and intended–actual behaviour gaps may then be explained by habits, social norms, and the use of prevalent technologies and material infrastructures. Consequently, simply providing new information and appealing to consumer preferences is at best ineffective, and at worst a distraction from the necessary means required for bringing about behavioural change towards more sustainable consumption patterns. In addition, people simplify complex decisions by employing a variety of mental shortcuts or loosely defined rules, called heuristics, that can operate subconsciously.

The concept of heuristics has been adopted by behavioural economists to explain systematic behavioural bias, i.e. relative to the expected actions of rational economic man. Behavioural economics integrates findings from psychology (e.g. bounded rationality), and more recently neuroscience, with microeconomic theory, which is then updated by considering the impact of cognitive, affective and social factors on the decisions of economic agents. This would appear to offer a potentially radical critique of economics. However, the dominant position, driven by economists from the United States of America (USA), has become one in which the mainstream economic model employs psychology to bolster the core concept of *homo œconomicus* by placing psychology within economics, rather than learning why this core is fundamentally flawed and placing economics within the context of psychology (Earl, 2005).

Thus, behavioural economics maintains the methodological individualism of mainstream economics and its preference utilitarianism. Humans are regarded as being predictably 'irrational', so that their behaviour can be corrected (Earl, 2016: 5). In that context, addressing environmental problems is a matter of getting all the autonomous self-interested *homo œconomicus* to cooperate for the common good. The research links with new institutional economics to engage in mathematical models, set up games and conduct social 'experiments' to show how carrots (benefits) and sticks (costs) can work to counter free-riders and rule breakers. They extend preferences to social and 'other regarding' behaviour, and squeeze in concepts, such as fairness, in the guise of commodities providing utility. Under such assumptions, a better, more caring, society requires education, creating empathy for others and making people feel that others are part of their 'in-group', so that they gain more personal benefits from helping those others (Spash, 2016).

Arising from this literature is a popularised concept called nudging (Thaler and Sunstein, 2009). This combines choice architecture and libertarian paternalism. Choice architecture under an evolutionary approach connotes: "the design of complex structures or systems that consumers construct as a means for coping with life" (Earl, 2016: 6). It might then have some correspondence with critical institutional economics [Chapter 3]. However, it tends to be reduced down, by authors like Thaler and Sunstein, to subtle use of psychological signals in the presentation of simple options to get a desired outcome. Libertarian paternalism conforms to the neoclassical economic idea that government can help perfect the institutions of the market, while leaving individual freedom to choose undisturbed. The key proposal is to adjust the choice architecture in order to nudge people towards making pro-environmental choices 'voluntarily'. The nudging approach has been adopted as a policy tool in countries where neoliberal politics was pioneered and has become most dominant, such as Australia, Canada, the United Kingdom and the USA.

Although psychologically based approaches to sustainable consumption have gained much popularity, they rely on a narrow understanding of human behaviour. The approach ultimately individualises responsibility as an act of finding 'solutions' to 'problems'. The complexity of institutions and social issues surrounding consumption is removed and human volition may be trivialised as a simple choice between corporate products. Sustainable consumption then means that individualised everyday actions and decisions—such as buying organic, eating less meat or composting waste—are meant to be positioned in relation to their role in causing, or alleviating, environmental problems as evaluated in terms of individual costs and benefits. The burden of social ecological transformation is placed on the individual who, as sovereign consumer, is solely accountable for achieving sustainability.

What this consumer choice model fails to recognise is that humans are neither perfect calculating machines maximising their own utility, nor are they best converted into such machines, via nudging or otherwise. People are fallible and struggle with everyday choices including what they should, or should not, buy. They face value conflicts that confront them with incommensurable options [see Chapter 22]. Changing embedded and group reinforced norms of purchasing is a far cry from a simple cost-benefit exercise for the achievement of efficient personal welfare gains. Indeed, consumption patterns are not explained by 'preferences' because preferring something offers no explanation of why (Spash, 2008). A deeper explanation requires understanding consumption as a conglomerate of acts embedded in social and cultural practices that are constitutive of personal identity.

Theories of social practice

In the journal *Ecological Economics*, Røpke (1999) provides an introduction to a social psychological perspective that explains consumption as interwoven with perceptions of living well. In effect, she argues that individuals are willing participants in the game of consumption because it meets several social and cultural functions and is necessary for participation in modern consumer society. This involves a complex of causal mechanisms ranging from the social technological (e.g. having the latest gadgets) to the way in which family life is conceptualised. The meaning of consumption then involves conflict between identity as defined in modernity and its negative environmental, social and economic consequences [see Chapter 15]. Røpke (2009) has advocated theories of social practice as the potential route by which ecological economists could improve their understanding of consumption.

In sociology, theories of practice offer an alternative to the individualistic perspective on consumption. Such theories regard the structure of social systems as both constraining and enabling agency, and as both the medium and outcome of the practices it recursively organises. In his theory of 'structuration', Giddens (1984) describes the domain of study for social sciences as being social practices ordered across space and time. Theories of social practice focus on the daily "doings and sayings" in which people are engaged (Welch and Warde, 2015), rather than on individual choices, consumption decisions or behaviours (Reckwitz, 2002; Røpke, 2009). Attention is redirected, away from individual decision-making and treating people as consumers, towards regarding them as 'practice carriers'. As Welch and Warde (2015: 85) state:

> Practice theories' central claim is to move beyond problematic dualisms like structure and agency, methodological individualism and holism, determinism and voluntarism, and subject and object.

The laudable aim is to use aspects of both sides of these dualisms to create a different understanding, although the extent to which practice theories have fulfilled this promise is questionable. As also noted by Welch and Warde (2015: 97): "Practice theories at present lack persuasive theoretical or conceptual answers."

Indeed, there is no single, coherent social practice theory, but rather a range of different theories unified by the focus on social practices as the unit of analysis. Also, there is no agreement as to how to delimit a social practice. Social practices are regarded as comprising a set of specific elements. For example, Reckwitz (2002: 249) talks about "forms of bodily and mental activities, things and their use, background knowledge in the form of understanding, know-how and notions of competence, states of emotion and motivational knowledge". Shove et al. (2012: 24) offer a simpler framework where social practices consist of "active integrations of material, competence, and meaning". They argue that the source of changing behaviour lies in the development of practices—how they emerge, persist and disappear. They integrate theories of social practice with innovation studies to address the active and interactive relationship between consumers and producers. Such accounts discuss the mechanisms underlying changing practices and outline how specific practices emerge (e.g. a daily shower) and disappear (e.g. a weekly bath). Other scholars have integrated social practice theory with transition studies (Rauschmayer et al., 2015). Spaargaren (2011), for example, employs social practices as connecting elements between individual lifestyles and social technical systems of provisioning. Environmental applications of social practice theories to sustainable consumption include: food waste, heating, fair trade and energy use. The vast majority of studies focus on domestic (and thus primarily inconspicuous) consumption practices of everyday life, rather than shopping. The emphasis is on mundane subconscious practices (e.g. showering) that are often habitual.

Groves et al. (2016) argue for a better grounding in psychology. They dismiss theories of practice that employ simplistic formulations of individual psychology, e.g. individuals defecting from or engaging in practices on the basis of internal rewards from doing so. They demonstrate how participation in particular practices is not simply about instrumental outcomes. They reject regarding practices as third-person explanatory variables and instead explain how practices matter to subjects. They emphasise that the relationships humans form during their lifetimes create associations that are constitutive of their identity. Through a set of examples, Groves et al. (2016) go on to explain how unsustainable practices are maintained because of a person's psychosocial biography. Attachment is described as helping individuals live with vulnerability and uncertainty, but this also means that removing practices can break attachments and (re) create vulnerability. Agents are formed in part by their approaches to handling attachment and this shapes their perspectives on what is desirable and rational. The implications for social ecological transformation are that any policy intervention will involve changing practices that are part of a person's identity, and successful intervention will need to recognise the complexity of why people are attached to manifestly unsustainable practices (Spash, 2016). As Earl (2016) notes, people create complementarities in their construction of lifestyles based on sets of organising principles (e.g. coherence, order, consistency) that lead them to actualise their conceptualisations of self and self-worth.

Structure, corporations and market institutions

What the social and psychological literatures around consumerism have revealed over recent decades is how people themselves buy into consumerism and unsustainable practices. In part this is the great success of marketing departments and their expert psychologists who have targeted self-image, identity formation, in-group selection and childhood development (Bakan, 2011). Yet, the desire to recognise a richer social psychological understanding of why humans opt into the consumer society has led to an almost wilful neglect of structural factors.

For example, the appeal of 'nudging' for the neoclassical economists, neoliberals and classic liberals is that coercion is supposedly avoided in the attempt to get people to do what is wanted. The fear that coercion might take place is directed at government intervention, although 'nudging' is in fact most prevalent in society today due to corporate advertising, marketing and product placement. Corporate nudging of people is pervasive and occurs through social media, creating norms of computer and mobile phone use, changing language to corporate speak (e.g. through branding), subliminal placement of products in films and on television, and so on (Spash, 2016).

The idea that there is more to consumption than individual choice, or freely adopted social practices, goes back a long way (Spash, 2009). For example, Devas (2009 [1899]) notes that the competitive industrial system can create "misdirected consumption"—supply of inferior goods—due to the profit motive. The consumer is not sovereign because they lack both information and power. Production needs regulation by the State to ensure quality, but a deeper issue concerns manipulation of wants to encourage turnover, e.g. fashion. Economics must then combine the technical and moral if the aim is to explain how to supply what achieves good ends for society. As Devas remarks, "so little it avails to speak of the satisfaction of wants unless we can distinguish those that are leading us to destruction, and unless we know what is the true good of man" (2009 [1899]: 272).

Here he is referring to a lengthier treatise by his contemporary Mackenzie. The relevant passage in Mackenzie explains the concern further as follows:

> If our wants themselves should happen to be leading us to destruction, the means of satisfying them will hardly in fairness be regarded as wealth. Such objects would be more correctly styled, in the language of Mr. Ruskin, 'illth'. We must distinguish, in

fact, between what we really want and what we only think we want, before a true conception of what we mean by wealth can be attained.

(Mackenzie, 1895: 347)

Ruskin (1907 [1862]: 88–89) in turn explains wealth as combining both possession of the valuable and the character of the possessor. This means:

> that many of the persons commonly considered wealthy, are in reality no more wealthy than the locks of their own strong boxes are; they being inherently and eternally incapable of wealth; and operating for the nation [...] as mere accidental stays and impediments, acting not as wealth, but (for we ought to have a correspondent term) as 'illth', causing various devastation and trouble around them in all directions.

Today, the economy might well be regarded as creating an illusion of wealth by operating an economic system that aims to create possessions without regard to individual character or the self-destructive aspects of want satisfaction. Devas (2009 [1899]) explains "depraved consumption" as resulting from the encouragement of excessive and unnecessary debt via credit systems, popular mass media (then music halls) appealing to the lowest common denominator, the profit motive encouraging gambling and drug abuse (e.g. alcohol, opium). To these, luxury and extravagance might be added in line with Veblen's (1991 [1899]) conspicuous consumption.

Hirsch (1977) explains the importance of asking and answering the "what for?" question, with respect to consumption, in order to be able to understand whether it contributes to well-being. In modern economics, the term 'growth' has replaced the earlier concern for 'wealth' as the determinant of economic success. As production and consumption become more complex so the range of "intermediate" goods and services increases, and although these may add nothing to overall well-being they are added to measures of successful growth. In a world of increasing environmental degradation, expenditures to protect oneself and family from harmful consequences are not a sign of progress, and neither are such "defensive expenditures" by governments. Similarly, spending to protect one's social position—conspicuous consumption, fashion, keeping up with neighbours—adds to the waste of the competitive market economy and not to well-being.

In line with these arguments, Kapp (1978) combines institutional, ethical, social and psychological factors in his analysis of consumerism. On the supply side Kapp, like Galbraith (1969 [1958]), recognises the oligopolistic power of suppliers that enables them to place their own concerns above those of the State. This goes well beyond merely pushing products on consumers. Kapp (1978) cites firms in the USA respecting contracts with German firms during World War II, and others have documented corporate involvement in supporting the Nazi regime and operationalising the holocaust to make profits (see Bakan, 2004; Black, 2001).

Galbraith (1969 [1958]) has a structured institutional theory describing how powerful firms operate outside of the market's regulatory controls—competition, profit motive, shareholder control—that are typically cited by economists as restrictions on firms' activities. The large corporations create a power elite of professional managers that Galbraith terms the technostructure. He refers to such corporations as operating a "planning system"; a term which many relate to government, not the corporate world, but actually reflects how corporations are internally organised. The technostructure allies itself with government to create a mutually supporting system of political economy, embedded in the rhetoric of free market economics while actually being a totally different beast.

The myth of consumer sovereignty plays an important role in avoiding a realistic economic analysis of the firm and regulation of corporate activities. The ultimate effect of advertising is to provide sustained propaganda on the importance of goods while no similar case is made on behalf of artistic, educational, or other humane achievement (Galbraith, 1970: 476). Promotion of consumer 'wants' by producers works in an affluent society because consumer goods in such a society are not necessities, but frivolous pleasures to be thrown away whenever fashions change. Power in the market then easily extends to pushing products to encourage mass consumption and throughput.

Mishan (1969) adds to the critique of consumer sovereignty by raising the lack of choice an individual has over their work. He also argues that perceived wants are socially and culturally constructed, and can easily be changed through legislation given the political will to do so. Later in life, Galbraith actually thought regulation was effectively controlling the corporation. Like others of his generation he failed to recognise the power of neoliberalism and the extent to which regulatory capture has persisted and spread. Indeed, the myth of the sovereign consumer has re-emerged with the rise of neoliberalism which has allied with neoclassical economics to perpetuate the deception (Fellner and Spash, 2015).

Future directions

While (un)sustainable consumption scholars commonly agree that individual consumption patterns are embedded in social, cultural and material contexts, and widely acknowledge the importance of adhering to the structural dynamics of consumption, studies still widely employ the simple frame of the individual. Maniates (2014) argues that consumption research is often trapped in an analytic framework that overemphasises the individual, because this is the main unit of analysis within the field's dominant disciplines (i.e. economics, psychology, business studies). He also notes the prevalence of the concept of consumers' sovereignty in traditional policy approaches as a contributing factor.

This methodological affinity for the individual might also explain why issues of power [see chapter 14] have so far scarcely been addressed in sustainable consumption debates. Addressing power is essential for understanding how institutions (i.e. conventions, norms, rules) reinforce practices of unsustainable consumption and how such practices evolve and can be changed. Such an investigation should encompass the power exhibited by governments, corporations and the modern marketing machine, as well as socio-cultural institutions, and span ecological, ethical and social aspects of consumption. Future research needs to connect the historical literature on consumption with the modern to rectify the overemphasis on agency to the detriment of understating the institutions that structure our society.

A better understanding of the determinants of (un)sustainable consumption practices would be provided by an analytical (dialectical) dualism connecting social agents and society (duality of structure and praxis, see [Chapter 2]). This means that the specific set of institutional arrangements within which humans operate, and try to find meaning in their lives, become even more important, both as empowering and constraining. The institutional domination of human society by markets and materialism creates a dynamic that promotes a limited range of means, or satisfiers, by which a select set of humans' social and psychological needs are met [see Chapter 24], but wherein agents are empowered in and through their consumer practices. The affluent society creates and promotes a very specific and narrow set of human values that are to be achieved through product purchase and accumulation. Research in social ecological transformation must identify how environmentally and socially just alternative satisfiers can be institutionalised.

Concluding remarks

A basic ontological premise of ecological economics is that biophysical reality imposes limits on human action. Social ecological economics extends the analysis to the social reality of how economies are structured and the institutions they employ. In studying consumer behaviour, this complex interrelationship between the individual consumer and biophysical and social realities becomes central. This requires looking beyond individual dimensions of consumption and addressing its social and material contexts. Individual choices and behaviours are interwoven in the respective social domains that implicitly and explicitly determine the dynamic and rationale of everyday life.

Societal transformation to sustainable consumption means implementing policies that deliberately aim at shaping consumption, and in the restrictive model of mainstream economists that can only mean shaping people's preferences. In the standard behavioural model there is no option but to change what motivates choice, i.e. attitudes, norms. Yet, creating formal and informal institutions to achieve these ends conflicts with a model where preferences are assumed fixed *a priori* and sacrosanct. There is then an inevitable tension between the idea that individuals have freedom to do as they please and the recognition that, as social animals, humans create institutions that impose constraints on such freedom in order to achieve communal goals and coordinated action (Spash, 2016).

Thus, the ongoing debate in the social sciences over whether human agency or social structure is more salient in determining human behaviour is also reflected in the discourse on (un)sustainable consumption and its alternative (disciplinary) perspectives on the causal mechanisms determining the decisions of consumers. Sustainable consumption research and policy requires a synthesis and integration of economic, psychological and sociological accounts. Measures to foster sustainable consumption have to acknowledge that, despite good intentions and pro-environmental attitudes, consumers are often locked in to habits, social norms and prevalent technologies. Hence, a purely individualistic approach is insufficient and ignores the simple truth that individual behaviours are embedded in social and institutional contexts and hence bound to larger institutional dynamics of consumption and production. Targeting the individual consumer as responsible for the economic system contradicts the notion that a social ecological transformation of the current consumption system demands collective action. Put bluntly, an individualistic approach simply fails to reflect social reality as comprising interconnected networks of social relations that form personal identity. Hence, there is no way to nudge our way out of a systemically induced environmental crisis. A new synthesis is required that brings together the institutional analysis of the dominant role played by the modern corporation and the marketing machine in consumption dynamics; the State as regulator, innovator and facilitator of institutional arrangements; an understanding of the social psychological formation of personal identity; the role of needs and their satisfaction relative to wants; and the ethical basis for judging what is of value. Ultimately, consumption must be put in the context of the reproduction of society.

Key further readings cited

Fellner, W. and Spash, C.L. (2015). The Role of Consumer Sovereignty in Sustaining the Market Economy. In: Reisch, L.A. and Thørgersen, J. (eds.). *Handbook of Research on Sustainable Consumption* (pp. 394–409) Cheltenham: Edward Elgar.

Maniates, M. (2014). Sustainable consumption: Three Paradoxes. *GAIA*, 23(1), 201–208.

Røpke, I. (1999). The dynamics of willingness to consume. *Ecological Economics*, 28(3), 399–420.

Røpke, I. (2009). Theories of practice: New inspiration for ecological economic studies on consumption. *Ecological Economics*, 68(10), 2490–2497.

Welch, D. and Warde, A. (2015). Theories of practice and sustainable consumption. In: Reisch, L.A. and Thørgersen, J. (eds.). *Handbook of Research on Sustainable Consumption* (pp. 84–100) Cheltenham: Edward Elgar.

Other literature cited

Bakan, J. (2004). *The Corporation: The Pathological Pursuit of Profit and Power*. New York: Free Press, Simon & Schuster Inc.

Bakan, J. (2011). *Childhood Under Siege: How Big Business Ruthlessly Targets Children*. London: The Bodley Head.

Black, E. (2001). *IBM and the Holocaust: The Strategic Alliance Between Nazi Germany and America's Most Powerful Corporation*. New York: Crown Publishers.

Devas, C.S. (2009 [1899]). The moral aspect of consumption. In: Spash, C.L. (ed). *Ecological Economics: Critical Concepts in the Environment, 4 Volumes*. London: Routledge, 265–274.

Earl, P.E. (2005). Economics and psychology in the twenty-first century. *Cambridge Journal of Economics*, 29(6): 909–926.

Earl, P.E. (2016). Lifestyle changes and the lifestyle selection process. *Journal of Bioeconomics* Forthcoming: 1–18.

Easterlin, R.A. (2003). Explaining happiness. *PNAS*, 100 (19): 11176–11183.

Galbraith, J.K. (1969 [1958]). *The Affluent Society*. Boston: Houghton Mifflin.

Galbraith, J.K. (1970). Economics as a system of belief. *The American Economic Review*, 60 (2): 469–478.

Giddens, A. (1984). *The Constitution of Society: Outline of the Theory of Structuration*. Cambridge: Polity Press.

Groves, C., Henwood, K., Shirani, F., Butler, C., Parkhill, K. and Pidgeon, N. (2016). Invested in unsustainability? On the psychosocial patterning of engagement in practices. *Environmental Values*, 25 (3): 309–328.

Hirsch, F. (1977). *Social Limits to Growth*. London: Routledge and Kegan Paul Ltd.

Kapp, K.W. (1978). The Social Costs of Cutthroat Competition, Planned Obsolesence and Sales Promotion. In: Kapp, K.W. (ed.). *The Social Costs of Business Enterprise, 3rd edition*. Nottingham: Spokesman, 224–247.

Mackenzie, J.S. (1895). *Introduction to Social Philosophy*. Glasgow: James Maclehose and Sons.

Mishan, E.J. (1969). The Myth of Consumers' Sovereignty. In: Mishan, E. J. (ed.). *Growth: The Price We Pay*. London: Staples Press, 89–96.

Polimeni, J.M., Mayumi, K.T., Giampietro, M. and Alcott, B. (2008). *The Jevons Paradox and the Myth of Resource Efficiency Improvements*. London: Earthscan.

Rauschmayer, F., Bauler, T. and Schäpke, N. (2015). Towards a thick understanding of sustainability transitions: Linking transition management, capabilities and social practices. *Ecological Economics*, 109 (0): 211–221.

Reckwitz, A. (2002). Toward a Theory of Social Practices: A Development in Culturalist Theorizing. *European Journal of Social Theory*, 5(2): 243–263.

Ruskin, J. (1907 [1862]). 'Unto This Last': Four Essays on the First Principles of Political Economy. London: George Routledge & Sons Limited.

Shove, E. (2004). Changing human behaviour and lifestyle: A challenge for sustainable consumption? In: Reisch, L. and Ropke, I. (eds.). *The Ecological Economics of Consumption*. Cheltenham: Edward Elgar, 111–131.

Shove, E., Pantzar, M. and Watson, M. (2012). *The Dynamics of Social Practice. Everyday Life and How It Changes*. London: Sage.

Southerton, D., McMeekin, A. and Evans, D. (2011). International Review of Behaviour Change Initiatives: Climate Change Behaviours Research Programme. Social Research. Edinburgh: Scottish Government Social Research, 41.

Spaargaren, G. (2011). Theories of practice: Agency, technology, and culture. *Global Environmental Change*, 21: 813–822.

Spash, C.L. (2008). How much is that ecosystem in the window? The one with the bio-diverse trail. *Environmental Values*, 17 (2): 259–284.

Spash, C.L. (2009). Sustaining Well-being: Introduction. In: Spash, C.L. (ed). *Ecological Economics: Critical Concepts in the Environment, 4 Volumes*. London: Routledge, 1–8.

Spash, C.L. (2016). Social ecological transformation. *Environmental Values*, 25 (3): 253–258.

Thaler, R.H. and Sunstein, C.R. (2009). *Nudge: Improving Decision About health, wealth and happiness.* London, England: Penguin

Veblen, T. (1991 [1899]). *The Theory of the Leisure Class.* Fairfield, New Jersey: Augustus M Kelley.

Vermeir, I. and Verbeke, W. (2008). Sustainable food consumption among young adults in Belgium: Theory of planned behaviour and the role of confidence and values. *Ecological Economics*, 64(3), 542–553.

21

WORK AND LEISURE

Money, identity and playfulness

Wolfgang J. Fellner

Introduction

The discipline of economics is commonly subdivided along two lines: (i) production and consumption with a commodity focus; (ii) micro and macro economics depending upon whether the focus is households and firms or the economy as a whole. The concept of the labour market seems to resist these divisions. It can be thought of as the bridge between production and consumption, representing both, labour as a factor of production and leisure as the realm of consumption. Whether labour market outcomes are determined at the micro or macro economic level is one of the most heavily contested issues in economics since the Keynesian [Chapter 7] revolution in the 1940s. Thinking of these two lines of division as a two-dimensional space, the idea of the labour market can be located at, and thought of as, the very centre of the discipline. Reviewing the labour market model more closely reveals important features and shortcomings of economic theory, which allow us to sketch a new way of conceptualising paid work and other spheres of life in line with contemporary psychological models of human motivation.

A key feature of how economics conceptualises human activity is the splitting of life into two opposing uses of time: work and leisure. People are assumed to select the combination of work hours and leisure that maximise their level of satisfaction or utility. This entails an entirely instrumental conceptualisation of work that rules out other benefits derived from work and motives to work.

This chapter explains and examines features of this model and identifies (non-instrumental) benefits of paid work that it ignores. Problems resulting from these omissions are illustrated. I then explain the necessity for future conceptual and empirical research as well as political activity, before drawing concluding remarks.

The orthodox model and its critics

The labour market model in a nutshell

Economists tend to describe the world in terms of markets. Although Gary Becker's notion of a market for marriages has created some resistance, even among economists, the concept of a labour market seems to be perfectly legitimate and uncontested, at least at first sight. An essential analytical element involved in the model can be traced back to Jevons. His major contribution to orthodox neoclassical economics is the 'disutility theory of labour'. Jevons argues that labour has a positive value on account of its irksomeness. Labour will be provided by workers as long as the marginal utility from income equals the marginal disutility of effort. The incentive for paid work is entirely attributed to its ability to buy commodities. Higher wages are consequently supposed to increase the incentive for workers to supply labour.

One might wonder why economists adopted this utterly negative and instrumental notion of work. Neoclassical economics has a strong analytical focus on markets that makes prices (i.e. for labour wages) the major phenomena to be explained. Consequently, economists must specify supply and demand functions. Where there are several determining factors for labour supply that act in opposite directions, pretending there exists a relatively stable upward sloping labour supply curve is impossible, without several auxiliary assumptions.[1] Another reason for this reductionist view of work lies in the concept of 'consumer sovereignty' that assumes producers always act in the interests of consumers (see critique by Fellner and Spash, 2015; and also [Chapter 20]). This implies that people acting in their role as producers or workers do not have any interests or preferences for what to do or how to do it. Work is entirely equated to the amount of money it pays. Put differently, an individual's identity is encapsulated entirely in what they buy and not what work they do. Consumer sovereignty is associated with a fragmentation of life into opposite spheres. As consumers people are described as a bundle of interests, or preferences, and as producers or workers they become (human) capital with a rate of return.

The upward sloping supply curve in combination with a technically determined downward sloping demand curve allows the creation of an unambiguous market clearing wage rate. From a macroeconomic perspective, the labour market model explains the level of (un)employment and the level of wages. From a microeconomic perspective it explains the allocation of peoples' time. The labour supply decision of individual workers is described as the choice between work and leisure. Whereas work yields disutility, leisure is assumed to be an unlimited source of utility or pleasure. The resulting optimisation problem of workers is to choose the utility maximising amount of products and leisure at a given wage rate.

Criticisms

Keynes and Post-Keynesian economists [Chapter 7] have rejected the idea that the labour market can be described in analogy to markets for commodities. They assume that wages and working conditions are predominantly determined by social customs and norms rather than the conditions of demand and supply. Consequently, supply for labour will show a very weak correlation with wages, and demand for labour will depend on aggregate commodity demand or expected future sales. This undermines the smooth operation of the price mechanism with respect to the allocation of labour in the economy. The orthodox microeconomic model of the labour market then becomes a socially and politically dangerous illusion that may cause involuntary unemployment due to a lack of demand.

Critical institutional economists [Chapter 3] have also raised doubts about labour market theory. Rosenbaum (2000) analyses this theory based on four criteria: (i) voluntary, (ii) specificity, (ii) regularity and typification, and (iv) competition. He states that:

> to claim, as Gary Becker does, that a market for marriages exists, obscures the fact that marriages are largely unspecified exchanges and hence violate the condition of specificity. […] There are also reasons to suggest that labour markets fulfil only in part

the criteria for markets which I have developed above. While competition, regularity and typification would seem common features of many segments of the labour "market" both voluntarity and specificity are more problematic.

(Rosenbaum, 2000: 479)

Lack of voluntarity occurs when other available ways to ensure a decent level of subsistence are absent. Labour contracts are relational contracts. Where they are long-term relationships specifying *ex ante* all rights and duties in the contract is impossible [see also theory of the firm in Chapter 19], which undermines specificity. Rosenbaum concludes that methods of analysis which presuppose specificity in order to explain prices and quantities are inapplicable.

Karl Polanyi's (1957) criticism of labour, land and capital as fictitious commodities is by far the most fundamental. He explains how industrialisation and commercialisation combined to achieve commodification.

> The extension of the market mechanism to the elements of industry—labour, land, and money—was the inevitable consequence of the introduction of the factory system in a commercial society. The elements of industry had to be on sale. [...] labour, land, and money had to be transformed into commodities in order to keep production going. They could, of course, not be really transformed into commodities, as actually they were not produced for sale on the market. But the fiction of their being so produced became the organizing principle of society. Of the three, one stands out: labour is the technical term used for human beings, insofar as they are not employers but employed; it follows that henceforth the organization of labour would change concurrently with the organization of the market system. But as the organization of labour is only another word for the forms of life of the common people, this means that the development of the market system would be accompanied by a change in the organization of society itself. All along the line, human society had become an accessory of the economic system.
>
> *(Polanyi, 1957: 78–79).*

Despite his insightful analysis of social and ecological decay, Polanyi provides very little instruction on how to avoid commodification of labour. Phrases like "labour is the technical term used for human beings", or "labour is only another word for the forms of life", have to be clarified in order to get a grip on how to reshape society in favour of human beings and life in general.

Specific features of the labour market model

The absence of power

The absence of power [Chapter 14] in economic models is a major criticism of orthodox economics by critical institutional economists [Chapter 3] (e.g. Galbraith, 1970). Rational choice theory assumes away power exercised by all kinds of social relations, institutions or organisations. According to individual preferences, workers are assumed to freely choose their working hours..

A vast amount of empirical literature about the mismatch of actual and preferred working hours, at the current wage rate, shows substantial deviations. Even though the measurement of preferred working hours poses a considerable challenge for empirical research this result is hardly surprising because most jobs are available only on a full-time or half-time basis. Looking at the volume of preferred and current working hours of the working age population in European economies, Bielenski et al. (2002: 21) find that many countries show a higher level of current than preferred working hours. This brings into question growth oriented policies in favour of a redistribution of working time.

Another aspect of power is dealt with in organisational theory: how to align the interests of firms/employers and employees. In order to conceptually grasp this aspect of power one has to deviate from the orthodox assumptions that labour power is a homogeneous good and people in their role as workers are only interested in the amount of money they earn. If workers have an interest in their work (e.g., what tasks they perform, for whom they work) then quality of work becomes an issue. Good jobs provide workers with such things as interesting tasks, social recognition and respect. If the interests of an employer are not in line with employees' interests (e.g., workers see no point in the tasks they perform or disagree with business practices) power issues arise. In his theory of the firm, Galbraith (1971: 128–39) identifies four relevant motivational forces to reconcile interests: compulsion, pecuniary incentives, identification and adaptation. He also illustrates their changing form and relevance in the course of economic history (Galbraith, 1971: 140–58).

Working to consume

Quality of work is also at the heart of this criticism. Based on Jevons' disutility theory of labour:

> The 'first neoclassical synthesis' was engineered by Alfred Marshall, who brought Bentham into economic theory now with both feet. Demand represented pleasure (utility) and supply represented pain (disutility).
>
> *(Hamilton, 1987: 1537)*

Such a hedonistic approach overemphasises spontaneous feelings, leaves questions about their sources unanswered and replaces them with crude and oversimplifying assumptions.

One of those sources, or neglected aspects, is that paid work is an important part of personal identity. The question 'who am I' is indivisible from all the activities a person engages in and that includes paid work. Imagining everybody as being indifferent about their profession or work life is hardly realistic. A good job can provide humans with a variety of feelings, such as pride in what they do, and social status, such as respect from other people. However, even bad jobs that are devoid of prestige, physically exhausting, demeaning, trivial in nature or mindlessly repetitive provide a badge of identity (Gini, 1998: 709).[2] To grasp this aspect, paid work has to be conceived as a basic requirement of adult life, necessary in order to fulfil ourselves as persons and important for mental health. In a positive sense, paid work has the ability to provide us with a sense of meaning. To do so, interests like moral, political and social attitudes have to be met to at least some extent to avoid deprivation and alienation. A sense of meaning is incommensurable with compensation by money. Even if people are willing to compromise their values for additional income, there are natural limits to this substitution. Otherwise society becomes nothing more than a grouping of ruthlessly greedy and corrupt individuals.

Work is also very important for 'who I become'. Gini (1998: 707) argues that "the business of work is not simply to produce goods, but also to help produce people". At the individual level, this argument renders the decision, what to do for a living, of paramount importance for personal development. A good job allows a person to exercise realised capacities and to extend faculties. John Rawls calls this aspect 'the Aristotelian principle' (Sayer, 2009: 5). It acknowledges curiosity as an innate non-instrumental driver of human activity and renders skilled, varied and complex activities superior to simple, repetitive ones because they provide the means to realise curiosity and competence. Competence and the ability to use talents and abilities also feature very prominently in Schumacher's conception of good work (Gini, 1998: 709). At the social level, the quality of available jobs becomes a key indicator for future mental and physical faculties in society. In a similar vein the Aristotelian conception of work emphasises the importance of quality of work for well-being and *eudaimonia*, because work shapes the worker's self-development and character (Sayer, 2009: 4–5).

Besides a sense of meaning various authors have emphasised a sense of belonging as an important aspect of identity and good work. Ideally, people have a sense of belonging at all levels: to others they work with, to the organisation they work for and to society as a whole. While a sense of belonging and community might vary in strength at different levels, spending a substantial part of a lifetime in an environment where there is no sense of belonging at any level would appear inhumane. According to Schumacher work provides us with an opportunity to overcome our natural egocentricity by working in conjunction with others (Gini, 1998: 709). Sympathy for the goals of an organisation allows an employee to perceive their own work as part of a bigger project that goes beyond individual capacities. Paid work provides a chance to experience oneself and be recognised as a valuable member of society. Based on the high relevance of paid work for peoples' identity Paul Gomberg put forward the concept of contributive justice, that stresses what people are expected and able to contribute to society in terms of work (Sayer, 2009). Providing people with the ability to contribute to society in ways that incorporate a sense of meaning and belonging fulfils an important social goal.

A sense of meaning and belonging as non-instrumental, irreducible and existential benefits of paid work has severe consequences for economic theory. They call into question one of the most important causal relationships in orthodox economics: the idea that people decide about the amount of hours they work depending on the desired level of consumption. Non-instrumental benefits render paid work as an end in itself and raise issues about the role of wage rates for the allocation of labour and the balance of power between employers and employees. Schor (1991) argues that a power asymmetry in the labour market, where employers have the dominant say over work hours, means that increases in wages are favoured over reductions in working hours. The mechanism behind this "work-and-spend cycle" causes productivity gains to be channelled into rising incomes and production, but fails to generate lasting improvements in well-being and plays a major role in ecological degradation (Schor, 1991). Consequently, workers in affluent societies (particularly in the USA) remain trapped in a pattern of long working hours and increasing levels of consumption.

This argument is similar to Galbraith's explanation of large business corporations under his term the "revised sequence" (Galbraith, 1971: 213-220). Whereas the "accepted sequence" claims that the economic process is entirely driven by interests of people in their role as consumers (i.e. consumer sovereignty), the revised sequence assumes that producers' interests predominate.[3] The potential conflict of interests resulting from the dominance of producer interests in economic relations and change is mitigated or disguised via subversive persuasion and advertising. Galbraith argues that in affluent societies commodities are largely designed and directed to satisfy psychological needs, which are, contrary to physical needs, limitless and subject to persuasion (Galbraith, 1998). Looking at the economy through this lens deconstructs the predominant orthodox economic narrative where unlimited economic growth appears as the path of economic development which is supposed to be in everyone's best interest. In reality, growth in affluent societies sustains an established monetary system of production and income distribution in the interest of the modern corporation and the financial sector at the expense of people and the environment. According to Schor (1991), a successful path to ecological sustainability and mental and physical health of workers will entail a stabilisation of consumption through taking productivity increases as reductions in hours of work. Ecological economists have recently shown increasing interest in this topic. Several authors have contributed to literature in favour of reductions in working hours, e.g. Buhl and Acosta (2015), Kallis et al. (2013) and Zwickl et al. (2015).

The concept of leisure

Whereas work is associated with irksomeness, discomfort or pain, leisure is described as a state of idleness, inactivity and pleasure derived from it. Yet, what is the substance of this notion of leisure? A typical image of leisure might be of someone lying on the beach in some exotic location with a glass of wine in their hand. Clearly such a characterisation of leisure fails to meet the reality of everyday non-work experience. The emptiness of the concept results from the lack of interest in something that falls outside the explanatory power of the orthodox economic model of markets and prices.

Household economics has introduced a third category of time use or sphere of life: home production, e.g. Gronau (1977). This additional category acknowledges the vast amount of time dedicated to subsistence activities in the household. It raises the question: under which 'non-work' time-use category (i.e. leisure or home production) should activities be placed? For example, raising children or taking care of family members are usually attributed to home production.[4] The underlying dichotomy of painful production and pleasurable consumption, which is at the root of the emptiness of the concept of leisure, is maintained in household economics. This dichotomy relies on the highly problematic assumption that humans are idle and passive by nature. In radical opposition to this proposition, critical institutional economics conceives of people as curious and active by nature.

> Life is an on-going active process with nothing that can be substantively distinguished as a consummatory end from a productive means. Means and ends are such only in a temporal sequence. Life is an active continuum.
>
> *(Hamilton, 1987: 1540)*

This approach transcends the work–leisure distinction and emphasises doing rather than having in line with the Aristotelian *eudaimonia* (Sayer, 2009: 4). While states of exhaustion and the need for recreation clearly exist, the point here is to stress the intrinsic human capacity and motivation to be active as part of peoples' life force.

Similarly, Adina Schwartz has argued that adults need to work, in the same way that children need to play, in order to fulfil themselves as persons (Gini, 1998: 709). Of course, the intrinsic capacity to be active might get lost, for example through traumatic experiences or in the process of socialisation. One of the problems resulting from the misconception of human nature as passive and idle is that it may render economic incentive structures favourable which foster exhaustion, overwork or even burnout. This has to do with the omission of another important non-instrumental aspect of paid work and all other spheres of life: playfulness.

By playfulness I mean a state of authenticity that is free from fear and enables one to live fully in the present. This state is characterised by feelings of curiosity and expansion. Achievements resulting from an activity become a by-product of the activity or the process itself. Physical, emotional and mental growth are by-products of intrinsic impulses to engage in play. Writing this chapter requires effort, but it also entails episodes dominated by playfulness which are not just free from irksomeness but empowering and nourishing. Every university teacher knows the difference between students for whom the degree is a by-product of their curiosity and interest in the subject, and those for whom the primary concern is a certificate called a degree. I suspect that well-being in countries and cultures dominated by a strong focus on achievement would benefit greatly from facilitating playfulness.

Dismissing the dichotomous work and leisure categorisation of time use raises the question: Are there useful ways to categorise time use differently in economics? Unfortunately there is little literature about this issue. Empirical time use research is usually based on comprehensive lists of activities, ranging from several hundred activities to condensed lists with around 30 activities, e.g., the Harmonised European Time Use Survey (HETUS) guidelines. Fischer-Kowalski et al. (2010) aggregated HETUS activities to reflect four subsystems of the social system: the personal system, the household system, the economy system and the community system.

> The advantage of this systemic rather than individualistic perspective on time use should be to draw attention to the specific possibilities and constraints a community has in its interaction both with its natural environment, and for its members among one another.
>
> *(Fischer-Kowalski et al., 2010: 7)*

From a social reformist perspective, Frigga Haug suggests distinguishing four areas of human activity that should get equal representation in peoples' life: paid work, care, culture, politics (Haug, 2008). Without going into details, such time use oriented approaches clearly provide a new lens for discussing social relations and priorities, responsibilities, and justice.

Future directions

This section briefly suggests what can and should be done in order to overcome the previously described challenges. It is subdivided into three areas: conceptual research, empirical research and political activity.

Conceptual research

Previous sections have shown that economics is in need of a new way of conceptualising time use. Research about paid work must not ignore non-instrumental benefits. Rational choice theory and utility theory have been identified as barriers to such a research agenda that overcomes the work–leisure dichotomy (Fellner and Seidl, 2015). Similarly, people are misconceptualised as merely consumers and producers (i.e. workers). They are social and political beings, who desire more than income and look for the non-instrumental benefits of meaning, belonging and playfulness in paid work and other spheres of life.

A multi-dimensional concept of incentives and benefits entails substantive reconceptualisation of behaviour, well-being and development. The relationship between well-being, or a good life, and development has been on the agenda of critical social science such as the work of Skidelsky and Skidelsky (2012) and Novy (2015). This has also appeared in critical welfare economics including the writings of Sen and the Stiglitz-Sen-Fitoussi, Commission on the Measurement of Economic Performance and Social Progress. In order to release their potential, such critical approaches to have to change economic methodology and the overall direction of economic research, something that has not been on the critical welfare economists' agenda.

Empirical research

The existence of hours mismatch (i.e. deviations between current and preferred working hours) provides strong evidence for power issues between employers and employees, e.g., Otterbach (2010). The high variance in data about hours mismatch indicates the need for methodological progress in measuring preferred working hours. Besides this, empirical research should provide suggestions for means as to how to reduce employers' power over working hours and the excessive consumption it creates.

Another interesting area for empirical research is to analyse the potential effects of an unconditional basic income in terms of instrumental and non-instrumental benefits. How would an unconditional basic income affect the allocation of time? Which spheres of life would be extended and reduced?

Besides research on the amount of working hours and their distribution, further research is also necessary on the quality of paid work and how to increase or redistribute it more equally. Sayer (2009: 2) poses the criticism that:

> as long as the more satisfying kinds of work are concentrated into a subset of jobs, rather than shared out among all jobs, then many workers will be denied the chance to have meaningful work and the recognition that goes with it.

Political activity

In accordance with a scientific debate about how to reduce/redistribute working hours and increase/redistribute quality of work, there is the need for political support for measures and the creation of institutions allowing people to reap non-instrumental benefits from work and other spheres of life. This requires engaging in and supporting discourse about social and environmental values and supportive time use structures.

Concluding remarks

As a cornerstone of economic theory, the labour market model illustrates central aspects of why orthodox economics fails. Heterodox economics has raised various critiques of this theory. A central proposition is then to conceive of paid work, and other spheres of life or activity categories, in terms of their composition as instrumental and non-instrumental benefits. Three essential non-instrumental benefits have been identified in this chapter: a sense of meaning, a sense of belonging (together they can be thought of as identity) and playfulness. Together with the instrumental benefit, earning income, they form four potential benefits. This formulation allows researchers to overcome the work–leisure dichotomy, and the reductionist concept of paid work as well as the empty notion of leisure contained in it. It also renders the production–consumption dichotomy obsolete.

People are conceived as social and political beings in all spheres of life, rather than as schizophrenic will-less, submissive workers exclusively interested in earning income and becoming sovereigns though consumption. This raises a comprehensive new research agenda, dealing with redistribution/reduction of working time to tackle unemployment, hours mismatch and to reduce ecological impacts of excessive consumption. In addition, there is the question of how to increase quality of work in terms of non-instrumental benefits. The findings suggest new concepts of well-being and a revised form of understanding work in social ecological economic development.

Notes

1 The notions of work and paid work are used interchangeably in this chapter. Even though work comprises many more activities than paid work (e.g. housework) the strict focus of orthodox economics on prices, implies that work, in orthodox economic terminology, typically gets reduced to paid work.
2 Editor's Note: This is exemplified by coal miners in the UK who built a strong sense of personal and community identity around a job that was physically demanding and led many to an early grave. The destruction of their industry under Thatcherism left many without any sense of meaning. Similarly, there is a high rate of suicide amongst subsistence farmers who lose their livelihoods due to the ongoing 'modernisation' in India and China that replaces unpaid subsistence with wage labour in factories or industrial agriculture.
3 Galbraith does not interpret this as a mere political issue. It largely results from technical requirements of the modern corporation. Securing the production of capital intensive, technologically advanced corporations requires at least some control over prices and quantities.
4 Editor's Note: Ecofeminism has also emphasised the failure of economics to address the role of care giving, and more generally social reproduction because this is 'women's work'. There are then serious issues in the failure of modern economics to address the reality of how the economy operates on the basis of the role played by women, their exploitation by men and the conceptualisation of what constitutes work [See also Chapter 5.]

Key further readings cited

Fellner, W.J., Spash, C.L. (2015). The role of consumer sovereignty in sustaining the market economy, in: Reisch, L.A., Thøgersen, J. (eds.), *Handbook of Research on Sustainable Consumption* (pp. 394–409). Cheltenham: Edward Elgar Publishing.

Gini, A. (1998). Work, identity and self: How we are formed by the work we do. *Journal of Business Ethics* 17, 707–714.

Sayer, A. (2009). Contributive justice and meaningful work. *Res Publica* 15 (1), 1–16.

Other literature cited

Bielenski, H., Bosch, G., Wagner, A. (2002). Working time preferences in sixteen European countries. *European Foundation for the Improvement of Living and Working Conditions*, Ireland, Dublin.

Buhl, J., Acosta, J. (2015). Work less, do less? *Sustainability Science,* 11 (2), 261–276.

Fellner, W.J., Seidl, R.J. (2015). Satiated consumers: Allocation of consumption time in an affluent society. *Metroeconomica* 66, 534–563.

Fischer-Kowalski, M., Singh, S.J., Ringhofer, L., Grünbühel, C.M., Lauk, C., Remesch, A. (2010). Sociometabolic regimes in indigenous communities and the crucial role of working time: A comparison of case studies. *Social Ecology Working Paper*. Institute of Social Ecology, Faculty for Interdisciplinary Studies, Klagenfurt University.

Galbraith, J.K. (1970). Economics as a system of belief. *The American Economic Review* 60 (2), 469–478.

Galbraith, J.K. (1971). *The new industrial state.* Boston: Houghton Mifflin Company.

Galbraith, J.K. (1998). *The affluent society.* Boston, MA: Mariner Books.

Gronau, R. (1977). Leisure, home production, and work: The theory of the allocation of time revisited. *Journal of Political Economy* 85 (6), 1099–1123.

Hamilton, D.B. (1987). Institutional economics and consumption. *Journal of Economic Issues* 21 (4), 1531–1554.

Haug, F. (2008). *Die Vier-in-einem-Perspektive.* Hamburg: Argument-Verlag.

Kallis, G., Kalush, M., O'Flynn, H., Rossiter, J., Ashford, N. (2013). Friday off? Reducing working hours in Europe. *Sustainability* 5 (4), 1545–1567.

Novy, A. (2015). A Good Life for all. A European development model. *Discussion Papers Series, Institute for Multi-Level Governance and Development*, No. 3, http://www-sre.wu.ac.at/sre-disc/sre-disc-2015_03.pdf. Accessed 10 September 2015.

Otterbach, S. (2010). Mismatches between actual and preferred work time: Empirical evidence of hours constraints in 21 countries. *Journal of Consumer Policy* 33 (2), 143–161.

Polanyi, K. (1957). *The great transformation: The political and economic origins of our time.* Boston: Beacon Press.

Rosenbaum, E.F. (2000). What is a market? On the methodology of a contested concept. *Review of Social Economy* 58 (4), 455–482.

Schor, J. (1991). *The overworked American: The unexpected decline of leisure*. New York: Basic Books.

Skidelsky, R.J.A., Skidelsky, E. (2012). *How much is enough? Money and the good life*. New York: Other Press.

Zwickl, K., Disslbacher, F., Stagl, S. (2015). Work-sharing for a sustainable economy. *Ecological Economics Working Papers Series* 4/2015.

PART VI

Value and ethics

22

PLURALISM AND INCOMMENSURABILITY

John O'Neill

Introduction

A central point of contention between social ecological economics and standard environmental economics concerns the question how far, if at all, markets and market mimicking procedures are appropriate for solving environmental problems. Standard neo-classical environmental economics claims that the source of environmental problems lies in the fact that preferences for environmental goods are not reflected in monetary prices, and correspondingly that their solution requires the pricing of all environmental goods and bads. The extension of markets can take place directly through the construction of markets (e.g., tradable emissions permits). Alternatively, it can occur indirectly by calculating shadow prices for environmental goods for the purposes of cost-benefit analysis (CBA), employing either preferences revealed in market behaviour (e.g. travel costs or property markets), or stated preferences about hypothetical changes (e.g. contingent valuation).

Social ecological economists argue that environmental problems reveal the limits of market based approaches to policy making. A clear statement of this view is that of Kapp:

> The formulation of environmental policies, the evaluation of environmental goals and the establishment of priorities require a substantive economic calculus in terms of social use values (politically evaluated) for which the formal calculus in monetary exchange values fails to provide a real measure [...] [E]nvironmental values are social use values for which markets provide neither a direct measure nor an adequate indirect indicator.
>
> *(Kapp, 1974: 38)*

An important strand of argument in the debates between these different views concerns value commensurability, and in particular whether the measuring rod of money could capture all the different dimensions of value at stake in environmental decision-making.

This chapter opens with an account of commensurability and the assumption of mainstream economists that money can serve as a universal measure for valuation. It then considers meaning of value monism and value pluralism and their relationship to commensurability. The final sections outline the central problems with the mainstream economists' approach and consider alternative approaches to environmental decision-making that do not assume monetary commensurability.

Commensurability, ethics and economics

One central argument for use of markets and market-mimicking procedures in environmental policy is that it offers a single metric for measuring the value of different policy options. It brings the value of different options under 'the measuring rod of money'. Pearce and his colleagues offer a typical formulation: "CBA is the only [approach] which explicitly makes the effort to compare like with like using a single measuring rod of benefits and costs, money" (Pearce et al., 1989: 57). Other approaches fail to offer "a common unit of measurement" to gauge the relative importance of environmental goods "to each other and non-environmental goods and services" (Pearce et al., 1989: 115).

The view that rational decision-making requires a single measure of the value of different options has its basis in the utilitarian background to welfare economics. The classical utilitarian approach to ethics argues that the right action is that which maximises the welfare of affected agents. The approach has three components:

1   welfarism: the only thing that is good in itself and not simply a means to other goods is the welfare of individuals;
2   consequentialism: whether an action is right or wrong is determined solely by the consequences of the action;
3   aggregation and maximisation: the best action is that which results in greatest total value.

The third component is typically taken to require a common measure of value, so that the value of different outcomes can be calculated and the option with the greatest total value ascertained. The first component requires that this be a measure of welfare. Ideally, then the utilitarian approach requires that there be a measure of welfare that can be used to calculate the total value of different options.

The founders of utilitarianism assumed a hedonic account of well-being, according to which well-being consists in pleasure and absence of pain, and suggested a direct measure of their value or disvalue. Bentham, for example, argued that pleasures could be measured through their intensity, duration, certainty and propinquity (Bentham, 1970 [1789]: chapter 4). The hedonic account of well-being and its direct measurement has seen a revival under the influence of hedonic psychology (Kahneman et al., 1997). However, in economic theory monetary measures remain predominant. In the early development of marginal economics, willingness to pay for a good at the margin was still understood as an indirect measure of expected pleasure (O'Neill, 1998: Chapter 3). In more recent economic literature willingness to pay measurements are combined with a commitment to a preference satisfaction theory of well-being. Well-being consists in the satisfaction of preferences, the stronger the preferences satisfied the greater the improvement in well-being: "the entire body of 'welfare economics' centres round the formal identity of the statement 'X prefers A to B' and the statement 'X has higher welfare in A rather than B'" (Pearce et al., 2003: 121). Willingness to pay at the margin for a good is a direct measure of the strength of the preference for that good. Well-being is directly brought under the measuring rod of money.

Given this assumption, rational choices about the environment require the extension of the measuring rod of money to include preferences for environmental goods which are unpriced in actual markets.

> The preferences for the environment, which show up as gains in welfare to human beings, need to be measured [...] In benefit estimation money is used as a measuring rod, a way of measuring preferences.
>
> *(Pearce et al., 1989: 52–3)*

Money offers a way of measuring the welfare gains and losses of environmental changes by capturing the preferences for environmental goods. This view makes three assumptions.

1 Value commensurability: There is a common measure of value through which different options or states of affair can be ordered;
2 Welfarism: The value in question is welfare understood in terms of preference satisfaction;
3 Monetary commensurability: Changes in welfare can be measured by money.

Value commensurability is the claim that there is a common measure of value through which different options can be ordered. Classical utilitarians assumed a *cardinal* scale; that is, a scale that provides information on precisely how much value different options offer. A cardinal scale needs to be distinguished from an *ordinal* scale; i.e. a scale that simply ranks 1st, 2nd, 3rd and so on—the value that different options offer without assigning them any specific value that would indicate how much they differ. Monetary valuation promises a cardinal scale of measurement for comparing the welfare value of different options.

The term commensurability is used in a variety of different ways. A cardinal scale of measurement is sometimes taken to define commensurability (Chang, 1997; Aldred, 2006). On this account commensurability should be distinguished from comparability which promises only an ordering of options according to some covering value. This usage is not uniform and sometimes the terms commensurability and comparability are used interchangeably (Raz, 1986: chapter 13). I have previously distinguished between weak and strong commensurability to mark the difference between ordinal and cardinal scales and between weaker and stronger forms of comparability (O'Neill, 1993: chapter 7). This chapter focuses on monetary commensurability and, for the purposes of this chapter, I use the term commensurability to refer to strong forms of commensurability that assume a single cardinal scale.

Value monism and pluralism

Classical utilitarian proponents of value commensurability were also value monists. Value monism is the view that there is only one kind of good that is valued for its own sake and is intrinsically valuable in this sense. Value monism contrasts with value pluralism, the view that there are a number of distinct intrinsically valuable goods, such as autonomy, knowledge, justice, equality and beauty which are irreducible either to each other or to some other ultimate value. For classical utilitarians, the only thing that is intrinsically valuable is pleasure. All other goods, social and environmental, have only instrumental value as a means to pleasure. If one assumes, as did Bentham, that this ultimate value can be measured by a single cardinal measure, then value monism offers one route to commensurability: different outcomes of actions can be compared by measuring how much total pleasure they produce.

Why assume value monism? One argument offered for value monism is that a single standard of value is required to make rational choices. John Stuart Mill offered an influential argument of this kind:

> There must be some standard to determine the goodness and badness, absolute and comparative, of ends, or objects of desires. And whatever that standard is, there can be but one; for if there were several ultimate principles of conduct, the same conduct might be approved of by one of those principles and condemned by another; and there would be needed some more general principle, as umpire between them.
>
> *(Mill, 1884, Book 6)*

Mill argues that, given a number of different standards of value, where these conflict another principle invoking a distinct standard of value is required to adjudicate that conflict. Hence a rational resolution of the conflict will always require an appeal to some single ultimate principle that calls upon a single standard of value.

There are a number of problems with this argument. First, even given the assumption that all value conflicts require some single umpiring principle to adjudicate conflicts between values, the conclusion does not follow that this principle must call upon just one standard value. An umpiring principle could for example appeal to many standards of value, v_0, v_1...v_n but have some ordering principle to decide which has priority. It might appeal to a lexicographic ordering amongst values v_0, v_1...v_n, such that v_1 comes into play only after v_0 is satisfied, and in general any standard of value v_n can be consider only if values v_0, v_1...v_{n-1} are already satisfied (Rawls, 1972: 42ff. and 61ff).[1]

Second, the argument commits a logical error involving a shift in the scope of a quantifier. One might grant Mill that the following is true:

UE. Rationality requires that, for any practical conflict, there is a principle that resolves the conflict.

Mill's claims that there must exist a single general umpiring rule that resolves any conflict does not follow. This is to make a distinct claim:

EU. Rationality requires that there is a principle such that for any practical conflict the principle resolves the conflict.

The inference of **EU** from **UE** involves an invalid shift in the scope of the quantifiers. There is no reason to conclude from Mill's argument that there is some single umpiring principle that resolves all conflicts (Wiggins, 1980; O'Neill et al., 2008: Chapter 5).

While value commensurability and value monism were both defended by classical utilitarians, there is no necessary relationship between the two claims. On the one hand, one might hold a version of value monism but deny commensurability. For example, one might hold that pleasure is the only ultimate intrinsic value but deny that there is a single cardinal measure that can capture the variety of different pleasures (Neurath, 1983 [1912]). On the other hand, one might reject value monism for some version of value pluralism, but still hold there is a single measure of value through which the value of different options can be ascertained. A significant argument for this view appeals to the claim that different values can be traded off with each other in a particular sense of trade-off.

The argument from trade-offs runs as follows: There is a plurality of ultimate intrinsic values—beauty, knowledge, autonomy, achievement, pleasures, relationships to friends and kin, etc.—but we can make comparisons across different values by considering how much a loss in one dimension of value can be compensated for by a gain in another. In making comparisons of this kind we could arrive at a trade-off schedule that says that a loss of so much in one value is equal to a gain of so much in another. Indeed, when making choices between different options individuals are implicitly trading off different values, whether or not they recognise this. The existence of such trade-offs allows the possibility of commensurability back in. One can posit a currency through which such exchanges across different dimensions of value can be made. This currency is not a different value to which others are reduced. It is a measure through which losses and gains across different dimensions of value can be measured and compared. What might this currency be? Economists generally claim it is money. As Pearce et al. (1989: 115) put it, money is "a common unit of measurement" through which it is possible to gauge the relative importance of environmental goods with "each other and non-environmental goods and services". In the next section I critically examine this argument.

Commensurability, money and trade-offs

There are two grounds for criticism of the trade-off position just presented. First, there are arguments specifically against monetary commensurability—the claim that money could offer a universal currency for measuring losses and gains across different dimensions of value. Second, there are reasons for suggesting that the very concept of a trade-off in values might be mistaken.

What happens if one asks people to use the 'measuring rod of money' to value environmental goods and bads? One response is that people protest. Here is a protest by a person over the attempt to put a price on the place where they live in the Narmada Valley, India, for the purposes of calculating the compensation for their being displaced by a dam:

> You tell us to take compensation. What is the state compensating us for? For our land, for our fields, for the trees along our fields. But we don't live only by this. Are you going to compensate us for our forest? […] Or are you going to compensate us for our great river—for her fish, her water, for vegetables that grow along her banks, for the joy of living beside her? What is the price of this? […] How are you compensating us for fields either—we didn't buy this land; our forefathers cleared it and settled here. What price this land? Our gods, the support of those who are our kin—what price do you have for these? Our adivasi life—what price do you put on it?
>
> *(Bava Mahalia, 1994)*

The point of the question 'what is the price of this?' is rhetorical. The possibility of putting a price on the goods involved is being rejected. Note that rejecting the possibility of pricing a good is not the same as saying that it has a zero or infinite price. Indeed, to say that a good has a price of zero or infinity would contradict the claim that a price could not be put on the good.

What rules out the possibility of putting a price on an environmental good or bad? One reason is what Raz (1986: 345ff.) calls constitutive incommensurability (see also O'Neill, 1993: 118–122). Certain relationships and commitments are constituted by a refusal to treat them as tradable commodities that can be bought or sold. For example, given the nature of relationships of love and friendship, and given the nature of market exchanges, it is not possible to buy love or friendship. A person who tried to buy a friendship would not understand what friendship is. A person who could say to his putative lover 'I love you so much it would take a £1000 to pay me to leave you' would not express love but its absence. Similarly, ethical value-commitments are also constituted by a refusal to price them. To show that strength of one's ethical commitments by saying how much it would take to break them would not be to show the extent of one's commitments, but rather to reveal their limits.

The protests in the case of Narmada valley in part express constitutive incommensurabilities. The place embodies relationships to past and present kin and community which are constituted by a refusal to a put a price on them. More generally, to the extent to which relationships to environments embody, in particular places, our relation to the past and future of communities to which we belong, or express ethical commitments, then they will be constituted by a refusal to put a price on those goods.

A problem here lies in the treatment of monetary prices as a 'measuring rod' for welfare gains and losses akin to metres as a measure of gains or losses in length, or grams as a measure of gains and losses in mass. Putting a price on an object is a social act with a social meaning in a way that is different from measuring length and mass. Money is not simply a 'measuring rod'. It embodies particular kinds of social relationships which are incompatible with other social relationships and ethical commitments.

These arguments point to the limits of monetary measures of gains and losses for the purposes of trade-offs between different values. They point to a problem with monetary commensurability. They do not rule out the possibility of trade-offs between different values, nor that some other universal measure might do the job of supplying a suitable metric. However, they give us reason to pause about how far the very idea of a trade-off between values is the appropriate way of thinking about conflicts between them. The concept of a 'trade-off', as Lukes (1997: 187) notes, uses a particular commercial metaphor to approach conflicts. What is implied by this commercial framing of choice?

The idea of a common currency for trading off values suggests a particular maximising consequentialist framing of choices. Rational choice should aim to bring about that state of affairs which has the greatest total value. Given value pluralism, this cannot be done through some single value like pleasure that can be measured and then maximised. However, by comparing the gains and losses of different dimensions of value and trading these off one can still calculate the outcome that produces the greatest gains in values over losses in value and hence has the greatest value.

There are problems with approaching choices in this manner. One cannot always trade off different dimensions of value in the manner suggested. Consider again well-being. An approach to well-being distinct from both hedonic and preference satisfaction approaches is the objective state account. On the objective state account, well-being is to be understood in terms of the ability to realise particular objective states—physical health, personal relations, autonomy, knowledge of the world, aesthetic experience, accomplishment and achievement, sensual pleasures, a well-constituted relation with the non-human world, and so on. Needs-based accounts of well-being (Wiggins, 1998) and capabilities-based accounts (Sen, 1987, 1993; Nussbaum, 2000) offer influential examples [see also Chapter 24].

Two features of this kind of approach are of importance here. First, they are typically pluralist: there a number of different dimensions of well-being that are not reducible to each other or to some other value. Second, the concepts of needs and capabilities are threshold concepts: if a person falls below thresholds on some dimensions then she or he will be harmed. Together these rule out certain kinds of trade-offs across different dimensions of value. If someone suffers a loss that takes them below the threshold of minimal levels of physical health, it is not the case that there is a trade-off to be made such that a gain well above the threshold in another dimension, say pleasure, can compensate for loss and keep total well-being unchanged. In such cases, restoring a person to well-being can only be properly addressed by the provision of goods in that dimension. To the extent there are measures of well-being in these different dimensions, they are unconvertible into some single currency through which gains and losses in different dimensions can be calculated and compared.

Second, the trade-off model assumes a consequentialist framing of choices that can be contested. A deontological framing for example would be different: a choice is a matter of what obligations for an individual or community have greater stringency in a particular context. An environmental activist who takes an evening off activism to spend time with her children does not necessarily approach this in terms of which action produces the state of affairs with greatest value. Rather her obligations to her children as their mother in some cases over-ride her other obligations as an activist and citizen. In other contexts, where the risks to community are great, she might reasonably decide obligations as a citizen take priority. Outcomes matter in all of this. However, the idea of trading off values in order to arrive at the outcome with the highest value does not adequately describe her deliberations in making those comparisons. Rather she will be considering the *relationships* in which she stands with respect to different individuals and groups and the competing obligations they impose.

Another framing might appeal to virtues. This asks: What kind of person do I want to be? What kind of community are we? Consider cases in which members of a fishing community risk their lives and resources to save fellow workers lost in a storm at sea. From a cost-benefit approach, such actions can make little sense in terms of the additional lives and resources put at risk. However, what is at stake in the choice cannot be captured by some trade-off schedule which produces the greatest total value. Rather, individuals act in accordance with values of solidarity that define their relationships to each other as a community. There are limits to what this requires and outcomes do matter. If the risks are extreme and likelihood of success is low then attempts at rescue are no longer courageous but foolhardy. However, the choice is not simply a matter of calculating the expected values of outcomes. Self-understandings about the kinds of individuals and communities to which we belong do work here.[2]

Future research directions

> There is great pressure for research into techniques to make larger ranges of social value commensurable. Some of the effort should rather be devoted to learning—or learning again, perhaps—how to think intelligently about conflicts of value which are incommensurable.
>
> *(Williams, 1972: 103)*

The promise of monetary valuation and commensurability more generally is the possibility of a method for rationally choosing between options through a calculative process. One is able to calculate which of a set of policy options produces the state of affairs with greatest value. It promises what Max Weber (1978 [1921–22]: 85) called 'formal rationality':

> The term 'formal rationality of economic action' is used to designate the extent of quantitative calculation or accounting which is technically possible and which is actually applied.

However, as Weber recognised, it is a mistake to confuse formal rationality with rationality as such.

How is rational choice possible in the absence of commensurability? The arguments in the preceding section point to some possible answers. Consider the objection that, given different dimensions of well-being with minimal thresholds, a loss in one dimension of value cannot be compensated for by a gain in another. Kapp (1970) offers a 'substantive' concept of rationality that is more sensitive to these dimensions of well-being. Environmental choices require an appeal not to "formal welfare criteria" but rather "concepts defining a substantive rationality reflecting actual human needs and requirements of human life" (Kapp, 1970: 847). Kapp borrows the concept of substantive rationality from Weber. In contrast to formal rationality, substantive rationality is defined as:

> the degree to which the provisioning of a given group of persons (no matter how delimited) with goods is shaped by economically orientated social action under some criterion [...] of ultimate values, regardless of the nature of these ends
>
> *(Weber, 1978 [1921–22]: 85).*

Kapp employs a needs based account of well-being to fill this account out. In contrast to the monetary measures invoked for formal rationality, substantive rationality requires the definition of "existential minima representing minimum adequate levels of satisfaction of essential human needs" (Kapp, 1965: 77). Given the plurality of needs, and the minimal thresholds associated with them, choice requires not a single measure of value to trade-off across different dimensions of value, but distinct measures associated with those different dimensions.

The other arguments of the last section also point to distinct dimensions of rational choice. Consider the claim that some social relations and value commitments are constituted by a refusal to trade. Refusing to trade is a way of expressing an evaluative or relational commitment. Actions are not just instrumental means to ends, but also ways of expressing attitudes to people and things. This suggests that rationality also governs the ways relations are expressed: "Practical reason demands that one's actions adequately express one's rational attitudes towards the people and things one cares about" (Anderson, 1993: 18). Protests to monetary valuation of environmental goods can rationally express the values put at risk in environmental choices.

Finally, consider the way that choices can be a matter of considering competing claims that individuals in different relations make on us. This is not a matter of calculation. It is a matter of judging which competing claims have significance in the context of choice. A general point can be made here. In most decisions agents are faced with competing reasons or grounds that tell for or against conflicting options. The problem is that of ascertaining which reasons make the strongest claim in that choice. This involves public deliberation not calculation. Rational action is that which is justified by deliberation that meets appropriate norms of reason. Rational public choice requires deliberative institutions that allow citizens to transform preferences through reasoned dialogue, rather than measuring through money given preferences for the purposes of aggregating them to arrive at an 'optimal' outcome (Elster, 1986; Smith, 2003; O'Neill, 2007). Indeed monetary measurement captures only the intensity of preferences not the soundness of the reasons for them. As such it precludes rational choice rather than enables it.

Once one moves beyond a narrow formal account of rationality, value commensurability in general and monetary commensurability in particular are not conditions of rational choice. Correspondingly research needs to shift from the development of techniques and procedures that assume value-commensurability to the development of multicriteria and deliberative procedures and institutions that enable participants to deliberate across the plural values that inform environmental choices (Martinez-Alier et al., 1998; Burgess et al., 2007).

Concluding remarks

The view that environmental choices require monetary valuation of unpriced environmental goods informs a great deal of current environmental economics and policy. It is founded in part on the assumption that rational choice requires value commensurability. This assumption is false. Rational environmental policy requires the development of procedures and institutions that recognise that values are plural and incommensurable.

Notes

1 For a discussion of lexicographic preferences in the context of environmental valuation see Spash (2000).
2 For more detailed discussion of the difference between consequentialist, deontological and virtues framings of choices see O'Neill et al. (2008: chapter 5).

Key further readings cited

Aldred, J. (2006). Incommensurability and Monetary Valuation, *Land Economics* 82, 141–161.
Chang, R. (ed.) (1997). *Incommensurability, Incomparability and Practical Reason*, Cambridge, MA: Harvard University Press.
O'Neill, J., Holland, A. and Light A. (2008). *Environmental Values*, London: Routledge.

Other literature cited

Anderson, E. (1993). *Value in Ethics and Economics*, Cambridge Mass: Harvard University Press.
Bentham, J. (1970 [1789]). *Introduction to the Principles of Morals and Legislation*, London: Methuen.
Burgess, J., Stirling, A., Clark, J., Davies, G. and Eames, M. (2007). Deliberative Mapping: A Novel Analytic-deliberative Methodology to Support Contested Science-policy Decisions, *Public Understanding of Science* 16(3), 299–322.
Elster, J. (1986). The Market and the Forum: Three Varieties of Political Theory, in J. Elster and A. Hylland (eds.). *Foundations of Social Choice Theory*, Cambridge: Cambridge University Press.
Kahneman, D., Wakker, P. and Sarin, R. (1997). Back to Bentham? Explorations of Experienced Utility, *The Quarterly Journal of Economics* 112, 375–405.
Kapp, K. W. (1965). Economic Development in a New Perspective: Existential Minima and Substantive Rationality, *Kyklos* 18(1), 49–79.
Kapp, K.W. (1970). Environmental Disruption and Social Costs: A Challenge to Economics, *Kyklos* 23, 833–848.
Kapp, K.W. (1974). *Environmental Policies and Development Planning in Contemporary China and Other Essays.* The Hague: Mouton.
Lukes, S. (1997). Comparing the Incomparable: Trade-Offs and Sacrifices. In R. Chang (Ed.) *Incommensurability, Incomparability and Practical Reason* (pp. 184–195). Cambridge, MA: Harvard University Press.
Mahalia, B. (1994). Letter from a Tribal Village. *Lokayan Bulletin* 11(2/3), Sept.–Dec.
Martinez-Alier, J., Munda G. and O'Neill, J. (1998). Weak Comparability of Values as a Foundation for Ecological Economics, *Ecological Economics* 26(3), 277–286.
Mill, J.S. (1884). *A System of Logic*, New York: Harper and Brothers.
Neurath, O. (1983 [1912]). The Problem of the Pleasure Maximum. In Cohen R.S. and Neurath M. (Eds.) *Otto Neurath: Philosophical Papers*, Dordrecht: Reidel.
Nussbaum, M. (2000). *Women and Human Development: The Capabilities Approach*, Cambridge: Cambridge University Press.
O'Neill, J.F. (1993). *Ecology, Policy and Politics: Human Well-Being and the Natural World*, London: Routledge.
O'Neill, J.F. (1998). *The Market: Ethics, Knowledge and Politics*, London: Routledge.
O'Neill, J.F. (2007). *Markets, Deliberation and Environment*, London: Routledge.
Pearce, D., Groom, B., Hepburn, C., and Koundouri P. (2003). Valuing the Future: Recent Advances in Social Discounting, *World Economics* 4, 121–141.
Pearce, D, Markaandyam A. and Barbier, E. (1989). *Blueprint for a Green Economy*, London: Earthscan.
Rawls J. (1972). *A Theory of Justice*, Oxford: Oxford University Press.
Raz, J. (1986). *The Morality of Freedom*, Oxford: Clarendon.
Sen, A. (1987). *On Ethics and Economics*, Oxford: Blackwell.
Sen, A. (1993). Well-Being and Capability. In Nussbaum, M. and Sen, A. (Eds.) (1993) *The Quality of Life*, Oxford: Clarendon Press.
Smith, G. (2003). *Deliberative Democracy and the Environment*, London: Routledge.
Spash, C.L. (2000). Ecosystems, Contingent Valuation and Ethics: The Case of Wetlands Re-creation, *Ecological Economics* 34, 195–215.
Weber, M. (1978[1921–22/]). *Economy and Society*, Berkeley: University of California Press.

Wiggins, D. (1980). Weakness of Will Commensurability and the Objects of Deliberation and Desire. In A. Rorty (ed.) *Essays on Aristotle's Ethics*, Berkeley: University of California Press.
Wiggins, D. (1998). The Claims of Need. In *Needs, Values, Truth*, 3rd edition, Oxford: Clarendon Press.
Williams, B. (1972). *Morality*, Cambridge: Cambridge University Press.

23

INTRINSIC VALUES AND ECONOMIC VALUATION

Katie McShane

Introduction

The issue of intrinsic values is often a point of disagreement and sometimes confusion between ethicists and economists. Ethicists often criticise economic modes of valuation for failing to take account of intrinsic values. In response, economists have proposed a number of different types of value meant to account for intrinsic values within an economic framework. However, many ethicists have criticised these notions as inadequate substitutes for ethical understandings of intrinsic value. One reason for confusion about this issue is that there are many different meanings of 'intrinsic value' within ethics. This chapter will identify those meanings and the differences among them, and then go on to consider how well the types of value proposed within economics can capture them.

Ethics and value

Understanding the debate requires some background on ethical theories and their differences. There are three primary theoretical approaches within ethics:

1   *Utilitarianism* is a version of consequentialism, which is the view that the right action is that which produces the best consequences. Utilitarians are those consequentialists who evaluate consequences in terms of their utility, which they take to be the equivalent of welfare or well-being. Some theories of welfare define utility as a matter of preference satisfaction/ frustration; other theories define it as a matter of pleasure/pain or happiness/suffering; still others define it as a matter of the gain/loss of certain specified components of human flourishing. (Note: ethicists define 'utility' as welfare, leaving it open whether welfare consists in preference satisfaction or something else, while economists define 'utility' as preference satisfaction. Hereinafter, I will assume the economists' definition.)
2   *Deontology*, or duty-based ethics, evaluates the rightness of an action by looking at the type of action it is rather than by looking at its consequences. Deontologists regard the right action as that which conforms to a particular set of duties, often lexicographically ordered and sometimes conceived of as issuing from rights. On this view, certain kinds of action can be wrong independently of the amount of utility they produce in the world.

3 *Virtue ethics* evaluates the rightness of an action by looking at which character traits the actor expresses through undertaking the action. Virtue ethicists regard the right action as one that expresses virtuous character traits. As in deontology, an action's rightness or wrongness is not just a matter of how much utility it produces in the world. In virtue ethics, an action can fail to be virtuous because it is performed out of vicious motives, even though it produces high levels of utility.

Thus, for example, a utilitarian might object to lying on the grounds that it produces disutility, a deontologist on the grounds that it violates an ethical duty to tell the truth, and a virtue ethicist on the grounds that it is disrespectful or manipulative.

Mainstream economic valuation is most consistent with utilitarianism, particularly versions of utilitarianism that understand welfare to be a matter of preference satisfaction. Economic valuation compares courses of action in terms of the aggregate utility they produce. It neither accepts lexicographically ordered principles nor evaluates actions in terms of their motives or expressive meanings. Thus economists and non-utilitarian ethicists often disagree about which aspects of a course of action to evaluate and how conflicts should be resolved and possible trade-offs assessed.

The standard versions of all three types of ethical theory include claims about intrinsic values. Utilitarians take welfare to be intrinsically valuable; deontologists take individuals or the conformity to principles of right action to be intrinsically valuable; virtue ethicists take virtue (or, in some versions, the good life that it is said to produce) to be intrinsically valuable. However, intrinsic value plays different roles in each of these theories. Not only are such differences significant among these three basic theoretical approaches, there are also important differences among particular theories within each approach. As a result, the claim by ethicists that something has intrinsic value can have very different meanings in different contexts (Jamieson, 2008; McShane, 2007; O'Neill, 1992). In ethics, the most common meanings associated with intrinsic value, attributed to an entity X, are:

- *Overriding value*: the value of X should override or trump non-intrinsic values in cases where they conflict.
- *Special value*: the value of X has greater importance than non-intrinsic values simply because of the kind of value it is.
- *Moral considerability*: moral agents have a duty to treat the interests of X as morally important.
- *Inherent worth*: moral agents have a duty to treat X with respect.
- *Unconditional value*: X has value in every circumstance; its value does not depend on any of its contingent features.
- *Internal value*: X is valuable because of its intrinsic properties alone.
- *Objective value*: the value of X does not come from being valued by valuers.
- *Nonanthropocentric value*: the value of X does not come from serving human interests.
- *Noninstrumental value*: X has value beyond merely being a means to an end.
- *End value*: X is properly cared about for its own sake rather than for the sake of some other good.

While this list treats these forms of intrinsic value as distinct from one another, in practice they are often combined in different ways within particular ethical theories. For example, theories utilizing the concept of inherent worth typically treat it as a value that is also objective and non-instrumental. However, none of these conceptions posit a notion of value that is entirely 'valuer independent' (cf. Justus et al., 2009). While each denies a particular kind of relationship to valuers, none denies all such relationships. For example, all of the conceptions above are compatible with the view that values are nothing more than social norms governing the attitudes of valuers.

There is a difference worth noting between the way that philosophers use the term 'value' and the way that it is used by mainstream economists and social scientists more generally. Philosophers accept a conceptual distinction between what is valued and what actually has value—between the valu*ed* and the valu*able*. When philosophers discuss 'value', they mean by this 'the valuable' rather than 'the valued'. This usage differs from that in the social sciences, where value is more typically used to mean the valued (Lockwood, 1999). Regarding the valuable as distinct from the valued is important within ethics in order to preserve the conceptual possibility that valuers can be mistaken in their valuations. If 'to be valuable' just meant the same thing as 'to be valued', it would be conceptually impossible to be mistaken in one's valuations, for anything that was valued would by definition be valuable. Distinguishing between the valued and the valuable as a conceptual matter does not rule out the substantive position that 'all and only that which is valued is valuable'. Within philosophy, however, this is a substantive claim (and not a very well-accepted one); it is not a claim derived from the very meaning of the concepts involved.

This terminological point might seem to be a mere technicality, but it is the root of important disciplinary differences in the way that economists and philosophers discuss value, and it is responsible for at least some of the misunderstandings between the two disciplines. Philosophers view value as 'the good' and often raise questions about whether people's actual desires, preferences, and so on, are in fact preferences for what is good [see also Chapter 22]. Social scientists more typically claim to be agnostic about which things in the world are good, and instead simply study how people's behaviour reveals what they take to be good. Ethicists recommend that people subject their preferences to critical scrutiny and reform their desires to better conform to what really is good in the world, while economists take the content of preferences as a given and scrutinise instead the efficiency with which individuals, institutions, and policies satisfy them.

When addressing policy, direct conflict between ethicists and economists tends to emerge. Assessments of policy that consider options only in terms of their utility miss a great deal of what ethicists think should guide policy choice—consideration of what would be good, not just of what people desire. As a result, the expansion of economic modes of assessment to non-market values, due to the increased interest in cost-benefit analysis as a tool for policy choice, has caused ethicists great concern. Insofar as cost-benefit analysis aims to offer a comprehensive analysis of the advantages and disadvantages of policies, and insofar as it uses economic methods of valuation to do so, ethicists worry that it fails to capture many features of policies that are relevant to the choice among them. In particular, economic modes of valuation have difficulties capturing some of the types of intrinsic value listed above.

Value in environmental economics

Value, from a standard economic perspective, is just utility—the satisfaction of a human preference—where the amount of value is determined by the strength of the preference, represented by a utility function. This is closest to the view of anthropocentric preference-satisfaction utilitarianism. Utilitarianism assumes a welfarist theory of the value—it reduces 'the good' to 'the good for'. Goodness or value, on this view, *just is* welfare or well-being (Sen, 1979). Preference-satisfaction utilitarianism further accepts an account of welfare whereby welfare consists entirely in the satisfaction of preferences. Anthropocentric preference-satisfaction utilitarianism involves the additional claim that only human preferences matter morally. Thus, anthropocentric preference-satisfaction utilitarians identify preference satisfaction with individual human welfare, and they identify individual human welfare with goodness itself.

Many economists, however, do not wish to identify utility with welfare or with goodness, and for understandable reasons. Anthropocentric preference-satisfaction utilitarianism is not regarded by most philosophers as a plausible ethical view, nor is the preference-satisfaction account of welfare regarded as a plausible theory of welfare (Griffin, 1986; Parfit, 1984). Not only do many economists not want to take on implausible ethical assumptions, many of them wish to avoid doing ethics altogether. Thus some economists have argued that utility should be treated as a technical term within economics, representing the satisfaction of preferences but presupposing no view about whether satisfying preferences is good for individuals or good in general (for discussion, see Broome, 1999). Treating utility as merely a technical term, however, has drawbacks. Although assuming no necessary connection between utility and welfare, or goodness, might be compatible with sophisticated analyses of consumer behaviour, why would anyone want to assess public policies in terms of their utility unless utility had some connection to welfare or goodness? Choosing policies with greater expected utility only makes sense if utility is a good thing.

One way out of this problem is to claim that there is a significant but contingent overlap between: (i) what people prefer (utility) and what is good for them, and (ii) what is good for people and what is good, all things considered. So understood, utility would be something necessarily valu*ed*, but not always valu*able*. Accepting this view of utility would avoid relying on implausible ethical views about the nature of welfare or goodness. Most ethicists do accept that as an empirical matter people often (though not always) prefer what is good for them and that having at least some of one's preferences satisfied is part of what makes up a good life for humans. They also typically accept that what benefits humans is good, though perhaps not the only good. Accepting these relationships among utility, welfare, and goodness as a contingent and empirical matter would at least make clear why utility is something one might want choices and policies to generate. However, this acceptance would clearly leave open the possibility that utility is not the only aspect of choices and policies worth caring about.

In any case, if economic value is understood as a matter of preference satisfaction, it is clear why market goods would not be the only bearers of value: people have preferences about a great many things in the world (clean air, friendship, endangered species) that are not traded in markets. Among these non-market goods, some are valued for the ways they might be used; others are valued independently of how they might be used. This difference has been the basis for distinguishing between use and non-use values in economics. As many writers have noted, however, the distinction between use and non-use is a blurry one—exactly what constitutes 'using' a good is not always clear. Does enjoying a beautiful sunset constitute 'using' it? Some theorists think that what constitutes use is a matter of how direct a person's interaction with the good is or where the person is when the benefits are acquired (Krutilla, 1967; Madariaga and McConnell, 1987; More, Averill and Stevens, 1996; Turner, 2004). Others classify all intangible goods as having non-use value on the assumption that they cannot be 'consumed' in the same way as can physical goods (Turner, 2004).

To avoid debate about what constitutes a 'use', the term 'passive use value' has been introduced as an alternative to 'use value' (Arrow et al., 1993). On this model, all economic values are assumed to involve some kind of 'use'; the question is just whether that use is active or passive, direct or indirect (Spash, 2008). However, the assumption that all economic values must concern some sort of use is unjustified. There is no reason to think that a preference that tigers continue to exist for their own sakes must really involve a passive 'use' of tigers or their existence. While it is true that the satisfaction of preferences has utility, this does not mean that all preferences must involve use, whether active or passive. Whatever their etymological relationship, utility is not the same thing as use. (To avoid confusion, in what follows, I will refer to the alternative to use values with the combined term 'non/ passive use values'.)

In an effort to make cost-benefit analyses more comprehensive, mainstream environmental economists have developed a rich typology of non/passive use values and associated methodologies for measuring them. The most common of these are:

- *existence value*: the existence value of X is the satisfaction of one's preference that it continues to exist, independently of any use (or active use) one might make of it (Krutilla, 1967).
- *bequest value*: the bequest value of X is the satisfaction of one's preference that future generations be able to continue to benefit from X (Krutilla, 1967).
- *option value*: the option value of X is the satisfaction of one's preference that one's option to use X in the future be preserved (Weisbrod, 1964). Option value is sometimes classified as a use value, since one's own future use is the basis of the preference (Crowards, 1997).
- *altruistic/philanthropic value*: the altruistic/philanthropic value of X is the satisfaction of one's preference that others be able to benefit from X (Kolstad, 2000).[1]

The relationships among these types of value are not always clear. Some environmental economists classify bequest and option value as forms of existence value that simply specify particular (non/passive use) reasons for preferring the continued existence of a thing (Brookshire et al., 1986). Others treat existence value as a preference that something exist 'for its own sake' and the other categories of value as preferences that it exist for other (ultimately use-related) reasons (Gowdy, 1997; Turner et al., 2003). Some consider existence value (Aldred, 1994) or even all non/passive use value (Crowards, 1997) to be by definition forms of altruistic value; yet others define existence value as a kind of non-altruistic value (Davidson, 2013). Furthermore, the legitimacy of these values as forms of economic value has been controversial within the economics literature (Aldred, 1994; Brookshire et al., 1986). Nevertheless, empirical studies suggest that these forms of value often play an important role in the preferences people have regarding the natural environment, and so understanding them is crucial to understanding conservation values (Crowards, 1997).

Current assessment of major issues

Existence value is the type of non/passive use value that is usually claimed to be an adequate substitute for intrinsic value (Pearce, Markandya and Barbier, 1989: 62; Aldred, 1994; Davidson, 2013). Assuming this to be correct, how well does existence value capture the various kinds of intrinsic value listed earlier? If by 'intrinsic value' we mean overriding or special value, then existence value will not be able to capture what is meant when intrinsic value is attributed to an object. To see something as special, perhaps overridingly so, does not imply that one values its continued existence. As Elizabeth Anderson points out: "it may make sense for me to love a person, but this does not imply that I must want that person to continue living. If he is gravely ill, it may be the best expression of my love for him to wish that he die quickly and mercifully (1993: 26)".

Overriding value and special value indicate how conflicts among different kinds of value should be handled. However, how one should handle cases of conflict among values is an entirely different question from whether one should prefer that a bearer of value continue to exist. Furthermore, overriding and special value come from deontological ethical theories that treat values lexicographically rather than aggregatively; they cannot be captured within a framework that treats values as utilitarians do (Davidson, 2013; Spash, 1997).

Likewise, moral considerability and inherent worth are moral statuses that concern how one is to treat something in one's moral deliberations, not whether one prefers the continued existence of that thing. To say that a thing is morally considerable is to say that its interests ought to matter to one, not to make a claim about the content of those interests. Of course, some things do have an interest in their own continued existence, but even then, this will be only one interest of many. To say that a thing has inherent worth is to make a claim about how one ought to treat it (namely, with respect), not to make a claim about whether one should want it to exist. One can respect people while at the same time being perfectly comfortable with the fact of human mortality. Again, how one ought to treat something and whether its continued existence is a good thing are different issues.

Attributions of unconditional and internal value are claims about the metaphysical status of a thing's value. They are meant to capture the idea that some things do not get their value from contingent facts about their circumstances or from their relations to other things, but rather they have value in their own right. The philosopher G.E. Moore (1873–1958) was most closely associated with this conception of intrinsic value. He proposed an 'isolation test' to determine whether things have it: if a universe containing only the object would be better than a completely empty universe, Moore claimed, then we know the object has intrinsic value (Moore, 1903/1993). Moore's understanding of value has been criticised on meta-ethical grounds too complex to take up here, but there are very few environmental goods that people value in this way. Extrinsic properties such as rarity or ecosystemic function are much more common bases of environmental values (O'Neill, 1992). Biodiversity is probably the best candidate for this kind of valuation—some people do seem to think that a biodiverse world is simply a better world. Yet, even in that case, if biodiverse environments were harmful to the individual organisms within them, or if biodiversity were associated with ecosystemic degradation rather than resilience, the reason for continuing to value biodiversity would be unclear.

Objective value is also a claim about the independence of a thing's value: for a thing to be objectively valuable is forr it to be valuable regardless of whether valuers in fact value it. At first it might seem as though objective value is wholly incompatible with economic valuation, since one of the presuppositions of economic valuation is that value comes from being the object of a preference. However, three points are worth noting in this regard. First, economic valuation need not be committed to the view that welfare (or goodness) is a matter of preference satisfaction. As seen above, the most plausible understanding of utility regards it as contingently associated with welfare and goodness rather than as constituting those things. Second, even if economics were to accept preference-satisfaction utilitarianism, that theory does accept the objectivity of at least one value, namely the satisfaction of preferences. So claims about objective value being incompatible with preference-satisfaction utilitarianism are wrong; the disagreement is not about whether values can be objective, but rather about which values are so. Third, it is not necessarily a problem for economists if the *content* of the preferences they are measuring involve different presuppositions about value than their own presuppositions. Just as virtue ethicists can judge the character of utilitarians who are indifferent to character, so economists can take account of the preferences of people who are unconcerned with preference satisfaction. That said, existence value still fails to capture intrinsic value in the sense of objective value. I can prefer that polar bears continue to exist independently of any (active) use I might make of them but also think that my preference is what makes their continued existence valuable. The existence value of things is compatible with objectivism about value *and* with subjectivism about value.

Existence value also fails to capture intrinsic value in the sense of nonanthropocentric value. Whether a thing should continue to exist and whether its interests are morally important are distinct matters. As with humans, one can think that a nonhuman's interests matter morally and yet think that in some cases those interests tell in favour of a merciful death rather than continued existence.

One might think that the clearest way in which existence value could serve as an adequate proxy for intrinsic value is if intrinsic value were understood as non-instrumental value or end value. Non-instrumental value is the value that a thing has beyond its value as a means to an end, and end value is a matter of how a thing ought to be cared about (for its own sake, rather than for the sake of something else). Existence value also seems to be a way of valuing things for reasons other than their (active) uses and so might seem to fit both conceptions nicely. However, even here, one must be careful. While wanting something to continue to exist might be involved in valuing it non-instrumentally, such a desire is not required for non-instrumental valuation. As Robin Attfield has pointed out, what many people who care about the welfare of nonhuman animals prefer is their *flourishing* rather than simply their *existence* (Attfield, 1998). While there might be some environmental preferences for the mere existence of particular things, more typically people want individuals, species, or ecosystems to flourish; they want ecological relationships maintained; and they want to prevent damage and harm. Further, many preferences for the continued existence of endangered species, for example, are really preferences their extinction not be caused by humans. Natural extinctions are disvalued far less than anthropogenic extinctions. So even existence itself is often valued in a way that is sensitive to causal context (Brookshire et al., 1986; Crowards, 1997).

Moreover, things can have existence value without non-instrumental or end value, and things can have non-instrumental or end value without existence value. For an example of the former, I might value spotted owls as a means to preserving old-growth forest ecosystems, and care about them for the sake of those ecosystems, but still prefer their continued existence independently of any (active) use I will make of them. For an example of the latter, a Buddhist can value her friends as ends in themselves and care about them for their own sakes while accepting the impermanence of all things and not forming desires that oppose this doctrine. As the earlier discussion noted, loving someone and preferring their continued existence are different matters.

Future directions

Existence value is thus a poor way to represent most claims about intrinsic value. This is unsurprising; capturing all the senses of 'intrinsic value' within the same concept, when they operate so differently, is difficult (perhaps impossible). Yet if public policies are to be assessed in part by looking at their effects on what people value, then understanding the nature of those values is a very important task.

Some instruments of policy choice have already been formed to try to address this problem. Multiple criteria decision analysis [Chapter 30], qualitative and semi-qualitative evaluation methods [Chapters 31 and 32], and deliberative models [Chapters 33 and 34] all aim to inform policy choice in a way that does not require the use of existence values as a proxy for intrinsic values. In this respect, they are superior to methods that do. Such methods need further development, however, and their adequate treatment of intrinsic values requires that they be developed in such a way that they remain sensitive to the differences among different types of intrinsic value.

Concluding remarks

People's preferences sometimes operate differently from the way that economic analyses assume they do: standard economic assumptions about commensurability, aggregation, and substitution are often rejected by those whose preferences are being assessed. Understanding intrinsic values can help us to see why this is so. Some senses of intrinsic value are really claims about lexicographic ordering of values; others invoke complex social norms about how we should respond to an object; others are claims about the sources of an object's value or its metaphysical status; others aim to present an object as something we have responsibilities to rather than something that should be regarded as a resource. These are not differences in how much we value things but rather differences in how we value things.

In order to understand the effects that policies will have on the things that people care about, understanding the differences in the ways that they care about these things is important. In this regard, policy analysis needs good psychology, sociology, and anthropology as much as it needs good economics. (It might also need good ethology: after all, humans are only some of the creatures with preferences.) However, policy analysis must consider not only what we do prefer, but also what we ought to prefer. Actual preferences are often short-sighted, destructive, and ignorant, making them a poor basis for policy choice. A sense of what constitutes human flourishing and the flourishing of other species, as well as what moral responsibilities we bear to one another and to other things in the world, is crucial for the formation of wise environmental policies.

Note

1   Editor's Note: Option, existence and bequest value were originally employed by environmental economists working on contingent valuation to explain the substantial non-equivalence of use value and willingness to pay. There was no altruism beyond that for future generations (i.e. bequest value), which logically is a subcategory of altruistic value (a much later addition). All economic altruism is paradoxically selfish, i.e. self rewarding (Spash, 2006).

Key further readings cited

Aldred, I. (1994). Existence value, welfare and altruism. *Environmental Values*, 3, 381–401.
Attfield, R. (1998). Existence value and intrinsic value. *Ecological Economics*, 24, 163–160.
Davidson, M.D. (2013). On the relation between ecosystem services, intrinsic value, existence value and economic valuation. *Ecological Economics*, 95, 171–177.

Other literature cited

Anderson, E. (1993). *Value in Ethics and Economics*. Cambridge, Massachusetts: Harvard University Press.
Arrow, K., Solow, R., Portney, P. R., Leamer, E.E., Radner, R. and Schuman, H. (1993). *Report of the NOAA Panel on Contingent Valuation*.
Brookshire, D. S., Eubanks, L. S. and Sorg, C. F. (1986). Existence Values and Normative Economics: Implications for Valuing Water Resources. *Water Resources Research*, 22(11), 1509–1518.
Broome, J. (1999). Ethics out of Economics. Cambridge: Cambridge University Press.
Crowards, T. (1997). Nonuse values and the environment: Economic and ethical motivations. *Environmental Values*, 6(2), 143–167.

Gowdy, J.M. (1997). The value of biodiversity: Markets, society and ecosystems. *Land Economics*, 73(1), 25–41.

Griffin, J. (1986). *Well-Being: Its Meaning, Measurement, and Moral Importance*. Oxford: Clarendon Press.

Jamieson, D. (2008). *Ethics and the Environment: An Introduction*. Cambridge: Cambridge University Press.

Justus, J., Colyvan, M., Regan, H. and Maguire, L. (2009). Buying into conservation: Intrinsic versus instrumental value. *Trends in Ecology and Evolution*, 24(4), 187–191.

Kolstad, C. D. (2000). *Environmental Economics*. Oxford: Oxford University Press.

Krutilla, J. (1967). Conservation reconsidered. *American Economic Review*, 57(4), 777–786.

Lockwood, M. (1999). Humans valuing Nature: Synthesising insights from philosophy, psychology and economics. *Environmental Values*, 8(3), 381–401.

Madariaga, B., McConnell, K.E. (1987). Exploring existence value. *Water Resources Research*, 23(5), 936–942.

McShane, K. (2007). Why environmental ethics shouldn't give up on intrinsic value. *Environmental Ethics*, 29(1), 43–61.

Moore, G.E. (1903/1993). *Principia Ethica* (2nd rev. ed.). Cambridge: Cambridge University Press.

More, T.A., Averill, J.R., Stevens, T.H. (1996). Values and economics in environmental management: A perspective and critique. *Journal of Environmental Management*, 48(4), 397–409.

O'Neill, J. (1992). The varieties of intrinsic value. *The Monist*, 75(2), 119–137.

Parfit, D. (1984). *Reasons and Persons*. New York: Oxford University Press.

Pearce, D.W., Markandya, A., Barbier, E.B. (1989). *Blueprint for a Green Economy*. London: Earthscan.

Sen, A. (1979). Utilitarianism and welfarism. *Journal of Philosophy*, 76(9), 463–489.

Spash, C.L. (1997). Ethics and environmental attitudes with implications for economic valuation. *Journal of Environmental Management*, 50(4), 403–416.

Spash, C.L. (2006). Non-economic motivation for contingent values: Rights and attitudinal beliefs in the willingness to pay for environmental improvements. *Land Economics*, 82(4), 602–622.

Spash, C.L. (2008). Contingent valuation design and data treatment: If you can't shoot the messenger, change the message. *Environment and Planning C: Government and Policy*, 26(1), 34–53.

Turner, R.K. (2004). Economic Valuation of Water Resources in Agriculture: From the Sectoral to a Functional Perspective of Natural Resource Management *Water Reports* (no.27). Rome: Food and Agriculture Organization of the United Nations.

Turner, R.K., Paavola, J., Cooper, P., Farber, S., Jessamy, V., Georgiou, S. (2003). Valuing nature: lessons learned and future research directions. *Ecological Economics*, 46(3), 493–510.

Weisbrod, B.A. (1964). Collective-consumption services of individual-consumption goods. *Quarterly Journal of Economics*, 78(3), 471–477.

24

NEEDS AS A CENTRAL ELEMENT OF SUSTAINABLE DEVELOPMENT

Felix Rauschmayer and Ines Omann

Introduction

Needs play a central role for sustainable development (SD), both in its most famous definition in the Brundtland report and, more generally, as a concept of wellbeing across the globe and into the future (Gough, 2015). The Brundtland report of the World Commission on Environment and Development defines SD as "development that meets the needs of the present without compromising the ability of future generations to meet their own needs" (WCED, 1987). The report also states that giving overriding priority to the needs of powerless people implies the acceptance of limitations when meeting present needs. However, the report's concept of needs is rather vague when referring to 'essential needs' (e.g., jobs, food, shelter) of the world's poor and future generations.

Despite such a prominent role, the concept of needs has not really been taken up in subsequent discussions (Gough, 2015). The debate has rather focused on strong or weak sustainability, the number and content of columns or dimensions of sustainability, or questions of assessment and decision making. The main school of practice within ecological economics that uses needs as a central concept builds on the seminal work of Manfred Max-Neef (1991) on human development, relating his concept of Human-Scale Development Approach (HSDA) to SD (Guillen-Royo, 2010; Rauschmayer et al., 2011a).

In this chapter we acknowledge the importance of needs for SD, but provide a specification that differs from the Brundtland report and SD literature. The following sections cover (i) different notions of needs, distinguishing needs from preferences; (ii) the centrality of needs in Max-Neef's HSDA, (iii) insights into current approaches on needs and SD, and (iv) emerging directions related to needs and SD.

The defining aspects of needs

The Brundtland definition uses the then dominant concept of basic needs, specifying individual needs (e.g., shelter, food) and societal needs (e.g., high growth rate of protein availability). This conception, also used by the World Bank and the International Labour Organisation, was criticised for its materialism and paternalism, as it easily leads to elites specifying measures, such things as square metres and calories for living, delivered through top-down administration.

According to Gasper (1996), the term needs has three generic meanings which feed into three types of analysis:

1 descriptive analysis: needs are understood as positive entities related to some form of want or desire;
2 instrumental analysis: needs are understood as requisites for meeting a given end;
3 normative analysis: needs are understood as justified, or priority, requisites.

Many studies rely on all three meanings at the same time and try to draw normative legitimacy from an empirically observed importance of instrumental needs (Rauschmayer et al., 2011b). In everyday language needs is a term often used descriptively in two senses. First, it may refer to goods or services that satisfy some form of want or desire (e.g., 'I need a job'). Here, the clear instrumental relation and the normative quality of the operative entity (job) are not spelled out. Second, when human wellbeing, as a multidimensional concept, is the given end, then some minimum fulfilment of each of these dimensions is instrumental for achieving wellbeing. The normative content of this end has to be specified further: Which needs? Whose needs? Which degree of needs fulfilment? For governments, a minimum fulfilment of individual needs, both *intra*generationally and *inter*generationally, is the goal of SD.

O'Neill differentiates between instrumental and categorical uses of the needs concept. For the latter the ends are not optional, but a "condition of living a minimal level of human flourishing at all, such that a person can be said to be harmed if they are not met" (O'Neill, 2011: 26). A categorical need is different from a biological need, but of course some of the categorical needs are biological. In this sense, a categorical use of needs requires the definition of dimensions of human flourishing,[1] as well as thresholds of harm.

Following Alkire (2002) we believe needs should refer to the final requisites individuals have for achieving human flourishing. In this sense, jobs are relevant to us insofar as through work we can earn money to buy necessary things for our survival (need for subsistence), find a place in society (identity), express our creativity (creation), or be part of a community (affection, participation). People can realise these (or further) needs to different degrees because there are differences between types of jobs, their institutional and cultural embedding, and individuals [see also Chapter 21].

Within the last 30 years, many different lists of needs, values or dimensions of human development have been created through empirical or conceptual research. Alkire (2002) compares a number of them, derived from the fields of moral philosophy, psychology, economics, and development studies. She refers to authors such as Nussbaum (2000: ten basic human capabilities directed to national legislative bodies), Finnis (1997: ten basic reasons for action), Max-Neef (1991: nine basic human needs; HSDA), Narayan et al. (2000: five dimensions of wellbeing, gathered from a cross-cultural study in 23 countries including primarily poor, illiterate or remote respondents), and Schwartz (1994: ten human values). Alkire names three reasons for specifying dimensions of human development: (i) they give secure epistemological and empirical footing to the multidimensional objective of human development; (ii) they are practical to use for communities to evaluate trade-offs; (iii) they help groups to make more informed and reflective choices as a non-paternalistic tool. Those lists share the idea that the dimensions which we further call 'needs', are incommensurable [see Chapter 22], non-hierarchical, and irreducible, but nonetheless interrelated and interactive. Alkire found few basic differences between them. Several authors claim these needs are universal (e.g. Max-Neef et al., 1991; Nussbaum, 2000; Gough, 2015; in a weaker sense also Alkire, 2002), whereas opinions differ with regard to the finiteness of the categories.

Much of the discussion on SD has been held in terms of preferences, a concept central to modern welfare economics. O'Neill (2011: 26) proposes the concept of needs as an "alternative to that of preferences in the characterisation of the concepts of welfare and sustainability". Gough (2015: 1) goes even further when stating that "only a concept of human needs can do the theoretical work required" to conceive of human wellbeing across space and time. Both authors list differences between needs and preferences, including: needs claims are objective, while preference claims are subjective; not meeting a categorical need might harm a person, whereas not giving a person what they prefer does not necessarily harm them; meeting needs leads to satisfaction (never disappointment), whereas satisfying a preference can lead to disappointment.

Following O'Neill (2011) and Gough (2015), needs rather than preferences should be used in characterising SD or human wellbeing for at least four reasons.

1   If SD means maintaining or improving the wellbeing of the next generation, and if wellbeing means meeting needs, then SD requires that the current generation bequests goods to future generations that allow them to meet all their different needs. However, "[e]nvironmental goods are not substitutable by goods that satisfy distinct needs and preferences because they answer to quite distinct dimensions of human wellbeing" (O'Neill, 2011: 33ff.). A preference-based approach would allow for substitutability of these goods.

2   A needs-based approach, relating to the universality of needs, better addresses the ethical obligations wealthy people owe to poor current and to future generations, because they owe them the freedom to achieve a decent quality of life which can be expressed through needs as fundamental dimensions, but not through preferences or goods. The degree to which certain needs are met may well constitute a criterion for intragenerational and intergenerational justice (cp. Gutwald et al., 2014).

3   Needs provide a more adequate starting point for the acknowledgement of forms of human dependence and vulnerability that informs basic concerns with sustainability.

4   Needs are satiable, preferences and desires are not, and as such are used in neoclassical economics where agents are assumed to be non-satiable. The satiability of needs, and herewith the limitation in the use of goods it implies, is an important characteristic supporting sufficiency and degrowth policies.

Gough (2015: 20) concludes that "[a] sound concept of universal basic human needs is now more essential than ever to guide policies that simultaneously sustain the planet and human wellbeing".

Needs as central to HSDA

In the 1980s, Max-Neef and his colleagues developed the needs-based HSDA as a concept and tool empowering communities to develop their future. Basing this development on their individual and societal needs in a participatory manner enables a community to interpret its own situation holistically and to improve wellbeing without depending on economic growth (Max-Neef, 1991). The HSDA's basis is a list of nine needs, which were developed in many small-scale workshops in Latin America, Asia and Europe (Max-Neef et al., 1991). The nine needs are: subsistence, protection, affection, understanding, participation, idleness, creation, identity, freedom.[2]

These needs are realised through satisfiers, which exist in four axiological categories: being, having, doing, and interacting (see Table 24.1 for a matrix including needs and satisfiers). The 'being' column lists personal or collective attributes. The 'having' column lists such things as institutions, norms, mechanisms and laws. The 'doing' column lists personal or collective actions. The 'interacting' column lists locations and milieus. Max-Neef considers needs as universal and non-hierarchic, whereas satisfiers differ from case to case, dependent on culture, situation, education, institutions and further factors. The satisfiers can be classified as singular, synergetic, destructive, inhibiting or as pseudo-satisfiers, according to the way in which they fulfil one or several needs. In Max-Neef's framework needs are abstract; they neither substitute for each other, nor do they conflict. Typically, conflicts arise at the level of specific negotiable satisfiers or strategies.

Table 24.1 Matrix of needs and satisfiers

	Existential categories			
	Being (qualities)	Having (things)	Doing (actions)	Interacting (settings)
Fundamental human needs				
Subsistence	physical and mental health	food, shelter, work	feed, clothe, rest, work	living environment, social setting
Protection	care, adaptability, autonomy	social security, health systems, work	co-operate, plan, take care of, help	social environment, dwelling
Affection	respect, sense of humour, generosity, sensuality	friendships, family, relationships with Nature	share, take care of, make love, express emotions	privacy, intimate spaces of togetherness
Understanding	critical capacity, curiosity, intuition	literature, teachers, policies, educational	analyse, study, meditate, investigate	schools, families, universities, communities
Participation	receptiveness, dedication, sense of humour	responsibilities, duties, work, rights	cooperate, dissent, express opinions	associations, parties, churches, neighbourhoods
Idleness	imagination, tranquillity, spontaneity	games, parties, peace of mind	day-dream, remember, relax, have fun	landscapes, intimate spaces, places to be alone
Creation	imagination, boldness, inventiveness, curiosity	abilities, skills, work, techniques	invent, build, design, work, compose, interpret	spaces for expression, workshops, audiences
Identity	sense of belonging, self-esteem, consistency	language, religions, work, customs, values, norms	get to know oneself, grow, commit oneself	places one belongs to, everyday settings
Freedom	autonomy, passion, self-esteem, open-mindedness	equal rights	dissent, choose, run risks, develop mindfulness	anywhere
Transcendence	inner centredness, presence	religions, rites	pray, meditate, develop mindfulness	places for worship

Source: adapted from Max-Neef et al. (1991: 32–33).

Such a matrix of needs and satisfiers can be used, and developed further, to assess the extent to which existing goods and services—or the social or natural systems providing them—contribute to or inhibit the fulfilment of needs. Depending upon context, 'goods and services' can be seen as strategies to meet one specific need (singular satisfier) or they can simultaneously meet several needs (synergetic). They can also fail to meet a need, or simultaneously impede several other needs (inhibiting satisfier). For example, at an individual level, owning a car may meet a person's needs for affection, idleness and freedom, but it may also inhibit their need for identity in the sense that after having bought a car, the person might not consider herself as living sustainably.

The matrix has been used by academics and practitioners both as a theoretical framework in desktop studies and as a participatory tool with groups of people or communities (Guillen-Royo, 2015). A workshop typically takes two to three days and consists of several phases in which participants co-generate: (i) a matrix with negative/harmful satisfiers which impede needs satisfactions; (ii) a utopian matrix with synergic satisfiers that allow optimal fulfilment of needs; (iii) a set of synergic bridging satisfiers, both exogenous and endogenous, that allow a transition from unmet needs to meeting needs and improving wellbeing (Guillen-Royo, 2015). Such a process, by focusing on needs and linking satisfiers to needs, "allow[s] for the discovery of unexpected facets of a problem, thus increasing awareness about what [is] relevant" (Max-Neef et al., 1991: 43). A clear dynamic evolves in the process of clarifying the relationship between satisfiers and needs. For example, clarifying the reasons why I might want to buy a car (i.e. the needs it addresses), and the reasons that inhibit me from doing so (i.e. my unmet needs), enables me to consider whether other satisfiers might be better suited to meeting my needs. This thought process encourages self-reflection and consideration of whether a set of needs are as important as assumed at first.

Max-Neef's original methodology requires many people and much time. Therefore, the HSDA has been developed to create less resource intensive formats and adapted to a multitude of contexts. The HSDA is well-known among ecological economists, but rarely analysed scientifically or used in academic contexts. María del Valle Barrera has established a growing database (http://hsdnetwork.org) with more than 400 HSDA entries from all over the world (when accessed September 2015).

Needs, HSDA and SD

The HSDA has been developed to improve the fulfilment of the needs of (mainly poor) citizens, but it is not explicitly linked to SD as a normative call for intragenerational and intergenerational justice. It is designed as a group-process around a common discussion concerned with identifying appropriate strategies for satisfying individual needs in a community setting. Yet Gough (2015) claims needs-based conceptions of wellbeing match the normative core of SD. So, let us turn to asking a central question: Does HSDA, by giving an explicit account of needs and satisfiers, provide the necessary, or even sufficient, conditions for furthering SD?

HSDA strengthens SD's normative core through a universal understanding of needs that induces empathy between the participants of such processes and beyond. More specifically, spelling out four different categories of how to satisfy needs reminds participants in countries with a high level of material throughput that 'having' is not the only way of meeting one's needs (e.g., for idleness). Moving away from 'having' towards other ways of meeting one's needs is certainly a significant way to reduce resource consumption and protect Nature.

Guillen-Royo (2015) argues that the HSDA provides a framework and methodology to support SD policy making at the grass-roots levels. She parallels the HSDA with alternative perspectives such as degrowth [Chapter 44] or steady-state economics [Chapter 45], both of which reject the necessity of economic growth. The HSDA is ambivalent on economic growth, but experience shows that participants of HSDA workshops identify satisfiers supporting economic growth—competitiveness, individualism, hectic lifestyles, consumerism—as being harmful (i.e., hindering fulfilment of needs). In contrast, Guillen-Royo associates SD with synergic satisfiers—values, attitudes, actions, institutions, infrastructures and natural environments—that address more than one of the ten fundamental human needs. She (2015: 14) regards the synergic satisfiers that participants identify, to be by definition sustainable, because "they cannot satisfy more than one need if they destroy or harm the natural environment" (Guillen-Royo, 2015: 14).

Starting from the political discussion on SD, Rauschmayer, Omann and Frühmann (2011b) link the discussions on capabilities, needs and wellbeing to that of sustainability. Their central argument is that a needs-based search for an increase in wellbeing (e.g. through HSDA) has a great potential to increase *eudaimonic* wellbeing (e.g. self-acceptance, autonomy, social contribution) and normally shifts the focus away from hedonic wellbeing. In this way, such a process reduces participants' hedonic treadmills and increases their capabilities to lead a valuable life. While the first effect is directly related to decreased materialism, both effects increase the participants' wellbeing; making constraints on consumption less susceptible to reducing the participants' overall wellbeing. Apart from these sustainability related effects, Rauschmayer, Omann and Frühmann (2011b) treat SD as a value that can (and should) be translated to needs-based processes in the form of decision constraints, knowledge inputs about human dependency or persuasion concerning intragenerational and intergenerational justice.

Capabilities and needs: Different or similar approaches?

Discussions on needs and SD often refer to Amartya Sen's capability approach (Lessmann & Rauschmayer, 2014), either to draw a distinction with or make a link to needs-based approaches (Costanza et al., 2007, Robeyns and van der Veen, 2007, Rauschmayer et al., 2011a, Gough, 2015). Two standard complaints from capability theorists against needs-based theories, referring to the basic needs approaches of the 1980s, are: (i) that needs are defined in terms of some bundle of goods, and (ii) needs-based approaches are paternalistic (O'Neill, 2011: 28). The argument runs that in contrast to the goods-focus of needs, the capability approach focuses on the functionings, relating to what people value doing and being; that specifying goods paternalistically is in contrast with Sen's concern for people's freedoms to achieve valuable doings and beings.

Confronting the capability approach with a fundamental and not goods-related needs approach such as the HSDA, the distinctions narrow down substantially: differentiating between needs and strategies opens up space to people for freely defining their own valuable doings and beings. Following Alkire (2002) needs can be understood as the basic dimensions of human flourishing, along which capabilities and functionings can be measured. Gough (2015: 21) even states that in order to deal with SD "the capability approach needs the underpinning of a rigorous theory of human need". In the light of transformative research, the HSDA offers a procedural frame for the elaboration of valuable functionings. As mentioned above adding the categories of doing and interacting to Sen's categories of having and being, incites people to consider immaterial alternatives to having things to meet their needs aka achieve their functionings.

Substantial, procedural and motivational sustainability

HSDA's link to SD can be summarised through differentiating between substantial, procedural and motivational sustainability (Schäpke and Rauschmayer, 2014). These can be described as follows:

1   Substantial sustainability refers to the factual consequences of actions on the world's poor's and future generations to lead a decent life;
2   Procedural sustainability addresses the ways in which actors deal with the factual and moral complexities inherent in SD, such as irreducible ignorance with regard to substantial sustainability or trade-offs between intergenerational and intragenerational fairness;
3   Motivational sustainability relates to the intentions that actors have for their action with regard to these possibilities.

The HSDA does not *per se* capture substantial sustainability, because it assesses neither consequences of strategies for the needs satisfaction of the world's poor or future generations, nor any proxies for the latter (such as effects on ecosystems, climate change). Omitting these aspects from assessment means it also fails to enhance procedural sustainability, because factual and moral complexities are not addressed. With regard to motivational sustainability, we would argue (but no studies are known to the authors) that using a needs-based setting for developing utopias and concrete strategies increases participants' empathy, as all humans, and partially also other beings (Jolibert et al., 2011), have the same fundamental needs which can be experienced and integrated into the process.

Putting all this together, we agree with Gough (2015) that needs-based conceptions are well suited to deal with SD problems and we think, but do not have evidence for it, that needs-based processes such as the HSDA have the potential to create sustainable policies. At the same time, needs-based processes do not automatically result in SD, and work is required to increase the suitability of HSDA and similar processes for SD. Related to substantial sustainability, spelling out intragenerational and intergenerational justice in terms of needs and satisfiers is an important task—Gough's work (2015) provides an excellent basis. Concepts known from other fields (e.g. Leach et al., 2010) could be adapted to address procedural sustainability. With regard to motivational sustainability, needs-based approaches are more intuitive than those based on preferences or capabilities. They offer more space for developing empathy and for dealing with conflicts and emotions—two components that are relevant especially for sustainability decision-making.

Future directions

The lack of attention to the motivational dimension of sustainability is, in our eyes, the most important flaw in the current discussion on sustainability transitions. This is especially the case for affluent people where there is a moral duty to adapt their impacts to norms of intragenerational and intergenerational justice. How can individuals in their various roles—citizens, consumers, change agents, change refusers—adapt their agency so that it includes the consideration of the world's poor and future generations?

This can be exemplified with respect to degrowth [Chapter 44] where sufficiency is heavily discussed as a concept that—based on the recognition of a moral duty—seeks to combine low material consumption with a high level of wellbeing. The concept of needs allows the reintroduction of the idea of satisfaction into consumption because needs can be satisfied unlike preferences. Understanding satisfiers in their relation to needs allows rediscovering and appreciating personal and societal limits to growth; not as external constraints, but as internal satisfaction. At the same time, the HSDA (as with other needs-based approaches) does not guarantee a move towards degrowth (at least, we are unaware of any such analysis). HSDA was developed for furthering community development of the poor, and the methodology would have to be adapted for application to the rich people for studying degrowth. This adaptation would have to address the inherent danger of paternalism—as for all transformative methods aiming at furthering sustainability or degrowth. Additionally, addressing motivational sustainability requires that HSDA applications to sustainability transition involve questions of substantive as well as procedural sustainability. How to use the needs concept on the level of whole economies also remains an open question; Nunes et al. (2016) have proposed a conceptual model linking needs to sustainability indicators.

Above we claimed that needs do not conflict with each other, but that conflicts may arise at the level of specific satisfiers that are perceived to be incompatible. Such conflicts are evident on a societal level, but here we focus on the phenomenon at an individual level. Selecting a satisfier that meets some need while harming another, while both are currently important to an individual, entails such an intrapersonal conflict. For example, if a person values SD highly (the needs of protection and identity can be associated with it), they might want to satisfy their needs in a way that also allows for intragenerational and intergenerational justice. At some point, this person will most likely experience intrapersonal conflicts due to conflicting motivations, such as, taking an airplane where a need for idleness might conflict with the need for protection and identity. Such intrapersonal conflicts may hinder personal attempts to live more sustainably and may even lead to psychological lock-in—a state in which an intrapersonal conflict has been present for a long time and where no resolution is in sight.

The discussion on categorical and imperfectly substitutable needs is relevant for the intrapersonal level as well: There are no substitutes for needs *per se*, but they may exist on the level of strategies. The need for idleness, for instance, can be met in a variety of ways, some using more resources than others. This substantial substitutability of satisfiers is highly relevant for sustainability. Although, while substituting satisfiers might sound easy, it is sometimes difficult to recognise the possibilities or achieve. For example, the conflicts experienced between different modes of idleness, are rarely evident or easily traced back to the needs or values underlying them. Rather people experience a vague feeling of unease with regard to their lifestyles (such as a person regarding themselves caring for SD because they are taking the plane).

In order to support recognising, addressing and eventually overcoming conflicts related to the wish of living sustainably, we have developed a tool—thriving through awareness for non-conflicting strategies (THANCS)—that employs a four-step process; ideally this is applied within a group in which the participants share the same or similar intrapersonal conflicts (Omann and Rauschmayer, 2011; Rauschmayer and Omann, 2015). The process aims at supporting individuals to effectively change their behaviour by implementing new strategies that should be supported through political change and backed up by knowledge on how this newly elaborated strategy can contribute to sustainability transitions. It supports participants in four ways: (i) acknowledging tensions; (ii) reflecting upon the internal reasons for the conflict in terms of needs and values (what needs are met or harmed; which values are concerned); (iii) communicating this reflection to others; and (iv) finding ways of dealing with or even overcoming the conflict(s).

Such processes combine individual reflection with group sharing and co-creation and combine reflection on motivational issues with those on substantial sustainability. They thereby can lead to increased sustainability as well as individual wellbeing, because they increase the coherence between one's own identity and action, and/or create synergies by realising several needs instead of achieving one and frustrating others. Yet, they only address substantial and procedural sustainability on a rather superficial level, because neither in-depth analysis of the satisfiers' consequences, nor the elaboration of societally more complex strategies to deal with the complexities are possible in such a setting.

Concluding remarks

Needs-based concepts, as defined in this chapter, offer an appropriate frame to deal with issues of intragenerational and intergenerational justice that are at the core of sustainability. To talk about needs is to talk about things that matter and basing assessments of SD on needs offers several advantages compared to preference based concepts. Relearning about limits of needs' satisfaction may further sufficiency and facilitate the emergence of degrowth. Within ecological economics, Max-Neef's HSDA is the most prominent and still most promising needs-based approach, close to Sen's capability approach. Max-Neef's differentiation between needs and satisfiers opens up space for linking inner and outer, individual and collective transformation processes. Although, in order to use it unambiguously for SD modifications in its design are required to create an individually and collectively enabling perspective. Modifications concern substantial references to intergenerational and intragenerational justice on a global scale, to procedural allowance on how to handle the implied complexities and to the question on why HSDA participants should acknowledge their moral duty towards future generations and the world's poor. This last question is of prime importance for sustainability transitions in countries with a high environmental impact and has to be addressed with much more intensity than has been the case to date.

Notes

1 We do not distinguish here between good life, human flourishing, quality of life or human wellbeing.
2 Following Costanza et al. (2007) and suggested by Max-Neef and colleagues (Max-Neef et al., 1991: 27), we add transcendence as a tenth need.

Key further readings cited

Alkire, S. (2002). Dimensions of human development. *World Development*, 30(2): 181–205.
Gough, I. (2015). Climate change and sustainable welfare: The centrality of human needs. *Cambridge Journal of Economics*, 39(5): 1191–1121.
Guillen-Royo, M. (2015). *Sustainability and Wellbeing. Human-Scale Development in Practice*. London: Routledge.
Max-Neef, M. (1991). *Human Scale Development: Conception, Application and Further Reflections*. London, New York: The Apex Press.
Rauschmayer, F., Omann, I., Frühmann, J. (eds.). (2011a). *Sustainable Development: Capabilities, Needs, and Well-Being*. London: Routledge.

Other literature cited

Costanza, R., Fisher, B., Ali, S., Beer, C., Bond, L., Boumans, R., Snapp, R. (2007). Quality of life: An approach integrating opportunities, human needs, and subjective well-being. *Ecological Economics*, 61 (1–2): 267–276.
Finnis, J. (1997). Commensuration and public reason. In R. Chang (ed.), *Incommensurability, Incomparability, and Practical Reason* (pp. 215–233). Boston: Harvard University Press.

Gasper D. (1996). Needs and basic needs: A clarification of meanings, levels and different streams of work. *Working Papers of the Institute of Social Studies*. The Hague: Institute of Social Studies.

Gutwald, R., Leßmann, O., Masson, T., Rauschmayer, F. (2014). A capability approach to intergenerational justice? Examining the potential of Amartya Sen's ethics with regard to intergenerational issues. *Journal of Human Development and Capabilities*, 15(4): 355–368.

Jolibert, C., Max-Neef, M., Rauschmayer, F., Paavola, J. (2011). Should we care about the needs of non-humans? Needs assessment: a tool for environmental conflict resolution and sustainable organisation of living beings. *Environmental Policy and Governance*, 21, 259–269.

Leach, M., Scoones, I., Stirling, A. (2010). *Dynamic Sustainabilities: Technology, Environment, Social Justice*. London: Earthscan.

Lessmann, O., Rauschmayer, F. (eds.). (2014). *The Capability Approach and Sustainability*. London: Routledge.

Max-Neef, M., Elizalde, A., Hopenhayn, M. (1991). Development and Human Needs. In M. Max-Neef (ed.), *Human Scale Development: Conception, Application and Further Reflections* (pp. 13–54). London, New York: The Apex Press.

Narayan, D., Chambers, R., Shah, M.K., Petesch, P. (2000). *Voices of the Poor: Crying Out for Change*. New York: Oxford University Press for the World Bank.

Nunes, B., Alamino, R.C., Shaw, D., Bennett, D. (2016) Modelling sustainability performance to achieve absolute reductions in socio-ecological systems. *Journal of Cleaner Production*, 132(September): 32–44.

Nussbaum, M. C. (2000). *Women and Human Development: The Capabilities Approach*. Cambridge: Cambridge University Press.

Omann, I., Rauschmayer, F. (2011). Transition towards sustainable development: Which tensions emerge? How do deal with them? In F. Rauschmayer, I. Omann, J. Frühmann (eds.), *Sustainable Development: Capabilities, Needs, and Well-Being* (pp. 144–163). London: Routledge.

O'Neill, J. (2011). The overshadowing of needs. In F. Rauschmayer, I. Omann, J. Frühmann (eds.), *Sustainable Development: Capabilities, Needs, and Well-Being* (pp. 25–42). London: Routledge.

Rauschmayer, F., Omann, I. (2015). Well-being in sustainability transitions - Making use of needs. In K.L. Syse, M.L. Mueller (eds.), *Sustainable Consumption and the Good Life: Interdisciplinary perspectives* (pp. 111–125). London: Routledge.

Rauschmayer, F., Omann, I., Frühmann, J. (2011b). Needs, capabilities, and quality of life. Re-focusing sustainable development. In F. Rauschmayer, I. Omann, J. Frühmann (eds.), *Sustainable Development: Capabilities, Needs, and Well-Being* (pp. 1–24). London: Routledge.

Robeyns, I., & van der Veen, R. J. (2007). *Sustainable Quality of Life: Conceptual Analysis for a Policy-relevant Empirical Specification*. Bilthoven: Netherlands Environmental Assessment Agency (MNP).

Schäpke, N., Rauschmayer, F. (2014). Going beyond efficiency: including altruistic motives in behavioral models for sustainability transitions to address sufficiency. *Sustainability: Science, Practice, & Policy*, 10(1): 29–44.

Schwartz, S.H. (1994). Are there universal aspects in the structure and contents of human values? *Journal of Social Issues*, 50(4): 19–45.

WCED (World Commission on Environment and Development) (1987). *Our Common Future*. Oxford: Oxford University Press.

25

FUTURE GENERATIONS

Richard B. Howarth

Introduction[1]

A concern for future generations is fundamental to the theory and practice of ecological economics, which Costanza (1991) defined as the "science and management of sustainability". As a field, ecological economics was formulated as an integrative, interdisciplinary response to the perceived limitations of natural resource and environmental economics—a branch of applied economics that strongly emphasises the criterion of Pareto efficiency as a guide to the "optimal" design of public policies. Following the publication of the Brundtland Report (WCED, 1987), issues of *intra*generational and *inter*generational fairness were given an essential role in the definition and achievement of sustainable development. Moreover, operationalising sustainability was seen to require an approach that linked economics (and its emphasis on efficiency) with the insights provided by ecosystem science, ethics, and a range of social science disciplines concerned with the analysis of institutions and governance.

In a deep sense, the concept of sustainability is a simple restatement of the conservation ethic that lay at the heart of the 'Progressive' approach to natural resource management that emerged in the United States of America (USA) during the early 1900s. In the USA, the acquisition of private property rights by corporate entities in the late 1800s led to the widespread clear-cutting of primeval forests across much of the country.[2] To conservationists, the physical overexploitation of resource stocks was seen as a threat to the interests of future generations. In this historical context, Gifford Pinchot—who had studied the principles of scientific forestry in Europe—led in the creation of the US Forest Service in 1905. Pinchot's management philosophy emphasised the public ownership and governance of natural resources based on sustained yield principles to meet the 'needs' of both present and future generations (Pinchot, 1910: 80) [see Chapter 24 on needs]. This conservation ethic strongly anticipated the definition of sustainable development set forth by the Brundtland Commission that focused on meeting "the needs of the present without compromising the ability of future generations to meet their own needs" (WCED, 1987). Yet, despite this continuity and the intuitive plausibility of this approach, issues of intergenerational fairness have remained controversial.

In this chapter, I cover the broad outlines of this debate in an attempt to summarise the current state of scholarly understanding, updating and extending the arguments presented in Howarth (2007). In the next section, I explain the core arguments concerning the perceived rights of future generations. I then focus on the concepts of weak and strong sustainability—competing frameworks for operationalising duties to posterity in policy analysis and decision-making. Finally, I discuss several promising directions that have emerged in the recent literature before presenting some closing remarks.

Are there duties to future generations?

A first set of issues concerns the basic moral status of future generations. Taken at face value, Pinchot's conservation ethic is based on the premises that: (i) natural resources should be understood as the joint property of all members of society; and (ii) future generations have rights that are commensurate with those held by the present generation. The first premise is supportive of a democratic approach to resource governance that ensures that the benefits of resource use are widely shared amongst members of society. This is expressly egalitarian, contrasting with the implications of pure private ownership, under which resource rents might be concentrated in the hands of the few.

This begs the question as to whether future generations have rights that are morally binding on the present. Beckerman (1994) has argued that future generations indeed should be afforded moral standing in social decisions about natural resources and the economy. However, he rejects the view that social choice should be grounded in a rights-based or deontological moral framework. Instead, decision-makers should aim to maximise the total summed welfare of present and future generations without an *a priori* focus on the concepts of rights or needs. Beckerman's approach to environmental management—grounded in Classical Utilitarianism—can support aggressive steps to conserve natural capital and the sustained provisioning of ecosystem services [see Chapter 43]. This is seen in the economics of climate change, where attaching equal weight to the utility of present and future generations supports aggressive actions to reduce greenhouse gas (GHG) emissions under plausible assumptions about the costs and benefits of climate stabilisation and the relationship between material affluence and experienced wellbeing (Broome, 2008). Still, Beckerman's approach rejects the moral intuition that future generations have rights that go beyond a consequentialist weighing of costs and benefits.

Parfit's (1983) argument against the conservation criterion is even more foundational. Suppose for the sake of argument that we adopt a deontological conception of individual rights, stipulating that actions are morally wrong if they inflict uncompensated harms on innocent third parties (Shue, 1999). This principle seems to entail a duty to avoid degrading the environment in ways that would impose catastrophic risks on posterity. Parfit, however, notes that the identities of future persons (i.e., the question of which set of *potential* persons becomes *actual*) is determined by the minute details of present decisions. In choices between futures involving high versus low environmental risks, Parfit's point is that the present generation is not deciding on the risks faced by a single, well-defined set of future people. On the contrary, the people who would be born into the "high risk" future would simply not exist if aggressive policies were implemented to protect the environment. According to this argument, those who come into existence would have reason to thank us for choosing the "high risk" outcome on which their very being depended, as long as they had lives that were minimally worth living, i.e. they were not prepared to commit suicide. (This contrasts with the classic utilitarian position whereby actions should be chosen to maximise total utility regardless of the identities of those to whom utility accrues.)

How pertinent is Parfit's critique to the real-world application of sustainability concepts? One point is that the children of today's world will have lives that will last many decades or even a century into the future. Based on the principle that an action is wrong if it benefits adults while impoverishing their living children and grandchildren, a straightforward conclusion is that each generation has a duty to ensure that life opportunities are sustained from one generation to the next. Moreover, our children and grandchildren will face duties to secure the flourishing of subsequent generations, resulting in a chain of obligation that stretches from the present to the indeterminate future (Howarth, 1992). The key to a conservation or sustainability ethic is the basic premise that the Earth's resources are in some sense the joint property of all members of society. An ethical contradiction arises if we provide our children with the capability to match our pattern of living but not the capacity to raise and adequately take care of their own children, which is after all a major dimension of human flourishing.

Weak sustainability

The foregoing discussion suggests that a coherent argument supports viewing questions of intergenerational fairness in terms of the rights of future generations, at least if one accepts a deontological approach to questions of justice and social choice. How can we then understand the specific content of those rights and their implications for ecological economics and governance? This question has generated a robust literature in which there are two major streams of thought focusing on the concepts of weak and strong sustainability (Neumayer, 2003).

In natural resource and environmental economics, the focus is typically on a weak sustainability that emphasises:

> an obligation to conduct ourselves so that we leave to the future the option or the capacity to be as well off as we are … [It] is an injunction not to satisfy ourselves by impoverishing our successors.
>
> *(Solow, 1993: 180–181)*

In succinct terms, the weak sustainability criterion requires that the welfare or utility experienced by a typical member of society should be constant, or increasing, from one generation to the next. Utility, not the conservation of ecosystems and natural capital *per se*, is the object of analysis.

Under certain idealised conditions, an economy is sustainable in this sense as long as investments in manufactured capital exceed the monetary value of natural resource depletion at all points in time—known as "Hartwick's rule" (Hartwick, 2000). In this characterisation, the definition of natural resources is all inclusive, involving any form of natural capital that contributes directly or indirectly to present or future human flourishing. Critics charge that this approach is problematic because it assumes that manufactured capital is substitutable for (and commensurable with) natural resources. Note, however, that the degree of substitutability is captured by the prevailing shadow prices that are employed in resource accounting. As the degree of substitutability approaches zero, the shadow price for a given resource approaches infinity and conserving natural capital becomes the only way to operationally satisfy the weak sustainability standard. Despite its popularity amongst mainstream economists, the axiomatic conditions under which Hartwick's rule holds true are strenuous and empirically problematic. In its basic form, the approach assumes that technology, population, and terms of trade are all constant over time, and that resources are allocated in a Pareto efficient manner so that there is no opportunity to improve the wellbeing of one generation without leaving another worse off (Pezzey, 2004). These assumptions are by no means innocuous, nor are they straightforward to address in generalisations of the approach.

In a world of technological change greater output can be derived from each unit of input, reducing the level of capital investment required to offset resource depletion. In contrast, population growth entails a need for increased investment to maintain a given level of welfare. Changing terms of trade can have complex effects. Consider the case of an agrarian economy that imports agrochemicals and equipment to produce commodities that are exported. If the price of chemicals and equipment increases relative to commodity prices on world markets, the level of domestic production must be increased to maintain a given standard of living.

Brekke (1997) casts doubt on the use of Hartwick's rule in practical applications of the weak sustainability criterion. In the face of changes in the state of technology, population and terms of trade, calculating the rate of investment needed to achieve sustainability requires both a suitably specified welfare metric and a model that projects economic, ecological and social trends into the long-run future. Technically, the welfare metric must be commensurable in the sense that it aggregates the various contributors to wellbeing into a single indicator [see Chapter 22 on incommensurability]. While the application and analysis of forward looking models may be important in understanding trade-offs between the welfare of present and future generations, one conclusion is that—in the short run—an economy can satisfy the accounting metrics associated with Hartwick's rule and yet be unsustainable (Pezzey, 2004).

The recent literature on the economics of climate change sheds further light on the practical limitations of the weak sustainability criterion as an approach to ecological governance. Models such as Nordhaus' (2013) dynamic integrated model of climate and the economy (DICE) suggest that climate 'externalities' have major implications for the standard of living enjoyed by future generations. This model is structured to represent the current state of knowledge concerning the costs of GHG emissions reductions, the impacts of human activity on climate, and the impacts of climate change on the future economy. Yet, under baseline assumptions, DICE suggests that deep cuts in GHG emissions are unnecessary to ensure that human welfare improves over intergenerational time scales. In this analysis, climate stabilisation may be justified in a utilitarian framing that attaches sufficient weight to the welfare of future generations (Broome, 2008), but issues of (weak) sustainability do not arise *per se*.

Of course, DICE is strongly assumption driven, and plausible changes in assumptions that are within the range of scientific opinion can change the results of DICE in qualitative terms. For example, Gerst et al. (2013) calculate a 0.3 per cent probability that climate change will cause a catastrophic collapse of the future economy in a stochastic version of DICE that accounts for statistically characterisable (or 'weak') uncertainties in climate damages and the sensitivity of climate with respect to GHG concentrations. This result does not account for 'strong' uncertainties linked to indeterminacy and ignorance that cannot be reduced to the language of probability measures (Spash, 2002, chapters 4 and 5). In a similar vein, Dietz and Stern (2015) find that climate change leads to outcomes that violate the weak sustainability criterion if climate damages fall on the capital stock and if technological change is endogenous.

On the one hand, such studies are examples of thought experiments that probe the scenarios that arise in alternative hypothetical worlds. On the other hand, the results of these studies show clearly that the basic conclusions of DICE and related models are not robust (Spash, 2002, chapter 7). The models support the conclusion that a phased transition to a low-carbon economy can minimise risks to the future economy at a relatively low short-run cost. They cast doubt, however, on the view that the damages caused by substantial changes in global climate can be compensated through increased capital investment, especially in the face of strong uncertainty.

Strong sustainability

An alternative approach to operationally defining the rights of future generations focuses on the concept of strong sustainability (Ekins et al., 2003). In its basic form, this criterion begins with the conservationist view that future generations have a right to share in the benefits provided by specific natural resources. Superficially, this conception might imply that ecological resources should be conserved and subject to minimal utilization. More deeply, however, the challenge is to manage resource stocks in ways that generate a sustained flow of services over time. The strong sustainability approach then specifies conditions that allow the fair distribution of benefits between generations.

In an attempt to flesh out the strong sustainability criterion in concrete terms, Daly (1991: 45) proposes a framework for 'environmental macroeconomics' that incorporates the following three-part rule:

1 Harvesting rates for renewable resources should not exceed regeneration rates.
2 Waste emissions should not exceed the renewable assimilative capacity of the environment.
3 Non-renewable resources should be exploited, but at a rate equal to the creation of renewable substitutes.

Daly suggests that utility is an experience that cannot be bequeathed *per se* to future generations and instead uses the concept of throughput based on the seminal work of Georgescu-Roegen (1971). Broadly, Daly's concern is to limit the use of the source and sink services provided by the biosphere to a scale that is ecologically sustainable. Daly believes that this has implications for the maximum level of aggregate throughput and for the forms of technological change that should be regarded as sustainable. In the same breath, however, these three conditions leave room for decision-makers to rely on cost-benefit analysis and other consequentialist valuation schemes as long as attention is paid to the needs of future generations. In this sense, the strong sustainability approach mirrors the Kantian distinction between duty and prudence in the theory of rational action.

The case of non-renewable resources is instructive and is worth exploring in some detail. Consider, for example, the case of fossil fuel extraction. Leaving all fossil fuel resources in the ground for all time would result in an outcome in which no present or future person derived benefits from an inherently valuable resource. This speaks to Hotelling's (1931) argument against government intervention in energy markets to slow the rate of resource extraction. Hotelling reasoned that achieving Pareto efficiency requires maximising the net present value of resource rents—an outcome that would (in theory) arise in a world of perfectly competitive markets. In Hotelling's model, property rights must be fully defined, and economic agents must be substantively rational with perfect foresight concerning future prices, resource scarcity and the state of the economy. These theoretical conditions are, of course, never fully satisfied in actual markets, and departures from them are then used as arguments for collective policy interventions to achieve an idealised market economy. Still, deriving benefits from fossil fuels requires the depletion of non-renewable resources. The question is then what resource management strategy Daly's criterion would support.

If we abstract away from the environmental impacts of energy production and use, the answer is an approach to energy policy in which economic efficiency—measured using the conventional metric of the present value of net monetary benefits—is maximised subject to the constraint that the availability of *energy services* is maintained over time. In practice, this entails a sector-based strategy in which fossil fuel depletion is offset by specific investments in improved energy efficiency and renewable technologies such as wind power and photovoltaics.

The application of this approach is by no means mechanical or easily reduced to simple biophysical accounting. Nor is it a matter that could be left to the workings of the market. If future generations have a rights-based (deontological) claim to the benefits provided by low-cost energy services, then this right imposes duties of trusteeship or stewardship specifically on governments (Brown and Garver, 2009). The duty is to implement policies and programs that—with reasonable certainty—ensure the achievement of a smooth transition to a post-fossil fuel economy. While the strong sustainability criterion is silent on the choice of policy tools, it does imply a need for sector-level planning based on scenario analysis and modelling. Moreover, the focus on rights implies a precautionary approach [Chapters 26 and 27] involving a high burden of proof, especially in situations involving strong uncertainty and potential irreversibilities (Ekins et al., 2003).

To see this, consider the case of climate stabilisation policy. On the one hand, members of the present generation have a *prima facie* right to engage in activities that provide benefits in terms of comfort, mobility and material sustenance. Given present technologies and market conditions, the provision of these services entails the combustion of fossil fuels, and reductions in fossil fuel combustion would result in some loss of benefits over the short run. On the other hand, if future generations have a *prima facie* right to protection from harms, and in particular the adverse effects imposed by GHG emissions, the question is then how to balance these conflicting rights.

One answer to this question is provided by the literature on safe minimum standards [see Chapter 27]. In this approach, the conservation of ecosystems and environmental quality is mandated unless the costs of conservation are unacceptably large. In the case of climate change, a phased transition to a post-carbon energy system would slow the rate of economic growth by roughly 0.06 per cent per year according to the most recent review by the Intergovernmental Panel on Climate Change (IPCC, 2014: 15). This cost is notably small in the context of the global economy, implying a 2 per cent reduction in aggregate output in the year 2050 relative to baseline levels.

Deciding whether this cost is unacceptably large requires the application of reasoned judgement (Mavrommati et al., 2016). However, as Schelling (1997: 10) frames this point, "If someone could wave a wand and phase in, over a few years, a climate mitigation program that depressed [economic output] by two percent in perpetuity, no one would notice the difference". In contrast, failing to stabilise climate would impose potentially catastrophic costs on future generations. Stern and Dietz (2015), for example, produce simulations in which climate change might lead to much larger impacts, and Gerst et al. (2013) show that climate change presents a small but clearly non-zero probability of long-run economic collapse. That probability is reduced to effectively zero when GHG emissions are sufficiently controlled.

Based on this style of reasoning, the 1992 United Nations Framework Convention on Climate Change calls for preventing "dangerous anthropogenic interference" (Art. 2) with the Earth's climate, while the Paris Agreement of 2015 embraces the normative goal of:

> Holding the increase in the global average temperature to well below 2 °C above pre-industrial levels and to pursue efforts to limit the temperature increase to 1.5 °C above pre-industrial levels, recognizing that this would significantly reduce the risks and impacts of climate change.

The achievement of this goal is in doubt since the system of Intended Nationally Determined Contributions negotiated in Paris will be insufficient to reduce GHG emissions enough to avoid larger temperature increases. In this sense, there is a gap between principles and current commitments, illustrating the role of politics and the difficulties of collective action in addressing global environmental challenges. Still, the core aim of the Paris Agreement follows the outlines of the strong sustainability framework, pointing to the salience of this approach in providing an ethical anchoring point.

Future directions

The preceding sections have outlined an approach to intergenerational fairness that emphasises a need to secure both the well-being and opportunities of future generations. Arguably, there is a need for:

1   Forward-looking models and scenarios that, to the extent possible, construct society wide indicators of human flourishing and that account for the great uncertainty over the needs and preferences of future generations.
2   Sectoral strategies that maintain the source and sink services provided by ecological systems, along with the aesthetic qualities and benefits provided by natural environments, which allow each generation to shape its preferences free from environmental constraints.

While this framing is in one sense anthropocentric, it certainly does not rule out a pluralist approach in which nonanthropocentric values might play a role in decision-making. With this in mind, what key issues remain to be addressed in this area of research?

First, Brown and Garver (2009) argue that a focus on "reverence for life" might provide an ethical framework that blurs the distinction between anthropocentric and nonanthropocentric ethics. In this perspective, the despoliation of the environment is caused in part by a craving for material goods that leads people to view Nature in mainly instrumental terms. From this, a logical conclusion follows that a transformation of values and metaphysical commitments could foster a less consumptive lifestyle, establishing a "right relationship" with Nature that provides mutual benefits to the present generation, future generations and, what Brown and Garver term, the "commonwealth of life".

For ecological economists, this approach offers exciting possibilities, returning to the core substance of Aldo Leopold's (1949) call for a land ethic for regulating the links between economic activity and the biotic community. Quite generally, Leopold's contribution is underappreciated in ecological economics, which is unfortunate given the sophistication of his ecological and moral reasoning. In this context, Brown and Garver point towards a path that— while exploratory and leaving many questions unanswered—is well worth further consideration and development in terms of its underpinnings and implications for institutions and governance.

A second key need is for a deeper and more integrative engagement between the fields of ecological economics and political ecology [Chapter 4]. While ecological economists have led the way in terms of the theory and measurement of sustainability [Chapter 37], political ecologists have emphasised the ways in which the sustainability discourse can reflect power relations [see Chapter 14] that are tied to issues of systemic injustice (Sneddon et al., 2006) [see also Chapter 13]. A concern for the rights of future generations is deeply linked to the concept that members of the present generation are entitled to equality of opportunity (Howarth, 1992). Yet in a world of inequality marked by the impacts of neoliberalism and globalisation, the achievement of a future that is just and sustainable may require the development of new frameworks for international cooperation and governance. A focus on the intergenerational dimension that abstracts away from questions of power can yield outcomes that are deeply problematic. Sorting out such conflicts is the home turf of political ecology.

Finally, the recent work of Raworth (2012) integrates Rockström et al.'s (2009) emphasis on planetary boundaries with a multi-dimensional suite of indicators on the social and economic foundations of human flourishing. Raworth's concept of a "safe and just space for humanity" emphasises the need to limit the use of the source and sink services provided by the biosphere to levels that are ecologically sustainable while simultaneously alleviating poverty, advancing wellbeing, and achieving gender equality and social justice. In a similar vein, Mavrommati et al. (2016) suggest that the concept of planetary boundaries can be invoked to define ethical constraints on the pursuit of utilitarian objectives and to provide the opportunity for equal treatment across generations. Through a pragmatic formulation that emphasises indicators that are tied to specific areas of policy and governance, this general approach can serve as a model for the important translational work that lies at the boundary between scholarship and praxis. Of course, no set of indicators or approach to policy analysis is ever complete, and Raworth's work is arguably more suggestive than conclusive. Still, it represents a potentially very promising way forward that integrates a concern for future generations with other dimensions of values and ethics.

Concluding remarks

This chapter has reviewed the treatment of future generations within the context of the concept of sustainability and its relationship to the theory of intergenerational fairness. Interestingly, the view that natural resources are the shared property of present and future society has a long history that is well institutionalised in conservationist approaches to natural resource management. Deeply, the conservationist stance emphasises equity both between and within generations, supporting a governance framework that focuses on public ownership and management rather than reliance on private property regimes and the market mechanism.

In an age of globalisation and the pervasive transformation of ecosystems by human activity, the challenge of sustainability stretches beyond the mere conservation of timber, fisheries, mineral and fossil energy resources. Key threats relate to the interplay between environmental problems. The example of climate change was employed to explore the character of problems that are driven by complex and multi-scalar processes in which causes are often far removed from their effects. In this environment, reasoned responses will require public policies and institutional schemes that align the incentives faced by individuals and organisations at scales ranging from the local to the global. Nonetheless, the basic concept of intergenerational fairness remains robust and applicable, even as the realities of the twenty-first century require new ways of thinking about justice, particularly in the international context.

Notes

1   I thank Georgia Mavrommati and Clive Spash for providing valuable comments on a draft version of this chapter.
2   This contrasts with Canada, where most land remained publically owned in the form of provincially held Crown Lands.

Key further readings cited

Brown, P.G. and Garver, G. (2009). *Right Relationship: Building a Whole Earth Economy*. San Francisco: Berrett-Koehler Publishers.

Ekins, P., Simon, S., Deutsch, L., Folke, C., and De Groot, R. (2003). A Framework for the Practical Application of the Concepts of Critical Natural Capital and Strong Sustainability. *Ecological Economics* 44(2–3): 165–185.

Neumayer, E. (2003). *Weak versus Strong Sustainability: Exploring the Limits of Two Opposing Paradigms*. Cheltenham: Edward Elgar Publishing.

Parfit, D. (1983). Energy Policy and the Further Future: The Identity Problem. In D. MacLean and P. G. Brown (eds.), *Energy and the Future* (pp. 166–179). Totowa, New Jersey: Rowman and Littlefield.

Sneddon, C., Howarth, R.B., and Norgaard, R.B. (2006). Sustainable Development in a Post-Brundtland World. *Ecological Economics* 57: 253–268.

Other literature cited

Beckerman, W. (1994). Sustainable Development: Is It a Useful Concept? *Environmental Values* 3: 191–209.

Brekke, K.A. (1997). *Economic Growth and the Environment: On the Measurement of Income and Welfare.* Cheltenham: Edward Elgar.

Broome, J. (2008). The Ethics of Climate Change. *Scientific American* 298: 96–102.

Costanza, R. (1991). *Ecological Economics: The Science and Management of Sustainability.* New York: Columbia University Press.

Daly, H.E. (1991). Elements of Environmental Macroeconomics. In R- Costanza (ed.), *Ecological Economics: The Science and Management of Sustainability.* New York: Columbia University Press.

Dietz, S., and Stern, N. (2015). Endogenous Growth, Convexity of Damage and Climate Risk: How Nordhaus' Framework Supports Deep Cuts in Carbon Emissions. *The Economic Journal* 125: 574–620.

Georgescu-Roegen, N. (1971). *The Entropy Law and the Economic Process.* Cambridge, Massachusetts: Harvard University Press.

Gerst, M.D., Howarth, R.B., Borsuk, M.E. (2013). The Interplay between Risk Attitudes and Low Probability, High Cost Outcomes in Climate Policy Analysis. *Environmental Modelling and Software* 41: 176–184.

Hartwick, J.M. (2000). *National Accounting and Capital.* Cheltenham: Edward Elgar.

Hotelling, H. (1931). The Economics of Exhaustible Resources. *Journal of Political Economy* 39: 137–175.

Howarth, R.B. (1992). Intergenerational Justice and the Chain of Obligation. *Environmental Values* 1: 133–140.

Howarth, R.B. (2007). Towards an Operational Sustainability Criterion. *Ecological Economics* 63: 656–663.

Intergovernmental Panel on Climate Change (IPCC) (2014). *Climate Change 2014: Mitigation of Climate Change.* New York: Cambridge University Press.

Leopold, A. (1949). *A Sand County Almanac.* New York: Ballantine.

Mavrommati, G., Bithas, K. Borsuk, M.E., Howarth, R.B. (2016). Integration of Ecological-Biological Thresholds in Conservation Decision Making. *Conservation Biology.*

Nordhaus, W.D. (2013). *The Climate Casino: Risk, Uncertainty, and Economics for a Warming World.* New Haven: Yale University Press.

Pezzey, J. (2004). One-Sided Sustainability Tests with Amenities, and Changes in Technology, Trade and Population. *Journal of Environmental Economics and Management* 48: 613–631.

Pinchot, G. (1910). *The Fight for Conservation.* New York: Doubleday, Page and Company.

Raworth, K. (2012). A Safe and Just Space for Humanity: Can We Live Within the Doughnut? *Oxfam Policy and Practice: Climate Change and Resilience* 8: 1–26.

Rockström, J., Steffen, W., Noone, K., Persson, Å., Chapin, F.S., Lambin, E.F., Lenton, T.M., Scheffer, M., Folke, C., Schellnhuber, H.J., Nykvist, B., de Wit, C.A, Hughes, T., van der Leeuw, S., Rodhe, H., Sörlin, S., Snyder, P.K., Costanza, R., Svedin, U., Falkenmark, M., Karlberg, L., Corell, R.W., Fabry, V.J., Hansen, J., Walker, B., Liverman, D., Richardson, K., Crutzen, P., Foley, J.A. (2009). A Safe Operating Space for Humanity. *Nature* 461: 472–475.

Schelling, T.C. (1997). The Cost of Combating Global Warming. *Foreign Affairs* 76: 8–14.

Shue, H. (1999). Bequeathing Hazards. In M. H.I. Dore and T.D. Mount (eds.), *Global Environmental Economics: Equity and the Limits to Markets.* Oxford: Blackwell.

Solow, R.M. (1993). Sustainability: An Economist's Perspective. In R. Dorfman and N. S. Dorfman (eds.). *Economics of the Environment* (pp. 179–187). New York: Norton.

Spash, C.L. (2002). *Greenhouse Economics: Value and Ethics.* London: Routledge.

World Commission on Environment and Development (WCED) (1987). *Our Common Future.* Oxford: Oxford University Press.

PART VII

Science and society
Uncertainty and precaution

26

PRECAUTIONARY APPRAISAL AS A RESPONSE TO RISK, UNCERTAINTY, AMBIGUITY AND IGNORANCE

Andy Stirling

Introduction

Across a wide range of sectors and under a host of different terminologies, few issues addressed in the field of ecological economics are more contentious or more momentous than the diverse challenges of incertitude. In seeking to tackle global imperatives like climate change, ecological degradation or social injustice, the intractabilities of uncertainty present an ever present obstacle to progress. In order to develop robust and practical responses that do justice to the full depth and scope of these challenges, no field of policy research is richer than the vast literature concerned with precaution. Key issues are held in common, for instance, with the discussion in Chapter 27 around the topic of safe minimum standards for addressing strong uncertainty. This chapter provides a complementary review of this literature in order to illuminate the fundamental relevance of precaution for the appraisal (as well as the management) of the challenge of the uncertainty, and identify a range of practical policy responses.

The first point to note is that precaution is one of the most hotly contended issues in environmental governance (O'Riordan and Jordan, 2001). Various interpretations of the Precautionary Principle (hereafter the PP) have been a longstanding interest in ecological economics (Dovers, 1995; Spash et al., 2005; Aldred, 2013; Common and Stagl, 2005; Persson, 2016). Related issues feature prominently in mainstream political discourse on technological risk as well as in academic literatures on science policy, environmental science, product regulation and international law (Fisher, 2002).

Originating in the earliest international initiatives for environmental protection in the 1970s, precaution first came to legal maturity in German environmental policy in the 1980s (O'Riordan and Cameron, 1994). Since then, it has been championed by environmentalists and public health advocates and strongly resisted by some of the industries they criticise (Raffensperger and Tickner, 1999). Diverse formulations of associated principles proliferate across a variety of international instruments (Trouwborst, 2002), national jurisdictions and policy areas (de Sadeleer, 2002). From a guiding theme in European Commission (EC) environmental policy (Commission of the European Communities, 2000), the PP has become a general principle of European Union (EU) law and a repeated focus of attention in high-stakes international disputes (Bohanes, 2002). The PP has been applied in a variety of areas including food safety, chemicals regulation, genetic modification, telecommunications, nanotechnology, climate change and general health protection; proving especially contentious in the United States of America (USA) (Martuzzi and Tickner, 2004).

As scientific uncertainty has become increasingly important in policymaking, and recognised to be a common feature of scientific knowledge, so the influence of the PP has extended, moving from environmental regulation to wider policymaking on issues of risk, emerging technologies and world trade (Harding and Fisher, 1999). In ecological economics, the PP has been discussed in relation to a diverse range of issues including: inequality and collective action (Basili et al., 2006), the nature of irreversibility (Verbruggen, 2013), conservation and national resource management (Cooney, 2004), degrowth economics (Garver, 2013) and co-operative transdisciplinary research (Healy et al., 2013). As associated issues have expanded in scope, so the PP has grown in profile and authority and in its general implications for the governance of science and technology (Felt et al., 2007).

This chapter reviews global policy debates over the PP as a response to uncertainty in environment and technology policy and assess some general policy implications. The next section defines the topic. This is followed by a discussion of some key concerns raised about the PP. In order to address these, the PP is highlighted as a rational response to aspects of incertitude that go beyond the relatively tractable condition of quantified risk. A variety of relevant, readily operationalised appraisal methods are mentioned, that are too-often neglected in the dominant fixation with risk assessment to the exclusion of all else. The chapter ends by pointing to a general operational framework for implementing more precautionary forms of regulatory appraisal.

Defining the topic

A widely influential early formulation of the PP was provided in the United Nations (UN) 1992 Rio Declaration, accepted even by many otherwise sceptical states like the USA (Myers and Raffensberger, 2006). Principle 15 states that: "Where there are threats of serious or irreversible damage, lack of full scientific certainty shall not be used as a reason for postponing cost-effective measures to prevent environmental degradation" (UN Conference on Environment and Development, 1992). This is sometimes characterised as an injunction, to "look before you leap" or remember that "it is better to be safe than sorry", with other versions of precaution characterised as being stricter, or more far-reaching (Randall, 2011). However, the simple wording of Principle 15 authoritatively exemplifies four key general features of the PP, underscoring its centrality in ecological economics.

1   The PP hinges on the presence in decision-making of two quite particular properties: a potential for particularly serious (for instance, irreversible) harm and a lack of scientific certainty.
2   The normative presumption is also very particular: favouring the interests of the environment (and human health) rather than economic, sectoral or strategic institutional interests (Fisher et al., 2006).
3   The PP refers to reasons for justifying action, not to the nature or stringency of the actions themselves.
4   In principle, the PP applies symmetrically to all policy alternatives in any given context, including 'doing nothing'.

In these terms, the PP is a succinct distillation of more than a century of experience with the unexpected consequences of new knowledge and technologies (Harremoës, 2001). In particular, it embodies an awareness of the asymmetries and inequities of power relationships in society [see Chapter 14]. As such, precaution bears close relationship with other parallel principles (with which it is sometimes compared and elided), like those concerning prevention, polluter pays, no regrets, participation, substitution and clean production. Similarly, precaution serves to enrich and reinforce appreciation of the duties of care on the part of commercial firms and the protective responsibilities of sovereign governments and regulatory administrations. In short, the PP requires more explicit, scientifically rigorous and socially sophisticated attention to the implications of incomplete knowledge, than is routinely provided in the conventional regulatory assessment of 'risk' (Funtowicz and Ravetz, 1990; EEA, 2013).

Past debate and main issues

Given the nature of the issues and the powerful interests at stake, the PP has been subject to vehement rhetorical criticism (Sandin et al., 2002). One frequent concern is that it is ill-defined. In the formulation given above, for instance, how serious is 'serious'? What exactly does 'irreversible' mean? Does 'full scientific certainty' ever exist? Such concerns seem well-founded if the PP is presented as a sufficient, comprehensive or definitive procedural rule. Yet legal scholars point out that, as with any general legal principle (like proportionality or cost effectiveness), no given wording of precaution can in itself be entirely self-sufficient as a decision rule (Fisher, 2002; Bohanes, 2002). Just as these other principles rely on specific methods and procedures (e.g., risk assessment, cost-benefit analysis) in order to make them operational, so too should precaution simply be seen as a general guide to the development and application of more detailed complementary practices (Stirling, 1999). This point is returned to at the end of this chapter.

A further criticism is that the explicitly normative character of the PP somehow renders it irrational (Sunstein, 2005). In one form, this concern rests on the (usually implicit) assumption that conventional 'science based' procedures manage somehow to transcend normative content. However, this neglects the ways in which practical applications of methods like risk assessment and cost-benefit analysis also require inherent exercise of evaluative judgements (Stirling, 2010). For instance, values are intrinsic to the setting of levels of protection in risk assessment, the weighing of different forms of harm and their balancing with countervailing benefits (Klinke et al., 2006).

Beyond this, an extensive literature documents how the claimed 'sound scientific' methods so often contrasted with precaution are typically subject to serious uncertainties concerning divergent possible 'framings' (Stirling, 2010). As a consequence, 'evidence based' results obtained in areas such as climate, energy, chemicals, genetic modification and industrial regulation often display strong sensitivity to assumptions, that can vary radically across different equally authoritative studies (Government Office for Science, 2014). When all analysis is acknowledged necessarily to be subject to such framing by value judgements, then it emerges that the explicit normativity of the PP is actually more, rather than less, rational (Klinke et al., 2006). As illuminated by other critiques of the fact–value dichotomy [e.g., Chapter 2], what is irrational, is denial by many critics of the PP, that there are inherent normativities in all risk assessment.

On this basis, there remains (for those so inclined) scope for criticism of the PP on the grounds of its particular normative orientation in favour of the environment and human health (Sunstein, 2005). This is understandably challenging for interests that prioritise economic competitiveness or have a partisan association with the particular technologies or policies that are subject to regulation by the PP. Under these views, it is of course politically expedient to stigmatise precaution as being somehow self-evidently unreasonable. However, while explicable as political polemics, such attempts to deny even the legitimacy of alternative values are actually themselves not only irrational but profoundly anti-democratic.

In these kinds of political debates between contending values, there is a key general rationale for the PP that can be appreciated even by those who might otherwise be sceptical. This lies in understanding the ever-present politics of technology and the environment, in which incumbent interests in any given sector are often in the position of 'capturing' regulation and asserting their own most expedient framings (EEA, 2001, 2013). In this bigger picture, the the PP can be recognised simply as a means to resist over privileged incumbency and restore a more reasonable balance of interests in appraisal (Stirling, 1999). In any case, adoption of the PP does not necessarily negate the possibility that other normative values might be applied. All it does is help ensure that—where scientific knowledge is insufficient to settle an issue on its own—decisions will be subject to more explicitly open deliberation and argument about which values to prioritise in the face of uncertainty (Funtowicz and Ravetz, 1990; Klinke et al., 2006).

A related set of concerns focus on the political implications of the PP. Cases are sometimes cited in which precaution itself appears to have been applied in an expedient fashion, to achieve outcomes that are actually pursued for rather different reasons; for example, the rejection of particular disfavoured technologies or the protection of national industries from international trade competition (Sunstein, 2005). At one level, this simply highlights a regrettable general tendency found on all sides in actual political situations concerning technology and its adoption. Reasonable advocacy should acknowledge that the PP is no more intrinsically immune to manipulation than any other principle. For example, as noted above, a principle of rational utility maximisation in risk assessment can end up asserting particular partisan framings as if these were synonymous with 'rationality' (Stirling, 1999).

There do nonetheless remain reasonable grounds for concern in cases where the PP is invoked selectively or opaquely (Klinke et al., 2006). For instance, imposing precaution selectively to particular policy options, whilst not doing so to alternative options (including 'business as usual') is illegitimate. Where this occurs perverse environmental or health outcomes may arise (Sunstein, 2005; Klinke et al., 2006). The fact that precaution applies in principle to all decision options means that this is not an inherent fault, but a matter of inadequate application (Stirling, 1999).

In considering such criticisms, it is wise to reflect upon some fundamental features of the PP. The PP is discriminating in its application, explicitly applying only under specific conditions of serious or irreversible threat about which there is a lack of scientific certainty. This does not render precaution immune to expediency, but it does help militate against arbitrary usage. There is also no shortage of examples of the expedient usage of conventional risk assessment as a means to protect the technologies or policies favoured by incumbents or to inhibit their competitors. A wide literature shows such expedient manipulation of risk assessment to be endemic in regulatory politics (EEA, 2001, 2013). Critics and proponents of the PP therefore hold tacit common ground here, in aiming for a situation in which the particular methods adopted in the implementation of regulatory appraisal are more rigorous, systematic and transparent about challenges of incomplete knowledge and potentially irreversible harm, than is normally the case in established practice of regulatory assessment (Stirling, 1999, 2010; Klinke et al., 2006)

There are many loudly voiced, but typically seriously under-substantiated, assertions that precaution can be motivated by, or might lead to, a blanket rejection of all new technological innovation (Sunstein, 2005). This is the point underlying increasingly intense rhetorics around various 'proactionary' or 'pro-innovation' principles dreamed up by individual enthusiasts, as if they can be compared with the outcome of decades of cumulative practice in international governance on the PP. The serious problem here is that such political interventions are based on fundamental misunderstandings (or misrepresentations) not only of precaution, but also of the nature of innovation (Stirling, 2010).

Precaution focuses on the reasons for intervening, and carries no necessary implications for the substance or stringency of the interventions themselves (de Sadeleer, 2002). Rather than bans or phase-outs, precautionary actions may as readily take the form of strengthened standards, containment strategies, licensing arrangements, monitoring measures, labelling requirements, liability provisions or compensation schemes (Stirling, 1999). General 'anti-innovation' accusations fail to address the fundamental point that technological and social change are branching evolutionary processes (Government Office for Science, 2014). As repeatedly shown in the application of precaution, the inhibition of one particular trajectory (e.g., nuclear or genetically modified organisms) becomes an advantage for another (e.g., renewables or marker assisted breeding) (EEA, 2001, 2013). Precaution is about steering, not stopping, innovation. The selective branding of specific concerns over particular technologies as if they represent an undifferentiated general anti-technology position can be recognised simply as political rhetoric.

Assessment of major issues

Perhaps the most important practical outcome of all these critical debates is a recognition that the substantive significance of the PP rests largely in the specific institutional frameworks, deliberative procedures and analytical methods through which it is implemented. In other words, precaution is more important as a process, than as a supposedly self-sufficient decision rule (Stirling, 1999). With the PP as a cue to such a process, a key ensuing purpose is to help address a lack of scientific certainty by expending more effort in hedging against unknown possibilities and investing in social learning—exploring a wider and deeper array of salient types of knowledge (Funtowicz and Ravetz, 1990; Wynne, 1992; Stirling, 1999). Much of the ostensible support currently afforded to the PP by governmental bodies (e.g. the EC in the past) is explicitly predicated on the qualification that precaution is purely a risk 'management' (rather than an 'assessment') measure (CEC, 2000). When the implications of precaution are understood for processes of regulatory appraisal, however, it can be seen that such a position threatens to undermine the real logic and value of precautionary responses to strong uncertainty (Voss et al., 2006) [see also Chapter 27].

This point is also relevant to arguments, to the effect that precaution is somehow unscientific or anti-scientific (Sunstein, 2005). Again, such accusations can be shown themselves to be ironically irrational (Stirling, 1999). In short, they involve an assumption that sound scientific regulation is synonymous with probabilistic risk analysis. This is perhaps the most serious of all misrepresentations around the PP. In the paragraphs that follow, I will explain how it is not precaution *per se*, but the underlying recognition of intractable forms of incertitude (Stirling, 2010), that inevitably entail a move away from exclusive reliance on conventional risk assessment.

The bottom line here is that precaution points to the necessity for different kinds of appraisal processes under uncertainty. Where these apply, they are not necessarily instead of risk assessment, but supplemental to it in particular ways. In order to appreciate this, a more detailed understanding is required of the practical relationships between the PP and conventional risk assessment. Here, an especially significant contribution has been made by an extensive literature in the social and policy analysis of science (Wynne, 1992; Felt, 2007). This shows that a lack of scientific certainty of the kind formally triggering precaution, can typically take a variety of forms. Extending well beyond the narrow technical characterisation of 'risk' governing orthodox risk assessment, many of these cannot be satisfactorily addressed by the conventional method of aggregating probabilities. To try to do this implies claims to precisely the kinds of scientific confidence that are precluded by uncertainty. So insistence that risk assessment is sufficient under a lack of scientific certainty is itself a profoundly unscientific assertion.

In conventional risk assessment, the many different real world complexities are reduced to just two parameters. First, there are the magnitudes of the things that may happen (hazards, possibilities or outcomes). Second, there are the likelihoods (or probabilities) associated with each. These are then aggregated across all possible dimensions, contexts, aetiologies and perspectives. The resulting reductive-aggregative style lends itself to an apparently transcendent quantitative idiom (Stirling, 2010). This can then be asserted as objective authority that effectively sidelines and implicitly denies deeper forms of incertitude (Wynne, 1992). It is this political body language that offers the sought after policy commodity of decision justification and offers to help secure trust, procure acceptance, channel accountabilities and manage blame. Whilst such discursive effects are politically expedient, this has little to do with science (Stirling, 2010). What is typically neglected in conventional risk assessment, then, is that both magnitudes and probabilities may each be subject to variously incomplete or problematic knowledge, of kinds that are (by definition) not susceptible to probabilistic analysis (Funtowicz and Ravetz, 1990).

This was first recognised in the strict (now canonical) sense of the term 'uncertainty' introduced nearly a century ago by the economist Frank Knight (1921). Much elaborated in the field of post-normal science [see Chapter 28], this makes very clear the difference between uncertainty and the relatively tractable state of 'risk'—under which it is held to be possible confidently to determine both the probabilities and the magnitudes of contending forms of benefit and harm (Stirling, 2010). Under Knight's more intractable state of uncertainty, there may be confidence in characterising a range of possible outcomes, but the available empirical information or analytical models simply do not present a definitive basis for deriving probabilities. This prompts consideration of a further contrasting condition—which might be called ambiguity—where it is the characterisation of outcomes that is problematic, rather than the probabilities. Ambiguity arises where there are contradictory certainties, applying even to outcomes that have occurred already. Disagreements may persist, for instance, over the selection, partitioning, bounding, measurement, prioritisation, interpretation and aggregation of different forms or understandings of benefit or harm (Arrow, 1963). Then, beyond both uncertainty and ambiguity, there lies the even less tractable predicament of ignorance, where neither probabilities nor outcomes can be fully characterised (Dovers and Handmer, 1995). Ignorance is where "we don't know what we don't know", thus facing the ever-present prospect of surprise.

The point in distinguishing these contrasting aspects of incertitude is not to assert particular terminologies.[1] In a vast and complex literature, each of the above terms can be used in radically divergent ways. The point here, for the purpose of illustrating practical precautionary responses to incertitude, is simply to emphasise the diversity of dilemmas. What they are each called is secondary. What is crucial is to avoid the present situation in technology governance, in which all forms of incertitude beyond probabilistic risk are effectively denied even a name.

Figure 26.1 organises these four contrasting aspects of lack of scientific certainty, as logical permutations under the two basic parameters that structure risk assessment: knowledge about outcomes and likelihoods. In practice, of course, these four ideal-typical states of knowledge tend to occur together. The scheme is thus not a taxonomy, but a heuristic distinction between different aspects of incertitude, each spanning a variety of specific implications, contexts and causes. The crucial point for considering precaution as a process of appraisal is that this illuminates in its own terms, why risk assessment is not enough. Each aspect of incertitude is susceptible (in overlapping ways) to treatment by different kinds of institutional frameworks, deliberative procedures or analytical methods, as indicated in Figure 26.1.

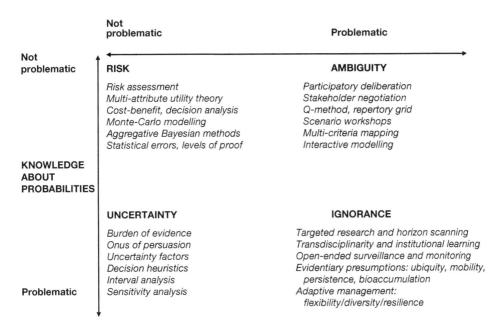

Figure 26.1   Responses in technology appraisal to different aspects of incertitude.

A key feature of the methods highlighted lower down and to the right in Figure 26.1, is that they are less reductive or aggregative than those that are appropriate under the strict condition of risk in the upper left. However, these more precautionary alternatives are no less systematic or scientific in nature than is risk assessment. By drawing attention to this diversity of practical responses in appraisal, the direct relevance of precaution can more readily be appreciated, not just for the management but also for the appraisal of risk. Precaution is also seen to be both consistent with fundamental principles of scientific rigour under incertitude, while offering the most robust way to respect these principles (Funtowicz and Ravetz, 1990; Wynne, 1992; Stirling, 1999). In particular, this framework shows how, contrary to much criticism, precaution does not imply a general rejection of risk assessment, but instead prompts attention to a variety of alternative methods that are more robustly applicable under uncertainty, ambiguity and ignorance.

Of course, none of this negates any relevance of precaution under narrow conditions of risk. Here precaution can still hold important implications for setting protection standards, striking a balance in avoiding different kinds of statistical errors and informing requirements for necessary strengths of evidence, levels of proof, onus of persuasion and burden of resourcing analysis. Beyond this a key challenge of precaution lies in considering how to implement this greater diversity of approaches under uncertainty, ambiguity and ignorance, and articulate them together in a more broad-based process of appraisal.

Drawing on a body of recent theoretical, empirical and methodological work (e.g., Stirling, 1999; EEA, 2001, 2013), Table 26.1 summarises a series of key considerations, which together help in responding to this challenge. Each represents a general quality, of a kind that should be displayed in any process of technology appraisal that may legitimately be considered to be precautionary in a general sense. Each is briefly illustrated by reference to an example drawn from regulatory experience. In many ways, the qualities listed in Table 26.1 are simply common sense. As befits their general nature, they apply equally to the implementation of any approach to technology appraisal, including risk assessment. This underscores that precaution represents

Table 26.1 Key features of a precautionary appraisal process

Feature	Examples
Independence from vested institutional, disciplinary, economic and political interests	Long constrained attention to problems caused to industrial workers by asbestos
Examine a greater range of uncertainties, sensitivities and possible scenarios	Early attention to risks of antimicrobials in animal feed, but later neglected
Search for 'blind spots', gaps in knowledge and divergent scientific views	Assumptions over dynamics of dispersal of acid gas emissions
Attend to proxies for possible harm, e.g., ubiquity, mobility, bioaccumulation, persistence	Managing chemicals like the ostensibly benign fuel additive MTBE
Contemplation of full life cycles and resource chains as they actually occur	Failures in PCB containment during decommissioning of electrical equipment
Consider indirect effects, e.g., decomposition, additivity, synergy, accumulation	Long neglected in the regulation of occupational exposures to ionizing radiation
Include industrial trends, institutional behaviour, strategic issues, non-compliance	Latter featuring prominently in the large scale misuse of antimicrobials in animal feed
Explicitly discuss appropriate levels and burdens of proof	Systematic neglect of 'Type II errors' in risk assessment
Compare a series of technology and policy options and potentially favourable substitutes	Overuse of diagnostic X-rays in health care
Deliberate over social justifications and possible wider benefits, risks and costs	Insufficiently considered in licensing of the drug DES for pregnant mothers
Drawing on relevant knowledge and experience beyond specialist disciplines	Knowledge gained by birdwatchers concerning the dynamics of fish stocks
Engage with the values and interests of all affected stakeholders	Experience of local communities on pollution episodes in the Great Lakes
Citizen participation in order to provide independent validation of chosen framings	Significantly neglected in checking assumptions adopted for management of BSE
Shift from reliance on theoretical modelling to systematic monitoring and surveillance	Address conceptual limitations, such as those affecting regulation of PCBs
Prioritise clear responsibilities for targeted research to address unresolved questions	Omitted for long periods over the course of the development of the BSE crisis
Initiate process at earliest stages 'upstream' in an innovation, strategy or policy process	Cleaner innovation pathways before lock-in occurs to less benign options
Examine strategic qualities e.g., reversibility, flexibility, diversity, resilience, robustness	Hedge against even the most intractable aspects of ignorance

an enhancement, rather than a contradiction, of accepted principles of scientific rigour under uncertainty.

Of course, important questions remain over the extent to which fully implementing the array of methods identified in Figure 26.1 is possible in existing institutional contexts in a fashion that displays all the qualities summarised in Table 26.1. While forestalling costs of environmental or health risks that might have been missed in risk assessment, this may incur more immediate and visible demands on money, attention, time and evidence in regulatory appraisal. This raises a number of tricky issues but suggest a focus for more constructive discussions than is evident in existing polarised debates over precaution.

Future directions

Building on recent analysis and adapted from a series of stakeholder deliberations, Figure 26.2 offers a schematic outline of one illustrative general framework for the articulation, alongside conventional risk assessment, of what might be termed precautionary appraisal (Klinke et al., 2006). By providing for an initial screening process, this deals with concerns over proportionality in appraisal. Only the most appropriate issues are allocated to treatment by more broad-based (and onerous) processes of precautionary appraisal. Subject to a set of detailed screening criteria applied in stakeholder deliberation, other cases are variously allocated to more inclusive and participatory forms of appraisal (in the case of ambiguity) or more straightforward and familiar forms of risk assessment (where these are held to be sufficient). In this way, established notions of proportionality are reconciled with precaution through the employment of more targeted approaches to appraisal. Since the screening applies to all cases, the resulting analytic-deliberative framework as a whole remains precautionary.

Of course, these kinds of operational frameworks can look highly simplified, instrumental and potentially counterproductive. A fear is that their compatibility with existing practices simply serves to reinforce current institutional inadequacies. However, such frameworks at least refute the blanket assertions over the non-operational status of precaution (Sunstein, 2005). They offer a way to provoke greater policy attention to crucial wider political issues concerning the governance of science and the steering of directions for innovation in any given field.

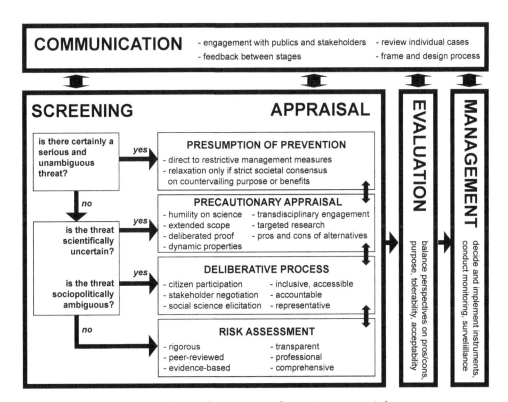

Figure 26.2 A framework articulating risk assessment and precautionary appraisal.
Source: adapted from Klinke, A. et al., 2006.

Concluding remarks

There is a crucial general promise offered in these kinds of emerging frameworks for more precautionary regulatory appraisal. This aims to help 'broaden out' attention to greater diversities of options, practices and perspectives in policy debates over technology. Beyond this, they can also open up more vibrant, mature and robust political debates over the steering of technology (Stirling, 2010). In this sense, the ultimate contribution of the explicitly normative character of precaution in response to otherwise scientific risk debates is to help foster a more deliberate and accountable innovation democracy.

Note

Editor's Note: Indeed, the more nuanced framework here is also totally compatible with the use in social ecological economics of the terms strong uncertainty (covering ignorance and social indeterminacy), and weak uncertainty (covering risk as probability assessment). This approach also references much the same literature. See Spash (2002, chapters 4 and 5).

Key further readings cited

EEA (2013). *Late Lessons from Early Warnings: science, precaution, innovation*. Copenhagen: EEA.

Fisher, E., Jones, J., von Schomberg, R. (eds.) (2006). *Implementing the Precautionary Principle: perspectives and prospects*, Cheltenham: Edward Elgar.

Stirling, A. (2010). Keep it complex. *Nature, 468*, 1029–1031.

Wynne, B. (1992). Uncertainty and Environmental Learning: reconceiving science and policy in the preventive paradigm, *Global Environmental Change*, 2(2), 111–127.

Other literature cited

Aldred, J. (2013). Justifying precautionary policies: Incommensurability and uncertainty. *Ecological Economics*, 96 132–140.

Arrow, K. (1963). *Social Choice and Individual Values*. New Haven CN: Yale University Press.

Basili, M., Franzini, M., Vercelli, A. (2006). *Environment, Inequality and Collective Action*. London: Routledge.

Bohanes, J. (2002). Risk Regulation in WTO Law: a procedure-based approach to the precautionary principle, *Columbia Journal of International Law*, 40(2), 323–390.

Commission of the European Communities (2000). Communication from the Commission on the Precautionary Principle, *COM (2000)1 final 2* February 2000, Brussels.

Common, M.S., Stagl, S. (2005). *Ecological Economics: an introduction*. Cambridge: Cambridge University Press.

Cooney, R. (2004). *The Precautionary Principle in Biodiversity Conservation and Natural Resource Management: an issues paper for policymakers, researchers and practitioners*. Cambridge: IUCN.

de Sadeleer, N. (2002). *Environmental Principles: from political slogans to legal rules*. Oxford: Oxford University Press.

Dovers, S.R. (1995). A framework for scaling and framing policy problems in sustainability. *Ecological Economics*, 12, 93–106.

Dovers, S.R., Handmer, J.W. (1995). Ignorance, the precautionary principle, and sustainability, *Ambio*, 24(2), 92–97.

EEA (European Environmental Agency) (2001). *Late lessons from early warnings: the precautionary principle 1896–2000*. Copenhagen: EEA.

Felt, U., Wynne, B., Callon, M., Goncalves, M., Jasanoff, S., Jepsen, M., Joly, P.B., Konopasek, Z., May, S., Neubauer, C., Rip, A., Siune, K., Stirling, A., Tallachini, M. (2007). Science and Governance: taking European Knowledge Society Seriously, *Report of the Expert Group on Science and Governance to DG Research*. Luxembourg: European Commission.

Fisher, E. (2002). Precaution, precaution everywhere: developing a "common understanding" of the precautionary principle in the European Community, *Maastricht Journal of European and Comparative Law*, 9, 7–28.

Funtowicz, S., Ravetz, J. (1990). *Uncertainty and Quality in Science for Policy*, Amsterdam: Kluwer.

Garver, G. (2013). The rule of ecological law: The legal complement to degrowth economics. *Sustainability (Switzerland)* 5(1), 316–337.

Government Office for Science (2014). *Innovation: Managing Risk, Not Avoiding It. Evidence and Case Studies*. London: UK Government Office for Science.

Harding, R., Fisher, E. (eds.) (1999). *Perspectives on the Precautionary Principle*. Sydney: Federation Press.

Harremoës, P. et al. (eds.) (2001). *Late Lessons from Early Warnings: the precautionary principle 1896-2000*. Copenhagen: European Environment Agency.

Healy, H., Martinez-Alier, J., Temper, L., Walter, M., Gerber, J.-F. (2013) *Ecological Economics from the Ground Up*. London, Routledge.

Klinke, A., Dreyer, M., Renn, O., Stirling, A. and Van Zwanenberg, P. (2006). Precautionary risk regulation in European governance. *Journal of Risk Research*, 9(4), 373–392.

Knight, F. (1921). *Risk, Uncertainty and Profit*. Boston: Houghton Mifflin.

Martuzzi, M., Tickner, J. (eds.) (2004). *The Precautionary Principle: protecting public health, the environment and the future of our children*, Copenhagen: World Health Organisation.

Myers, N., Raffensberger, C. (eds.) (2006). *Precautionary Tools for Reshaping Environmental Policy*. Cambridge: MIT Press.

O'Riordan, T., Cameron, J. (1994). *Interpreting the Precautionary Principle*. London: Earthscan.

O'Riordan, T., Jordan, A. (2001). *Reinterpreting the Precautionary Principle*. London: Cameron May.

Persson, E. (2016). What are the core ideas behind the Precautionary Principle? *Science of the Total Environment*, 557–558, 134–141.

Raffensperger, C., Tickner, J. (eds.) (1999). *Protecting Public Health and the Environment: implementing the precautionary principle*. Washington, D.C.: Island.

Randall, A. (2011). *Risk and Precaution*. Cambridge: Cambridge University Press.

Sandin, P., Peterson, M., Hansson, S.O., Rudén, C., Juthe, A. (2002). Five Charges against the Precautionary Principle. *Journal of Risk Research*, 5(4), 287–299.

Spash, C.L. (2002). *Greenhouse Economics: Value and Ethics*. London: Routledge.

Spash, C.L., Stagl, S., Getzner, M. (2005). Exploring Alternatives for Environmental Valuation. In: Getzner, M., Spash, C.L., Stagl, S. (eds.), *Alternatives for Environmental Valuation* (pp. 1–20). London: Routledge.

Stirling, A. (1999). *On Science and Precaution in the Management of Technological Risk – Volume I: a synthesis report of case studies* (Vol. I), Seville: European Commission.

Sunstein, C. (2005). *Laws of Fear: beyond the precautionary principle*. Cambridge: Cambridge University Press.

Trouwborst, A. (2002). *Evolution and Status of the Precautionary Principle in International Law*. Amsterdam: Kluwer Law International.

UN Conference on Environment and Development, Final Declaration, Rio de Janeiro, 1992.

Verbruggen, A. (2013). Revocability and Reversibility in Societal Decision-making. *Ecological Economics*, 85, 20–27.

Voss, J., Bauknecht, D., Kemp, R. (eds.) (2006). *Reflexive Governance for Sustainable Development*. Cheltenham: Edward Elgar.

27

SAFE MINIMUM STANDARDS

Addressing strong uncertainty

Irmi Seidl

Introduction

Ecological and environmental destruction is advancing rapidly worldwide; this is in part because the harmful effects of human activity are either underestimated or ignored. Knowledge about current and future harm can be lacking due to uncertainty, caused by ignorance and/or indeterminacy (see Spash, 2002). This strong uncertainty cannot be overcome. Additionally, harmful processes may be irreversible. Hence, concepts have been devised that capture strong uncertainty and thus justify and allow limiting or redirecting potentially harmful or irreversible human activities. The first economic concept to capture such uncertainty and irreversibility in the field of resource use was the Safe Minimum Standard (SMS). Related concepts that have been developed are the Precautionary Principle (PP) [see also Chapter 26], a political instrument focussing on protecting the environment and human health, and planetary boundaries, proposing limits not to be transgressed in Earth system processes. The SMS will be discussed in detail, then the PP and planetary boundaries will be presented and compared, and concepts to help achieve them (e.g. reversal of the burden of proof, as well as intragenerational and intergenerational justice) will be briefly introduced.

Understanding the SMS and its development

SMS was developed by Siegfried von Ciriacy-Wantrup (1906–1980), hereafter CW, in his book *Resource conservation. Economics and Policies* (1963, [1952]). CW was then Professor of Agricultural Economics, University of California, Berkeley. His writings focused on resource conservation and, in particular, agricultural resources. CW defined SMS as a state of conservation with the "primary objective [...] to maintain the economic possibility of halting and reversing a decrease of flow and use" (ibid.: 254), and at a level that "should actually be realized under all conditions" (ibid.: 261). He understood conservation not as non-use but as a change in the intertemporal distribution of physical rates of use (ibid.: 51).

SMS was devised for flow resources. The future flow can be negatively affected by human action, and the resources exhibit a critical zone which is "a more or less clearly defined range of rates below which a decrease in flow cannot be reversed economically under presently foreseeable conditions" (ibid.: 39), and which would result in depletion and destruction. The critical zone takes into account uncertainty about whether depletion is economically irreversible (ibid.: 252) and/or technologically (biologically) irreversible.

Before explaining the SMS of CW in more detail, the reader should note that Bishop's (1978) understanding of SMS has become the well-known version rather than CW's original conceptualisation, and this has triggered some debate as to the appropriateness of Bishop's reinterpretation (Seidl and Tisdell, 2001). Bishop justified SMS with game theory and he suggested that SMS should be adopted to avoid extinction unless the social costs were unacceptably high. He proposed a procedure to apply SMS reliant on the calculation of social costs, although he emphasised that such an economic analysis would be insufficient because accounting for intergenerational equity requires social decision-making. In what follows the original position of CW is presented.

Application of SMS

Examples of flow resources with a critical zone include: animal and plant species, scenic resources, land, and storage capacity of ground-water basins (CW, 1963 [1952]: 42). The utilisation of these resources is heavily influenced by economic and social institutions, and hence conservation policy is important. In contrast, the utilisation of stock resources (e.g. ores, coal, oil, gas, plant nutrients), its intensity and effects are largely ignored by CW, because he sees them as determined by the state of technology and to a lesser extent by institutions. This idea is rather untenable today.

In spite of the focus on particular resources, CW considered it "impractical to define a safe minimum standard for each resource simply in terms of a single flow rate which is to be maintained" (ibid.: 259); "it is more practical to define a safe minimum standard in terms of conservation practices" (ibid.: 257) or performances. His examples of the flow rate concept include: the avoidance of gullies in soil conservation, the maintenance of a given plant association in forest conservation, a maximum degree of water pollution, contour cultivation and mulching. Similarly, Ostrom (1990) identifies and recommends adaptation practices for successful management of the commons. Examples of performance are maximum water use rates, maximum rates of stocking or maximum admission of people in recreational facilities. This sort of limit on economic activity is similar to Daly's (1992) concern for the scale of the economy, which requires determining the level of overall economic activity that is permissible.

Basic assumptions of SMS: uncertainty, irreversibility, critical zone

The concept of uncertainty draws on Knight's (1992 [1921]) definition of uncertainty which is ignorance about the outcome of a process or action (called partial ignorance by Spash, 2002) and the impossibility of calculating the probability of an outcome (indeterminacy, Spash [2002]; see same author for similarity of Knight's and Keynes' definitions of uncertainty). This kind of strong uncertainty is dominant in both natural and social systems, and in conservation contexts. Reasons for uncertainty are varied, including: complexity, time and time-lags, unforeseeable reactions and processes, novelty, hazards, mutations, non-linear processes or emergence.

Irreversibility means both economic and biological/technical irreversibility. According to CW (1963 [1952]) economic irreversibility is a relative concept and depends on "technology, wants and social institutions" (ibid.: 39). In contrast, biological or technical irreversibility is absolute and value free. The relationship between economic and biological irreversibility is depicted in Figure 27.1 (Seidl and Tisdell, 2001). Economic irreversibility may start at a lower level of resource use compared to when biological irreversibility sets in, but the latter implicates economic irreversibility, and even ample economic means cannot reverse resource depletion. Note that irreversibility is uncertain too!

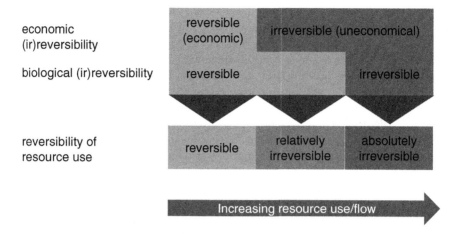

Figure 27.1 Heuristic displaying SMS, threshold and critical zone.

Given uncertainty and irreversibility, CW introduced the critical zone to make the decision problem more tangible. The term stands for a "more or less clearly defined range of rates [of resource use] below which a decrease in flow cannot be reversed *economically* under presently foreseeable conditions" (CW, 1963 [1952]): 39). CW focused mainly on economic—and less on biological—irreversibility. He also avoided the term threshold in favour of critical zone, which better reflects uncertainty and allows for flexibility in conservation.

A critical zone is characterised by a physical condition: it can be the destruction of a breeding stock or of protective plant cover, the development of gullies or the spoliation of recreational resources by improper buildings (e.g. roads, dams). Figure 27.2 indicates the critical zone of use (ZT) with economic irreversibility starting at Z and biological irreversibility in the area right of T. As SMS avoids the critical zone of use, the flow of resource may remain below Z. Economic irreversibility, and hence the critical zone, is contextual and depends upon technology, wants and social institutions (ibid.: 39), which are undergoing constant change.

Role of costs, revenues and institutional setting

Costs and revenues (CW does not use the word benefits) and the institutional setting play an important role in CW's reasoning about the SMS. The objective of conservation policy is, according to CW, to reach an optimum state of conservation in social economics (covering the public realm, institutions, society and politics) which contrasts with private economics. This is to be achieved by maximising social net revenues in resource utilisation over time.

Yet, both private and social costs and revenues are biased by institutional settings; for instance by particular market conditions such as monopoly, or by credit availability, interests, property, taxation, price relations and the overall economic situation. The fact is that even costs and revenues are biased because they are partly private and partly public, often costs and revenues are unrecognised as such or there can be extra-market values and goods. (Note: CW dismissed the neoclassical distinction between internal and external costs and benefits.) By proposing and critically discussing some procedures to identify the correct social costs and revenues (ibid.: 230–250), CW laid the groundwork for the advancement and critique of economic resource valuation.

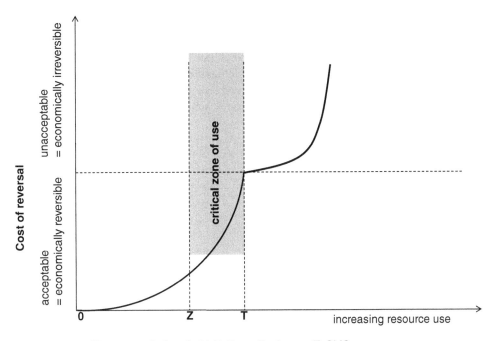

T = economic threshold; Z–T = critical zone, Z: SMS

Figure 27.2   The critical zone of use.

However, CW considered correct valuation procedures to be a less important problem than identifying and correcting "social weighting" which stands for (un)equal economic and political opportunities. Identifying social weighting is important as it provides the reference point needed to identify distortions in the social optimum state of conservation (ibid.: 244ff). However, equality was not proposed or recommended as a tool (even indirectly) to be incorporated into conservation policy.

Despite, or maybe because of, the awareness of the theoretical and formal difficulties involved in identifying socially weighted revenues and costs, and hence the social optimum of conservation, CW considered these ideas to be of limited practical interest. Instead he believed that:

> the practical goal in conservation policy is [...] a step-by-step improvement of the existing [time distribution of use rates] through trial and error. The improvement is made by [...] an increase of present total social net revenues.
>
> *(ibid.: 249)*

He thereby rejected the optimum time distribution of use rates.

CW considered the costs of adopting SMSs as low compared to the high costs of not adopting it. This conclusion might be due to most conservation problems still being considered mainly local or regional in the 1950s. In addition, he conceptualised conservation policy as being both societal and institutional, involving practice, routines, habit, knowledge, property, tenancy and taxation. Changes in these factors could make conservation cheap. However, as explained further below, realisation of conservation projects could be insufficient or untimely to achieve their intended goals.

Tools for realising SMSs

CW proposed an array of possible tools and means by which to realise SMSs, ideally "with minimum total social costs" (ibid.: 259). Indirect tools involved social institutions and economic forces and they comprised interest rates, prices, taxation, property, tenure, monopolistic conditions and economic stability. Although these forces and institutions are supposed to have an important impact on conservation, their effects might be uncertain regarding degree, extent and timing. Still he claims that:

> conservation policy may attempt to bring the social institutions affecting the state of conservation into agreement with each other and with changing economic conditions. This aim may involve the weakening or elimination of some social institutions and the strengthening of others.
>
> *(ibid.: 228)*

Direct tools on the other hand are education, subsidies, penalties, zoning and regulation. These are considered to be fairly effective and may impact only a few enterprises. Thereby, CW came back to his claim that adopting SMSs implies low costs even for the private sector.

Finding theoretical foundations for the SMS concept

The SMS concept is a pragmatic deduction of an institutional economic analysis of conservation. However, it lacks a theoretical basis and its application has no conceptual framework. From the late 1970s to the 1990s attempts have been made to fill these theoretical inadequacies. While referencing CW's contribution, SMS was reconceptualised to conform to environmental economics and its mainstream (neoclassical) theory. The three most far-reaching attempts to do this were to fit and apply the SMS within: (i) game theory, (ii) cost-benefit analysis and (iii) cost-effectiveness analysis.

Bishop (1978) framed the decision problem of a resource flow involving the SMS concept as a game between society and nature and suggested the minimax principle (minimisation of maximum possible loss) as a decision rule. Yet, he conceded that the minimax principle was inadequate and concluded that the rule should be modified so that a SMS be adopted unless the social costs were unacceptably high (ibid.: 13). Ready and Bishop (1991) introduced a lottery game but did not come to unambiguous results because the outcome depended on the framing of the game. They concluded: "Rejection of game theory does not necessarily imply rejection of the SMS as a decision-making policy, although it does leave us without a theoretical foundation for that policy" (ibid.: 311). Palmini (1999) reassessed the debate and proposed the 'minimax regret' decision rule that emphasises risk aversion, thus capturing only weak uncertainty. Therewith he claimed to provide a game theoretical justification for SMS. However, two problems remained: the choice of the games is an arbitrary judgement of the analyst, and also the minimax regret rule has not removed the problems linked to (strong) uncertainty and valuation of costs and benefits.

CW (1963 [1952]) made no reference to cost-benefit analysis, although costs, revenues and social optima of resource conservation played an important role in his analysis. Moreover, both conservation policy and the SMS were *prima facie* not supposed to reduce the private optima of economic activity. CW was very aware of the problems in identifying social costs and revenues, and was ambiguous about cost-benefit analyses; in 1955 he judged cost-benefit analyses critically but favourably (CW, 1955). However, elsewhere he proposed a qualitative standard for water quality to "avoid the most difficult aspects of benefit-cost analysis, namely the evaluation, in quantitative, pecuniary terms, of extra market and collective benefits of pollution abatement" (CW, 1961: 1143).

Bishop (1978) plainly linked evaluation of SMSs and cost-benefit analysis in his game theoretical trial to provide a theoretical foundation for the SMS concept. He coined the term "safe minimum standard approach" (in contrast to "safe minimum standard of conservation") and described the approach as a "decision rule that should be adopted unless the social costs of doing so are unacceptably large" (1978: 10). Although he conceded that "unacceptably large" exceeds the domain of economics, the result was from then onwards for analysts to apply cost-benefit analysis to decide the applicability of any specific SMS policy. Another proposal is to consider setting SMSs on the basis of cost-effectiveness evaluation rather than a full-fledged cost-benefit analysis (Chisholm, 1988: 199).

Other related concepts

The concept of the SMS has hardly advanced in recent years, yet it is frequently evoked as being related to, or a basis and inspiration for, threshold concepts such as PP and planetary boundaries (Röckstrom et al., 2009). Further to these related concepts are those that contribute to realising SMSs and PP (and, partially, planetary boundaries). These are the reversal of the burden of proof, and intergenerational and intragenerational justice. Each will be addressed in turn but the last three will be only briefly outlined.

Precautionary Principle (PP)

Precaution is common sense, though it was only introduced in 1976 as a norm of conduct in the environmental program of the German government (the Vorsorgeprinzip) [Chapter 27 covers the theory of PP, here political applications are discussed]. In the 1990s PP was introduced in international environmental and health policies, based on Swedish and German law. The 1992 Rio Declaration on Environment and Development and the Maastricht Treaty on European Union of the same year incorporated it within the context of the environment (Principle 15 in the Rio Declaration, and Art. 130r in the Maastricht Treaty). Later the European Commission (2000) concretised and enlarged its application as follows:

> The precautionary principle enables rapid response in the face of a possible danger to human, animal or plant health, or to protect the environment. In particular, where scientific data do not permit a complete evaluation of the risk, recourse to this principle may, for example, be used to stop distribution or order withdrawal from the market of products likely to be hazardous.

Additionally it has been taken up in treatises and regulations regarding biodiversity, biosafety, pharmaceutical research, health, chemicals and chemical pollution (e.g. Montreal-Protocol to protect the ozone layer). The Wingspread Statement on the Precautionary Principle of 1998, was a call to the government of the USA to strengthen precaution in law and states that "when an activity raises threats of harm to human health or the environment, precautionary measures should be taken even if some cause and effect relationships are not fully established scientifically" (cited in Raffensperger and Tickner (1999)).

The wide application of PP has triggered a vast body of literature and interpretations which led some to claim that PP is a heterogeneous idea rather than a unified doctrine. Indeed, comparisons of political enforcement of PP within Europe show that member states have different legal interpretations and try to influence the Commission's decisions on whether and how to invoke PP. The EU and corporations use their own experts to challenge decisions (Tosun, 2013). Furthermore, whether the European Commission invokes PP seems to be a matter of which Directorate General is responsible and whether a topic has a high degree of politicisation (Tosun, 2013).

According to Steel (2015), PP might be constructed as a meta rule (i.e. a constraint on decision-taking), as a decision rule (selecting among policy options), or as an epistemic rule (requiring standards of evidence before accepting an activity or technology). In debates around the PP there is the concern about false positives; that is, overregulation of alleged risks and harms, and hence encumbrance of innovation and economic activities. The European Environmental Agency (EEA) has followed up on these concerns. Their two investigations (EEA, 2001, 2013) show that most of the cases examined revealed false negatives. That is, most cases were ones where early warnings of harm existed but prevention was delayed or not taken at all.

The focus on strong uncertainty and the aim of avoiding serious or irreversible consequences of an activity links SMS and PP. SMS provides a more precise indication of where to set a minimum inviolable standard. This is due to the fact that SMS only focuses on flow resources whereas the application of PP is much broader. Also, PP does not suggest how to define barriers to the potentially harmful activity and what tools can help avoid transgressing the critical zone. Yet, since PP has been strongly developed and expanded with regard to applications, there are detailed procedures on how to apply PP in particular fields (e.g. Raffensperger and Tickner, 1999). Finally, compared to SMSs, PP lacks an analysis of why a problem or harmful activity occurs and hence it fails to address institutional dimensions. Yet, science technology assessments that have been proposed as an element of an application of PP, may involve institutional dimensions.

Planetary boundaries

The concept of planetary boundaries (Rockström et al., 2009) explicitly builds on the concept of SMS and PP amongst others. Planetary boundaries involve thresholds, defined as non-linear transitions in human–environmental systems. Thresholds are "intrinsic features of those systems and often defined by a position along one or more control variables" (ibid.: 3). Additionally, there are boundaries that are recognised by human-determined values of the control variable set at a safe distance from a dangerous level (ibid.). Dangerous level is defined as a reference point which, if transgressed, triggers unacceptable global environmental change in Earth system processes established during the Holocene during which present societies and cultures have evolved. The determination of a safe distance requires normative judgements as to risk and uncertainty.

Similar to SMS and PP, planetary boundaries assume uncertainty due to a lack of scientific knowledge and the dynamics of complex systems. This necessitates a 'zone of uncertainty' that will encompass an identified threshold. Rockström et al. (ibid.) have identified nine planetary boundaries. Four of these planetary boundaries have already been transgressed by humanity, namely those relating to: climate change, genetic diversity loss, land system change, and biochemical flows, comprising the global nitrogen cycle and the global phosphorus cycle (Steffen et al., 2015). On the basis of defined planetary boundaries, humans should use only a safe operating space for development. Planetary boundaries and SMSs also share the idea of a zone of uncertainty—in the language of SMS, 'critical zone'—and this depends on three aspects:

the kind of uncertainty, the degree of damage and a society's capabilities to deal with threats and strong uncertainty.

Reversal of the burden of proof

Advocates of PP support a reversal of proof for potentially harmful activities before obtaining approval for entry into the marketplace (Steel, 2015: 197) or consider it a part of PP (Randall, 2011). The EU considers the reversal of burden of proof as one possible measure in case of an action being taken under PP. Hence, "the producer, manufacturer or importer may be required to prove the absence of danger. This possibility shall be examined on a case-by-case basis" (European Commission, 2000). Reversal of burden of proof has also been claimed for SMS. Bererens et al. (1998: 149) even think that the SMS "can perhaps best be conceptualised as a burden-of-proof switching device. [...] The burden of proof lies in demonstrating that the opportunity costs of preservation activities are intolerable." Yet, it could also be a proof that an activity will not involve irreversibility. Otherwise, there may be good grounds to apply SMS, which means that the agent's harmful activity will be restricted. There are two questions relating to proof: Who provides the burden of proof? What is the standard of proof required? Absolute proof is impossible. Therefore, judgement is required to determine answer to both.

Intergenerational and intragenerational justice

Any interest in uncertainty and irreversibility involves considering the future. The limits to activities advocated by SMS or PP in cases of ecological or economic irreversibility and/or harmful effects are aimed at conserving resources for the future, and thus, at realising some degree of intergenerational and intragenerational justice. Moreover, as soon as costs and benefits of precautionary measures are calculated, the issue of discounting arises, which in turn involves judgements about intergenerational justice.

Any discussion about unacceptably high costs of conservation or precaution highlights also the question of intragenerational justice, as for instance Hampicke (1992: 312ff.) has shown. The question that arises is: For whom are the costs unacceptable? Using, as an example, conservation conflicts in developing countries, he suggests that in many cases a more equitable distribution of wealth would make the question about unacceptable cost superfluous and would thus remove any doubt about the usefulness of a proposed standard. Hampicke (ibid.: 313) concludes: "Thus, future generations only seemingly ask for sacrifices of the present generation; in reality they ask for a fairer distribution, which has to be considered as much more legitimate" (translation by the author). So, SMS and PP not only contribute to intergenerational justice but also involve intragenerational justice. CW was well aware of the equality issue when stating that social weighting determines the reference point to identify distortions in the social optimum state. However, these reflections did not lead to recommendations or claims regarding equality.

Future directions

CW's recommendation to address "the institutional perspective on conservation problems" has remained largely unheeded by those discussing and developing the SMS concept after him. Instead, conservation problems have been addressed within a neoclassical and game theoretical frame of analysis, reducing these problems to a question of monetary values and market prices. Yet, the roots and dynamics of many conservation problems point to institutional and equality dimensions such as monopolistic or oligopolistic situations, financial and monetary policies, subsidies and taxing, corruption, missing law enforcement, inequality in income and wealth, and many more. We often superficially know of these factors but miss deeper understanding with regard to particular conservation problems and implications for problem solution.

Another of CW's topics that has been ignored is the role of conservation practices, e.g. harvest and use practices. He considered these easy and cheap means for conservation in many instances. However, introducing advantageous practices and breaking with established routines and interests is often challenging, because this usually involves more issues than simply knowledge and awareness. Many of these issues need to be addressed within the context of interdisciplinary and transdisciplinary methodology.

Regarding PP, a challenge is to reduce false negatives. These are the cases, as noted by the EEA, where harm was forecast but action delayed or not taken. The reasons for such inaction and delay may be economic, political and/or institutional. Precaution may be enhanced by understanding the various multiple causal mechanisms.

Concluding remarks

SMS is an appealing concept that has been referred to frequently. However, the critical institutional analysis it entailed as fundamental has been stripped off, and the concept has been adapted to neoclassical economics. The related concept of PP is foremost a general political principle that addresses politics and administration but also fails to address the institutional aspects of conservation and other problems. Planetary boundaries are mainly concerned with boundaries to human activities leaving open the question of how environmental destruction is constrained politically and institutionally. In the face of strong uncertainty, there is an urgent need to take up the thinking and work of CW and extend his view, with further analysis and instruments appropriate for our present pressing social, ecological and environmental problems.

Key further readings cited

Ciriacy-Wantrup, S.V. (1963 [1952]). *Resource Conservation. Economics and Policies.* Berkeley: University of California Press.

Seidl, I. and Tisdell, C. (2001). Neglected features of safe minimum standard: Socio-economic and institutional dimensions. *Review of Social Economy,* 59(4), 418–442.

Steel, D. (2015). *Philosophy and the Precautionary Principle. Science, Evidence, and Environmental Policy.* Cambridge: Cambridge University Press.

Other literature cited

Berrens, R.P., Brookshire, D.S., McKee, M., Schmidt, C. (1998). Implementing the safe minimum standard approach: Two case studies from the U.S. Endangered Species Act. *Land Economics,* 74(2), 147–161.

Bishop, R.C. (1978). Endangered species and uncertainty: The economics of a safe minimum standard. *American Journal of Agricultural Economics,* 57(Feb.), 10–18.

Chisholm, A.H. (1988). Sustainable resource use and development: uncertainty, irreversibility and rational choice. In C. Tisdell & P. Maitra (eds.), *Technological Change, Development and the Environment: Socio-economic Perspectives* (pp. 188–216). London: Routledge.

Ciriacy-Wantrup, S.V. (1955). Benefit-cost analysis and public resource development. *Journal of Farm Economics,* 37(4), 676–689.

Ciriacy-Wantrup, S. V. (1961). Water quality, a problem for the economist. *Journal of Farm Economics,* 43(5), 1133–1144.

Daly, H.E. (1992). Allocation, distribution, and scale: towards an economics that is efficient, just, and sustainable. *Ecological Economics*, 6(3), 185–193.

EEA (European Environmental Agency) (2001). *Late Lessons from Early Warnings: The Precautionary Principle 1896–2000*. Copenhagen: EEA.

EEA (European Environmental Agency) (2013). *Late Lessons from Early Warnings: Science, Precaution, Innovation*. Copenhagen: EEA.

European Commission (2000). *Communication from the Commission on the Precautionary Principle*, Brussels, COM(2000)1.

Hampicke, U. (1992). *Ökologische Ökonomie. Individuum und Natur in der Neoklassik, Natur in der ökonomischen Theorie: Teil 4*. Opladen: Westdeutscher Verlag.

Knight, F.H. (1992 [1921]). *Risk, Uncertainty and Profit*. New York: Houghton Mifflin.

Ostrom, E. (1990). *Governing the Commons. The Evolution of Institutions for Collective Action*. Cambridge: Cambridge University Press.

Palmini, D. (1999). Uncertainty, risk aversion, and the game theoretic foundations of the safe minimum standard: a reassessment. *Ecological Economics*, 29(3), 463–472.

Raffensperger, C., Tickner, J. (Eds.). (1999). *Protecting Public Health & the Environment: Implementing the Precautionary Principle*. Washington: Island Press.

Randall, A. (2011). *Risk and Precaution*. Cambridge: Cambridge University Press.

Ready, R.C., Bishop, R.C. (1991). Endangered species and the safe minimum standard. *American Journal of Agricultural Economics*, 73(2), 309–312.

Rockström, J., Steffen, W., Noone, K., Persson, Å., Chapin III, F.S. (2009). A safe operating space for humanity. *Nature*, 461, 472–475.

Spash, C.L. (2002). *Greenhouse Economics. Value and Ethics*. London: Routledge.

Steffen, W., Richardson, K., Rockström, J., Cornell, S. E., Fetzer, I., Bennett, E.M., Biggs, R., Carpenter, S.R., de Vries, W., de Wit, C.A., Folke, C., Gerten, D., Heinke, J., Mace, G.M., Persson, L.M., Ramanathan, V., Reyers, B., Sörlin, S. (2015). Planetary boundaries: Guiding human development on a changing planet. *Science*, 347(6223), 736.

Tosun, J. (2013). How the EU handles uncertain risks: Understanding the role of the precautionary principle. *Journal of European Public Policy*, 20(10), 1517–1528.

28

POST-NORMAL SCIENCE

Roger Strand

Introduction

Post-normal science (PNS) is a critical concept originally developed to describe situations in which there are important or controversial public decision problems informed by an incomplete, uncertain or contested knowledge base. In this chapter, such problems are called "post-normal problems". Writings on PNS are descriptive in the sense that they describe the characteristics of post-normal problems and how the relationship between science and policy changes in the face of such post-normal problems. They are frequently also normative in the sense that they interpret the situations created by post-normal problems and propose how the relationship between science and policy ought to change, above all in the direction of what has been called the democratisation of expertise.

This chapter introduces and explains the theoretical context of, and contribution by, PNS as a critical concept. The concept is briefly compared to similar developments in post-empiricist history, philosophy and sociology of science before I end the chapter with a look at the practice dimension of PNS [see also Chapter 29]. The objective of this chapter is to indicate what the concept may have to offer ecological economists now and in the future.

Post-normal science: origin and overview

The philosophers Silvio Funtowicz and Jerome Ravetz (1990) coined the term "post-normal science". It has since caught on as an analytical concept but also as a label for a style of research practice. A growing community of researchers state that they are doing PNS; that is, producing knowledge or practising problem-solving strategies better suited for post-normal problems. These strategies are then seen as being logically implied, or at least legitimised, by analyses based on PNS as a critical concept. Often, the strategies include elements of public participation— "extension of the peer community"—and/or innovative approaches to the characterisation, communication and management of scientific uncertainty.

Research that claims to do PNS in practice attends to a wide range of concrete topics and decision problems. However, the main focus is on public governance of the natural environment, sustainability and climate change. Figure 28.1 provides a rough indication of topics covered. This is a word cloud representing words in the title or abstract of explicitly "post-normal" research papers registered in Web of Science.

Figure 28.1   Post-normal science word cloud.

This reveals a considerable overlap between the topics of ecological economics and writings on PNS. That is no coincidence. After an initial focus mainly on technological risk, the seminal writings of Funtowicz and Ravetz (to be explained below) rapidly broadened their scope to the risks, uncertainties and complexities of environmental governance. Notably, Funtowicz and Ravetz (1994) themselves proposed that ecological economics is, or could become, a post-normal science. Silva and Teixeira (2011) performed a bibliometric analysis of all articles in the journal *Ecological Economics*, 1989–2009, and concluded "at least through the lens of EE [the journal], ecological economics has evolved towards a post-normal science" (ibid.: 849). Their conclusion is a matter of some contestation because they employ a definition that includes much which is actually rejected by Funtowicz and Ravetz; as Spash (2013: 356) states, their claims "that ecological economics is now a post-normal science appear based upon the antithesis of the post-normal philosophy (e.g., the spread of mathematical formalism, abstract expert modelling, and low quality uncritical monetary quantification)". This indicates some confusion on the part of Silva and Teixeira as to what constitutes PNS. Still, as also noted by Spash (2012: 42–43), the concept of PNS has definitely played a role in the modern history of ecological economics.

The theory of PNS by Funtowicz and Ravetz

Three types of risk assessment

In 1985, five years before the first mentioning of "post-normal science", Funtowicz and Ravetz published a paper called "Three Types of Risk Assessment: A Methodological Analysis" (Funtowicz and Ravetz, 1985). The three types were:

1   applied science;
2   technical consultancy (to be called "professional consultancy" in later works);
3   total-environmental assessment (to be called "post-normal science" in later works).

They explained these concepts in a diagram reproduced here as Figure 28.2 and discussed further below.

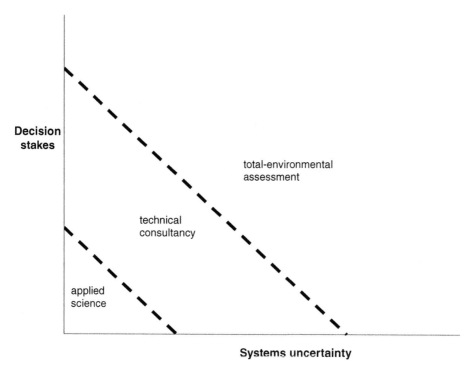

Figure 28.2   The original diagram of three types of risk assessment.
Notes: "Total-environmental assessment" would later be relabelled as "post-normal science".
Source: redrawn after Funtowicz and Ravetz (1985).

The typology is better understood as a heuristic than a set of exact definitions. The underlying idea is that applied science works well only under conditions of relatively low uncertainty and decision stakes. For instance, one might be faced with technological risks (or rather hazards) for which there is no historical record that validly warrants probability estimates, or that result from interactions in systems that are too complex or too poorly characterised to be reliably captured in a model. This might be a trivial problem if the risk or hazard is quite small and there can be a cumulative learning cycle based on repeated failures, accidents and improvements. Ever more decision problems are, however, connected to issues of a larger magnitude and with higher decision stakes. The risk of major nuclear accidents is one example.

Decision stakes are rightly seen as a subjective property in the sense that they cannot be assessed without applying value judgements. Not by logical necessity but as a matter of fact, high decision stakes also tend to be connected to disagreements about the stakes and the underlying value judgements between different stakeholders and affected parties. Funtowicz and Ravetz (1985) note that there is a type of practical risk assessment (and management) taking place that may be heavily informed by science but still different from it: the type of work being done by engineers, medical doctors and other professional consultants who combine scientific training with practical skills and experience. This style of work may tackle higher uncertainties along the facts and values dimensions, in part because of a more flexible and adaptive work mode than allowed by the standards for scientific rigour and in part because they reduce the uncertainty in the value dimension by loyalty. Those undertaking such work, by adopting the values and goals of their client—patient, company, governmental organisation—may reduce the scope of relevant concerns and accordingly exclude relevant system uncertainties.

290

The partly descriptive, partly normative claim of Funtowicz and Ravetz is that there is a growing class of decision problems in modern societies that belong to the top-right sector of Figure 28.2, characterised by high stakes and high system uncertainties. Energy supply is one of their examples. The analysis accepts that societal choices about energy supply can be informed by numerous rigorous facts and analyses. However, the choices cannot be reduced to questions that can be answered by applied science or technical consultancy, because the content of the choices themselves depends upon: the framing of the decision alternatives; the value judgements on the relevance and importance of the various risks and benefits; the time frame; the delimitation of affected parties; and similar factors. In other words, the definition of the issue itself is (or should be) a matter of continuous value-laden deliberations and negotiations. This is so for two reasons, regarded as inextricably linked concerns: democracy and the quality and effectiveness of knowledge. The recommended process of ongoing deliberation—framing and reframing the issue—is what Funtowicz and Ravetz originally call the "total-environmental assessment", because it cannot be reduced to a technical exercise, or a political decision. Potentially, any kind of descriptive or normative input to the process may be relevant.

The concern for democracy is readily justified if interpreted on the grounds of justice. We may imagine an industry that produces a certain product for profit and at the same time exposes its workforce and its surroundings to emissions with unclear consequences for human health and the environment. The industry itself may hire consultants to investigate the risks as defined from their perspective, for instance in terms of current occupational health standards, and with a view to liabilities and reputational risks. However, affected parties might be dissatisfied with this scope and insist on the need for an independent inquiry where they have a say in the choice of risks to consider and the standards employed for comparison. In academic communities, such as that of ecological economics, as well as in the regulatory set-up of most modern states, there is little need to argue why these affected parties may rightly make such claims.

Clearly the concern for democratic principles is often neglected in reality—war, torture, oppression, exploitation. Risk assessment and management may often take place as an expert, closed-down exercise within a narrow frame, excluding the concerns of affected parties, and without much transparency. Within the theory of PNS this is also seen as a quality problem. If the risk assessment fails to address relevant concerns of legitimate stakeholders, it is not fit for the purpose. The definition of the purpose is a matter of the framing of the problem, which is a democratic—deliberative, inclusive and participatory—concern, and consequently the judgement on quality is also, in this particular sense, a democratic concern. The scope of the risk assessment (or indeed any other production of knowledge relevant for a decision problem) is a function of the over-all decisions on problem framing, but typically also a myriad of smaller or larger methodological decisions, such as: the exact choice of variables, metrics and indicators, resolution of spatial and temporal grids, inclusion and exclusion of data variables, and so on. All of these decisions potentially involve value judgements of a partially political character. A key concept in PNS is therefore the extension of the peer community, defined as the inclusion for the production of knowledge of 'other' (non-expert) actors in methodological decisions and quality judgements.

A frequent criticism of the argument just presented is that it is too idealist in the sense of being too optimistic about the prospects of involving non-experts in processes of knowledge production. Believers in 'objective science' typically argue that stakeholders might be guided by their own interests and accordingly subjective and biased. Furthermore, following this line of argument, stakeholders may lack the knowledge required to make competent contributions to the deliberations upon methods and knowledge quality. One can find different stances towards this objection in the writings on PNS. One line of response is to see the objection as a question open to empirical inquiry. Wikipedia, for example, is an online encyclopaedia with a virtually open peer community and with a relatively light structure to organise and manage author inputs. In this sense it can be seen as an experiment of PNS that can help with casting light on the conditions under which an extension of the peer community appears to work well (or not so well). The response closest to the core of the analysis provided by Funtowicz and Ravetz, however, is to remind the critics of the direness of many post-normal situations. PNS is not about piece-meal improvements in the methods of risk assessment—enriching an already fine scientific risk assessment with valuable facts and values from the citizens and thereby also improving its democratic legitimacy. The theory of PNS focuses on the social reality of controversy, conflict and erosion of trust between experts and non-experts. Extension of the peer community is not an extra to improve chances of success but a necessity. It is required to address the implication of acknowledging that—under conditions of high uncertainty, high decision stakes and values in dispute—a number of dichotomies, central to the imaginary of modern societies, simply fail to match reality. A range of dichotomies and their divisions cannot be justified in an absolute sense: facts and values; science and politics; expertise and non-expertise. So in cases where a strict separation between "objective" expertise and "subjective" non-expertise is seen to be impossible or dysfunctional—in the sense that controversies are unresolved, trust is absent and important decisions are stalled—refusing to extend the peer community is unjustified (Funtowicz and Strand, 2007).

The theory of PNS is less about providing recipes for success and more about understanding why success recipes and technical fixes often prove inadequate and why the desire for technical fixes is part of the dysfunctionality encountered in post-normal situations. In this sense, the word science in PNS is misleading because it indicates a focus on science alone. The scope of this theoretical perspective is more correctly seen as the interface between science and (modern) society and, in particular the institutions and culture(s) that govern the interface between science and policy. Rather than a technical solution, PNS advocates institutional change and a change of individual and group mentality.

Normal and post-normal science

Why then, should we call it "post-normal science" rather than total-environmental assessment? In addition to being catchy, the term "post-normal science" offers a useful contrast to "normal science", which is a central concept in the philosophy of science associated with Thomas Kuhn in his *The Structure of Scientific Revolutions* (1962). There are many good alternatives to Kuhn's description of scientific practice—indeed, Ravetz (1971) himself offered a much more detailed description and explanation of the workings of science—so the main advantage of Kuhn's work is its wide dissemination. *Structure* is widely cited and has sold more than one million copies, and (even amongst those who have never read or heard of the book) the concepts of normal science, paradigm, paradigm shift, scientific revolution and incommensurability have made their way into popular as well as academic culture. Didactically, the comparison of Kuhn's normal science with PNS allows a set of easily explained contrasts, as shown in Table 28.1.

Didactics are important in this respect. To my knowledge, there are no educational programmes entirely devoted to PNS. It has been included as one of several theoretical frameworks in some study programmes within interdisciplinary environmental science (including ecological economics). A very important role for PNS, however, is its inclusion as a critical concept in normal science education. In the typology of research related to PNS provided by Turnpenny et al. (2011), one of the main genres of PNS is that of being a challenge for scientists. One may argue with Kuhn that science education is designed to socialise students

Table 28.1 Normal science and post-normal science compared

Normal science	Post-normal problems	Post-normal science maxims
.. takes time	.. call for urgent decisions	Focus on knowledge quality in terms of fitness for purpose!
.. replaces ignorance and uncertainty with certainty	.. may have irreducible uncertainties	Communicate and manage the uncertainties (rather than trying in vain to eliminate them)!
.. focuses on simple and idealized systems	.. emerge in complex systems (non-linear; nature–culture)	Include a multitude of perspectives!
.. is puzzle-solving	.. have high stakes	Extend the peer communities!
.. is practiced within a paradigm of agreed methods and shared values	.. may involve both facts and values in dispute	Acknowledge that methods and facts are value-laden!

into the normal science paradigms, teaching them not only skills, theories and other forms of positive knowledge, but also discipline; that is, disciplining them to focus their cognitive efforts inside the borders of the paradigm and discouraging reflection and questions critical to or outside of the paradigm.

In Kuhn's analysis, this state of affairs is simply a matter of fact, an inevitable effect of the organisation of normal science. For his interlocutors Karl Popper (1963) and Paul Feyerabend (1975), the repressive and dogmatic character of normal science was something that could and should be fought by open criticism. They thought this could be achieved either by cherishing the classic scientific ideals of fallibilism and humility (Popper) or opening up established science to what currently falls outside of it (Feyerabend). The role of PNS, in normal science education, can then be thought of as akin to Feyerabend's philosophy, trying to open up scientific minds by showing them how important sources of uncertainty and complexity remain invisible from within their paradigms.

PNS and the science–policy interface

The theory of PNS places itself among several other theoretical developments that criticise empiricist and objectivist portrayals of scientific practice and scientific knowledge. There are several sources and origins of these strands of thought. In non-anglophone philosophy of science, post-empiricist/post-positivist thinking has been around for a long time (since Husserl and Heidegger and the Frankfurt School in Germany; with Bachelard, Canguilhem and Foucault in France; Ortega y Gasset in Spain; and in various shapes in Russian philosophy). In the 1960s, neo-Marxist influence was present in the critical science/radical science movements with which PNS shares its theoretical and practical interests. Similarly there is cross-over of interest with early science studies and "Science, Technology and Society" (STS), in the 1960s (Sardar and van Loon, 2011). STS later became more theoretically sophisticated and institutionalised into "Science and Technology Studies", a research field of its own, with study programmes and research departments around the world. Within (and around) STS, the typical topics of PNS—strong uncertainty, complexity, the importance of the framing of issues and the value of knowledge outside of normal science—are by no means underrepresented in theoretical and empirical work. When I teach courses on PNS I always include work by STS researchers such as Sheila Jasanoff and Brian Wynne, and frequently also the actor-network theory with reference to Bruno Latour or Michel Callon.

Furthermore, one can encounter critical concepts in STS and the history, philosophy and sociology of science that share the heuristic and didactic value and some of the content of PNS. One prominent example is the "Mode 1/Mode 2" distinction made by Gibbons et al. (1994). Mode 1 is a mode of knowledge production quite close to normal science: disciplinary, taking place within academic institutions, motivated by curiosity at the research forefront as defined by the discipline itself, and subject to quality standards defined and sanctioned by the disciplinary peer community. Mode 2, on the other hand, is conceived as transdisciplinary problem-solving by scientific researchers outside of academia; for example, in industry and the service sector, where quality is a matter of solving the problem to the satisfaction of the employer or client rather than meeting disciplinary standards. In their original work, Gibbons et al. (1994) hardly touched the aspect of civil society and the democratisation of expertise. However, their follow-up (Nowotny et al., 2001), does cover the issue of accountability and interaction with broader society, and develops their concept of "socially robust knowledge", thereby providing a suite of concepts that are similar to professional consultancy and PNS.

In sum, there is no strict demarcation between the theory of PNS and these areas of STS and related work. PNS is also a moving target, depending upon which authors are read, and which of their texts. The texts by Funtowicz and Ravetz also, unsurprisingly, developed throughout the 1980s, 1990s and 2000s, departing from a focus on exceptionally complex cases of technological risk and towards a general diagnosis of late modern societies. As a rule of thumb, PNS has tended to place itself somewhere between scientific realism and the full-blown social constructivism of, say, early Sociology of Scientific Knowledge (SSK). This is not so extraordinary any more either, because several of the radical SSK researchers later modified their positions to more moderate constructivist positions in the course of the 1990s. One might perhaps conclude that a weak, overlapping consensus on moderate constructivist positions is gradually emerging from the diversity of research on science and technology (Sardar and van Loon, 2011). Perhaps the main difference between PNS and STS is that the former has been much more engaged in the development of concrete problem-solving practices; taking part in practice and not just studying it.

Future directions

As noted above, the Web of Science (as of 1 August 2015) counts 259 research papers with the words "post normal" or "post-normal" in the title or abstract. Ten per cent of these papers were published in the 1990s. Most of them can be classified as philosophical or conceptual in their outlook, and most of them were published either by Funtowicz, Ravetz or their close collaborators. In the 2000s, this changed. More and more of the post-normal research papers (in the sense that they call themselves post-normal) are predominantly empirical and practical in their orientation, claiming to apply or do PNS in some sense, in particular in order to improve some aspect of environmental governance (e.g., concerning climate change, ecosystem or natural resource management, nature preservation).

This change is quite in line with the recommendations of the early writings of Funtowicz and Ravetz. Indeed, in their much cited book *Uncertainty and Quality in Science for Policy*, Funtowicz and Ravetz (1990) developed the NUSAP system, which is a flexible notational system for the characterisation, communication and management of scientific uncertainty. NUSAP is an acronym for numeral, unit, spread, assessment and pedigree [see also Chapter 29]. Normal statistical notation can provide options for NUSA (no P)—for example, standard deviation would be a measure for spread while p-values or confidence levels provide information on assessment. Pedigree, however, is the post-normal or mildly constructivist innovation in this system. The pedigree of a number or a fact can be elicited and communicated through tailored sets of descriptors; for instance, on the level of expert agreement, quality of data, the use of models, and the level of maturity of underlying scientific theory. Some of those conducting PNS apply the NUSAP system or similar methodological developments along that line (for instance Petersen et al., 2011). The other major type of work on PNS consists of attempts at extending the peer community by including local knowledge, stakeholder involvement and/or citizen participation in some way. The types may of course be (and often are) combined in the same study or exercise.

Extending the peer community means moving towards transdisciplinarity in the sense of including non-academic knowledge sources and methods. The use of Web of Science in this chapter as a source of data on PNS can therefore be criticised as being far too narrow. Indeed, while Web of Science provides only 259 "hits", a similar search on Google Scholar gives 11,000. Furthermore, if one wanted to write a handbook on PNS, relevant methods and experiences go beyond those who use the label or reference PNS in their writings. From an (explicit) PNS perspective, practice is becoming increasingly post-normal, regardless of whether the actors are aware of that label or the underlying theory. For example, one may interpret the phenomenon of wikis (such as Wikipedia.org) as typical of PNS in the sense of being transdisciplinary knowledge production that essentially relies on a wide extension of the peer community. For some proponents of the theory of PNS, it is this broader trend that is important and not the label of "post-normal science" itself. Others are more active and eager to promote PNS as an identity marker in order to develop and consolidate a community of researchers and practitioners at the science–policy interface. If I were to make guesses about the future, however, I would not expect a similar development as that of STS; that is, going from a quite hetero-geneous community who shared a broad concern to a disciplinary project of building academic institutions. After all, the core of PNS is that it is not normal science. It is unlikely that a majority of its proponents will forget this core.

Concluding remarks

Funtowicz and Ravetz (1994) proposed in their paper "The Worth of a Songbird: Ecological Economics as a Post-normal Science" that the main challenge for ecological economics is not to provide yet another attempt at a technical solution to reduce and eliminate the descriptive and normative uncertainties and complexities involved in human interaction with Nature, but rather to identify, understand and manage them. In that sense, they envisioned ecological economics as an opportunity not to become just another normal science. One may discuss the extent to which ecological economics in fact is post-normal. On one hand, we may observe that with the exception of *Futures*, no journal has published more papers on PNS than *Ecological Economics*. However, as noted earlier, while Silva and Teixeira (2011) concluded that ecological economics is indeed becoming post-normal, their analysis appears to be based upon a different and perhaps somewhat superficial concept of PNS. Furthermore, the extent to which publications in *Ecological Economics* actually pay attention to the messages of PNS is highly debatable. For example, Spash (2007) provides an example applying the framing of PNS to critically appraise the Stern review on climate change, but the majority of climate research published in *Ecological Economics* appears to adopt a mainstream neoclassical economic framing (Anderson and M'Gonigle, 2012), and thus remains within normal science.

We have argued above that PNS is a term that is used in a variety of ways; and while one can meaningfully say that one is "doing post-normal science" for instance by applying methods of strong uncertainty management or extending peer communities, describing PNS as a type of science or research is inappropriate. PNS is a term, a convenient label for a description and a diagnosis of the science–society interface, and for providing some ideas of how to improve that interface. In order to say something more specific about what PNS "is", the best option is to employ the initial term "total-environmental assessment", meaning the ongoing negotiation, framing and reframing of decision issues. Along this line of argument it does not make much sense to ask if ecological economics is "a post-normal science". PNS is not science; if ecological economics pretends to be a scientific discipline, it is not PNS.

What makes sense, however, is to analyse how actors and institutions of ecological economics envision the interface between their own production of knowledge and the society (and Nature) for and in which it is produced, notably institutions of policy and governance. To the extent that ecological economics offers, or wishes to offer, venues at the science–policy interface for keeping fundamental philosophical debates open—What are problems? What may count as solutions? Who should judge and assess? What are the quality criteria?— we can call it a "post-normal science". Rather than a set of techniques and practices, at least some of us who identify with the label "post-normal", identify with a certain engagement, mentality and attitude. A main dimension of that attitude is reflexivity and humility (Strand and Cañellas-Boltà, 2006). This, I believe, poses a challenge. Clearly this challenges orthodox economists who may have been socialised into the belief that they are producing "Truth in order to speak to Power". However, the challenge may be found equally demanding for ecological economists of all heterodox colours who have had to build such hard stratgies against the hegemony of orthodox thought that they can only rarely allow themselves to doubt their own epistemic and moral virtues. This, however, is at the core of PNS: the willingness to open up one's cherished facts and values to inclusive processes of total-environmental assessment.

Acknowledgements

I thank the editor, Clive Spash, for comments that significantly improved this contribution. I also wish to express my gratitude to Ina Hannestad Nygaard for editing text and figures.

Key further readings cited

Funtowicz, S., Ravetz, J. (1990). *Uncertainty and Quality in Science for Policy,* Dordrecht: Kluwer Acad. Press.

Funtowicz, S., Ravetz, J. (1994). The worth of a songbird: Ecological economics as a post-normal science. *Ecological Economics* 10, 197–207.

Funtowicz, S., Strand, R. (2007). Models of Science and Policy, in Traavik, T. and Lim, L.C. (eds.), *Biosafety First: Holistic Approaches to Risk and Uncertainty in Genetic Engineering and Genetically Modified Organisms* (pp. 263–278). Tapir Academic Press, Trondheim.

Sardar, Z. and van Loon, B. (2011). *Introducing Philosophy of Science: A Graphic Guide.* London: Icon Books.

Turnpenny, J., Jones, M., Lorenzoni, I. (2011). Where now for post-normal science? A critical review of its development, definitions, and uses. *Science, Technology, & Human Values* 36, 287–306.

Other literature cited

Anderson, B., M'Gonigle, M. (2012). Does ecological economics have a future? Contradiction and reinvention in the age of climate change. *Ecological Economics* 84 (December), 37–48.

Feyerabend, P. (1975). *Against Method.* London: Verso.

Funtowicz, S., Ravetz, J. (1985). Three types of risk assessment: a methodological analysis, in: C. Whipple, V. T. Covello (eds): *Risk Analysis in the Private Sector* (pp. 217–231). New York and London: Plenum Press.

Gibbons, M., C. Limoges, H. Nowotny, S. Schwartzman, P. Scott, M. Trow (1994). *The New Production of Knowledge. The Dynamics of Science and Research in Contemporary Societies*. London: Sage.

Kuhn, T. (1962). *The Structure of Scientific Revolutions*. Chicago, IL: University of Chicago Press.

Nowotny, H., Scott, P., Gibbons, M. (2001). *Re-Thinking Science. Knowledge and the Public in an Age of Uncertainty*. Cambridge: Polity Press.

Petersen, A.C., A. Cath, M. Hage, E. Kunseler, J.P. van der Sluijs (2011). Post-normal science in practice at the Netherlands Environmental Assessment Agency. *Science, Technology, & Human Values* 36, 362–388.

Popper, K. (1963) *Conjectures and Refutations: The Growth of Scientific Knowledge*. London: Routledge.

Ravetz, J. (1971), *Scientific Knowledge and Its Social Problems*. Oxford: Clarendon Press.

Silva, C.M., Teixeira, A. (2011). A bibliometric account of the evolution of EE in the last two decades: Is ecological economics (becoming) a post-normal science? *Ecological Economics* 70, 849–862.

Spash, C.L. (2007). The economics of climate change impacts à la Stern: Novel and nuanced or rhetorically restricted? *Ecological Economics* 63(4), 706–713.

Spash, C.L. (2012). New foundations for ecological economics. *Ecological Economics* 77(May), 36–47.

Spash, C. L. (2013). The shallow or the deep ecological economics movement? *Ecological Economics* 93(September), 351–362.

Strand, R., Cañellas-Boltà, S. (2006). Reflexivity and Modesty in the Application of Complexity Theory. In A. Guimarães Pereira, S. Vaz, S. Tognetti (eds.), *Interfaces between Science and Society* (pp. 100–117). Sheffield, UK: Greenleaf Publishing.

PART VIII

Methods

29

THE NUSAP APPROACH TO UNCERTAINTY APPRAISAL AND COMMUNICATION

Jeroen P. van der Sluijs

Introduction

The knowledge base available for decision-making on contemporary environmental and sustainability issues is often characterised by an imperfect understanding of the complex systems involved. Decisions will need to be made before conclusive scientific evidence is available, while at the same time the potential error costs of wrong decisions can be huge. This societal context of knowledge production and use for decision-making and risk management implies an urgent need for explicit appraisal and consideration of all dimensions of scientific uncertainty (Funtwicz and Ravetz, 1990, 1993; Van der Sluijs, 2002; Van der Sluijs et al., 2008, Saltelli et al., 2013); [see also Chapters 26–28].

The transdisciplinary nature of science for sustainability poses additional requirements with regard to the systematic analysis, documentation and communication of uncertainty. When quantitative information is produced in one disciplinary context and used in another, we often see that important caveats tend to be ignored, uncertainties compressed and numbers used at face value (Wynne, 1992). Knowledge utilisation for sustainability issues requires a full and public awareness of the various sorts of uncertainty and underlying assumptions. Knowledge needs to be robust both technically and socially (Nowotny, 1999).

The past record of science for policy has shown that omitting uncertainty assessment and communication can undermine public trust in the science (e.g. Keepin and Wynne, 1984). An example concerns the Netherlands National Institute for Public Health and the Environment (RIVM). In early 1999, De Kwaadsteniet, a senior statistician, accused the RIVM of "lies and deceit" in their State of the Environment Reports and Environmental Outlooks. In a quality newspaper (*Trouw*) he criticised RIVM for basing their studies on the 'virtual reality' of poorly validated computer models, while RIVM presented these results as point values with unwarranted significant digits and without elaborating the uncertainties. A vehement public debate was triggered on the credibility and reliability of environmental numbers and models. The case got front page and prime time coverage in the mass media and led to a debate in the Netherlands parliament (Van der Sluijs, 2002). The RIVM went through a learning process that led to the development of guidance for uncertainty management in the institute (Van der Sluijs et al., 2008; Petersen et al., 2011).

In this chapter I explain how such incidents have led to a revision of the approach to uncertainty. The next section outlines how the understanding of uncertainty has changed and the implications this has for policy. This background explains why new transdisciplinary methods for evaluating uncertainty have been developed. The chapter then focuses on the Numeral, Unit, Spread, Assessment and Pedigree (NUSAP) framework and explains its key features. Pedigree is given particular attention as the innovative aspect of this post-normal science system [see Chapter 28].

Understanding uncertainty

In the early phase of its development, the field of uncertainty analysis mainly evolved around mathematical statistical methods such as sensitivity analysis and Monte Carlo techniques for the assessment of error propagation in model calculations. These tools address quantitative dimensions of uncertainty using sophisticated algorithms (Saltelli et al., 2000, 2008). Although these quantitative techniques are essential in any uncertainty analysis, they provide only a partial insight into what usually is a very complex mass of uncertainties involving technical, methodological, epistemological and societal dimensions. Quantitative methods can however be complemented with new qualitative approaches addressing aspects of uncertainty that are hard to quantify and were therefore largely under addressed in the past. In their combination, the quantitative and qualitative methods provide a richer diagnosis of uncertainty than each of these methods alone.

Over the past decades, an increasing body of conceptual and theoretical work in the field of uncertainty management has been compiled. Key insights from the field include the following:

- Uncertainty is partly socially constructed and its assessment always involves subjective judgement.
- More research does not necessarily reduce uncertainty; it often reveals unforeseen complexities;
- Some uncertainty is irreducible (intrinsic or practically).
- High quality scientific knowledge for policy making does not require low uncertainty.
- Uncertainty is a multi-dimensional concept involving quantitative (technical inexactness) and qualitative dimensions (i.e., methodological unreliability, epistemological ignorance and societally limited robustness), and it can manifest itself at different locations (e.g., context, indicator choice, model structure, parameters and data).
- In problems that are characterised by high systems uncertainties, ignorance, and high decision stakes, the qualitative dimensions of uncertainty may well dominate the quantitative dimensions.

Most of present day methodologies and practices for addressing uncertainty focus exclusively on quantitative uncertainty in model parameters and input data. Methods to address qualitative and societal dimensions of uncertainty are absent or in their early stage of development. Uncertainties relating to model structure, model assumptions and model context are largely ignored.

Scientists, policymakers and stakeholders now widely hold that uncertainty management in environmental assessment is essential. However, in the practice of uncertainty management there is little appreciation for the fact that uncertainty is more than a number. There are many different dimensions of uncertainty and there is a lack of understanding about their different characteristics, relevance and relative importance. Even within the different fields of decision support (such as integrated assessment, environmental risk assessment, environmental impact assessment, policy analysis, engineering risk analysis and cost-benefit analysis), there is neither a commonly shared terminology nor agreement on a generic typology of uncertainties (Walker et al., 2003).

A better understanding of the various dimensions of uncertainty is needed in order to provide an improved theoretical foundation for uncertainty assessment. Improved conceptualisation of uncertainty is desirable for a number of reasons. First, it will aid better communication amongst the many disciplines involved. In the current situation, different analysts use different terms for the same kinds of uncertainty, and some use the same term to refer to different kinds. This makes it difficult for those who have not participated in the actual work to understand what has been done. Improved conceptualisation of uncertainty will further provide for better communication among scientists, policymakers and stakeholders. A common belief is that policymakers expect scientists to provide certainties and hence dislike uncertainty in the scientific knowledge base. However, uncertainty is a fact of life and a better understanding of its key dimensions and their implications for policy choices would be likely to lead to more trust in the scientists providing decision support, and ultimately to better policies. Finally, a better understanding of the different dimensions of uncertainty and their potential impact on the relevant policy issues at hand would help in identifying and prioritising effective and efficient research and development activities for improving the knowledge base.

Van der Sluijs (1997) concludes that in the practice of uncertainty management in integrated modelling of climate change, major gaps exist in the systematic analysis of unreliability of the knowledge about input data, model parameters and model assumptions, and also in the analysis of uncertainty about model structure. A major obstacle is that tools for assessing these types of uncertainty and how these might affect the outcomes of assessments, are either not available or in their early stage of development. Only recently have new tools been developed that focus on the qualitative (methodological and epistemological) dimensions of uncertainty using methods of expert elicitation, quality assistance checklists (Risbey et al., 2005), Pedigree analysis (using multiple criteria [Chapter 30]) assessing the strength of various underpinning components of the knowledge base by self-review, peer review or extended peer review (Funtowicz and Ravetz, 1990; Van der Sluijs et al., 2005a, 2005b, 2005c), and methods for the systematic identification and characterisation of critical assumptions in models (Kloprogge et al., 2011).

Addressing the multiple dimensions of uncertainty

Whereas quantitative methods are well developed, standardised and supported by handbooks (Morgan and Henrion, 1990; Saltelli et al., 2000, 2008) and software (@Risk, Crystal ball, Simlab, Analytica), qualitative and multi-dimensional methods have been demonstrated and tested but have not yet been widely disseminated and adopted. Multi-dimensional methods are those that address qualitative and quantitative aspects in a coherent way. They do so by assessing the technical (inexactness), methodological (unreliability), societal (social robustness) and epistemological (border with ignorance) dimensions of uncertainty, as shown in Table 29.1.

Numeral, Unit, Spread, Assessment, Pedigree (NUSAP)

NUSAP is a notational system, proposed in the context of post-normal science by Funtowicz and Ravetz (1990), which aims to provide an analysis and diagnosis of uncertainty in science for policy. The NUSAP system structures the systematic appraisal and communication of the various dimensions of uncertainty. It provides an heuristic for good practice addressing uncertainty in quantitative information. NUSAP has extended the statistical approach to uncertainty with methodological and epistemological dimensions by adding expert judgement of reliability (Assessment) and systematic multi-criteria evaluation of the underpinning of numbers (Pedigree). Examples of Pedigree criteria are empirical basis, methodological rigour, theoretical understanding, degree of validation and peer acceptance.

Table 29.1 Dimensions of uncertainty

Dimension	Type	Can stem from or can be produced by
Technical	Inexactness	*Intrinsic uncertainty:* Variability; stochasticity; heterogeneity *Technical limitations:* Error bars, ranges, variance; Resolution error (spatial, temporal); Aggregation error; Linguistic imprecision, unclear definitions
Methodological	Unreliability	*Limited internal strength of the knowledge base in:* Use of proxies; Empirical basis; Theoretical understanding; Methodological rigour (including management of anomalies); Validation
Epistemological	Ignorance	*Limited theoretical understanding* *System indeterminacy:* Open-endedness of system under study; Chaotic behaviour *Intrinsic unknowability with active ignorance:* Model fixes for reasons understood; Limited domain of validity of assumptions; Limited domains of applicability of functional relations; Numerical error; Surprises type A (some awareness of possibility exists) *Intrinsic unknowability with passive ignorance:* Bugs (software error, hardware error, typos); Model fixes for reasons not understood; Surprises type B (no awareness of possibility)
Societal	Limited social robustness	*Limited external strength of the knowledge base in:* Completeness of set of relevant aspects; Exploration of rival problem framings; Management of dissent; Extended peer acceptance/stakeholder involvement; Transparency; Accessibility *Bias/Value-ladenness:* Value laden assumptions; Motivational bias (interests, incentives); Disciplinary bias; Cultural bias; Choice of (modelling) approach (e.g. bottom up, top down); Subjective judgement

The NUSAP framework provides a means for synthesis and integration of findings on each of these dimensions, combining formal Monte Carlo and mathematical sensitivity analysis techniques with systematic qualitative uncertainty assessment. NUSAP enables providers and users of knowledge to be clear and transparent about its various uncertainties. This promotes critical reflection on the strengths and weaknesses of the underlying knowledge base by users of all sorts (e.g., experts, lay public) and thereby supports an extended peer review process. It aims to provide those who produce, use and are affected by policy-relevant knowledge with a set of diagnostic tools for a critical self-awareness of their engagement with that knowledge.

NUSAP extends the statistical approach to uncertainty (inexactness) by incorporating the methodological (unreliability) and epistemological (ignorance) dimensions using expert judgement of reliability (Assessment) and systematic multi-criteria evaluation of the process by which numbers are produced (Pedigree). Numbers are provided with a separate qualification for each dimension of uncertainty, allowing nuances of meaning about quantities to be conveyed concisely and clearly, to a degree that is quite impossible with reliance on statistical methods alone. NUSAP captures both quantitative and qualitative dimensions of uncertainty and enables one to display these in a standardised and self-explanatory way. The basic idea is to qualify quantities using the five aspects of the NUSAP system: (i) Numeral, (ii) Unit, (iii) Spread, (iv) Assessment and (v) Pedigree. Each of these dimensions, or numeric qualifiers, is discussed in turn.

First is the Numeral, which is normally an ordinary number, but, when appropriate, can be a more general quantity, such as the expression 'a million' (which is not the same as the number lying between 999,999 and 1,000,001). Second is the Unit, which may be of the conventional sort, but which may also contain extra information, such as the date on which the Unit is evaluated (e.g. a common qualification for monetary values subject to inflation). The third category is Spread, which is a generalisation from the 'random error' of experiments or the variance of statistics. Although Spread is usually conveyed by a number (either +, % or 'factor of'), it is not an ordinary quantity, because its own inexactness is of a different sort from that of measurements. Methods to address Spread can be statistical data analysis, sensitivity analysis or Monte Carlo analysis, possibly in combination with expert consultation.

The remaining two qualifiers constitute the more qualitative side of the NUSAP framework. 'Assessment' expresses qualitative judgements about the information. In the case of statistical tests, this might be the significance level; in the case of numerical estimates for policy purposes, it might be the qualities of optimism or pessimism. In some experimental fields, information is supplied qualified by two + terms, of which the first is the Spread, or random error, and the second is the systematic error which must be estimated on the basis of the history of the measurement, and which corresponds to the use of Assessment in NUSAP. A frequently observed pitfall is to wrongly think that systematic error must always be less than any experimental error, or else a stated error bar would be meaningless or misleading. However, in many real life cases systematic error can be well estimated only in retrospect, and then it can produce surprising results that are far outside the error bar of the previously published number(s).

The fifth and final aspect of NUSAP is the Pedigree. This conveys an evaluative account of the production process of information, and indicates different aspects of the underpinning of the numbers and scientific status of the knowledge used. Pedigree is expressed as a set of criteria and assessed using qualitative expert judgement. Risbey et al. (2001) document a method to draft Pedigree scores by means of expert elicitation, on which Knol et al. (2010) provide guidance as to good practice. Arbitrariness and subjectivity in measuring strength are minimised by using a Pedigree matrix to code qualitative expert judgements for each criterion into a discrete Numeral scale from 0 (weak) to 4 (strong) accompanied by linguistic descriptors or modes.

Pedigree and its assessment

Each special sort of information has its own aspects that are key to its Pedigree, so different Pedigree matrices using different criteria can be used to qualify different sorts of information. An overview of the literature on Pedigree matrices and examples of questionnaires for eliciting Pedigree scores is available online at http://www.nusap.net. Ellis et al. (2000) have developed a Pedigree calculator to assess propagation of Pedigree in a calculation in order to establish Pedigree scores for quantities calculated from other quantities. Table 29.2 gives an example of a Pedigree matrix for emission monitoring data. Next I briefly elaborate the four criteria employed.

Proxy

Sometimes measuring the thing we are interested in directly, or representing it by a parameter, is impossible, so some form of proxy measure is used. Proxy refers to how good or close a measure of the quantity that we measure or model is to the actual quantity we seek or represent. Examples are first order approximations, over simplifications, idealisations, gaps in aggregation levels, differences in definitions, non-representativeness and incompleteness issues.

Table 29.2 Example Pedigree matrix for emission monitoring data

Score	Proxy	Empirical basis	Methodological rigour	Validation
4	An exact measure of the desired quantity	Controlled experiments and large sample direct measurements	Best available practice in well-established discipline	Compared with independent measurements of the same variable over long domain
3	Good fit or measure	Historical/field data, uncontrolled experiments, small sample direct measurements	Reliable method common within established discipline Best available practice in immature discipline	Compared with independent measurements of closely related variable over shorter period
2	Well correlated but not measuring the same thing	Modelled/derived data Indirect measurements	Acceptable method but limited consensus on reliability	Measurements not independent, proxy variable, limited domain
1	Weak correlation but commonalities in measure	Educated guesses, indirect approx. rule of thumb est.	Preliminary methods unknown reliability	Weak and very indirect validation
0	Not correlated and not clearly related	Crude speculation	No discernible rigour	No validation performed

Source: Risbey et al. (2001) adapted from Ellis et al. (2000).

Empirical basis

This typically refers to the degree to which direct observations, measurements and statistics are used to estimate a parameter. Sometimes directly observed data are unavailable, and the parameter or variable is estimated based on partial measurements or calculated from other quantities. Parameters or variables determined by such indirect methods have a weaker empirical basis and will generally score lower than those based on direct observations.

Methodological rigour

Parameter or variable estimates employ a method to collect, check, and revise the data. Methodological quality refers to the norms for methodological rigour in this process, as applied by peers in relevant disciplines. Well-established and respected methods for measuring and processing data would score high on this metric, while untested or unreliable methods would tend to score low.

Validation

This metric refers to the degree to which the analyst has been able to cross-check the data and assumptions used to produce the Numeral of the parameter against independent sources. In many cases, independent data for the same parameter over the same time period are unavailable and other data sets must be used for validation. This may require a compromise in the length or overlap of the data sets, or may require use of a related, but different, proxy variable for indirect validation, or perhaps use of data that has been aggregated on different scales. The more indirect or incomplete the validation, the lower it will score on this metric.

Visualising Pedigree analysis

In general, Pedigree scores will be established using expert judgements from more than one expert. Two ways of visualising results of a Pedigree analysis are discussed here: radar diagrams and kite diagrams (Risbey et al., 2001; Van der Sluijs et al., 2002), as exemplified in Figure 29.1. Both representations use polygons with one axis for each criterion, having 0 in the centre and 4 on each corner point. In the radar diagrams a coloured line connecting the scores represents the scoring of each expert, whereas a black line represents the average scores.

The kite diagrams follow a traffic light analogy. The minimum scores by a group of experts for each Pedigree criterion span the green kite; the maximum scores span the amber kite. The remaining area is red. The width of the amber band represents expert disagreement on the Pedigree scores. In some cases the size of the green area can be strongly influenced by a single deviating low score given by one of the experts. In those cases the light green kite shows what the green kite would look like if that outlier had been omitted. Note that the algorithm for calculating the light green kite is such that outliers are evaluated per Pedigree criterion, so that outliers defining the light green area need not be from the same expert. A web-tool to produce kite diagrams is available from http://www.nusap.net.

The kite diagrams can be interpreted as follows: the green coloured area reflects the (apparent minimal consensus) strength of the underpinning of each parameter. The more green, the stronger is the underpinning. The orange coloured zone shows the range of expert disagreement on that underpinning. The remaining area is red. The more red, the weaker is the underpinning (all according to the assessment by a group of experts). A kite diagram captures the information from all experts in the group without the need to average expert opinion. Averaging expert opinion is a controversial issue in elicitation methodologies (Knol et al., 2010). Another advantage is that it provides a fast and intuitive overview of parameter strength, preserving the underlying information. However, kite diagrams can be misleading because the amount of red and green surface area can be sensitive to the order of the criteria in the diagram. As an alternative, bar charts can be used with error-bars to reflect the range of expert opinion; see Kloprogge et al. (2007) and Wardekker et al., (2008) for further guidance.

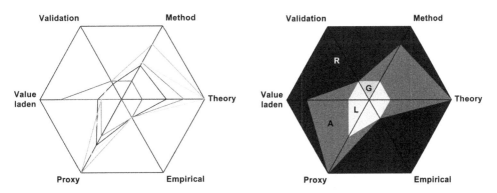

Figure 29.1   Graphic representation of Pedigree scoring.
Notes: Example of representations of same Pedigree results as scored by six different experts by radar diagram (left) and kite diagram (right); G=green, L=light green, A=amber, R=red.
Source: Van der Sluijs et al (2002).

Diagnostic diagrams

There are two independent metrics that can be used for diagnostic purposes. First is the method chosen to address the Spread qualifier (typically sensitivity analysis or Monte Carlo analysis) which provides, for each input quantity, a quantitative metric of uncertainty contribution, or sensitivity (e.g., the relative contribution to the variance in a given model output). Second are the Pedigree scores that can be aggregated (by dividing the sum of the scores of the Pedigree criteria by the sum of the maximum attainable scores) to produce a metric for parameter strength. These two independent metrics can be combined in a NUSAP diagnostic diagram (see Figure 29.2).

The diagnostic diagram is based on the notion that neither Spread nor strength can alone provide a sufficient measure of quality. Robustness of model output to parameter strength could be good even if parameter strength is low, provided that the model outcome is not critically influenced by the Spread in that parameter. In this situation our ignorance of the 'true value' of a parameter has no immediate consequences because it has a negligible effect on calculated model outputs. Alternatively, model outputs can be robust against parameter Spread—even if its relative contribution to the total Spread in a model is high—provided that parameter strength is high. In the latter case, the uncertainty in the model outcome adequately reflects the inherent irreducible uncertainty in the system represented by the model. In other words, the uncertainty then is a property of the modelled system and does not stem from imperfect knowledge about that system. Mapping model parameters in the Assessment diagram thus reveals the weakest critical links in the knowledge base of the model with respect to the model outcome assessed and helps in setting the priorities for model improvement.

Most of the Pedigree assessments in the literature have addressed uncertainties located in inputs and parameters, thereby focussing on the internal strength of the knowledge base. Kloprogge et al. (2011) extended Pedigree analysis to assess assumptions in models. Examples of putting the approach into practice include Laes et al. (2011) for evaluating the external costs of nuclear energy, De Jong et al. (2012) for quantified health risks of overhead power lines, and Boone et al. (2009) and Bouwknegt et al. (2014) for quantitative microbial risk assessment. Van der Sluijs et al. (2015) have further extended the application of NUSAP to assess modelling assumptions in a chain of integrated models in the context of decisions concerning local adaptation to climate change impacts.

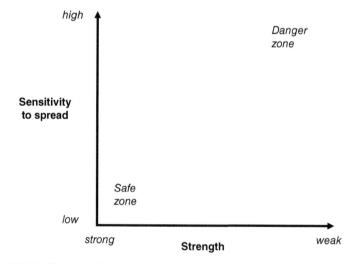

Figure 29.2   NUSAP diagnostic diagram.

Corral (2000), in his Ph.D. thesis, extended the Pedigree scheme to address uncertainties located in the sociopolitical context, focussing on the external strength of the knowledge base (i.e., its relationship to the world outside of science). The criteria that Corral used to assess the Pedigree of the processes of knowledge utilisation and institutional context of the analysts were *inter alia*: accessibility, terminology, completeness, source of information, verification, colleague consensus, extended peer acceptance, legitimation, experience, and flexibility.

Future directions

The NUSAP approach has a great potential to systematise the appraisal and consideration of uncertainty at the science–governance interface. Further tailoring and standardisation of Pedigree matrices and procedures for the elicitation of Pedigree scores is desirable but the main challenge is in dissemination. Successful pilots with inclusion of NUSAP in M.Sc. and Ph.D. teaching curricula at the universities of Utrecht, Bergen and Versailles Saint-Quentin-en-Yvelines can be scaled up. An open access course in knowledge quality assessment is also now available online (https://proxy.eplanete.net/galleries/broceliande7/KQA).

Concluding remarks

Overall, NUSAP has a strong foundation in the theory of knowledge and the philosophy of science connecting to post-normal science [see Chapter 28]. It provides a framework to systematically and coherently address and communicate three of the dimensions of uncertainty, namely: technical (inexactness), methodological (unreliability) and epistemological (bordering with ignorance). It provides a framework for synthesising qualitative and quantitative assessments of uncertainty and can act as a bridge between the quantitative mathematical disciplines/traditions and the qualitative discursive and participatory disciplines/traditions in the field of uncertainty management.

Key further readings cited

Funtowicz, S.O. and Ravetz, J.R. (1990). *Uncertainty and Quality in Science for Policy*. Dordrecht: Kluwer.

van der Sluijs J.P. and Wardekker, J.A. (2015). Critical appraisal of assumptions in chains of model calculations used to project local climate impacts for adaptation decision support: The case of Baakse Beek. *Environmental Research Letters* 10, 045005.

van der Sluijs, J.P., Craye, M., Funtowicz, S.O., Kloprogge, P., Ravetz, J.R. and Risbey, J. (2005a). Combining quantitative and qualitative measures of uncertainty in model based environmental assessment: the NUSAP system. *Risk Analysis* 25(2), 481–492.

van der Sluijs, J.P., Risbey, J. and Ravetz, J.R. (2005b). Uncertainty assessment of VOC emissions from paint in the Netherlands. *Environmental Monitoring and Assessment* 105, 229–259.

van der Sluijs, J.P., Petersen, A.C., Janssen, P.H.M., Risbey, J.S. and Ravetz, J.R. (2008). Exploring the quality of evidence for complex and contested policy decisions. *Environmental Research Letters*, 3, 024008 (9 pp.).

Other literature cited

Boone, I., Van der Stede, Y., Bollaerts, K., Vose, D., Maes, D., Dewulf, J., Messens, W., Daube, G. Aerts, M. and Mintiens, K. (2009). NUSAP method for evaluating the data quality in a quantitative microbial risk assessment model for Salmonella in the pork production chain. *Risk analysis* 29(4), 502–517.

Bouwknegt, M., Knol, A.B., van der Sluijs, J.P., Evers, E.G. (2014). Uncertainty of population risk estimates for pathogens based on QMRA or epidemiology: a case study of Campylobacter in the Netherlands. *Risk analysis*, 34(5), 847–864.

Corral Quintana, S.A., (2000). Una Metodología integrada de exploración y compensión de los procesos de elaboración de políticas públicas. Ph.D. thesis, University of La Laguna.

De Jong, A., Wardekker, J.A., van der Sluijs, J.P. (2012). Assumptions in quantitative analyses of health risks of overhead power lines. *Environmental science & policy* 16, 114–121.

Ellis, E.C., Li, R. G., Yang, L. Z. and Cheng, X. (2000). Long-term change in village-scale ecosystems in China using landscape and statistical methods. *Ecological Applications* 10, 1057–1073.

Funtowicz, S.O. and Ravetz, J.R. (1993). Science for the post-normal age. *Futures* 25(7), 735–755.

Keepin B. and Wynne, B. (1984). Technical analysis of IIASA energy scenarios. *Nature* 312, 691–695.

Kloprogge, P., van der Sluijs J.P., and Wardekker, A. (2007). *Uncertainty communication: issues and good practice*, Report NWS-E-2007-199, Department of Science Technology and Society, Copernicus Institute, Utrecht University. 60 pp.

Kloprogge, P., van der Sluijs J.P., and Petersen A.C. (2011). A method for the analysis of assumptions in model-based environmental assessments. *Environmental Modelling & Software* 26(3), 289–301.

Knol, A.B., Slottje, P., van der Sluijs, J.P., and Lebret, E. (2010). The use of expert elicitation in environmental health impact assessment: a seven step procedure. *Environmental Health* 9, 1–16.

Laes, E., Meskens G., and van der Sluijs, J.P. (2011). On the contribution of external cost calculations to energy system governance: The case of a potential large-scale nuclear accident. *Energy Policy* 39(9), 5664–5673.

Morgan, M.G., and Henrion, M. (1990). *Uncertainty: A Guide to Dealing with Uncertainty in Quantitative Risk and Policy Analysis*, Cambridge: Cambridge University Press.

Nowotny, H. (1999). The place of people in our knowledge. *European Review* 7(2), 247–262.

Petersen, A.C., Cath, A., Hage, M., Kunseler, E., and van der Sluijs, J.P. (2011). Post-normal science in practice at the Netherlands Environmental Assessment Agency. *Science Technology & Human Values* 36(3), 362–388.

Risby, J. S., van der Sluijs, J.P., Ravetz, J. (2001). *Protocol for Assessment of Uncertainty and Strength of Emission Data*, Department of Science Technology and Society, Utrecht University, report nr. E-2001-10, 22 pp.

Risbey, J., van der Sluijs, J. P., Kloprogge, P., Ravetz, J., Funtowicz, S. and Corral Quintana S. (2005). Application of a checklist for quality assistance in environmental modelling to an energy model. *Environmental Modelling & Assessment* 10(1), 63–79.

Saltelli, A., Chan, K., Scott, E.M. (eds.). (2000). *Sensitivity Analysis*. Chichester: John Wiley & Sons.

Saltelli, A., Ratto, M., Andres, T., Campolongo, F., Cariboni, J., Gatelli, D., Saisana, M. and Tarantola, S. (2008). *Global Sensitivity Analysis: The Primer*. Chichester: Wiley.

Saltelli, A., Guimarães Pereira, Â., van der Sluijs, J.P. and Funtowicz, S. (2013). What do I make of your Latinorum? Sensitivity auditing of mathematical modelling. *International Journal of Foresight and Innovation Policy* 9(2/3/4), 213–234.

Van der Sluijs, J.P. (1997). *Anchoring Amid Uncertainty: On the Management of Uncertainties in Risk Assessment of Anthropogenic Climate Change*, Ph.D. dissertation, Utrecht: Utrecht University.

Van der Sluijs, J.P. (2002). A way out of the credibility crisis around model-use in Integrated Environmental Assessment. *Futures* 34, 133–146.

van der Sluijs, J.P., Potting, J., Risbey, J., van Vuuren, D., de Vries, B., Beusen, A., Heuberger, P., Corral Quintana, S., Funtowicz, S., Kloprogge, P., Nuijten, D., Petersen, A., Ravetz, J. (2002). *Uncertainty assessment of the IMAGE/TIMER B1 CO2 emissions scenario, using the NUSAP method*, Dutch National Research Program on Climate Change, Report no: 410 200 104, Bilthoven (available from www.nusap.net).

van der Sluijs, J. P., Craye, M., Funtowicz, S., Kloprogge, P., Ravetz, J. and Risbey, J. (2005c). Experiences with the NUSAP system for multidimensional uncertainty assessment in Model based Foresight Studies. *Water Science and Technology* 52(6), 133–144.

Walker, W.E., Harremoës, P., Rotmans, J., van der Sluijs, J.P., van Asselt, M.B.A., Janssen, P, Krayer von Krauss, M.P. (2003) Defining uncertainty, a conceptual basis for uncertainty management in model-based decision support. *Integrated Assessment* 4(1), 5–17.

Wardekker, J.A., van der Sluijs, J.P., Janssen, P.H.M., Kloprogge, P., Petersen, A.C. (2008). Uncertainty communication in environmental assessments: Views from the Dutch science-policy interface. *Environmental Science and policy* 11, 627–641.

Wynne, B. (1992). Uncertainty and environmental learning: Reconceiving science and policy in the preventive paradigm. *Global Environmental Change* 2(2), 111–127.

30

MULTIPLE CRITERIA EVALUATION IN ENVIRONMENTAL POLICY ANALYSIS

Salvatore Greco and Giuseppe Munda

Introduction

In the context of policy analysis and project appraisal, cost-benefit analysis (CBA) is often considered (especially by economists) as the best evaluation tool with its focus on efficiency criteria. However, any policy decision affects the welfare of individuals, regions or groups in different ways. As a consequence, public support for any policy decision depends upon the distributional effects it entails. CBA is based on the Kaldor-Hicks hypothetical compensation principle, which is grounded in preferences expressed in the market place (or which would be expressed if there were a market), not on preferences expressed by a political vote. The main underlying idea of using such preferences is that individuals can be compared by virtue of being consumers. The market provides a single unit of measurement (i.e., money values) expressed via an individual's willingness to pay (or accept payment) for a good or service. The validity of money values is then connected to the objective of economic efficiency and the institution of the market. However, this approach fails to incorporate other objectives and values, such as equity or sustainability.

This means that a policy option may appear preferable just because some dimensions (e.g., the environment) or some social groups (e.g., the poor) are not taken into account. There is no obvious reason why this issue of the existence of a plurality of values should be considered a problem that can only be 'solved' by considering consumers' preferences as the only relevant social value (Lo and Spash, 2013). Our point here is not to argue against giving economic value to natural resources, human health (or even lives) or cultural heritage, but rather that social decisions involve multiple and incommensurable values. Therefore, since different values are related to different objectives and institutions, plural values cannot be reduced to a single metric (Martinez-Alier et al., 1998; Munda, 2016; O'Neill, 2001).

For example, urban well-being is not evaluated as good or bad as such, but rather, as good, bad, beautiful or ugly in relation to different descriptions or indicators. It can involve at one and the same time a good average income and a bad social inclusion, a beautiful skyline and an ugly cultural heritage. This basic idea of multi-criteria evaluation (MCE) is to achieve the comparability of incommensurable values (Figueira et al., 2016) [see also Chapter 22]. From an operational point of view, the major strength of MCE is its ability to deal with policy issues characterised by various conflicting evaluations, thus allowing for an integrated assessment of the problem at hand.

In the next section, we will present the basic ideas of MCE considering the technical, empirical and epistemological aspects. That is followed by a section dealing with the main mathematical aggregation procedures that are employed in MCE. We then present some future research directions before concluding.

Key aspects of multi-criteria evaluation

A multi-criteria method is an aggregate of all dimensions, objectives (or goals), criteria (or attributes) and criterion scores. This implies that what formally defines a multi-criteria method is the set of properties underlying the convention it uses for mathematical aggregation of these different aspects. MCE proceeds on the basis of defining four concepts, namely: objectives, evaluation criterion, goals and attributes. Objectives indicate the direction of change desired, e.g. growth has to be maximised, social exclusion has to be minimised, carbon dioxide emissions have to be reduced. An evaluation criterion is the basis for evaluation in relation to a given objective (any objective may imply a number of different criteria). It is a function that associates alternative actions with a variable indicating its desirability according to expected consequences related to the same objective. Examples in economics would be national income, savings and inflation rates under the objective of economic growth maximisation. A goal is synonymous with a target and is something that can be either achieved or missed, e.g. reducing nitrogen pollution in a lake by at least 10 per cent. If a goal cannot, or is unlikely to, be achieved, it may be converted to an objective. An attribute is a measure that indicates whether goals have been met or not, on the basis that a particular decision will provide the means of evaluating various objectives.

A discrete multi-criterion problem can be formally described as follows. A is a finite set of N feasible actions or alternatives. M is the number of different points of view or evaluation criteria, gm, that are considered relevant to a specific policy problem. Where action a is evaluated to be better than action b (both belonging to the set A), by the m-th point of view, then $gm(a)>gm(b)$. In this way a decision problem may be represented in an N by M matrix P called an evaluation or impact matrix. In such a matrix, the typical element pmn $(m=1, 2, \ldots, M; n=1, 2, \ldots, N)$ represents the evaluation of the n-th alternative by means of the m-th criterion. As shown in Table 30.1, the impact matrix may include quantitative, qualitative or both types of information. In general, in a multi-criterion problem, there is no (ideal or utopian) solution optimising all the criteria at the same time, and therefore compromise solutions have to be found.

Historically the first stage of the development of MCE is characterised by the so-called methodological principle of multi-criteria decision-making. The main aim of this is to elicit clear subjective preferences from a 'mythical' decision-maker, and then try to solve a well-structured mathematical decision problem by means of a, more or less, sophisticated algorithm. In this way a multi-criterion decision problem can still be presented in the form of a classical optimisation problem (Keeney and Raiffa, 1976).

The limitations of the classical concept of an optimum solution and the consequential importance of the decision process were emphasised by authors such as Herbert Simon and Bernard Roy. According to Roy (1996) saying that a decision is a good or bad one is in general impossible on the basis of referring only to a mathematical model. All aspects of a decision process which leads to a given decision also contribute to its quality and success. Thus, establishing the validity of a procedure is impossible, either based on a notion of approximation (i.e., discovering pre-existing truths) or on a mathematical property of convergence (i.e., does the decision automatically lead, in a finite number of steps, to the optimum a^*?). The final

Table 30.1 Example of an impact matrix for a wind farm

Criteria	Units	A	B	C	D	E	F
Owners' income	€/year	48	33	99	132	78	72
Economic Activity Tax	€/year	~12.750	~15.470	~46.410	~61.880	~36.570	~33.750
Construction tax	€	~61.990	~55.730	~96.520	~152.250	~81.890	~67.650
Number of jobs		2	1	4	5	3	3
Visual impact	km²	76.57	71.46	276.550	348.01	220.400	163.290
Forest lost	ha	8.4	8.1	6.6	14.7	3.9	2.6
Avoided CO_2 emissions	ton CO_2/ year	4.68	6.01	19.74	25.75	14.74	13.76
Noise	dB(A)	14.64	23.86	18.6	23.84	20.88	14.66
Installed capacity	MW	13.6	16.5	49.5	66.0	39.0	36.0

Source: adapted from Gamboa and Munda (2007).

solution is more like a creation than a discovery. Under the framework of 'multiple criteria decision aid', the principal aim is not to discover a solution, but to construct or create something that is viewed as liable to help an actor taking part in a decision process either to shape, argue and/or transform her/his preferences, or to make a decision in conformity with his/her goals (Roy, 1996).

The need for public participation has been increasingly recognised in MCE. In particular, Social Multi-Criteria Evaluation (SMCE) recognises the need to extend multiple criteria decision aid by incorporating the notion of the social actor. Thus, a SMCE process must be as participative and as transparent as possible; although, participation is a necessary but not a sufficient condition for successful evaluation (Munda, 2004). This is the main reason why the concept of SMCE is proposed in place of participatory MCE or stakeholder approaches (Banville et al., 1998). The strength of SMCE is the fact that the use of various evaluation criteria has a direct translation in terms of the plurality of values used in the evaluation exercise. In a SMCE framework, the pitfalls of the technocratic approach can be overcome by applying different methods of sociological research.

In operational terms, the application of a SMCE framework involves the following seven main steps (Munda, 2008):

1   Description of the relevant social actors. For example, institutional analysis [Chapter 3] may be performed on historical, legislative and administrative documents to provide a map of the relevant social actors.
2   Definition of social actors' values, desires and preferences can be achieved using focus groups and used to develop a set of policy options. The main limitations of focus groups are lack of statistical representation of the population and occasional reluctance of people to participate or state publicly what they really think (e.g., in small towns and villages). For this reason anonymous questionnaires and personal interviews are an essential part of the participatory process.
3   Generation of policy options and selection of evaluation criteria is a process of co-creation resulting from a dialogue between analysts and social actors. For example, potential sites for the location of wind parks generating renewable energy could be found by considering factors relevant for investors only, such as technical and economic feasibility depending on wind availability. However, local people will raise other concerns such as visual impact or

closeness to places of a high symbolic value for the community (e.g. an ancient monument or a peculiar landscape). Should the evaluation criteria then come directly from the public participation process or be mediated by the research team? We think that the rough material collected during interviews and focus groups could be used as a source of inspiration but the technical formulation of criteria is a job for expert researchers. In this way, evaluation criteria become a technical translation of social actors' needs, preferences and desires. For example, if a local community has worries about the possible noise produced by windmills, a possible evaluation criterion is sound pressure computed in decibels; if a desire is to keep younger generations in a rural area, a clear relevant criterion is the number of people employed by the wind park, and so on. Of course, in this step, judgement is unavoidable, e.g. which is the best way of measuring visual impact? For this reason a widespread information campaign—including local people, regional and national authorities, international scientists and even children at school—covering the assumptions and conclusions of the study is, in our opinion, always highly recommended.

4   Construction of the multi-criteria impact matrix synthesises the scores of all criteria for all alternatives, i.e. the performance of each alternative according to each criterion. For example, the location of windmills can be evaluated according to a set of criteria as exemplified in Table 30.1 (see Gamboa and Munda, 2007 for more details).

5   Construction of an equity impact matrix. Criteria and criterion scores are not determined directly by social actors. The impact matrix is a result of a technical translation operationalised by expert analysts. Even if the criteria are exactly the ones agreed with the social actors the determination of the criterion scores is independent of their preferences. For example, an interest group can accept the use of a criterion measuring the effects of the various alternatives on employment, but the determination of the figure cannot be (at least not completely) controlled by them. This is the main reason why we recommend combining a social impact matrix with a technical impact matrix (Munda, 1995).

6   A mathematical procedure (or algorithm) is applied in order to aggregate criterion scores and obtain a final ranking of the available alternatives. Many multi-criteria methods have been formulated since the 1960s, each with its own advantages and disadvantages (Figueira et al., 2016). We return to this point in the next section.

7   Sensitivity and robustness analysis aims to address aspects of abstraction from reality required of any modelling exercise, i.e., checking the relevance and the explicative capacity of the theoretical framework used to structure and understand a policy problem. One approach is to look at the sensitivity of results to the exclusion/inclusion of different criteria, criterion weights and dimensions (see Saltelli et al., 2008). While such analysis may look very technical, in reality a social component is also present. That is, inclusion/exclusion of a given dimension, or set of criteria, normally involves a long story of social, political and scientific controversy as well as social values and social actors.

These seven steps are not rigid. On the contrary, flexibility and adaptability to actual situations are among the main advantages of SMCE. As a tool for policy evaluation and conflict management, SMCE has demonstrated its applicability to problems in various geographical and cultural contexts (e.g., Gamboa, 2006; Garmendia and Stagl, 2010; Monterroso et al., 2011; Munda and Russi, 2008; Özkaynak, 2008; Scolobig et al., 2008; Soma and Vatn, 2009; Straton et al., 2010; Zendehdel et al., 2010).

The main mathematical approaches to MCE

The importance of mathematical approaches in MCE is their ability to allow a consistent aggregation of diverse information. Otherwise, even if everybody agreed upon the considerations contained in the previous section, their implementation in an actual evaluation exercises would be impossible. There is no perfect aggregation procedure, thus, unlike other mathematical fields, neither approximation nor convergence criteria can be used, and only reasonable mathematical procedures can be developed in this framework. Reasonable here means that algorithms can be evaluated not only according to the formal properties they respect, but, overall, according to the empirical consequences implied by their use. Three main methodologies have been proposed to solve the discrete multi-criterion problem: (i) multi-attribute value and utility theory,[1] (ii) outranking methods and (iii) the decision rule approach.

Multiple attribute value theory (MAVT)

From a theoretical point of view, MAVT is a very elegant and attractive solution to the discrete multi-criterion problem. From the operational point of view, it is the most important theory behind multi-criteria decision-making, which assumes a decision-maker who always "believes that in a specified decision context there is a particular preference structure that is appropriate for him" (Keeney and Raiffa, 1976: 80). MAVT is based on the following hypothesis: in any decision problem there exists a real value function V defined on the set A of feasible actions, which a decision-maker wishes, consciously or not, to examine. This function aggregates the different criteria (generally referred to as attributes) to be taken into consideration, so that the problem can be formulated as:

max $V(\boldsymbol{g}\ (a_n))$ such that a_n belongs to A (1)

where $\boldsymbol{g}\ (a_n)=[g_1(a_n),\ldots,g_M(a_n)]$ and $V(\boldsymbol{g}\ (a_n))$ is a value function aggregating the M criteria. The role of the analyst is to determine this function. One of the most important policy consequences of using MAVT functions is that complete compensability is always assumed. As stated clearly by Keeney and Raiffa (1976: 66) "our problem is one of value trade-offs". Since there exists a function V by which criteria (attributes) $g_1, g_2,\ldots,g_M$, can be aggregated, there must also exist functions $w_{mm'}$ (called trade-offs between the *m-th* and the *m'-th* criteria) measuring the amount that a decision-maker is willing to accept on the *m-th* criterion to compensate the loss of a unit on the *m'-th* criterion (an amount which may vary according to the point considered in the criteria space). This means that, for example, in the wind farm location problem described in Table 30.1, an improvement in the "Economic Activity Tax" criterion can easily compensate a worsening in "Forest lost" or "Visual impact". From an environmental policy point of view, this always implies a philosophy of weak sustainability [see Chapter 25]. That is, a good economic value function assessment can always compensate for a bad environmental assessment.

In practice determining such trade-offs in precise terms is difficult. Often trade-offs are the basis for discussions between the analyst and the decision-maker towards the construction of the function V. The simplest, and most commonly used, analytical form is the linear aggregation rule. An important point to consider is that each criterion can have its own value function because of the existence of preference independence. This property is a necessary condition for the existence of a linear aggregation rule. From an operational point of view this means that an additive aggregation function permits the assessment of the marginal contribution of each criterion separately (as a consequence of the preference independence condition). The marginal contribution of each criterion can then be added together to yield a total value. This implies that, for example, among the different aspects of an ecosystem there are no phenomena of synergy or conflict, e.g. interaction among different pollutants. This is rather unrealistic from a scientific point of view [see Chapter 12]. Thus, an interesting research topic for environmental policy analysis is the study of interactions between criteria, when the preference independence condition is inapplicable. Such research is related to the use of non-additive integrals, e.g., the Choquet integral (see Grabisch, 1996).

A particular application of MAVT, that is also completely compensatory, is the analytic hierarchy process (AHP) as developed by Saaty (1980). AHP structures the decision problem into levels which correspond to the decision-maker's understanding of the situation: objectives, criteria, sub-criteria and alternatives. The decision-maker can focus on smaller sets of decisions by breaking the problem up into levels. The AHP is a very widespread approach with many applications and is one of the few methods that explicitly deals with the issue of hierarchy in decision problems. However, we think that AHP is an adequate decision tool only when the decision-maker is clearly identifiable and expresses her/his preferences and takes responsibility for the decision outcome. This may be the case in entrepreneurial decisions but is hardly ever so in social decisions.

Outranking methods

The concept of partial comparability is the basis for the outranking methods. The most representative ones are ELECTRE (Roy, 1996) and PROMETHEE (Brans et al., 1986). These methods entail aggregating the criteria into a partial binary relation S (an outranking relation) based on concordance and discordance indexes, and then 'exploiting' this relationship. Each of these two steps may be treated in a number of ways according to the problem formulation and the particular case under consideration.

To illustrate the method, consider parliamentary voting. The concordant coalition can be considered as the sum of the votes of the members in favour of a given option; according to a majority voting rule, this option will be approved if it obtains more than 50 per cent of the votes. According to the normative tradition in political philosophy, all coalitions, however small, should be given some fraction of the decision power. One measure of this power is the ability to veto certain subsets of outcomes. This explains the use of the condition of non-discordance. In practice, the effect of the discordance test is that even if M-1 criteria support the recommendation of choosing a over b, this recommendation must not be accepted if only one criterion is against it with a strength bigger than the veto threshold. This implies that in a situation where all economic criteria would support a policy option, this option cannot be accepted if one environmental criterion is very strongly against this option. Of course, this depends on the way in which 'very strongly' is defined, i.e. the definition of the veto threshold.

In the 1990s some outranking methods were especially designed to address environmental policy analysis. Among these methods a special place is taken by NAIADE (Munda, 1995). It is a discrete multi-criteria method whose impact matrix may include crisp, stochastic or fuzzy measurements of the performance of an alternative with respect to an evaluation criterion. Thus it is very flexible for actual applications. NAIADE can give the following information:

- ranking of the alternatives according to the set of evaluation criteria, i.e. technical compromise solution(s);
- indications of the distance of the positions of the various interest groups, i.e. possibilities of convergence of interests or coalition formations;

- ranking of the alternatives according to actors' impacts or preferences, i.e. social compromise solution(s).

A common property of all outranking methods is that they are partially non-compensatory; thus a weak sustainability philosophy is generally avoided and weights can be used as 'coefficients of importance', rather than trade-offs. Two issues are connected with all the outranking methods, as well as with other approaches based on pair-wise comparisons. First, the axiom of independence of irrelevant alternatives is not respected. Thus the phenomenon of rank reversal may appear (i.e. the preference between *a* and *b* can change due to whether a third option *c* is considered or not). Second, the 'Condorcet paradox' may appear, i.e. alternative *a* may be ranked better than *b*, *b* better than *c* and *c* better than *a*. In addition, there is a problem specifically connected with the outranking approach. That is the necessity to establish a large number of 'preference parameters', i.e. indifference and preference thresholds, concordance and discordance thresholds and weights. This may cause a loss of transparency and consistency in the model. In the framework of SMCE, outranking approaches look like an interesting assessment framework, but, to guarantee consistency with the social process behind the problem structuring, the mathematical aggregation rules need to be kept as simple as possible (see Munda, 2008 for a deeper technical discussion on this issue).

The decision rule approach

Another methodology that has gained interest within SMCE is the decision rule approach. This aims to elicit preference information and supplying a decision model in the simplest possible way. The preference information required can be:

- assignments of some reference alternatives to some predefined classes of merits, such as alternatives *a, b* and *c* are bad, alternatives *e, f* and *g* are medium, alternatives *h, j, k* are good; or,
- pairwise comparisons of some reference alternatives, such as alternative *a* is weakly preferred to alternative *b*, alternative *c* is fairly preferred to alternative *d*, alternative *e* is strongly preferred to alternative *f*.

The decision model supplied to the decision-maker is a set of easily understandable 'if then' decision rules induced from the above preference information, such as:

- if on attribute g_{m1} the evaluation is at most medium and on attribute g_{m2} the evaluation is at most good, then the overall evaluation is at least medium; or,
- if on attribute g_{m1} alternative *a* is at least fairly preferred to alternative *b*, and on attribute g_{m2} it is strongly preferred, then alternative *a* is comprehensively at least fairly preferred to alternative *b*.

The decision rules, induced from the preference information by using the 'dominance-based rough set approach' (Greco et al., 2001), give simple explanations to the preference information and can be critically discussed. A decision-maker can accept some of them and reject others, or modify the corresponding preference information. The final result of this process is a set of decision rules accepted as representative of preferences so that these rules can be applied to the whole set of alternatives. Decision rules not only permit the assignment of comprehensive evaluations to the alternatives, or drawing the conclusion that an alternative is preferred over another one, but also supply an explanation for this, thus increasing transparency.

An interesting advantage of the decision rule approach is that it does not entail the use of any preferential parameter such as weights, thresholds or value functions. As we have already observed, the use of these parameters is associated with many difficulties, and the possibility of getting rid of them may consequently constitute an interesting advance from a policy point of view. Another advantage of this approach is that it does not require fulfilment of demanding conditions such as preference independence.

Future directions

In the twenty-first century, a great deal of attention has been given to the problem of the robustness of the results supplied by MCE methods. This trend will continue because, as outlined above, sensitivity and robustness analysis are a key success factor for all MCE applications, including SMCE. In this context, robust ordinal regression, a generalisation of ordinal regression, has gained attention. The idea is to consider not only one value function compatible with the preference information expressed by the decision-maker, but instead the whole set of value functions compatible with the available preference information (Corrente et al., 2013). This idea has also been applied to outranking methods and the Choquet integral model to represent interaction between criteria (Angilella et al., 2015). Currently attention is focusing more and more on the possibility of coupling MCE approaches with big data sets; this might allow a much more widespread use of MCE in macroeconomic modelling and in dealing with global environmental issues such as climate change policy. MCE is a promising assessment framework for environmental policy analysis. SMCE in particular can be useful in dealing with the plurality of technical dimensions, values and interests always present in this type of problems. In our opinion, the prevalent future challenge of MCE is to make more and more operational all the main advances of the last couple of decades. From the theoretical point of view, MCE is a mature field, but clear cut operational guidelines still need to be developed. Achieving this could transform MCE into the key element of twenty-first-century welfare economics and public policy.

Concluding remarks

When a public policy needs to be implemented, there is a need for comparing different options and valuing and evaluating them to assess their social attractiveness. Each policy option is often characterised by conflicts between competing values, perspectives, interests and different groups and communities that represent them. A key requirement for public policies to be considered fair is thus to respect value pluralism.

The main achievement of SMCE is that the use of various evaluation criteria has a direct translation in terms of plurality of values and dimensions used in the evaluation exercise. SMCE can accomplish the goals of being inter/multi-disciplinary with respect to the research team and participatory with respect to the local community. It is also transparent because all criteria are presented in their original form without any transformations into a common measurement rod (e.g., money, energy or whatever).

Note

1   In this context, the terminology 'value function' is used when preferences are assumed to be certain and 'utility functions' when they are subject to probability distributions. Here we consider value functions only.

Key further readings cited

Figueira, J., Greco, S. and Ehrgott, M. (eds.) (2016). *Multiple-criteria decision analysis. State of the art surveys.* Springer International Series in Operations Research and Management Science, New York.

Keeney, R., Raiffa, H. (1976). *Decisions with multiple objectives: preferences and value trade-offs.* Wiley, New York.

Martinez-Alier, J., Munda, G., O'Neill, J. (1998). Weak comparability of values as a foundation for ecological economics. *Ecological Economics* 26, 277–286.

Munda G. (2008). *Social multi-criteria evaluation for a sustainable economy,* Heidelberg, New York: Springer.

Roy B. (1996). *Multicriteria methodology for decision analysis,* Dordrecht: Kluwer.

Other literature cited

Angilella, S., Corrente, S., Greco, S., Słowiński, R. (2016). Robust ordinal regression and stochastic multiobjective acceptability analysis in multiple criteria hierarchy process for the Choquet integral preference model. *Omega*, 63: 154–169.

Banville, C., Landry, M., Martel, J.M., Boulaire, C. (1998). A stakeholder approach to MCDA. *Systems Research and Behavioral Science* 15, 15–32.

Brans, J.P., Mareschal, B. and Vincke, Ph. (1986). How to select and how to rank projects. The PROMETHEE method. *European Journal of Operational Research* 24, 228–238.

Corrente, S., Greco, S., Kadziński, M. and Słowiński, R. (2013). Robust ordinal regression in preference learning and ranking. *Machine Learning* 93(2–3), 381–422.

Gamboa G. (2006). Social multi-criteria evaluation of different development scenarios of the Aysén region, Chile. *Ecological Economics* 59(1), 157–170.

Gamboa G., Munda, G. (2007). The problem of wind-park location: a social multi-criteria evaluation framework. *Energy Policy* 35(3), 1564–1583.

Garmendia, E., Stagl, S. (2010). Public participation for sustainability and social learning: Concepts and lessons from three case studies in Europe, *Ecological Economics* 69(8), 1712–1722.

Grabisch, M. (1996). The application of fuzzy integrals in multicriteria decision making. *European Journal of Operational Research* 89(3), 445–456.

Greco, S., Matarazzo, B., and Slowinski, R. (2001). Rough sets theory for multicriteria decision analysis. *European Journal of Operational Research*, 129(1), 1–47.

Lo, A.Y., Spash, C.L. (2013). Deliberative monetary valuation: In search of a democratic and value plural approach to environmental policy, *Journal of Economic Surveys* 27(4), 768–789.

Monterroso, I., Binimelis, R., Rodríguez-Labajos, B. (2011). New methods for the analysis of invasion processes: Multi-criteria evaluation of the invasion of Hydrilla verticillata in Guatemala, *Journal of Environmental Management* 92(3), 494–507.

Munda, G. (1995). *Multicriteria evaluation in a fuzzy environment.* Heidelberg: Physica-Verlag, Contributions to Economics Series.

Munda G. (2004). Social multi-criteria evaluation (SMCE): Methodological foundations and operational consequences, *European Journal of Operational Research* 158(3), 662–677.

Munda, G. (2016). Beyond welfare economics: some methodological issues. *Journal of Economic Methodology* 23(2), 185–202.

Munda, G., Russi D. (2008). Social multi-criteria evaluation of conflict over rural electrification and solar energy in Spain, *Environment and Planning C: Government and Policy* 26, 712–727.

O'Neill, J. (2001). Representing people, representing nature, representing the world, *Environment and Planning C: Government and Policy* 19(4), 483–500.

Özkaynak, B. (2008). Globalisation and local resistance: Alternative city developmental scenarios on capital's global frontier-the case of Yalova, Turkey, *Progress in Planning,* 70(2), 45–97.

Saaty, T.L. (1980). *The analytic hierarchy process.* New York: McGraw Hill.

Saltelli, A., Ratto, M., Andres, T., Campolongo, F., Cariboni, J., Gatelli, D., Saisana, M., Tarantola, S. (2008). *Global Sensitivity Analysis. The Primer*, New York: John Wiley & Sons.

Scolobig, A., Broto, V.C., Zabala, A. (2008). Integrating multiple perspectives in social multicriteria evaluation of flood-mitigation alternatives: The case of Malborghetto-Valbruna, *Environment and Planning C: Government and Policy* 26(6), 1143–1161.

Soma, K., Vatn, A. (2009). Local democracy implications for coastal zone management-A case study in southern Norway. *Land Use Policy* 26(3), 755–762.

Straton, A.T., Jackson, S., Marinoni, O., Proctor, W., Woodward, E. (2010). Exploring and evaluating scenarios for a river catchment in Northern Australia using scenario development, multi-criteria analysis and a deliberative process as a tool for water planning, *Water Resources Management* 25(1), 141–164.

Zendehdel, K., Rademaker, M., De Baets, B., Van Huylenbroeck (2010). Environmental decision making with conflicting social groups: A case study of the Lar rangeland in Iran, *Journal of Arid Environments* 74(3), 394–402.

31

MULTICRITERIA MAPPING

Rebecca White

Introduction

Multicriteria mapping (MCM) is an appraisal tool for use in cases where a range of possible options exist in the context of complexity, uncertainty and diverse values. Options in this instance can be defined as the set of practices, policies, strategies or technologies that are held under different perspectives to be broadly salient (directly or indirectly) to achieve some broadly shared societal aim, function, quality or value (Stirling and Coburn, 2014:14). However, rather than offering a means of definitively justifying a single decision through a narrowly defined, or indeed single (set of) metric(s), MCM is a heuristic. The aim is not to prescribe a particular best choice, but to explore the way in which the outcomes of strategic choice appraisal change, depending on the view that is taken and the values brought to bear in doing so (Stirling, 2005). The output is both a qualitative and quantitative 'map' of how different options look from different perspectives. MCM is therefore a method that speaks directly to a defining characteristic of ecological economics, that of taking pluralism and complexity of values seriously [see Chapter 22]. Spash (1999: 431) notes that:

> A central part of defining ecological economics as a distinct new subject rotates around the importance of incorporating moral values and being prepared to openly debate difficult issues, such as the set of morally considerable entities, the rights of future generations and treatment of the poor.

MCM is a means of doing this. The method is applicable to issues in multiple contexts and has been used in offices and field locations by academics, civil society organisations and government research organisations.

MCM was developed from a frustration with the nature of many decision support tools that 'close down' around narrow framings of the inputs to and outputs from appraisal (Stirling, 2005). Conventional appraisal methods, such as cost-benefit analysis, narrow forms of risk assessment, or life cycle analysis bring a potentially diverse set of predefined options into a directly comparable 'hard' common denominator, such as cost, probability or impact. In doing so, a number of assumptions and value-judgements have to be made because different sorts of impacts or characteristics are measured, translated, aligned and made directly comparable. This obfuscates the subjective and political decisions—often numerous with questions of environmental resource allocation—needed to achieve these translations. Any values that are not easily quantifiable (such as those linked to quality, identity, ethics or emotions like love) are often excluded, and plural or changeable values—those relating to the environment (cf. O'Neill and Spash, 2000)—that exist in many forms, are also omitted or held constant.

Similarly, the other options that respondents would like to have appraised, are commonly invisible. Often viewed as rigorous, being productive of reaching a single decision, and achieving comparability, conventional appraisal methods do so at the cost of excluding the immeasurable, disempowering participants, closing down diverse framings of the problem and possible responses, and hiding the considerable uncertainty that underlies assessments of impact. Different approaches have value depending on what you want to achieve and the ethical and ontological underpinning of your research. However, methods need to be "fit for purpose" (Davies et al., 2003: 31) with open communication about how appraisal closes down possibilities and the implications of doing so.

This chapter gives a brief step by step overview of MCM, and its approach to analysis, showing how the process seeks to account for broader contexts, diverse views and uncertainties of various kinds. This is followed by description of how MCM has developed over time—this is not comprehensive, but seeks to illustrate how MCM has been used and adapted in different settings. Future directions in the use and development of MCM are briefly discussed. Finally the concluding remarks re-emphasise some key links between what MCM enables the researcher to explore and critical tenets of ecological economics—pluralism of values, interdisciplinarity, transdisciplinarity and uncertainty.

How MCM works

Preliminary stages in MCM

There are two preliminary stages in any MCM process: (i) the development of options and (ii) sampling/selection of stakeholders. These activities are typically interdependent. The development of options should draw from a comprehensive understanding of the issue at hand, whether that be generated via engagement with literature, stakeholders or the issue more broadly. Options should account for the 'key dimensions of variation' shaping an issue or debate. Options should be well explained, easily understood by the stakeholders involved, and not too complicated or multifaceted (multifaceted options lead to difficulty in prescribing or attributing scores clearly).

MCM's ability to map how perspectives alter the way that options are appraised means that the process of creating stakeholder groups should seek to account for at least a diversity of relevant viewpoints or types of stakeholders, if not comprehensively cover this range. Studies vary in the number of participants involved from 12 people (pilot study by Stirling and Mayer, 2001) to 191 people (Lobstein and Millstone, 2006). How groups and individuals are identified for a study should be documented thoroughly.

MCM can be undertaken with counter based scoring and/or on paper if the field conditions or the circumstances of stakeholder engagement prevent using a computer. However, a computer and web connection is immensely helpful. It supports the use of an MCM software package which forms the basis of inputting respondent decisions and scores, providing visual feedback on the choices made, and allowing for easy manipulation by respondents who might wish to explore the implications of their scoring or weighting.

The interview process

The interview takes place around a four-stage process:

1 Option review and development: Here respondents illustrate that they understand the options presented, clarify any questions, and develop and add their own options if they feel that those presented are inadequate in scope. If respondents feel that certain options are ethically unjustifiable, they are also able to exclude these from consideration.

2 Criteria: Respondents then consider their own priorities and values against which they think the options should be appraised. The interviewer/facilitator helps guide the interviewee to develop these into criteria. While some studies predefine some criteria for inclusion, respondents should be allowed to add at least as many again to this basic list.

3 Scoring: Each option is then scored against each criterion. Rather than asking for a single score, respondents are able to give an optimistic and pessimistic score. This may illustrate either a sense of general uncertainty or how scores differ depending on contextual assumptions. For example, Stirling and Mayer (2001) conducted a study on genetically modified organisms in agriculture that compared different ways to grow and regulate oilseed rape production. They found that assumptions about low and high capacity in the farming and regulatory sectors determined optimistic and pessimistic scores for some options against some criteria. Respondents can choose not to score an option at all if they feel that it crosses a 'red line'—an ethical absolute/principle that they hold—or they consider this would be incompatible with their principles (e.g. putting a price on lives).

4 Assigning weights: The criteria are then weighted by the respondents to denote relative importance compared to each other. While respondents are assumed to choose criteria that are important to them personally, they are not always equally important and so can be weighted. Compared to the relatively more technical assessment of scores in the previous stage, weighting is a subjective expression of values. The weightings multiplied by the performance scores produce overall rankings of options against a criterion which respondents are encouraged to reflect upon. In doing so they can also explore how changes of weighting affect overall rankings. Once they agree that how the overall options are ranked reflects their perspective, the interview finishes.

Interviews vary in length, depending on the number of options and criteria, from between 1.5 and 3 hours. Respondents are asked to read aloud, and when making choices over the scoring and weighting are asked to provide reasons. This is captured by recording and then transcribing interviews.

Analysis of MCM data

The analysis undertaken in MCM brings together the results from all respondents and allows the analyst to explore how options have performed, what sorts of criteria were chosen and how they were weighted across the sample. A first stage of analysis is that of grouping all the criteria developed across respondents into 'issue groups'; that is, bringing similar criteria together and collating scores of options against those criteria in order to conduct analysis of the whole. Grouping criteria is a subjective process requiring judgement on the part of the researcher, but can be changed as the analysis progresses.

MCM analysis is very much an iterative process, requiring a log to be kept of approaches tried, observations made and avenues tested. Once an initial set of issue groups has been decided upon, the sample of respondents can be broken down into the different perspective groups to examine differences in scoring between these groups. This can be a matter of overall option ranks, the degree of uncertainty shown by individuals from that perspective scoring a particular option, or the variation between group participants in how they scored (ambiguity). The analyst can also examine how different perspective groups weighted criteria relative to each other.

Analysis seeks to characterise variation and convergence in relation to the specific topic being addressed. Using both the quantitative output and interview recordings, a range of questions can be explored, such as: How are options ranked across all the participants and with what level of certainty? Under what circumstances do some options perform better, or worse, than others? Did the choice of criteria differ between perspectives? How are criteria weighted and how are options ranked against particular criteria? Do the interview recordings help us to determine why? Is uncertainty higher when scoring against particular issues?

Figure 31.1 shows the MCM results from research conducted by the author into models for supporting urban food growing in a United Kingdom (UK) city. A–E are options scored by the

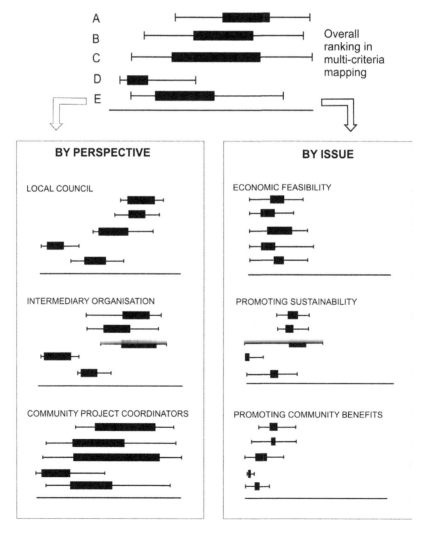

Figure 31.1   Illustration of the quantitative output of MCM.

respondents, and they represent different funding and support models for urban food growing. Rather than seeking to convey specific results, I use the scores to illustrate the nature of quantitative results from MCM and how they open up results. In Figure 31.1 the top chart shows the overall option rankings, and then, beneath this, disaggregation into rankings by 'perspective' and 'issue'. Within each chart the thick bars denote the range of scoring means, while the terminus bars show the lowest and highest scores given (for more information see Stirling and Coburn, 2014).

Importantly, in MCM the ranks of options can change considerably if the analyst takes the bottom or top of scoring ranges. Furthermore, the mid-point of any individual's scoring range cannot be assumed to be an average or most likely score. The 'by perspective' graphs in Figure 31.1 also highlight how uncertainty in scoring is quite different between different types of stakeholders, as are the order of options ranked, emphasising that narrowing participation in appraisal can skew the results. Ranks and the uncertainty of scoring are also altered when the options are scored against different issues, or groupings of criteria, as shown in the 'by issue' box. Outputs of more conventional multicriteria or single criteria analysis, where single scores are given for each option, potentially hide the nuance, contingency and variety revealed by MCM.

The development and use of MCM

The foundational study

The MCM approach was developed by Andrew Stirling, and was first piloted in a study conducted in 1998 by Stirling and Mayer (2001). They were discontented with the field of social risk appraisal and noted the need for: "appraisal methods […] which are: flexible and broad in scope; open to divergent interests and values; able to acknowledge uncertainty; whilst being systematic, transparent, verifiable, and accessible as well as practically feasible and efficient" (Stirling and Mayer, 2001: 531). At the time, the debate over the introduction of genetically modified crops into European agriculture was in full swing, and there was high uncertainty over the possible impacts. Confidence in regulatory appraisal in the UK was also low across stakeholder groups (non-governmental organisations, businesses and the general public). Stirling and Mayer (2001) used MCM to explore the introduction of genetically modified herbicide-tolerant oilseed rape alongside other crop production methods. This allowed a systematic mapping of the perspectives held on different production methods by leading protagonists in the UK debate over the use of genetically modified crops in food production. Participants represented a diverse range of interests and perspectives.

The limitations of the relatively narrow boundaries then being drawn around the regulatory appraisal of genetically modified crops were illustrated by their stark contrast with the very broad range of criteria developed by participants, including those working in the existing regulatory system. Some criteria were qualitative (aesthetics, farmers' rights, quality of life) and brought much more nuance to the traditionally narrower and more scientific categories of evaluation. Even similar criteria were found to be framed in slightly different ways, with consequent differences in option scorings. This calls into question, "the validity of aggregating criteria into an overarching 'value tree' spanning the perspectives of different participants" (Stirling and Mayer, 2001: 531) as is practiced in more traditional forms of multicriteria decision analysis.

Being able to express uncertainty in the scores was critical because performance was seen to be context dependent; for example, on the degree of good or bad practice and capacity amongst the farming and regulatory communities. However, Stirling and Mayer concluded that:

the consistent adoption of 'optimistic' and 'pessimistic' approaches to the scoring of options does not generally affect the picture of overall performance as much as do differences in framing assumptions (such as criteria choice, scoring and weightings)

(Stirling and Mayer, 2001: 548)

The strong influence of perspective and associated choices on performance against a broad range of (sometimes incommensurable) criteria, emphasises the mathematical and categorical arm wrenching that takes place in appraisal methods seeking to align these factors across a common denominator, or towards a single outcome.

MCM and participatory deliberation

Since this pilot study, MCM has been adopted in a number of settings to interrogate some diverse issues. Its modular structure has also made it amenable to use in slightly different ways. The rest of this section reviews some particularly contrasting examples of MCM use and the outcomes of mapping different perspectives in these instances.

In 2001 an MCM approach was integrated into a two-stage 'deliberative mapping' exercise (Burgess et al. 2007; Davies et al. 2003). Deliberative mapping is a form of Participatory Technology Assessment which seeks to broaden appraisal of technological innovations beyond narrow expert-led framings and approaches, and towards dialogue and mutual learning based models that bring together members of the public, interest groups, 'experts' and policy actors. In this study possible approaches to reducing or closing the UK's 'kidney-gap'—the difference between demand for donor kidneys and their supply—were mapped by four citizen panels, (n=34), differentiated by gender and socio-economic group, and an expert panel (n=17), comprising people working in different areas of the transplant 'field'. This was supported by high quality facilitation, which was essential to the success of the project.

The citizen panels recruited people from a diversity of backgrounds and with no prior experience or knowledge of transplant issues. MCM was used symmetrically across the citizen and expert panels in two waves, prior to a specialist workshop and then afterwards. The workshop enabled citizens and specialists to engage in discussion and explore questions arising in the first wave of MCM. Six 'core options' were identified by the research team for appraisal, and four 'prompted options' could be scored by the citizen panels if desired. The specialists involved could develop their own further options. In the first wave panels collectively discussed and then scored each option against the criteria they developed. During the second wave the citizen panels considered rescoring options in light of discussions they had in the workshop. The criteria were then also weighted. In a final meeting the results of each panel's mapping were discussed, as were the overall results of the study.

This study found a high degree of consistency in option rankings across the different panels (i.e., citizen and specialist), despite the participants having come to the exercise with very different perspectives. The issue groups, to which both perspectives contributed, also tended to be weighted in a similar order by these two groups. Through a well-managed process and with good quality facilitation, MCM brought a systematic, auditable and transparent approach allowing a deliberative appraisal of the options in this highly technical and ethically conflicted field. The mix of qualitative and quantitative modes of recording judgements was seen to be critical; the study authors noted that "purely discursive analysis would likely have been dominated by a picture of contrasts and tensions. By the same token, quantitative analysis alone would have missed important nuances of difference" (Burgess et al., 2007: 8).

A study on envisioning the future

A multicriteria sustainability appraisal of different visions of possible hydrogen-based energy systems was undertaken by 15 people in the UK, as part of a larger back-casting scenario project (McDowall and Eames, 2006). This study differed from previous MCM studies by evaluating a set of visions—"credible, transparent and internally consistent end points [with] coverage of the hydrogen 'possibility space'" (McDowall and Eames, 2006: 11). The visions comprised narrative storylines describing infrastructural and technological configurations; quantitative indicators providing a sense of the scale of technological change implied; and systems diagrams of each vision. A status quo option was also added to the set so that visions could be compared to a known baseline.

MCM was useful in this instance because of the huge uncertainties inherent in appraising visions, and the contested values underlying different people's views on how the UK's energy system might develop. Another alteration to the method involved setting four core criteria groups based around sustainability and energy security, with all respondents then defining particular criteria within these. An 'other' category then allowed for further types of criteria. Finally, in recognition that "while an MCM study attempts to record framing assumptions, these are often implicit and often remain tacit" (McDowall and Eames, 2006: 14), two 'side swipe' scenarios were provided to participants at the end of the MCM process. These presented respondents with a considerable change in circumstance underlying the visions (rapid climate change and a sustained oil and gas crisis). Participants were asked for brief comments on how the scenarios might change their appraisal in terms of criteria selected, their weightings and how visions performed against these. The study authors, reflecting on the use of these scenarios, noted that "participants had explored future states in terms of current society's assessment of the importance of climate change and energy security" and this "demonstrates the difficulties of thinking through the implications of a radically altered future" (McDowall and Eames, 2006: 32).

European policy appraisal

A policy appraisal considering how best to tackle Europe's growing obesity crisis was conducted with nearly 200 people across nine European Union member states (Lobstein and Millstone, 2006). There is a paucity of well-evidenced interventions shown to successfully reduce obesity levels in a population. In light of this, the European Commission funded project PorGrow sought to gain insight into possible policy interventions from those on the front-line of this issue across nine European Union countries. MCM was chosen because it allowed for a transparent engagement with different options for reducing obesity by the diverse actors who, when policies are introduced, need to 'buy-in'.

Participants formed seven perspectives groups: public interest non-governmental organisations; large commercial operators in the food chain; small food and fitness operators; large non-food commercial operators; policy makers; public providers; public health specialists. They were given 20 options: seven core options that everyone scored, and 13 discretionary options. If participants wanted they could add further options.

The PorGrow MCM generated appraisals of how well interventions were thought to reduce levels of obesity, and how they performed against other aspects (e.g., cost, acceptability) stakeholders consider when appraising policy. Importantly, the use of range scoring allowed exploration of the role played by context. This generated a rich output for further policy deliberation. The study concluded that:

policy-makers can be assured by the PorGrow findings that a comprehensive portfolio of policy measures, integrated into a coherent programme, would be well-supported by a broad coalition of stakeholders, and that the costs of such a programme are not considered as important as the potential costs of not taking action.

(Lobstein and Millstone, 2006: 1)

MCM in a Global South context

An MCM study was undertaken as a way to examine alternative pathways in and out of maize intensive cultivation practices in Kenya (STEPS Centre and ACTS, 2010). In Kenya maize security has come to be equated with food security; the crop dominates this country's national agricultural research and development leading to 'lock-in' to maize as the answer to food security. Given the already high levels of food insecurity in the country, climate change presents a challenge to large proportions of the country's population who rely on this single crop. Maize was used as the gateway through which to explore how agricultural practices, across the local agricultural innovation system, might alter in response to climate change.

The Kenyan study was novel in method because when interviewing some respondents, the interview was conducted using paper and scoring beans in mixed individual and group deliberations. People across the innovation system were interviewed including a diversity of farmers, government officials, researchers, plant breeders, agricultural input suppliers and donor organisation representatives. Option ranks varied between perspective groups across the agricultural innovation system; for example, around the stress tolerance of high maize pathways (a continued central role for maize rather than diversifying away from it). Where farmers saw maize reliant options as performing poorly against stress tolerance criteria, high maize options were seen to perform well by the other perspective groups, illustrating very different views of how best to deal with stresses. High maize options, despite being strongly promoted in Kenya's public discourse, consistently had wider uncertainty ranges and low rankings under pessimistic conditions across all the groups interviewed. Altogether the use of MCM here both challenged the dominant discourse around maize, opening up a much more nuanced picture of uncertainty and maize's ability to deal with future change, as well as illustrating why maize nevertheless continues to dominate the Kenyan agricultural sector.

Future directions

The software supporting MCM has recently been updated and is now available as a web-based package—available at http://www.multicriteriamapping.com. Also available are newly updated interview and analysis manuals (Stirling and Coburn, 2014) which take a prospective user through the process and include a lot of detailed guidance. MCM is suited for use in different contexts and for different problems of appraisal. The modular nature of MCM and its flexibility of use suggests an abundance of exciting new ways it can be mobilised.

I will highlight two possibilities. First, there is the prospect of improving the process of opening up the use of MCM. This might be achieved in a number of ways—for example: larger sample sizes that enable the examination of diversity within perspective groups; more studies that engage the general public or lay experts (with reference to the studies reviewed above this might include farmers, the obese, those affected by kidney donation); improving the responsiveness of analysis to different kinds of hypothesis testing; longitudinal use of MCM to explore the stability of values expressed in MCM; and better differentiation of the sources of uncertainty within MCM scoring, both in terms of good interview technique and communication of results, and through the use of prompting tools like the 'side swipe' scenarios. Second, research could explore how MCM can be integrated into larger decision-making processes that maintain its commitment to participation and systematic opening up. Not all use of MCM is as a decision support tool. Its utility in this vein will, however, be enhanced if more studies, and accounts of its use, include its integration into decision-making processes.

Concluding remarks

Let me briefly re-emphasise how I think the studies reviewed here illustrate how MCM links to ecological economics. First, MCM's commitment to value pluralism is evident in requiring participation by a range of stakeholder perspectives coupled with their shaping of the appraisal process, by choosing extra options and the criteria on which all options are appraised. Measures of ambiguity in MCM analysis illustrate how these perspectives vary in their appraisal of options against certain criteria. Consequently MCM has been used to show the limitations of traditional regulatory appraisal in terms of who is involved, how, and how their decision-making process is represented. This is a position supported by the post-normal science community [see Chapter 28]. Stirling and Mayer (2001), in their founding study of MCM, and Davies et al. (2003), through participatory deliberation, illustrate how perspectives and their associated framings strongly shape the nature of appraisal outcomes. Many framings of a problem bring with them criteria that are traditionally seen as outside the scope of regulatory appraisal, and are incommensurable. When excluded, this narrows the terms of appraisal to the degree that it does not reflect the priorities of the populace. Decisions made in this way are vulnerable to different or changing viewpoints, and to being unsupported by a broad range of stakeholders.

A closely linked outcome of MCM is that it produces interdisciplinarity and transdisciplinary insights. This is nicely exemplified in the PorGrow (Lobstein and Millstone, 2006) and Kenyan maize studies (STEPS Centre and ACTS, 2010). MCM specifically seeks to understand how different stakeholder groups view possible responses to a problem. Judgements drawn from different disciplinary/work-based/cultural or experiential worldviews can be integrated into a single analytical (but not disciplinary!) framework. The potential for expression of people's multiple rationales is also possible.

MCM promotes consideration of uncertainty in appraisal. It is now well known that ecological systems have non-linear dynamics [Chapter 12]. Ecological economics seeks to integrate this dynamism with its associated uncertainty into considering problems of environmental resource use and distribution (Spash, 1999). Ecological economics similarly acknowledges the complex ethics and uncertainty and ignorance when thinking about the future [Chapters 26–28]—whether that be with respect to resource distribution between current and future generations [Chapter 25], or how different socio-technical systems might be valued in 30 years (Spash, 1999, 2011). The possibility of contingent scoring against multiple criteria enables this to be expressed, as shown through the studies on hydrogen futures by McDowall and Eames (2006) and the Kenyan maize study (STEPS Centre and ACTS, 2010).

In summary, there are a number of ideals integral to ecological economics which the design of MCM promotes. These include MCM's commitment to plural values, the related promotion of interdisciplinarity and transdisciplinarity, and engagement with uncertainty. The method is especially well placed for inclusion in the social ecological economist's tool box.

Key further readings cited

Stirling, A. (2005). Opening up or closing down? Analysis, participation and power in the social appraisal of technology. *Science and Citizens*. Ed. M. Leach, I. Scoones and B. Wynne. London: Zed Books.

Stirling, A., Coburn, J. (2014). *Multicriteria Mapping Manual*. Brighton: SPRU, University of Sussex.

Stirling, A., Mayer, S. (2001). A novel approach to the appraisal of technological risk: a multicriteria mapping study of a genetically modified crop. *Environment and Planning C: Government and Policy* 19(4): 529–555.

Other literature cited

Burgess, J., Stirling, A., Clark, J., Davies, G., Eames, M., Staley, K., Williamson,S. (2007). Deliberative mapping: a novel analytic-deliberative methodology to support contested science-policy decisions. *Public Understanding of Science* 16(3): 299–322.

Davies, G., Burgess, J., Eames, M.. Mayer, S., Staley, K., Stirling, A., Williamson, S. (2003). *Deliberative Mapping: Appraising Options for Addressing the 'Kidney Gap'*. Final Report to the Wellcome Trust. London, UK.

Lobstein, T., Millstone, E. (2006). *Policy Options for Responding to Obesity: Evaluating the Options*. Summary Report to European Commission. Brighton: SPRU, University of Sussex

McDowall, W., Eames, M. (2006). *Towards a Sustainable Hydrogen Economy: A multi-criteria mapping of the UKSHEC hydrogen futures*. London, Policy Studies Institute.

O'Neill, J.F., Spash, C.L. (2000). Conceptions of value in environmental decision-making. *Environmental Values* 9(4): 521–536.

Spash, C.L. (1999). The development of environmental thinking in economics. *Environmental Values* 8(4): 413–435.

Spash, C.L. (2011). Social ecological economics: Understanding the past to see the future. *American Journal of Economics and Sociology* 70(2): 340–375.

STEPS Centre and ACTS (2010). *Environmental Change and Maize Innovation in Kenya: Exploring Pathways In and Out of Maize*. UK and Kenya, STEPS Centre and ACTS.

32

Q METHODOLOGY

Ben Davies

Introduction

Founded in the 1950s by psychologist William Stephenson (1953) Q methodology has since been adopted across a wide range of social science research domains. The objective of Q methodology is to reveal different opinions or perspectives on a topic of study by exploring how respondents judge the relative importance to them of different dimensions of a problem or situation. To achieve this insight, Q methodology identifies a set of key items, typically short statements, that represent different opinions and viewpoints about the topic, and asks respondents to create a partial ranking of these items in a process known as a Q sort. The purpose of the Q sort ranking is to show the relative significance that respondents attribute to each item presented. Factor analysis is then employed to identify commonalities and differences between the Q sorts produced by different respondents, with the aim of summarising these into a small number of archetypal sorts that represent common viewpoints held by groups of similarly minded individuals. These archetypal sorts provide the framework for discussion of the different viewpoints held, and identification of points of coherence and divergence in opinions between groups.

This chapter focuses on the aims and application of Q methodology within ecological economics research, excluding wider debates across the whole field of Q studies. In ecological economics Q methodology has responded particularly effectively to three key interests:

1   the construction of pluralist viewpoints on matters of both political and scientific debate, which seek to identify differences in opinion on matters of public concern;
2   the desire for holistic evaluation, which rejects a reductionist scientific approach based on objectively measurable criteria (i.e., naïve empiricism) and instead requires a more openly subjective assessment of relative importance based on individualised perspectives;
3   the search for processes of public participation to address areas of value conflict and public policy controversy, and that enable respondents to evaluate such issues.

For these reasons Q methodology offers both a method and a philosophy well suited to the transdisciplinarity of ecological economics. Barry and Proops (1999) make a clear statement of the potential for the method in the field, while Addams and Proops (2000) report a selection of case studies on its use for environmental discourse analysis.

This chapter proceeds with a section on the background to the development of Q methodology. The conduct of a Q study and the various stages involved are then explained. This is followed by pointers on data analysis and some key issues that arise. The chapter concludes with future directions and some closing remarks.

Theoretical development of Q methodology

Before reviewing the key practical steps in undertaking a Q study, it is useful to reflect briefly on the theoretical justifications for the approach. The central concern of Q methodology was to provide a robust approach to the scientific study of subjectivity (Stephenson, 1953). The methodology seeks to place the individual interests of research subjects at the centre of the research process, and in this sense reverse the classical scientific perspective on knowledge generation. Rather than the research community deciding on the variables and measurements that need to be investigated, in Q methodology the researcher seeks to hand the topic of study over to the research participants and asks them to identify what is of central importance to them in a particular topic area.

To explore subjectivity effectively, a critical concern was that the mind of a single individual should holistically judge the relative importance of all the features of the topic under study, and revealing how each element of this set was relatively more or less important than any other to the respondent undertaking the evaluation. What was provided in the Q sort itself, as the ordered pattern of relative importance of different stimuli, was the visible operation of an otherwise hidden human mind. This meant that the respondent was required to perform a particular kind of operation—make judgements about the relative importance of matters pertaining to the outside world—by providing a rank ordering of the key features of that world from his or her own perspective. This highlights the emancipatory intentions of the Q approach, which sought to enable research participants themselves to determine the domain of contested ideas that ought to be subject to investigation.

Following the work of Stephenson, Q studies have been undertaken in numerous fields including education, nursing, social care, politics, human geography, development studies, sociology, and business and management. Political scientist Stephen Brown's detailed treatment of the method in his book *Political Subjectivity: Applications of Q Methodology in Political Science* (Brown, 1980) is widely credited with broadening the method's appeal, although it is still perceived by many as a controversial approach. Early pioneers helped to found the International Society for the Scientific Study of Subjectivity (ISSS), which holds an annual conference, maintains a Q listserv, and publishes the quarterly journal *Operant Subjectivity* (for which an extensive back catalogue is available on CD). An excellent practical introduction to Q methodology is now available (Watts and Stenner, 2012), which provides a user-friendly complement to the earlier work by McKeown and Thomas (1988).

Steps in undertaking a Q study

There are several key steps that are typically undertaken in a Q study, starting with data gathering and leading into analysis.

Defining the concourse

Setting the boundary to a Q study is the first critical step, and this requires establishing the appropriate sources of material which will provide a stimulus for judgements about the topic at hand. With this in mind, Stephenson suggested that this material should be based on an assessment of what the commonly communicated ideas are related to the topic of study, as evidenced by the myriad articles, reports, and discussions that relate to it. All these forms of communication flow into what is called a concourse of mutually competing and challenging ideas. The concourse represents the visible outward expression of multiple different viewpoints, entailing the co-mingling of several different discourses. This is the field of ideas about which the researcher wishes to create understanding and learn about associated subjective judgements.

The concourse has no set or clear boundaries, and is, in any case, undergoing constant development at any moment in time. It can also be defined by the researcher in relation to any number of different interests and source materials. The central concern in defining the concourse is to delimit appropriately the range of the topic, and from a wide choice of source material to extract a small number of stimulus items. The range of items reflects the focus of the study, and consideration of the concourse forces the researcher to establish more clearly what are the key areas for consideration. Short statements (of both fact and opinion) have been the predominant form for items extracted from the concourse, and a typical starting phase would involve gathering hundreds of candidate statements as source material.

As an example, in his study of attitudes to a carbon offset project, Lansing (2013) takes the concourse to cover material from two sources: (i) published documents on the role of carbon offset projects, including materials from the United Nations Framework Convention on Climate Change, and (ii) transcriptions and notes from in-depth personal interviews with project staff and stakeholders involved in the offset project under study. This is clearly only a minute fraction of all the material dedicated to the topic, but it nevertheless provides a pertinent and manageable source for the extraction of a body of claims and arguments centred around carbon offsetting.

Production of Q set

While the concourse can be conceived of as a flow of interweaving human communication around a topic of interest, making this web of communicative elements manageable for evaluation involves a necessary step of communicative reduction. This is achieved by the production of a discreet Q set, which involves the choice of a relatively small number of stimulus items carefully selected from the concourse. The Q set will be evaluated by individual respondents through inter-comparison of the items with the aim of enabling them to make a judgement on the relative importance of different items.

The typical stimuli or items used in a Q set are short written statements drawn from available sources which express opinions or views about the topic under consideration. In theory there is no restriction on the kind of items that can be used in a Q set, as long as they enable the respondent to make comparisons of their subjective importance; visual stimuli such as photographs can clearly also be suitable for this purpose. In practice, short written statements are utilised in the vast majority of studies, since they are the most direct way of capturing attitudes and opinions regarding matters of interest.

The typical process of Q set production proceeds by first generating a large number of candidate statements from concourse sources, frequently hundreds of statements. This large array is subsequently whittled down to a number between 30 and 60 through a necessarily judgemental process on the part of the researcher. The final Q set is transparent for all to see, and all study outcomes are necessarily circumscribed by its breadth. As Watts and Stenner (2012) note, the Q set selection process, although foundational to the conduct of any study, received very little attention from Stephenson himself and the criteria employed frequently remain opaque. The final set simply emerges from the concourse through a process of considered professional judgement. Some studies do specify a formal matrix block design. For example, Urquhart et al. (2012) assign statements to eight component categories given labels such as 'moral' and 'pragmatic', and cross-reference these with three main effects yielding a final Q set of 36 statements. Many studies however adopt an open design in which there is no determinate structure. Overall, the critical feature of a Q set is that it should provide a balanced reflection on the kind of debates ongoing in public discourse, and it should be amenable to evaluation by the respondent.[1]

A Q set of more than 60 items tends to become unwieldy, although studies have been successfully undertaken using 80 items. Fewer than 30 items makes it difficult both to represent a topic adequately and to identify broad enough variations to map clear differences between sorts. During a respondent's sorting of items a reasonable time frame is roughly a minute per item in arriving at a finished sort (allowing time for revisions), and hence such practicalities may determine the necessary size of the Q set. A substantial number of sets fall in the region of 40 items.

Selection of the P set

The participants in a Q study are known as the P set. Since the objective in a Q study is to identify the dominant discourses existing around a topic, but not to make claims about the proportions of these existing in a wider population, this can be achieved with quite small numbers of participants. A key concern is that there should be sufficient diversity of views represented in the P set to allow representation of all relevant perspectives, and as a rule of thumb at least two similar viewpoints are required to form a viable factor (explained further below). Studies have been effectively conducted with fewer than 10 and more than 100 participants, but the majority of P sets lie between 20 and 50.

The rationale underlying the selection of small numbers of participants is that the number of identifiable viewpoints regarding a particular Q set, and existing in the population, is in reality quite limited, in the order of two to five. Within most Q studies, this accounts for similarities and differences around the majority of views held across the P set, regardless of how many respondents take part. There are typically a few individuals who seem to bear no similarity to anyone, and a more significant number who may share characteristics from two core perspectives rather than being captured by just one. Nevertheless, overall, a relatively small number of discursive positions capture the bulk of the viewpoints presented.

In order to identify these core perspectives, the recruitment of participants typically follows a purposive selection strategy, inviting respondents who are anticipated to provide a range of interesting perspectives. These choices will determine the breadth of opinions that can emerge from a study, and are necessarily referenced to the overall study locations. The choice of P set will therefore be guided by knowledge gained in developing the Q set. Some studies used interview material with participants as the source of Q set material which is subsequently sorted by the interviewees themselves. Again, the choice of P set is necessarily directed by the overall aims of the study being undertaken.

Q sorting

The process of sorting the Q set items into an arrangement that reflects a personal evaluation of the relative importance of the items, considered holistically, is at the heart of knowledge generation within Q. Two features of this process are critical: (i) the terms of instruction, and (ii) the sorting grid.

Terms of instruction

In a Q sort, the respondent is asked to arrange the Q set items so that they reflect the subjective evaluation of the respondent in response to the instructions suggested for sorting. The most common terms of instruction are to arrange the items across a scale reflecting the spectrum from 'strongly agree' to 'strongly disagree', allowing for several items at each level across a nine or eleven point spectrum. This approach is very commonly employed, but the Q approach is open to a wide range of variations on this theme. For example, the respondent can vary his or her sorting persona, so that they can present sorts that they think would be agreeable or disagreeable to others— perhaps family and friends, or political opponents. This would generate several sorts produced by a single individual but representing their subjective assessments of what others perceive.

Similarly, 'agree/disagree' may be changed to any polar spectrum such as 'like most/dislike most' or 'hate most/love most'. What is important is that the range of the spectrum represents equally powerful opposing forces. A rising scale, such as 'most interesting/least interesting', does not capture this range, because 'least interesting' occupies the centre of a distribution where there are no compelling items. The terms of instruction therefore need to specify poles with positive and negative valence, but beyond this can be adapted to the needs of a specific study.

The Q sorting grid

The terms of instruction are applied to placing the Q items into a grid arrangement spanning the evaluative spectrum. This grid guides the placement of items across the range, and is most typically presented in a quasi-normal distribution as shown in Figure 32.1. Much controversy surrounds the choice and shape of the Q grid, but again in practice less hangs on this choice than is often claimed. Stephenson (1953) himself felt the normally shaped Q grid was simply appropriate since it was generally the case that only a few items would really excite attention whilst sorting and much else would be of more middling importance. Brown (1980) later demonstrated that the shape of the grid itself made relatively little difference to the emergent results from a set of Q sorts; regardless of whether flatter or steeper curves, or even flat stacks, were employed, similar patterns of association between sorts could still be observed and extracted.

Therefore the researcher can employ what are known as forced (grid-constrained) or free distributions, or indeed distributions that start out initially as forced but that are allowed to become freer as sorting progresses. Overall, the large majority of studies tend to follow a forced distribution, but vary the curve used from relatively flat curves, requiring finer judgements between a wider range of rankings (better suited to more knowledgeable and engaged

strongly disagree						neutral				strongly agree
−4	−3	−2	−1	0	+1	+2	+3	+4		
−4	−3	−2	−1	0	+1	+2	+3	+4		
	−3	−2	−1	0	+1	+2	+3			
		−2	−1	0	+1	+2				
			−1	0	+1					

Figure 32.1   A Q sorting grid.

respondents) to relatively steep curves, requiring fewer judgements across a smaller range (better suited to unfamiliar topics or less engaged respondents).

Analysis of Q sort data

The analysis of Q sort data involves a considerable degree of researcher judgement. The objective is to reduce the range of subjective perspectives represented by the individual Q sorts into a smaller and more manageable set of archetypal sorts which reflect the main dimensions evident within the whole set. The statistical approach of factor analysis is employed to this end and helps in achieving data reduction by establishing dimensions that capture key aspects of variation between sorts. The degree of association between each individual sort and each explanatory factor can thereby be estimated. Sorts which are significantly associated with a single factor are those that share common characteristics, and these significantly correlated sorts are then aggregated to create a single criterion or factor sort which represents this grouping as a whole.

The software package PQMethod is the most well established of the programs available for undertaking this analysis and generates a wide range of statistics and raw data. Standard statistical packages can also be applied to obtain some of these outputs, but the benefits of a specialised programme greatly assist in exploring alternative interpretations of the data. Two critical technical steps in the analysis are: (i) the choice of number of factors to extract, and (ii) the rotation of factors to provide the clearest representation of these groups within the sample.

Choosing the number of factors

Q methodology aims for some way of identifying, with the minimum number of representative sorts, the maximum amount of coherent variation existing across the whole sample. The number of sorts required to do this effectively will depend on the degree of variation present within the data, and this cannot be known in advance. As a factor is extracted, this captures a certain portion of the total variation present in the data, and each subsequent factor extracted takes another portion. Initially, when there is a lot of variation present, each factor can summarise a significant portion, but this declines as more factors are extracted and relatively quickly the new factors cease to summarise variation effectively. The objective here is to extract a sufficient number of factors to summarise the data usefully, with each factor representing a coherent set of shared ideas as evidenced by groups of similarly ordered Q sorts. However, the fact remains that there is frequently no clear number of factors that ought to be retained; the choice will come down to the researcher and the interpretation that can be made of the factors chosen. Three common rules employed are the scree test (which stops extracting factors when there is a clear drop in the variance being explained by additional factors), retaining factors with eigen values greater than one (which at least ensures that each factor explains more variance than study of any single item), and retaining only factors which have at least two significantly loading sorts (which ensures that there is a core grouping of individuals which is being adequately represented by the factor array). Further details on these and other approaches can be found in Watts and Stenner (2012).

Factor rotation

Once factors have been extracted, the fit between factors and cases can often be improved by rotation of the factors. The effect of rotation is to change the distribution of variance explained by a factor. Rotating the factors makes it possible to align them more closely with specific clusters of similar cases, thereby describing these cases through their high loadings on a single factor rather than moderate loadings on two factors. The rotation of factors can be undertaken either manually using visual inspection of the data (available in PQMethod), or automatically using the varimax operation. Either method can be employed and the choice of final rotation, as in the choice of factors, needs to be guided by close inspection of the possible solutions. The factor arrays change markedly under rotation, and the critical choice of a final array is whether it helps to illuminate the shape of the responses amongst a subset of the sorts.

Generation of criterion sorts

Once the final rotated factor solution has been settled upon, the relationship between factors can be explored in a number of ways. The single most useful outcome is to create a representative Q sort for each factor, known as a criterion sort. This is a weighted aggregation of all the sorts which load significantly on the factor. These criterion sorts enable cross-comparison between different groups as well as close study of individual group perspectives. Underlying the criterion sort placements are z-scores assigned to each of the Q set items, which are standardised scores indicating how each item was scored collectively by the members of its contributing group. The criterion sort for a factor is generated by first ranking all Q items by their factor z-scores and then entering the items by rank order into the Q scoring grid. This generates a Q sort which acts as the representative sort for the factor, and it is this criterion sort which forms the anchor for subsequent analysis. A section of a summary table showing criterion sort scores for a five factor solution is shown in Table 32.1.

Table 32.1 Example of item scores for five criterion Q sorts

Statements	Criterion Q scores*				
	E	P	CC	J	Y
2. There should be more access routes onto farmland to help people to visit the countryside.	0	−4	0	−1	−3
6. Beyond earning a reasonable income, the main joy in farming is the lifestyle.	1	0	−3	2	4
7. It is important to help smaller farmers stay on the land.	2	−3	−1	4	0
22. Farmers should feel guilty if they cause a water pollution incident, whatever the cause.	2	3	−2	−1	0
24. Maintaining an attractive-looking countryside should be an important goal of farmers.	1	1	3	0	3
31. All the earth's resources, such as minerals, fuels, forests, should be used as sparingly as possible.	4	1	0	1	2
33. Financial viability has to be the judge of everything you do on a farm.	0	2	4	3	−4

Notes: *E: Environmentalists; P: Progressives; CC: Commodity Conservationists; J: Jeffersonians; Y: Yeomen.

Source: Davies and Hodge (2007).

Interpretation of the results

Once a small number of factors have been identified that describe the shape of the perspectives evident amongst all the Q sorts, the researcher is then engaged in interpreting these sorts. This is by no means an easy task. Although the technical analysis is complete and a satisfactory factor solution has been reached, the researcher now has the equally challenging task of making sense of the final criterion sorts. Why do these patterns of items emerge? What are the core attitudes, beliefs and values underlying the external evidence presented by the final sorts? How can the researcher summarise the basic positions presented to capture their key characteristics?

These questions are not simple to answer. There is no set procedure for interpreting Q sorts, bearing in mind that the sorts themselves involve hundreds of judgements between items. The task for the researcher is to find the common themes that underlie these judgements and bring attention to these. In this task the discussions held with respondents, during sorting itself, can be particularly valuable in contextualising the choices made in individual sorts.

A critical step in the analysis is to decide on a name for each factor that tries to capture its essential character. Once a name is assigned, it subsequently colours our interpretation and for that reason it should only be chosen once the researcher is satisfied with a coherent narrative underlying the factor. Reaching this point involves a substantial work of interpretation, and reflecting back on the choice of factors in this process is worthwhile. Perhaps a five factor solution produces two factors that are simply very hard to interpret, and which have small numbers of loadings and relatively weak significance. These may prove to be ultimately uninterpretable and fail to really capture solid themes in the social reality of groups of respondents. A rotated three factor solution on the other hand, may provide a much more robust fit.

During interpretation the researcher must bear in mind that the scores assigned are aggregates of individual sorts, and observation of the z-scores may often show that the difference between column scores can be extremely marginal. Within a criterion sort, a rule of thumb is that items placed more than two columns apart are likely to have a significant difference in underlying z-scores, and can therefore be taken as genuinely ranked differently.

In summarising a criterion sort, a common form of presentation is a short narrative description with presentation of a small number of particularly illuminating scores. These capture the essential differences between groups whilst keeping the analysis to a minimum. Some interesting examples of environmental studies using a varying number of factor solutions can be seen in Dryzek and Braithwaite (2000), Sandbrook et al. (2013), Venables et al. (2009) and Wolf et al. (2009).

Future directions

The above summary indicates the principal steps undertaken in Q studies. There are some interesting emerging results in test-retest experiments with Q; for example, Hobson and Niemeyer (2011) investigate the effect of deliberation on public attitudes by comparing responses between participant Q sorts completed before and after a focus group discussion of the adaptive capacity to climate change. This revealed that there was some significant movement towards a preferred discourse around collective action after a four-day workshop. In another repeat study, Davies and Hodge (2012) identified some key changes in environmental emphasis amongst groups of farmers over a seven-year interval, including particularly marked retreats from some environmentalist perspectives. These studies indicate the potential for using Q in dynamic research settings and for engaging respondents in reflection on their own changes in orientation in comparison with the evidence from previous studies of their views.

As the concourse of public debate is itself ever-changing, the opportunity for revisiting the topics studied in earlier Q studies is always present, in addition to explorations into new areas. The activity of the Q sort itself is typically well received by respondents, being flexible and under the control of the respondent until they are fully satisfied with their completed sort.

Concluding remarks

The role of Q methodology in ecological economics continues to expand, illuminating competing discourses on topics from local to global levels. The methodology is well suited to small-scale studies drawing on the thoughts and experiences of practitioners and analysts involved in environmental debates, and these results themselves generate further opportunities to reflect on and further interrogate the presentation of competing arguments. The approach now benefits from an extensive catalogue of past studies as well as several guidance manuals and an active community of research practitioners maintaining a discussion list and holding regular annual meetings.

The outline of Q methodology presented here has focused on the key features of the approach and much greater depth can be found in the key readings. Although Q methodology employs the mathematics of factor analysis to extract discourses from the sorts, it is best described as grounded in a weak constructivist epistemology, seeking to make sense of the complex perspectives of others through a careful and reflective analysis of shared orderings of the Q set. The claims made in any study are necessarily circumscribed by many researcher-led choices, most notably the selection of initial concourse sources and material, Q and P sets, factor extraction and final factor interpretation. Ultimately the final discourses identified in any study remain open to further interrogation and critique, whilst at the same time remaining tied to the expressions generated by the participants themselves. The method continues to illuminate the plurality of social perspectives held on issues of environmental concern, and provides valuable insights into this diversity shaped by the views of participants themselves.

Note

1 Editor's Note: Researchers undertaking such a process will bring with them a conceptual model which must bear-up to social reality. If it fails to do so this will result in misrepresentation of the topic being addressed and if substantive will produce negative respondent reaction. Thus social reality limits the extent to which any such process is open or any researcher comes forward without preconceptions of what is relevant.

Key further readings cited

Addams, H., Proops, J. (2000). *Social Discourse and Environmental Policy: An Application of Q Methodology*, Cheltenham: Edward Elgar.

Brown, S. (1980). *Political Subjectivity: Applications of Q Methodology in Political Science*, New Haven: Yale University Press.

Watts, S., Stenner, P. (2012). *Doing Q Methodological Research: Theory, Method and Interpretation*, London: Sage Publications Ltd.

Other literature cited

Barry, J., Proops, J. (1999). Seeking sustainability discourses with Q methodology, *Ecological Economics* 28(3), 337–345.

Davies, B.B., Hodge, I.D. (2007). Exploring environmental perspectives in lowland agriculture: A Q methodology study in East Anglia, *Ecological Economics* 61(2–3), 323–333.

Davies, B.B., Hodge, I.D. (2012). Shifting environmental perspectives in agriculture: Repeated Q analysis and the stability of preference structures. *Ecological Economics* 83, 51–57.

Dryzek, J., Braithwaite, V. (2000). On the prospects for democratic deliberation: values analysis applied to Australian politics', *Political Psychology* 21(2), 241–266.

Hobson, K., Niemeyer, S. (2011). 'Public responses to climate change: the role of deliberation in building capacity for adaptive action', *Global Environmental Change* 21(3), 957–971.

Lansing, D.M. (2013). Not all baselines are created equal: a Q methodology analysis of stakeholder perspectives of additionality in a carbon forestry offset project in Costa Rica, *Global Environmental Change* 23(3), 654–663.

McKeown, B.F., Thomas, D. (1988). *Q Methodology: Quantitative Applications in the Social Sciences*, London: Sage.

Sandbrook, C.G., Fisher, J.A., Vira, B. (2013). What do conservationists think about markets? *Geoforum* 50, 232–240.

Stephenson, W. (1953). *The Study of Behaviour: Q Technique and its Methodology*, Chicago: University of Chicago Press.

Urquhart, J., Courtney, P., Slee, B. (2012). Private woodland owners' perspectives on multifunctionality in English woodlands, *Journal of Rural Studies* 28(1), 95–106.

Venables, D., Pidgeon, N., Simmons, P., Henwood, K., Parkhill, K. (2009). Living with nuclear power: a Q method study of local community perceptions, *Risk Analysis* 29(8), 1089–1104.

Wolf, J., Brown, K., Conway, D. (2009). Ecological citizenship and climate change: perceptions and practice, *Environmental Politics* 18(4), 503–521.

33

PARTICIPATION IN THE CONTEXT OF ECOLOGICAL ECONOMICS

Kirsty L. Blackstock

Introduction

Ecological economics is the study of interactions between human societies and the ecosystems in which human activities are embedded. Spash (2011) has emphasised the need to raise the profile of the human aspect and refers to social ecological economics. Therefore, understanding how individuals and social groups participate in the decisions that affect social ecological systems is central. Participation seems intuitively simple, but is loosely defined in academic literature; resulting in many different understandings. I define participation as the process of actively involving anyone who might affect, or be affected by, a process or decision [see also Chapter 50]. It is doing research with, rather than about, the population in question. Understanding participation means considering the processes by which people participate, and the consequences of their participation (Creighton, 2005). Thinking about participation helps to prevent the ecological economist from taking the stance of an objective observer 'outside' their study. Instead they are a participant within the research process, where their own positions and subjectivities matter.

This chapter will discuss the meaning of participation, who might participate and rationales for participation, before focussing on current issues and future directions. These insights are relevant for two areas of research:

1   why and how to study participation in environmental policy processes; and
2   why and how to involve participants in ecological economic research.

These are different things—studying the participation involved in policy making or implementation is perfectly possible without the research being, itself, participatory. Equally, a common approach is to involve people in research as interviewees, questionnaire respondents or expert commentators, but unless these people are actively involved in all facets of the research, including defining the research objectives and agreeing outcomes, this is not participatory research (Bergold and Stefan, 2012).

What is participation?

Direct participation by individuals in aspects affecting their lives, rather than through indirect means such as electing official representatives or through consumer choices, became a hallmark of Western societies in the late twentieth century. It has become increasingly common in other nation states in the twenty-first century. Participation is part of a shift from technocratic approaches towards polycentric and multi-level governance, and chimes with transformative and sustainable development. What differentiates this from social protest [Chapter 17] is the formal institutionalisation of the practice. Thus, whilst there remain strong bottom-up demands for active involvement in public policy (e.g., neighbourhood planning, health care and education), there are also top-down drivers that mandate participation in policy making and implementation. For example, Principle 10 of the 1992 United Nations (UN) Rio Declaration states that "environmental issues are best handled with participation of all concerned citizens, at the relevant level", and the UN Aarhus Convention (2001) on Access to Information, Public Participation in Decision-making and Access to Justice in Environmental Matters has 47 signatories, including the European Union.

However, there are many debates about what exactly constitutes participation. Participation is often connected to action research (i.e. research that generates change beyond the academic sphere; Kemmis and MacTaggart, 2005). Whilst some note participation can focus on co-production of knowledge, without necessarily leading to changes in practice (Bergold and Stefan, 2012), the majority view remains that what defines participation is the co-production of "knowledge for action" (Cornwall and Jewkes, 1995: 1667). The degree of participation is central to the above debate (Luyet et al., 2012). Some proponents equate this to the extent and quality of representation (discussed further below).

Other proponents equate this to the degree of empowerment experienced by participants, such as found in Arnstein's (1969) ladder of participation. There have been subsequent debates regarding whether all participation should, or could, aspire to achieving the top rung, namely citizen power. Alternatives, such as Davidson's (1998) wheel of participation have been promoted to acknowledge situations where a more practical or desirable approach may be to implement information or consultation processes properly, rather than promise empowerment but be unable to deliver it. Most recently, Hurlbert and Gupta (2015) have proposed a split ladder of participation, which combines Arnstein's ladder with the wider political context and associated social learning dynamics.

These refinements of the ladder of participation are a response to critiques regarding the tyranny of participation (Cooke and Kothari, 2001). This is the situation whereby participatory processes have promised devolution of power to citizens yet often became co-opted by elites to sustain the status quo. Participation has tended to allow power-sharing within manifest forms of power (i.e., direct changes to specific policies or plans), but elites still tend to control the agenda of what is discussed (latent power) and condition the way problems and solutions are framed (ideological power) (Baum, 2015; [Chapter 14]). Dominant responses to Cooke and Kothari have recognised the constraints on the ability of participatory processes, singlehandedly, to achieve social transformation and place participation explicitly within its wider organisational and institutional contexts.

Often, the outcomes of a participatory process will be one factor among many in the final decision or implementation process. To avoid stakeholder fatigue research should illustrate to what extent the participatory process influenced final outcomes and recognise where other factors, such as statutory requirements or resource limitations, resulted in an alternative choice (see Drazkiewicz et al., 2015). Participatory researchers cannot ensure their findings are implemented, and researchers of participation should consider to what extent the objectives were achieved and the reasons for this, rather than solely focussing on the participatory process itself.

Who participates?

Participation is normally prefixed by public, citizen, or community, and it is often used synonymously with the concept of stakeholder engagement. There are some essential distinctions that need to be considered. In some participatory processes, any individual who wishes to participate does so and represents themselves. With the right to participate come responsibilities, such as the responsibility to contribute to well-informed and civilised public debate (see below). Some participatory processes lend themselves to this view of participation, such as public consultations or public hearings.

However, inviting citizens to participate does not automatically result in equitable representation. There are many structural issues associated with participation, such as being unable to attend meetings during working hours or without childcare, ability to access and download large documents, translating specialist information and understanding the procedures. Participatory processes then tend to disadvantage low-income, less educated citizens and often result in the overrepresentation of high-income, well-educated and time-rich people, often middle-aged, white males. Thus, researchers and policy analysts should consider the consequences of non-participation on the decision or actions taken (Larson and Lach, 2008).

In other cases, face-to-face participatory processes may work with selected citizens in small groups. These participants may be self-selecting, often reflecting the biases discussed above. Additionally, they may be those most exercised by the issue, which can affect their ability to conduct dispassionate deliberations on the topic. Participation is often premised on the Habermasian ideal of rational deliberation (Habermas, 1984), but this has been critiqued as culturally specific and failing to acknowledge other discursive styles (Gambetta, 1998). More recent literature highlights the emotion involved and limits to 'rationality' in public debate (Bergold and Stefan, 2012). Finally, participants may be selected to have a representative mandate, and be actively involved on behalf of a wider group (O'Neill, 2001). As Davies et al. (2005) and Blackstock et al. (2014) have highlighted, representation is often understood as discrete and static categories where identities are generally multifaceted and fluid. This can conflate someone being from a community of place or interest with someone representing this community, without ensuring sufficient resources or time are put in place to allow appropriate soundings of their constituency. More attention should be paid to the way representation is enacted in participatory processes.

Adult citizen participants do not necessarily represent all aspects of the social ecological system that may affect, or be affected by, decisions. Both future generations and non-human actors tend to be neglected in decision-making processes (O'Neill, 2001; [Chapter 25]). Young people and environmental NGOs are sometimes explicitly invited to participate to redress these gaps, but, as discussed above, one person may be unable to represent the diversity of these constituents. Furthermore, where participatory processes seek consensus, a single voice representing the environment, or the future, can easily be silenced (Drazkiewcz et al., 2015).

There is also a difference between presence and influence within participatory processes. Participants may be strategic in their framing of issues or contest evidence that goes against their interests, because most participants will have their own private objectives for the process. Organised interest groups tend to have more experience, and more resources to draw on, in strategically positioning themselves within public debates, than members of the unorganised public. Thus, participants may oppose the spirit of rational deliberation for the public good.

Rationales for participation

There are multiple potential benefits arising from participation. These can be categorised into three rationales: (i) substantive, (ii) instrumental and (iii) normative (Pellizoni, 2001). Each is discussed here in turn.

Substantive rationale

The substantive rationale covers complexity and multiple perspectives. This has two aspects. First, most issues being tackled through a participatory process are complex. They are therefore not easily understood by an individual. Instead, to understand the issue and devise an appropriate solution requires pooling knowledge from a variety of sources. Traditionally, pooled knowledge came from a variety of academic technical experts. However, increasingly, there is recognition of traditional, indigenous and experiential knowledge, whereby non-professionals may have extremely relevant insights into the nature of a problem, the way in which a problem manifests itself, potential solutions and/or the impacts of any potential solutions on themselves or their communities (Fischer, 2000; [see also Chapter 28]).

Second, most issues are contested, and there are multiple views on what the problem is and therefore the best way to resolve it. This adds additional complexity that requires recognising the multiple readings of the situation and multiple responses to any potential solution, rather than just eliciting knowledge to generate an optimal solution. Scientific and lay experts may disagree on how to interpret insights, and many aspects of a complex social ecological system remain uncertain or even unknowable [Chapter 26 and 27]. Participation therefore will increase the ability to understand and define the dimensions of a problem, and generate more robust solutions. It will illuminate, but not necessarily resolve, conflicting perspectives.

Instrumental rationale

The instrumental rationale covers efficiency and legitimacy. Although participation, when done well, is resource intensive and can prolong a decision-making process, ultimately, it should be more efficient in terms of providing an easily implemented solution. If the process by which a decision has been made is transparent and represents a consensus based on all available information, then it is much less likely to be resisted or subject to legal contestation. Furthermore, when individuals or groups are involved in generating solutions, they are more likely to wish to contribute to their implementation, such as providing volunteers or changing their own behaviours. Thus, public funds can be supplemented by in-kind or private donations, and the costs of incentives or regulation reduced or avoided.

A well-run participatory process should increase public confidence in the legitimacy of the decision made, by ensuring that all relevant evidence and views are considered. Thus, participation becomes a way of making public institutions more accountable, which can help address the prevalent lack of trust in many public institutions in the twenty-first century (Fischer, 2000). However, in order to achieve consensus for effective implementation, and appear legitimate in terms of representing the majority, certain knowledge claims or problem framings may be excluded, resulting in disillusioned individuals and screening out more radical solutions (Beierle and Cayford, 2002). Given the ability for participatory processes to be co-opted, or for participatory outcomes to be ignored in wider political decision-making, legitimacy may be hard to achieve.

Normative rationale

The normative rationale covers several issues regarding benefits to society, but also to individuals. Those involved should have a greater understanding of how governance processes function and feel more confident about their ability to participate in public life in the future. All participants gain new insights about the topic under discussion and gain greater understanding of different perspectives and interests. This allows previously atomised sectors of society to be connected via bonds of respect and reciprocity that help increase community cohesion (i.e., social capital). Citizens are provided with enhanced capabilities for future governance processes that, in turn, should result in a rejuvenated civic democracy. However, where participatory processes are co-opted or ignored, participants may become more distrustful of public institutions, more antagonistic to other sectors of society and more cynical about the practice of democracy.

There has been insufficient awareness of the synergies, or incommensurabilities, between these three rationales, yet this is essential for truly understanding how participation works in practice. The normative and instrumental rationales intersect with interests in political science related to debates over the merits of deliberative or representative democracy. However, participation can also be closely related to social protest [Chapter 17], social learning and action research, with a strong commitment to transformation, and less focus on the outcomes for individuals or social networks. Therefore, practitioners must have clarity of purpose in conducting participation and acknowledge the relative weightings they place on each of these three rationales (Wesselink et al., 2011).

Key aspects of a participatory process

Design and facilitation

Achieving the promise of participation and avoiding its pitfalls relies on good participatory design and expert facilitation [see also Chapter 35]. There is little academic research—but a plethora of grey literature and good practice guides—on these topics, despite research showing that the quality of the participatory process greatly affects the outcomes (Shirk et al., 2012). Participatory design requires that a suite of methods that will suit a range of participants, are matched to the objectives of the process and suit the available resources and timescales (Rowe and Frewer, 2000). Participatory processes should accommodate various forms of knowledge. The philosophy behind the design is as fundamental as the selection of techniques. As Figure 33.1 illustrates, participatory design covers much more than the interaction itself. It requires a full analysis of the context and feedback loops.

Facilitators can assist with many aspects of participation. For example, they can help:

- consider what form of participation might be appropriate given the history and geography of the community or social group;
- manage expectations, set realistic objectives and identify local resources to support the process;
- identify participants that represent the diversity of the social group or community of place and encourage new voices to attend and influence the discussions.

However, some 'gate-keepers' can restrict access and perpetuate local power imbalances.

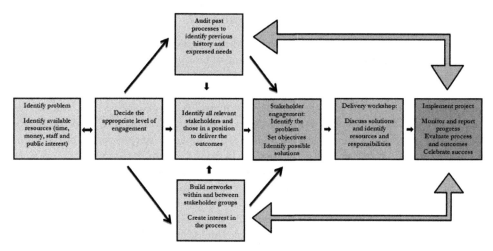

Figure 33.1 Designing a participatory process.
Source: Richards et al. (2007).

Many participatory methods rely on face to face interaction and increased recognition of internal group dynamics in participatory processes is needed. Skilled facilitators can ensure that all participants are able to voice their opinions, through tactfully handling dominant characters and encouraging more reticent participants. Facilitators need a blend of: strong technical skills with regard to data collection and rapid analysis techniques; practical skills associated with running workshops and handling equipment; and interpersonal qualities of being approachable, flexible, calm yet enthusiastic. Most of all they have to be perceived as neutral to facilitate a safe communicative space for expressing conflicting views. The facilitator remains an under-researched actor in the participatory process, although reflexive accounts of participatory research increasingly explore the roles of all participants in their projects.

Participation in time and space

Social ecological economics highlights the interdependencies of social and ecological systems through time and space [Chapter 1]. Figure 33.1 emphasises the need to acknowledge previous participatory processes and build on their legacies in order to avoid consultation fatigue (Barreteau et al., 2010). Much of the literature highlights the time needed to build trust between participants, but sometimes statutory requirements or environmental crises do not allow for this (Waylen et al., 2015; Mackenzie and Larson, 2010). Different forms of participation might be required at different stages. At times, opening up deliberation to inform problem framing is required, while at other times, consensus is needed to come to a final decision (Macleod et al., 2008). Participatory processes are often focussed on resolving immediate and visible problems rather than considering the long-term consequences of slow change variables in social ecological systems. The growth of future methodologies in participatory projects is one response to this problem.

There has been insufficient consideration of the role of space and place in understanding the dynamics of participation. Participation is often most viable at the local scale, building on local knowledge and a shared sense of place. However, if the issue is a national or global governance problem, then bespoke local solutions may become lost in global political negotiations. There have been two responses. The first is the scaling up of participatory processes such as twenty-first-century town hall meetings (Lukensmeyer and Brigham, 2003). However, Brandt and Svendsen (2013) question the benefits of increased numbers. The second is the consideration of any individual participatory project as part of a wider patchwork of cross-level processes occurring across multiple spaces (Klinke, 2012).

Future directions

The debates regarding the purpose and problems of participation have become more diverse and nuanced in a variety of disciplines, from participatory geography to town planning. Four issues seem most relevant in terms of both researching participation and undertaking participatory research. These are: (i) the influence of new media and online tools; (ii) the democratisation of expertise; (iii) attention to the corporate sphere; and (iv) the importance of ethics, emotions and justice.

The majority of Western citizens now have constant and affordable access to the internet. In theory this can help overcome many of the hurdles disadvantaging certain participants, as it allows people to participate in their own homes, at times that suit them. Anonymous participation in a virtual arena can be more egalitarian, promoting a focus on the content of the message rather than the identity of the messenger. Online communities can span geographical space, enabling shared learning from project participants who would not normally know about each other, empowering projects and lending them international credibility. However, a digital divide exists (even in industrially developed countries) with many rural or deprived urban areas lacking high speed broadband access, and low-income households or community groups unable to afford the hardware required to access internet materials. Online participation tends to be biased to the young, well-educated and men (Nyerges and Agguirre, 2011).

There has been a rapid growth in visual methods, some of which are used in a participatory manner. One is to train participants to shoot and edit videos or photographs; this allows participants to collect and analyse data themselves and present their views. The results can be made available to a wide range of future participants (e.g. via social media) and can often include evidence that may not be easily accommodated in traditional written reports. However, whilst they appear democratic, there is still the potential for manipulation in terms of what material is discarded and how the outputs are used (Chalfen, 2011).

Participatory geographic information systems (PGIS) allow participants to make their lived experiences spatially explicit, and can enable more citizens to participate in land or environmental planning. In the past, the expense and complexity of the technology tended to restrict participants to providing data to an expert GIS technician, but the growth of open source GIS programs and easy-to-use interfaces has made control of the technologies possible for participants themselves. However, use of these online tools remains low (Brown, 2012). As above, the degree to which GIS is participatory depends on how the data are analysed and used within a democratic process. Too often, projects labelled participatory GIS remain data elicitation for the benefit of scientific discovery and are of little benefit to the participants.

The democratic potential of visual or spatial technologies connects to the democratisation of expertise, in particular, what is termed 'citizen science'. There has been increasing interest in the use of 'big data' to better understand the dynamics of social ecological systems and new online tools have enabled citizens to assist with the collection of data and increase the extent and quality of data sets. This can achieve substantive benefits (i.e., increasing the sum of knowledge) and normative benefits (i.e., increasing individual skills and awareness of ecological processes). However, in many cases, participation is limited to provision of data, not extending to shared analysis or joint action (Shirk et al., 2012). To me, this is not participation because the citizen scientist is not actively involved in decision-making nor the implementation processes. Ecological economists might consider how to rethink the notion of expertise to make these processes more democratic [see also Chapters 26 and 28].

Participation research tends to study processes initiated by public or non-governmental organisations. However, transformative sustainable development involves the corporate sector (and hybrids between public, corporate and third sector). Ecological economists could highlight the impact of citizen participation in corporate governance. This raises questions about whether one participates as a citizen through politically engaged debate, or as a consumer through ethically engaged purchasing. Equally, greater attention should be paid to the influence of powerful corporate interests who avoid public debates, but nevertheless have considerable influence on final policy decisions and/or ability to implement the outcomes.

Positioning participatory projects in their wider institutional contexts also requires a more reflexive approach by the ecological economist. There should be renewed regard for positionality and subjectivity when considering how multiple and fluid identities may influence the ethical practice of participation. This is not to psychologise participation, but to account for the emotional effect of participation in order to better understand changes in public trust in democracy.

Finally, research on participation, or participatory research, should scrutinise its outcomes and impact. These may be intermediate outcomes, in terms of new knowledge, conceptual ideas or social capital, or final outcomes in terms of concrete changes in policy, plans or practices. There is a wealth of literature on participatory evaluation (e.g., Whitmore, 1998), but how to evaluate participatory research remains surprisingly under researched (see Blackstock et al., 2007). One of the problems for evaluation has been the time lag before outcomes are achieved. Therefore, future researchers should consider longitudinal embedded research relationships that allow an understanding of the influence of the participatory project as part of a dynamic social ecological system. This requires the participatory investigator to occupy a hybrid role as researcher, colleague and engaged citizen, and it means they will be held to account for the consequences of their research over a far longer period. Such sustained interaction is more likely to result in social transformation as it increases the salience, legitimacy and credibility of research (Cash et al., 2003).

Concluding remarks

An interest in participation is fundamental if ecological economics is concerned with the interactions between Nature, social justice and time. Participation draws on a number of different academic disciplines (e.g., political science, geography) and multiple practice domains (e.g., community development, health), resulting in a huge literature and ongoing debates about definitions and application. This chapter has drawn attention to the debates over what is participation, who participates, and the synergies or conflicts between different rationales for participation. It has highlighted insights for those wishing to practice, research or evaluate participation and for those wishing to practice participatory research, but the chapter is not a 'how to do' manual (see key readings for such guidance). Future directions highlighted include: the influence of new media and online tools; the democratisation of expertise; awareness of the corporate sphere and the importance of ethics, emotions and justice. Whilst acknowledging debates around how to conceptualise and operationalise the degree and quality of participation, the chapter firmly locates participation within post-normal science [Chapter 28], highlighting multiple perspectives, uncertainty, subjectivity and power. In common with concepts such as sustainable development and adaptive management, participation is part of a long-term process rather than a task-and-finish activity. This provides challenges for the social ecological economist, but also many rich rewards.

Key further readings cited

Creighton, J.L. (2005). *The Public Participation Handbook: Making Better Decisions Through Citizen Involvement.* London: John Wiley and Sons.

Richards, C., Sherlock, K. and Carter, C.E. (2007). *Practical Approaches to Participation, 2nd edition.* In SERP Policy Brief Series, Spash, C.L. and Carter, C.E. (eds.). Aberdeen: Macaulay Institute.

Whitmore, E. (ed.) (1998). Special Issue: Understanding and Practicing Participatory Evaluation, *New Directions for Evaluation* 80: 1–99.

Other literature cited

Arnstein, A.S. (1969). A ladder of citizenship participation, *Journal of the American Institute of Planners* 26(4): 216–233.

Barreteau, O., Bots, P.W.G., Daniell K.A. (2010). A framework for clarifying "participation" in participatory research to prevent its rejection for the wrong reasons. *Ecology and Society* 15(2), 1–22.

Baum, H.S. (2015). Citizen Participation. *International Encyclopaedia of the Social & Behavioral Sciences*, 2nd Edition. J.D. Wright. Oxford: Elsevier, pp. 625–630.

Beierle T.C., Cayford C. (2002). *Democracy in Practice: Public Participation in Environmental Decision Making.* Washington DC: Resources of the Future, pp. 1–158.

Bergold, J., Stefan T. (2012). Participatory research methods: A methodological approach in motion. *Qualitative Social Research* 13 (1). Art. 30, http://nbnresolving.de/urn:nbn:de:0114-fqs1201302

Blackstock, K.L., Kelly, G.J., Horsey, B.L. (2007). Developing and applying a framework to evaluate participatory research for sustainability, *Ecological Economics* 60(4), 726–742.

Blackstock, K.L., Waylen, K.A., Marshall, K.M., Dunglinson, J. (2014). Hybridity of representation: insights from river basin management planning in Scotland. *Environment and Planning C: Government and Policy* 32, 549–566.

Brandt, U.S., Svendsen, G.T. (2013). Is local participation always optimal for sustainable action? The costs of consensus-building in Local Agenda 21, *Journal of Environmental Management* 129(0), 266–273.

Brown, G. (2012). Public Participation GIS (PPGIS) for regional and environmental planning: Reflections on a decade of empirical research. *URISA Journal* 25 (2), 7–18.

Cash, D.W., Clark, C.W., Alcock, F., Dickson, N.M, Eckley, N., Guston D.H., Jager, J., Mitchell, R.B. (2003). Knowledge systems for sustainable development. *Proceedings of the National Academy of Science* 100(14), 8086–8091.

Chalfen, R. (2011). Differentiating practices of participatory visual media production. In E. Margolis and L. Pauwels (eds.), *Visual Methods.* London: Sage Publications Ltd, pp. 186–201.

Cooke, B., Kothari, U. (Eds.) (2001). *Participation: The New Tyranny?* London: Zed Books.

Cornwall, A., Jewkes, R. (1995). What is participatory research? *Social Science and Medicine* 41(12), 1667–1676.

Davidson, S. (1998). Spinning the wheel of empowerment. *Planning* 1262: 14–15.

Davies, B.B., Blackstock, K.L., Rauschmayer, F. (2005). 'Recruitment', 'composition', and 'mandate' issues in deliberative processes: should we focus on arguments rather than individuals? *Environment and Planning C: Government and Policy* 23(4), 599–615.

Drazkiewicz, A., Challies, E., Newig, J. (2015). Public participation and local environmental planning: Testing factors influencing decision quality and implementation in four case studies from Germany, *Land Use Policy* 46(0), 211–222.

Fischer, F. (2000). *Citizens, Experts and the Environment: The Politics of Local Knowledge.* Durham, N.C.: Duke University Press.

Gambetta, D. (1998). Claro! In: Elster, J. (ed.), *Deliberative Democracy* (pp. 19–43). Cambridge: Cambridge University Press.

Habermas, J. (1984). *The Theory of Communicative Action.* Boston, MA: Beacon Press.

Hurlbert, M., Gupta, J. (2015). The split ladder of participation: A diagnostic, strategic, and evaluation tool to assess when participation is necessary, *Environmental Science & Policy* 50(0), 100–113.

Kemmis, S., McTaggart, R. (2005). Participatory Action Research: Communicative Action and the Public Sphere. In Denzin, N. and Lincoln, Y. (eds.), *The Sage Handbook of Qualitative Research* (pp. 59–604). London: Sage.

Klinke, A. (2012). Democratizing regional environmental governance: Public deliberation and participation in transboundary ecoregions. *Global Environmental Politics* 12(3), 79–99.

Larson, K.L., Lach, D. (2008). Participants and non-participants of place-based groups: An assessment of attitudes and implications for public participation in water resource management. *Journal of Environmental Management* 88(4): 817–830.

Lukensmeyer, C.J., Brigham, S. (2003). Taking democracy to scale: Creating a town hall meeting for the twenty-first century. *National Civic Review* 91(4): 351–366.

Luyet, V., Schlaepfer, R., Parlange, M.B., Buttler, A. (2012). A framework to implement Stakeholder participation in environmental projects. *Journal of Environmental Management* 111, 213–219.

Mackenzie, B.F., Larson, B.M.H. (2010). Participation under time constraints: Landowner perceptions of rapid response to the Emerald Ash Borer. *Society & Natural Resources* 23(10), 1013–1022.

Macleod, C.J.A., Blackstock, K.L., Haygarth, P.M. (2008). Mechanisms to improve integrative research at the science-policy interface for sustainable catchment management. *Ecology and Society* 13(2), 1–17.

Nyerges, T., Agguirre, R.W. (2011). Public participation in analytic-deliberative decision –making evaluating a large group online field experiment. *Annals of the Association of American Geographers* 101 (3), 51–586.

O'Neill, J. (2001). Representing people, representing nature, representing the world, *Environment and Planning C: Government and Policy* 19(4), 483–500.

Pellizzoni, L. (2001). The myth of best argument: power, deliberation and reason. *British Journal of Sociology* 52 (1), 59–86.

Rowe, G., Frewer, L.J. (2000). Public participation methods: A framework for evaluation *Science Technology and Human Values* 25(1), 3–29.

Shirk J, Ballard H, Wilderman C, Phillips T, Wiggins A, Jordan R, McCallie E, Minarchek M, Lewenstein B, Krasny M, Bonney R. (2012). Public participation in scientific research: A framework for deliberate design. *Ecology and Society* 17(2), 1–29.

Spash, C.L. (2011). Social ecological economics: Understanding the past to see the future. *American Journal of Economics and Sociology* 70(2), 340–375.

Waylen, K. A., Blackstock, K.L., Marshall, K., Dunglinson, J. (2015). The participation-prescription tension in natural resource management: The case of diffuse pollution in Scottish water management. *Environmental Policy and Governance* 25(2), 111–124.

Wesselink, A., Paavola, J., Fritsch, O., Renn, O. (2011). Rationales for public participation in environmental policy and governance: practitioners' perspectives. *Environment and Planning A* 43(11), 2688–2704.

34

DELIBERATIVE MONETARY VALUATION

Jasper O. Kenter

Introduction

Deliberative Monetary Valuation (DMV) encapsulates a range of approaches that integrate participation, reflection, discussion and social learning into monetary valuation of environmental and other public goods, or budgetary decisions relating to provisioning of such goods. The term was first employed by Spash (2007, 2008a). In DMV, small groups of participants explore values and preferences for different policy options through a process of reasoned discourse. DMV has developed as a critical response to more established valuation methods, particularly the contingent valuation method (CVM) and cost-benefit analysis (CBA), which have been challenged both by ecological complexities and the intricacies and multidimensionality of human values. DMV has also been advocated as a more 'democratic' approach to valuation that can enhance the perceived legitimacy of policy making, as a result of increased public participation and better understanding of values (Howarth and Wilson, 2006). Others have used DMV to work with participants with limited formal education and literacy, and have pointed out that group-based, rather than individual/household, decisions and shared values are the norm in many parts of the world, especially for managing public goods (Kenter et al., 2011). Thus there are a range of different motivations for DMV that shape how it is put into practice.

In the next section, I discuss some of these motivations, key issues facing environmental valuation and how different values come into play. I then consider different DMV approaches divided in two categories: deliberated preferences (DP), which enhance neoclassical economic valuation, and deliberative democratic monetary valuation (DDMV), which elicits group values to directly establish value to society. The final sections discuss future directions and provide concluding remarks.

Deliberation and challenges to valuation

While DMV is not limited to environmental issues, the discussion around how deliberation might benefit valuation has been most pronounced in the environmental field. Reasons for environment valuation include: improving policy and project appraisal, incorporating natural capital into financial accounts, informing decisions around trade-offs and awareness raising. A key idea is to compare the relative importance of the environment to other private and public goods with the aim of evaluating different policy options and informing decision-making.

In the context of valuation, the terms 'value' and 'values' can have different meanings across different dimensions, including the concept of value, the value provider, scale, intention and elicitation process (Kenter et al., 2015). I distinguish three types of value: transcendental, contextual and indicators. Transcendental values transcend specific contexts. They are values in the sense of guiding principles and life goals that shape the way we live our lives, e.g., enjoyment, honesty, social status, security and harmony with nature. Transcendental values help shape contextual values, which express opinions about the importance of particulars, e.g., where protecting a wetland is judged more important than developing it, or where a wetland protecting the coast is judged a better reason than that it provides food for seabirds. Value indicators provide a measure of importance, e.g., the maximum willingness to pay (WTP) of a valuing agent to protect a wetland.

These different concepts can be expressed through different value providers, including:

• individuals;
• groups of people, such as in a valuation workshop (group values);
• different geographical communities or communities of practice (communal values);
• societies and cultures as a whole (societal and cultural values).

Values can also be distinguished in terms of an individual and/or societal scale, be self-regarding and/or other-regarding, and be elicited through deliberative and/or non-deliberative processes. Valuation, broadly defined, involves a wide range of methods—depending on what type of values are targeted—including: cultural-historic document analysis, geographic mapping, psychological surveys, questionnaire-based and qualitative social research, and monetary valuation (Kenter, 2016a). As depicted by the grey arrows in Figure 34.1, the choice of process for eliciting values and the type of value provider will influence the values articulated in terms of concept, intention and scale.

Neoclassical environmental economic valuation is focused on individual contextual values and value indicators, ignoring the values considered by other disciplines as shared or social values; indicated in Figure 34.1 in italic font. It assumes transcendental values are completely reflected in contextual values, and communal, societal and cultural values are fully reflected in individual values. In neoclassical economics, whether something has value to an individual depends on his or her wants, and these wants are expressed as preferences for one thing over another within different contexts, where individuals are assumed to maximise satisfaction of these preferences through rational choice. The framework of what constitutes valid wants has been extended to a concept termed 'total economic value', which is conceived of as including such things as altruistic values (valuing something for the sake of another), bequest values (valuing something for the sake of future generations) and existence values (valuing knowing that something will continue to exist regardless of its human use) [see Chapter 23]. Nonetheless, these values are still considered self-regarding and founded upon the personal satisfaction that an individual gains. That this satisfaction can be traded off with any other good is taken as unquestioned and doing so is equated to being rational [see Chapter 22].

Finally, value to society is equated with the aggregate of individual values. However, when creating societal values from individual values, further assumptions are necessary to address how to aggregate within dimensions of valuation (i.e. how much does each individual count?), and across dimensions of valuation (i.e. how are different value criteria to be made commensurate?). For example, consider the appraisal of a hypothetical mining project proposed in a local area

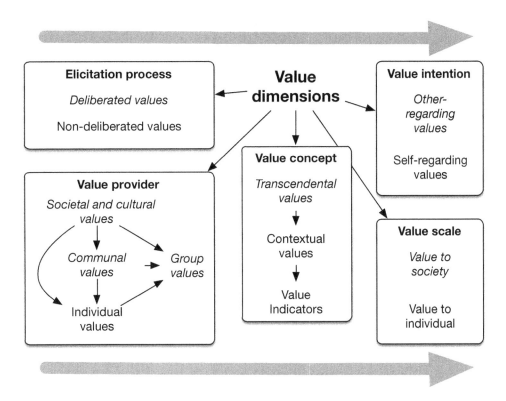

Figure 34.1 Dimensions and types of values.
Source: adapted from Kenter et al. (2015).

where traditional people have historical rights. There are many different dimensions of value that might be considered, including the internal costs and benefits of the project, livelihoods of people, cultural impact of the project and impacts on local biodiversity. The environmental and social impacts would need to be valued in monetary terms to be included in a cost-benefit analysis (CBA). In theory, this would then enable people who suffer negatively from the mining project to be compensated for environmental damage and impacts on livelihoods and culture. If the benefits outweigh the costs, after compensation, the project would be 'efficient' in the sense that it would deliver a net economic welfare value to society. Typically compensation is not actually paid but the hypothetical possibility of a welfare improvement (a potential Pareto improvement) is judged adequate by economists (called the Kaldor-Hicks criteria).

The neoclassical framework requires the idea that the ecological, social and cultural dimensions of value are substitutable, commensurable and can be fully compensated if lost [see Chapter 22]. Such compensation is assumed to be just or ethical if the result is that no one is made worse-off and someone is made better-off (the Pareto criteria). Implicitly this ethical criteria assumes that there exists an accepted mechanism for aggregating values. However, this means that the property rights of local people can be trumped by the collective net social benefit, or the poor by the rich. Moreover, unless all parties completely agree about how different dimensions of value should be traded off against each other, there can be no single conclusion as to the scenario that might deliver the highest net value to society, and the valuation question is inherently a political one.

The neoclassical perspective thus models values as individual, preference utilitarian and their aggregation as utility maximising social value. The critique posed by advocates of DMV has focused on three things:

1   people often lack clearly defined preferences, especially when dealing with complex and unfamiliar entities, concepts and scenarios;
2   equating value with satisfying individual, self-regarding preferences excludes broader shared and plural values; and
3   value to society should be established through debate rather than an arbitrary technical procedure for aggregating individual preferences.

In terms of the first issue, much of the public appears to be unsure about the meaning of environmental concepts, such as biodiversity (Spash and Hanley, 1995). Group discussion can then be a useful tool to help participants become more familiar with the environmental goods they are being asked to value (Christie et al., 2006). This concern was the main motivation for some of the first empirical DMV papers, where DMV was conceptualised as a 'market stall' whereby analogy participants would be able to 'browse' (i.e. become familiar with the goods they were asked to value) before stating their WTP (Macmillan et al., 2002). Lack of understanding and absence of preformed preferences is even more of an issue for habitats that are unfamiliar to respondents, such as many marine habitats (Spash, 2002). A recent DMV study with scuba divers and sea anglers demonstrated that even such expert participants, who were much more familiar with marine habitats than the general public, lacked well-developed preferences, but they were able to develop habitat-specific preferences through group discussion (Kenter et al., 2016c).

However, uncertainty over values goes beyond familiarity with the objects of value. Even those with expert knowledge are still faced with the complexity of social ecological systems. As a consequence, projecting trajectories of change with any kind of certainty is impossible, and scenarios harbour unknown risks. Analysis involves incomplete representation of systems and what to include/exclude requires researcher judgement. From this perspective—linking to post-normal science [Chapter 28]—the role of deliberation goes beyond merely increasing respondent familiarity with an object of study. The complexities, uncertainties and risks of the policy options need to be taken into consideration along with how they impact on values. So far, no DMV studies have attempted this, although some studies have been conducted that engage systems thinking (Kenter, 2016b; Orchard-Webb et al., 2016).

The second argument for deliberation is that values are often not individualistic, self-interested and utilitarian, and monetary values reflect a variety of motivations. For example, Desvousges et al. (1993)—studying WTP for wire-nets to reduce bird mortality in oil companies' waste oil settling ponds—found differences in what participants considered their WTP represented, including it being a consumer benefit, charitable contribution, signal for their moral or political beliefs, and a made-up number. Values are often multifaceted, particularly in situations where costs and benefits are less straightforward to grasp. Their incorporation in CBA is then problematic because they may consist of a mix of transcendental and contextual values, norms, attitudes, concerns and beliefs that are incommensurable. Thus there is a need for a different approach to valuation, where participants can discuss their transcendental values including considerations such as equity, fairness, rights and responsibilities, alongside discussions of costs, benefits and trade-offs, uncertainties and risks, in order to come to a more meaningful constitution of their contextual values. Next, these contextual values need to be translated into a weighing of the options or issues at stake. From this perspective, valuation is a shared social process of value construction (Kenter et al., 2015).

This brings us to the third argument to support deliberation, which concerns the theoretical difficulty of aggregating values. This is a problem long recognised in economics going back to Arrow's (1950) claim that there is no logically infallible way to aggregate the preferences of individuals that can lead to a single consistent ranking of policy alternatives. Economists make value laden decisions in CBA about the distribution of property rights, and who counts and how much. Economic analysis implicitly supports the rich and powerful by basing decisions on the status quo because, in monetary terms, they will have the largest WTP and the most to lose. For example, take a hypothetical CBA about two locations for a waste incineration: either near a well-off neighbourhood or social housing project. Economic analysis based on the likely impact on house prices (i.e., hedonic pricing) will favour placing it near the social housing, despite the higher population density meaning more people are affected. Adjustments to such CBA calculations can be made but this requires deliberation over what should constitute alternative assumptions and ethical criteria.

A further issue with aggregation is that self-interested preferences may have little correspondence to the good of society as a whole. As Mauss (1954: 75) states:

> The mere pursuit of individual ends is harmful to the ends and peace of the whole [...] and hence in the end to the individual.

Mauss distinguishes a group morality that exists separately from individual preferences, which Sagoff (1986) calls public or shared values. Both authors consider that the public good should be derived directly from shared values rather than through aggregated individual preferences. Sagoff points out that many individual preferences are sadistic, envious, racist, unjust, coercive or related to addictions. There are philosophical and practical problems in determining whether such preferences truly reduce well-being, or reflect genuinely divergent preferences. However, even for 'normal' consumer preferences there is no self-evident reason for taking the maximisation of preference satisfaction as equating with social good. Sagoff (1986: 303) asks:

> Why is it good in itself that a person who wants a Mercedes succeeds in getting one? Having a preference is a reason for the person who has it to try to satisfy it. Why should it be a goal of public policy, however, to satisfy that preference?

There is also a literature critiquing the basis for calling upon preferences as the defining reference point for determining environmental policy (see Spash, 2008b).

In summary, the maximisation of social welfare cannot be equated with simply allocating resources to those with the highest WTP. Instead, evaluating the public good requires a deliberative process that can go beyond a simple preference based frame of decision-making.

Deliberated preferences and democratic valuation

Depending on whether and how DMV studies aim to address the issues outlined above—familiarity and complexity, value plurality, and the need for deliberation to establish social value—they can be placed on a spectrum between two archetypal approaches. These are the approaches I term DP and DDMV. Table 34.1 provides an overview of key areas of difference between the two, which will be discussed here in some detail. So far, almost all empirical studies can be located at the DP end of the spectrum, and thus the characterisation of DDMV is mostly theoretical.

Table 34.1 Two archetypes of DMV and their properties

	DP	DDMV
Conception of deliberation	Informing preferences through group discussion	Deliberating on plural values to consider public good
Issues the approach addresses	Familiarity; Weak value plurality	Complexity and uncertainty; Strong value plurality; Value aggregation
Means of establishing value to society	Aggregation of individual utility	Deliberation and negotiation
Value concept focus	Contextual and indicators	Transcendental, contextual and indicators
Value provider	Individual in group setting	Group
Rationality assumptions	Instrumental	Communicative
Conception of representativeness	Statistical	Statistical or political
Scale of value and value indicators used	Value to individual (individual WTP or fair price)	Value to individual (fair price); Value to society (deliberated social WTP)

DP: preference economisation

DP approaches focus on providing research participants time to discuss and think about their preferences, to ease the respondent's cognitive burden, something that Lo and Spash (2012) call preference economisation. Discussions are primarily focused on nurturing value elicitation at the individual level. Values are reflected as individual WTP, analysed and aggregated to the societal scale using econometric approaches. While nominally DP, as in conventional stated preferences studies, focuses upon eliciting contextual values, nonetheless there is a weak form of value plurality. That is, in practice, discussion rarely limits itself to information, and the deliberation provides space for transcendental values and non-utilitarian perspectives. I term this weak value plurality because ultimately participants are asked to make their judgements solely on the basis of maximising their individual utility. Those who decide on their WTP in a different way are excluded from the sample as protest voters.

DDMV: moralisation and democratisation

In DDMV studies the primary focus is on providing a platform for people to deliberate directly on the public good. DDMV is a structured process where participants consider benefits and costs of different policy options alongside non-instrumental concerns, including: deontological motivations such as social norms, rights and duties, virtues such as fairness or responsibility, and narratives—stories that explain the past but may also express values on how to move forward. While this process has been termed preference moralisation (Lo and Spash, 2012), the transcendental values involved are more than just moral values because they address broader conceptions of what is important in life. These life goals relate to broad sets of shared communal, cultural and societal values, and also to the relations between environment and culture. These values are often latent, emphasising the need for explicit consideration in deliberation. Evaluation in DDMV takes place through communicative rather than instrumental rationality, where the common good is conceived of as ultimately a question of communication and negotiation.

There is yet little evidence on how this might work in practice. There has been only one DDMV study where participants directly established value to society, involving a single group of stakeholders in a deliberation on hypothetical policy options for strategic local development (Orchard-Webb et al., 2016). This demonstrated that participants can indeed set their individual utility aside in order to negotiate social WTP for policy options that reflect a range of value types and concerns. The key ground on which to evaluate whether such valuations are rational is whether participation has been inclusive—all salient perspectives and interests have been included—and outcomes are not distorted by power relationships [Chapter 14]. DDMV may lead to 'aggregation by mutual consent' (Howarth and Wilson, 2006) in the sense of value convergence, but could also lead to '"agreement to pay under value disagreement" (Lo, 2013). The purpose of DDMV in valuation is not to moralise values towards any specific moral premise, or to create an artificial divide between the 'I' and the 'We'; something criticised by Lo and Spash (2012). The aim is to create a democratic platform for evaluating options across different types of ethical and practical stances. The deliberative-democratic nature of the process is that participants decide for themselves which values and value dimensions are considered and how these are reconciled, enabling what I term strong value plurality.

Representativeness, power, institutions and legitimacy

Not just the outcomes but also the legitimacy of DMV rests on how key institutional issues are addressed. This is particularly salient given some of the challenges of deliberative methods relating managing issue of power within the deliberative process and who is represented around the table. DP approaches tend to rely on statistical representativeness, using traditional quantitative social science sampling approaches, and verifying whether a sample represents a wider population (most often the public, sometimes specific user groups, such as tourists visiting an area) through social, economic and demographic variables (e.g. age, income and education level). DDMV studies may follow this approach (e.g. a citizens' jury constituted to represent a geographically specific public to deliberate directly on the value to society of a set of policy options), but they may also undertake a valuation with a group of stakeholders.

Regardless of the approach taken, unequal social relations and institutions outside of the valuation setting will influence participants' ability to voice their opinions and concerns. There are likely to be differences in terms of social status, political influence, class, education and experience with deliberation and discussion. This can lead to participants' failing to express or adjusting their views under the pressure of power dynamics, or as a result of perceived social desirability. Questions might also be raised in relation to competence: are participants able to assess the issues at stake? While these issues can be managed to some degree through professional facilitation, they also need explicit consideration in designing the process [see Chapter 33].

In DDMV valuations on the basis of political (as opposed to statistical) representativeness, legitimacy rests on whether all relevant interests are able to participate. This means that, in addition to managing internal dynamics of the group process, there is also the need for rigorous stakeholder analysis. Here, the question may also be asked whether representation should counterbalance the type of political and institutional biases described above (Fish et al., 2013). While there are well-developed processes for stakeholder selection (see Reed et al., 2009), a challenging issue in the selection of participants is the inevitably subjective character of the process and the influence this may have on outcomes. Social power of participants (e.g. expertise or experience) is hard to fully even out by careful process design and facilitation. For example, in the study by Orchard-Webb et al. (2016) unequal power appeared to steer the discussion towards pragmatism and the status quo of the current institutional environment. This could be addressed by under-representing the powerful, or developing a more explicit process for transformative social ecological change, or one might simply accept that, when following accepted stakeholder selection processes, democratic valuation processes are likely to reflect the status quo.

Types of value indicators

As shown in Table 34.2, for both DP and DDMV, the outcome of the DMV process is some kind of monetary value indicator. Spash (2007) distinguished these as 'payment terms' across two dimensions: the value provider (individual vs. group) and scale (individual vs. societal). This schematic thus suggests four main types of monetary value indicator: (i) a deliberated individual WTP, (ii) a 'fair price', and a deliberated social WTP (i.e. value to society) determined by either (iii) individuals or (iv) the group.

DP studies have almost exclusively used individual WTP. DDMV is conceived of as establishing a pre-aggregated value to society, and thus will most likely focus on social WTP established on a group basis. What this means in practice is that participants deliberate on how much they think society should spend on one thing over another, by deciding how much of a budget should be allocated to the provisioning of different public goods through various policy options. A fair price payment term asks participants about what they think both others and themselves should pay. There have been a small number of fair price studies, with group value providers (Kenter, 2016b; Kenter et al., 2011, 2016c) as conceived in the original schematic by Spash (2007), or with individually expressed fair prices (Szabó, 2011). These can be placed in the middle of the DP–DDMV spectrum, because asking about what people should pay by definition explicitly brings out transcendental values (characteristic of DDMV). However, the individual scale of fair prices does not address questions around aggregation (e.g. Should everyone pay a fair price or are some people exempt? Should the fair price be adjusted for those who have a higher income?). All the fair price studies so far have used econometric means of analysis based on utility models (characteristic of DP).

Table 34.2 Types of value indicators

		Scale of value	
		Individual	*Society*
Value provider	*Individual in group setting*	Individual WTP/WTA: interpreted as informed exchange price or charitable contribution (e.g., Lienhoop and Völker 2016) Fair price (e.g. Szabó 2011)	Deliberated social WTP/WTA; no empirical studies
	Group (vote or consensus)	Fair price (e.g. Kenter et al., 2011)	Deliberated group social WTP/WTA (e.g. Orchard-Webb et al., 2016)

Notes: WTA = willingness to accept compensation; WTP = willingess to pay.
Source: adapted with modifications from Spash (2007, 2008a).

Future directions

DMV has been advocated by ecological economists in recognition of value plurality, the aggregation problem, and the complexity and uncertainty associated with understanding, managing and governing social ecological systems. These are crucial issues that define social ecological economics and differentiate it from environmental economic approaches; especially in linking the natural and social worlds. While there has been substantial theorising around DMV, there have been only a limited number of empirical studies, almost all DP. These have demonstrated that deliberation can be an effective tool to (in)form peoples' preferences, and make their WTP more robust. Most are small-scale studies, but there has also been research showing that deliberation can be effective with larger sample sizes (Torres et al., 2012; Kenter et al., 2011). A key issue for future DP research is how to resolve the tension inherent in its weak plurality, i.e. between the potential for plurality within deliberation and the utilitarian constraints around what value terms are acceptable and how values should be aggregated.

DDMV uses deliberation directly to establish aggregate values, where participants, rather than the analyst, set the terms of what is socially optimal. However, there is an almost complete lack of empirical studies that demonstrate how this is done. Notably, the non-monetary, analytical-deliberative method that is perhaps most similar to DMV, social/participatory multi-criteria analysis [Chapter 30], has faced fundamentally the same issues around value aggregation, and despite having a much broader base of past application, few studies have addressed the issue. Ultimately, for both DDMV and DP, procedures are needed for deliberating on not just values but also the rules of the game in terms of how to aggregate values (Kenter et al., 2016b).

More broadly, the formats for different types of DP and DDMV approaches are widely divergent, including workshops, structured and unstructured focus groups and citizens' juries. Within the DP arena, the market stall format has been used in the United Kingdom, Iceland and Germany, but this only focuses on informing values, largely ignoring transcendental values (Lienhoop and Völker, 2016). These have been more explicitly recognised by the deliberative value formation model (Kenter et al., 2016a) used to underpin some recent studies. A relevant question is how different process designs, protocols and modes of facilitation impact on outcomes. In mainstreaming DMV for use in decision-making, standardised approaches that also pay attention to such issues as power relations, representation and inclusivity, are essential.

Concluding remarks

DMV is a method proposed to address a substantial number of challenges to monetary valuation, but there is tension between theoretical concerns that relate to core issues in social ecological economics and the empirical work on DMV. Rather than trying to perfectly rhyme theory and practice, this tension could be a creative one. DMV could be conceived as a reflection of democratic decision-making with its constant conflicts between utilitarianism and other ethical and political concerns, and questions such as how to aggregate the values of different stakeholders. Policy-making can be seen as a form of DMV through allocation of budgets, which inevitably involves balancing value for money with deliberation over what constitutes the public good, involving different types of ethical and political questions, negotiation and compromise, and reconciling different dimensions of value. Thus DMV, as an economic method, sits between research and politics. This is the fruitful post-normal, transdisciplinary space more broadly occupied by social ecological economics, with its recognition that all research has value connotations. Through further empirical research, innovative process design, and practical protocols, DMV can become an effective tool for democratising valuation and achieving more sustainable and equitable decisions.

Key further readings cited

Kenter, J.O., Reed, M., Fazey, I. (2016). The Deliberative Value Formation model. *Ecosystem Services* 21(October), 208–217.

Kenter, J.O., O'Brien, L., Hockley, N., Ravenscroft, N., Fazey, I., Irvine, K.N., Reed, M.S., Christie, M., Brady, E., Bryce, R., Church, A., Cooper, N., Davies, A., Evely, A., Everard, M., Fish, R., Fisher, J.A., Jobstvogt, N., Molloy, C., Orchard-Webb, J., Ranger, S., Ryan, M., Watson, V., Williams, S. (2015). What are shared and social values of ecosystems? *Ecological Economics* 111, 86–99.

Lo, A.Y., Spash, C.L. (2012). Deliberative monetary valuation: in search of a democratic and value plural approach to environmental policy. *Journal of Economic Surveys* 27(4), 768–789.

Orchard-Webb, J., Kenter, J.O., Bryce, R., Church, A. (2016). Deliberative Democratic Monetary Valuation to implement the Ecosystems Approach. *Ecosystem Services.* 21(October), 308–318.

Other literature cited

Arrow, K. (1950). A difficulty in the concept of social welfare. *Journal of Political Economy* 58(4), 328–346.

Christie, M., Hanley, N., Warren, J., Murphy, K., Wright, R., Hyde, T. (2006). Valuing the diversity of biodiversity. *Ecological Econonomic* 58(2), 304–317.

Desvousges, W.H., Johnson, F.R., Dunford, R.W., Hudson, S.P., Wilson, K.N. (1993). Measuring natural resource damages with contingent valuation: tests of validity and reliability, in: Hausman, J.A. (ed.), *Contingent Valuation: a Critical Assessment* (pp. 91–164) New York: North Holland Press.

Fish, R., Winter, M., Oliver, D., Chadwick, D., Hodgson, C., Heathwaite, A. (2014). Employing the citizens' jury technique to elicit reasoned public judgments about environmental risk: insights from an inquiry into the governance of microbial water pollution. *Journal of Environmental Planning and Management* 57(2), 233–253.

Howarth, R.B., Wilson, M.A. (2006). A theoretical approach to deliberative valuation: Aggregation by mutual consent. *Land Economics* 82, 1–16.

Kenter, J.O. (2016a). Deliberative and non-monetary valuation, in: Potschin, M., Haines-Young, R., Fish, R., Turner, R.K. (eds.), *Routledge Handbook of Ecosystem Services*. London: Routledge.

Kenter, J.O. (2016b). Integrating deliberative choice experiments, systems modelling and participatory mapping to assess shared values of ecosystem services. *Ecosystem Services* 21(October), 291–307.

Kenter, J.O., Raymond, C., Christie, Bryce, R., Cooper, N.M., Hockley, N., Irvine, K.N., O'Brien, L., Orchard-Webb, J., Ravenscroft, N., Tett, P., Watson, V. (2016b). Shared values and deliberative valuation: Future directions. *Ecosystem Services* 21(October), 358–371.

Kenter, J.O., Hyde, T., Christie, M., Fazey, I. (2011). The importance of deliberation in valuing ecosystem services in developing countries—Evidence from the Solomon Islands. *Global Environmental Change* 21(2), 505–521.

Kenter, J.O., Jobstvogt, N., Watson, V., Irvine, K., Christie, M., Bryce, R. (2016a). The impact of information, value deliberation and group-based decision-making on values for ecosystem services: integrating deliberative monetary valuation and storytelling. *Ecosystem Services* 21(October), 270–290.

Lienhoop, N., Völker, M. (2016). Preference refinement in deliberative choice experiments for ecosystem service valuation. *Land Economics* 92(3), 555–577.

Lo, A.Y. (2013). Agreeing to pay under value disagreement: Reconceptualizing preference transformation in terms of pluralism with evidence from small-group deliberations on climate change. *Ecological Economics* 87(March), 84–94.

Macmillan, D.C., Philip, L., Hanley, N., Alvarez Farizo, B. (2002). Valuing the non-market benefits of wild goose conservation: A comparison of interview and group-based approaches. *Ecological Economics* 43(1), 49–59.

Mauss, M. (1954). *The gift: forms and functions of exchange in archaic societies.* 2000 edition, New York: W.W. Norton & Company.

Reed, M.S., Graves, A., Dandy, N., Posthumus, H., Hubacek, K., Morris, J., Prell, C., Quinn, C.H., Stringer, L.C. (2009). Who's in and why? A typology of stakeholder analysis methods for natural resource management. *Journal of Environmental Management* 90(5), 1933–1949.

Sagoff, M. (1986). Values and preferences. *Ethics* 96(2), 301–316.

Spash, C.L. (2002). Informing and forming preferences in environmental valuation: Coral reef biodiversity. *Journal of Economic Psychology* 23(5), 665–687.

Spash, C.L. (2007). Deliberative monetary valuation (DMV): Issues in combining economic and political processes to value environmental change. *Ecological Economics* 63(4), 690–699.

Spash, C.L. (2008a). Deliberative monetary valuation and the evidence for a new value theory. *Land Economics* 84(3), 469–488.

Spash, C.L. (2008b). How much is that ecosystem in the window? The one with the bio-diverse trail. *Environmental Values* 17(2), 259–284.

Spash, C.L., Hanley, N. (1995). Preferences, information and biodiversity preservation. *Ecological Economics* 12(3), 191–208.

Szabó, Z. (2011). Reducing protest responses by deliberative monetary valuation: Improving the validity of biodiversity valuation. *Ecological Economics* 72(December), 37–44.

Torres, A.B., MacMillan, D.C., Skutsch, M., Lovett, J.C. (2012). The valuation of forest carbon services by Mexican citizens: The case of Guadalajara city and La Primavera biosphere reserve. *Regional Environmental Change* 13(3), 661–680.

35

PARTICIPATORY MODELLING IN ECOLOGICAL ECONOMICS

Lessons from practice

Nuno Videira, Paula Antunes and Rui Santos

Introduction

Participatory modelling approaches build on deliberative principles, which have been defended by social ecological economists as a way to open up debates in the science policy interface and engage societal actors in learning and knowledge co-creation processes. Over the past decade, deliberative methods have been referred to as value articulating institutions [Chapter 3], offering alternative rule structures to standard economic appraisal techniques by accounting for multiple values, uncertainty in information and asymmetries between individuals (Antunes et al., 2009; Vatn, 2009). The rationale for deliberative methods that engage extended peer communities in planning and assessment processes also builds on the critique of expert determined decisions made by post-normal science [Chapter 28]. Participatory approaches contribute to achieving three essential goals (De Marchi and Ravetz, 2001):

1   widening the framings of policy issues by including representation of multiple sectors of society;
2   delivering a decision-making mode which is responsive to democratic principles and encourages commitment throughout the several stages of the policy-making cycle; and
3   improving the quality of decisions by accommodating multiple perspectives that expand the scope of problem definition, as well as design and selection of alternative solutions.

Calls for active democracy in environmental and sustainability decision-making have increased interest in the development and testing of different participatory methods [Chapter 33]. Participatory modelling contributes a structured deliberation, involving stakeholder groups in problem scoping activities and the sustainability assessment of alternative policy pathways.

   In this chapter we present the fundamentals of participatory system dynamics modelling (PSDM) and a set of applications in ecological economics. We start by defining the main features of this approach and providing an overview of the main stages in a generic participatory modelling process. Subsequently, we provide an overview of case studies to derive a set of lessons from practice in six different projects covering six distinct topics: maritime policies, sustainable food consumption, degrowth, river basin governance, coastal zone management and protected areas management. Finally, we advance future directions for the development of the method.

Defining features of PSDM

We define participatory modelling broadly as any deliberative approach aiming to engage a group of participants in a bottom-up model building process, or in a collaborative experience where previously built models are used for the purpose of addressing a complex issue. Although the term participatory modelling is found in the literature referring to a suite of modelling methods and tools (Voinov and Bousquet, 2010)—Bayesian networks, fuzzy cognitive mapping, agent-based modelling—our focus here will be on participatory modelling approaches based on the system dynamics method.

System dynamics, which was developed in the 1960s by Jay Forrester, is grounded in the theory of non-linear dynamics and feedback control. It constitutes a problem-oriented method for understanding complex issues that are dynamic (i.e., which can be expressed in terms of behaviour of relevant variables over time) and exhibit feedback (i.e., a sequence of causes and effects between variables defining closed loops). Recognising that ecological, economic and social systems form interconnected sets of feedback loops, the PSDM approach focuses on building models that capture the feedback structure responsible for a problematic behaviour over time, and subsequently uses those models to experiment with alternative management policies (Richardson and Pugh, 1981).

The two main tools for building system dynamics models are Causal Loop Diagrams (CLDs) and Stock-and-Flow Diagrams (SFDs). CLDs are drawings of a system that map it by representing names of relevant variables and arrows depicting the cause–effect relationships and feedback loops established between them. In SFDs the structure of the model is visually represented in terms of stocks, flows and auxiliary variables or parameters that are formalised with sets of integral equations. With the support of user-friendly software packages such as STELLA (http://www.iseesystems.com), POWERSIM (http://www.powersim.com), or VENSIM (http://vensim.com), SFDs may be quantified and operationalised to simulate model behaviour over a chosen time horizon.

System dynamics has been used for a long time in ecological economics, providing a synthesis framework in problem-solving processes (Farley et al., 2005) and powerful tools for scenario based analysis. More recently, with stakeholder engagement becoming widespread and indispensable to environmental assessment and modelling efforts (Voinov and Bousquet, 2010), PSDM has been applied to several topics, such as nature and biodiversity conservation, sustainable consumption, sustainable river basin governance and degrowth (e.g. Antunes et al., 2006; Sedlacko et al., 2014; van den Belt, 2004; Videira et al., 2009, 2014). As a systems science approach, PSDM brings a powerful contribution to address many features of complex human–nature interrelationships, while enabling the kind of transdisciplinary and integrated analyses defended in ecological economics. In Table 35.1 we specify the characteristics of PSDM matching fundamental principles of the ecological economics approach. On one hand, the participatory nature of the method meets several problem-solving requirements arising from the social and ecological characteristics of environmental issues (van den Hove, 2000). This involves the adoption of a transdisciplinary approach to tackle uncertainties, diffused responsibilities and conflicts of interest among stakeholders. On the other hand, the system dynamics method provides a modelling language that explicitly accounts for the complexity, non-linearities and delays underpinning social ecological systems (Sterman, 2012). System dynamics models also allow the integration of plural metrics, thus accepting multiple standards of valuation (Victor, 2015).

System dynamics approaches for modelling with stakeholders and clients in public or private organisations have evolved since the second half of the 1970s (Andersen et al., 2007). Currently, there are several variants of participatory system dynamics, including group model building

Table 35.1 Why is PSDM suitable for environmental and sustainability issues?

Ecological economics argues for…	PSDM contributes by…
Transdisciplinarity for analysis of interactions between economic, social and ecological systems	Integrating plural perspectives through involvement of participants from multiple stakeholder groups, with different academic and practice backgrounds, in the construction of models representing a holistic and shared view of a dynamic problem.
Dealing with uncertainty of environmental phenomena	Addressing uncertainty sources and measurement, by, for instance, designing and testing alternative scenarios in a participatory setting, implementing peer-reviewed quality assurance protocols, performing sensitivity analysis and model validation tests.
Recognition of complexity, non-linearity and dynamic nature of social ecological systems	Supporting the identification of tight couplings and feedback processes typical of ecological-economic systems. Model simulation allows identification of unintended consequences and counterintuitive behaviour, thus generating impact through surprise, and dealing with the root causes of policy resistance arising from linear worldviews. Finding the structures that create path dependence is also a way to address system lock-ins and decisions leading to irreversible effects.
Looking out for long-term impacts of issues with unequal social, ecological, economic consequences and causing political controversies	Adopting a long-term perspective through simulation. Explicitly consideration of time delays is a key tenet of the method.
Recognition of incommensurability of values	Accepting plural metrics (e.g., monetary and biophysical), providing a tool for synthesis of a wide range of data and multiple standards of valuation.

(Richardson and Anderson, 1995; Vennix, 1996), mediated modelling (van den Belt, 2004) and participatory systems mapping (Sedlacko et al., 2014; Videira et al., 2012). The differences between the different typologies are often subtle and have been detailed by several authors, such as Voinov and Bousquet (2010). Instead we focus here on the set of features held in common in order to profile the characteristics of a typical PSDM project. There are three main aspects:

1   A stakeholder analysis is performed to identify and select the participants. The selection procedures are usually based on achieving a broad representation of multiple perspectives and interested parties (rather than a representative or random sample of an affected population). This aims to reveal a richer understanding of the feedback processes underlying the problem being studied.

2   Modelling workshops are the main platform for deliberation. Participants are invited to facilitated sessions where they are guided through a collaborative model building process. They may be actively involved in one or several tasks of the system dynamics approach, including the conceptualisation of the model's structure (e.g., suggesting variables and causal links), the specification of the model (e.g., discussing mathematical representation of variables) and the analysis of alternative policy solutions (e.g., designing or testing model-based scenarios). Antunes et al. (2015) describe these different modes of application at different stages of the modelling process.

3   The tools used to facilitate deliberation. Eliciting stakeholders' knowledge and perceptions involves the translation of participants' mental models into a common language through the use of visually oriented modelling techniques. This is essentially promoted through system dynamics qualitative and quantitative modelling tools, such as CLDs and SFDs, respectively. Mediated modelling is typically focused on the construction of SFDs and computer simulation models, participatory systems mapping focuses on the collaborative development of CLDs, while group model building uses both tools.

The use of these system dynamics tools is critical in differentiating PSDM approaches from other participatory methods, since they structure the deliberative process and the type of outputs to be delivered (Kallis et al., 2006). Furthermore, the collaborative model building exercise usually pays as much attention to the participatory process as to the modelling outputs. This means aiming to produce useful models that capture the feedback structure and dynamic behaviour of the problematic issues being studied and, at the same time, envisaging co-production of knowledge, improved communication among participants, and a broad commitment for action and policy implementation.

PSDM as a three-stage process

A generic participatory modelling project typically develops in three stages (Antunes et al., 2006; van den Belt, 2004; Videira et al., 2011).

Stage 1: preparation

Participatory modelling projects have been promoted by research institutes, governmental agencies, local sponsors, stakeholder advisory groups, and consortia with a combination of representatives from these organisations. There are a number of skills and roles that need to be fulfilled (Richardson and Anderson, 1995), and in particular, the facilitator and modeller roles are especially critical. The facilitator is required to conduct group discussions during the modelling workshops, while modellers with system dynamics skills are needed to guide the process of model construction. These two roles may be performed by the same person, whom van den Belt (2004) describes as the mediating modeller, or by different members of the modelling team. In anticipation of the modelling workshops, preliminary questionnaires or interviews with participants are very useful to collect individual perceptions on the problem under study, present the modelling objectives and process, and build rapport with participants (van den Belt, 2004; Vennix, 1996).

Stage 2: workshops

The outline of participatory modelling workshops is very flexible and may be adjusted to several criteria, including the type of tools being used, the size of the participant group, the desired level of stakeholder involvement in the model building process, and the resources available to the steering group. Several cases have been described in the literature where this participatory method has been conducted with 5–12 participants in small group sessions and 40–70 participants in plenary sessions (Kallis et al., 2006). A one-day workshop may allow the development of a CLD with a stakeholder group. However, several days are required where the aim is to involve participants more intensively in the construction of computer simulation models (Kallis et al., 2006; Sedlacko et al., 2014; van den Belt, 2004; Videira et al., 2011). When a sequence of multiple workshops is planned, modellers usually perform several supporting tasks in-between (Stave, 2002), which entail the preparation of workbooks to report on changes made in the model (Vennix, 1996), and collecting historical data on model variables, as well as verification and validation tests to build confidence in the model.

Stage 3: follow-up and evaluation

The follow-up of participatory modelling workshops involves dissemination, evaluation and implementation activities. Dissemination deals with reporting the process and final results back to participants and a larger audience. In some cases, training of stakeholders in the autonomous use of the models is also promoted (van den Belt, 2004). Evaluation of outputs and outcomes of the participatory modelling process is also a critical task, performed through observations, questionnaires or post-workshop interviews with participants. A systematic evaluation is recommended shortly after the workshops to assess effects at three levels (Rouwette et al., 2002; van den Belt, 2004; Videira et al., 2009). First, the methodological level assesses if the models are useful and how well the method performed as a participatory process. Second, the individual level evaluates participants' reaction to the process and learning effects. Third, the group level collects perceptions on whether a shared view of the problem was developed and if the process improved communication among participants. A fourth dimension of analysis may be added, which deals with measurement of effects at the organisational level. This entails monitoring the mid- and long-term impacts arising from the implementation of modelling results in practice, and measuring changes in procedures and rules of stakeholder's organisations, as a consequence of the lessons learned throughout the PSDM process.

Lessons from the field: an overview of PSDM applications

PSDM has been applied to a wide range of environmental and sustainability topics. Beall and Ford (2010) compared nine participatory modelling case studies, dealing with diverse environmental issues (e.g., biodiversity protection, sustainable fisheries, water management), to extract patterns in the application of the method. They discuss participatory modelling in terms of a spectrum with contrasting profiles at the extremes. On one end of the spectrum, applications have addressed well-defined problems using computer simulations to study alternative management policies. This required large sets of empirical quantitative data and a model built by experts with input from participants in the workshops. At the opposite extreme, studies have been conducted where the problem was poorly defined and the process assisted primarily in problem scoping, with stakeholders contributing directly to mapping of relevant variables and feedback loops.

Next, we provide a reflection on lessons learned from six case studies selected from research projects in which we have collaborated. The lessons reflect on the trends presented by Beall and Ford (2010) and bring forth additional insights. The case studies involved are:

- Study 1: Sustainability assessment of maritime policies in Portugal (Videira et al. 2012);
- Study 2: Sustainable food consumption and conflicts with economic growth (Sedlacko et al., 2014; Videira et al., 2013);
- Study 3: Mapping degrowth pathways (Videira et al., 2014);
- Study 4: River basin management in the Baixo Guadiana (Videira et al., 2009);
- Study 5: Coastal zone management in Ria Formosa (van den Belt, 2004);
- Study 6: Management of the Ria Formosa Natural Park (Videira et al., 2003).

Lesson 1: purpose, resources and problem definition influence the selection of modelling tools and approach

Case studies 1–3 followed a participatory systems mapping approach with the use of CLDs as the modelling tools facilitating deliberation. A participatory systems mapping approach seems to be most useful in the early stages of policy formulation and assessment, or in situations where there is only a sketchy understanding of the problem. CLDs offer a promising entry point, where the problem being studied is poorly defined and ill-structured, by facilitating collective understanding and scoping of the underlying feedback structure. This approach is also useful when there are limited resources and time available, since a draft CLD can be created in sessions of 1.5 to 4.0 hours. This is evidenced by case studies 1–3, where participants played an active role in the systems mapping process. Following a brief initial explanation on the relatively straightforward notation of the method, those cases unfolded in such a way that facilitators encouraged participants to actively contribute to the construction of diagrams, first identifying the problem variables, then drawing the problem causes and consequences, and subsequently the possible feedback loops (Vennix, 1996). The resulting CLDs connected the piecemeal perceptions of individual participants and delimited the factors and feedback mechanisms that were deemed as more important for describing the problem.

The main limitation of qualitative models (CLDs) is that they cannot simulate the dynamic behaviour of the problem and compare alternative policy scenarios. If this is the purpose, and resources are available, the process may proceed to the collaborative construction of SFDs and computer simulations. That was the approach followed in case study 4, while scoping river basin management issues in the Baixo Guadiana. On the other hand, cases 5 and 6 skipped the CLD construction step and promoted conceptualisation of the problem through SFDs. Participants helped in delimiting the problem to be modelled directly through the identification of stocks and flows with the support of system dynamics software. This tool was chosen *a priori* since the purpose was to build scoping simulation models for testing 'what if…?' policy scenarios. The fact that case studies 4–6 were developed at the local scale, and addressed less abstract or aggregated issues than cases 1–3, also goes along with the deployment of quantitative modelling tools.

Lesson 2: managing stakeholders' involvement is a tough job… but someone's got to do it

A critical mass of participants for the group modelling exercises was achieved in all the case studies. This required a significant time investment from the research teams for stakeholder selection, invitation and communication. Stave (2002) refers to this as a critical challenge when applying PSDM to environmental and sustainability issues. She argues that in these situations, stakeholders are much more "loosely bound" (2002: 160) to the process as opposed to those group model building applications where participants belong to the same organisation. Furthermore, since most participants are volunteers, ensuring continuous engagement is difficult (Stave, 2002). We found this to be particularly relevant in cases 4–6, where a sequence of multiple events changed group composition from workshop to workshop. To avoid these fluctuations from limiting the potential for participants' involvement in the model building process, several strategies have been deployed. For example, reporting results from each workshop and keeping a permanent communication channel with participants, both by e-mail and phone, worked well and increased the turnout in the final workshops after a decline in intermediate sessions. Attracting particular stakeholder groups, such as civil servants and politicians, may be difficult. That was especially observed in case 2, where modelling sessions were integrated into multinational knowledge brokerage events, which required a dedicated recruiting of international participants.

Several factors are expected to play an influence in the recruitment challenge. First, if the modelling process addresses a well-defined, locally relevant, or 'urgent' policy issue, the chances for securing involvement of participants are higher (case study 6). Second, we found that preliminary face-to-face interviews (cases 1, 4–6) are valuable tools to build rapport with participants before the workshops, fostering their interest and clarifying the purpose and proceedings of the process. Third, the more institutionalised the participatory process is, in terms of being backed up by a legal mandate or aiming to deliver agency or government goals, the more chance there is of engaging stakeholders with higher decision-making responsibility throughout the entire PSDM experience (Kallis et al., 2006).

Lesson 3: modelling workshops are a groundswell for collaborative learning

Participant evaluation of the six cases generally provided very positive feedback with respect to the method, process and aiding participant understanding of the modelled issues. The PSDM tools offered a powerful, transparent, and insightful language for deliberation during the workshops, and all cases provided rich evidence of learning outcomes. For example, in the systems mapping workshops (cases 1–4), the construction of CLDs offered a creative platform for exchanging participants' perceptions and co-producing knowledge regarding the causal structure of the problem. The achievement of systemic insights is a function of the method's focus on closed-loop thinking, which enables the collective discovery of previously unnoticed interrelationships, showing how parts of the system are connected and how changes in one variable ripple towards other parts and return (i.e., feedback loops). The potential learning outcomes arising from the use of SFD tools are even stronger, since model simulations show how the system responds to policy levers and allow a direct comparison of trade-offs among alternative options. This was verified in case studies 4–6, where the majority of participants agreed that the participatory process showed more sides to the problem than they originally thought, and that they could better interrelate different system components.

The modelling tools helped 'level the playing field' by allowing all participants to contribute to the model building process, regardless of their background and capacity to influence decisions. All the case studies mixed small group sessions with plenary debates, which worked well to avoid discussions being controlled by stakeholders with better oral skills and a propensity for public interventions. The modelling tools structured deliberations around the process of model construction, and at the same time, these directed possible initial disagreements towards an open conversation about what the policy outcomes should be (Stave, 2002). System dynamics models allow representing and simulating competing views on the problem and its solutions. For example, in case study 4, water quality issues were mapped together with nature conservation conflicts in the same CLD, accommodating different perspectives of stakeholder groups on what were the main river basin issues. Moreover, quantitative tools, cases 4–6, allow different simulation experiments in the same model, which may be regarded as a way to articulate different values and stakeholder perceptions on what the policy scenarios should be and how alternative policies impact on key system indicators.

Lesson 4: disseminate and integrate; the process does not end with the modelling outputs

In case study 1, the CLDs were the point of departure for a visioning workshop where stakeholders selected variables from each system map to define objectives, quantified targets and a desired vision for the future of marine and coastal systems. In case study 2, participants of the second knowledge-brokerage event did not make substantial changes to the CLDs from the first workshop. Instead, they used the previously developed system maps as a platform to guide additional deliberation on research gaps, job effects and policy instruments related with sustainability issues in food chains and reduction of food waste. Showing yet another possibility, emblematic degrowth proposals (e.g., work sharing, resource sanctuaries) depicted in the system maps of case study 3 were subsequently analysed with a cross-impact matrix to evaluate synergies and outline causal pathways for implementation. These experiences indicate that there are several options for exploring outputs from systems mapping workshops, which also underlines the importance of multi-method approaches wherein participatory modelling is integrated with other assessment tools in broader deliberative decision-making processes.

Another technique that we found useful in providing a synthesis of results is the leverage points framework developed by Meadows (1999). Leverage points are "places in complex systems where a small shift in one thing can produce big changes in everything" (Meadows, 1999). We used this concept in case studies 1, 3 and 4 by asking participants to vote on variables that they perceived as fundamental levers in the system. At the end of the process, the most voted for places for intervention provide instant takeaway messages, which may be explored by participants in further research or in the development of action plans.

Finally, when simulation models are built, a user-friendly interface should be developed to distribute the final output to participants and encourage them to further experiment with the model. In case study 6 an interactive learning environment was created for users to explore the Ria Formosa Natural Park model. The interface allowed an easy navigation through the model's stock-and-flow structure and dynamic behaviour graphs, and it also offered a control panel for running alternative management scenarios for the protected area.

Future directions

One open topic that remains to be fully understood is the effect of institutionalising PSDM within existing policy-making structures. When a participatory modelling process is initiated and maintained by governmental institutions, does this increase the effectiveness of the method with respect to organisational impacts? Does institutional responsibility strengthen the engagement of stakeholders throughout the process? Answers to these questions, which could only be hypothesised in the described case studies, would shed light on the conditions for further uptake and expansion of the method.

On a related topic, PSDM researchers have increasingly paid attention to the investigation of long-term effects of these processes. On one hand, establishing a reference control system to measure outcomes is difficult and additionality of results hard to verify—had the participatory modelling process not been implemented. On the other hand, evaluating lasting effects is often limited by the fact that research programmes neglect funding for long-term monitoring and evaluation activities. All parties involved need to commit time and energy. These are necessary to get the most out of workshop deliberations and, after the modelling process ends, for implementing the lessons learned, which requires tackling policy resistance and avoiding short-term fixes.

Finally, since every method has its own biases and limitations, multi-method approaches might bring the potential for combining tools and improve deliberative processes. As shown in some of the applications mentioned in this chapter, a PSDM process may be linked, for example, with scenario and visioning workshops for creative exploration of desired futures, with cross-impact analysis tools as a means to systematise stakeholder judgements and gain insights into interdependencies between system variables, or with multiple criteria analysis methods [Chapters 30, 31] to support appraisal of alternatives simulated with the system dynamics model.

Concluding remarks

PSDM has developed as a promising method to facilitate the engagement of stakeholders in environmental and sustainability decision processes. It offers a platform for structured deliberation, involving stakeholder groups in problem conceptualisation, policy formulation and assessment. The lessons presented in this chapter build on the experience from over 15 years of practice, showing how PSDM places the participatory exercise within a collaborative learning environment, expanding problem views, promoting consensus and extending multi-stakeholder dialogues on the dynamic complexities arising in social ecological systems.

Key further readings cited

Antunes, P., Stave, K., Videira, N., Santos, R. (2015). Using participatory system dynamics in environmental and sustainability dialogues. In M. Ruth (ed.), *Handbook of Research Methods and Applications in Environmental Studies* (pp. 346 374). Cheltenham, UK: Edward Elgar Publishing.

Sedlacko, M., Martinuzzi, A., Røpke, I., Videira, N., Antunes, P. (2014). Participatory systems mapping for sustainable consumption: Discussion of a method promoting systemic insights. *Ecological Economics* 106, 33–43.

van den Belt, M. (2004). *Mediated Modeling: A System Dynamics Approach to Environmental Consensus Building*. Washington DC: Island Press.

Vennix, J. (1996). *Group Model-Building: Facilitating Team Learning Using System Dynamics*. Chichester: John Wiley & Sons.

Videira, N., Antunes, P., Santos, R. (2009). Scoping river basin management issues with participatory modelling: The Baixo Guadiana experience. *Ecological Economics* 68(4), 965–978.

Other literature cited

Andersen, D., Vennix, J., Richardson, G., Rouwette, E. (2007). Group model building: problem structuring, policy simulation and decision support. *Journal of the Operational Research Society* 58(5), 691–694.

Antunes, P., Kallis, C., Videira, N., Santos, R. (2009). Participation and evaluation for sustainable river basin governance. *Ecological Economics* 68(4), 931–939.

Antunes, P., Santos, R., Videira, N. (2006). Participatory decision making for sustainable development: The use of mediated modelling techniques. *Land Use Policy*, 23(1), 44–52.

Beall, A.M., Ford, A. (2010). Reports from the field: assessing the art and science of participatory environmental modelling. *International Journal of Information Systems and Social Change* 1(2), 72–89.

De Marchi, B., Ravetz, J.R. (2001). *Participatory approaches to environmental policy*. EVE-Concerted Action, Policy Research Brief Number 10. Cambridge: Cambridge Research for the Environment.

Farley, J., Erickson, J., Daly, H. (2005). *Ecological Economics. A workbook for problem-based learning*. Washington DC: Island Press.

Kallis, G., Videira, N., Antunes, P., Guimarães Pereira, A., Spash, C.L., Coccossis, H., Corral Quintana, S., del Moral, L., Hatzilacou, D., Lobo, G., Mexa, A., Paneque, P., Pedregal, B., Santos, R. (2006). Participatory methods for water resources planning and governance. *Environment and Planning C: Government and Policy* 24(2), 215–234.

Meadows, D.H. (1999). *Leverage Points: Places to Intervene in a System*. Hartland: The Sustainability Institute.

Richardson, G., Anderson, D. (1995). Teamwork in group model-building. *System Dynamics Review* 11(2), 131–137.

Richardson, G., Pugh, A. (1981). *Introduction to System Dynamics Modeling with Dynamo*. Portland: Productivity Press.

Rouwette, E., Vennix, J., Mullekom, T. (2002). Group model building effectiveness: a review of assessment studies. *System Dynamics Review* 18(1), 5–45.

Stave, K. (2002). Using system dynamics to improve public participation in environmental decisions. *System Dynamics Review* 18(2), 139–167.

Sterman, J.D. (2012). Sustaining Sustainability: Creating a Systems Science in a Fragmented Academy and Polarized World. In M.P. Weinstein and R.E. Turner (eds.) *Sustainability Science: The Emerging Paradigm 21 and the Urban Environment* (pp. 21–58). New York: Springer.

van den Hove, S. (2000). Participatory approaches to environmental policy-making: the European Commission Climate Policy Process as a case study. *Ecological Economics* 33(3), 457–472.

Vatn, A. (2009). An institutional analysis of methods for environmental appraisal. *Ecological Economics* 68(8–9), 2207–2215.

Victor, P. (2015). Ecological economics: A personal journey. *Ecological Economics* 109(January), 93–100.

Videira, N., Antunes, P., Santos, R., Gamito, S. (2003). Participatory modeling in environmental decision-making: the ria Formosa natural park case study. *Journal of Environmental Assessment, Policy and Management* 5(3), 421–447.

Videira, N., Lopes, R., Antunes, P., Santos, R. (2012). Mapping maritime sustainability issues with participatory modelling. *Systems Research and Behavioural Science* 29(6), 596–619.

Videira, N., Rubik, F., Sedlacko, M., Antunes, P., Santos, R., Müller, R. (2013). *Shaping the future of Sustainable Food Consumption: Challenges and opportunities for policy and science integration*. Background paper to the RESPONDER 2nd Multinational Knowledge Brokerage Event on Sustainable Food, Lisbon, 18–19 April 2013.

Videira, N., Schneider, F., Sekulova, F., Kallis, G. (2014). Improving understanding on degrowth pathways: An exploratory study using collaborative causal models. *Futures* 55(January), 58–77.

Videira, N., van den Belt, M., Antunes, P., Santos, R., Boumans, R. (2011). Integrated modeling of coastal and estuarine ecosystem services. In E. Wolanski and D.S. McLusky (eds), *Treatise on Estuarine and Coastal Science* (pp. 79–108, vol. 12). Waltham, MA: Academic Press.

Voinov, A, Bousquet, F. (2010). Modelling with stakeholders. *Environmental Modelling & Software* 25(11), 1268–1281.

36

INPUT-OUTPUT ANALYSIS

Jon D. Erickson and Melinda Kane

Introduction

A consistent concern of ecological economics has been the biophysical and institutional foundations of the economy. During the formalisation of the field, scholars such as Daly (1968), Victor (1972), and Herendeen (1974) helped align questions over the energy, materials and pollution basis of the economy with methodological approaches of input-output analysis. Through providing a framework of interdependency, input-output provided one of the early empirical bases for studying the relationships of the macro-economy including its supporting institutions and environmental stocks, flows and sinks. For instance, Daly (1968) sketched the economy as a system embedded in social institutions and sustaining ecosystems, building on the foundational work of Leontief (1936) and Stone (1961). The early work included an important exchange of ideas between economists and ecologists—on the structural properties of (economic and ecological) systems, the complementarity of inputs in the production process (particularly energy) and an early attention to embodied pollution in trade flows—critical to understanding the difference between relative and absolute decoupling of the economy from energy and materials [Chapter 11].

This chapter introduces the methodological foundation of this structural approach to economic analysis. The basic input-output model is presented, followed by a number of extensions relevant to ecological economics. These include the development of social accounts, hybrid environmental input-output tables, total flows analysis and the supply-side model. The chapter concludes with a short assessment of structural economic models as a renewed platform for a methodological approach for ecological economics.

The standard input-output model

Nobel laureate Wassily Leontief (1936) is credited with having developed input-output analysis in the 1930s, a time when economists were researching the root causes of the Great Depression and concerned with supply bottlenecks as nations prepared to enter World War II. However, the examination of interdependence between economic sectors is much older than Leontief's work, dating back to Quesnay's 1758 *Tableau Economique*, while the notion of production coefficients, a familiar feature of the input-output system, dates back to Léon Walras' work in

1874. Today virtually all developed countries maintain input-output accounts to complement their national income accounts, while the United Nations has supported a standardised system of economic accounts in order to facilitate the use of input-output analysis as a planning tool for less developed countries.

The most basic input-output framework is the static model, which shows the flows between industries during a one-year time period. The core of the model is a set of linear relationships describing each industry both as a producer and consumer of goods and services. Industries purchase inputs from other industries (inter-industry transactions), and also from other factors of production including payments to labour, government taxes, interest payments on capital, profits and adjustments to inventories. The input-output system also shows final demand for an industry's output, generally consisting of household consumption, government demand, private investment and foreign demand (the components of gross domestic product).

The heart of input-output modelling is the transactions table, showing the purchase and sale of intermediate inputs between industries. Each cell of the matrix represents both a sale (reading across rows) and a purchase (reading down columns). Figure 36.1 illustrates the basic form of the static input-output model. Total economic output equals total input, calculated as the sum of inter-industry transactions (Z) and final demand (Y), as well as the sum of Z and value added inputs (W).

Much of the literature on input-output analysis is described through linear algebra, so a brief mathematical description of the core model is helpful in preparation for further exploration. With n industries and aggregated final demand and value-added, Figure 36.1 can be organised in a set of linear equations in matrix form. Assuming an index i for selling sector (row), and

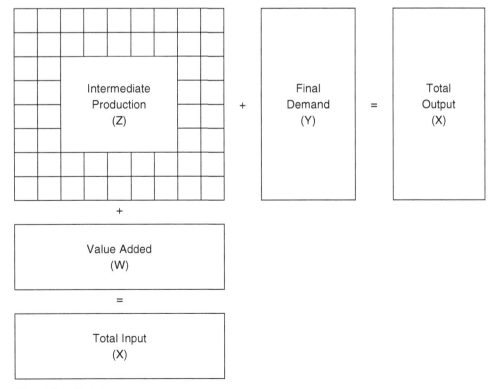

Figure 36.1 Basic input-output system.

index j for purchasing sector (column) each inter-industry transaction is denoted as z_{ij}. Total output of any particular industry sector is then defined as the sum of all sales to both intermediate (industry) and final consumers:

$$X_i = z_{i1} + z_{i2} + \ldots + z_{in} + Y_i \qquad (1)$$

or, in more general terms,

$$X_i = \sum_{j=1}^{n} z_{ij} + Y_i \qquad (2)$$

In order to analyse the impacts of changes in a particular sector on the larger economy, information on the ratio of various inputs to the level of outputs is needed. These ratios, denoted a_{ij}, are the technical coefficients of the model and are calculated as:

$$a_{ij} = \frac{z_{ij}}{X_j} \qquad (3)$$

For example, if in producing €1000 of output for the livestock sector, farmers spent €300 on cattle feed, the technical coefficient would be €300/€1000 or 0.3. The coefficient is interpreted as the amount of input i required for the output of €1 of sector j. These technical coefficients are assumed fixed in nature (i.e. constant returns to scale) so that if livestock output were tripled, purchases of feed by farmers would also triple. Also, inputs are assumed to be used in fixed proportions (i.e. strictly complimentary), such that if more feed was purchased but additional labour was not available, the amount of livestock output could not be increased. Only when all inputs are increased in constant proportions can total output increase.

Critics of the input-output approach most often cite the limitations of this fixed proportion assumption. However, the assumption of complementarity of inputs (particularly over short-term planning horizons) allows for very detailed description of economic production and empirical study of technological and resource constraints. Compared to the popular Cobb-Douglas production function, typically with only a single labour and single capital input, an input-output approach is able to show detailed flows within a large production system. If the assumption of fixed technical coefficients is accepted, equation 1 can be rewritten substituting for each z_{ij}:

$$X_i = a_{i1}X_1 + a_{i2}X_2 + \ldots + a_{in}X_n + Y_i \qquad (4)$$

A system of n such equations, one for each sector, then fully describes the inter-industry transactions within the economy. By further manipulating each equation, grouping the Xs and leaving final demand on the right-hand side, the following form is reached:

$$(1 - a_{11})X_1 - a_{12}X_2 - \ldots - a_{1i}X_i - \ldots - a_{1n}X_n = Y_1$$
$$-a_{21}X_1 + (1 + a_{22})X_2 - \ldots - a_{2i}X_i - \ldots - a_{2n}X_n = Y_2$$
$$\vdots$$
$$-a_{i1}X_1 - a_{i2}X_2 - \ldots + (1 - a_{ii})X_i - \ldots - a_{in}X_n = Y_i$$

$$\vdots$$

$$- a_{i1} X_1 - a_{i2} X_2 - \ldots + \left(1 - a_{ii}\right) X_i - \ldots - a_{in} X_n = Y_i$$

$$\vdots$$

$$- a_{n1} X_1 - a_{n2} X_2 - \ldots - a_{ni} X_i - \ldots + \left(1 - a_{nn}\right) X_n = Y_n$$

$$(5)$$

The entire system can be rewritten in matrix form as

$$\left(I - A\right) X = Y \tag{6}$$

where

$$A = \begin{bmatrix} a_{11} & a_{12} & \cdots & a_{1i} & \cdots & a_{1n} \\ a_{21} & a_{22} & \cdots & a_{2i} & \cdots & a_{2n} \\ \vdots & \vdots & & \vdots & & \vdots \\ a_{n1} & a_{n2} & \cdots & a_{ni} & \cdots & a_{nn} \end{bmatrix}, \; X = \begin{bmatrix} X_1 \\ X_2 \\ \vdots \\ X_n \end{bmatrix}, \; Y = \begin{bmatrix} Y_1 \\ Y_2 \\ \vdots \\ Y_n \end{bmatrix}$$

and I is the $n \times n$ identity matrix. The standard input-output system of equations is then represented by pre-multiplying each side of the equation by $(I - A)^{-1}$ to show the entire output of the economy as a function of final demands:

$$X = \left(I - A\right)^{-1} Y \tag{7}$$

where $(I - A)^{-1}$ is known as the Leontief inverse.

This inverse captures both the direct and indirect requirements of production. For example, in producing one Euro's worth of grain for final consumption, the agricultural sector requires inputs from both itself (perhaps in the form of seed and other inputs) and from other sectors (perhaps a tractor or fencing). In producing those requirements, each sector uses inputs from other sectors; e.g., the tractor producer needs steel and tools and fuel, while the seed company needs sorting equipment and labour among other things. These are the indirect requirements for producing grain. In the standard model, the inverse captures both direct and indirect requirements in calculating the total amount of production necessary to fulfil any extra final demand.

National databases are constructed with industry survey data that characterise these relationships. In the United States of America (USA), the Bureau of Economic Analysis (BEA) publishes national benchmark tables every five years using the North American Industry Classification System (NAICS). Private companies such as IMPLAN (www.implan.com) and REMI (www.remi.com) assemble data into software packages used for national, state, and regional analysis (down to the USA postal code level). Disaggregated models typically include over 500 sectors, the majority of which are part of manufacturing, but data can be built in standard one and two-digit aggregations, or custom aggregation to suit the questions at hand. Since each industry may produce more than one commodity, data is published and incorporated into models as both make and use tables.

Extensions of input-output analysis

Descriptions of the standard Leontief model and its many extensions are covered in texts such as Miller and Blair (1985), Miller et al. (1989), and Rose and Miernyk (1989). Extensions have dealt with both the limits of the strict technological assumptions and applications to broader research questions, including the foundations of dynamic economic approaches such as computable general equilibrium models (Rose, 1995). A few extensions with significance to central research questions in ecological economics are summarised here.

Social accounting matrix

Traditional input-output analysis focused on the structure of production, the matrix in the upper left corner of Figure 36.1, but provided less detail for final demand, described only in terms of the four major components of household consumption, investment, government consumption, and trade. While the input-output table can describe production in terms of hundreds of industries, in the standard model households are represented by a single sector, even though they account for most of final demand. This restricted treatment of households limits the ability of the input-output model to address such issues as income distribution or more specific impact analysis of changing patterns of household spending.

The need for a more detailed treatment of households in order to address major economic policy questions led researchers, beginning with the work of Richard Stone in the 1960s, to expand the input-output system to a fuller social accounting matrix. Figure 36.2 provides a simplified version of a social accounting matrix. As consumers, households are disaggregated from one column into many according to criteria relevant to the policy question at hand, such as income level or educational status. As suppliers of labour and capital, the value-added block is also disaggregated, often by different wage or occupation groups. The connection between the source of income (household supply of labour and capital) and consumption (household purchases in final demand) is represented by a new matrix of the flows between final demand and value-added.

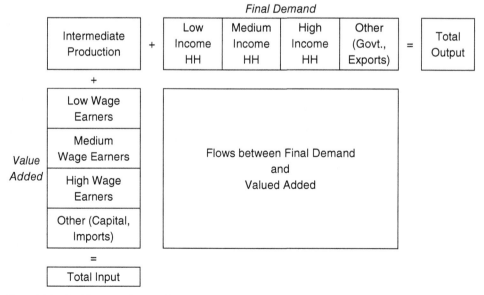

Figure 36.2 Social accounting matrix.

In the typical social accounting matrix model, when industries employ new labour, households then spend this new income in the economy, contributing to new rounds of inputs and outputs. An induced component is added to economic multipliers by including households in the endogenous part of the model, and this supplements the direct and indirect impacts of new demand. For a full overview, history and application of social accounting matrix models to planning, see the World Bank publication by Pyatt and Round (1985).

Regional models

Early input-output studies reflected concern with the national economy, however the framework has been extended to apply to sub-national regions and to explore the inherent openness and trade between regions. In the absence of regional tables, much of this research has involved various approaches to regionalise national accounts. Miller and Blair (1985) summarise non-survey techniques that have estimated regional input coefficients through the adjustment of national technical coefficients using published information on regional employment, income or output by industry. For example, regional supply percentages can be calculated as a ratio of the locally produced available amount of an input to the total amount of the input available in the region. The national technical coefficients matrix (A) is thus transformed into a matrix of regional input coefficients. Techniques have also been developed to estimate location quotients, supply–demand pooling, and regional purchase coefficients.

The importance of feedback between open regional models has also led to the development of interregional and multiregional models. To overcome severe data constraints in these models, research has incorporated non-survey and partial survey (or hybrid) methods to account for changes in spatial coverage (e.g., regionalising national tables) or temporal situations (e.g. accounting for changing technologies or the introduction of completely new products). A number of commercial software packages use various incarnations of regionalisation techniques, described in part by Brucker et al. (1990). Isard (1951) and Leontief (1951) are credited with the seminal work in development of regional models. Jensen (1990) offers an excellent discussion of more recent progress in applying an input-output approach to regional economies.

Environmental input-output analysis

The policy questions of the 1960s and 1970s presented a growing need for analysis that linked economic and environmental effects, and the basic input-output/social accounting matrix framework was expanded to incorporate environmental and natural resource accounts (Victor, 1972). This additional set of information includes resource use, such as land of different kinds or location, and various kinds of environmental pollution associated with production by each industry and final use designed to fit with the input-output/social accounting matrix framework (United Nations, 1993; Lange, 1998, 1999).

The first environmental models were framed as interregional models based on the notion that the human economy and the natural environment could be treated as two 'regions'. Isard (1967) and Daly (1968) both conceptualised fully integrated models that encompassed inter-sectoral flows within and between the economy and the regional environment. However, data limitations have led to more modest efforts at showing the links between the economy and certain environmental media by adding vectors to account for the by-products of pollution and additional input requirements from natural resources. These vectors are incorporated into the transactions matrix and have multipliers in the corresponding inverse (i.e., pollution or natural resource multipliers) that show the total pollution output, or resource requirements, associated with a given level of final demand.

Kane (2003) reviewed research on water quantity and quality illustrative of these integrated approaches. For example, through the development of water use and pollution coefficients, analysts have calculated direct, indirect, and induced demands on the resource, total outputs of waste products, and interregional trade in water. These integrated approaches have also expanded beyond analysis of money flows alone. For example, input-output approaches have also been developed with physical measures of flows, particularly in the analysis of economic dependence on energy inputs. This approach was pioneered by Herendeen (1974) and Hannon and Blazeck (1984) in the Energy Research Group at the University of Illinois. Also of interest is the application of decomposition analysis using an input-output table based on British thermal units (Gowdy and Miller, 1987; Ang, 1995; Casler and Blair, 1997; Rose, 1999).

Supply-side model

In the traditional Leontief model, demand is viewed as the limiting factor and the source of any impacts on the economy. However, a mirror image of this demand-driven process must also hold on the supply-side. Often called a Ghoshian model, after Ghosh (1958), the source of economic change can also derive from changes in value-added inputs (W). Here W becomes the limiting factor and the source of economic change, and Y is now the sink. Technical coefficients are again fixed, but are derived by dividing output into rows of the transaction matrix, rather than down columns as in the Leontief system. In contrast to the fixed input requirements in the demand-driven Leontief system, the supply-driven Ghoshian system assumes fixed output coefficients.

While the Leontief model is most useful when describing a short-run economic system with idle resources and thus very elastic factor-supply curves, the Ghoshian system is plausible under conditions of resource scarcity and very inelastic factor-supply curves, as in the case of supply-side shocks. For instance, Giarratani (1976) estimated a Ghoshian input-output model to investigate supply linkages associated with energy production in the USA and the impact of oil supply allocation schemes on the economy of the USA. While energy shocks are often estimated in monetary units, the model can be easily transformed into energy units such as quads or British thermal units by incorporating sector and fuel specific energy intensities.

Future directions

The 1970s and early 1980s were the heyday of input-output research related to energy and environmental issues. Changing political priorities in the USA and Europe resulted in funding cuts for research in regional planning and environmental conservation, and input-output tables required to further develop environmental applications lost support. Research and data collection fell to international bodies, including the development of the System of Integrated Environmental and Economic Accounting of the United Nations (http://unstats.un.org/unsd/envaccounting/seea.asp). Input-output approaches also found a home in fields such as industrial ecology, including overlapping research in life-cycle analysis such as the Economic Input-Output Life Cycle Assessment method developed at Carnegie Mellon University (see http://www.eiolca.net). New collaborations and research on material flows is also returning to some of the original questions of the physical basis of economic transactions, including collaboration between research institutes in Austria and Germany under the title of the Global Material Flows Database (http://www.materialflows.net).

The application of the input-output model with physical units highlights distinct parallels between structural analysis of ecological and economic systems, an early theme within input-output research dating to Isard (1967) and Daly (1968), and today an important direction for ecological economics. For example, the assumption of no net storage in ecological systems parallels the assumption of no net investment, or no net change in inventories, in economic systems. Also, energy transfers in ecosystems are modelled in much the same way as inter-industry transfers in economies. However, the straightforward application of the economic principles of input-output to ecological questions has also been faced with several problems, because ecology has no analogous concept to final demand. As Szyrmer (1984: 40) notes:

> in ecology the 'useful' intrasystem flows are regarded as much more important than the 'useless' respiration outputs, while in economic systems the main emphasis is placed upon the final demands rather than upon the internal transactions, the latter being valuable only insofar as they provide directly or indirectly the goods and services for final consumption.

Thus, an ecologist may place greater importance on the total flows (direct and indirect) from one system element to another (e.g., between Sun and zebra in the African savannah ecosystems) or between one system element and the system as a whole (e.g., the impact of lion extinction on the African savannah ecosystem).

With these corollaries in mind, one particular future direction of input-output to highlight can be found in Szyrmer's work on total flow analysis (Szyrmer, 1984, 1992; Szyrmer and Olanowicz, 1987). Total flow analysis is an underutilized method for quantifying the relationship between any two system elements, or between any one element and the system as a whole. A central question, from a total flow perspective, is: what happens to element i activity or to total system activity if element j is decoupled from the system? In an economic context, the question arises as to what happens to other sectors in a regional economy, and the system as a whole, if one of its sectors begins importing all of its input requirements? Such a hypothetical extraction technique can be used to determine the dependence of a particular sector, or the region as a whole, on another given sector. This technique is equivalent to zeroing all the entries in a given sector's column, re-computing the Leontief inverse and total output, and subtracting the new total output figures from the previous case.

In terms of impact analysis, total flow can be viewed as an upper bound for the perturbation that a system element may exert upon itself, upon other elements, or upon the system as a whole. When considered from the perspective of the entire system, this impact can be expressed as a scalar measure of sectoral significance. In other words, if all sector inputs from a particular sector are externalised, estimates can be made for the decline of total system activity. Beyond the traditional Leontief output multiplier, total flow provides many additional ways to rank sectors, depending on one's perspective of what constitutes a 'key' sector characteristic. Sectors with high transit flows may be key in that they function to maintain the connections between other sectors, while those with large total flows might be considered key by virtue of the sheer magnitude of flows, or the share of total throughput, that are embodied in them as sectors.

Analysis of total output dependence is important in economic systems, especially in highly specialised production structures, such as, when commodity production is completely dependent on processing sectors (e.g., crude oil producers and refineries). Connecting the method of total flow analysis with new databases on resource and energy inputs could provide an empirical basis for addressing the resilience of social ecological systems, a common concern in ecological economics.

Concluding remarks

Input-output analysis and its various extensions have generally aligned with central questions of ecological economics. The method provides an empirical approach to applied research on the structure of national and regional economies, energy requirements and pollution embodiment in economic transactions, and dependency between economic sectors, institutions and the environment. It has also provided a research platform that is less concerned with market efficiency and prices, and more suited for questions of economic scale and distribution. In fact, the use of input-output for economic planning has stood in opposition to the mainstream's *laissez faire* approach to economics. Throughout the 1980s and 1990s input-output was systematically displaced by computable general equilibrium models in mainstream economics, putting concerns over the price sensitivity of consumer demand above those of the structure and function of economic production.

Today, pressing environmental issues—climate change, land use change, biodiversity loss and natural resource depletion—all point to a renewed focus on measuring economic interdependencies and planning economic and social ecological transformation. Structural approaches to studying economic change first came into use in response to the extraordinary circumstances of the Great Depression and World War II, then again during the economy-wide disruptions of the Arab oil embargoes of the 1970s. Along with the call for a social ecological economics (Spash, 2011), input-output might again come into favour in response to the integrated social, economic and environmental challenges of our time.

Key further readings cited

Daly, H. (1968). On economics as a life science. *The Journal of Political Economy* 76(3), 392–406.

Lange, G. (1999). How to make progress toward integrating biophysical and economic assessments. *Ecological Economics* 29(1), 29–32.

Miller, R.E., Blair, P.D. (1985). *Input-Output Analysis: Foundations and Extensions*. Englewood Cliffs, New Jersey: Prentice-Hall, Inc.

Miller, R.E., Polenske, K.R.. Rose, A.Z. (1989). *Frontiers of Input-Output Analysis*. New York: Oxford University Press.

Rose, A.Z., Miernyk, W. (1989). Input-output analysis: The first fifty years. *Economic Systems Research* 1(2), 229–271.

Other Literature Cited

Ang, B.W. (1995). Multilevel decomposition of industrial energy consumption. *Energy Economics* 17(1), 39–51.

Brucker, S.M., Hastings, S.E., Latham, W.R. (1990). The variation of estimated impacts from five regional input-output models. *International Regional Science Review* 13(1&2), 119–139.

Casler, S. and Blair, P. (1997). Economic structure, fuel combustion, pollution emissions, *Ecological Economics*, 22(1), 19–27.

Ghosh, A. (1958). Input-output approach to an allocative system. *Econometrica* 25(97), 58–64.

Giarratani, F. (1976). Application of an interindustry supply model to energy issues. *Environment and Planning A* 8(4), 447–454.

Gowdy, J. and Miller, J. (1987). Technological and demand change in energy use: An input-output analysis. *Environment and Planning A*, 19(10), 1387–1398.

Hannon, B. and Blazeck, T. (1984). The marginal cost of energy goods and services. *Energy Systems and Policy* 8(4), 85–112.

Herendeen, R. (1974). Affluence and energy demand. *Journal of Mechanical Engineering* 96, 1–16.

Isard, W. (1951). Interregional and regional input-output analysis: A model of a space economy. *Review of Economics and Statistics* 33(4), 318–328.

Isard, W., Bassett, K., Choguill, C., Furtado, J., Izumita, R., Kissin, J., Romanoff, E., Seyfarth, R., Tatlock, R. (1967). On the linkage of socio-economic and ecologic systems. Papers and Proceedings of the Regional Science Association, 21, 79–99.

Jensen, R.C. (1990). "Construction and use of regional input-output models: Progress and prospects." *International Regional Science Review* 13(1&2), 9–25.

Kane, M. (2003). *Shared Futures of City and Country: a Total Flows Analysis of Urban-Rural Ecological Economic Dependence in New York City's Catskill Delaware Watershed.* Ph.D. Dissertation, Department of Economics, Rensselaer Polytechnic Institute, Troy, NY.

Lange, G. (1998). From data to analysis: The example of natural resource accounts linked with input-output information. *Economic Systems Research* 10 (2), 113–134.

Leontief, W. (1936). Quantitative input-output relations in the economic system of the United States. *Review of Economics and Statistics* 18(3), 105–125.

Leontief, W. (1951). *The Structure of the American Economy, 1919–1939.* New York: Oxford University Press.

Pyatt, G. and Round, J. (1985). *Social Accounting Matrices: A Basis for Planning.* Washington, DC: The World Bank.

Rose, A. (1995). Input-output economics and computable general equilibrium models. *Structural Change and Economic Dynamics*, 6 (3), 295–304.

Rose, A. (1999). Input-Output Structural Decomposition Analysis of Energy and the Environment. In: van den Bergh J. (ed.), *Handbook of Environmental and Resource Economics* (pp. 1164–1179), Cheltenham: Edward Elgar.

Spash, C.L. (2011), Social ecological economics: Understanding the past to see the future, *American Journal of Economics and Sociology*, 70(2), 340–375.

Stone, R. (1961). *Input-Output and National Accounts.* Paris: Organisation for Economic Cooperation and Development.

Szyrmer, J.M. (1984). Total Flow in Input-Output Models. Ph.D Dissertation submitted to the Department of Regional Science, University of Pennsylvania.

Szyrmer, J.M. (1992). Input-output coefficients and multipliers from a total flow perspective. *Environment and Planning A* 24(7), 921–937.

Szyrmer, J.M. and Ulanowicz, R.E. (1987). Total flow in ecosystems. *Ecological Modeling* 35(1–2), 123–136.

United Nations (1993). *The System of Integrated Environmental and Economic Accounts.* UN, New York.

Victor, P. (1972). *Pollution: Economy and the Environment.* London: Allen & Unwin.

37

SUSTAINABILITY INDICATORS

Philippe Roman and Géraldine Thiry

Introduction

Sustainability has undoubtedly become an almost consensual normative horizon, in the academic and policy making spheres, despite its numerous interpretations. No consensus has been reached on a definition and there is heterogeneity on the matter. However, ecological economics proposes a specific ontological standpoint regarding sustainability, which is well encapsulated in the picture of three concentric circles—the economy is part of a social system which is itself a part of ecosystems and the biosphere—conveying the idea of an ordered hierarchical system (Spash, 2012: 43–44). Such a preanalytic vision bears consequences for the type of indicators used to assess sustainability.

There are a plethora of indicators aiming to quantify sustainability rather than measuring societal success by Gross Domestic Product (GDP)—the "beyond GDP" debate. In this chapter, we focus on those indicators relating to ecological economics. After briefly reviewing the founding principles of ecological economics, we classify sustainability indicators. The core of the chapter is a review that identifies seven families of indicators and summarises their aims and problems. Some normative issues are briefly mentioned before we suggest further research avenues and make a few concluding remarks.

Ecological economics and sustainability indicators

From its inception as a specific field of inquiry, ecological economics has attempted to go beyond scholarly research, and achieve social change under the broad goal of sustainability. The organisers of the first conference of the International Society for Ecological Economics promoted "measurement and policy" and defined the subject area as "the science and management of sustainability" (Costanza, 1991). No wonder then that indicators, as conveyors of knowledge and policy tools, became prominent in ecological economics.

The ecological economics' lens

Sustainability indicators promoted by ecological economists put special emphasis on scale, distribution and value pluralism. Concerns over the scale of economic activity have led to a host of indicators that address the (material) size of the economy and bring to light the pressures on ecosystems and limits that should be respected to maintain the structure, functioning and integrity of ecosystems [Chapter 12]. Ecological economists accept strong sustainability [Chapter 25],[1] and want to include indicators covering both the social and biophysical foundations of the economy. Distributional inequity is addressed by providing indicators of the extent to which natural resources and environmental amenities, and scarcities and environmental impacts, are equally/unequally distributed between social classes, income or ethnic groups [Chapters 4 and 15]. As far as value pluralism is concerned [Chapter 22], particular emphasis is put on procedural issues like participation [Chapter 33], deliberation [Chapter 34] and multiple criteria analysis [Chapter 30]. Indicators are then normative, political and value-laden tools. Their reflexive critical assessment is therefore of paramount importance (Kovacic and Giampietro, 2015).

Sustainability indicators within the 'beyond GDP' debate

Limits and pitfalls of traditional indicators of prosperity, especially GDP, have been amply revealed. The main deficiencies of traditional economic indicators are: i) the inclusion of defensive expenditures, undertaken to correct problems such as pollution, as something positive; ii) the neglect of numerous environmental and social impacts of production and consumption; iii) the disregard of distributional issues and inequalities; and iv) the absence of goods and services produced outside the market economy (Cassiers and Thiry, 2015; Gadrey and Jany-Catrice, 2006).

Various attempts have then been made to correct such problems. The computation of the Measure of Economic Welfare (MEW) by Nordhaus and Tobin (1972) is widely recognised as a pioneering contribution to the sustainability indicators debate. Following on from this, Daly and Cobb (1994 [1989]) created the influential and broadly implemented Index of Sustainable Economic Welfare (ISEW), which was slightly modified and renamed the Genuine Progress Index (GPI) in 2004. The adoption in 1992 of Agenda 21 during the first United Nations Conference on Environment and Development gave a strong impetus to the sustainability indicators movement. The main criteria for sustainability indicators to respect were stated in the 1996 Bellagio Principles. At this time, the ecological footprint gained increasing media-coverage. In 2009, the Stiglitz-Sen-Fitoussi Report provided an authoritative synthesis and appreciation of the extensive literature on beyond GDP indicators (Stiglitz et al., 2010).

Despite these and numerous other endeavours—approximately 900 initiatives are registered in the Compendium of Sustainable Development Indicator Initiatives (IISD, n.d.)—consensus on a comprehensive and robust (set of) sustainability indicator(s) is still beyond reach. Cleavages appear along several lines: format, unit of account, link to national accounts, building process, actors supporting or using indicators, scale, and articulation of the dimensions of sustainability. In order to address this complexity, we propose a typology of sustainability indicators as shown in Figure 37.1 (for alternative typologies, see Hezri and Dovers, 2006, or Bartelmus, 2013).

We distinguish indicators along two main dimensions: aggregation and monetisation. Following these criteria, we identify seven families of sustainability indicators. Only some of the most iconic indicators are displayed (for more see UNECE/Eurostat/OECD, 2013). Beside the construction of sustainability indicators, a key issue is the way in which they are articulated within a framework that makes sense of them. Most of these sets (such as the indicators of the joint UNECE/Eurostat/OECD Task Force on Measuring Sustainable Development) and frameworks (such as the OECD driving forces, pressure, state, response framework) encompass several indicators displayed in Figure 37.1.

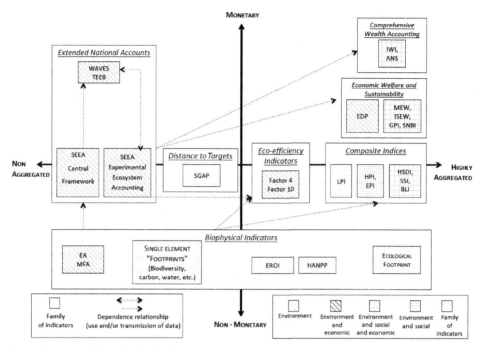

Figure 37.1 A guide to the family of sustainability indicators.

Families of sustainability indicators and their related issues

Extended national accounts

The strength of standardised national accounts, whose key indicator is GDP, comes from their internal coherence, consistency and integration. Many experts therefore believe that beyond GDP indicators have to be compatible with national accounting. This is the ambition of the System of Environmental-Economic Accounting (SEEA), first proposed in 1993. This statistical framework creates a satellite account which is a comprehensive set of tables and accounts that aims at "understanding the interactions between the economy and the environment" and "describing stocks and changes in stocks of environmental assets" (United Nations, 2012: vii). The objective is to measure imputed environmental costs (not supported by the economy or the society).

Some, such as Bartelmus (2013), would like (monetary) environmental degradation accounts to be mainstreamed and so go beyond the marketed natural resources accounted for in SEEA. There are also debates over the inclusion of ecosystem accounts. The objective is to integrate non-marketed natural assets in the form of ecosystem assets and their services. Such an exercise is ridden with difficulties: the boundaries of ecosystems do not necessarily fit with national boundaries, and complex and uncertain dynamics and interactions are pervasive. Difficulties are compounded in monetary accounts.

Yet, despite fundamental problems, the monetary valuation of ecosystems and their services has received strong endorsement through international initiatives such as the Wealth Accounting and Valuation of Ecosystem Services (WAVES), and The Economics of Ecosystems and Biodiversity (TEEB), that aim at mainstreaming monetary valuation of ecosystems [Chapter 43]. The monetary valuation of 'natural capital' and ecosystems is criticised for lacking robustness and scientific credibility (e.g., Spash, 2008), especially when using contingent valuation and benefit transfers to create money numbers (Spash and Vatn, 2006). Such doubts help explain why the approaches are put in an "Experimental Accounts" section of the SEEA. Besides lacking scientific credibility, the TEEB project aims to capture values and so raises concerns over creating market competition, disturbing previous (common) property rights, and commodifying ecosystems (Gómez-Baggethun et al., 2010).

Economic welfare and sustainability

Among endeavours to build upon national accounting aggregates (e.g., consumption, investment), one finds indicators of economic welfare and sustainability, which were among the first sustainability indicators proposed. The MEW of Nordhaus and Tobin (1972) adds 'desirables' of leisure and non-market outputs to GDP and deducts 'regrettables' from GDP. Regrettables are defensive expenditures, requirements for production and capital from population growth, and environmental 'externalities'. One important critique of the MEW is that it relies upon a strong faith in economic growth. Social and environmental costs are understated because of large positive imputations for leisure and non-market subsistence, and relatively low deductions for environmental and social deterioration (see Bartelmus, 2008: 128).

Daly and Cobb (1994 [1989]) addressed the pitfalls of the MEW by proposing their own ISEW indicator—in a self-admitted attempt at provocation for awareness-raising purposes (see Ziegler, 2007; Daly and Cobb, 2007). This makes adjustments for income inequalities and includes more defensive expenditures, environmental damages and degradations of the human quality of life. Evidence for the longitudinal decoupling between the ISEW and GDP was considered to validate a threshold hypothesis, according to which "for every society there seems to be a period in which economic growth […] brings about an improvement in the quality of life, but only up to a point—the threshold point—beyond which, if there is more economic growth, quality of life may begin to deteriorate" (Max-Neef, 1995: 117). Daly calls such divergence 'uneconomic growth'. However, Neumayer (2000) casts doubt on such a threshold hypothesis which he regards as very sensitive to computational aspects of the ISEW/GPI that rely upon doubtful theoretical grounds. In response to this critique, Lawn (2003) has dedicated efforts to establishing strong theoretical foundations to the indicator, on the basis of Irving Fisher's notion of 'net psychic income'.

While the useful role of the ISEW/GPI as an alert to GDP flaws is recognised, confusion is pointed out about combining, within one single indicator, sustainability of economic production—conceived as the maintenance of forms of capital—with welfare effects from the consumption of goods and services (Bartelmus, 2008, 2013, Stiglitz et al., 2010). Lawn (2013) argues that ISEW and GPI are not about sustainability *per se*, but economic welfare, and as such they need to be supplemented with biophysical indicators.

Alleging a more consistent use of national accounting categories, Bartelmus (2008: 151) proposed the Environmentally-adjusted net Domestic Product (EDP), defined as "the sum of environmentally adjusted value added of industries, with a further deduction of environmental costs generated by households". It aims both to account for the maintenance of produced and natural capital assets and to deduct the costs of natural capital consumption.

Comprehensive wealth accounting

Environmentally adjusted production (and/or income) indicators have been harshly criticised by neoclassical environmental and resource economists for their theoretical inconsistency. Instead they advocate wealth (i.e. stock) rather than flow indicators. The two most significant initiatives are the Adjusted Net Savings (ANS) (World Bank, 2006) and the Inclusive Wealth Index (IWI) (UNU-IHDP and UNEP, 2012). These indicators are embedded within the capital theory approach to sustainability, whereby sustainability requires the maintenance of stocks of extended wealth, valued in monetary terms, and including manufactured, human and natural entities as 'capital assets'.

From an ecological economics perspective, these indicators suffer from strong drawbacks (Munda, 2014). First, in the ANS the depletion of non-renewable resources is mostly imputed to resource exporting developing countries. This implies that developed countries, that are generally less endowed in natural resources but richer in human and physical capital, appear incorrectly sustainable (Stiglitz et al., 2010). Second, the ANS and IWI rely upon unrealistic assumptions about the future. In the computation of the ANS, the flow of current and future consumption is supposed *ex ante* to be known and sustainable, which is paradoxical. The authors of the IWI try to overcome this shortcoming by getting rid of the sustainable consumption path assumption. Yet they still assume that the intertemporal resource allocation mechanism of all assets in the economy is known and correctly reflected in shadow prices. Indeed, for the IWI (and, to a lesser extent, ANS) shadow prices are the keystone of the indicator. While the use of shadow prices is motivated by pragmatic arguments, it actually bears a certain *weltanschauung*, a series of (potentially contentious) implicit assumptions (Munda, 2014). In addition, shadow prices are supposed to synthesise a very wide array of information including the degree of substitution across the different forms of capital, the contribution to well-being by each capital asset, future scarcities and all 'externalities' (Roman and Thiry, 2016). Last but not least, by cardinally classifying the capital assets on the basis of a unique unit of account, the ANS and IWI assume strong commensurability between these assets, a case of value monism which is unwarranted from an ecological economics perspective (Martínez-Alier et al., 1998) [Chapter 22].

Composite indices

Within the composite indices family, one can distinguish between those accounting for the environment exclusively, e.g. Living Planet Index (LPI), for environmental and social dimensions of sustainability, e.g. Happy Planet Index (HPI), and Environmental Performance Index (EPI), and for environmental, social and economic dimensions, e.g. Human Sustainable Development Index (HSDI), Sustainable Society Index (SSI), and Better Life Index (BLI) (see Costanza et al., 2009). Composite indices are often praised for their integrative endeavour, their communicative virtues, the simplicity of their message and their comparability. However, these qualities have their drawbacks. First, most of the composite indices are considered as atheoretical or as relying upon doubtful conceptual foundations. Neoclassical economists often stress the unclear definition of sustainability. Second, the way dimensions are weighted and normalised is controversial. Who weights and according to what principles or methods? Third, normalisation and weighting imply commensurability and value monism.

Biophysical indicators

Physical indicators attempt to shed light on the biophysical pressures created by human activities in the modern economy. They relate to the limits of ecosystems [Chapter 12], and the scale of material and energy throughput, e.g., through the quantification of social metabolism [Chapter 11]. This subsection starts from the material based indices, moves to the energy based ones and then to ecological footprints.

Material and energy flows accounting

Physical accounting rests upon the first law of thermodynamics, the conservation of mass and energy [Chapter 9]. There is much debate over which unit of energy should be used in such accounts. Material Flow Analysis (MFA) uses mass. According to Fischer-Kowalski et al. (2011: 856): "With materials, mass (e.g., tonnes) […] is a very robust measure, immutable across time and space in classical physics." MFA offers an account of the extraction of biomass, fossil fuels, industrial metals and minerals, as well as imports and exports of goods. Water and air are not included. While indicators tend to be exclusively based upon material throughput of the domestic economy, there have been recent attempts to extend MFA of domestic consumption to the environmental impacts it involves that occur beyond the national boundaries of the consuming nation State [Chapter 11]. This is increasingly important as nations shift the social and environmental costs of their consumption onto other nations, e.g. by relocating manufacturing.

While the accounting systems of MFA generate highly aggregate information, they are also built up from, and can be broken down into, more detailed information. Another advantage is that the scope of MFA fits the SNA, which permits the integration of monetary and physical information within the same accounting framework. MFA is also praised for its internal consistency since it is grounded on physical laws and comprehensive accounting (Bartelmus, 2008). In spite of these virtues, MFA has been described as 'ton ideology'. Measuring dimensions according to the weight of materials implies ignoring different impact potentials of materials, excluding other environmental functions and inadequately reflecting resource depletion. MFA studies show that attempts to reduce material and energy use in the modern economy have only resulted in reductions relative to GDP, or relative decoupling [Chapter 11]. They also identify a trend in environmental damage 'cost-shifting' to other countries, revealed by computing indirect and international resource flows. This is unsurprising in light of the 'imperial mode of living' being promoted [Chapter 15].

Energy return on energy investment (EROI)

The EROI is defined as "the ratio between the energy obtained and the energy spent in the process geared to supplying energy to the economy. The EROI is the inverse of the energy cost of obtaining energy" (Martínez-Alier, 2011: 147). Murphy and Hall (2010) offer a review of the several definitions and implementations of the EROI. From an ecological economics perspective, the EROI is a good indicator of the energetic dependence of human activities. Recent EROI-like studies shed doubt on the sustainability of the 'Green growth' paradigm, by revealing the poor energetic return of new energy sources, e.g., biofuels, wind and solar energy. The results can have large standard deviations due to the decision as to where to draw the boundaries of analysis, e.g. oil and gas including the energy associated with extraction, refining, transport, and associated infrastructure.

Human Appropriation of Net Primary Production (HANPP)

The HANPP designates the aggregate impact of land use on biomass available each year in ecosystems (Haberl et al., 2007). This is a good indicator of humanity's 'colonisation' of natural processes of biomass creation. The indicator is computed as the difference between potential net primary production without human activities and what actually remains in ecosystems (i.e. neither harvested nor altered by land use changes). High HANPP is deemed to indicate less biomass availability for non-human species and, as hypothetical corollaries, biodiversity losses and interference in geochemical cycles. While HANPP aims to provide an indicator of material limits to growth, no unequivocal relationship between HANPP and GDP growth has yet been demonstrated (Krausmann et al., 2013).

Ecological footprint

The ecological footprint is a synthetic indicator of ecological sustainability which converts consumption into standardised land area units, global hectares (Wackernagel and Rees, 1996). If the land area required for consumption exceeds biocapacity of the studied entity or a normatively defined global average, consumption is unsustainable (there is overshoot). A typical statement is that "humanity used the equivalent of 1.5 planets to provide the resources we use and absorb our waste" (Global Footprint Network, n.d.). Beyond this global picture of unsustainability, the ecological footprint is useful for shedding light on the distribution of the ecological burden [Chapter 4].

While the indicator has performed a useful awareness raising role, because of its simplicity and its straightforward message, its scientific reliability and utility as a policy tool have been questioned (Giampietro and Saltelli, 2014: 610). The global hectare unit of account has received ample criticism for its false concreteness, lack of robustness (productivity can change over time, so the biocapacity of a global hectare is not constant), and focus on land scarcity as the foremost concern, overruling all other problems. Common issues of aggregation (commensurability and weighting) are also raised as objections (van den Bergh, 2014). The ecological footprint is often criticised for its lack of distinction between sustainable and unsustainable uses of soils (the footprint-biocapacity diagnosis is indeed not altered by intensification of agriculture, in spite of potential disturbance of bio-geochemical cycles) and its inherent anti-trade bias. Finally, the ecological footprint is over-determined by carbon dioxide emissions, which leads many to advocate a simpler carbon footprint.

Single element footprints

A series of footprint measures has been developed for the quantification of specific human pressures on the Earth. Though they are usually called footprints, the principle of their computation is different from the ecological footprint. They are actually measures of one element's requirements and/or degradation in the consumption of goods and services, expressed in the element's unit, without conversion into global hectare equivalents. Carbon footprints have benefited from the development of large multi-regional input-output tables [Chapter 36], and life-cycle assessment studies. Interesting work addresses distributional relationship of carbon footprints revealing the role of income and expenditure (Papathanasopoulou and Jackson, 2009). Similarly, water footprints quantify the amount of water necessary for the production of consumption goods. Other footprints focus on such things as materials or even biodiversity. Material footprint analyses put into perspective the fallacy of material decoupling of industrialised nations. Research is thus heading toward the construction of a series of footprint measures, a footprint family of indicators.

Eco-efficiency indicators

These indicators answer the question: is the economy on a trend to produce more income or wealth with less material/energetic input/throughput? They are expressed in energy/material units per monetary unit of GDP (eco-efficiency), or GDP per unit of energy/material (eco-productivity). Such relative measures indicate the extent to which the economy is dematerialising in value terms, or treading a path of 'Green growth' (Weizsäcker et al., 1997; Schmidt-Bleek et Klüting, 1994). Ecologically, this relative decoupling does nothing to address the environmental crisis, which ecological economists have emphasised requires absolute reductions in energy and material throughput.

Sustainability gaps

The sustainability gap approach consists in comparing environmental performance with environmental standards (Ekins and Simon, 2001). These standards are built on the principle that what should be sustained is a wide range of environmental functions to maintain the basic integrity of natural systems that are a pre-requisite for the continued performance of the functions that provide direct benefits for humans. The gaps may be measured in physical units, in money costs or in years to sustainability.

Current assessment of major issues

There are as many indicators of sustainability as there are normative definitions of what we want to sustain (Stiglitz et al., 2010). Pillarisetti and van den Bergh (2010) show that different sustainability indicators can give rise to very different rankings of nations. However, such divergence is unsurprising: many sustainability indicators actually target specific and distinct objectives (e.g., critical natural capital preservation, non-decreasing welfare, compliance costs assessment). They also rely upon different ontological underpinnings. Unveiling this hidden ontology is a key issue for future research.

Davis et al. (2012: 4) believe that the "use of indicators in global governance has the potential to alter the forms, the exercise, and perhaps even the distributions of power in certain spheres of global governance". If indicators are assumed to have such transformative power, then they must be critically assessed. Besides internal coherence they require external consistency, which implies considering the social process surrounding their creation, the power balances at stake in their adoption and use, and the value systems underlying their methodology. As Gasparatos and Scolobig (2012: 1) rightly note, while tools to assess sustainability are plethoric, "what is really lacking, however, are guidelines and criteria on how to choose between these tools".

Sustainability indicators "deal with systems characterised by open causal chains, where the outcome space is unknown and changing at all times" (Kovacic and Giampietro, 2015: 56). Their measurement schemes reveal implicit values, and the complexity of sustainability issues entails a plurality of legitimate standpoints on what should be taken into account. Post-normal science [Chapter 28] might provide some basic guidelines in this context and criteria for quality assessment [Chapter 29]. Thus, based on posit-normal science, Kovacic and Giampietro (2015: 54) advocate a reflexive posture in the assessment of indicators: "in this framework, quality is defined as fitness for purpose."

Future directions

An important research avenue consists in revising the official criteria assessing the quality of indicators. Usual official quality criteria (relevance, accuracy and reliability, timeliness and punctuality, coherence and comparability, accessibility and clarity) do not provide enough guidance for the selection of indicators that would respect the tenets of social ecological economics: value pluralism, recognition of incommensurability, interdisciplinarity, empiricism, rejection of mechanistic reductionist approaches, acceptance of strong uncertainty.

This review has revealed the need for quality assessment and opening up the indicator field to critical analysis while building on the foundational messages of ecological economics. Deliberative multiple criteria analyses are a bold endeavour in that direction, since they respect value pluralism, are built on incommensurability assumptions and carry a strong sustainability vision. Deliberation is important insofar as "the goal is not so much to create a certain final set of technical indicators, as it is to engage a range of stakeholders in society in discussions about what it is that we value" (Garnåsjordet et al., 2012: 330). Indicators are means to (ideally) socially debated ends. Participatory deliberation can be time intensive and non-deliberative multiple criteria analysis may also be fruitful. By proposing a dynamic multi-dimensional assessment of sustainability at the macroeconomic level for Austria, Schmelev and Rodríguez-Labajos (2009) have pioneered the application of multiple criteria tools to the dynamic analysis of sustainability.

Concluding remarks

The elaboration of sustainability indicators by ecological economists has been instrumental in raising awareness of environmental issues both within academia and amongst the larger public. The work on indicators needs to be steadily pursued. However, a balance must be struck between i) further statistical quality and theoretical sophistication, ii) immediate and straightforward usability and iii) respect for ontological and procedural principles. Navigating the complex 'beyond GDP' ocean requires keeping in mind that indicators are both theoretical constructs, conventional objects and cogs in the machinery of governance structures.

Note

1   Weak sustainability relates to high, or even perfect, substitutability between different kinds of capital (social, human, natural, produced). Strong sustainability allows for incommensurability and non-substitutability as well as rejecting reduction of all things to forms of capital.

Key further readings cited

Bartelmus, P. (2008). *Quantitative Eco-nomics. How Sustainable Are Our Economies?* New York: Springer.
Gadrey, J., Jany-Catrice, F. (2006). *The New Indicators of Well-being and Development.* Basingstoke: Palgrave Macmillan.
Stiglitz, J. E., Sen, A., Fitoussi, J.P. (eds.). (2010). *Mismeasuring our Lives: Why GDP Doesn't Add Up.* New York: New Press.

Other literature cited

Bartelmus, P. (2013). The future we want: Green growth or sustainable development? *Environmental Development* 7, 165–170.
Cassiers, I., Thiry, G. (2014). A High-Stakes Shift: Turning the Tide From GDP to New Prosperity Indicators, in Cassiers, I. (ed.). *Redefining Prosperity.* New York: Routledge.
Costanza, R. (1991). *Ecological Economics: The Science and Management of Sustainability.* New York: Columbia University Press.
Costanza, R., Hart, M., Posner, S., Talberth, J. (2009). *Beyond GDP: The Need for New Measures of Progress.* Boston University Creative Services.
Daly, H.E., Cobb, J.B. (1994). *For the Common Good: Redirecting the Economy Toward Community, the Environment, and a Sustainable Future* (2nd ed., updated and expanded). Boston: Beacon Press.

Daly, H.E., Cobb, J.B. (2007). ISEW the "debunking" interpretation and the person-in-community paradox: Comment on Rafael Ziegler. *Environmental Values* 16(3): 287–288.

Davis, K. E., Fisher, A., Kingsbury, B., Engle Merry, S. (eds.) (2012). *Governance by Indicators: Global Power through Classification and Rankings*. Oxford: Oxford University Press [in association with] Institute for International Law and Justice, New York University School of Law.

Ekins, P., Simon, S. (2001). Estimating sustainability gaps: methods and preliminary applications for the UK and the Netherlands. *Ecological Economics* 37(1), 5–22.

Fischer-Kowalski, M., Krausmann, F., Giljum, S., Lutter, S., Mayer, A., Bringezu, S., Weisz, H. (2011). Methodology and indicators of economy-wide material flow accounting: State of the art and reliability across sources. *Journal of Industrial Ecology* 15(6), 855–876.

Garnåsjordet, P.A., Aslaksen, I., Giampietro, M., Funtowicz, S., Ericson, T. (2012). Sustainable development indicators: From statistics to policy. *Environmental Policy and Governance* 22(5), 322–336.

Gasparatos, A., Scolobig, A. (2012). Choosing the most appropriate sustainability assessment tool. *Ecological Economics* 80, 1–7.

Giampietro, M., Saltelli, A. (2014). Footprints to nowhere. *Ecological Indicators* 46, 610–621.

Global Footprint Network (2015), *World Footprint. Do we fit on the planet?* consulted on 15 October 2015, http://www.footprintnetwork.org/ar/index.php/GFN/page/world_footprint.

Gómez-Baggethun, E., de Groot, R., Lomas, P. L., Montes, C. (2010). The history of ecosystem services in economic theory and practice: From early notions to markets and payment schemes. *Ecological Economics* 69(6), 1209–1218.

Haberl, H., Erb, K. H., Krausmann, F., Gaube, V., Bondeau, A., Plutzar, C., Fischer-Kowalski, M. (2007). Quantifying and mapping the human appropriation of net primary production in earth's terrestrial ecosystems. *Proceedings of the National Academy of Sciences* 104(31), 12942–12947.

Hezri, A.A., Dovers, S.R. (2006). Sustainability indicators, policy and governance: Issues for ecological economics. *Ecological Economics* 60(1), 86–99.

IISD, International Institute for Sustainable Development (2015), *Compendium. A global Directory to Indicator Initiatives,* consulted on 15 October 2015, https://www.iisd.org/measure/compendium/searchinitiatives.aspx.

Kovacic, Z., Giampietro, M. (2015). Beyond 'beyond GDP indicators': The need for reflexivity in science for governance. *Ecological Complexity* 21, 53–61.

Krausmann, F., Karl-Heinz, E., Gingrich, S., Haberl, H., Bondeau, A., Gaube, V., Lauk, C., Plutzar, Ch., Searchinger, T.D. (2013). Global human appropriation of net primary production doubled in the 20th century. *PNAS* 110(25), 10324–10329.

Lawn, P. (2003). A theoretical foundation to support the Index of Sustainable Economic Welfare (ISEW), Genuine Progress Indicator (GPI), and other related indexes. *Ecological Economics* 44(1), 105–118.

Lawn, P. (2013). The failure of the ISEW and GPI to fully account for changes in human-health capital—A methodological shortcoming not a theoretical weakness. *Ecological Economics* 88, 167–177.

Martínez-Alier, J. (2011). The EROI of agriculture and its use by the Via Campesina. *Journal of Peasant Studies* 38(1), 145–160.

Martínez-Alier, J., Munda, G., O'Neill, J. (1998). Weak comparability of values as a foundation for ecological economics. *Ecological Economics* 26(3), 277–286.

Max-Neef, M. (1995). Economic growth and quality of life: a threshold hypothesis. *Ecological Economics* 15(2), 115–118.

Munda, G. (2014). On the use of shadow prices for sustainable well-being measurement. *Social Indicators Research* 118(2), 911–918.

Murphy, D.J., Hall, C.A.S. (2010). Year in review: EROI or energy return on (energy) invested. *Annals of the New York Academy of Sciences* 1185(1), 102–118.

Neumayer, E. (2000). On the methodology of ISEW, GPI and related measures: some constructive suggestions and some doubt on the "threshold" hypothesis. *Ecological Economics* 34(3), 347–361.

Nordhaus, W., Tobin, J. (1972). Is Growth Obsolete? in Nordhaus and Tobin (eds.) *Economic Research: Retrospect and Prospect*, Volume 5, Economic Growth (pp. 509–564). Cambridge, MA: NBER.

Papathanasopoulou, E. Jackson, T. (2009). Measuring fossil resource inequality: A case study for the UK between 1968 and 2000. *Ecological Economics* 68, 1213–1225.

Pillarisetti, J. R., van den Bergh, J. (2010). Sustainable nations: what do aggregate indexes tell us? *Environment, Development and Sustainability* 12(1), 49–62.

Roman, Ph., Thiry, G. (2016). The inclusive wealth index. A critical appraisal. *Ecological Economics* 124, 185–192.

Schmidt-Bleek, F., Klüting, R. (1994). Wieviel Umwelt braucht der Mensch? MIPS – das Maß für ökologisches Wirtschaften. Berlin: Birkhäuser.

Shmelev, S.E., Rodríguez-Labajos, B. (2009). Dynamic multidimensional assessment of sustainability at the macro level: The case of Austria. *Ecological Economics* 68(10), 2560–2573.

Spash, C.L. (2008). How much is that ecosystem in the window? The one with the bio-diverse trail. *Environmental Values* 17(2), 259–284.

Spash, C.L. (2012). New foundations for ecological economics. *Ecological Economics* 77(May), 36–47.

Spash, C.L., Vatn, A. (2006). Transferring environmental value estimates: Issues and alternatives. *Ecological Economics* 60(2), 379–388.

UNECE/Eurostat/OECD (2013). *Framework and suggested indicators to measure sustainable development*. Prepared by the Joint UNECE/Eurostat/OECD Task Force on Measuring Sustainable Development. Geneva: UN Economic Commission for Europe.

UNECE/Eurostat/OECD (2014). *Conference of European Statisticians on Measuring Sustainable Development*. New York and Geneva: United Nations.

United Nations (2012). *System of Environmental-Economic Accounting 2012*. New York: United Nations.

UNU-IHDP, UNEP (2012). *The Inclusive Wealth Report 2012. Measuring Progress Toward Sustainability*. Cambridge: Cambridge University Press.

van den Bergh, J. (2014). Ecological Footprint Policy? Land Use as an Environmental Indicator. *Journal of Industrial Ecology* 18(1), 10–19.

Wackernagel, M., Rees, W.E. (1996). *Our ecological footprint: reducing human impact on the earth*. Gabriola Island, BC ; Philadelphia, PA: New Society Publishers.

Weizsäcker, E.U., Lovins, A.B., Lovins, L.H. (1997). *Factor Four: Doubling Wealth, Halving Resource Use: The New Report to the Club of Rome*. London: Earthscan.

World Bank. (2006). *Where is the wealth of nations? Measuring capital for the 21st century*. Washington, D.C: The World Bank.

Ziegler, R. (2007) Political perception and ensemble of macro objectives and measures: The paradox of the index for sustainable economic welfare. *Environmental Values* 16(1), 43–60.

PART IX

Policy challenges

38

COMMONS

Bengi Akbulut

Introduction

Recent times have witnessed the resurgence of the term commons, invoked from various different, and often radically opposed, positions. Some relate commons to efficient use and governance of resources in a rather sterilised fashion, de-contextualised from the broader processes of capital accumulation, spread of markets and power relations. International organisations, such as the World Bank—in a move that (implicitly) acknowledges the destructive impact of the relentless spread of markets and market relations—have been emphasising the need for community-based management of the commons to ensure their efficient and sustainable use. Somewhat similarly, an increasingly popular approach posits the commons as a third way between the State and market, sitting side-by-side (peacefully) with them. This takes for granted that certain fields of the social economic landscape should be organised *via* the market (such as private production and consumption) and others by the State (such as public goods and services), but those arenas where the State–market duo is either ineffective or undesirable are commons to be governed by communities. On the other hand, social mobilisations all around the world, whether resistance movements [Chapters 16 and 17], or concrete practices of alternatives, are increasingly framing their discourses with reference to the commons: defending, reclaiming and/or building them. These social mobilisations often adopt the term as a conceptual tool to help participants imagine non-capitalist ways of organising their material life and creating solidarity.

In its contemporary reincarnations, commons can be found to refer to a resource to be exploited, a group of people cooperating for their interests or forms of social relationships that constitute a need-based organisation of social economic life. Such uses of the term are undoubtedly tied to different approaches to and conceptualisations of the commons, and different understandings of the physical and social reality in which they are embedded, that often remain implicit in the narratives surrounding the concept. Critically discussing different approaches to commons and conflicts over them emerges as a crucial necessity.

In this chapter, I initiate such a discussion by critically reviewing the contributions of major schools of thought on the commons. While I start with an exploration of the literatures inspired by two canonical figures, well-known to ecological economists, Garrett Hardin and Elinor Ostrom, I will then turn to a much older tradition, Marxian political economy and the more recent reformulations of the commons within that tradition. I conclude with a brief consideration of potential ways to further the ecological economics agenda on the commons.

From Hardin's tragedy to Ostrom's community

The literature on the commons has long been influenced, if not dominated, by the (in)famous framework laid out by Hardin (1968) in his "The Tragedy of the Commons". This invokes the example of a pasture collectively used by a group of herders, whose income is directly and positively related to the number of sheep they graze. Every herder decides on the number of sheep they keep individually and there is no collective limit on this individual decision. The problem faced by each and every herder is thus deciding the number of sheep they keep in their individual herds. An individual herder captures the whole of the extra income (utility) from an additional sheep in his/her herd. However, the amount of available pasture decreases for all herders with such an addition, and the cost (disutility) of the intensified use of the pasture is shared by all herders, i.e. only a fraction of the disutility associated with the pasture's overuse is faced by the individual herder. That is to say, every herder is motivated to increase his/her extraction from the pasture without taking into account the costs associated with such an increase on other users. Since each and every herder goes through the same calculation and reaches the same decision, the total number of sheep that is kept collectively ends up being beyond the ecological carrying capacity of the pasture.

Hence a tragedy is asserted to exist: the collective use of a resource by a group of individuals will lead to its inevitable overexploitation. An often-overlooked point here is signified by the precise choice of the word 'tragedy'. Hardin (1968: 1244) argues that, very much like the Greek tragedies, the outcome he foreshadows cannot possibly be averted within a context that combines freedom and commons: "[f]reedom in a commons brings ruin to all". Thus, the solution lies in dispensing with either the freedom or the commons, i.e. centralisation or privatisation. Against the image that he depicts, of helpless individuals trapped in their self-interested behaviour, Hardin claims that commons should either be managed by a central authority who will formulate and enforce regulations of use (e.g. the number of herders who can use the pasture, the number of sheep they can keep, the amount of grass they can use to feed their sheep), or that a regime of well-defined private property rights should replace them (every herder would have their private plots of pasture to graze their sheep).

However, both centralisation and privatisation have been demonstrated to be highly problematic policy prescriptions. The former suffers from issues related to operating a central agency in terms of the costs of its creation and maintenance, the nature and limits of its authority, the effectiveness with which it obtains information, and the potential of free-riding by its agents who would presumably collect information about use and enforce sanctions in case of trespassing. The latter faces the difficulties of assigning clear private property rights (difficult for non-stationary resources such as water), which paradoxically require a public institution for their maintenance and enforcement. Indeed, despite appearing as two extremes of the institutional policy space, both prescriptions share the central idea that institutional change must come from outside the social system of the commons and be imposed upon it.

Both the empirical validity of this narrative and its theoretical foundations have been criticised (e.g. Ostrom, 1990, Harvey, 2011). The argument has been made that what Hardin referred to was in fact an open-access resource and not a common-pool one (Dasgupta, 1996, Ostrom, 1990). Yet, the central dilemma that Hardin's piece focused on was still embraced in these criticisms; namely the dilemma between the difficulty of excluding users from extracting benefits from a resource (non-exclusion of users) and the decrease in benefits that an extra user's extraction implies for the remainder of the group (rivalry in consumption). That many groups who use a common-pool resource find self-devised solutions to this dilemma, without resorting to either a centralised authority or private property rights, was the invaluable contribution made by the works of Ostrom (1990, 1994, 1999, 2005), but also by others such as Fikret Berkes (1989, 2009), Arun Agrawal (2003), and Robert Wade (1987).

Ostrom starts her seminal book *Governing the Commons: The Evolution of Institutions for Collective Action* by examining and subsequently refuting influential models of thinking on the commons—ideas placing the free-rider problem at the centre much like Hardin's "Tragedy"—and argues that the users of natural resources are in fact capable of changing the constraints (on engaging in collective action) that they face. Her argument refocuses the debate on how to enhance the capabilities of those involved and "lead to outcomes other than remorseless tragedies" (Ostrom, 1990: 7). This work and the subsequent literature it inspired thus mark the start of a broader shift in scholarly thinking about the commons and policy making. Research here shows not only the failure of the privatisation-or-statisation duo as the 'only way' of managing the commons, but also illuminates the existing policy space, where interventions can be reoriented towards supplementing and maintaining the ways in which communities can successfully govern the commons, and have done so in the past.

Such research highlights the prevalence of cases where communities can indeed craft their own rules of access and enforce them through mutual monitoring to successfully avert the 'tragedy'. The case studies cited range from fisheries to forestry, from meadows to irrigation systems in various parts of the world including India, Philippines, Spain, Japan, Canada and the United States of America. Researchers have focused on identifying the conditions under which community management emerges successfully. Among the factors highlighted within this context, some are related to the specifics of the commons being studied—size, ease of monitoring, predictability of the benefit streams, importance for users—while others relate to the group of users—number, local knowledge, existence of collective-choice rules, prevalence of social norms, mutual trust within the group. Accordingly, the importance of the resource increases the pay-offs associated with a co-operative solution to the management problem for the group and thus provides an incentive. A clearly defined and bounded resource implies that use and access can be more easily monitored, overuse can be more quickly detected and/or management rules can be more adequately adapted. Stronger norms of reciprocity and intra-group trust are identified as factors that enhance the users' ability to monitor and effectively impose sanctions on each other.

The rich tradition of scholarship produced within this vein holds immense value as it has effectively challenged and pushed the boundaries of the entrenched thinking on the commons. Perhaps the most critical and far-reaching contribution made by this line of work has been related to its unearthing of the assumptions underlying Hardin's tragedy narrative. The Ostrom School has replaced Hardin's conceptualisation, shared widely by mainstream economists, of the individual as an agent motivated (solely) by economic incentives, with that of the individual constrained by social norms and rules [Chapter 3]. The widespread recognition that individuals are social beings who act upon values, concerns, incentives and preferences that extend beyond narrowly defined economic self-interest, and that factors such as mutual trust, altruism, reciprocity and cooperation should become key elements in any debate on the commons, is a major accomplishment; especially given that the zeitgeist was Hardin's tragedy.

However, the Ostrom School's framework might actually have more in common with Hardin's approach than meets the eye. While their work is ground-breaking in many senses, it does not go far with respect to incorporating a vision of the social beyond an aggregation of individuals, or of a form of relationships that is not based on extraction of benefits between communities and commons. The methodological individualism that this approach shares with Hardin's narrative implies a notion of community that is the sum of strategically interacting individuals, albeit responding to both economic and social incentives, and an additional set of constraints (e.g. trust figures into their utility functions in the form of expected costs). Moreover, while the individuals are not narrowly defined *homo economici*, they still primarily relate in economic terms to a resource. Put in a vocabulary familiar to ecological economists, the valuation language that this analytic mobilises remains often implicit, but it is one of material benefits and not much else.

On the other hand, this approach—much like Hardin's—is largely silent on the ways that different dimensions of inequality and relations of power [Chapter 14] interact with the commons. In a related vein, the Ostrom School ignores the political-economic context within which the commons are embedded. In an era marked with expanding commodification, deepening of markets and expropriations of common wealth, the Ostrom School's approach lacks a satisfactory analytic to address many of the issues emerging around the commons today. A radically different, and much older, literature speaks precisely to this lack, namely, Marxian political economy and the notion of primitive accumulation.

From Marxian political economy to anti-capitalist commonings

In the last few chapters of *Capital Volume I*, Marx (1967 [1867]) locates the origins of and the conditions that enable capitalist accumulation, i.e. the existence of capital and wage-labour, within the enclosure of the commons. Accordingly, the process of capitalist accumulation presupposes the ready availability of a population divorced from their means of subsistence and thus forced to sell their labour power, and a surplus wealth that can be put to production as capital. Writing on land enclosures and usurpation of common property in England from the fifteenth to the eighteenth-century, Marx illustrates how direct producers were divorced from their means of production by a variety of means, ranging from individual acts of violence to legal restructuring that removed the remaining barriers to the expropriation of the commons (e.g. the Acts for Enclosures of Commons passed in Parliament). Accordingly, lands cultivated in common or held by communities—pastures grazed communally, forests from which communities had customary rights of use and extraction—were passed into the hands of landlords who now gained exclusionary rights over them. Through enclosures, commons were transformed into capital and 'immediate producers' were turned into wage-labourers;[1] this process, coined famously as 'primitive accumulation', yielded the original surplus that enabled subsequent capitalist production. As Marx (1967: 500) states: "[t]his primitive accumulation plays in Political Economy about the same part as original sin in theology".

Although Marx did not explicitly attribute a specific temporality (such as pre-capitalism) to the concepts of primitive accumulation and enclosures, the Marxian tradition has often operationalised them in the context of geographies that capitalism has not yet penetrated and/ or periods predating the advent of capitalism. The concept has been reworked under different names, such as 'accumulation by extra-economic means' and 'accumulation by dispossession', to show that primitive accumulation is ongoing, both in the global North and the Global South, in different forms with new twists (De Angelis, 2001, Glassman, 2006, Harvey, 2003, Midnight Notes Collective, 1990) [Chapters 4 and 15].

Perhaps the most notable among these is David Harvey's notion of 'accumulation by dispossession'. According to Harvey (2003), enclosures of the commons are not limited to a specific geography or temporality, but rather represent a strategy employed when capital accumulation slows down, hits barriers and/or is in crisis. Enclosing of the commons restores accumulation by opening outlets of investment (new venues of capital accumulation) and providing cheap input supplies. Analysing the rise of neoliberalism in these terms, Harvey mentions a series of processes as means of accumulation by dispossession, including the commodification and privatisation of land and the forceful expulsion of peasantry; conversion of various forms of property rights (common, collective, State) into exclusive private property rights; suppression of rights to the commons; commodification of labour power and the eradication of alternative forms of production and consumption; privatisation of public assets; colonial, neo-colonial and imperial asset appropriation (including natural resources); licensing of bio-genetic material under intellectual property rights; commodification of nature and culture; and the use of the credit system (Harvey, 2003, 2005). In a similar vein, De Angelis (2004) lists the imposition of intellectual property rights on culture and collective knowledge; depletion of the global commons due to commodification of nature and negative externalities such as pollution; commodification of cultural forms, histories and intellectual creativity; privatisation of public assets; and the reversion of common rights to State pensions, welfare and national health systems as forms of new enclosures.

The Marxian reincarnations of the concept of the commons (and enclosures), by Harvey and others, have effectively posited the notion in relation to capital accumulation. These scholars have revealed the ways in which the expropriation of commons is inherent in contemporary (as well as historical) processes of capital accumulation, and how commons have served, and continue to serve, as a support and/or enabling mechanism for capitalism. For them, the broader political-economic landscape, in which commons are embedded, is not to be taken as an exogenous variable but rather the founding ground of analysis. In this sense, the Marxian framework speaks to the ever-present tension between the process of capital accumulation and the commons, so conveniently skirted around both by the tragedy narrative of Hardin and the new institutional economics of the Ostrom School.

The works within this literature have also contributed to expanding the boundaries of conventional understandings of the commons to include social entitlements—welfare and pension systems—urban space, knowledge, and cultural and intellectual commons, most of which are now in our collective imaginary as intangible commons. They also revealed new forms of enclosure. The licensing of the genetic material contained in seeds, for instance, can be regarded as a fencing-off of an historical wealth of knowledge produced and held collectively. The land pollution due to negative 'externalities' similarly forms an expropriation of a portion of commons as an environmental sink for private use and barring its other uses. They are thus put *on par* with other forms of enclosures, such as privatisations of public and communal lands or of water resources. As such, the Marxian literature on new commons and new enclosures has provided an analytical toolbox for addressing some of the most pressing issues of our era, such as commodification of nature and culture, privatisation of natural resources, pollution and contamination, and urban gentrification. In doing so, it has illuminated the thread that ties these distinct processes together and provided a shared language and line of struggle to the oppositions against them.

Within the Marxian literature on the commons, the Autonomist Marxist approach epitomised by the works of Caffentzis (2010), Federici (2010), De Angelis (2001, 2006) and more broadly the Midnight Notes Collective (1990), among others, is particularly noteworthy for the purposes of this chapter. This vein of thought defines both the concepts of commons and enclosures in a rather distinct way from the traditional Marxian line, most of all due to its explicit reference to the set of social relationships in and around the commons. In particular, this approach conceptualises the commons as social spheres of life the main characteristics of which are to provide various degrees of protection from the market. That is, the commons form modes of social reproduction and accessing social resources that are not mediated by the market. They are non-commodified forms of fulfilling social needs such as obtaining social wealth and organising social production (De Angelis, 2004, Harvie, 2004). Enclosures, in turn, are acts directed towards the expropriation, fragmentation and destruction of the autonomy of social reproduction by the market (and/or the State).

Seen this way, commons are no longer limited to shared forms of natural and social wealth, but include forms of relationships, networks, practices and struggles that provide (varying degrees of) access to means of material and social reproduction outside of the mediation of the market. This conceptualisation goes beyond an understanding of commons as existing, pre-defined entities, and, rather, points to the amalgam of social relations and practices that produce and reproduce commons. Linebaugh (2008), and others, term this 'commoning'. Moreover, this emphasises not only the commons as process but also the particular characteristics of their constitutive social practices. Accordingly, commons are forms of non-commodified wealth to be used by all, sites of collective cooperative labour and regulated non-hierarchically. More specifically, then, commons emerge as spaces of social reproduction accessed equally by all, autonomous of intermediation of the State or the market, where reproduction and production takes place under collective labour, equal access to means of (re)production and egalitarian forms of decision-making (Federici and Caffentzis, 2014, De Angelis, 2006).

Within this context, time banks, urban gardens, land and urban squats, food co-ops, local currencies, 'creative commons' licenses and bartering practices, in addition to communal control and use of resources, emerge as contemporary forms of commons (Federici and Caffentzis, 2014). These examples represent practices in self-provisioning outside the logic of markets and, to varying extents, embody a collective form of self-reproduction. For example, urban squats are a form of commons to the extent that they organise their reproduction outside of State and market control and provide access to the means of such reproduction on a collective, democratic and egalitarian basis. Urban gardens serve as vehicles of regaining control over food production, regeneration of the environment and provision for subsistence. They are also venues of knowledge production, intergenerational transmission/exchange and of reproduction of social relationships, as well as a medium for the encounter of diverse cultural practices. Similar examples of commoning are: appropriations of unused plots of public land for subsistence farming by landless rural and urban women; local currencies and bartering practices that represent networks of exchange outside of market relations; and community governance of water through committees, such as those set up in Cochabamba, Bolivia (Dwinell and Olivera, 2014, Federici, 2011, Federici and Caffentzis, 2014).

As the examples above suggest, this approach defines commons not necessarily (or exclusively) by their common-pool resource characteristics (rivalry in consumption and non-exclusion of users), but rather by the degree of autonomy they provide from capital and State, and the type of social relationships that constitute them. As a consequence, this approach lends itself to a distinguishing commons as milieus of non-commodified reproduction not driven by the profit motive of commodity-producing commons—an implicit dimension of both Hardin's and Ostrom's frameworks (Caffentzis, 2010, Federici and Caffentzis, 2014). In contrast to a vision of the commons as a 'third sector', between the State and the market, this perspective envisions the commons as empowering and enabling social struggles against the two. This does not deny a potential role for the State in helping carve out support for the struggles to defend, reclaim and construct commons. Examples where this has been important include the sanctioning of the right of the indigenous people to use the natural resources in their territories by the Venezuelan Constitution in 1999, and the recognition of communal property by the Bolivian Constitution in 2009.

Future directions

Commons, despite being generally used interchangeably with common property resources, has always been a substantial topic of interest within ecological economics. While there is neither a unified nor clearly defined approach to the commons shared by the diversity of strands within it, most debates within ecological economics have focused on either refuting Hardin's tragedy framework and/or (somewhat uncritically) celebrating the work of Ostrom and her colleagues. Indeed, the refutation is critical and valuable given that Hardin's work has served to legitimise widespread privatisation and the imposition of a specific, Western, form of property relations on the commons. Consequently, ecological economists working on the commons have predominantly been concerned with (re)emphasising Hardin's mistake when conceptualising the commons as an open-access resource and further documenting cases of successful commons management by self-devised local institutional arrangements.

Such work has demonstrated several important aspects of the policy prescriptions stemming from Hardin's work:

1   privatisation and 'statisation' have resulted in devastating social and ecological outcomes in different settings;
2   institutions, social groups and the non-human environment co-evolve [Chapter 13];
3   related to the preceding point, the key to successful management of the commons is to achieve a correct match between institutions and the cultural and the biophysical environments;
4   assumption of *homo economicus* as a behavioural foundation is misconceived.

Ostrom and her colleagues' work struck a chord with ecological economists especially regarding the last point, because of their long tradition of stressing that the motivation and behaviour of human beings are endogenously determined by social structures.

This research, however, suffers from many of the same issues that plague the Ostrom School. Ecological economists have certainly been concerned with the equity implications associated with private or State expropriations of the commons and the unequal appropriations of global commons, as encapsulated in the notion of ecological debt [Chapter 16]. However, in the absence of a coherent analytical framework on the political economy of the commons, these issues have often been addressed as single-standing instances of misinformed or ill-conceived policy. As such, the more structural conflict between the commons and the political-economic context (i.e. capitalism), within which they are embedded, is rendered invisible in most ecological economics writing on the commons. Thus the dimensions of inequality within the commons and the power dynamics that shape them have gone largely unaddressed, except for the notable work done primarily by feminist ecological economists (e.g. Agarwal, 2001).

More generally, ecological economics would benefit from a broader engagement with the burgeoning commons literature. While there is much to incorporate from analyses of non-traditional commons that fall outside of the ecological economics radar, the most significant contribution of such an engagement would perhaps be in terms of the agenda of social and ecological justice that has always been fundamental to ecological economics [Chapter 16]. One notable line of correspondence, for instance, is that between the literature on multiple valuation languages (e.g. Martinez-Alier, 2002)—that problematises the imposition of the language of monetary exchange values to the detriment of other value systems within ecological economics—and the understanding of commons as non-commodified sites of social reproduction. Similarly, the existing interaction of the literature on the commons and on degrowth [Chapter 44] would benefit from the inspiring formulation of commons as spaces of collective and democratic social reproduction. De Angelis and Harvie (2014) make the assertion that today the demands for social and ecological justice and calls for alternative forms of living cannot be meaningfully met without a vision of how to organise the terrain of commons as non-commodified systems of social reproduction.

Concluding remarks

This chapter has laid out different approaches to conceptualising the commons and the connected understandings of the physical and social reality in which they are embedded. Grasping the different frameworks underlying the uses of the notion is important beyond its value as an analytical exercise, because these frameworks are tied to different visions of politics and policies regarding the commons.

The framework mobilised by Autonomist Marxists that rescues the notion of the commons from being frozen as a tragedy or conflicted production unit is noteworthy. By positing commons as a process based and relational concept, this framework envisions commons as constituted in part by social relationships, collective practices, struggles over access and control, and the forms of subjectivity that are (re)configured. It thus opens up space to recognise the diversity of forms that commons and commoning practices can take as well as their dynamism; it helps illuminate the existing and proliferating forms of commons and commoning practices. This reveals the many forms of contemporary social struggles that are continuously constructing and reproducing the commons, and thus sheds light on the potential of political action.

The framework also highlights relationships between the social and the commons that are not resource-centric (e.g. being self-sufficient, autonomous reproduction of life, guaranteeing subsistence rather than profit-generation) and incorporates the bases on which social relationships of commoning arise (e.g. solidarity, collectivity, cooperation, self-governance, egalitarianism, democracy). This invigorates a fundamentally social ecological notion of the commons, rather than an understanding of the commons as purely physical ecological entities. Social ecological economics can thus gain a lot from such an understanding.

Note

1   This refers to a statement by Marx that:

> The process, therefore, that clears the way for the capitalist system, can be none other than the process which takes away from the labourer the possession of his means of production; a process that transforms, on the one hand, the social means of subsistence and of production into capital, on the other, the immediate producers into wage labourers,
>
> *(1967 [1867]: 507–508)*

Key further readings cited

De Angelis, M. (2004). Separating the doing and the deed: Capital and the continuous character of enclosures. *Historical Materialism*, 12 (2): 57–87.

Hardin, G. (1968). The tragedy of the commons. *Science*, 162 (3859), 1243–1248.

Harvey, D. (2003). *The New Imperialism*. Oxford: Oxford University Press.

Ostrom, E. (1990). *Governing the Commons: The Evolution of Institutions for Collective Action*. Cambridge: Cambridge University Press.

Other literature cited

Agarwal, B. (2001). Participatory exclusions, community forestry and gender: An analysis for South Asia and a conceptual framework. *World Development* , 29(6), 1623–1648.

Agrawal, A. (2003). Sustainable governance of common-pool resources: Context, methods, politics. *Annual Review of Anthropology*, 32, 243–262.

Berkes, F. (1989). The benefits of the commons. *Nature*, 340(July), 91–93.

Berkes, F. (2009). Revising the commons paradigm. *Journal of Natural Resources Policy Research*, 3 (1), 261–264.

Caffentzis, G. (2010). The future of 'the commons': Neoliberalism's 'Plan B' or the original disaccumulation of capital? *New Formations*, 69 (Summer), 23–41.

Dasgupta, P. (1996). The economics of the environment. *Environment and Development Economics*, 1(04), 387–428.

De Angelis, M. (2001). Marx and primitive accumulation: The continuous character of capital's 'enclosures'. *The Commoner*, N2.

De Angelis, M. (2006). Enclosures, commons and the outside. Paper presented at the annual meeting of the International Studies Association, Town & Country Resort and Convention Center, San Diego, California.

De Angelis, M. and D. Harvie (2014). The Commons. In M. Parker, G. Cheney, V. Fournier and C. Land (Eds) *The Routledge Companion to Alternative Organization* (280–294) New York: Routledge.

Dwinell, A. and M. Olivera (2014). The water is ours damn it! Water commoning in Bolivia. *Community Development Journal*, 49 (S1), 44–52.

Federici, S. (2010). Feminism and the politics of the commons in an era of primitive accumulation. In The Team Colors Collective (Ed.), *Uses of a Whirlwind: Movement, Movements, and Contemporary Radical Currents in the United States* (pp. 283–293). Oakland, CA: AK Press.

Federici, S. (2011). Women, land struggles, and the reconstruction of the commons. *WorkingUSA: The Journal of Labour and Society*, 14 (1), 41–56.

Federici, S. and G. Caffentzis (2014). Commons against and beyond capitalism. *Community Development Journal*, 49 (1), 92–106.

Glassman, J. (2006). Primitive accumulation, accumulation by dispossession and accumulation by extra-economic means. *Progress in Human Geography*, 30 (5), 608–625.

Harvey, D. (2005). *A Brief History of Neoliberalism*. Oxford: Oxford University Press.

Harvey, D. (2011). The future of the commons. *Radical History Review*, 109 (Winter), 101–107.

Harvie, D. (2004). Commons and communities in the university: Some notes and some examples. *The Commoner*, N4 (Autumn-Winter), 1–10.

Linebaugh, P. (2008). *The Magna Carta Manifesto: Liberties and Commons for All*. Berkeley: University of California Press.

Martinez-Alier, J. (2002). *The Environmentalism of the Poor: A Study of Ecological Conflicts and Valuation*. Cheltenham: Edward Elgar.

Marx, K. (1967 [1867]). *Capital: A Critique of Political Economy. Volume 1: The Process of Capitalist Production*, edited by Frederick Engels, translated from the third German edition by Samuel Moore and Edward Aveling. New York: International Publishers.

Midnight Notes Collective (1990). *The New Enclosures*, New York: Autonomedia.

Ostrom, E. (1994). *Neither market nor state: Governance of common-pool resources in the twenty-first century*. Washington, DC: International Food Policy Research Institute.

Ostrom, E. (1999). Coping with the tragedies of the commons. *Annual Review of Political Science*, 2(June), 493–535.

Ostrom, E. (2005). *Understanding Institutional Diversity*. Princeton: Princeton University Press.

Wade, R. (1987). The management of common property resources: Collective action as an alternative to privatisation or state regulation. *Cambridge Journal of Economics*, 11 (2), 95–106.

39

UNEVEN DEVELOPMENT AND RESOURCE EXTRACTIVISM IN AFRICA

Patrick Bond

Introduction

Neoliberal ideology has expanded into environmental management and Africa has suffered as a result. The most serious eco-social contradiction may well be the extraction of non-renewable resources—minerals, oil, gas and old-growth forest resources—at a pace far in excess of returns to source countries, especially in the wake of the catastrophic commodity price crash from 2011 to 2015. Even during the 2002–2011 commodity super-cycle, extraction left a net negative 'adjusted net savings' once natural capital accounting is applied; in other words, countries are demonstrably poorer the more they face resource extraction by multi-national corporations. Most serious of all environmental problems is the extreme vulnerability Africans face due to human induced climate change, with estimates of unnecessary deaths approaching 200 million and large parts of the continent expected to be unliveable by the end of the twenty-first century, if not well before. In addition, African climate justice advocates and progressive conservationists have often found themselves confronting the adverse impacts not only of resource 'extractivism' and neoliberal socio-economic policies, but also of specific market-environmentalist strategies such as Clean Development Mechanism projects, forest offsets and proposed trading systems for rhinoceros horn and elephant ivory (Bond, 2012).

Signs of dissent across Africa are the main hope—far greater than top-down Sustainable Development Goals or the United Nations Paris Agreement on climate—for a dramatic reversal in Africa's eco-social development prospect. Though there are few ecological economists and political ecologists in Africa doing research and developing a pedagogy at present (aside from the Council for the Development of Social Science Research in Africa and a few non-governmental organisation [NGO] initiatives mainly aimed at resource-related transparency), such intellectual work is urgently needed by grassroots dissidents. The period ahead requires revitalised political economy research, with more sensitivity to gender [Chapter 5], race and identity as central facets of uneven development [Chapters 4 and 15], alongside a critique of capitalism's widespread environmental damage (Bond, 2006).

This chapter introduces the reader to some of the central problems facing Africa today. The next section gives a brief general background to the political, social and economic situation. This is followed by a more specific account of debates over eco-social development in which ecological economics concepts are usefully invoked.

Background to development in Africa

The conditions for reproduction of daily life, sustainable economic development and ecological conservation in Africa have not improved as a result of the frenetic expansion of global capitalism over the past third of a century. In many ways conditions have worsened. The period has been characterised by the fall, rise and crash of commodity prices; the Soviet Union's collapse and hence the 1990s' dramatic shrinkage of overseas development aid (earlier so closely tied to the Cold War); persistent civil wars and regular cross-border conflicts; structural adjustment austerity imposed by the Bretton Woods institutions, carried out by dictatorships or at best semi-democratic regimes; the intensification of export-oriented macroeconomic policy; deepening of extractive industry super-exploitation, in which profits are captured by local rentiers and multi-national corporations, both using tax-avoidance techniques known as 'Illicit Financial Flows' (IFFs); worsening relative deindustrialisation; AIDS, Ebola and other preventable diseases; and the resulting amplification of various political, economic and ecological injustices.

Simultaneously, though paradoxically, a cacophony of 'Africa Rising' rhetoric emerged from business journalists, mainstream think tanks and financial institutions. Some of the rhetoric was based on the post-2000 arrival of new fixed capital investment, including mega-infrastructure projects, emanating from the BRICS (Brazil, Russia, India, China and South Africa) countries. Some was based upon microeconomic innovations, such as cellular telephony 'leapfrog technology,' or micro-credit's role in 'financial deepening' (i.e. higher domestic debt loads). Some celebration was justified by the continent's Gross Domestic Product (GDP) growth rate, which initially appeared relatively unscathed by the 2008–2009 'Great Recession'. In 2015 there were also partial celebrations of Millennium Development Goal (MDG) achievements, including nominal declines in the numbers of people suffering 'poverty' (depending upon definitions). Minor progress on the social welfare front in some African countries can indeed be traced to slightly more generous public education and health system spending—including free AIDS medicines that before 2000 cost $10,000/year, until desperate health activists compelled change (hence resulting in dramatic African life expectancy increases from the mid-2000s)—as well as cash transfer redistribution schemes. However, while some have 'developed', others still suffer dramatic declines in living standards and ecological conditions, for the African continent remains the world's most extreme site of uneven development.

A period of even harsher conditions lies ahead, not least due to the growing contradictions within and between markets, States, societies and the environment. The 2011 peak of world commodity prices followed by crashes of 50 per cent or more for many African raw materials by 2016, left most of Africa suffering from global capitalism's vicissitudes. Symptoms included fast-rising current account deficits and foreign debt. Yet there are many residues of the 'Africa Rising' rhetoric that remain to be contested.

African eco-social development, from above

Overconfidence in a top-down 'development' model coincides with pressure on Africa to further extract and export raw materials, tighten State budgets as revenues shrink, and continue financial and trade liberalisation, ultimately emphasising GDP growth above all else. To define development as GDP leaves out factors that are especially vital in Africa: non-renewable resource depletion, the pollution of air and water, loss of farmland and wetlands, unpaid women's and community work, and family breakdown due to widespread migrant labour systems (Fioramonti, 2014).

Technocratic interventions promoting Keynesian and basic-industrial strategies, such as the 1980 Lagos Plan of Action for the Economic Development of Africa and 1989 African Alternative Framework to Structural Adjustment Programmes, were useful as semi-official reform proposals. These were ignored in practice as neoliberalism dominated policy-making, but in any case did not highlight environmental values. As a result, subsequent debate centred on whether the export-oriented, resource-intensive strategy could be improved by new counting techniques, greater transparency, attention to IFFs, and the incorporation of nature into the market. Advocating the latter, the World Bank (2012: 12) argues that:

> green growth is about good growth policies—addressing market failures and 'getting the price right' by introducing environmental taxation, pricing environmental externalities (such as carbon pricing), creating tradable property rights, and reducing inappropriate subsidies.

Environmental considerations are apparently a lower priority, however, now that the commodity price super-cycle is definitively over. As a result, foreign investors are more frenetically extracting resources from existing mines, oil fields and plantations across the continent, raising output levels where possible to offset the commodities' lower profitability. There is limited incentive to reinvest, to engage seriously in Corporate Social Responsibility or environmental protection, or to open new production facilities. Tens of thousands of Africa's resource-sector workers have lost their jobs in several of the countries most adversely affected. These contradictions may well lead to more social and political explosions.

Debates over Africa's resource dependency

The most powerful statements concerning uneven eco-social and cultural development in contemporary Africa are from the diaspora's critical intellectuals and political visionaries (e.g., Ake, 2001; Amin, 1976; Fanon, 1963; Nkrumah, 1966; Onimode, 1988; Rodney, 1974). Many such works reflected on how Africa's comprador classes emerged to lubricate transnational corporations' value transfers to the West. These transfers included not just undercompensated labour values, but also under-priced natural resources, as commodity prices fell steadily after the 1973 oil price spike, through the early 2000s. Moreover, the continent's residual pre-capitalist patriarchal, ethnicist, xenophobic, homophobic and other oppressive narratives were often amplified during the postcolonial transition (Mama, 2002).

Reflecting the lost decades associated with structural adjustment, three International Monetary Fund (IMF) economists (Salinas, Gueye and Korbut, 2011: 3) recognised the reality of postcolonial economic decline:

> The apparent stagnation of Sub-Saharan Africa (SSA) (the poorest region in the world) in an era of freer markets has fuelled strong criticisms against market reforms. Indeed, condemnation of economic liberalization has become part of mainstream development thinking, and several commentators urge SSA countries to accelerate growth by modifying their comparative advantage on natural resources. But does SSA stagnation imply the failure of market reforms and of the natural resource-based model in the region?

Reflecting the dominant discourse, however, they answered firmly in the negative:

SSA countries can *grow sustainably without changing their comparative advantage in natural resources*. The growth experience of SSA countries that dismantled the Import Substitution Industrialisation model and avoided major political instability provides further evidence that a natural resource-based model can be consistent with sustained economic growth. [emphasis added]

(Salinas, Gueye and Korbut, 2011: 3)

This ideologically charged claim was made in 2011, at the peak of the commodity price cycle, and entailed a misleading characterisation of high-growth African countries to include those that were recovering (rapidly in GDP terms) from ubiquitous civil wars, while the majority of the continent still suffered (Weeks, 2010). Similarly, a decade earlier, the New Partnership for Africa's Development (NEPAD) strategy adopted by the African Union also decried historic underdevelopment processes and, as a solution, proposed even more integration into the world economy (Bond, 2005). According to standard liberal doctrine, this was meant to be accompanied by democratisation, but in 2016 the African Peer Review Mechanism—a continental agreement promoting freedom and human rights that was meant to undergird NEPAD's economic strategy—was also at risk of "breathing on life-support in a coma, while effectively brain-dead", according to one of its main NGO supporters (Fabricius, 2016). In other words neither neoliberalism nor its liberal political veil were suitable frameworks to prevent the rise of resource-related super-exploitation during the commodity super-cycle, nor to prevent adverse exposure to global economic volatility and crashing markets in the subsequent period. Moreover, notwithstanding claims to the contrary about a 'rising middle class' in Africa, there was a decline in the proportion of Africans spending at least \$20/day, from 6.5 to 4.8 per cent of the population from 2000 to 2010 (African Development Bank, 2011). Claims made by advocates of the MDGs and Sustainable Development Goals are just as misleading (Amin, 2006; Brewer, 2015).

The case for export-led growth is further weakened when ecological economists introduce calculations of Africa's changes in 'natural capital', i.e., physical resource endowments. The removal of non-renewable minerals, oil and gas—and the failure to reinvest profits from these resources—leaves Africa far poorer in net terms than anywhere else on Earth. That bias towards non-renewable resource depletion without reinvestment meant the continent's net wealth fell rapidly after 2001. Even the World Bank (2014: vi) admits that 88 per cent of sub-Saharan African countries suffered net negative wealth accumulation in 2010. (In contrast, what is termed 'Adjusted Net Savings' rose in Latin America and East Asia.) Although the end of the commodity super-cycle means a lower rate of value extraction, this should not blind Africans to the dangers of extractivism where transnational corporations primarily benefit, in contrast to Australia, Canada and Norway, whose resource extraction generates profits to home-based corporations, and hence reinvestment.

The failure of the resource-based model is reflected in declining African exports after 2011, a (small) trade deficit, a near doubling of foreign debt from \$200 billion in 2005 to \$400 billion a decade later, and an annual current account deficit in excess of \$50 billion by 2015 (largely driven by the payments account, i.e. export of profits and dividends). Most aspects of the neoliberal model covered below—Foreign Direct Investment (FDI), IFFs and also *licit* (legal) financial flows, manufacturing deindustrialisation, land-grabs, climate change and militarisation— still prove destructive to any reasonable expectations the African citizenries may have about their eco-social development prospects.

Current assessment of major issues

The situation facing an Africa increasingly dependent upon the world economy after 2000 became dire once the commodity crash gathered pace in 2014. According to the United Nations Conference on Trade and Development (2016), "FDI inflows to Africa fell by 31% in 2015 to an estimated $38 billion, due largely to a decline of FDI in Sub-Saharan Africa". Subtracting mergers (i.e., not the more desirable 'greenfield' investments) from FDI, the 2014–2015 drop was from $50 billion to $18 billion. The most developed economy, South Africa, in 2015 witnessed only $1.5 billion in new FDI, a 74 per cent decline from 2014 levels.

On the other hand, the slowing of FDI inflows means the extractive industries' extreme pressures on people and environments will probably slow, although in some cases, corporate desperation will intensify site-specific extractive industry malpractices, more extreme forms of ecological degradation, social depravity and labour exploitation. Traumatic job losses were announced in 2015—with the Anglo American Corporation (the largest on the continent over most of the prior century) revealing it would scale down mining employment by more than half—but on the positive side, that could also mean less financial disinvestment from Africa and hence less pressure on the balance of payments from profit repatriation (as occurred in 2008–2010 when prices and profits were also lower).

However, aside from licit profit outflows facilitated by the relaxation of exchange controls across the continent, there are huge IFFs—thanks to transfer pricing, mis-invoicing and various other tax avoidance gimmicks—which an African Union commission headed by Mbeki recorded at a minimum of $80 billion annually (Mwiti, 2016). Global Financial Integrity (Kar and Spanjers, 2015: 8–9, 23) measured annual average IFFs from 2004 to 2013 at $21 billion in South Africa alone (rising to $29 billion in 2013) and $18 billion in Nigeria. Sub-Saharan Africa as a whole lost at least 6 per cent of GDP annually to IFFs, more than 50 per cent higher than the rate for other continents' poor countries. Out of every dollar in capital flight, 80 per cent comes from: metals (26 per cent); oil (25 per cent); natural gas (11 per cent); minerals (10 per cent); and petroleum and coal products (6 per cent). Specific examples abound:

- In South Africa, Bracking and Sharife (2014) reported that De Beers mis-invoiced $2.83 billion of diamonds over six years, while even Zimbabwean President Robert Mugabe claimed $15 billion in missing revenues from diamonds mainly mined by Chinese capital and local military officials from 2008 to 2015 (Saunders and Nyamunda, 2016).
- The Alternative Information and Development Centre (2014) showed that Lonmin's platinum operations—notorious at Marikana not far from Johannesburg, where the firm arranged a massacre of 34 of its wildcat-striking mineworkers in 2012—has also spirited hundreds of millions of dollars offshore to Bermuda since 2000
- The Indian mining house Vedanta's chief executive arrogantly bragged at a Bangalore meeting how in 2006 he spent $25 million to buy Zambia's Konkola Copper Mines, which is Africa's largest, and then reaped at least $500 million profits from it annually (*Lusaka Times*, 2014).

Sustained analyses of IFFs at continental scale have been carried out by Ndikumana, Boyce and Ndyiaye (2014), demonstrating how Africa is both more integrated but more marginalised in world trade due to exploitation. There are also policy-oriented NGOs working against IFF across Africa and the South, including several with northern roots like Trust Africa's 'Stop the Bleeding' campaign, Global Financial Integrity, Tax Justice Network, Publish What You Pay, Open Society and Eurodad. Such institutions' studies of IFFs are a source of economic critique that gives hope to so many who want Africa's scarce revenues to be recirculated inside poor countries, not siphoned away to offshore financial centres. Nevertheless, the implicit theory of change adopted by the head offices of some such NGOs is dubious to the extent that they argue that because transparency is like a harsh light that can disinfect corruption, their task is mainly a matter of making capitalism cleaner by bringing problems like IFFs to light (a notable exception is the WoMin—African Women Unite Against Destructive Resource Extraction— which explicitly opposes extractive industries from ecofeminist and anti-imperialist standpoints).

Africa's growing current account deficit requires that State elites attract yet more new FDI or foreign debt, so as to have hard currency on hand to pay back profits and dividends on prior FDI, to overseas transnational corporate headquarters. Foreign debt in sub-Saharan Africa was in the $170–$210 billion range during 1995–2005, and was then reduced 10 per cent by G7 debt relief in 2006. However, when China stepped in as creditor, it rose to nearly $400 billion by 2015. Neoliberal conditionalities by the IMF never stopped, in spite of successful demands to give more voting power to leaders of the Global South in late 2015: China received a 37 per cent greater weight, Brazil 23 per cent, India 11 per cent and Russia 8 per cent. Simultaneously, every African State lost voting power, with six losing more than a quarter, including Nigeria at 41 per cent and even BRICS member South Africa losing 21 per cent (Bond, 2016).

In spite of rising Chinese corporate investment, the single biggest country-based source of FDI in Africa is internal, from the continent's largest foreign debtor (at nearly $140 billion), South Africa. A dozen companies with Johannesburg Stock Exchange listings draw out profits from the rest of the continent: British American Tobacco, SAB Miller breweries, the MTN and Vodacom cell phone networks, Naspers newspapers, four banks (Standard, Barclays, Nedbank and FirstRand), the Sasol oil company and the local residues of the Anglo American Corporation empire. The main retail chains—such as Walmart-owned Massmart and its affiliates—use the larger market in the south to achieve economies of scale in production that then swamps and destroys Africa's remaining basic-needs manufacturing sector.

As another reflection of 'sub-imperial' accumulation, South Africa's MTN cell phone service was reported by the Amabhungane (2015) investigative journalist network to have Mauritian and Dubai financial offices which systematically skim profits for dubious tax-avoidance purposes from high-profit operations (Mauritian company taxes are 3 per cent with no capital gains). This was a blatant practice when MTN's chairperson was Cyril Ramaphosa, subsequently South Africa's deputy president from 2014 and the likely president in 2019. In November 2015, MTN was fined $4 billion by Abuja authorities due to its failure to disconnect more than 5 million unregistered Nigerian customers during the State's crackdown on Boko Haram terrorists' cell phones. There were few MTN defenders and indeed, as South African corporations advance further in Africa, they carry the baggage of home: when xenophobia broke out in 2015, branch plants of Johannesburg firms became targets of protest by Nigerians, Zimbabweans, Malawians, Mozambicans and Zambians concerned about their relatives' safety.

Hostility to Johannesburg capital is logical because South African corporate leadership was named the world's most corrupt by the auditing firm PricewaterhouseCoopers (2016) on two occasions since 2014. That year, 80 per cent of managers admitted that they commit economic crimes, making them the "world leaders in money-laundering, bribery and corruption, procurement fraud, asset misappropriation and cyber crime" (Hosken, 2014). The profits do not stay in South Africa. Since the early 2000s the current account deficit has soared because nearly all the country's biggest companies relocated to London, New York or Melbourne, including: Anglo American and its historic partner De Beers, SAB Miller, Investec bank, Old Mutual insurance, Didata IT, Mondi paper, Liberty Life insurance and Gencor (now BHP Billiton). As a result, the South African Reserve Bank (2015: 39) revealed that Johannesburg firms were by 2012–2014 drawing in only 45 per cent as much in internationally sourced profits (dividend receipts) as TNCs were taking out of South Africa.

Is this withdrawal of Africa's surplus sustainable? In assessing the current direction of African eco-social development, a critical factor is the degree of popular discontent with the status quo. The end of the commodity super-cycle coincided with major public protests across Africa, rising from an index level of 100 in 2000 to nearly 450 in 2011, as measured by Agence France Press and Reuters (African Development Bank et al., 2016). Even after the end of the North African uprising ('Arab Spring')—especially in Tunisia, Egypt and Morocco—the index of Africa-wide protests rose still higher, to 520 in 2012 and 550 in 2013. In 2014 the protest rate fell back just slightly (to 540) and in 2015, according to the African Development Bank, there were several reasons for a substantial decline (to an index of 300).

> Ebola in West Africa and terrorist attacks in several countries led to reduced tolerance for public demonstrations by authorities. Temporary bans or restrictions were imposed on rallies in Guinea, Liberia and Sierra Leone and in the context of officially declared states of emergency in Chad, Egypt, Mali, Niger and Tunisia.
>
> *(African Development Bank et al., 2016: 118)*

A good share of the social turmoil in Africa prior to the 2011 upsurge took place in the vicinity of mines and mineral wealth, as reflected in mappings of Armed Conflict and Location Events Data (Berman et al., 2014) and the Environmental Justice Organisations, Liabilities and Trade (EJOLT) project (http://ejatlas.org). The World Economic Forum (2015) regularly cites African countries as having amongst the most militant workforces, including South Africa as the proletariat least cooperative with employers from 2012 to 2015.

Future directions

The central question for Africa's eco-social development in coming years is whether the world economy will continue to stumble—leading to further commodity price deterioration—in part because the Chinese infrastructure boom that required such bountiful raw materials from Africa has come to a grinding halt. If so, while new mining and petroleum projects are likely to be cancelled or postponed, there is a serious threat to the continent, of even more frenetic extraction from existing mines and wells. However, if, partly as a result of State subsidies, a new series of mines and oil rigs are financed, this will probably occur within the Programme for Infrastructure Development in Africa (PIDA). The donor-supported, trillion-dollar strategy is mainly aimed at providing new roads, railroads, pipelines and bridges, but they largely emanate from mines, oil/gas rigs and plantations, and are mainly directed towards ports. Electricity generation is already overwhelmingly biased towards projected mining and smelting needs. One route for further indirect financing subsidies to corporations (i.e., loans at preferential rates) is via the BRICS New Development Bank (Bond, 2016). The first loan in Africa, made in 2016, is to connect privatised electricity supply from solar plants that the State-owned firm Eskom refused to finance in spite of consistent advocacy by climate activists (and opposition to privatised supply by organised labour). Eskom's most influential customers are the Energy Intensive Users Group of 33 companies in the carbon-intensive mining and smelting sectors which consume nearly half the country's electricity, so the benefits of renewable supply are quickly overwhelmed by the extractive character of production.

That the first BRICS loan was 'green' in that limited sense would not be typical of a future portfolio anticipated to stress extractive-industry accumulation. Already, as the climate campaigning group 350.org Africa (2014) points out:

> South African banks are greenwashing their work while funding Africa's growing addiction to fossil fuels at the same time, [through financing] massive coal power stations, oil refineries and drilling rigs.

These include Nedbank, Barclays (owner of ABSA) and Standard Bank which together invested more than $1 billion in coal projects from 2005 to 2013. It is fair to predict that the BRICS bank and PIDA will amplify the problems of resource extractivism, given the prevailing power structure (Bond and Garcia, 2015).

The resulting intensification of climate change will affect the most vulnerable Africans in the poorest countries, who are already subject to extreme stress as a result of war-torn socio-economic fabrics in West Africa, the Great Lakes and the Horn of Africa. The Pentagon-funded Strauss Center of the University of Texas (2013) is acutely concerned about the extent to which social unrest will emerge, as a result. There is some potential for African leaders to access the United Nations Green Climate Fund for adaptation funds, though the fund will have nowhere near the $100 billion annually that was promised by USA's then Secretary of State, Hillary Clinton in 2009 (Bond, 2012). However, hopes that claims for climate-related 'loss and damage' could be made against those with the highest historic emissions were dashed at the Paris climate summit in 2015 when African leaders agreed to a 'no liability' clause insisted on by the USA and Europe. They were also pushed to accept non-binding and non-accountable emissions targets that in any case fall far short of addressing the crisis or reaching the 2°C maximum temperature increase, let alone 1.5°C aspirations (Spash, 2016).

Finally, land-grabs and militarisation are also threats to eco-social development, most urgently when faced by the African peasantry, especially women, and especially those in areas attractive to foreign investors whether in agri-corporate or extractive sectors (Hargreaves, 2014). Already, small farmers are being displaced in sites like Ethiopia and Mozambique as a result of land-grabs by Middle Eastern countries and Brazil, India, South Africa and China, a problem likely to be amplified as food shortages worsen (Ferrando, 2012). The growing role of the USA military's Africa Command in dozens of African countries bears testimony to Washington's overlapping desire to maintain control amidst rising Islamic fundamentalism from the Sahel to Kenya, sites which are, coincidentally, theatres of war in the vicinity of large petroleum reserves (Turse, 2014).

Concluding remarks

Africa's eco-social development is marred by numerous forces that reflect the continent's subordinate political-economic power relations. Excessive profits exit Africa as IFFs and as licit (legal) financial flows. FDI continues to leave Africa poorer in part thanks to the need to pay foreign corporations their profits and dividends in hard currency, a factor which recently raised Africa's foreign debt to unprecedented heights. Other emerging adverse factors include South African and other BRICS countries' sub-imperial accumulation; new State and donor subsidised extractive-oriented infrastructure and financing that will exacerbate African underdevelopment; uncompensated mineral and oil/gas depletion; and land-grabs, militarisation and climate change. Finally, on all fronts ranging from economy to climate to militarisation, global governance has failed.

Only *social* resistance [Chapter 17] can halt and reverse these trends. In most countries, the African people are not allowing these processes of eco-social underdevelopment to proceed without opposition. However, if protesters continue to challenge specific projects and sectoral problems without drawing links, and making common cause with others in their home countries and across their region, then the cycles of extraction, capitalist crises, heightened accumulation-by-dispossession and repression of dissent will continue. If the protesters do join forces with new movements and political parties, and adopt some form of post-extractivist developmental ideology, then there are indeed prospects for overthrowing the current eco-social system, that offers most Africans underdevelopment and environmental destruction, and replacing it with one more attuned to Ubuntu, the idea that 'we are who we are through others'.

Key further readings cited

Amin, S. (1976). *Unequal Development*. New York: Monthly Review Press.
Fanon, F. (1963). *Wretched of Earth*. Boston: Grove Press.
Mama, A. (2002). *Beyond the Masks*. London: Routledge.
Rodney, W. (1974). *How Europe Underdeveloped Africa*. London: Bogle-L'Ouverture Publications.

Other literature cited

350.org Africa (2014). '350 Africa.org launches Fossil Free Africa campaign with call on dirty South African banks to stop financing fossil fuel projects.' Johannesburg, http://350africa.org/2014/11/26/350-africa-org-launches-fossil-free-africa-campaign-with-call-on-dirty-south-african-banks-to-stop-financing-fossil-fuel-projects.
African Development Bank (2011). *The Middle of the Pyramid*. Tunis: African Development Bank.
African Development Bank, OECD Development Centre, UN Development Programme and Economic Commission for Africa (2016). *African Economic Outlook*. OECD: Tunis.
Ake, C. (2001). *Democracy and Development in Africa*. Owerri: Spectrum Books.
Alternative Information and Development Centre (2014). 'Lonmin, the Marikana Massacre and the Bermuda Connection.' Cape Town, http://aidc.org.za/lonmin-the-marikana-massacre-and-the-bermuda-connection-seminar-and-press-conference.
Amabhungane (2015). 'Ramaphosa and MTN's offshore stash.' *Mail & Guardian,* 8 October, http://amabhungane.co.za/article/2015-10-08-ramaphosa-and-mtns-offshore-stash.
Amin, S. (2006). 'The Millennium Development Goals: A Critique from the South.' *Monthly Review,* 57, 10. http://monthlyreview.org/2006/03/01/the-millennium-development-goals-a-critique-from-the-south.
Berman, N., Couttenier, M., Rohner, D., Thoenig, M. (2014). This Mine is Mine! How minerals fuel conflicts in Africa. Oxford: Oxford Centre for the Analysis of Resource Rich Economies. http://www.oxcarre.ox.ac.uk/files/OxCarreRP2014141.pdf.
Bond, P. (2005). *Fanon's Warning*. Trenton: Africa World Press.
Bond, P. (2006). *Looting Africa: The Economics of Exploitation*. London: Zed Books.
Bond, P. (2012). *Politics of Climate Justice*. Pietermaritzburg: University of KwaZulu-Natal Press.
Bond, P. (2016). 'BRICS Banking and the Debate over Sub-Imperialism.' *Third World Quarterly*, 37 (4), pp. 611–629.
Bond, P., Garcia, A. (eds.) (2015). *BRICS: An Anti-Capitalist Critique*. London: Pluto Press.
Bracking, S., Sharife, K. (2014). Rough and Polished, Manchester University Leverhulme Centre for the Study of Value, http://thestudyofvalue.org/wp-content/uploads/2014/05/WP4-Bracking-Sharife-Rough-and-polished-15May.pdf.
Brewer, J. (2015). Hacking the SDG Discourse. http://therules.org/hacking-the-sdg-discourse.
Fabricius, P. (2016). 26th African Union Summit *PoliticsWeb,* 28 January. http://www.politicsweb.co.za/news-and-analysis/26th-au-summit-time-to-take-the-aprm-off-life-supp.
Ferrando, T. (2012). 'BRICS, BITs and land grabbing,' Paris, Sciences Po Law School, http://papers.ssrn.com/sol3/papers.cfm?abstract_id=2174455.
Fioramonti, L. (2014). *How Numbers Rule the World*. London: Zed Books.
Hargreaves, S. (2014). Extractivism, its deadly impacts and struggles towards a post-extractivist future. Unpublished paper, Johannesburg: WoMin.
Hosken, G. (2014). World Fraud Champs. *The Times,* 19 February.

Kar, D., Spanjers, J. (2015). *Illicit Financial Flows from Developing Countries,* Washington, DC. http://www. gfintegrity.org/report/illicit-financial-flows-from-developing-countries-2004-2013.

Lusaka Times (2014). Video of Vedanta Boss Saying KCM makes $500 million profit per year. *Lusaka,* 13 May. https://www.lusakatimes.com/2014/05/13/video-vedanta-boss-saying-kcm-makes-500-million-profit-per-year.

Mwiti, L. (2016). $80 Billion not $50 Billion. *Mail & Guardian,* 27 April. http://mgafrica.com/article/2016-04-26-80-billion-not-50-billion-loss-of-african-funds-even-worse-than-thought-mbeki.

Ndikumana, L., Boyce, J., Ndyiaye, A. (2014). Capital Flight: Measurement and Drivers.' University of Massachusetts/Amherst Political Economy Research Institute, http://www.peri.umass.edu/236/hash/b3af64ea1d53b2a932a8b6cd57e45e6d/publication/653.

Nkrumah, K. (1966). *Neo-Colonialism.* New York: International Publishers.

Onimode, B. (1988). *A Political Economy of the African Crisis.* London: Zed Books.

PricewaterhouseCoopers (2016). Global Economic Crime Survey 2016: Adjusting the Lens on Economic Crime, Johannesburg. http://www.pwc.com/gx/en/services/advisory/consulting/forensics/economic-crime-survey.html.

Salinas, G., Gueye, C., Korbut, O. (2011). Growth in Africa Under Peace and Market Reforms. Washington, DC. https://www.imf.org/external/pubs/ft/wp/2011/wp1140.pdf.

Saunders, R., Nyamunda, T. (eds.) (2016). *Facets of Power.* Johannesburg: University of the Witwatersrand Press.

South African Reserve Bank (2015). *Quarterly Bulletin,* June. Pretoria.

Spash, C.L. (2016). This changes nothing: The Paris Agreement to ignore reality. *Globalizations,* 13(6): 928–933.

Turse, N. (2014). Africom becomes a war-fighting combatant command. *TomDispatch,* 13 April, http://www.tomdispatch.com/blog/175830/tomgram%3A_nick_turse,_africom_becomes_a_%22war-fighting_combatant_command%22.

United Nations Conference on Trade and Development (2016). *Global Investment Trends Monitor #22,* 20 January. http://unctad.org/en/PublicationsLibrary/webdiaeia2016d1_en.pdf.

University of Texas (2013). 'Climate change and African political stability,' Austin: Strauss Center, https://strausscenter.org/ccaps.

Weeks, J. (2010). Employment, Productivity and Growth in Africa South of the Sahara. Unpublished paper for the *Trade and Development Report 2010,* University of London Centre for Development Policy and Research, School of Oriental and African Studies.

World Bank (2012). *Inclusive Green Growth.* Washington, DC.

World Bank (2014). *The Little Green Data Book.* Washington, DC.

World Economic Forum (2015). *Global Competitiveness Report 2015–16.* Geneva: World Economic Forum, http://www.weforum.org/issues/global-competitiveness.

40

MINING CONFLICTS

Begüm Özkaynak and Beatriz Rodriguez-Labajos

Introduction

Mining is far from being a new activity, but its scale and nature have changed in recent decades. In earlier times, when working conditions and wages were the main source of social political struggles, mining gave rise to economic distribution debates. However, this changed from the 1980s onwards as the throughput of energy and materials in the world economy significantly amplified and the mining frontier expanded, driven by growth in consumption and production. Technological advances, along with increasingly favourable commodity prices and neoliberal reforms, have made previously uneconomical reserves accessible. As the industry has penetrated ecologically and socially vulnerable areas to extract resources, tensions between supporters and opponents of mining projects have intensified and focused increasingly on social ecological concerns in addition to economic ones. From a social metabolic perspective [Chapter 11], mining conflicts involve base metals (e.g. copper and zinc) and mineral commodities used by energy and construction industries (e.g. coal, uranium, and sand) that are needed for the growing material economy. Precious metals (e.g. gold and silver) are demanded for speculation, stores of value and social objects, rather than for production, although they do have industrial applications.

This chapter lays out mining activities as a universal political problem of social environmental justice [Chapter 16], using examples from landmark cases. The roots of these conflicts are explored alongside relevant social, economic, cultural, health and ecological impacts and related community claims. Since the world's extractive appetite obviously goes beyond mining, debates on mining issues have counterparts in other anti-extractivist controversies (e.g. oil, forestry) and mining is representative of policy challenges experienced in other social ecological struggles. The aim here is to link insights from empirical evidence with the social ecological economics approach ([Chapter 1]; Spash, 2011) and to underline why studying such conflicts is crucial in promoting transformations to sustainability. The role resistance movements [Chapter 17] play in introducing the issue of environmental liabilities into legislative and governance processes is also highlighted.

The mining industry and community resistance

The drivers of mining expansion can be traced to the three layers of the economy that ecological economics recognises (Kallis et al., 2012; Martinez-Alier, 1990), based on the work of Soddy

(1926): the financial economy, the real productive economy, and the real-real economy of energy and material flows [Chapters 10 and 11]. First, in terms of the financial economy, positive market price trends in mineral resources show that corporate benefits are one causal mechanism explaining new mining investments. Despite the global recession, the price of base metals, energy resources and precious metals have been on the rise during the past decade, with noticeable peaks in some periods, making mining equities an even more attractive investment. The particularly high prices of uranium oxide and gold have boosted interest in initiating projects in regions where they were previously unprofitable. The fact that developing countries adopted neoliberal reforms in the 1980s and 1990s helped investors overcome limitations imposed by national regulations and facilitated the rapid expansion of multinational mining capital [Chapter 39].

Second, on the real economy front, there are arguments in favour of mining centred on a strategy of commodity extraction and export, geared to economic growth as development. In this view, economic growth is a necessary step towards sustainable development, and the mining industry will offer new opportunities generating jobs and income. This was the basis on which the World Bank Group and other international financial institutions encouraged countries to embrace extractive industry growth as a development strategy in the 1990s (Campbell, 2009). The rise of resource nationalism in Africa [Chapter 39], and the adoption of extractivism in Latin American countries, even those that had undertaken counter-neoliberal reforms (Andreucci and Radhuber, 2015), corroborate the relevance of mining on the developmentalist agenda.

Third, and most fundamentally, is the basis of the economy in biophysical reality. As the physical economy grows, international investors easily promote their projects in a range of industries including energy, construction/housing, automobiles, shipbuilding, and consumer electronics. Hence, the metabolic profiles of countries (in terms of energy and material flows) have become highly dependent on stable imports of mineral resources. China, for instance, as a mining investor, intensifies the global pressure to acquire base metals. Even in a softened growth scenario, the Chinese demand for copper—not domestically satisfied and driven more by long-term strategic interests than the pursuit of quick profits—is expected to push new mining projects around the world (Rogich and Matos, 2008) [see also Chapter 11].

According to Bebbington et al. (2008), extensive conflicts related to mining are unsurprising. Compared to the few nuanced arguments of potential benefits, complaints against mining activities are numerous, complex and diverse. An overview of conflicts worldwide points to numerous underlying causes and highlights contested territories where industry and government experts are being opposed by impacted populations (Özkaynak et al., 2012). The conflicts mainly concern:

1   the distribution of burdens and benefits, and the struggle between knowledge, precaution and risk, given strong scientific uncertainties;
2   rights related to environmental conservation and the preservation of cultural integrity, indigenous rights and moral values; and
3   participation in decision-making on local development and environmental issues.

These categories are intertwined and support Schlosberg's (2003, 2007) analysis, which indicates that the demands of the global environmental justice movement are actually threefold: equity in the distribution of environmental risk, recognition of the diversity of participants and experiences in affected communities, and participation in policy-making.

In mining struggles, opposition groups use various means to protest. They organise awareness campaigns, create alternative reports in collaboration with experts and international non-governmental organisations (NGOs), orchestrate demonstrations, and strikes, appeal to the parliament and demand explanations from the government, appeal to judicial activism by filing court cases and objecting to Environmental Impact Assessments, and promote community consultations through alternative means and via referenda. Yet the uncertainties of environmental risk and the difficulties in gathering statistical data on, say, radioactivity or waste toxicity have produced a new practice of activism in mining conflicts whereby laypeople gather scientific data and other relevant information in citizen science [Chapter 33] or popular epidemiology (Brown, 1992). In Caetité, Brazil, for example, the risks and uncertainties related to uranium mining and milling were central to the conflict. After confirming that adequate information on human exposure to different levels of radioactivity and its possible health effects was lacking, activists and residents formed an alternative database, collecting extensive evidence on cancer-related deaths in the region to empirically counter the official discourse that denied the risks.

The main issues in mining conflicts

The literature on mining addresses diverse issues, but three trends emerge from the analytical perspectives of spatial, economic and ecological distribution. First is the universal displacement of investments from the global North toward the Global South (Bridge, 2004; [Chapters 5, 15 and 39]). Industries are relocating to developing countries where reserves are relatively unexploited, governmental intervention is minimal, environmental regulations are unenforced and labour rights are weak (Smith et al., 2012). In this context, a dramatic increase in mining activities in developing countries during and after the 1990s followed the adoption of domestic neoliberal economic reforms (Bebbington et al., 2008). The Latin American Observatory of Mining Conflicts cites more than 150 active mining conflicts in the region, most of which began in the 2000s.

Second, studies that examine the mining industry question the assumed link between development and mining expansion, and many associate mines with a spectacularly unequal distribution of wealth and unsustainable patterns of economic growth (Bebbington et al., 2008). This is closely related to the 'resource curse' argument, which suggests that economic development models dependent on natural resources generate economic and political distortions that ultimately undermine any positive contributions to development (Pegg, 2006).

Third, as mining conflicts multiply, scholarly research on mining resistance movements also expands. Today, mining activities are widely acknowledged to generate various negative environmental and social impacts, including deforestation, biodiversity loss, high water consumption, groundwater contamination and population migration (Urkidi, 2010). These all create discontent and conflict within communities. The basic rights of some groups are compromised and ecosystems suffer irreversible changes, resulting in a loss of livelihoods, culture, and even lives (Martinez-Alier, 2001; [Chapter 16]). Such losses lead communities to claim liabilities through court cases or direct action, either in terms of monetary compensation or other valuation languages, depending on the context.

As a result of the growing appetite of the world economy for incorporating new regions and commodities into the market system, a new trend seems to be emerging at the 'commodity frontiers'. One indicator of this expansion is the development of major mining projects in parts of the world the industry had previously avoided. Examples include the race to control new strategic minerals such as coltan, and other rare earth elements, which has led to deep-sea mining ventures receiving the green light (e.g. the recently approved Nautilus project in Papua New Guinea).

Actual and potential impacts

Table 40.1 categorises the ecological, social, economic, health and cultural impacts most frequently reported by activists relative to a specific time scale, namely, in terms of short/medium-term

Table 40.1 Impacts of mining activities

	Ecological	Socioeconomic	Health	Cultural
Short- or mid-term impacts	• Deforestation • Adverse impacts on air quality due to noise, dust and poisonous gas • Water depletion (underground and surface waters) • Water pollution due to waste dumping and waste rock disposal • Soil pollution • Soil erosion due to mechanized sand mining • Airborne dispersal of radioactive gas and dust	• Impact on grasslands and thus on cattle production because of mine dust • Endangerment of local agricultural activities and food provision due to water uptake by the mine and decrease in soil quality • Decrease in agricultural sales because of the risk of radioactive contamination • Impact on access to land due to the amount of mining rights appropriated by mining activities	• Adverse effects on health due to mine dust • Increase of illnesses such as cancer and central nervous disorders • Risks of poisoning due to cyanide use • Health effects caused by air, water and noise contamination • Dead livestock due to water and soil contamination	• Loss of livelihood due to displacement of neighbourhoods • Damage to the ancestral homeland of indigenous communities • Unequal distribution of environmental burden on some ethnic groups • Damage to historical and cultural values due to accumulation of waste rocks close to historical or sacred places
Long-term or potential impacts	• Changes in the water cycle (in the drainage regime, sedimentation and groundwater) • Displacement of glaciers and impacts on the permafrost • Irreversible impacts on landscape due to desalination plants, water pipe lines, power lines and roads • Degradation of the bio-physical environment, resulting in habitat and biodiversity losses	• Damage to glaciers which guaranteed irrigation • Risk of dam failure • Security and social problems such as increase in criminality and militarization • Income losses in tourism due to loss of natural landscape and damage to historical sites • Pressures on housing, schools, hospitals, and traffic as well as water and electricity supplies • Incompatibility of the extractivist development path with the regions' original development vision • Adverse impacts on social cohesion	• Higher mortality rates due to exposure to radioactivity because of toxic materials, contaminated wells, and re-use of radioactive waste rocks in buildings • Health impact due to decreasing water quality • Increase in HIV/AIDS infection rate in settlements around the mines	• Total/incompatible change in the regions' traditional way of life and vision • Adverse impacts on landscape qualities with historical and cultural importance

Source: adapted from Özkaynak et al. (2012).

versus long-term/potential impacts. These range from concerns about the distribution of income gains and losses and environmental burdens and risks, to adverse impacts on human and ecosystem health, and historical and cultural values. The issues raised by activists match Scholsberg's (2007) first category of justice demands—the distribution of burdens and risks. While mainstream neoclassical economics views such environmental impacts as externalities (outside the market) that should be integrated into the price system, social ecological economics [Chapter 1] follows Kapp (1978) in describing them as cost-shifting successes on the part of business enterprises. The injustice of the cost-shifting then gives rise to environmental movements.

Adverse health effects and risks are frequently related to air and water contamination, cyanide use and extraction of radioactive materials. Note that ecological impacts refer not only to local concerns, but also to global issues such as biodiversity loss, including irreversible extinction of endangered endemic species. Water impacts are also a major social and environmental concern. In some cases mining projects impair access to water where it is naturally scarce, while in others maintenance of the hydrological cycle and its ecological functioning are affected despite water being naturally abundant. Water depletion due to overuse (an ongoing problem in Latin America) and pollution (e.g. most cases of uranium mining) are the outcomes, and there is a high risk of both occurring simultaneously. Mining is also widely regarded as both environmentally and socially disruptive.

However, mining conflicts arise not only from physical impacts and distributional concerns. Bridge (2004) notes the problem is not always one of 'cleaner production' or 'environmental standards' but more a recognition of rights, closely linked to the second and third dimensions of justice in Schlosberg's categories. This goes beyond a definition of environmental justice that emphasises the disproportionate placement of environmental loads on disadvantaged communities, generally for reasons of race or income; see Bullard (1994, 2001), Agyeman et al. (2003) and Mohai and Saha (2007).

Recognition

As in other social movements, recognition as a legitimate partner in the debate is as important as distributional outcomes. In mining conflicts, lack of recognition is actualised by promoters of mining projects who devalue individual and collective rights. For example, affected communities in Adatepe, Bulgaria demanded their right to a peasant livelihood and agricultural production, while in el Mirador, Ecuador, locals asked that their communitarian lifestyles and indigenous territorial integrity be respected. Other causes of injustice and conflict stem from the violation of a right to healthy work conditions, particularly in uranium mining.

Table 40.2 lists rights-based arguments collected from case studies. These show how the environmental justice debates evolved from the consideration of fundamental rights of disregarded minorities and communities to the recognition of the rights of nature. Arguments often overlap, e.g. the health demands of the working class and environmental concerns. Recognition of the arguments has as its key reference points the right to alternative local visions of development and the right to development alternatives that are incompatible with mining. This is exemplified in the case of Esquel, Argentina, where the conflict revolved around two opposing views on mining and development. While one group of stakeholders saw mining as a beneficial local activity, the other opposed it. The latter group valued the small size and quiet lifestyle of the city, preferring strong, long-term sustainability to a project of uncertain environmental sustainability that privileged pecuniary income in the short run.

Table 40.2 Right-based claims in mining conflicts

Dimensions of recognition	Claims
Fundamental rights	Human rights
Health-related rights	Claims of adequate health care
	Claims of healthy labour conditions
	Claims of a healthy environment and ecological integrity
Rights to nature	Claims over clean water, access to water and water use
	Territorial rights of indigenous communities
	Right to property
Rights to livelihood security	Right to self-sustenance, work and livelihood
	Right to peasant livelihood and way of life; right to agricultural production
	Demand of recognition for local visions of development that are not compatible with mining
	Claims of communitarian lifestyles and indigenous livelihoods; *Buen Vivir*
Rights of nature and sacred places	Rights of nature
	Claims of the protection of religious and sacred places

Source: adapted from Özkaynak et al. (2012).

Participation

The third category of Schlosberg focuses on the political and institutional order of decision-making and the ability of communities to participate in decisions on local development with prior informed consent. Formalised participatory procedures often prove insufficient in terms of taking into account local views and concerns [see also Chapter 33]. In Conga, Peru, for instance, the many demonstrations, the general strikes, the police violence that led to the death of five activists and persistent criticism of mining by elected regional authorities were not enough. The Newmont-owned Yanacocha mining company suspended the project and the government in Lima lifted the state of emergency only after an opinion poll in August 2012 showed that the majority of the population opposed the project. Until the very end, the government and the company wanted to show they were in control, and they made explicit attempts to downgrade regional and local participation. In Esquel, Argentina, citizens realised that decision-making processes disregarded local values and interests, focusing instead on promoting alternative spaces for deliberation and participation. The successful call for a local referendum is a powerful indicator of how serious local communities were about participation, and how determined they were to have their say.

Mining conflicts as drivers of environmental sustainability?

Are mining resistance movements limited to preventing a project in a given area, or do they demand broader transformative policies and changes in the current political economy? This section reviews four main types of response from resistance movements to such projects and their role in forging pathways to sustainability.

Stop the project!

The foremost challenge of resistance movements is usually to stop a mining project that is perceived as problematic, ideally before it starts. Notable successes have occurred, including intense social opposition to a gold mining project in Crucitas leading to a moratorium on open-cast mining in Costa Rica (Carbonell, 2012), and the long running fight for survival by the Dongria Kondh tribe in Odisha, India against the bauxite mining plans of London-based Vedanta corporation that ended with protection of the tribes sacred mountain (Temper and Martinez-Alier, 2013). Although stopping a project is rare, because of the power imbalances involved [Chapter 14], these cases constitute major achievements when they do occur. Yet success is seldom permanent, as new projects usually appear, driven by the presence of mineral deposits in an area and their increasing scarcity.

Even if a campaign is unsuccessful in stopping a mining project, it can help problematise mining as an unsustainable activity and contribute to a greater awareness of the social ecological impacts that transcends geographical boundaries. In this respect, mining conflicts and opposition movements demonstrate that mineral extraction and the expansion of commodity frontiers result in a broad set of concerns about the scale of human intervention in the environment, and relate directly to the social and ecological costs of unequal exchange [Chapter 4] and globalisation [Chapter 15]. Inevitably, while some grassroots protests are closer to the so-called not-in-my-backyard (NIMBY) position, others are more aware that mining effects are not discrete or localised but global, and hence closer to a not-in-anyone's-backyard (NIABY) position. All in all, different movements play distinct and important roles in the quest for sustainability by forcefully articulating their demands via existing national and international networks and alliances, or establishing new alliances and platforms to deal with mining issues, such as the Observatorio de Conflictos Mineros de América Latina (OCMAL) in Latin America.

Building networks and linking with movements nationally and internationally are crucial not only for finding and circulating information, but also for sharing experiences and enhancing communal capacity for self-determination and strengthening a movement's agency and legitimacy. In the Argentinian Esquel case, the Mineral Policy Centre and Greenpeace were important international agents, writing reports and financing local activities, while the Autonomous People's Assembly (AVA) managed to become a real forum for deliberation and action. Later, the AVA promoted the establishment of the first national network against mining—the National Network of Communities Affected by Mining—and created the "No a la mina" website (www.noalamina.org), which has become a comprehensive source of news and reports on mining conflicts in Latin America and across the world.

Liabilities and compensation claims

If stopping an operating project is not an option, yet concerns about risk of pollution remain, then the attention is centred more on liabilities overlooked by the mining industry. One way to address environmental injustices is to focus on the damage caused by the project and later claim liability for it. In such cases, individuals or communities usually claim liabilities either *ex ante*, to prevent further damage—in the form of requests for improved transparency, care and technology standards, or reduced output—or *ex post*, to repair the harm done through remedial actions (Segerson, 2001). Depending on the circumstances, remedial actions may include monetary or in-kind compensation. Sometimes, however, an apology that acknowledges the wrongdoing becomes the most important outcome.

Here, the matter of whether all impacts in a given mining conflict can be assessed in a single dimension of value—money—and whether all costs and benefits are comparable and compensable becomes relevant [Chapter 22]. Since justice claims are broad and diverse, there are often discrepancies in the valuation standards used by companies and State and local communities. In conflicts where discussions focus on economic or technical aspects, especially if damage has already occurred, there may be room for economic valuation and monetary compensation. Monetary compensation through legal proceedings has a symbolic value that can reaffirm people's rights to their territory. Yet this strategy can be counterproductive; accepting compensation can undermine people's *de facto* rights to their own territory. Therefore, especially in non-technical and non-monetary conflicts, there is a need for evaluation tools such as multi-criteria analysis [Chapter 30] that can accept and incorporate the plurality of incommensurable values [Chapter 22]. In this context, opposition movements need to strategically distinguish which valuation standards are more appropriate, in which cases and types of contexts, and at what times.

Local developmentalism or a critique of development?

Communities often problematise the mining-imposed economic development in their territories. Alternatives that involve more control over local resources are often demanded in response to the argued benefits of mining to local or regional prosperity. This approach not only questions the top-down and extractivist model of development that is being forced on local territories, but it also requires discussion about the kind of change people desire for their communities. Proposals might involve creating protected areas, sometimes in combination with eco-tourism initiatives;[1] constructing local infrastructure; conserving sustainable agriculture; and strengthening local institutions through innovative schemes such as community planning.

Reading across these diverse ideas reveals that they sometimes resemble the underlying rationale of developmentalism. Many of the so-called alternatives can represent an unanticipated shift from the social and economic context that existed before the arrival of a mining project or its proposal, i.e. the imperative of 'development' in some form has become dominant. However, given the power imbalances (political and economic) between mining corporations and local communities, proposing alternative local projects is still a brave action that is in line with worldwide critical voices against developmentality (Deb, 2009; Escobar, 1992).

A post-extractivist systemic transformation

Alternatives to mining include unambiguously post-extractivist ideas that push for systemic transformation. Proposals to ban or place a moratorium on mining, often in combination with a call for major systemic changes such as boosting food sovereignty or an energy revolution, require an understanding of the metabolic nature of base and energy minerals at the societal level [Chapter 11]. Such proposals require re-scaling collective demands to Soddy's conceptualisation of the real-real economy and emphasise the importance of strengthening and promoting communication. For this reason, the likelihood of an alliance between post-extractivism and other systemic transformative ideas (e.g. socially sustainable de-growth [Chapter 44]) seems feasible.

Future directions

Mining conflicts offer a perfect setting for collaboration between social ecological economics and other interdisciplinary fields such as industrial ecology, environmental sociology, economic geography and political ecology. Combined, these fields may provide theoretical frameworks and methodological tools for explaining the social ecological dynamics of conflicts and 'glocal' (i.e. global to local) processes linked to mining. Although there are good examples of such collaborative work, there is still a need to better understand the link between mining conflicts and the social metabolism of economies [Chapter 11], and the role that the capitalist system and ecologically unequal exchanges play in this context [Chapters 4 and 15].

Close collaboration is also needed amongst scientists and activists to strengthen resistance movements and improve communication about alternatives. A good example of activism-led science is uranium mining in Namibia where the non-governmental organisation Earthlife Namibia worked with independent scientific experts to monitor radioactivity around mines and helped organise the data on environmental risks and health problems collected by local communities (Conde, 2014). There are numerous possibilities. Ecological economics promotes evaluation mechanisms that respect pluralism, incommensurability and the democratic process, and that need collaborative efforts in legislative and governance processes to be implemented. Multiple criteria analysis [Chapter 30], participatory methods [Chapter 33 and 35], deliberative valuation techniques [Chapter 34], action research, legal instruments and GIS mapping technologies are some of the tools that could aid activists and be pursued through scientist–activist engagement.

Additionally, despite the quantitative roots of early environmental justice studies, justice issues have so far been addressed mostly through a case study approach, and little has been done to examine them at the international level through the lens of statistical techniques. Careful analysis of activist practices as they appear in conflict databases and maps of mining conflicts would make possible a more precise definition of success and facilitate an understanding of associated conditions and causal mechanisms. Ultimately, success stories would become models for others, and disseminating and publicising them would help expand the environmental justice movement. This necessitates exploring how networking occurs in mining resistance movements—at the global, national and local levels—and how communities can learn from the experiences of others and become more self-confident in their own capacity. Such learning may offset to some extent the power imbalance between environmental justice movements and corporate initiatives. Globally shared discourses like 'sustainable mining' have already been used to legitimise access to resources and intervention in the social life of communities.

Above all, however, the mining versus environment debate should continue to be framed as a fundamentally political one shaped by perceptions and values, without losing sight of the material processes. This would help open a political space for negotiation and further broaden Schlosberg's environmental justice framework by better incorporating alternative visions of social ecological economic systems and guaranteeing people real power in decision-making.

Concluding remarks

The rise in mining activities is a product of both social metabolism and the capitalist economy, with varying consequences for health, social cohesion and the environment. Opposition movements that emerge in response to these consequences may thus be considered a part of the resistance against environmental injustices. A general look at opposition discourses in the mining debate reveals that justice claims are broad and diverse, and that they encompass distributional concerns, recognition of rights and participatory claims as well as alternatives to development or alternative visions of development.

We summarised these issues, explaining how the diverse dimensions of justice become manifest in mining conflicts. The chapter systematises how mining resistance movements have responded to policy challenges imposed by mining through a variety of proposals that sought to improve the well-being of affected communities and to intervene in the fundamental forces that drive mineral exploitation. It also underlines the political dimension of mining resistance movements and recognises mining activists as political actors at the 'glocal' level.

Ecological economics contributes in different ways to tackling debates on mining. First, it helps to clarify that mining conflicts are driven by different factors at different levels of the economy, particularly by the social metabolic rate of the global economy. Second, it strives to better understand the types of claim made by those opposing mining from a science in-and-with society perspective. To this end, and for some time now, ecological economics has been enjoying a fruitful dialogue with other interdisciplinary fields such as political ecology and environmental justice. Third, it plays a role in addressing issues related to liability valuation, with a broader perspective than the estimation of impacts in monetary terms. Ultimately, social ecological economics acknowledges that a truly social ecological transformation in resource extraction requires political action.

Note

1   Editor's Note: While being offered as a lesser evil than mining, tourism itself can have high impacts, depending on circumstances, both environmentally (e.g. long haul flights, infrastructure) and socially (corporate takeover of local economies, catering to non-indigenous desires and wants, commodification of labour). Tourism is not inherently eco-friendly or socially desirable.

Key further readings cited

Bebbington, A., Hinojosa, L., Bebbington, D. H., Burneo, M. L., & Warnaars, X. (2008). Contention and ambiguity: Mining and the possibilities of development. *Development and Change, 39*(6): 887–914.

Bridge, G. (2004). Mapping the bonanza: Geographies of mining investment in an era of neoliberal reform. *The Professional Geographer, 56*(3), 406–421.

Özkaynak, B., Rodriguez-Labajos, B., Arsel, M., Avcı, D., Carbonell, M.H., Chareyron, B., Chicaiza, G., Conde, M., Demaria, F., Finamore, R., Kohrs, B., Krishna, V.V., Mahongnao, M., Raeva, D., Singh, A.A., Slavov, T., Tkalec, T., Yánez, I., Walter, M., ,Živčič, L. (2012). *Mining conflicts around the world: Common grounds from an environmental justice perspective.* EJOLT Report No. 7. Retrieved from http:// www.ejolt.org/2012/11/mining-conflicts-around-the-world-common-grounds-from-an-environmental-justice-perspective. Accessed 20 December 2016.

Other literature cited

Agyeman, J., Bullard, R.D., Evans, B. (2003). *Just Sustainabilities: Development in an Unequal World.* Cambridge, MA: MIT Press.

Andreucci, D., Radhuber, I.M. (2015). Limits to "counter-neoliberal" reform: Mining expansion and the marginalisation of post-extractivist forces in Evo Morales's Bolivia. *Geoforum*, forthcoming.

Brown, P. (1992). Popular epidemiology and toxic waste contamination: lay and professional ways of knowing. *Journal of Health and Social Behavior 33*(3), 267–281.

Bullard, R.D. (1994). *Unequal Protection: Environmental Justice and Communities of Color.* San Francisco, CA: Sierra Club Books.

Bullard, R. (2001). Environmental Justice. In N. J. Smelser (ed.), *International Encyclopedia of the Social & Behavioral Sciences* (4627–4633). Oxford: Pergamon.

Campbell, B. (2009). *Mining in Africa. Regulation and Development.* New York: Pluto Press.

Carbonell, H. (2012). Gold mining suspended in Crucitas (Costa Rica) In Özkaynak, B., Rodriguez-Labajos, B. (coord.), *Mining Conflicts around the World: Common Grounds from Environmental Justice Perspective*, EJOLT Report No. 7.

Conde, M. (2014). Activism mobilising science. *Ecological Economics, 105*(September), 67–77.

Deb, D. (2009). *Beyond Developmentality: Constructing Inclusive Freedom and Sustainability.* London: Routledge.

Escobar, A. (1992). Imagining a post-development era? Critical thought, development and social movements. *Social Text 31/32,* 20–56.

Kallis, G., Kerschner, C., Martinez-Alier, J. (2012). The economics of degrowth. *Ecological Economics 84,* 172–180.

Kapp, K.W. (1978). *The Social Costs of Business Enterprise*, 3rd edn., Nottingham: Spokesman.

Martinez-Alier, J. 1990, *Ecological Economics: Energy, Environment and Society*, Oxford: Basil Blackwell.

Martinez-Alier, J. (2001). Mining conflicts, environmental justice, and valuation. *Journal of Hazardous Materials 86*(1-3), 153–170.

Mohai, P., Saha, R. (2007). Racial inequality in the distribution of hazardous waste: A national-level reassessment. *Social Problems 54*(3), 343–370

Pegg, S. (2006). Mining and poverty reduction: Transforming rhetoric into reality. *Journal of Cleaner Production 14*(3-4), 376–387.

Rogich, D.G., Matos, G.R. (2008). *The global flows of metals and minerals: U.S. Geological Survey Open-File Report 2008.*

Schlosberg, D. (2003). The justice of environmental justice: Reconciling equity, recognition, and participation in a political movement. In A. Light and A. De-Shalit (eds.), *Moral and Political Reasoning in Environmental Practice* (77–106). Cambridge, MA: MIT Press.

Schlosberg, D. (2007). *Defining Environmental Justice: Theories, Movements, and Nature.* Oxford: Oxford University Press.

Segerson, K. (2001). *Economics and Liability for Environmental Problems.* Aldershotand Burlington: Ashgate Publishing Co.

Smith, S.M., Shepherd, D.D., Dorward, P.T. (2012). Perspectives on community representation within the Extractive Industries Transparency Initiative: Experiences from south-east Madagascar. *Resources Policy 37*(2), 241–250.

Soddy, F. (1926). *Wealth, Virtual Wealth and Debt.* London: Allen and Unwin.

Spash, C.L. 2011, Social ecological economics: Understanding the past to see the future, *American Journal of Economics and Sociology 70*(2), 340–375.

Temper, L., Martinez-Alier, J. (2013). The god of the mountain and Godavarman: net present value, indigenous territorial rights and sacredness in a bauxite mining conflict in India. *Ecological Economics 96*(December), 79–87.

Urkıdı, L. (2010). A glocal environmental movement against gold mining: Pascua-Lama in Chile. *Ecological Economics 70*(2), 219–227.

41

PEAK-OIL AND ECOLOGICAL ECONOMICS[1]

Christian Kerschner and Iñigo Capellán-Pérez

Introduction

Peak-Oil as a concept was coined in 2002, when Collin Campbell and Kjell Aleklett founded the Association of the Study of Peak-Oil (ASPO).[2] Its early members used a curve-fitting method developed by fellow petroleum geologist K. Hubbert to forecast future oil production (e.g. Aleklett and Campbell, 2003; Campbell and Laherrère, 1998). In the mid-twentieth century, Hubbert empirically discovered that the maximum extraction rate of crude oil from the wells of a region follows a bell-shaped (Hubbert) curve, due to geological constraints. Hubbert applied his findings to forecast conventional oil extraction for the United States of America (USA) and globally.

The concept of peaking resources is now wide spread, but oil merits particular attention. Oil is the largest proportion of total global primary energy needs—33 per cent in 2014 (BP, 2015)—being critical for key economic sectors of industrialised economies such as transportation, agriculture and the chemical industry (Kerschner et al., 2013; Murphy and Hall, 2011). It is also expected to be the first global energy supply constraint.

Public interest in Peak-Oil (based on web search statistics) has declined since 2005, with a short-lived comeback around the 2008 financial crisis when oil prices reached over $140 per barrel. Critics celebrated the "death" of the concept and the victory of human ingenuity in the form of fracking technology (e.g., Maugeri, 2012). Within Peak-Oil circles however, the declining interest is attributed to the lack of news worthiness assuming that most stories about 'the problem' have already been told, and the fragmentation of the Peak-Oil community which split into divergent camps when addressing potential solutions. Some Peak-Oilists argue for the inevitable collapse of the current industrial economies, some defend the feasibility of shifting to a 100 per cent renewable energy system, while others favour nuclear power and/or the intensification of oil exploitation. Articles on Peak-Oil in academic publications (based on Web of Science) declined after 2008, but are now on the rise again. However, ecological economists so far have shown limited interest. In the journal *Ecological Economics*, for example, only 6 per cent of all articles between 2002 and 2015 mentioned "peak oil", compared to 48 per cent that mentioned "climate change".

In this chapter we explain why Peak-Oil is a relevant and useful concept for ecological economists. The next section presents a definition based on the distinction between a quantity and a quality dimension of the phenomenon. We then turn to explanations of the evolution of oil prices and their role in indicating scarcity. We finish with some reflections on future directions and concluding remarks.

Defining Peak-Oil: quality and quantity

Understanding Peak-Oil requires distinguishing between the available quantity and quality of existing oil (Kerschner, 2015, 2012; Murphy and Hall, 2011). The concept can then be defined as follows:

> Peak-Oil is the maximum possible production of petroleum fuels per unit of time given external constraints. These constraints can be geologic, economic, environmental or social and determine its available quantity and quality to society.

The quantity dimension of Peak-Oil

The quantity dimension can be further divided into a stock (resource in the ground) and a flow (extraction rate of this resource) dimension.

Oil stocks

A variety of metrics are used to describe the future availability of oil. The most common type of classification distinguishes between "resources" (amounts in the ground that might be exploitable in the future) and "reserves" (identified fraction of the resource-base estimated to be economically extractable at a given time). However, these estimates are affected by critical ambiguities and inconsistencies leading to considerable uncertainty as well as fluctuations over time. These are particularly problematic in long-term assessments, such as those required for the planning of an energy transition or the design of a sustainable economy (Capellán-Pérez et al., 2016; Miller and Sorrel, 2014).

For these reasons, Peak-Oil scholars have focused on the estimation of oil stocks in the light of the best available and transparent data, measured in terms of ultimately recoverable resources (URR). Table 41.1 compares the estimates of oil stocks available in terms of reserves and resources for conventional and unconventional oil according to three international agencies— the International Energy Agency (IEA), the German BGR and the Global Energy Assessment (GEA)—with a recent literature review of URR estimates (Mohr et al., 2015). The spread is in the range of around 1,300 Gigabarrels (Gb) for conventional oil and 2,350 Gb for unconventional oil. That is equivalent to approximately 40 and 75 years of current consumption, respectively (BP, 2015). The highest uncertainties relate to the potential of unconventional oils,[3] with various claims of no peak being in sight for 50 to 100 or more years (e.g. Maugeri, 2012).

Oil flows

As Laherrère (2010: 6) has stated, what matters most for economic activity is not "the size of the tank" (stocks) but "the size of the tap" (flows). Geology imposes certain physical constraints on the extraction rate of non-renewable energy resource stocks. Oil deposits are not underground lakes but consist mostly of porous rock impregnated with oil. Usually water is injected to maintain underground pressure and bring the oil to the surface. Thus, technology can help regulate the extraction rate, but is bound by physical reality. Indeed innovation has so far failed

Table 41.1 Global oil estimates from different sources (Gb)

	Reference	Conventional oil	Unconventional oil
Resources plus Reserves	GEA (Rogner et al. 2012)	1,590 to 2,410	2,630 to 3,570
Resources plus Reserves	BGR (2013)	2,413	2,310
Remaining Recoverable Resources	IEA (WEO 2014)	2,715	3,296
Remaining Ultimately Recoverable Resources	Mohr et al. (2015)	1,420; 1,490; 2,640 (low; best guess; high)	930; 1,810; 2,800 (low; best guess; high)

Notes: 1 gigabarrel = 5.7 exajoules.

Source: adapted from Capellán-Pérez et al., (2016).

to deliver substantial long-term increases in the flow rates of conventional oil wells without eventually damaging the well (Miller and Sorrell, 2014; Muggeridge et al., 2014). In addition, there are many factors (e.g. economic, political) "above the ground" that affect levels of investment in oil infrastructure (e.g. pipeline or refinery capacity) and so impact on flow rates.

Hence one key message of the Peak-Oil concept is that the most relevant limiting factor is not the remaining resource in-situ, but the constrained flow rates from deposits to consumers. Figure 41.1 illustrates the depletion over time of a non-renewable resource stock (grey dashed line) through flows (black solid line) in the absence of non-geologic restrictions. The maximum flow rate is reached much earlier than the full depletion of the stock. One of the reasons why mainstream economists struggle to grasp the concept of Peak-Oil is due to the fact that the notion of limits imposed by time is even more alien to them than absolute limits to materials and energy usage (Daly, 1992). In fact, they consider flow rates as technical details that can be changed at will.

Peak-Oil for conventional deposits was reached in the early 2000s. Current extraction rates have remained at an undulating plateau since about 2005—levels projected by ASPO already in 2002 (~85 megabarrels per day [Mb/d]). Since 2010 even the IEA—who previously ignored the work of ASPO and avoided even mentioning the term Peak-Oil—acknowledged the importance of supply constraints in its World Energy Outlooks (WEO). Extraction from operating conventional oil wells is declining at a global average rate of around 4 per cent to 7 per cent and eight of the top 20 producing nations have already peaked (BP, 2015). Among them are politically stable, advanced industrialised countries with the best available technology such as Norway in 1999 and the United Kingdom in 2002. Offsetting this decline would require adding, every year, an amount of production capacity equivalent to all current shale oil rigs in the USA (~4.2 Mb/d), and if adjusting for quality (as discussed below) then an even greater amount.

Flow rates are also a key variable for unconventional deposits. For example, the oil stocks from tar sands in Alberta, Canada, are comparable to Saudi Arabia's (second largest oil producer after USA), but reaching just a fifth of its flow rate (~2 Mb/d), with substantial future increases being highly unlikely. In fact, Brecha (2012) argues that the rates of production of new unconventional oil are unable to make up for declines of conventional oil flows globally. Flows also matter for the oil industry as higher extraction rates promise faster payback of investments. Indeed, high initial flow rates are one of the main reasons why hydraulic fracturing has caused a gold rush among oil companies and investors.

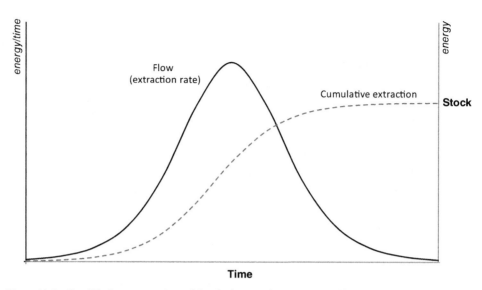

Figure 41.1 Simplified representation of the depletion of a non-renewable resource in the absence of non-geologic constraints. Stocks and flows of energy relative to time.
Source: own elaboration.

Shale oil and gas operations are easier to upscale than those of tar sands (given the absence of public opposition). The recent steep increase of shale oil and gas production was initially not foreseen by Peak-Oilists. So far, however, what Maugeri (2012) called the "shale oil revolution" has remained mostly a USA phenomenon with around 50 per cent of total current domestic oil production coming from shale (EIA, 2015). As a result, the USA became the world's top producer of oil liquids as of 2014, surpassing Saudi Arabia (BP, 2015). However, after reaching their peak, shale oil wells show exorbitantly high extraction decline rates of up to 70 per cent in the first year and between 55 per cent and 22 per cent thereafter, reaching their peak and being depleted much faster than conventional wells. In fact, total shale oil (and also shale gas) production in the USA is expected to peak by 2020 (Hughes, 2015, 2013). Meanwhile, the related environmental impacts are vast. Hence far from a revolution, the shale oil and gas phenomenon is more like "a dirty retirement party of the oil age". In fact, in many other regions like Europe, fracking faces strong public opposition, and is not expected to reach a significant scale.

Figure 41.2 depicts the estimated projections of total oil production (conventional plus unconventional) found in the literature from analyses considering URR estimates (stock limits) and taking into account geological constraints of extraction rates (flow limits). Leaving aside variations due to a lack of standardisation, the general trend indicates a stagnation of production in the near future, followed by a decline during the rest of the century. Note also the substantial drop between IEA projections of 2004 and one decade later, from over 120 Mb/day by 2030 to below 100 Mb/day by 2040 (WEO, 2004, 2014).

Ahead of geology, the possible flow rate is determined by economic, social, political and environmental parameters. Many oil producing countries have, for example, substantially reduced oil exports due to increases in (usually subsidised) domestic demand. Geopolitics—as in the standoff between the USA, Saudi Arabia and Russia since about 2014—is another causal mechanism. However, in the medium to long run the critical factor determining flow rates is the quality dimension of Peak-Oil, as it essentially changes the social metabolic profile [Chapter 11] of our energy–economy system.

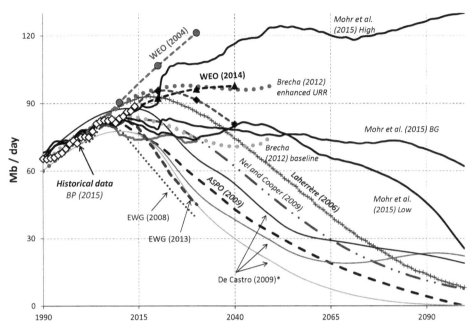

Figure 41.2   Estimations of total primary oil extraction (conventional and unconventional) by different authors (Mb/day).

Note: * Denotes estimates that account for resource quality (i.e. adjusted for net-energy via the EROI).

Source: figure updated from Capellán-Pérez et al (2014).

The quality dimension of Peak-Oil

According to resource economists, those resources with the highest quality will be extracted first—the 'best first principle'—in order to minimise costs and maximise profits. For the case of oil, the highest quality deposits are conventional giant fields (over 0.5 Gb of sweet light crude oil) situated on land, ideally in a desert with low population density and low environmental impacts and in a politically stable country willing to sell freely to global markets. Any deviation from this ideal case tends to increase economic, social, political and environmental costs and therefore reduces its 'quality'.

One parameter of resource quality is the net energy obtained. That is the available primary energy after subtracting the amount necessary to explore, extract and refine an energy resource. This is called the energy return on investment (EROI). If the EROI is 1, then as much energy is invested as finally recovered, and if it is less than 1, then more energy is invested than recovered (i.e. extraction results in creating a net energy sink instead of an energy source). According to Hall et al. (2014), the global EROI of oil has declined from 30 in 1995, to about 18 in 2006, while unconventional oil (e.g. tar sands, shale oil) is between 1 and 5. As the EROI of energy resources declines less net energy is available for our economic system (Dale et al., 2012). Similar to natural systems, our socio-economic systems have been conditioned by some key (energy) resources which have been accessible to us in a certain *quality* and *quantity*—they might be regarded as having co-evolved [Chapter 13]. The decline in EROI equates to a regime shift or metabolic change in our energy system (Murphy and Hall, 2011; Sorman and Giampietro, 2013), and Peak-Oil is such a change being actualised (Kerschner, 2015, 2012).

Most current energy–economy models ignore the "net energy" approach and thus are unable to detect or analyse its implications (Dale et al., 2012). For mainstream economists, natural resources are only scarce relative to another resource or the same resource of a different quality (Daly, 1992). They assume that the price mechanism will bring about new technological advances (like fracking) that will solve eventual scarcities (e.g. Barnett and Morse, 1963; Solow, 1974). Thus, Peak-Oil may occur sooner or later, but will not substantially affect world economies because oil can be replaced by perfect substitutes.

In contrast, the ontology of ecological economics incorporates biophysical reality (Spash, 2012). This includes the Laws of Thermodynamics and the absolute scarcity of low entropy matter and energy (Georgescu-Roegen, 1971). Low entropy materials (e.g. concentrated iron ore) and energy resources (e.g., light sweet crude oil) are the ultimate means of economic activity. In fact entropy could be seen as an indicator of quality of resources in general (Valero and Valero, 2014), however attempts to measure entropy have proven elusive and any claims of success have been highly misleading [Chapter 9].

Other physical properties also make oil a high quality resource. It is a liquid fuel with very high power density, of relatively little toxicity or explosiveness, and that can easily be transported (e.g. via pipelines or tankers). Hence Peak-Oil is also often seen as a liquid fuel problem rather than a general energy problem. This however does not reduce its relevance, on the contrary, our globalised economy requires cheap transport, 95 per cent of which currently depends upon oil. These qualities make oil very difficult to substitute (Capellán-Pérez et al., 2014; Miller and Sorrel, 2014). Substitution often depends on using alternative low entropy energy and/or materials which are subject to their own peaks (Valero and Valero, 2014). Moreover, leaving aside past dreams about a future hydrogen economy, only biofuels could currently be seen as relevant substitutes for liquid oil. However, they compete with food production, have low power density and an EROI of 2 or less depending on end use (Hall et al., 2014).

Economic costs

Unconventional oil, which accounts for most of the latest additions to global oil flows, currently becomes profitable at oil prices between $60 and $80 per barrel (Hughes, 2013). This seems very high considering that our present economic system has been built on oil prices oscillating between $10 and $40 per barrel from 1880 to 2000 (except for the two oil crises). Murphy and Hall (2011) have estimated that a 'real' price of around $60/barrel is the threshold of how much our global economy was able to take in the past before entering recession. Tverberg (2015) on the other hand emphasises the role of average wages. They tend to rise with low oil prices because this leads to high labour productivity and decrease with high prices that lead to low labour productivity. The threshold for the USA seems to be around $40/barrel. From that point wages start to decline, reducing peoples' discretional spending power and ability to pay mortgages, as during the 2008 financial crisis (Tverberg, 2012).

Environmental, social and political costs and impacts

Non-economic costs resulting from resource scarcities have been neglected in the Peak-Oil literature. The exception being a geo-political discourse emphasising the potential for direct conflicts over resources, both nationally and internationally. Klare (2004), for example, warns about a future intensification of wars over oil and other resources. Thus, the armed forces of the USA and Germany consider Peak-Oil in their planning while other public agencies ignore the issue. Securitisation and survivalism are emphasising domestic, national and individual resilience in the face of Peak-Oil achieved through eco-modernisation, securing international supply chains and by taking up a position of all-round defence. In contrast, a recent Austrian project concluded that areas with better social structures and networks would be more resilient to the inevitable energy crises (Exner, 2015).

An overall decline in the quality of a resource also causes increasing environmental costs, because declining ore grades increase the overburden (unwanted material) in both quantity and toxicity. In addition, the necessary extraction and refining activities are carbon intensive (e.g. natural gas is necessary for processing tar sands). In fact, some researchers have recently argued that at least a third of all oil reserves are unburnable if the international limit on climate forcing of 2°C is to be met with a 50 per cent chance. Thus, the development of unconventional fuels is totally inconsistent with such a climate goal (McGlade and Ekins, 2015). Others have argued these estimates are themselves serious underestimates, and that the actual excess of reserves is more likely 80 per cent and fossil fuel assets on company and State balance sheets are toxic (Anderson, 2015; Spash, 2016). Some policy-makers have challenged fossil fuel businesses to declare such stranded assets. Meanwhile activists have initiated a 'fossil fuel divestment' campaign. However, many fossil fuel companies (e.g. Petróleos de Venezuela SA, Saudi Arabian Oil, Statoil Norway) are State owned without public share trading. In addition, national oil companies control approximately 90 per cent of the world's oil reserves and 75 per cent of production, with similar numbers applying to gas (Tordo et al., 2011: xi).

Phases of high oil prices also lead to the advancement of 'commodity frontiers', a concept that has been developed in ecological economics [Chapter 16 and 40]. It means that resource extraction expands into industrially untouched/pristine ecosystems, biodiversity hotspots and remote communities. Extractive activities carried out in such areas can be disastrous for the environment and local inhabitants. This is exacerbated by accidents, such as the 2010 Gulf of Mexico oil spill. Social struggles in this context include the Inuit's fight against tar sand operations in Alberta, Ecuadorian tribes opposing the Yasuni-ITT project in the Amazon, and public opposition to fracking. Civil resistance to the advancement of commodity frontiers can bring about an earlier oil climax. This might restrict supply as well as induce environmentally motivated voluntary reductions that could lead directly to a demand decrease, in advance of the supply peak projections shown in Figure 41.2. Taxes or direct regulation would either increase production costs or decrease available quantity by restricting access (e.g. to the Arctic or to Amazonian biodiversity hot spots). The former is advancing a demand peak (unwanted oil), the latter a supply peak (unavailable oil).

Peak-Oil and oil prices

Oil demand and supply as well as its quality and quantity dimensions interact with prices in often complex and counter-intuitive ways. Interest in Peak-Oil as an explanatory concept tends to rise with high oil prices and fade with low ones. However, when entering the Peak and post-Peak-Oil era, it is rather price volatility that can be expected. Oil prices start rising as decreasing quality raises multidimensional costs (either directly via production costs or indirectly via attempts to govern non-economic costs) and decreasing quantity reduces market supply. As potential substitutes fail to achieve the necessary quantity and quality, oil prices rise far higher than the historical level upon which industrialised economies were built, causing widespread recession. Demand for oil falls and prices collapse again, which if combined with Keynesian expansionary policies may lead to a temporary recovery of the economy. However such policies only work if debts can be repaid by expanding economic activity fuelled by an expanding resource base, which is not the case after Peak-Oil (Douthwaite, 2012). Hence a new cycle starts with demand recovering and prices rising until hitting a ceiling again (e.g. Tverberg,

2012). The result is a business cycle wave-like development. Volatility in (and not consistently high) oil prices, happening over ever shorter intervals, are then to be expected (Murphy and Hall, 2011). This volatility creates uncertainty that is more difficult to handle economically than permanent high oil prices, hampering also the planning of an energy transition.

In recent years, such volatility seems particularly evident. After the historic spike in oil prices of US$ 140/barrel in 2008, the global economy entered a deep recession and oil prices declined to below US$ 40/barrel. Countries like the USA and China put together emergency Keynesian stimulus packages of historical dimensions. Oil prices recovered and rose to a record annual average of around $100/barrel between 2011 and 2014, and Wall Street was flooded with money from investors seeking safety in commodities (Rogers, 2013). Hence not only technological advances and lax environmental legislation, but also, and most importantly, the combined situation of low interest rates and high oil prices brought about the shale 'revolution' and economic recovery in the USA with annual Gross Domestic Product growth rates of +2.2 per cent since 2009.

However, the rest of the world only partly shared this recovery and government debts have been increasing substantially everywhere. Even China's period of relentless growth appeared to have ground to a halt amid the detrimental effects of its stimulus package, i.e. rising debts and a housing bubble (Wigglesworth et al., 2015). Meanwhile oil prices have once again collapsed to levels just above $40/barrel, because of a short- to medium-term oversupply of oil and decreasing demand due to a weakening global economy. Such low prices mean that most producers of expensive oil are making losses (e.g. from shale). Hence many analysts talk of a shale oil investment bubble that is bound to burst at any time, possibly causing a renewed financial crisis, recession or depression (Hughes, 2013).

Future directions

Uncertainty surrounds how our social economic system will respond to Peak-Oil and whether price volatility, conflicts and economic turmoil are already the first signs of the post-Peak-Oil era. In fact, relatively little is still known about the economy–energy nexus (Sorman and Giampietro, 2013). Hence vulnerability and impact analysis, as well as progressive energy–economy models are regarded as essential for designing effective policy responses (Capellán-Pérez et al., 2014; Kerschner et al., 2017). Special analytical attention is needed at the sectorial economic level such as transport (Kerschner et al., 2013).

To date, most of the empirical research related to Peak-Oil has focused on estimating future oil extraction consistent with geological constraints (Figure 41.2). However, these studies have usually applied simple models (often built ad hoc) without a full representation of the economy–energy interactions. They are incapable of consistently accounting for potential technology and fuel substitutions. Thus, future work could (i) expand these models to include these features, or (ii) introduce Peak-Oil assumptions into current energy–economy models. However due to the urgency of the situation, these efforts can only go hand in hand with attempts to study, design and implement biophysical degrowth strategies such as legislated resource limits and carbon taxes. Moreover experiments should be undertaken to explore alternative social ecological economic systems that are fossil fuel independent.

Concluding remarks

Reaching Peak-Oil is not the same as running out of oil. Neither does this imply long-term sustained and exorbitantly high oil prices, as is sometimes claimed. Instead, the concept of Peak-

Oil refers to a complex energy phenomenon framed by the interaction of a diversity of constraints that limit flow rates of oil to society both in quantity as well as in quality. The same concept is applicable to other non-renewable and renewable resources e.g. gas and water peaks.

Ecological economic theory is essential for understanding the relevance of resource peaks, because substitution of low entropy matter and energy is limited. Key resources like oil create use dependencies and as a result become difficult or impossible to replace in the quantity and quality required by our current industrial economic system. Moreover social ecological economics, with its concept of expanding commodity frontiers and environmental conflicts, directs the research to analyse the usually neglected environmental and social costs of resource peaks.

In response to Peak-Oil and other social and environmental factors, social ecological economists and the degrowth community [Chapter 44] argue in favour of a conscious downscaling of the economy, with some arguing in favour of a biophysical steady state [Chapter 45] (e.g. Kerschner, 2010). This goal could be seen as identical to that of a post-carbon transformation of our society. In terms of Peak-Oil it implies voluntarily bringing about an early peak or adapting to the post-Peak-Oil era quickly and proactively. As we have outlined, there are indications that our society has already entered this era because of persistent and substantial oil price volatility, economic turmoil and conflicts.

A radical post-carbon transformation provides the only long-term exit route out of Peak-Oil enhanced boom and bust cycles. Ill-conceived Keynesian stimulus packages for saving banks and the automobile industry or for feeding housing and infrastructure bubbles only postpone the peak and steepen the inevitable decline. Moreover, this transformation, which also means a reshuffling of the cards of global power relations should be seen as an opportunity for creating a more equal and just society as envisioned by the degrowth movement.

Notes

1   Research supported by the Czech Science Foundation under the project Vulnerability and Energy-Economy Nexus at the Sector Level: A Historic, Input-Output and CGE Analysis (no. 16-17978S).
2   The grammatically correct term would be oil peak; the change is like saying peak mountain as opposed to mountain peak. The reason for the incorrect usage was to change the acronym, because "a sop" is a derogatory term commonly used in the USA for drunkards or those easily bribed.
3   Unconventional oil (deep sea, heavy oils, tar sands, shale oil, oil shale and polar oil) is generally more technically difficult to extract, than conventional low-viscosity oils from subsurface reservoirs, requiring novel production technologies. Within the unconventional category there are several categories. Heavy or extra heavy oils are characterised by low flow and high viscosity. Shale oil (or light tight oil) is found in low permeability shale formations where flow requires stimulation via hydraulic fracturing or fracking. Tar sands (oil/bituminous sands, bitumen) is immobile in situ sometimes requiring mining.

Key further readings cited

Brecha, R.J. (2012). Logistic curves, extraction costs and effective peak oil. *Energy Policy* 51: 586–597.

Campbell, C.J., and Laherrère, J. (1998). The end of cheap oil. *Scientific American*, March 1998: 78–83.

Kerschner, C., Hubacek, K., Arto-Oliazola, I., Prell, C., Feng, K. (2017). Input-Output Models of Economic Vulnerability to Peak Oil, *SpringerBriefs in Energy Analysis*. Cham: Springer (forthcoming).

Miller, R.G., Sorrell, S.R. (2014). The future of oil supply. *Philosophical Transactions of the Royal Society of London A: Mathematical, Physical and Engineering Sciences* 372(2006): 1–27.

Murphy, D. J., Hall, C.A.S. (2011). Energy return on investment, peak oil, and the end of economic growth. *Annals of the New York Academy of Sciences* 1219: 52–72.

Other literature cited

Aleklett, K., Campbell, C.J. (2003). The peak and decline of world oil and gas production. *Minerals & Energy, Raw Materials Report* 18(1), 5–20.

Anderson, K. (2015). Duality in climate science. *Nature Geosciences* 8(12): 898–900.

ASPO (2009). *The Association for the Study of Peak Oil and Gas Newsletter* 100(April), 1–4, Cork: C.J. Campbell and S. H. Ballydehob.

Barnett, H., Morse, C. (1963). *Scarcity and Growth. The Economics of Natural Resource Availability*. Baltimore: John Hopkins Press.

BP (2015). *BP Statistical Review of World Energy 2015* (Annual No. 64). London: British Petroleum.

Capellán-Pérez, I., Arto, I., Polanco-Martínez, J., González-Eguino, M., Neumann, M.B. (2016). Likelihood of climate change pathways under uncertainty on fossil fuel resources availability. *Energy and Environmental Science*, 9 (8): 2482–2496.

Capellán-Pérez, I., Mediavilla, M., de Castro, C., Carpintero, Ó., Miguel, L.J. (2014). Fossil fuel depletion and socio-economic scenarios: An integrated approach. *Energy* 77(December): 641–666.

Dale, M., Krumdieck, S., Bodger, P. (2012). Global energy modelling — A biophysical approach (GEMBA) part 1: An overview of biophysical economics. *Ecological Economics* 73(January): 152–157.

Daly, H.E. (1992). *Steady-state Economics*, 2nd ed. London: Earthscan Publications Ltd.

De Castro, C. (2009). *Escenarios de Energía-Economía Mundiales con Modelos de Dinámica de Sistemas*. Unpublished Ph.D. Thesis. Valladoid: University of Valladolid. Available at: http://www.eis.uva.es/energiasostenible/wp-content/uploads/2011/11/Tesis-Carlos-de-Castro.pdf. Accessed 5th March 2017.

Douthwaite, R. (2012). Degrowth and the supply of money in an energy-scarce world. *Ecological Economics* 84(December): 187–193.

EIA (2015). *Annual Energy Outlook 2015 with projections to 2040*. Washington: U.S. Energy Information Administration.

EWG (2008). *Crude Oil: The Supply Outlook*. Berlin: Energy Watch Group. Available at: http://energywatchgroup.org/wp-content/uploads/2014/02/2008-02_EWG_Oil_Report_updated.pdf. Accessed 5th March 2017.

EWG (2013). *Fossil and Nuclear Fuels: The Supply Outlook*. Berlin: Energy Watch Group. Available at: http://energywatchgroup.org/wp-content/uploads/2014/02/EWG-update2013_short_18_03_2013.pdf. Accessed 5th March 2017.

Exner, A. (2015). *Resilienz gegenüber Energiekrisen*. Resilienz Österreich. Retrieved (date of access: September 18, 2015) from: http://www.umweltbuero.at/resilienz/?p=128.

Georgescu-Roegen, N. (1971) *The Entropy Law and the Economic Process*. Cambridge: Massachusetts, Harvard University Press.

Hall, C.A.S., Lambert, J.G., Balogh. S.B. (2014). EROI of different fuels and the Implications for Society. *Energy Policy* 64(January): 141–152.

Hughes, J.D. (2013). Energy: A reality check on the shale revolution. *Nature* 494: 307–308.

Hughes, J.D. (2015). *Shale Gas Reality Check: Revisiting the U.S. Department of Energy Play-by-Play Forecasts through 2040 from Annual Energy Outlook 2015*. Post Carbon Institute, Santa Rosa, CA, U.S.

Kerschner, C. (2010). Economic de-growth vs. steady-state economy. *Journal of Cleaner Production* 18: 544–551.

Kerschner, C. (2012). *A Multimethod Analysis of the Phenomenon of Peak Oil, Economic Degrowth and Attitudes towards Technology*. Barcelona: Universidad Autónoma de Barcelona.

Kerschner, C. (2015). Peak Oil. In D'Alisa, G., Demaria, F., Kallis, G. (eds.) *Degrowth: A Vocabulary for a New Era* (pp. 231–236). Abingdon and New York: Routledge.

Kerschner, C., Prell, C., Feng, K., Hubacek, K. (2013). Economic vulnerability to Peak Oil. *Global Environmental Change* 23 (6): 1424–1433.

Klare, M.T. (2004). *Blood and Oil: The Dangers and Consequences of America's Growing Dependency on Imported Petroleum*. New York: Metropolitan Books.

Laherrère, J. (2006). Oil and gas, what future? Unpublished paper presented at the Groningen Annual Energy Convention, 21st November. Available at: http://oilcrisis.com/laherrere/groningen.pdf. Accessed 5th March 2017.

Laherrère, J. (2010). *Peak Oil y Seguridad Energética*. Presented at the Segundo Simposio ASPO Argentina Buenos Aires, Buenos Aires (Argentina).

Maugeri, L. (2012). *Oil: The Next Revolution - the unprecedented upsurge of oil production capacity and what it means for the world*. Cambridge: Harvard Kennedy School

McGlade, C., Ekins, P. (2015). The geographical distribution of fossil fuels unused when limiting global warming to 2 °C. *Nature* 517: 187–190.

Mohr, S.H., Wang, J., Ellem, G., Ward, J., Giurco, D. (2015). Projection of world fossil fuels by country. *Fuel* 141: 120–135.

Muggeridge, A., Cockin, A., Webb, K., Frampton, H., Collins, I., Moulds, T., Salino, P. (2014). Recovery rates, enhanced oil recovery and technological limits. *Philosophical Transactions of the Royal Society of London A: Mathematical, Physical and Engineering Sciences* 372: 20120320.

Rogers, D. (2013). *Shale and Wall Street: Was the decline in natural gas prices orchestrated?* (No. 10). Energy Policy Forum. Retrieved (date of access: August 31, 2015) from http://shalebubble.org/wp-content/uploads/2013/02/SWS-report-FINAL.pdf.

Solow, R.M. (1974). The Economics of Resources or the Resources of Economics. Richard T. Ely Lecture, *American Economic Review* 64 (2): 1–14.

Sorman, A.H., Giampietro, M. (2013). The energetic metabolism of societies and the degrowth paradigm: analyzing biophysical constraints and realities. *Journal of Cleaner Production* 38(January): 80–93.

Spash, C.L. (2012) New foundations for ecological economics. *Ecological Economics* 77(May): 36–47.

Spash, C.L. (2016). This changes nothing: The Paris Agreement to ignore reality. *Globalizations*, 13 (6): 928–933.

Tordo, S., Tracy, B., S., Arfaa, N. (2011). *National oil companies and value creation,* World Bank working paper. Washington: The International Bank for Reconstruction and Development/The World Bank.

Tverberg, G.E. (2012). Oil supply limits and the continuing financial crisis. *Energy* 37(1): 27–34.

Tverberg, G.E. (2015). *A new theory of energy and the economy* - Part 1 - Generating economic growth. Our Finite World. Retrieved from https://ourfiniteworld.com/2015/01/21/a-new-theory-of-energy-and-the-economy-part-1-generating-economic-growth. Accessed 20 December 2016.

Valero, A., Valero, A. (2014). *Thanatia: The Destiny of the Earth's Mineral Resources : A Thermodynamic Cradle-to-Cradle Assessment*. New Jersey: World Scientific Publishing Company.

WEO (2004). *World Energy Outlook 2004*. Paris: OCDE/IEA.

WEO (2014). *World Energy Outlook 2014*. Paris: OECD/IEA.

Wigglesworth, R., McGee, P., Anderlini, J. (2015, August 24). China stocks sink lower as rout intensifies. *Financial Times*. http://www.ft.com/cms/s/0/855d2014-4a30-11e5-b558-8a9722977189.html#axzz4An4k1tAm.

42

HUMAN INDUCED CLIMATE CHANGE FROM A POLITICAL ECONOMY PERSPECTIVE

Max Koch

Introduction

Human induced climate change (CC) is one of the major and most encompassing threats in the world today (Dryzek et al., 2011). While the facts and highly consensual predictions amongst natural scientists are increasingly well-known, the understanding of CC as a social science subject is more unclear and controversial. This chapter briefly summarises the current state of climate science and then discusses the evolution of CC as a social ecological economic issue with emphasis on its parallel development with capitalism and highlighting past research and recent advances. The chapter concludes by outlining future directions both for research and policymaking.

Defining the topic

There is broad agreement in the natural sciences that observed increases in average global temperatures over the past century are due in large part to the anthropogenic emission of greenhouse gases (GHGs), primarily stemming from fossil fuel combustion and land use changes, such as deforestation. The Intergovernmental Panel on Climate Change (IPCC), in its Fifth Assessment Report on the *Physical Science Basis for Climate Change* (IPCC, 2014), highlights that atmospheric concentrations of CO_2 and other GHGs have risen to levels that are unprecedented in the last 800,000 years. The burning of fossil fuels is given as the main reason behind the 40 per cent increase in atmospheric CO_2 concentrations since the Industrial Revolution. In recent decades, changes in climate have caused impacts on natural and human systems on all continents and in the oceans. Climate expertise has linked extreme weather and climate events to human influences, including increases in the number of warm and cold temperature extremes and in heavy precipitation events in a range of regions. The IPCC forecasts that, by the end of the twenty-first century, the global surface temperature increase will exceed 1.5°C relative to the period 1850–1900 for a range of scenarios. Some scenarios predict that global temperatures will rise as much as 4.8°C. This is associated with uncontrollable CC, where there are frequent droughts, floods and storms plus largely unpredictable climate feedback effects. The higher end of this range—and particular the unprecedentedly high speed of the temperature rise—would be far outside the experience of human civilisation. The IPCC expects global mean sea levels to continue to rise during the twenty-first century. Heat waves are 'very likely' to occur more often and last longer, while extreme precipitation events will become more intense and frequent in many regions. Oceans are predicted to warm and acidify, and global mean sea level to rise further. Many aspects of CC and associated impacts will continue for centuries, even if anthropogenic emissions of GHGs are stopped fairly soon.

Capitalism is one of the major social structures of contemporary society, which historically developed almost simultaneously with CC. It creates particular social relations, discourses and ideologies through which social actors (including policymakers) make sense of society. Capitalist development takes different forms over space and time and involves different modes of regulation. Research in this area has been dedicated to the continuities and ruptures in the ways in which particular capitalist 'growth strategies' and corresponding institutional features affect the climate system.

Past research and recent advances

Capital accumulation and environmental exploitation

While the neoclassical perspective in economics focuses on the circularity and reversibility of the 'return' of monetary value and capital, ecological economists stress the fact that any economic activity involves physical flows and throughput of matter and energy, and that the Earth's reservoir of natural resources is limited [Chapters 9, 10, 11]. This is also at the heart of work by Marx, who—far from disregarding natural laws—made the pivot (*Springpunkt* in the German original) of his critique of political economy the dual nature of commodities as constituting both exchange value and use value. He saw work as producing both abstract value and concrete products through the transformation of raw materials and energy.

Understanding this 'double character' provides insight not only into further economic categories and the associated social relations, but also into the corresponding tensions between the capitalist economy and the ecological system that amplify the greenhouse effect (Koch, 2012: 33–35). Any further analysis of the dual nature of commodities and labour suggests that labour processes, under capitalist auspices, not only create abstract exchange value but that they must also be understood as concrete stocks of invested time-specific and place-specific assets of matter and energy. In general, the capitalist mode of production is oriented towards unlimited and short-term valorisation, quantitative and geographic expansion, circularity and reversibility, while the principles that guide the ecological system involve stable and sustainable matter and energy transformations and throughputs as well as irreversibility (Burkett, 1999).

Capital's expansionism tends to be accompanied by the degradation of the environmental conditions of production and especially reductions in their ability to act as sources and sinks for the permanently increasing flow and throughput of matter and energy (Clark and York, 2005). When these sources and sinks cease to function, their decelerating impact on the greenhouse effect is nullified, thus increasing the risk of negative feedback mechanisms within the climate system. Eco-Marxist authors [see also Chapter 6], such as Burkett and Clark and York, succeed in demonstrating that capitalist development proceeds in both socio-economically and ecologically contingent forms.

However, eco-Marxists sometimes seem to be unaware of the high level of abstraction in which Marx's mode of production is located. Though their research has generated the important result that the increase in material and energy throughput and the associated rise in GHG emissions are linked to capitalism's general and long-term trend towards an increased scale of production, existing variants of eco-Marxism often fail to consider what Poulantzas (1975) referred to as the distinction of 'mode of production' and 'social formation' (Koch, 2015). While the analysis of the mode of production allows for insights into the general tensions between economy and ecology that characterise all capitalist societies, it does not sufficiently consider how these structural tensions are articulated in actual societies and particular institutional circumstances (Koch, 2012: 39–45).

Capitalism, carbon and the policy response

A consideration of this more concrete level of abstraction is above all necessary to account for the fact that CO_2 emissions vary considerably across actual capitalist countries; for example, Sweden's CO_2 emissions per capita are considerably below that of the United States of America (USA). There is an emerging literature about if and why particular institutional and regulatory features of capitalism correspond to different amounts of GHG emissions. A world-system perspective has been able to reveal how CO_2 emissions are related to global stratification (Timmons Roberts et al., 2003). Nations within the core are the primary emitters due to their scale of production and consumption and influence on the global economy. However, particular nations in the periphery remain significant CO_2 polluters, and are unable to pursue more energy efficient development paths because their position in the global division of labour is characterised by debt, export dependency, outdated technologies and a narrow range of production. Uneven capitalist development and the corresponding enormous global inequalities also lie at the heart of the long running stalemate in climate negotiations, the results of which tend to reproduce the original structure of inequality (Roberts and Parks, 2006).

Due to their power and control over resources, delegations from Western countries have been able to define climate goals that avoid a transition from fossil fuels to renewable energy sources. The United Nations Framework Convention on Climate Change (UNFCCC) established procedures to meet the goals agreed in the Kyoto Protocol. This involved carbon trading and mostly European countries 'offsetting' CO_2 emissions by paying developing countries to reduce theirs. Such mechanisms constitute new investment opportunities for (financial) capital, but have contributed next to nothing to a reduction in the atmospheric concentrations of GHGs (Spash, 2011; Koch, 2014). The Paris Agreement of 2015 also changes nothing in this respect (Spash, 2016a, 2016b).

Institutional theories deployed in research on environmental regulation and climate performance include regulation theory and theories of capitalist diversity and change, as well as applications of the welfare regime approach. Core concepts of regulation theory (Boyer and Saillard, 2002) such as the 'accumulation regime' including operationalisations of production and consumption norms, 'mode of regulation' and 'institutional forms' have been complemented by the notion of 'energy regimes' and environmental regulation, which allowed for an empirical and comparative analysis of CO_2 emissions in accordance with the production and consumption patterns in the two main post-war capitalist growth strategies: Fordism and finance-driven capitalism (Koch, 2012: 49–136).

The regulation of nature varies and is to be understood as the temporary results of social struggles between various social actors. The choice and preference of certain environmental policies over others relies less on having the 'better argument' and more on wider societal power relations and asymmetries, including divisions within the capitalist class and the institutional traditions of different countries. Indeed, without an adequate concept of financialisation (and also of transnationalisation) of investment and capital accumulation, and the corresponding transnational actors, much of the current attempts to regulate CC in the form of commodification and carbon markets could not be fully understood (Lohmann, 2010).

Christoff and Eckersley (2011) found that domestic political institutions—proportional representation versus 'first past the post' electoral systems and the presence of Green parties in parliament and government—and corporatist systems that include business and labour have a statistically relevant impact on the level of GHG emissions. While national vulnerability to CC is a poor indicator, both reliance on fossil fuel extraction and energy-intensive industry heighten opposition to reducing carbon emissions. Meanwhile, hopes that social democratic welfare regimes, that are least unequal in social economic terms, would also perform best in ecological and climate terms (Gough et al., 2008) and gradually turn into 'eco-social States' remain unverified in comparative empirical research (Koch and Fritz, 2014). Since representatives of the social democratic, conservative and liberal welfare regimes were found among relatively well, medium and poor performing 'Green' states, the opposite might actually apply: The dialectics of the Western welfare state appears to lie in the fact that the same mechanism that defuses the socio-economic inequalities inherent in capitalist development ensures the inclusion of an increasing amount of people in environmentally problematic production and consumption practices [Chapter 15]. While most European Union (EU) countries perform poorly in combining economic development, social equity and environmental performance, including CO_2 emissions, there are non-European countries (e.g. Costa Rica and to a lesser degree Uruguay) that manage to perform relatively well on social indicators, such as life expectancy and subjective well-being, and at the same time display much lower levels of economic growth, CO_2 emissions and ecological damages (Fritz and Koch, 2014).

A clear pattern between ecological performance and environmental regulation, on the one hand, and welfare and other institutional features, on the other, remains unestablished. Conversely, a range of studies (Koch, 2012: 123–125; Koch and Fritz, 2014; Fritz and Koch, 2014) point to the close connection between economic development measured as Gross Domestic Product (GDP), material resource use and carbon emissions. While there is some evidence for the relative decoupling of GDP growth, material resource use and CO_2 emissions per unit of economic output in OECD countries, there is no evidence whatsoever for an absolute decoupling of these parameters [Chapter 11]. Yet such decoupling is regarded as necessary to make the internationally agreed 2°C climate target a realistic possibility. The failure of it to materialise seems to confirm Jevons' paradox [Chapter 9]: that increased efficiency in the use of fossil fuels results in an increase in demand for them. In fact, the only occasions where absolute GHGs fell in recent decades were during periods of major social economic crises such as in Cuba and Eastern Europe after the fall of the Berlin wall or, more recently, in the EU during the financial crisis.

In Europe reliance on the EU Emissions Trading Scheme (EU ETS) appears flawed due to its textbook orthodox economics that ignores power and lack of realism about markets (Spash, 2010; 2011). The argument that ETS can be refined ignores the fact that there is no time for empirical tests if emissions are to be curbed before damages become extreme. There is no indication whatsoever that existing carbon markets can be re-regulated—let alone expanded to the rest of the world—in ways that would make global carbon emissions peak in the foreseeable future. Hence, compared to its regulatory alternatives—direct regulation and Pigouvian taxes— carbon trading systems are the least best solution, unlikely to result in the extent of absolute decoupling of GDP growth, resource inputs and carbon emissions that would be necessary to meet the UNFCCC climate targets.

Worse still, the system's existence creates the deceptive appearance that "something is being done about the issue". By assuring the public that tackling CC does not contradict finance driven capitalism and can be handled within its institutional structures, resistance and the establishment of alternative ways of working and living become more difficult. On top of allowing corporations and associated governments to manage CC at the lowest financial cost and to open up a range of new career and investment opportunities, the existing CC governance edifice has a detrimental impact at the individual level, where it undermines a transformation of the fossil consumption norm (Spash, 2010). Carbon offsetting schemes offer a comfortable way of salving one's guilty conscience by maintaining the illusion that CC can be mitigated without behavioural change.

Future directions

Governance and institutional aspects of change

The type of changes in production and consumption processes, that scientists regard as necessary to mitigate CC, will be impossible to achieve within the framework of the current finance driven accumulation regime, consumption norm, mode of regulation and energy regime. In order to avoid catastrophic CC, capitalist development, global inequality and the climate crisis will need to be addressed as a whole. CC is a global issue that should be addressed and regulated at that level.

A sustainable economic strategy would, at the very least, involve the reconfiguration of social (including communal), State and market regulation and the establishment of international institutions—similar to Bretton Woods after World War II—powerful enough to limit and steer capital valorisation in accordance with ecological laws. In particular such institutions would need to specify boundaries and limit GHG emissions for companies, countries and individuals, in accord with expert climate science. They would need to be strong enough to enforce ecological standards in production and consumption in the developed countries and, if necessary, to abolish market steering, the profit motive and private property in areas where there is failure to meet emissions targets. Such an approach would create a mixed economy with different forms of property (private, communal, societal, State property) and a more important role for 'commoning' [Chapter 38] as a means of regulating behaviour.

The creation of such international institutions presupposes the building of trust at the international level. According to Roberts and Parks (2006: 24), this presupposes a 'greater stake' for developing countries in governance and decision-making of international financial institutions. Enough scenarios exist today that illustrate the kind of changes that would need to be implemented to transform dominant production and consumption patterns in ways that limit GHGs according to climate science expertise. For example, in order to tackle global inequality and CC in tandem, Robert and Parks (2006: 217) recommend the provision of: "greater 'environmental space' to late developers, supplying meaningful sums of environmental assistance, funding aid for adaptation and dealing with local environmental issues".

Further elements of a new environmental governance system would include strict regulation for setting efficiency and carbon use standards for buildings, vehicles, urban development and land use. Many authors and activists propose determining and monitoring a gradual reduction of the global annual output of fossil energy carriers, such as crude oil, on a worldwide scale. If this reduction amounted to 2 per cent a year, within 50 years there would be no more CO_2 emissions arising from oil combustion. A legally binding "keep the oil in the soil" approach would constitute a real incentive for companies to shift their energy supply to renewable, especially solar, energy sources in the foreseeable future.

Procedurally, Lohmann (2010) and Spash (2011) suggest that carbon taxes, 'Green' taxes on material intensity (e.g., metals, water, wood, plastics) and legal action would be most effective at steering the transition towards a low-carbon economy. Revenues from taxes could be used to fund low-carbon energy and increase efficiency, and the transitions of the economies of the currently oil-exporting countries. Hence, the exploration of the potential structure of global, national and local institutions to mitigate and regulate CC as well as their procedural particulars opens up a range of new research issues suggesting interdisciplinary cooperation.

Inequity and distribution

Environmental, and specifically climate, policy targets raise questions about fairness, because they have distributive consequences and hence implications for social justice and social policy. Often responsibilities and impacts do not coincide and constitute a 'double injustice' (Walker, 2012), since the groups and populations likely to be most harmed by CC are the least responsible for causing it and have the least resources to cope with the consequences. The ensuing distributional dilemma has so far largely been studied at global level with a focus on the responsibilities of developing and developed countries. Yet this dilemma also surfaces within European and other OECD countries (Büchs et al., 2011).

Due to their higher consumption levels, one must expect that households situated in the upper part of the income distribution contribute more to CO_2 emissions than lower income households, while poor households suffer most from environmental degradation (e.g., through poorer housing, risk of flooding) and are disproportionally burdened by the costs of CC policies. Future research should therefore address questions such as the following: How do the burdens of climate policies impact on household income across European countries? Are such burdens proportional to the impact on the environment of different lifestyles? How can countervailing social policies be designed such that unjust distributional effects are avoided?

A post-growth economy

The debate on the role of capitalist diversity and various institutions in the provision of economies, which produce and emit fewer GHGs, sustainability and welfare is still young and should be continued. A hypothesis that is worthwhile testing further results from recent comparative research into 'prosperity beyond growth'—operationalised as environmental sustainability, social inclusion and quality of life—which suggests a positive link between the extent of civic participation in a country and its environmental performance (Fritz and Koch, 2014). However, since ecological sustainability and particularly an absolute decoupling of carbon emissions and GDP growth seem unachievable in growing economies, the feasibility of providing ecological, social and individual prosperity in non-growing economies should be moved into focus. Here, the steady-state economy (SSE) [Chapter 45], advocated by Herman Daly (1977), may be a useful theoretical entry point for consideration of ecological sustainability in the economic cycle. Instead of the money measure of GDP growth, the point of departure of a steady-state economy is primarily physically based in terms of a relatively stable population and 'artefacts' (stock of physical wealth) and the lowest feasible rates of matter and energy throughput in production and consumption. Though I agree with Dale (2012: 440) that Daly's approach lacks "precision in locating the driving force" of the growth imperative—largely due to Daly's rather uncritical reading of John Stuart Mill—I would nevertheless concur with Daly that a transition from current growth economies to steady state economies is a goal worth achieving (Koch, 2015).

However, the original concept of a SSE was not developed at the global level. Yet environmental threats such as CC are global issues, because it does not matter from which part of the globe GHGs are emitted. Any institutional compromise for a SSE would therefore need to go beyond the national scale, on which post-war welfare arrangements were agreed, and encompass the entire globe. It is only at the global level that thresholds for matter and energy throughput can be determined in order to effectively mitigate global environmental challenges such as CC. At the same time, these biophysical terms achieved at the global level would delineate the leeway within which national and local economies and societies could evolve. This cannot be achieved via a simple top-down approach from the global to national and local levels. What is required is a new division of labour between regulatory scales where key and general features such as biophysical thresholds are agreed at the global level and local levels play a much greater role both in production and consumption and in the provision of welfare.

The goal of a global SSE is supported by much of the degrowth [Chapter 44] research community. Although some authors have stressed differences between the two approaches, the emerging consensus seems to be that degrowth is a process whose end goal is a SSE (Martínez-Alier et al., 2010; O'Neill, 2012). Kerschner (2010) came to the conclusion that both concepts are complementary, whereby the global North would need to embark on degrowth trajectories to a SSE, while the Global South would need to "follow a path of decelerating growth" (O'Neill, 2012: 222). In other words, there would be space for different national and local paths to post-growth economies and societies that represent different traditions and institutional patterns and that could provide prosperity in different ways. Such path-dependent degrowth trajectories would also reflect different divisions of labour between the market, State and the commons, which opens up new research areas.

However, according to Daly, any SSE would not only feature a statutory minimum income but also a maximum limit for income and wealth. Hence, post-growth economies and societies would not abolish the market as economic steering instrument, but this would operate within rather narrow political and ecological limits decelerating the capitalist accumulation dynamic considerably. The introduction of a global SSE would then presuppose a clear break with current regulatory modes of finance-driven capitalism.

The meaning of and justification for capitalist growth is increasingly questioned by a wide variety of disciplines including: epidemiology, consumption research, psychology of wellbeing and theories of human needs [see Chapter 24]. These all suggest that treating ecological sustainability, social equity as well as individual wellbeing is best done in the absence of economic growth (Koch, 2013). Epidemiologists have provided ample evidence that people in more equal and socially inclusive societies are better-off, and report greater amounts of wellbeing than in more unequal and growth-driven ones where status competition is particularly pronounced (Wilkinson and Pickett, 2010). Consumption researchers argue that in rich countries buying things has less to do with the goods themselves than the symbolic message that the act of purchase conveys (Røpke, 1999). The competition for positional goods is mediated through a genuinely social logic that Pierre Bourdieu referred to as 'distinction'. This general societal race to determine the legitimate taste is by definition short term, does not contribute anything to human wellbeing in the long term and contradicts the principal reproductive needs of the Earth as an ecological system, since consumption practices are normally bound to matter and energy transformations and necessitate the burning of fossil fuels.

Wellbeing and quality of life researchers assume that humans must have certain psychological needs satisfied in order to flourish and experience personal wellbeing. These needs include feeling safe and secure as well as competent and efficient. People also require love and intimacy and struggle under conditions of loneliness, rejection, and exclusion (Kasser, 2011). Ecological economists have discussed the role and meaning of human needs (e.g., Rauschmayer et al., 2011) [Chapter 24]. Koch and Buch-Hansen (2016) integrate need theories with the notions of a SSE and 'sustainable welfare'. The satisfaction of most basic human needs requires much fewer material resources than in the current wants-oriented capitalist growth economy, potentially allowing for a surplus in welfare and prosperity for one person or one generation while still leaving room for the development of others. While due to planetary limits and CC existing Western welfare systems cannot be generalised to the rest of the world, the issue of whether a global SSE and an according sustainable welfare system is capable of providing more than basic human needs is an empirical one or, in Gough's words, a matter of "policy auditing", during which critical thresholds for the universal provision of human needs (and wants) would constantly be redefined in light of the best available scientific knowledge (Gough, 2015). A great deal of work remains to integrate these diverse growth critical approaches into a coherent theory of prosperity, the 'good life' or 'sustainable welfare' (Koch and Mont, 2016).

Concluding remarks

This chapter has outlined the main features of CC and its link to capitalist development, past and present research agendas for and beyond ecological economics and delineated future challenges. Ecological economists, social scientists and other intellectuals can assist climate and related activists by jointly constructing development models that de-prioritise GDP growth and over-consumption as well as associated social, ecological and economic policies to defuse the 'double injustice' of CC and social inequality at global, national and local levels. The point of departure for any transition to an ecologically sustainable and socially just mode of regulation of the global economy is an academically sound analysis of what I elsewhere called the "twofold crisis of finance-driven capitalism" (Koch, 2012: 191). The chance of alternative thought and practice becoming hegemonic depends on the extent to which the 'objective' economic, political and cultural structures of contemporary society and the corresponding symbolic systems become themselves crisis prone, and on the extent to which actors are aware of this.

Human induced CC is a major social, ecological and economic issue. There is now a very short time frame within which GHG emissions reductions need to be implemented to avoid serious and accelerating harm. At the same time, there is a total lack of evidence for the possibility of absolutely decoupling of GHG emissions from GDP growth. The key political and research issue is therefore how to embark on effective CC mitigation and a corresponding wider social ecological economic policy strategy in the absence of economic growth.

Key further readings cited

Dryzek, J., Norgaard, R. and Schlosberg, D. (eds.) (2011). *Oxford Handbook of Climate Change and Society*. Oxford: Oxford University Press.
Koch, M. (2012). *Capitalism and Climate Change. Theoretical Discussion, Historical Development and Policy Responses*. Basingstoke: Palgrave Macmillan.
Roberts, J.T. and Parks, B.C. (2006). *A Climate of Injustice. Global Inequality, North-South Politics, and Climate Policy*. Cambridge, MA: The MIT Press.

Other literature cited

Boyer, R. and Saillard, Y. (eds.) (2002). *Regulation Theory. The State of the Art*. London: Taylor and Francis.
Büchs, M., Bardsley, N. and Duwe, S. (2011). Who bears the brunt? Distributional effects of climate change mitigation policies. *Critical Social Policy* 31(2), 285–307.
Burkett, P. (1999). *Marx and Nature. A Red and Green Perspective*. New York: St. Martin's Press.
Christoff, P. and Eckersley, R. (2011). Comparing State Responses. In J. Dryzek, R. Norgaard, and D. Schlosberg, D. (Eds.), *Oxford Handbook of Climate Change and Society* (pp. 431–448). Oxford: Oxford University Press.

Clark, B. and York, R. (2005). Carbon metabolism: Global capitalism, climate change, and the biospheric rift. *Theory and Society* 34(4), 391–428.

Dale, G. (2012). Critique of growth in classical political economy: Mill's stationary state and a Marxian response. *New Political Economy* 18(3), 431–457.

Daly, H. (1977). *Steady State Economics.* San Francisco: W.H. Freeman.

Fritz, M. and Koch, M. (2014). Potentials for prosperity without growth: Ecological sustainability, social inclusion and the quality of life in 38 Countries. *Ecological Economics* 108, 191–199.

Gough, I. (2015). Climate change and sustainable welfare: An argument for the centrality of human needs. *Cambridge Journal of Economics* 39, 1191–1214.

Gough, I., Meadowcroft, J., Dryzek, J., Gerhards, J., Lengfield, H., Markandya, A. and Ortiz, R. (2008). JESP symposium: Climate change and social policy, *Journal of European Social Policy* 18(4), 25–44.

Intergovernmental Panel on Climate Change (IPCC) (2014). *Climate Change 2014: Synthesis Report. Summary for Policymakers*, Geneva: IPCC; available online at www.ipcc.ch/pdf/assessment-report/ar5/syr/AR5_SYR_FINAL_SPM.pdf. Accessed 20 December 2016.

Kasser, T. (2011). Cultural values and the well-being of future generations: A cross-national study. *Journal of Cross-cultural Psychology* 42(2), 206–215.

Kerschner, C. (2010). Economic de-growth vs. steady-state-economy. *Journal of Cleaner Production* 6(8), 544–551.

Koch, M. (2013). Welfare after growth: Theoretical discussion, historical development and policy implications. *International Journal of Social Quality* 3(1), 4–20.

Koch, M. (2014). Climate change, carbon trading and societal self-defense. *Real-world Economics Review* 67, 52–66.

Koch, M. (2015). Climate change, capitalism and degrowth trajectories to a global steady-state economy. *International Critical Thought* 5(4), 439–452.

Koch, M. and Fritz, M. (2014). Building the eco-social state: Do welfare regimes matter? *Journal of Social Policy* 43(4), 679–703.

Koch, M. and Buch-Hansen, H. (2016). Human needs, steady-state economics and sustainable welfare. In Koch, M. and Mont, O. (Eds.) (2016). *Sustainability and the Political Economy of Welfare*. London: Routledge.

Koch, M. and Mont, O. (Eds.) (2016). *Sustainability and the Political Economy of Welfare*. London: Routledge.

Lohmann, L. (2010). Uncertainty markets and carbon markets: Variations on Polanyian themes. *New Political Economy* 15(2), 225–254.

Martínez-Alier, J., Pascual, U., Vivien, F.D. and Zaccai, E. (2010). Sustainable de-growth: mapping the context, criticism and future prospects of an emergent paradigm. *Ecological Economics* 69(9), 1741–1747.

O'Neill, D.W. (2012). Measuring progress in the degrowth transition to a steady state economy. *Ecological Economics* 84(December), 221–231.

Poulantzas, N. (1975). *Political Power and Social Classes*. London: Verso.

Rauschmayer, F., Omann, I. and Frühmann, J. (Eds.). (2011). *Sustainable Development: Capabilities, Needs, and Well-being*. New York: Routledge.

Røpke, I. (1999). The dynamics of willingness to consume. *Ecological Economics* 28(3), 399–420.

Spash, C.L. (2010). The brave new world of carbon trading. *New Political Economy* 15(2), 169–195.

Spash, C. (2011). Carbon Trading: A Critique. In J. Dryzek, R. Norgaard, and D. Schlosberg (Eds.), *Oxford Handbook of Climate Change and Society* (pp. 550–560). Oxford: Oxford University Press.

Spash, C.L. (2016a). The political economy of the Paris Agreement on human induced climate change: A brief guide. *Real World Economics Review* 75(July), 67–75.

Spash, C.L. (2016b). This changes nothing: The Paris Agreement to ignore reality. *Globalizations* 13(6): 928–933.

Timmons Roberts, J.T., Grimes, P.E. and Manale, J.L. (2003). Social roots of global environmental change: A world-systems analysis of carbon dioxide emissions. *Journal of World-Systems Research* 9(2), 277–315.

Walker, G. (2012). *Environmental Justice: Concepts, Evidence and Politics*. London: Routledge.

Wilkinson, R. and Pickett, K. (2010). *The Spirit Level. Why Equality is Better for Everyone*. London: Penguin.

43

ECOSYSTEM SERVICES

Erik Gómez-Baggethun

Introduction

In 1944, political economist and economic historian, Karl Polanyi wrote:

> The economic function is but one of many vital functions of land. It invests man's life
> with stability; it is the site of his habitation; it is a condition of his physical safety; it is
> the landscape.
>
> *(Polanyi, 1957 [1944]: 178)*

Looking beyond the conventional economic focus on money and markets, Polanyi paid
attention to the importance of land and its multiple functions in satisfying essential human
needs. Possibly too advanced for his time, Polanyi's ecological economic vision passed
underappreciated by his contemporaries. Half a century later, attention to the functions of land
would come back in the form of the ecosystem service approach (Daily, 1997) to become one
of the dominant frames in environmental science and policy at the turn of the twenty-first
century.

In recent years, the ecosystem services approach has been the subject of heated debates about
the framing concepts and institutions that ought to govern environmental and economic policy
(Norgaard, 2010). While many see in the concept a powerful communication tool and potential
driver of policy transformation, others conceive of it as a neoliberal and managerial vision of
environmental policy. The present chapter offers a synthesis of the origin, theoretical
developments and implementation of the ecosystem services approach, calling attention to the
controversies that surround the concept and its policy applications. I set the stage discussing the
way contemporary lifestyles affect capacity to appreciate societal dependence on natural
ecosystems. Next, I discuss the ecosystem services concept as an attempt to raise awareness of
societal dependence on ecosystems and biodiversity. A review of the ecosystem services concept
from theory to implementation follows. Next, the contested fields of ecosystem services
valuation and governance are discussed. The chapter ends with some brief concluding remarks
on the relation between ecological economics and the ecosystem services approach.

Valuing Nature in a technological era

We live in an urban and technological era. Since the early twenty-first century, and for the first time in history, more people live in cities than in rural areas [see Chapter 48]. By 2050, two out of every three of the world's inhabitants will be urban and in most developed countries, as much as 80 per cent to 90 per cent of the population already lives in cities. As urban areas absorb a growing share of the planet's population, more people grow up surrounded by technological landscapes where ecological life-support processes are hidden from view. Pyle (1978) hypothesised that as people drift away from personal contact with Nature, awareness and appreciation of the environment decline, which in turns breeds apathy towards Nature and, ultimately, environmental decline. He referred to this phenomenon as 'the extinction of experience' (see also Miller, 2005).

Divorce from Nature

Unless effectively counteracted—the hypothesis goes—the problem tends to worsen over time. As each new generation lives ever more separated from Nature, our capacity to miss biodiverse ecosystems and to struggle for their protection erodes. This leads to a generational environmental amnesia, where knowledge is lost and younger generations are unaware of past ecological conditions. The stars, which urban light pollution have turned invisible to many, illustrate this phenomenon. Over millennia, the night sky has inspired all of human kind's questions in religion, philosophy, science, and art. Today's city dwellers are the first generation of humanity to have missed their grandness and beauty. However, those who grew up without them do not know what they are missing, and so show no signs of concern. As Pyle (1993: 147) explains: "What is the extinction of a Condor to a child who has never seen a wren?". This raises serious concerns over economists' appeals to individual preferences as a basis for ecosystem valuation (Spash, 2008).

Another development in this direction stems from the fact that we increasingly live our lives through screens, an additional barrier for engaging with the intimacy of our social and physical environment. The point here is not moralising about screen time or urban lifestyles, but calling attention to the hypothesis that contemporary lifestyles may reduce the ability to perceive, understand, and appreciate the many ways in which we humans depend upon ecosystems and other species. Urban children in many parts of the world associate food and water more with corporate brands, supermarkets and built infrastructure, rather than watersheds, soil, plants and animals (Miller, 2005).

As the market economy globalises, less people obtain food, water, fibre or medicines from their immediate natural surroundings. Ecosystem 'goods' tend to be obtained as commodities, transported from increasingly distant areas through complex distribution chains. Societal alienation from ecological life-support systems has paved the way for the belief that technological progress will release humans from their historical dependence on Nature (e.g. Ausubel, 1996; Nordhaus et al., 2011; Kareiva et al., 2015).

Dependence on Nature

Technological innovation decoupling economic growth from resource use and pollution is a mainstay among many economists and policy makers (Gómez-Baggethun and Naredo, 2015). However, that humans can free themselves from dependence on Nature is one of the most prevalent myths of the industrial civilisation. As of today, empirical data do not hint of any symptoms of economic dematerialisation [Chapter 11]. Although some environmental indicators, particularly at the local and urban levels, have improved over the last decades, globally, growth in Gross Domestic Product (GDP) has run in parallel with mounting pressure on the environment (Krausmann et al., 2009). Our energy and material footprints were never larger than today and human demands on ecosystem services and biodiversity keep rising (Guo et al., 2010).

That today we depend on Nature *differently* from traditional small-scale societies does not mean we depend on it *less* (Gómez-Baggethun and de Groot, 2010). Cities, for example, depend on territories to supply them with resources and absorb their wastes that typically cover from 500 to 1,000 times their own size (Folke et al., 1997). Hence, societal decoupling from ecological systems has only occurred locally and partially, through increased appropriation of ecosystem services from distant areas and by shifting the social costs of economic growth to other regions and future generations.

Many conservationists and environmental scientists believe that in an era of generalised environmental amnesia, a prerequisite to achieving environmental sustainability is to re-establish awareness of the connections between people and ecological life-support systems. Here, we refer to connections between people and Nature in a very concrete way, namely, through the flows of energy, materials, and information from the environment that sustain long-term conditions for life, human well-being and economic prosperity.

Ecosystem services: from metaphor to market

Ecosystem services are defined as the benefits humans derive from ecosystem functions (MA, 2005) or as the contributions of ecosystems to human well-being (TEEB, 2010). First used in the late 1970s (Westman, 1977; Erlich and Ehrlich, 1981), the concept of ecosystem services was introduced precisely to emphasise societal dependence on natural ecosystems (Daily, 1997). The aim was to make visible the values that myopic economic analysis of the environment had turned invisible (Gómez-Baggethun et al., 2010). Since the late 1970s, ecosystem services and related concepts were used as a metaphor to emphasise societal dependence on nature (Norgaard, 2010).

In the 2000s, the release of the Millennium Ecosystem Assessment (MA) firmly established the ecosystem services concept in the policy agenda. This regarded the concept as being able to capture the many ways in which human society depends upon the existence and functioning of Nature, and aiming to cover the full variety of benefits that humans derive from ecosystems. The MA defined these as including i) physical goods like food and medicine, ii) indirect benefits from ecological processes like climate regulation and water purification, iii) immaterial benefits humans derive from their interaction with Nature, like sense of place and amenity benefits, and, iv) the core Earth functions responsible for maintaining evolutionary processes and life on Earth, including biogeochemical and energy cycles (MA, 2005).

The MA concluded that two-thirds of ecological life support systems worldwide had been degraded in the previous 50 years, noting that humanity was living beyond their means at the expense of biodiversity and future generations (MA, 2005). The assessment was primarily biophysical and monetary valuations held a marginal position in the reports. However, following the ecological and environmental economics literature of the 1990s, the MA framework adopted economic metaphors to conceptualise Nature as a 'stock of natural capital' providing 'flows of ecosystem services'.

The genie had been let out of the bottle and by the turn of the twentieth century, a growing number of environmentalists endorsed monetary valuation of ecosystem services as a strategy to communicate the societal value of Nature in the language perceived to dominate decisions in market driven economies. Costanza et al. (1997) produced the first attempt to come up with a monetary measurement of the value of the world's ecosystem services and natural capital. A growing body of literature on monetary valuation followed in the 2000s, often making the case that natural or semi-natural ecosystems produce more societal and economic benefits than converted ones, if the "monetary value of non-market ecosystem services" is taken into account (Heal et al., 2005).

The general claim was now that ecosystem services valuation was a necessary means for 'internalising externalities'. In the late 1990s monetary valuation was used mostly by economists. Over the 2000s, however, economic framing of environmental problems became increasingly popular among natural scientists too. Seduced by the alleged persuasive power of the money language, many ecologists and conservation biologists (e.g. Balmford et al., 2002; Daily and Ellison, 2002) replaced their traditional valuation languages (species rareness, richness, abundance, vulnerability, and intrinsic value) to endorse the money language in the name of pragmatism and emergency (Spash and Aslaksen, 2015).

The academic wave of what Spash (2009; 2013) terms "new environmental pragmatism" soon crashed on the shores of the policy agenda. In 2007, as the international community worked on preparations for the Conference of the Parties (COP) of the Convention on Biological Diversity (CBD) in Nagoya, state of the art knowledge on biodiversity status confirmed what most people feared: two decades after the launch of the CBD, biodiversity loss not only remained unabated, but had accelerated to an unprecedented pace. Many environmental scientists took this to mean that traditional conservation strategies—based on intrinsic values [Chapter 23] and ethical motivation—had miserably failed. They called for a shift towards the more pragmatic approaches to conservation. This shift was one factor leading to the publication of the report *The Economics of Ecosystem and Biodiversity* (TEEB), which aims to estimate the global unaccounted costs of biodiversity loss (TEEB, 2010).

The contested domain of valuation

Valuation of ecosystem services is a highly divisive question that has split ecological economists between those who accept it as a pragmatic choice, and those who reject it on ethical or political grounds (Spash, 2013). Some ecological economists suggest we should endorse monetary valuation of ecosystem services without commodifying them (Costanza, 2006). Others suggest that, given the governance structures in which environmental policy currently operates, monetary valuation leads to the "tragedy of well-intentioned valuation" (Gómez-Baggethun and Ruiz-Pérez, 2011: 624). That is, because commodification involves institutional changes as much as symbolic ones, monetary valuation of ecosystem services crafts discursive framings and metrical technology that paves the way for further degrees of commodification, even if this may happen against the original will of the valuator.

How then should value be qualified or quantified? Within the discourse about ecosystem services 'value' has been too often misread as merely denoting 'monetary value'. However, much of the ecosystem services literature endorse a broader understanding of value. The Oxford Dictionary defines 'value' as "the regard that something is held to deserve; the importance, worth, or usefulness of something" and as "[...] one's judgment of what is important in life". Two aspects deserve attention in these definitions. First, a key word when we deal with value is 'importance'. Second, values do not derive merely from preferences (Spash, 2008), but also from people's principles and convictions with regard to what is socially appropriate to do [Chapter 22].

Ecological economics' perspectives on ecosystem services valuation embrace the term value in its broader understanding as importance and as principles, or moral duties towards Nature (Gómez-Baggethun and Martín-López, 2015). This raises concerns over the incommensurability and pluralism of values [Chapter 22]. For centuries, value theorists have striven to find a common metric (money, energy, labour, or land) to measure value. Georgescu-Roegen (1975) criticised such monist theories of environmental valuation as a form of reductionism that capture only one of the several important dimensions of Nature's value. Ecological economists have embraced value pluralism as a core epistemological foundation.

Value pluralism is the idea that there are multiple values which in principle may be equally correct and fundamental. It departs from the premise that understanding the importance of ecosystems and the services they provide to humans involves dealing with multiple and often conflicting valuation languages. Different values may be considered to inform decisions, but not reduced to a single metric (Kapp, 1978). Ecological economics therefore acknowledges multiple values in ecosystem services, including ecological, economic, social, cultural and symbolic values (Chan et al., 2012; Dendoncker et al., 2013; Gómez-Baggethun et al., 2016). A key challenge for value pluralism however is to further develop coherent frames in which different valuation languages can be consistently combined to assist decision processes.

Clashes over ecosystem services governance

Another contested domain in ecosystem services concerns which governance structures should be used to articulate the value of ecosystem services in policy decisions. Different governance approaches have been proposed, including State, market- and community-based institutions, or a combination thereof. In practice, the market approach is the one that has received most attention in the literature.

The prominence of market approaches in debates on ecosystem services governance has to be understood in the context of the neoliberal political-economic context in which environmental policy has operated since the 1980s (Gómez-Baggethun and Muradian, 2015). Political-economic practices such as privatisation, reduction of State intervention in the economy, and expansion of market valuation to spheres formerly unaffected by trade, have gradually permeated all aspects of environmental governance. So-called 'market environmentalism' aims at conciliating economic growth, allocation efficiency and environmental conservation (McCarthy, 2004). Policy tools promoted by this approach include the establishment of well-defined property rights over ecosystem services, monetary valuation of the environment and market-based instruments for conservation (Gómez-Baggethun and Ruiz-Pérez, 2011).

Proponents of market environmentalism make the case that the most effective way of 'making ecosystem services count' is articulating them through markets and payments schemes. This approach has been implemented through two main families of economic instruments: markets for ecosystem services and payments for ecosystem services (PES). The former follows the polluter pays principle, and often frames environmental problems, such as atmospheric pollution and biodiversity loss, as 'negative externalities' to be internalised into market operations. Examples include carbon markets, wetland banking schemes and biodiversity offsets. The second family of instruments under PES refers to the various types of incentive schemes following the "provider gets principle", and frames ecosystem services as 'positive externalities' that should be paid for.

Criticism to market environmentalism has revolved around opposition to the commodification of Nature. The notion of commodification describes the phenomenon by which things that were not previously meant for sale enter the sphere of money and market exchange. Commodification of Nature has been criticised for privileging access to ecosystem services for those with the ability to pay (Martínez-Alier, 2002) or because duties towards the environment should not be for sale (McCauley, 2006; Spash, 2009; Sandel, 2012).

The extent to which different economic instruments involve commodification of ecosystem services is however under dispute. While carbon markets represent an obvious case of commodification, most schemes labelled as PES are far from meeting the conditions of a market transaction (Muradian and Gómez-Baggethun, 2013; Vatn, 2015). The largest existing PES schemes, whether measured in physical (land area) or economic terms (volume of payments), are run under public policy regulation frameworks, such as those found in Costa Rica, Mexico, China and Vietnam, and operating under the agro-environmental payment schemes of the United States of America and the European Union. Funds are collected through taxes or fees, and public authorities define the level of payments. Milder et al. (2010) found that the vast majority of funding to operate PES schemes comes from public bodies and Vatn (2015) notes that public funding of PES schemes amounts to 90 per cent of the total and up to 99 per cent of the PES schemes oriented at public goods. Hence, despite the market mythology that pervades much of the literature, actual PES schemes on the ground are variants of environmental rural subsidies whereby States pay landholders and communities to reward their stewardship or compensate opportunity costs from restrictions to land use changes (Gómez-Baggethun and Muradian, 2015).

Despite this the long-term impacts of PES remain unclear. A particular concern is the effects of PES on motivations for conservation. For example, Rode et al. (2015) found cases where conservation payments contributed to the erosion of intrinsic motivations for conservation, calling for caution in their implementation.

Future directions

What is the way forward for ecological economics in relation to ecosystem services? Contending views range from the support for monetary valuation and market-based instruments as a pragmatic choice, to an outright rejection of the ecosystem services approach as a whole. I contend that both of these responses may be misleading.

In the first case, we would be reinforcing the market ideology and political-economic institutions that ecological economics ultimately intends to overcome. The case for endorsing the market approach temporarily as a pragmatic short-term strategy is moreover unrealistic. Its benefits remain unproven, and possibly unprovable. In addition, market environmentalism drives policy away from the goals of ecological economics, namely long-term economic viability that is socially equitable and within planetary boundaries.

The second response may also be wrong to the extent it reproduces the misleading strategy of many critical theories of change over recent decades, namely, surrendering to their enemies all good ideas as soon as they gain attention from the mainstream. By retreating to the morally safe domain of criticism and deconstruction, theories of radical change are losing hegemony in the science and policy arenas. Whether or not the ecosystem services approach can serve the purposes of ecological economics depends entirely on whom appropriates the concept and its applications.

Ecosystem services are a misleading concept if used as an all-encompassing framework that displaces Nature's intrinsic values and non-utilitarian motivations for environmental protection. However, within given policy contexts and in co-existence with other framings of Nature, it can remind us that functioning ecosystems are not only the foundation of life, but also a prerequisite for sustaining human well-being and long-term economic prosperity. Likewise, valuation becomes a misleading tool if a single valuation language comes to dominate decision and planning. However, applied in a framework of value pluralism it can render visible social environmental costs that tend to be systematically overlooked in policy decisions. That the terms 'valuation' and 'monetary valuation' are used interchangeably by market environmentalists, as much as by their most determined critics, reflects how the latter have surrendered the framing of value and valuation to the former, letting their opponents define the terrain of the struggle.

Also economic valuation and economic policy instruments can be useful tools under certain conditions (Kallis et al., 2013). Economic growth bears many unaccounted costs e.g. pollution and associated health damages. These social environmental costs rarely appear in company balance sheets or macroeconomic accounts, unless they are claimed through court cases or unless State regulations mandate their internalisation. The dominant approach in ecosystem services valuation frames these costs as 'externalities' resulting from market failures, calling for their internalisation in the price system (e.g. through monetisation and market-based instruments). There is, however, a body of literature in institutional and ecological economics that, following Kapp (1978), does not frame externalities as accidental market failures, but as 'cost-shifting successes' through which powerful actors capitalise the benefits of their economic activity while imposing costs on others (Zografos et al., 2014). Framed from this perspective, economic valuation can inform liability claims for social ecological damages, serving both deterrence and corrective justice roles (Phelps et al., 2015). This perspective involves shifting the frames and institutions that guide monetary valuation so that the point is no longer 'getting prices right' but 'getting justice right'. Informing liability suits is a promising and yet under-exploited application of valuation that deserves further attention from ecological economists.

Concluding remarks

Ecosystem services have become an influential concept in science and policy, partly thanks to the contributions of ecological economists. The concept was originally introduced as a metaphor to emphasise societal dependence on functioning ecosystems. Much of the aim was drawing attention to the 'hidden' costs of growth and long-term effects of biodiversity loss on human well-being. As it gained popularity, the concept developed life of its own. Some applications then departed markedly from the spirit and purpose for which the concept was originally introduced, and the concept has in some cases been instrumentalised to further agendas of neoliberal environmental policy.

How to value and govern vital ecosystem services to sustain long-term conditions for life and social prosperity, is too important in its implications to be left to those who attempt to reduce it to market logics and the profit calculus. Change is already under way. Many scholars in the ecosystem service approach either ignore or actively oppose market environmentalism, and attention to monetary valuation and market instruments has lost leverage in the ecosystem services literature over recent years. Ecological economics should retain and expand the aspects of the approach that are consistent with its principles and purposes, while dismissing and actively opposing its counterproductive applications.

Key further readings cited

Gómez-Baggethun, E., de Groot, R., Lomas, P., Montes, C. (2010). The history of ecosystem services in economic theory and practice: from early notions to markets and payment schemes. *Ecological Economics* 69(6), 1209–1218.

Norgaard, R. (2010). Ecosystem services: From eye-opening metaphor to complexity blinder. *Ecological Economics* 69(6), 1219–1227.

Spash, C.L. (2008). How much is that ecosystem in the window? The one with the bio-diverse trail. *Environmental Values* 17(2): 259–284.

Other literature cited

Ausubel, J.H. (1996). The Liberation of the Environment, *Daedalus* 125(3): 1–17.

Balmford A., Bruner, A., Cooper, P., Costanza, R., Farber, S., Green , R.E., Jenkins, M., Jefferiss, P., Jessamy, V., Madden, J., Munro, K., Myers, N., Naeem, S., Paavola, J., Rayment, M., Rosendo, S., Roughgarden, J., Trumper, K., Turner, R.K. (2002). Economic reasons for conserving wild nature. *Science* 297, 950–953.

Chan, K., A. Guerry, P., Balvanera, S., Klain, T., Satterfield, X., Basurto, A., Bostrom, Chuenpagdee, R., Gould, R., Halpern, B.S., Hannahs, N., Levine, J., Norton, B., Ruckelshaus, M., Russell, R., Tam, J., Woodside, U. (2012). Where are cultural and social in ecosystem services? A framework for constructive Engagement. *BioScience* 62(8), 744–756.

Costanza, R. (2006). Nature: Ecosystems without commodifying them. *Nature* 443, 749.

Costanza, R., d'Arge, R., de Groot, R., Farber, S., Grasso, M., Hannon, B., Limburg, K., Naeem, S., O'Neill, R.V., Paruelo, J., Raskin, G.R., Sutton, P., van der Belt, M. (1997). The value of the world's ecosystem services and natural capital. *Nature* 387, 253–260.

Daily, G.C. (1997). *Nature's Services: Societal Dependence on Natural Ecosystems.* Washington, DC: Island Press.

Daily, G.C. and Ellison, K. (2002). *The New Economy of Nature. The Quest to Make Conservation Profitable.* Washington, DC: Island Press.

Dendoncker, N., Keune, H., Jacobs, S., Gómez-Baggethun, E. (2013). Inclusive Ecosystem Services Valuation. In Jacobs, S., Dendoncker, N., and Keune H. (eds.). *Ecosystem Services: Global Issues, Local Practices* (pp. 3–12). San Diego, CA, Waltham, MA: Elsevier.

Ehrlich, P R., Ehrlich, A.H. (1981). *Extinction: the Causes and Consequences of the Disappearance of Species.* New York: Random House.

Folke, C., Jansson, A., Larsson, J., Costanza, R., (1997). Ecosystem appropriation by cities. *Ambio* 26(3), 167–172.

Georgescu-Roegen, N. (1975). Energy and economic myths. *Southern Economic Journal* 41(3), 347–381.

Gómez-Baggethun, E., de Groot, R. (2010). Natural capital and ecosystem services: the ecological foundation of human society. In Hester, R.E., Harrison, R.M. (eds.), *Ecosystem services: Issues in Environmental Science and Technology* (pp. 118–145), Cambridge.

Gómez-Baggethun, E., Ruiz-Pérez, M. (2011). Economic valuation and the commodification of ecosystem services. *Progress in Physical Geography* 35, 613–628.

Gómez-Baggethun, E. and Martin-Lopez, B. (2015). Ecological Economics perspectives on ecosystem services valuation. In Martinez-Alier, J. & Muradian, R. (eds.), *Handbook of Ecological Economics* (pp. 260–282), Edward Elgar.

Gómez-Baggethun, E., Muradian, R. (2015). In markets we trust? Setting the boundaries of Market-Based Instruments in ecosystem services governance. *Ecological Economics* 117, 217–224.

Gómez-Baggethun, E., Naredo, J.M. (2015). In search of lost time: The rise and fall of limits to growth in international sustainability policy. *Sustainability Science* 10, 385–395.

Gómez-Baggethun, E., Barton, D., Berry, P, Dunford, R Harrison, P, (2016). Concepts and methods in ecosystem services valuation. In: Potschin, M., Haines-Young, R., Fish, R., Turner, R.K. (eds.), *Routledge Handbook of Ecosystem Services* (pp. 99–111). London and New York: Routledge.

Guo, Z., Zhang, L., Li, Y. (2010). Increased dependence of humans on ecosystem services and biodiversity. *PloS One*, 5(10), 1–8.

Heal, G.M., Barbier, E.E., Boyle, K.J., Covich, A.P., Gloss, S.P., Hershner, C.H., Hoehn, J.P., Pringle, C.M., Polasky, S., Segerson, K., Shrader-Frechette, K. (2005). *Valuing Ecosystems Services: Toward Better Environmental Decision-making.* Washington, D.C: National Research Council.

Kallis, G., Gómez-Baggethun, E., Zografos, K. (2013). To value or not to value. That is not the question. *Ecological Economics* 94(October), 97–105.

Kapp, K.W. (1978).*The Social Costs of Business Enterprise.* Nottingham: Spokesman.

Kareiva, P., Marvier, M., Lalasz, R. (2015). Conservation in the Anthropocene, *Breakthrough* August 3.

Krausmann, F., Gingrich, S., Eisenmenger, N., Erb, K.H., Haberl, H., Fischer-Kowalski, M., (2009). Growth in global materials use, GDP and population during the 20th century. *Ecological Economics* 68(10), 2696–2705.

MA, Millennium Ecosystem Assessment (2005). *Ecosystems and Human Well-being: Synthesis.* Washington, D.C: Island Press.

Martínez-Alier, J. (2002). *The Environmentalism of the Poor.* Cheltenham: Edward Elgar.

McCarthy, J. (2004). Privatizing conditions for production: Trade agreements as neoliberal environmental governance. *Geoforum* 35(3), 275–283.

McCauley, D.J. (2006). Selling out on nature. *Nature* 443, 27–28.

Milder, J.C., Scherr, S.J., Bracer, C. (2010). Trends and future potential of payment for ecosystem services to alleviate rural poverty in developing countries. *Ecology and Society* 15(2), 4.

Miller, J. R. (2005). Biodiversity conservation and the extinction of experience. *Trends in Ecology and Evolution,* 20, 430–434.

Muradian, R., Gómez-Baggethun, E. (2013). The institutional dimension of "market-based instruments" for governing ecosystem services. *Society & Natural Resources* 26(10), 1113–1121.

Nordhaus T, Shellenberger M, Mukuno J. (2011). Ecomodernism and the Anthropocene. *Nature.* 29 November.

Phelps, J., Jones, C.A., Pendergrass, J.A., and Gómez-Baggethun, E. (2015). Environmental liability: A missing use for ecosystem services valuation. *Proceedings of the National Academy of Sciences* 112(39): E5379.

Polanyi, K. (1957). *The Great Transformation: The Political and Economic Origins of Our Time.* Boston: Beacon Press. First published in 1944.

Pyle, R.M. (1978). The extinction of experience. *Horticulture* 56, 64–67.

Pyle, R.M. (1993). *The Thunder Tree: Lessons from an Urban Wildland.* Boston: Houghton-Mifflin.

Rode, J., Gómez-Baggethun, E., and Krause, T. (2015). Motivation crowding by economic incentives for biodiversity conservation: A review of the empirical evidence. *Ecological Economics* 117(September), 270–282.

Sandel, M.J. (2012). *What Money Can't Buy: The Moral Limits to Markets.* New York: Farrar, Strauss and Giroux.

Spash, C.L. (2009). The new environmental pragmatists, pluralism and sustainability. *Environmental Values* 18(3), 253–256.

Spash, C.L. (2013). The shallow or the deep ecological economics movement? *Ecological Economics,* 93 (September), 351–362.

Spash, C.L. and Aslaksen, I. (2015). Re-establishing an ecological discourse in the policy debate over how to value ecosystems and biodiversity. *Journal of Environmental Management,* 159 (August), 245–253.

TEEB (The Economics of Ecosystems and Biodiversity) (2010). *The Economics of Ecosystems and Biodiversity: Ecological and Economic Foundations.* London: Earthscan.

Vatn, A. (2015). Markets in environmental governance — from theory to practice. *Ecological Economics* 105, 97–105.

Westman, W. (1977). How much are nature's services worth? *Science* 197, 960–964.

Zografos, C., Rodríguez-Labajos, B., Aydin, C.İ., Cardoso, A., Matiku, P., Munguti, S., O'Connor, M., Ojo, G., Özkaynak, B., Slavov, T., Stoyanova, D., Živčič, L. (2014). Economic tools for evaluating liabilities in environmental justice struggles, the EJOLT experience. *EJOLT Report No. 16.*

TOPIC X

Future post-growth society

44

DEGROWTH AND DEMOCRACY

Daniel Hausknost

Introduction

Degrowth is a "political slogan with theoretical implications" (Latouche, 2009: 7) that has recently started to inspire an increasing number of social movements and academic debates in Europe and beyond. Degrowth signifies a radical critique of the growth paradigm, which is seen as holding modern societies captive. The rejection of growth as the blind driving force of modern society has several roots—ecological, cultural and political.

The ecological critique is rooted in the argument that infinite growth on a finite planet is physically impossible and that an absolute 'decoupling' of economic growth from resource use and environmental impact is an illusion (Meadows et al., 1972, Georgescu-Roegen, 1979, Jackson, 2009) [Chapter 11]. According to this view, modern civilisation has the alternative to face social ecological collapse or embark on a journey of politically steered degrowth. The latter has been defined as an "equitable and democratic transition to a smaller economy with less production and consumption" (Martínez-Alier et al., 2010: 1741; cf. Kallis, 2011, Victor, 2008, Jackson, 2009).

The cultural root is related to a radical critique of the development paradigm. This attacks the underlying anthropological assumption of a *homo oeconomicus* with its instrumental and utility-maximising rationality, that tends to commodify relations among humans and between humans and Nature (Martínez-Alier et al., 2010: 1743). Degrowth draws on earlier critiques of modern development as elaborated by Ivan Illich (1973) and Jacques Ellul (1980).

Finally, the political root comes from the idea that a structural growth imperative (as in capitalism) disables the potential of societies to become politically autonomous and free to determine their own fate (Castoriadis, 1975). This argument critiques the relations of domination among humans, and between humans and Nature, inherent in the capitalist accumulation regime (Brand, 2014) [see also Chapters 4, 15, 39 and 42]. It forms a critique of liberal democracy as an elitist instrument to manage the growth economy (Bonaiuti, 2012).

These different strands of reasoning have been articulated in recent years by academics and activists into what has been called a common degrowth paradigm, perspective, or movement (particularly in France). Central to this intellectual project is the common appeal to democracy as the *sine qua non* of any future degrowth society (Cheynet, 2008; Fournier, 2008; Asara et al., 2013). As Romano (2012: 582) observes, "[m]ost degrowth thinkers and advocates assume that degrowth and democracy are co-substantial and go hand in hand toward a shared destiny". Concrete proposals for democratic arrangements under degrowth conditions range from radically localist visions of autonomous democratic communities to reformist ideas of deliberative processes embedded in representative structures. The focus of most discussions rests on the emancipatory potential of democratic degrowth, while until now important questions about the functionality, stability and indeed legitimacy of post-growth democracies, as well as questions of internal and external power relations, have been side-lined. The ideological bias in the debate has left little room for a political or sociological analysis of the conditions necessary to achieve democracy under conditions of degrowth. This chapter aims to help start filling this gap.

Degrowth and democracy: some theoretical foundations

At the core of the debates that have occurred on degrowth and democracy are the interrelated concerns over questions of scale, technology and autonomy. These concepts are commonly related to the intellectual legacies of Ivan Illich, Jacques Ellul and Cornelius Castoriadis (Cattaneo et al., 2012). I will briefly note the main arguments of each in turn.

A central thesis in the work of Illich (1973, 1974) is the existence of an inverse relationship between scale and democracy. The larger a system, the more uneven the internal distribution of power, as a ruling class of 'experts' emerges, which knows best how to manage the complexities of the system. Complex systems rely on complex technologies and bureaucracies that require expert rule, which erodes democratic structures. Consequently, only small systems can be democratic. Truly participatory democracy, according to Illich, requires low-energy technologies, or what he called "convivial tools", i.e. unlike industrial tools, their use is flexible and decided by the user, and no other tools or energy-intensive and complexly organised processes are necessary for their production (Cataneo et al., 2012: 516). The term "conviviality" for Illich, is to designate the opposite of industrial productivity and refers to autonomous and creative intercourse among persons, and the intercourse of persons with their environment (Illich, 1973).

Jacques Ellul (1980) also focuses on the uncontrollable nature of modern technological society. He claims that technological change dictates the course of societal development, and disables democratic autonomy. Societies adapt their social arrangements and institutional configurations to the ever-changing requirements of technology, instead of subjecting technological change to their own ends.

The political philosophy of Castoriadis (1975) is associated with the quest for autonomy, understood as the 'self-institution' of society. Castoriadis (2010: 46) defines institutions as "the entire set of tools, language, skills, norms and values" of a society. Self-institution, then, means the capacity to collectively reflect upon and change institutions in a continuous double movement of instituting and being instituted. Autonomy does not refer to any extra-historical truth that is to be discovered and enacted, but to the self-empowerment to become aware of the underlying rules of society (which are always historically contingent) and to change them. Economic growth and development, according to Castoriadis, are institutions that are systematically excluded from public scrutiny and posited as non-negotiable preconditions of any social order. They dominate the "social imaginary" in a way that excludes the ability to effectively question them. Radical change in the social imaginary is needed—a type of change that can only be achieved, according to Castoriadis (2010: 3), in a revolutionary project of direct democracy in which "all citizens have an equal, effective possibility of participation in legislating, governing, and judging". However, Castoriadis did not develop any concrete contours or institutions for his direct democracy project.

The quest for sustainable and democratic degrowth is therefore understood as an emancipatory project that is predicated on three pillars that are shared by these authors: small organic scales, low or convivial technologies and democratic institutions that lead to the most comprehensive individual and collective autonomy. In sum, the project aims at an "escape from the economy" (Fournier, 2008), and the emancipation of democracy from economic determinism. The economy is to be "re-embedded"—to use the well-known term by Karl Polanyi (1944)—into society, which means it is to be turned into a means of achieving democratically defined ends rather than being an end in itself. As Fournier (2008: 533) points out:

> it is not enough to propose alternative economic models because the proposal of alternative economies does not in itself question the importance accorded to the economy; instead we need to start with value and politics, we need to oppose economic determinism or 'economism' by going back to the terrain of the political.

According to Serge Latouche (2003), a leading figure of the French *décroissance* movement, rejecting economism requires the "decolonisation of the imaginary". That is, the collective generation of new significations and practices that break up the reification of the economy as an autonomous sphere that controls the production of meaning and sense. However, this decolonisation, or "detoxification"—a recent problematic term used by Latouche (2015)—"is not fully possible if a degrowth society has not been already established" (Latouch, 2003: 119). Hence, we are faced with a chicken-and-egg quandary related to democratic degrowth: do we need a degrowth society in place in order to generate the alternative imaginary necessary for the exit of the growth paradigm? Obviously, there would have to be intermediary steps of decolonisation through the creation of niches from which local degrowth initiatives could gradually expand (Latouche, 2009). In the words of Fournier (2008: 541), the task is to "create as many spaces as possible where we would be defined in terms other than economic rationality".

Ulrich Brand (2014) sounds an important warning against adopting too idealist an understanding of a decolonisation of the imaginary as if it were a matter of consciousness alone. Drawing on the works of Antonio Gramsci [Chapter 17], he contends that what is understood as the colonisation of the imaginary by the economy is in fact the hegemony of particular capitalistic power relations that inscribe themselves into the common sense by establishing a material and ideological consensus about the existence of a reified, externalised economic sphere. Challenging that hegemony will inevitably mean challenging the existing power relations established by capitalist accumulation. Brand's sympathetic words of caution imply that creating alternative niches for decolonised imaginaries might prove insufficient to break the cycles of accumulation and commodification. Capitalism has shown a considerable capability to absorb and commodify even the most radical subcultural currents and turn them into niche markets.

Dimensions of a degrowth democracy debate

A key open question is: "What should a realistic and workable degrowth democracy look like?" As Asara et al. (2013) point out, different attributes have been attached to democracy in relation to degrowth, such as direct, inclusive, participatory, deliberative, real or representative. To this, we have to add the frequent appeals to the concepts of economic and ecological democracy. There are few concrete proposals and a range of more general suggestions for concrete institutional arrangements. The concrete proposals are usually the more radical and utopian ones, whereas the vaguer suggestions tend to concern themselves with the reform of existing institutions, or with the politicisation of civil society. In what follows, a few exemplary and influential proposals are discussed.

At one end of the spectrum, there are radically localist visions of direct democratic and self-sufficient communities. Much discussed examples are the proposal for an "Inclusive Democracy" by Takis Fotopoulos (2005, 2010) and voluntary simplicity termed "The Simpler Way" by Ted Trainer (2012, 1985). I will consider each in turn before discussing the alternative viewpoint from advocates of representative democracy.

Inclusive democracy

Fotopoulos' project of inclusive democracy refers to the integrated realisation of four forms of democracy: political, economic, social and ecological. The project is predicated on the equal distribution of all forms of power, particularly political and economic (Fotopoulos, 2005: 3). The polity is constituted as a confederation of communities ('*demoi*') that are run on the basis of direct political democracy. One such community may encompass the size of a town and surrounding villages. Political democracy means that "all political decisions (including those relating to the formation and execution of laws) are taken by the citizen body collectively and without representation" (Fotopoulos, 2005: 202). Furthermore, no structures embodying unequal power relations must be set up.

> This means, for instance, that where delegation of authority takes place to segments of the citizen body, in order to carry out specific duties (e.g., to serve as members of popular courts, or of regional and confederal councils, etc.), the delegation is assigned, on principle, by lot, on a rotation basis, and it is always recallable by the citizen body.
>
> *(Fotopoulos, 2005: 202)*

According to Fotopulos (2005: 218), economic democracy implies two things:

1   "[A]ll 'macro' economic decisions, namely, decisions concerning the running of the economy as a whole (overall level of production, consumption and investment, amounts of work and leisure implied, technologies to be used, etc.) are taken by the citizen body collectively and without representation."
2   The means of production and distribution are collectively owned and directly controlled by the demos.

In summary, economic democracy presupposes "a stateless, moneyless and marketless economy that precludes private accumulation of wealth and the institutionalisation of privileges for some sections of society" (Fotopoulos, 2005: 223). The core operative unit is the "demotic enterprise", some kind of collectively owned enterprise controlled by workplace assemblies. The allocation of resources is organised at the level of the confederation of *demoi* through mechanisms that combine elements of democratic planning (between workplace assemblies, demotic assemblies and a confederal assembly) and an artificial market based on the exchange of vouchers for non-basic goods. What constitutes basic and non-basic needs (and thus goods) is determined democratically by the citizens [on needs, see Chapter 24].

This leaves the social and ecological dimensions. The social dimension of democracy is the least elaborated in Fotopoulos' framework. It refers to the levelling out of hierarchical conditions in the household, workplace and educational realms. Ecological democracy aims at a society that is "re-integrated with Nature" (Fotopoulos, 2010: 3). However, there is no specification of ecological provisions or institutions. Instead he assumes that inclusive democracy is inherently ecologically sustainable due to its local, participatory and decentralised characteristics. Fotopoulos (2010: 3) believes that "every single component of an Inclusive Democracy leads to an ecological democracy".

A simpler way of life: voluntary simplicity and sufficiency

Trainer (2012) argues for a simpler way of life that has many similarities to the proposal for inclusive democracy. However, there are distinct elements. The proposal is predicated on the assumption that the collapse of the dominant social economic system is imminent, due to resource scarcity. Simplicity is therefore a proposal for a post-collapse world, which conveniently relieves the author from discussing the question of how to make the transition from liberal democracy to his model world.

Trainer (2012: 596) constructs certain features of his model as logical necessities in a post-collapse, scarcity stricken society. For example, representative democracy will have to be abandoned, as large-scale, centralised government structures will have insufficient resources for their operation. Instead, there will be an:

> intense dependence on the locality, on its ecosystems, soils, water catchments, infrastructures, and on its social systems and processes, morale and 'social capital'. [...]
>
> the premium will be on reaching consensus on what is in fact the best arrangement for the town,

which is in contradiction to

> the present adversarial, conflict and power ridden, and patriarchal conception of democracy.

The Simpler Way will therefore be a radically participatory democracy that requires and rewards cooperation and care. Due to the small scales and simple structures of communities, much of the work of government would take place informally "in the everyday conversations people engage in within workplaces, kitchens and cafes", and consequently "[v]oting would be a minor element and town meetings would often only confirm policies now recognised by all to be desirable" (Trainer, 2012: 596).

Constitutive of both proposals is an underlying assumption or trust that there is a necessary link between small scales, democracy and ecology. Both proposals also rely heavily on the assumption that the new political rationality and value system will be naturally shared by all citizens. Thus, "if a vote is split, it probably means it is not yet clear to all which option is technically best for the town" (Trainer, 2012: 596). Trainer accordingly admits that the Simpler Way will only work if very different attitudes and values come to be held from those of today (Trainer, 2012: 594). Deviations from shared values (e.g., frugality, cooperation, solidarity) are to be addressed by means of *paideia*, which means education in citizenship (Fotopoulos, 2005: 244; Deriu, 2012). Once again this reveals a trust that people will, once they start thinking about life in the proper way, come to see that the new values and institutions on offer are the only rational and desirable ones.

The representative and deliberative democratic approach

The other end of the spectrum of democratic degrowth proposals is characterised by an emphasis on the role of civil society and the public sphere within the representative democratic model. Representative democracy is argued for on two grounds:

1   Whilst direct democracy is appropriate at the local level, "it cannot be organised beyond small groups of 50 people, thus excluding the majority of citizens" (Fournier, 2008: 539; Cheynet, 2007).
2   If degrowth is to be transformed into a mass movement, there is a need to engage with a broader public, which involves entering parliamentary politics (Fournier, 2008; Ariès, 2007).

However, once the continuation of the institutional framework of growth societies (i.e., representative democracy) is accepted, the focus of attention must necessarily shift from institutional breaks to the utilisation and enhancement of existing institutions. Latouche, for example, bases his degrowth transition proposal on a "quasi-electoral programme" that can be realised within a representative democratic framework enhanced with elements of localisation and participatory democracy (Asara et al., 2013: 222). The programme includes measures like massive cuts in intermediate consumption (e.g., transport, energy, packaging), eco-taxes, the phase-out of pesticides and the reduction of working hours (Latouche, 2009: 68 ff.).

A "democratisation within existing democracy" is also the strategy favoured by Konrad Ott (2012: 577). He proposes a Habermasian model of deliberative democracy, with a strong role for civil society and "intermediate zones" between the political system (government, parliament, administration, parties) and civil society "in which NGOs, boards of scientific policy counselling, academia, concerned scientists, freelancers, pressure groups and other agents propose ideas on policy making" (2012: 578). The aim is deliberation (i.e. making use of communicative reason) about political proposals in a public sphere that is shared by civil society and the agents of the intermediary zone, with the result that such ideas that achieve some level of agreement start to infiltrate the political core and become enacted. Beyond this Habermasian ideal of democracy, Ott envisages institutional innovations in both the political core and the intermediate zones. At the core, he imagines the introduction of referenda on specific matters, while in the intermediary zones he thinks about the direct involvement of citizens through deliberative instruments like citizen juries. Ott makes clear that his proposal of beefed-up deliberative democracy would only work for a moderate degrowth perspective that is oriented at the concept of strong sustainability and a strong reduction of material throughput, but that is not *per se* anti-capitalist, localist or anti-market. However, he leaves unanswered the question of why his model should be in any way particularly favourable to the perspective of degrowth. Indeed, Ott (2012: 576) argues that: "theories of democracies must conceptually be neutral against specific political ideas and movements". Logically then, his proposed model may not lead to a degrowth trajectory.

The moderate proposals all have in common a certain emphasis on civic engagement and deliberation. They rely on the activation of citizenship ideals within existing (or mildly reformed) institutions rather than on the creation of new democratic models. According to Fournier (2008: 536), for example, the aim of the movement is to reclaim citizenship by replacing the consumer through the citizen, while citizenship is understood as collective or individual political practice within existing institutions. This focus on citizenship *as* democracy leaves two questions open, which Fournier (ibid.: 539) readily admits:

The first one concerns the mechanisms through which we are called upon as citizens (how do we get the call?), the second concerns our willingness to answer that call, in other words why should we want to be a citizen?

There is a striking void in the degrowth literature precisely relating to this gap between, on the one hand, radical and utopian proposals, that are detached from existing political reality, and, on the other hand, the activist appeal to the emancipatory ideal of the citizen, as being independent of the institutions in which citizenship is enacted and lived.

Several research questions then arise. Is there a middle ground to be discovered, where existing democracies are rebuilt and modified in a way that breaks their structural tie to the growth paradigm and opens up new trajectories of development beyond growth? Are transformative democratic institutions conceivable whose purpose is to enable a reflexive and wilful transition to a sustainable type of society that is not predicated on material growth? This middle ground, between the status quo and utopia, deserves more attention from both activists and scholars.

Future directions

So far, the debates on democratic degrowth have produced a variety of interesting positions, ideas and proposals. Most of them are characterised by an underlying assumption about an intrinsic complicity between degrowth and democracy. For example, the Castoradian notion of a 'decolonisation of the imaginary' suggests that there is something real, pure and authentic to be discovered beneath the layers of externally imposed imaginations. The growth paradigm is constructed as a kind of foreign rule (colonisation) of which we need to rid ourselves in order to be authentically 'us'. While this articulation of degrowth and democracy as a necessary condition of emancipation is not without appeal, it risks obstructing a more comprehensive and sober analysis of the conditions and possibility for democracy to operate after the age of economic growth. Such an analysis must include, but decisively go beyond, defining emancipatory ideals like autonomy or conviviality. Without including the sociological and political economic dimensions of democracy in the analysis, any resulting model of post-growth democracy is in danger of turning into a Potemkin village: a façade that does not stand the test of reality.

Two hitherto neglected areas of research require particular attention. The first concerns the relationship between stability and legitimacy in democratic regimes. This question requires moving beyond a purely normative understanding (in terms of moral justification) of legitimacy and including sociological explanations of regime stability. In particular, the stabilising role in modern democracies played by economic growth and an autonomous economic sphere need to be analysed without prejudice. The crucial questions arising here are: "What would happen to modern democracies if growth were taken away from the equation and the economy were re-embedded into the political sphere? If modern (i.e. parliamentary, large-scale) democracy turned out to be impossible under such conditions: what would that mean for the prospects of a new democratic order to emerge and to remain stable?" Only if we fully understand the stabilising functions of the growth paradigm can we identify the conditions of possibility of a stable post-growth democracy (Hausknost, 2012, forthcoming).

Marco Deriu (2012) is among the few within the degrowth camp who recognise the deep and structural connection in Western history between economic growth and political democracy. He acknowledges that the political emancipation Western mass democracy brought about was premised on the exploitation of fossil energy for a growth-driven industrialism that promised collective upward mobility (Deriu, 2012: 554). Can this promise credibly be replaced by a promise of conviviality? Will it suffice to switch from a socioeconomic (upward mobility) to a moral (conviviality) register in defining the societal promise? Are voluntary simplicity and frugality appropriate values to sway the masses for a new model of civilisation? What can we learn from the fact that emancipation has hitherto entailed a strong material component and that precisely this component turns out to be unsustainable? Will people prefer the emancipation from materialism (e.g. sustainable degrowth) or (unsustainable) material prosperity *at the expense* of emancipation? Put differently, what if people rather chose to emancipate themselves from the modern notion of emancipation (Blühdorn, 2011), in order to save the promise of upward mobility and consumption at all costs?

This leads directly to the second area of research in need of attention: power relations and conceptions of rule in degrowth democracy [Chapter 14]. The radical conceptions of degrowth democracy discussed here (Fotopoulos and Trainer) are both based on essentialist notions of power, while the deliberative and civil society–oriented conceptions (Ott, Fournier) eschew the problem of power by relying on some vague 'trickling-up' of the popular will into the core of the political system. The essentialist notions of power presume a logical co-extension of the democratic will with the substantive goals of degrowth as laid down by the authors. That way a stateless (Fotopoulos, 2005: 223) democracy can be envisioned, which is not regarded as a form of rule but as pure autonomy. Autonomy here can easily function as an empty signifier to which a particular set of meanings is attributed as a universal truth (which could then be referred to as the decolonised imaginary, for example). Democratic discord, according to these models, would in fact only arise about practical issues of the management and administration of those particular societies, as all the core values are assumed to be consensual. How would these democratic models deal with antagonism about the very meaning of autonomy? What is to be done with people or groups who do not share or who even undermine the very concept of degrowth? Liberal democracies have an easy answer to the question of defection: whoever does not share in growth and competition drops out and impoverishes (or survives in a social cultural niche like an eco-village). What do degrowth democracies do with people who do not share in degrowth and cooperation? Would there be competitive, capitalistic niches for dissenters? Alternatively, as Brand (2015: 19) problematises the situation: How can we be sure that the principle of 'less is more' does not turn out to be repressive?

Lastly, what is the conception of foreign relations and external power inherent to these models? How would the decentralised low-tech communities of a degrowth confederation react to the covetousness of a neighbouring region or country, which rejects the degrowth perspective and for which the voluntary simplicity of degrowth is nothing but a power vacuum to be filled (Tainter, 1988: 202)? This is not just a matter of employing a more 'realist' notion of power, but also one of a more realist notion of technological development. The idea that all regional powers worldwide would voluntarily restrict themselves to the development and application of only convivial technologies is rather implausible. Instead, the more reasonable assumption is that technologies of domination, warfare and mass production will be available and employed in the future, at least by some. This alone creates power imbalances that need to be addressed by any serious conceptualisation of degrowth democracy.

Concluding remarks

The vision of sustainable degrowth is commonly associated with a hope to renew and radicalise democracy. Real democracy, so the argument goes, will only be possible in a society that is not driven by the blind force of infinite economic growth. Proposals for degrowth democracies range from radically localist direct democratic communities to the implementation of degrowth policies within existing parliamentary structures. Most debates have a normative bias and focus on the institutional implementation of a core set of values including autonomy, conviviality and frugality. Degrowth and democracy are often presented as co-extensive and as a logical pairing in what is a major emancipatory project. However, the historical relationship of democracy with industrialism, and economic growth, is rather substantial, and the elimination of growth from the equation poses conceptual problems that have been insufficiently examined by scholars of democratic degrowth. The mechanisms (other than shared values, for which there are no guarantees) that would stabilise degrowth democracy remain unclear as does how political power is to be wielded in a non-repressive way.

The quest for workable models of democracy after the age of growth has only just begun and has so far yielded some exciting thought experiments and debates. However, upon closer inspection, the conceptual coupling of degrowth and democracy might be more precarious and unstable than the functional coupling of growth and democracy in the liberal democratic model. Solving the conundrum of how to effectively dissociate democracy from growth will therefore constitute a key challenge for political theory and practice in the twenty-first century.

Key further readings cited

Asara, V., Profumi, E., Kallis G. (2013). Degrowth, democracy and autonomy. *Environmental Values* 22(2), 217–239.

Cattaneo, C., D'Alisa, G., Kallis, G., Zografos, C. (2012). Introduction: Degrowth futures and democracy. *Futures* 44(6), 515–523.

Fotopoulos, T. (2010). Direct democracy and de-growth. *The International Journal of Inclusive Democracy* 6 (4) (accessible online at http://www.inclusivedemocracy.org/journal/vol6/vol6_no4_takis_direct_democracy_degrowth.htm). Accessed 20 December 2016.

Ott, K. (2012). Variants of de-growth and deliberative democracy: A Habermasian proposal. *Futures* 44(6), 571–581.

Trainer, T. (2012). De-growth: Do you realise what it means? *Futures* 44 (6), 590–599.

Other literature cited

Ariès, P. (2007). Adresse aux objecteurs de croissance qui veulent faire de la politique. *Les Cahiers de'l IEEDSS*, 1, 4–7.

Blühdorn, I. (2011). The sustainability of democracy. *Eurozine.* (accessed at http://www.eurozine.com/articles/2011-07-11-bluhdorn-en.html). Accessed 20 December 2016.

Bonaiuti, M. (2012). Growth and democracy; Trade-offs and paradoxes. *Futures* 44(6), 524–534.

Brand, U. (2014). Kapitalistisches Wachstum und soziale Herrschaft. Motive, Argumente und Schwächen aktueller Wachstumskritik. *PROKLA* 44 (2), 289–306.

Brand, U. (2015). Degrowth und Post-Extraktivismus: Zwei Seiten einer Medaille? Working Paper 5/2015 der DFG Kollegforscherinnengruppe Postwachstumsgesellschaften.

Castoriadis, C. (1975). *L'institution imaginaire de la societé.* Paris: Édition du Seuil.

Castoriadis, C. (2010). *A Society Adrift: Interviews and Debates, 1974–1997.* New York: Fordham University Press.

Cheynet, V. (2007). Pour une Décroissance civilise. *Les Cahiers de'l IEEDSS* 1, 8–11.

Cheynet, V. (2008). *Le choc de la décroissance.* Paris: Seuil.

Deriu, M. (2012). Democracies with a future: Degrowth and the democratic tradition. *Futures* 44(6), 553–561.

Ellul, J. (1980). *The Technological System.* New York: Continuum.

Fotopoulos, T. (2005). The multidimensional crisis and inclusive democracy. *The International Journal of Inclusive Democracy.* Special Issue (accessible online at http://www.inclusivedemocracy.org/journal/ss/ss.htm). Accessed 20 December 2016.

Fournier, V. (2008). Escaping from the economy: the politics of degrowth. *International Journal of Sociology and Social Policy* 28 (11-12), 528–545.

Georgescu-Roegen, N. (1979). *Demain la décroissance: entropie-écologie-economie*. Lausanne: P.M. Favre.

Hausknost, D. (2012): 'The "Epistemic Legitimacy" of Liberal Democracy as a Structural Constraint for Radical Politics', in: J. Gijsenberg, T. Houwen, S. Hollander, W. de Jong (eds.), *Creative Crises of Democracy*. Brussels: Peter Lang.

Hausknost, D. (forthcoming). *The Limits to Change: Liberal Democracy, Agency, and the Environment*. London: Routledge.

Illich, I. (1973). *Tools for Conviviality*. New York: Harper & Row.

Illich, I. (1974). *Energy and Equity*. New York: Harper & Row.

Jackson, T. (2009). *Prosperity Without Growth*. London: Earthscan.

Kallis, G. (2011). In defence of degrowth. *Ecological Economics* 70, 873–880.

Latouche, S. (2003). *Décoloniser l'imaginaire: La Pensée creative contre l'économie de l'absurde*. Lyon: Parangon.

Latouche, S. (2009). *Farewell to Growth*. Cambridge: Polity Press.

Latouche, S. (2015). Imaginary, decolonization of. In G. D'Alisa, F. Demaria, G. Kallis (eds.), *Degrowth: A Vocabulary for a New Era*. London and New York: Routledge.

Martínez-Alier, J., Pascual, U., Vivien, F.-D., Zaccai, E. (2010). Sustainable de-growth: Mapping the context, criticisms and future prospects of an emergent paradigm. *Ecological Economics* 69(9), 1741–1747.

Meadows, D.H., Meadows, D.L., Randers, J., Behrens III., W.W. (1972). *The Limits to Growth*. New York: Universe Books.

Polanyi, K. (1944). *The Great Transformation*. New York: Farrar and Reinhart.

Romano, O. (2012). How to rebuild democracy, re-thinking degrowth. *Futures* 44, 582–589.

Tainter, J. (1988). *The Collapse of Complex Societies*. Cambridge: Cambridge University Press.

Trainer, T. (1985). *Abandon Affluence*. Zed Press, London.

Victor, P. (2008). *Managing Without Growth. Slower by Design, Not Disaster*. Cheltenham: Edward Elgar.

45

THE STEADY STATE ECONOMY

Brian Czech

Introduction

One of the primary reasons for the development of ecological economics was the gradual realisation during the latter half of the twentieth century that economic growth was starting to cause more problems than it solved. Arguments about limits to economic growth and the relationship between economic growth and environmental protection proliferated in the 1960s and especially the 1970s. Many of the arguments stemmed from the publication of *The Limits to Growth* (Meadows et al., 1972). Some readers refused to acknowledge limits to growth; others asked: What are the alternatives to growth? Fortunately the answer to that question, at least, is quite straightforward, because there are only two basic alternatives: degrowth [Chapter 44] and the steady state economy. The focus here is the latter.

Defining the topic

To understand what a steady state economy is, entails, and connotes, requires understanding what economic growth is, i.e., increasing production and consumption of goods and services in the aggregate (Czech and Daly, 2004). Economic growth, normally measured as Gross Domestic Product (GDP), entails increasing population multiplied by per capita consumption, higher throughput of materials and energy, and a growing ecological footprint. Economic growth is distinguished from 'economic development', which, at least in ecological economics, refers to qualitative change independent of quantitative growth (Daly and Farley, 2010). For example, economic development may refer to the attainment of a more equitable distribution of wealth, or a sectoral readjustment reflecting the evolution of consumer preferences or newer technology. (However, readers should also be aware that, outside of ecological economics, growth and development are often conflated. In neoclassical economics, 'development' often implies increasing GDP/capita.)

Degrowth, then, is most readily defined as decreasing production and consumption in the aggregate as indicated by decreasing GDP. Decreasing population and/or per capita consumption is required. Degrowth tends to carry many social and political connotations in addition to a smaller economy, and is especially discussed as such in Europe [Chapter 44]. As with economic growth, degrowth, in the sense of a shrinking economy, is ultimately unsustainable. While it occurs, however, degrowth may occur within or without the context of economic development.

The steady state economy is the sustainable alternative to unsustainable growth and degrowth. It is an economy with stabilised production and consumption of goods and services in the aggregate. (Stabilised means mildly fluctuating around a sustainable level.) A steady state economy has stabilised population and/or per capita consumption. Throughput and the ecological footprint are gradually stabilised—in the aggregate and also per capita—as the limits to productive efficiency are reached (Czech, 2008). Therefore, and all else being equal, a steady state economy is indicated by stabilised GDP (Czech and Daly, 2004). The 'all else being equal', described in detail by Czech (2013), includes level of technology, inflation, the propensity to use money relative to other means of exchange, and environmental conditions.

Theoretically and temporarily, a steady state economy may have a growing population with declining per capita consumption, or vice versa, but neither of these scenarios is sustainable in the long run. Therefore steady state economy connotes constant populations of people (and, therefore, stocks of labour) and constant stocks of capital. In a stable environment and a given technological framework, these constant stocks will yield constant flows of goods and services.

Technological progress may yield a more efficient 'digestion' of throughput, resulting in the production of more, or more highly valued, goods and services. However, as emphasised in biophysical assessments of economic activity [e.g., Chapters 9 and 11], there are limits to productive efficiency imposed by the Laws of Thermodynamics, and therefore limits to the amount and value of goods and services that may be produced in a given ecosystem. In other words, technological progress does not allow for perpetual growth, and there is a maximum size at which a steady state economy may operate (Czech, 2008). Conflicts with ecological integrity and environmental protection occur long before a steady state economy is maximised (Czech, 2000a).

Some attention to the linguistics of steady state economy is in order. In neoclassical economics, the hyphenated phrase "steady-state economy" is used to refer to an economy with steady ratios of variables, with an emphasis on the capital:labour ratio. Therefore, in neoclassical economics, a steady state economy may be growing, shrinking, or steady, and only in the latter case does it also constitute the steady state economy of ecological economics. In ecological economics, the unhyphenated phrase "steady state economy" is used to describe an economy of stable size because "State" (as in political State) is an adjective of "economy" (as in a State's economy), and "steady" is an adjective of this State economy. In other words, "steady state economy" typically refers to a national State economy of stable size, although it may also refer to an economy of a city, province, or other political unit. (It may also refer to a regional economy or the global economy, and in such cases political units are aggregated.) In neoclassical economics, the conjoined "steady-state" is a heuristic tool to imply stable ratios of factors and, linguistically, is an adjective of "economy".

Past research and main issues

The steady state economy was the focus of one of the founders of ecological economics, Herman Daly (e.g., Daly, 1974). Daly's case for a steady state economy may be viewed as the foundation of ecological macroeconomics, if not ecological economics at large. While ecological microeconomics, such as estimating the value of natural capital and ecosystem services [Chapter 43], comprises much of the ecological economics literature, social ecological economists argue that such exercises are not fundamentally distinct from conventional or neoclassical economics (Spash, 2013). Recognising limits to growth, based on Laws of Thermodynamics [Chapter 9] and principles of ecology [Chapter 12], is what clearly distinguishes ecological from neoclassical economics (Czech, 2013).

Daly did not invent the basic idea of a steady state economy. Classical economists of the early nineteenth century such as Thomas Malthus and David Ricardo focused on limits to growth, and John Stuart Mill indicated a preference for the "stationary state". However, most references by classical economists to the stationary state were brief, general and pointed towards a relatively distant future (Heilbroner, 1992).

For Daly, however, writing primarily in the late twentieth century, sustainability had become the key economic issue of the times (e.g. Daly, 1973, 1974, 1997). He called for a movement towards steady state economies, especially in nations with a relatively high standard of living. In addition to his familiarity with the writings of John Stuart Mill, Daly was a student of Nicholas Geoergescu-Roegen, who wrote *The Entropy Law and the Economic Process* (1971). Geoergescu-Roegen had gone to great lengths to explain the relevance of the Second Law of Thermodynamics—the Entropy Law—to economic growth. He also displayed a very long-term philosophy, describing for example how the universe was heading towards thermodynamic dissipation, while Daly applied the Laws of Thermodynamics to a politically and policy-relevant timeframe.

In effect, the first two Laws of Thermodynamics are both necessary and sufficient for establishing limits to growth, short-term and long-term. The First Law—the Law of Conservation of Energy—can be stated in economic terms as 'you can't make something from nothing'. Production of goods or services requires energy and materials, and since neither of these may be created (all energy and matter already exists; it may only be transformed), there is a fundamental limit to growth. The Second Law—the Entropy Law—can be stated as 'there's no such thing as 100% efficiency in the transformation process'. This limiting of efficiency to something less than 100 per cent, applied macroeconomically, means there is a limit to the decoupling of GDP from material and energy throughput.

The steady state economy was, from the beginning of Daly's scholarship, as much a normative as a technical economic pursuit. In the tradition of the classical economists, Daly's economics were steeped in moral philosophy. Given limits to growth, which were becoming evident at a planetary scale, was it fair for the wealthiest nations to pursue even higher per capita consumption and greater GDP while others struggled in widespread poverty? This line of questioning could be applied within nations as well, at all levels of society. Daly teamed at times with theologians to explore the issues of equity resulting from limits to growth (e.g. Daly and Cobb, 1989).

At the same time, Daly and many of the figures influencing the early development of ecological economics (such as Georgescu-Roegen, Kenneth Boulding and Richard Norgaard) were economists *per se*. Therefore the efficiency with which resources were allocated among producers was also a key concern for ecological economics. Daly described how the primary issues for ecological economics, then, were scale, distribution, and allocation, and in that order of concern.

- Scale referred to the size of the economy relative to its containing, sustaining ecosystem. The goal pertaining to scale was, at the least, sustainability, and ideally optimality.
- The goal pertaining to the distribution of wealth was fairness or equity.
- The goal pertaining to allocation was, as in conventional economics, efficiency.

Combining the three provides a clear focus for the basic goal of applied ecological economics, i.e. the steady state economy with an equitable distribution of wealth and efficient allocation of resources.

Current assessment of major issues

Assessing sustainable scale

Always at the fore in ecological macroeconomics is the issue of limits to growth. Meadows et al. (1972) set the stage for comprehensive scholarship pertaining to limits, albeit with an emphasis on the biophysical. They also set the precedent of combining actual-world, actual-time data with computerised modelling of future prospects. The most likely scenarios indicated by their modelling included global limits to growth being reached in the twenty-first century. Their efforts have been analysed and re-analysed numerous times, most notably by Graham Turner (2008) and also by Dennis Meadows in *Limits to Growth: The 30-Year Update* (Meadows et al., 2004). These analyses have largely corroborated projections from the initial analysis.

Recent related scholarship has addressed such concepts and issues as the ecological footprint, Peak-Oil [Chapter 41] and planetary boundaries. These efforts continue to come primarily from the biological and physical sciences, with scientists becoming increasingly concerned with the lack of acknowledgement in mainstream economics of limits to growth, and concerned as well with the preponderance of microeconomic methods and findings in the ecological economics literature.

The ecological footprint

The ecological footprint is a direct approach to assessing sustainable scale. It represents the ratio of humans' demand on Nature to the biophysical capacity of Nature to support humans. The leading organisation for developing such calculations is the Global Footprint Network, which describes the ecological footprint as "the productive area required to provide the renewable resources humanity is using and to absorb its waste" (Global Footprint Network, 2015). Their calculations indicate a condition of 'overshoot' since the 1970s, meaning that human economic activity has required more resources than can be renewed. This chronic condition of overshoot has been possible only because humans have been liquidating stocks of natural capital and funds of ecosystem services. Ecological footprint accounting is highly complex and entails numerous assumptions [see Chapter 48]; while debated (e.g., Fiala, 2008; Giampietro and Saltelli, 2014; van den Bergh and Grazi, 2014, 2015), it remains for many an attractive approach to assessing the sustainability of the economy. It has also been very effective for purposes of educating the public and policy makers about limits to growth, ecological macroeconomics and sustainable scale, with numerous reports issued on countries as well as those summarising the global ecological footprint.

Peak-Oil

Peak-Oil refers to the geological and economic availability of petroleum, the energy source for a large proportion of global economic activity [Chapter 41] (see also Gates et al., 2014). Petroleum is the primary fossil fuel in general and especially for transportation. The phrase Peak-Oil has also come to connote fossil fuels in general, including, for example, the study of Peak Coal. The general concept has been applied to other types of natural resources, and at least one book represented an attempt to summarise "Peak Everything" (Heinberg, 2010). The concept of Peak-Oil is somewhat self-explanatory. It refers to maximum level of per capita oil production, and usually on a global scale. The study of Peak-Oil can be traced back to Marion King Hubbert, who in 1956 predicted the peak of American oil production to occur in the early 1970s. In fact, 1970 was the year per capita American crude oil production started falling. Kenneth Deffeyes built upon Hubbert's model and extrapolated it to the world, reporting his findings in *Hubbert's Peak*. He predicted the peak in world oil production to occur between 2004 and 2008. In 2007 oil prices were pushing $100/barrel for the first time in history. Since then, extremely complicated technical and political developments have challenged scholars in this field and the simplistic expectations about oil prices [Chapter 41], but the phrase Peak-Oil and the irrefutable logic behind it have served to raise awareness of limits to growth.

Planetary boundaries

Another aspect of oil production is the effects of its subsequent combustion on Earth's climate. Serious attempts to curb the rate and extent of human-induced climate change [Chapter 42] hinge largely on limiting the combustion of fossil fuels in general. Fossil fuel combustion has been the primary source of the rapid increase (since the Industrial Revolution) in atmospheric carbon dioxide, the primary greenhouse gas behind global warming (IPCC, 2000). How much climate change can the human economy withstand? Theoretically, global warming and other effects of climate change could become the limiting factor for GDP. Climate change and other ubiquitous aspects of environmental deterioration motivated scholars to assess the planetary boundaries of economic activity (Rockström et al., 2009).

The planetary boundaries described by Rockström et al. (2009) pertained to climate change, biodiversity loss, biogeochemical processes, ocean acidification, land use, freshwater depletion, ozone depletion, atmospheric aerosol levels, and chemical pollution. Any of these environmental problems could constitute the limiting factor for economic growth, and each problem interacts with the others, setting up unpredictable feedback loops, thresholds, and tipping points. Although the methodology was controversial, and researcher judgement cannot be eliminated from such assessments, Rockström et al. (2009) concluded that climate change, biodiversity loss, and some aspects of biogeochemistry were especially problematic, worsening, and increasingly likely to cause catastrophic and irreversible damage to human development prospects. Czech (2000b, 2004) described the proliferation of human economic activity during the Industrial Revolution as a fundamental transformation marking the end of "ecological integrity" for conservation policy and management purposes pursuant to the National Wildlife Refuge System Improvement Act of 1997.

Policy issues

Ecological economics is looked to for policy solutions to the problems of unsustainable scale and uneconomic growth (i.e., growth beyond optimal scale), and there have been some original policy tools proposed in the ecological economics literature. However, the most important terrain in the policy arena, as it pertains to sustainable scale, is the myriad already existing policies designed to stimulate economic growth. These may be categorised as fiscal, monetary, and trade policies. Fiscal and trade policies generate the most attention in ecological economics. Not much is said in the literature about reforming particular monetary policies, such as money supplies and interest rates, presumably because the proper reforms for sustainable scale are too obvious, and also because the challenge is so daunting politically. Monetary authorities are expected to cut interest rates and increase money supplies to stimulate sluggish economies. However, if an economy has grown beyond maximum sustainable scale, monetary policy to stimulate economic growth does more societal harm than good. In this context, higher interest rates and tighter money supplies are appropriate. As of the second decade of the twenty-first century, though, ecological economics was not known widely enough in public and policy-making circles to precipitate a serious dialogue about monetary policy towards a steady state economy. Monetary authorities typically favour higher interest rates and restrictive money supplies only when inflation threatens.

Monetary policy has limited effects, too. For example, when an economy is operating at full capacity, lowering interest rates and flooding the economy with money will only result in inflation. Similarly, as economic capacity diminishes due to the liquidation of natural capital (i.e. as limits to growth are reached) the economy must become sluggish and will almost certainly be forced to contract in the wake of major and global supply shocks such as Peak-Oil. No amount of monetary tinkering can change this biophysical reality.

If a polity is determined to have economic growth, however, the monetary authority may resort to drastic measures and, more importantly, fiscal policy will also be geared towards growth. Taxes will be lessened with the hope that consumers will spend more. Budgets will be reallocated in a manner also designed to stimulate the economy. An early twenty-first-century example is the subsidising of corn farming to increase the production of ethanol, a hoped-for alternative to petroleum as a primary energy source for economic growth.

These traditional and expected responses of fiscal and monetary policy authorities are not consistent with ecological economics and a steady state economy. The ecologically economic approach would be to readjust fiscal and monetary levers downward. As yet, however, this type of policy reform is not politically feasible, which may explain to a large extent why the ecological economics literature lacks such policy recommendations. This also points to the primacy of identifying the appropriate policy 'goal', in contrast to particular policy tools. Until the steady state economy becomes a widespread policy goal within and among nations, policy reforms towards a steady state economy are extremely unlikely.

New policy prospects

Reforming existing policies is a necessary but probably insufficient condition for establishing a steady state economy. New policies will almost surely be required, including policies designed to help with stabilising population, per capita production, per capita consumption, throughput, and natural capital stocks. The most direct approach in all cases is legislative regulation, whereby the State imposes behavioural and commercial limits. Direct regulation has been made into something of a pariah in Western countries under neoliberalism and is often described as a threat to liberty by both neo- and classic liberals. However, it is a necessity for any economy and even the market system to operate. This does not diminish concerns over how States and regulators operate in practice.

In addition to direct regulation, Pigouvian taxes and subsidies may be designed to contribute to sustainable scale. What distinguishes Pigouvian policies (after Arthur C. Pigou, 1877–1959) from other taxes and subsidies is their focus on correcting for market failures. This makes them palatable to most economists and useful for social justice as well. Particular Pigouvian instruments may contribute substantially to sustainable scale, too. For example, if polluters are taxed the full social cost of the pollution, the rate of the pollution will decrease.

The most distinctive form of policy regulation with regard to sustainable scale is the cap, which in recent times has been made into a market mechanisms via cap-and-trade, or tradable emissions permits. In theory, cap-and-trade policies allow for microeconomic freedom more than direct regulations because polluting firms can trade permits within the limits established by the cap. Markets are established, permits are allocated among firms, and thenceforth some of the allocative advantages of relatively free markets are engaged. A cap-and-trade policy is regarded by some as an effective policy mechanism that can be applied to most stocks of natural capital and many pollutants. However, emissions trading has also proven problematic in practice and has been heavily criticised in relation to carbon markets (see Spash, 2010).

The relevance to scale is exhibited by the word 'cap'. When the use of a material or energy source that is integral to the economy is capped, the cap puts up a *de facto* sideboard to economic growth. The clearest example is with greenhouse gas emissions, especially from the combustion of fossil fuels. The global economy is primarily fossil-fuelled; capping greenhouse gas emissions in this context is tantamount to capping economic growth. The primary objective of policy makers in favour of capping, or attempting to cap, greenhouse gas emissions is not to stop economic growth, but rather (outside of political motives) to protect the atmosphere and prevent catastrophic levels of global warming. Yet the predictable economic dampening effects of a strict cap on greenhouse gas emissions may be the most important reason behind why some of the wealthiest nations have for a long time avoided participating in international agreements to lower greenhouse gas emissions. This experience demonstrates the primacy of macroeconomic policy goals in the policy arena.

Theoretically, starting from the perspective of ecological economics, one could prescribe a cap on greenhouse gas emissions explicitly for scale-limiting purposes. However, this would only be feasible if the international community agreed, consistent with the tenets and findings of ecological economics, that global economic growth was no longer an appropriate goal. A precautionary approach [Chapters 26 and 27] is called for, too, so that any benefit of the doubt would be applied to environmental protection and future generations. Applying a cap gradually— if there is time for gradualism to be effective—would prevent shocks to the economic system. Policies to cap throughput must also be flexible in design and allow for adjustment; their aim is to make self-evident limits to growth and optimum scale, while recognising that throughput issues are global in character and require initiatives at the international policy level.

Future directions

Research directions

The topics for steady-state research are potentially as numerous as the researchers available to pursue them. However, at least three lines of questioning stand out as warranting substantial attention.

First, how tight is the linkage between GDP and throughput? The trophic theory of money (Czech, 2013: 171–194) leads to the conclusion that the linkage is inevitable and inflexible, distorted only by inflation, technological progress, the propensity to use money as a means of exchange and environmental conditions. This linkage is not widely acknowledged, however, leading some to reject the use of GDP as an indicator of throughput and stabilised GDP as an indicator of a steady state economy. If GDP is not a solid indicator of throughput (or ecological footprint), what is the difference between neoclassical and ecological interpretations of GDP? After all, neoclassical economists have long advocated 'smart' growth, i.e. growth of GDP that is reconciled (somehow) with environmental protection and social justice.

Second, how can we ascertain not only maximum sustainable scale, but optimal scale within and among nations? In simple economic terms, optimal scale would be where the marginal utility of growth equals the marginal disutility thereof. However, what exactly are the components of utility and disutility, and how do we measure them? This line of questioning requires a synthesis of natural (biological and physical) and social sciences. Development of the Genuine Progress Indicator and research pertaining to happiness has helped lay the foundation, but much remains to be identified and reasonably quantified [see also Chapter 37 on sustainability indicators]. Compelling research on optimal scale would help people and polities to see the advantages of a steady state economy.

Third, what is the ecologically economic approach to interest rates? This line of questioning stems from a conundrum: High interest rates motivate landlords (private and public) to liquidate stocks of natural capital, while low interest rates stimulate investment including in natural capital liquidating ventures. Where is the sweet spot conducive to a steady state economy? Czech (2013) suggested that there is a natural interest rate balancing depreciation with solar income (and primary productivity), but extensive research on this topic is needed to resolve the interest rate conundrum.

Policy directions

In ecological economics, the goal of fair distribution is largely dependent on sustainable scale. As limits to growth are breached, history shows that conflict invariably ensues and the victors claim the natural resources, including the land itself (Klare, 2002). Peaceful and equitable coexistence requires a social contract in which citizens agree to live sustainably, as a society, and to share, within reason, natural resources and other wealth. In ecological economics, this social contract would be manifest in caps on income and wealth, minimum income, and the distribution of returns from the factors of production, especially natural capital.

Given a global economy exceeding its maximum sustainable scale, the only ethical and ecologically economic approach to alleviating poverty while moving closer to sustainable scale is the capping of income and wealth, with pre-existing excess used to alleviate poverty. Precisely at what level to cap income or wealth is a matter to be determined, ideally in a democratic manner (according to policy design theory), whereby the majority of citizens understand the need for caps on throughput and therefore caps on income, and support the goals of sustainability and social justice [see also Chapter 44 on democracy and degrowth]. Presumably a gradualist approach would entail formal but voluntary capping, followed if necessary by imposed capping. Data pertaining to the existing scale of the economy, a range of optimal scales, and the ecological footprints associated with different levels of income and wealth would be necessary for determining appropriate capping levels.

At the other end of the distributional policy spectrum is minimum income. A minimum income policy has logical and ethical foundations pertaining to scale and distribution. Logically, impoverished individuals are unlikely to prioritise environmental protection, which is crucial for establishing sustainable scale. For example, landless, unemployed peasants may resort to poaching timber from public lands. Poor people typically have been victims of circumstance rather than lazy, and the ethical response is to help them without jeopardising the environment and future generations.

Normally the policy reforms of ecological economics are envisioned as operating at national levels, and appropriately so. However, ultimately for global economic sustainability, the sum total of a nation's economic activity must result in a global steady state economy. Few would have a vision of such a global economy operating smoothly and with no international strife. This points to the need for 'steady statesmanship' in international diplomacy. A framework for steady statesmanship would presumably rest heavily on social metabolism [Chapter 11], ecological footprint accounting, input-output analysis [Chapter 36] and other measures that hold nations accountable for their proportionate use (and waste) of natural resources. Ecological economists will need to team with like-minded thinkers in the world of international diplomacy, e.g. in the United Nations where international conventions are discussed and formulated.

Concluding remarks

The steady state economy—stabilised production and consumption of goods and services in the aggregate—is the macroeconomic highlight of ecological economics.[1] It is the natural recommendation resulting from the ecological critique of growth. It is at once an academic concept and policy alternative. Pursuit of a steady state economy means movement towards a stabilised population and per capita consumption. Virtually all other economic goals—full employment, stable monetary conditions, fair terms of trade—may be reconciled with a steady state economy. Indeed the long run, the only truly sustainable economy is a steady state economy.

Note

1 Editor's Note: Some contention surrounds the extent to which steady state economic theory, especially that of Herman Daly, is actually compatible with ecological economics as an heterodox school. Pirgmaier (2017) argues it is internally flawed, relies upon neoclassical economic theory and so contradicts basic positions and directions in ecological economics. A broader engagement on such issues is necessary within the context of social ecological economic transformation to a future post-growth society.

Key further readings cited

Czech, B. (2013). *Supply Shock: Economic Growth at the Crossroads and the Steady State Solution*. Gabriola Island, British Columbia: New Society Publishers.

Czech, B. and Daly, H. (2004). The steady state economy: What it is, entails, and connotes. *Wildlife Society Bulletin* 32(2), 598–605.

Daly, H.E. (ed.) (1973). Toward a steady-state economy. San Francisco: W.H. Freeman.

Daly, H.E. (1974). The economics of the steady state. *American Economics Review* 64(2), 15–21.

Daly, H.E. and Farley, J. (2010). *Ecological Economics: Principles and Applications*. Second edition. Washington, DC: Island Press.

Other literature cited

Czech, B. (2000a). Draft policy on maintaining the ecological integrity of the National Wildlife Refuge System. *Federal Register* 66(10), 61356–61362.

Czech, B. (2000b). Economic growth as the limiting factor for wildlife conservation. *Wildlife Society Bulletin* 28(1), 4–14.

Czech, B. (2004). A chronological frame of reference for ecological integrity and natural conditions. *Natural Resources Journal* 44(4), 1113–1136.

Czech, B. (2008.) Prospects for reconciling the conflict between economic growth and biodiversity conservation with technological progress. *Conservation Biology* 22(6), 1389–1398.

Daly, H. and Cobb, J. (1989). *For the Common Good: Redirecting the Economy Towards Community, the Environment and Sustainable Development*. Boston: Beacon Press.

Daly, H. E. (1997). *Beyond Growth: The Economics of Sustainable Development*. Beacon Press, Boston, MA.

Deffeyes, K.S. (2001). *Hubbert's Peak: The Impending World Oil Shortage*. Princeton, NJ: Princeton University Press.

Fiala, N. (2008). Measuring sustainability: Why the ecological footprint is bad economics and bad environmental science. *Ecological Economics* 67(4): 519–525.

Gates, E., Trauger, D. and Czech, B. (eds.) (2014). *Peak Oil, Economic Growth, and Wildlife Conservation*. New York: Springer.

Georgescu-Roegen, N. (1971). The entropy law and the economic process. Cambridge, Massachusetts: Harvard University Press.

Giampietro, M. and Saltelli, A. (2014). Footprints to nowhere. *Ecological Indicators*. 46(November): 610–621.

Global Footprint Network. (2015). Footprint Basics: Overview. Online at http://www.footprintnetwork. org/en/index.php/GFN/page/footprint_basics_overview. Accessed 21 December 2016.

Heilbroner, R.L. (1992). *The Worldly Philosophers: The Lives, Times, and Ideas of the Great Economic Thinkers*. Sixth edition. New York: Simon and Schuster.

Heinberg, R. (2010). *Peak Everything: Waking Up to the Century of Declines*. Gabriola Island, British Columbia: New Society Publishers.

IPCC (Intergovernmental Panel on Climate Change) (2000). Special report on emissions scenarios: Working Group III of the IPCC. Geneva: IPCC.

Klare, M.T. (2002). *Resource Wars: The New Landscape of Global Conflict*. New York: Holt Paperbacks.

Meadows, D.H., Meadows, D.L., Randers, J. and Behrens, W.W. (1972). *The Limits to Growth: a Report to the Club of Rome*. New York: Universe.

Meadows, D.H., Randers, J. and Meadows, D.L. (2004). *Limits to Growth: The 30-Year Update*. White River Junction, Vermont: Chelsea Green.

Pirgmaier, E. (2017). The neoclassical Trojan horse of steady-state economics. *Ecological Economics*, 133(March): 52–61.

Rockström, J., Steffen, W., Noone, K., Persson, Å., Chapin III, F.S., Lambin, E., Lenton, T. M., Scheffer, M., Folke, C., Schellnhuber, H., Nykvist, B., De Wit, C.A., Hughes, T., van der Leeuw, S., Rodhe, H., Sörlin, S., Snyder, P.K., Costanza, R., Svedin, U., Falkenmark, M., Karlberg, L., Corell, R.W., Fabry, V. J., Hansen, J., Walker, B., Liverman, D., Richardson, K., Crutzen, P. and Foley, J. (2009). Planetary boundaries: exploring the safe operating space for humanity. *Ecology and Society* 14(2): 1–32.

Spash, C.L. (2010). The brave new world of carbon trading. *New Political Economy* 15(2), 169–195.

Spash, C.L. (2013). The shallow or the deep ecological economics movement? *Ecological Economics* 93 (September), 351–362.

Turner, G. (2008). *A Comparison of The Limits To Growth with Thirty Years of Reality*. Canberra: Commonwealth Scientific and Industrial Research Organisation.

van den Bergh, J.C.J.M. and Grazi, F. (2014). Ecological footprint policy? Land use as an environmental indicator. *Journal of Industrial Ecology* 18(1): 10–19.

van den Bergh, J.C.J.M. and Grazi, F. (2015). Reply to the first systematic response by the Global Footprint Network to criticism: A real debate finally? *Ecological Indicators* 58(November): 458–463.

46
POST-GROWTH ECONOMICS

Niko Paech

Introduction

Today's sustainability concepts are mostly based on ecological modernisation. Modern societies follow this trend and tend to shift the necessity of changing their consumption habits to a point later in time, or even deny the necessity of change completely. This is based on the hope that technological progress can solve the sustainability problem without having to go through difficult changes in lifestyle and a moderation of consumption habits. However, many of those 'Green' innovations intensify material and energy overexploitation by making use of previously unspoilt landscapes and untouched resources. As long as decoupling by technological means turns out to be impossible, sustainable development can only be understood as a programme for economic reduction rather than conjuring Green Growth solutions.

In this chapter I will explore an alternative to this popularised approach. That is a world that no longer clings to the growth imperative and makes the post-growth economy its goal. I start by defining what is meant by post-growth economics and how it has developed. This is followed by an exploration of the case for limits to growth and why decoupling runs into problems, including the rebound effect. I then outline some key aspects of a post-growth economy, before briefly identifying future directions and finishing with some concluding remarks.

The development and meaning of post-growth economics

Development of post-growth economics

The terms post-growth economics (as an analytical framework) and post-growth economies (as a concrete draft for the future) arose in debates over sustainability held at Carl von Ossietzky University in Oldenburg during 2006. Since then numerous publications, events and networks have devoted themselves to this topic, although they might have different foci and specific interests. Post-growth economics can be seen as a further development of a first wave of growth critical discourses. These include the works of Kohr (1957), Mumford (1967), Georgescu-Roegen (1971), Meadows et al. (1972), Illich (1973), Schumacher (1974), Daly (1977), Hueting (1980), and Gronemeyer (1988). This first wave arose in the late 1960s and peaked in the 1970s. However, since the turn of the century, a second wave of growth critical discourses has arisen and is associated with a variety of terms and authors, including: "Ökosozialismus" (Sakar, 2001), La Decrescita Felice (Pallante, 2005), Décroissance (Latouche, 2006/2009), Degrowth (Martínez-Alier, 2009), Postwachstumsökonomie (Paech, 2008, 2012), Managing without Growth (Victor, 2008), Prosperity without Growth (Jackson, 2009), Vorwärts zur Mäßigung (Binswanger, 2009), Exit (Miegel, 2010), Plenitude (Schor, 2010), and Postwachstumsgesellschaft (Seidl and Zahrnt, 2010).

Definition of post-growth economics

Post-growth economics is a sub-discipline in the field of economics. Subject areas of post-growth economics are the connection between sustainable development and economic growth. In contrast to environmental economics which aims at the ecological decoupling of the Gross Domestic Product (GDP), post-growth economics focuses on economic systems, subsystems and even lifestyles with the aim of reducing the quantities of supply and demand. This field of economics aims to describe the rationales which justify the approach of an economy without growth (post-growth economy) and generates knowledge for action in order to practically implement the overcoming of the growth orientation.

There are three major topics within the study of post-growth economics, as shown in Figure 46.1, namely, limits to growth, growth mechanisms and the post-growth economy. First, limits to growth, or growth criticism, analyses several things including failures of decoupling, unjustified wealth, peak everything, social inequality, peak happiness and also financial crises. The approach makes clear that further growth of GDP is not an option for shaping modern societies. Second, supply side and cultural forces are analysed as part of the mechanisms that drive growth. One of the main concerns here are the factors leading to division of labour in

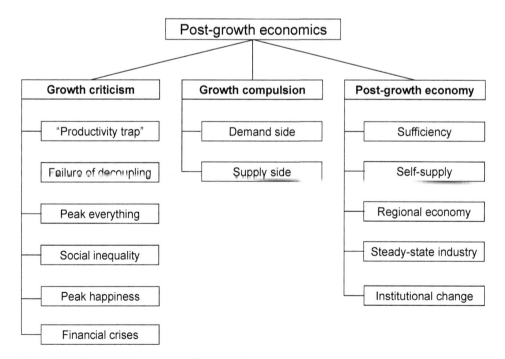

Figure 46.1 Understanding post growth economics.

industrial societies. Third, the post-growth economy is analysed with a focus on concepts like sufficiency, subsistence, regional economies, zero sum games and institutional change. A major issue covered in this discussion is the derivation and justification of the conditions for an economy without growth (post-growth) as a combination of complementary supply systems, which are characterised by the different degrees of industrial division of labour and have to be stabilised without growth of GDP.

Limits to growth

Green Growth depends on decoupling modern consumption and mobility practices from ecological damages [see Chapter 20]. This fails due to the deeply rooted misconception that individual objects or activities can be linked with attributes of sustainability. For example, why should a 3-litre car for example be more climate-friendly than a 25-litre guzzling Opel Admiral if the owner of the first one commutes 150 miles every day whereas the Admiral owner uses his vehicle only five times per year and the rest of the time cycles? To which extent does a passive house contribute to sustainable development if its inhabitants possess as many flat screens, computers, coffee machines and hi-fi systems as they have rooms? How many human lifetimes would be required to compensate the carbon dioxide (CO_2) emissions of a single intercontinental flight through constant consumption of organic lemonade, waste separation and car-sharing? Only individual CO_2 balances are a reliable target value. The central question here is: what amount of material freedom can a single individual be allowed to appropriate without living beyond his or her means? In relation to a 2°C temperature target, this means that every individual can have an annual budget of 2.7 tons of CO_2 emissions (WBGU, 2009). In comparison, the current average rate of emissions per capita in Germany, for example, is about 11 tons (Umweltbundesamt, 2015).

Seemingly sustainable single practices and products increasingly reveal mere symbolism utilised to morally compensate for something else, unsustainable and pursued by the same individual: 'Recently I've only bought organic T-shirts and participated in every climate-meeting, so I don't also have to give up my vacation in India, do I?' In the twenty-first century, whoever is unable to project his or her own lifestyle with respect to global transferability can never contribute to sustainable development, let alone to a post-growth economy. In order to encourage and enable sustainable lifestyles, companies could be obliged to label all their products and services with information about their lifecycle environmental impacts (e.g. CO_2 emissions, ecological footprint). Apart from the problem that Green Growth fails because it focuses on the wrong target, there are even more serious doubts to be raised about the decoupling strategy.

Decoupling is not an option

Increasing GDP requires additional production that, as an economic activity, has to be transferred from at least one provider to a demander, thereby inducing a cash-flow. Consequently, this added value splits up into a material origin side and a financial use side of the additional income [see also Chapter 40 on the real-real economy]. Both impacts would have to be neutralised in order to keep the economy growing without causing additional ecological damages. This means that, even if the generation of a monetarily measurable and hence GDP-relevant performance transfer could be technically dematerialised—which is not foreseeable as of now, apart from a few laboratory experiments—the problem of decoupling would remain unsolved as long the additional income can be used for purchasing any goods that are not completely dematerialised. Let me explain both issues a bit further.

Material rebound effects

What would goods look like that can be transferred from at least one provider to a demander as a service worth money, and that are, at the same time, free from any consumption of land, material or energy in production, physical transfer, use and disposal? All Green Growth solutions proposed up until now most evidently do not fulfil these requirements, regardless of whether they are passive houses, electronic vehicles, eco-textiles, photovoltaic systems, organic food products, offshore wind power stations, heat and power cogeneration units, solar thermal heaters, cradle-to-cradle drink packages, car sharing, digital services, and so on. Nothing of all this can exist without physical input and new production capacities and in particular infrastructure.

Perhaps 'Green' efficiency or consistency solutions could simply replace any less sustainable output instead of causing a material addition? In order to achieve a substitution that actually reduces ecological impact, simply replacing output-flows is inadequate, as long as this goes along with increases in material stock sizes and land use (as is the case with passive houses and renewable energy facilities). In addition, the previous capacities and infrastructures would have to be dismantled and the embodied energy and material resources largely wasted. There seems no way that the materials of whole industries and building complexes can be made to disappear in an ecologically neutral manner.

On top of this comes a second dilemma: how could GDP permanently grow if the profit from each act of creating 'Green' value added is countered by a non-sustainable value added loss due to the deconstruction of old structures? This can be traced with the example of the German Energiewende (a government scheme that subsidises Green energy sources for electricity generation). For a start, the contribution of renewable energies to economic value added, which the Green Growth community is currently praising, on closer inspection turns out to be, at best, a flash in the pan. After the installation of additional energy capacity is finished, the contribution to the added value is reduced to an energy flow that, in comparison, does not create a great deal of value added and cannot be increased easily—unless the production of new facilities is continued without limits. In this case, there would be further environmental damages. For example, landscape destruction, which is already oppressive, would increase due to the expansion of material stock sizes. Here the problem of material relocation effects becomes obvious. In most cases Green technologies do not solve ecological problems, but rather they only transfer them to other physical, spatial, temporal and systemic dimensions. For this reason, the attempts to empirically prove the success of decoupling are only valid if they consider all such relocation effects.

Financial rebound effects

Even if dematerialised production increases were possible, someday, the unavoidable corresponding income increases would also have to be ecologically neutralised. Yet, keeping the basket of goods that those consumers who benefit by obtaining additional income—generated in the Green sectors—free from being spent on resource intensive, globally produced items has proven simply unthinkable. These people will buy homes, travel by plane, drive cars and pursue conventional consumption activities that increase in-line with the growth in available income. Another financial rebound effect lurks behind Green investments when they raise the overall level of output, owing to the fact that old capacities are not simultaneously deconstructed to the same extent—additional passive houses increase net dwelling area and new photovoltaic systems increase net energy output—a situation that tends to cause price reductions leading to increases in demand. The fossil sector cannot be ruled out from also benefiting. A third financial rebound effect occurs wherever efficiency gains reduce the operating costs of certain objects (e.g., houses, cars, lights).

Theoretically, these rebound effects could be avoided by absorbing all the income increases that are generated by efficiency improvements and the income effect of investment, but then it would be needless to stimulate growth. What could be more absurd than generating growth just to neutralise the intended effects of growth, namely the increase of income? Accordingly, the assertion that through investment in Green technologies, growth could be associated with an absolute decrease in environmental burdens is not only flawed, but actually results in the exact opposite. That is, from the perspective of financial rebound effects, Green technologies can only relieve the ecosphere of environmental harm under conditions of non-growing GDP. Even this is not a secure condition, given the unaccounted for material effects on the generation side—especially the relocation impacts. Furthermore, the strategy of decoupling also brings an ethical problem. The fate of humanity would be at the mercy of a technological progress that has not yet been realised and whose future realisation is impossible to prove—notwithstanding that it might cause more additional problems than it is able to resolve.

Economic, psychological and social limits to growth

Material prosperity in modern industrial societies is based on endless availability of low price fossil energy sources and other essential resources. Already today the maximum extraction of crude oil (Peak-Oil [Chapter 41]) is foreseeable as well as the shortage of other production factors. Peak-Oil has already become 'peak everything'. Against this background, an increase of the purchasing power of new middle classes, in countries like China and India, leads to an escalating demand meeting a stagnating supply of resources [Chapter 11].

Besides scarce resources, such as lithium for rechargeable batteries and coltan for mobile phones, there is increasing technological dependency on rare Earth metals [Chapter 10]. These are appearing in more products that we seem no longer to be able to do without and upon whose mass marketing modern economies have long become dependent. The recent waves of growth in demand can be traced back to innovative, sometimes even Green, technologies. Mobile phones, computers and flat screens cannot be produced without rare Earth metals, and the same applies to LED lamps, and electronic and hybrid cars. Similar to wind power generating facilities, such vehicles depend on neodymium for the production of permanent magnets. A hybrid vehicle contains up to 12 kilograms of rare Earth metals. Every social sub-system, product and infrastructural element is at least indirectly dependent on fossil fuel energy carriers, rare Earth and scarce metals. So, unleashing substantial growth in purchasing power by means of worldwide networked production chains that exploit cost differences is bought at the cost of unprecedented instability [see also Chapter 15]. External supply dependency maximises the risk of social decline—if jobs fall, price rises reduce purchasing power or the external provision of essential or critical inputs is interrupted. The term sustainability therefore can increasingly be interpreted as the requirement for increased resilience. These are precautions that could soften the expected fall. This perspective also shows that reducing the by now exorbitant level of external supply is the last chance we have. It is the only way to reduce the social drop from the height we have reached today.

Limits to growth are not only seen in production systems but also in the hedonic overstimulation of people, causing mental illnesses and stress. Important results from happiness research suggest that an increase of materialistic wealth at a certain level does not increase subjective well-being (Easterlin, 1995). Consumer activities are only beneficial if people devote a minimum of their time to them. This causes psychological stress, because an individual's time budget cannot be exceeded, so an increase of the consuming option leads to overstimulation and stress instead of self-realisation [see Chapter 21]. Stress, disorientation and burn-out effects characterise the normal conditions of modern and wealthy societies. Reducing the number of potential consumer goods might then be understood as self-protection.

Causal mechanism of growth

Structural growth

Supply systems dependent upon imports into an economy are based on steadily increasing the distance between consumption and production. If production processes that were formerly bound to one location are dissected into many specialised production stages, their locations can be flexibly shifted, depending on cost and quality advantages. However, every stage of specialisation must finance the required input factors in advance, i.e., investment is needed upfront. Third party capital costs interest, while one's own capital assets demand a sufficient yield. In addition, the change in spatial boundary from local to global has led to a greater demand for physical infrastructure and facilities that are subject to constant wear. So for each period in each company that is part of an industrialised supply chain, an excess (after subtracting 'pure' production costs) must be achieved that is no lower than the sum of third party interest, own capital asset yield and costs for maintenance and reproduction of physical assets. Therefore, the minimum growth in the value added chain required to stabilise the overall process tends to increase with every specialisation, i.e., the number of separate companies and their relevant excess requirements.

Binswanger (2007) has analysed the structural growth compulsion in connection with the income and capacity effect of an investment. The income effect begins before the capacity effect, because initially capital is invested and the sale of production is only possible afterwards. Investment today immediately increases the income of households. However, the production volume resulting from the investment can only be bought later, in the following period. Households can only buy today what was produced yesterday. In this way, increased demand precedes an increased supply. Balancing the system of monetary payments within a single period is only possible if the payment gap on the demand side is balanced out by additional net investment to generate the appropriate income. The process described by Binswanger as a "growth spiral" would not be conceivable, or at least only in a much milder form, if corporate banks were unable to constantly generate new money to provide companies with credits for investment. This creation of money generation practically comes from nowhere because banks do not simply pass on savings one-to-one, but can instead transform debt into money. The debt money system allows unlimited increases in cash generation and turns money into materialised growth.

Another structural growth mechanism has already been mentioned, namely increased labour productivity. The less work necessary to create a specific output, the more output there must be to require all current employees to the same extent, at least under the same ownership conditions. Interestingly, the same conclusion follows, namely that reducing the structural growth compulsion means producing with less capital.

Cultural growth

Under which conditions does consumption create happiness? An unqualified answer to this key question cannot be made, owing to Gossen's famous first law (Gossen, 1854). This states that the utility an additional consumer good provides is reduced in relation to the increasing quantity. That encourages constantly new increases in consumer self-realisation options through qualitative changes. The permanent reinvention of the consumer society protects it from saturation symptoms and boredom.

As mentioned, happiness research has shown that from a certain level onwards, increased per capita income does not lead to any further increase in happiness. Hirsch (1977) offers as an explanation that the use of many goods is symbolic or demonstrative, i.e. based on distinction, social prestige or membership of a specific social group. Consumption is therefore characterised by competition, whereby the aim is to attain a higher place in the social hierarchy. One person's gain can only be achieved through another person's loss. An initially achieved advantage erodes with the number of people who are initially overtaken but catch up as a result of further growth. The resulting dynamism is like an arms race, as ever higher consumption efforts are required to maintain or regain a specific, but by no means higher, level of happiness. From an abstract perspective, this logic of growth can be described as the dominant development principle in modern consumer society. The never ending source of a social political need to act is fed by uncovering social differences, which are then transformed into the imperative of their removal through additional action and growth. In this way, all political and economic activities achieve a perpetual, self-strengthening legitimation. Enough is never enough. Growth creates differences that cause further growth in the attempts to remove those differences.

A post-growth economy

The alternative to an economy based on growth dependency would correspond to a socially acceptable dismantling and conversion of the industrial system. Mechanisms of growth, both on the supply and the demand side, would have to be overcome by supply infrastructures which would on the one hand be less capital-intensive, less specialised, and spatially confined (more subsistence) and on the other hand more frugal (more sufficiency). From this, five transformation steps can be derived.

First is sufficiency. From the point of view of an individual who is overstrained by the variety of options available, reduction does not equal loss but an exemption from time demanding excess. Sufficiency comprises the identification and discarding of those burdens that use up time, money, space and ecological resources, but only gain a minimum of usefulness for the individual. Sufficiency therefore equals time economic optimisation (Paech, 2013). Simultaneously this results in more independence from volatile market developments, and therefore helps achieve economic resilience.

Second is subsistence. A readjustment of the interrelation between self-sufficiency and external resource supply would aim to gradually abolish industrial production systems. Different external supply levels exist between pure subsistence and consumption of industrial goods. An average of 20 weekly working hours would release time resources that could be dedicated to non-market activities, like crafting, parenting, neighbourly help, participation in community gardens and care and repair of goods, as well as sharing of products. Three de-commodified resources take the place of material resources being used for new production: (i) manual skills for own production and extension of product lifetimes, (ii) own time that is needed to accomplish (i), and (iii) social relationships for the purpose of joint use and exchange of services. With these inputs urban subsistence generates three output categories, consisting of own production, extension of product lifetimes and intensification of uses, which reduce the need for industrial production and thus capital requirements. The corresponding industrial deconstruction would have to be designed in a way that the free time could feed into those subsistence services, which can absorb the decline in production.

Third is the regional economy. In between the two extremes of local subsistence and global division of labour, regional economies can be developed as another complementary supply system. Complementary currencies could stabilise the regional economy and bind demand to the region. Entrepreneurial advantages due to specialisation could be used, but would be based on de-globalised and work intensive technologies.

Fourth is material zero sum games as a production mode. After a partial dismantling of industry the remaining industrialised production systems would have to be reshaped in a way that goods should only be newly produced if the old goods cannot be reused. Focus would be on preservation, conservation, optimisation, extension of lifetimes and intensification of benefits. Defective goods could be refitted by reparation services. By following renovation strategies that have their focus on reconstruction, instead of new construction, existing goods would gain additional benefits by adjusting them to people's functional and aesthetic needs to keep them useful as long as possible. Markets for used, processed and overhauled goods would also add to the reduction of new production. If the average lifetime and intensity of use of some goods could be doubled, by combining long-life designs with urban subsistence and supplementing corporate services, then output could be halved without having to reduce the availability of the possibilities to consume.

Fifth is institutional innovation. Land, monetary and financial market reforms could mitigate the growth compulsion that is inherent in the system. Regional currencies could be combined with a circulation safeguard that brings the interest levels close to zero. Changed types of enterprises could have a dampening effect on the dynamics of profits. The present confusing structure of government subsidies could be revised to reduce ecological damages and public debts. Soil sealing moratoriums and programmes to deconstruct infrastructures would be most useful—especially industrial parks, highways, parking areas and airports would have to be unsealed and re-naturalised. Plants that use renewable energies could be installed in their place, to reduce the use of space and natural areas for these technologies. Sustainable development should be oriented towards the individual life cycle assessment and carbon footprint. Each person would have the right to emit a certain amount of CO_2 per year (approx. 2.7 tons) and companies would have to label the carbon emissions on their products. Precautions against planned obsolescence should be taken and an education system, that would enable urban subsistence, implemented.

Further driving forces are social processes, which create platforms for testing resilient lifestyles. Resulting templates for lifestyles can be used for orientation by other members of the community as needed. An ecologically and socially sustainable economy must therefore be free from all dependency on growth and subsequent pressure for growth, including the innovation orientation of modern market economies, the present monetary and interest-earning system, expectations of high profit, external supplies of resources based on a model of global division of labour, and a culture of unquestioning pursuit of material self-actualisation.

Future directions

Further research should concentrate on the communication and diffusion of post-growth compatible lifestyles. Why? If the thesis described above is taken seriously, whereby no technical solution to the growth problem is in sight, there is no alternative except reduction strategies. They would inevitably affect our lifestyles since sufficiency cannot be delegated to machines nor the political system. Who would choose a policy that questions the continued execution of a lifestyle that one does not wish to give up voluntarily? Therefore, growth-critical models of the future that are completely dependent on political agendas for their implementation are simply a waste of time. No democratically elected government is a pioneer of social change and instead always lags behind in order to avoid risk [see also Chapter 44 on degrowth democracy]. Political decision-makers will only feel encouraged to move towards a post-growth policy if there are enough convincing signals for the readiness and ability of society to cope with that change.

Concluding remarks

Could a life under the conditions of a post-growth economy, unburdened from excess, consisting of a paid 20-hour job, complemented by a wealth of subsistence practices, already be rewarding enough to begin now?

- Relieving the burden of as much third party supply as possible, which makes one needy and controllable, frees us from the fear of an increasingly insecure future. Needing little and being able to shape as much as possible by ourselves, or together with others, is an expression of strength and economic sovereignty.
- The almost overwhelming overstimulation we are exposed to from all communication channels could be eased in a simpler, more easily manageable world. That allows concentrated enjoyment instead of pale superficiality.
- Modern subsistence creates success experiences, especially through self-production, by repairing objects or undertaking works of art. Completed results of work, which can be tangibly perceived as such, are positively distinct from the transience of abstract performance in a labour dividing sphere.
- Buying less and instead organising more together with others, exchanging, using or producing, means reintegrating the social into the economic. Reliable and stable social coherence can replace individualisation. If simple manual work regains its status then this will open up the possibility of integrating those who are ostracised due to a lack of money, education or communicative abilities. That gives greater self-respect to those whose contributions are no longer in demand in a specialised competitive environment.
- Extreme forms of social imbalance are a logical consequence of the third party supply model. Since only monetary performance can be infinitely increased, the differences in income and wealth can grow accordingly. A high degree of wealth that is no longer based on money, but instead on one's own ability to produce, levels out differences in material equipment, and we have long known that unfair distribution is detrimental to all happiness.

Key further readings cited

Georgescu-Roegen, N. (1971). *The Entropy Law and the Economic Process.* Cambridge/London: Harvard University Press.
Paech, N. (2012). *Liberation from Excess. The Road to a Post-Growth Economy.* Munich: Oekom-Verlag.
Schor, J.B. (2010). *Plenitude. The New Economics of True Wealth.* New York: Penguin Press HC.

Other literature cited

Binswanger, H.C. (2007). *Die Wachstumspirale.* Marburg: Metropolis. Translated in 2012: *The Growth Spiral: Money, Energy, and Imagination in the Dynamics of the Market Process.* Berlin: Springer.
Binswanger, H.C. (2009). *Vorwärts zur Mäßigung.* Hamburg: Murmann Verlag GmbH.
Daly, H. (1977). *Steady-State Economics.* Washington: Island Press.
Easterlin, R.A. (1995). Will raising the income for all increase the happiness for all? *Journal of Economic Behavior and Organization*, 27(1), 35–47.

Gossen, H.H. (1854). *Entwicklung der Gesetze des menschlichen Verkehrs und der daraus fließenden Regeln für menschliches Handeln.* Braunschweig: Friedrich Vieweg & Sohn.

Gronemeyer, M. (1988). *Die Macht der Bedürfnisse.* Reinbek: WBG.

Hirsch, F. (1977). *Social Limits to Growth.* Cambridge: Harvard University Press

Hueting, R. (1980). *New Scarcity and Economic Growth.* Amsterdam: Elsevier Science Ltd.

Illich, I. (1973). *Tools for Conviviality.* Cornell: Harper & Row.

Jackson, T. (2009). *Prosperity Without Growth: Economics for a Finite Planet.* London: Routledge.

Kohr, L. (1957). *The Breakdown of Nations.* London: Green Books.

Latouche, S. (2006). *Le pari de la décroissance.* Paris: Fayard. Translated in 2009: *Farewell to Growth.* New York: John Wiley & Sons.

Martínez-Alier, J. (2009). Socially sustainable economic de-growth. *Development and Change* 40(6), 1099–1119.

Meadows, D., Meadows, D., Zahn, E., Milling, P. (1972). *Limits to Growth – A Report for the Club of Rome's Project on the Predicament of Mankind.* London: Universe Books.

Miegel, M. (2010). *Exit – Wohlstand ohne Wachstum.* Berlin: Propyläen Verlag.

Mumford, L. (1967). *The Myth of the Machine.* London: Secker & Warburg.

Paech, N. (2008). Regionalwährungen als Bausteine einer Postwachstumsökonomie. *Zeitschrift für Sozialökonomie* (ZfSÖ) 45 (158-159), 10–19.

Paech, N. (2013). Eine zeitökonomische Theorie der Suffizienz, in: *Umweltpsychologie*, 17. Jg., Heft 2/33, 145–155.

Pallante, M. (2005). *La decrescita felice. La qualità della vita non dipende dal PIL.* Roma: Ediz. per la Decrescita Felice.

Sakar, S. (2001). *Die nachhaltige Gesellschaft. Eine kritische Analyse der Systemanalysen.* Zürich: Rotpunktverlag.

Schumacher, E.F. (1974). *Small is Beautiful.* London: London Abacus.

Seidl, I., Zahrnt, A. (2010) (eds.). *Postwachstumsgesellschaft. Konzepte für die Zukunft.* Marburg: Metropolis.

Umweltbundesamt (2015): *Europäischer Vergleich der Treibhausgas-Emissionen* (https://www.umweltbundesamt. de/themen/klima-energie/klimaschutz-energiepolitik-in-deutschland/treibhausgas-emissionen/ europaeischer-vergleich-der-treibhausgas-emissionen). Accessed 21 December 2016.

Victor, P.A. (2008). *Managing Without Growth: Slower by Design, Not Disaster.* Cheltenham: Edward Elgar Publishing Ltd.

WBGU (2009). *Kassensturz für den Weltklimavertrag – Der Budgetansatz.* Sondergutachten, Berlin.

47

THE BIOREGIONAL ECONOMY

Celebrating the local in production and consumption

Molly Scott Cato

Introduction

Our economic decisions need to be taken within the limits provided by biophysical reality [Chapters 9–13]. This requires a radical rethinking of the key questions of economics: how we work, produce and consume goods, and forge our individual and social identities. For many Greens and environmentalists, the conclusion is that we must relocalise our economies and that the trend of the past century towards increasing trade volumes, travelling greater distances, relying on extended supply chains and fossil fuel dependency must all be reversed. The cry has been for strengthened local economies and yet little work has been undertaken to define what a local economy might look like and how local our economic relationships are likely to become in an environmentally sustainable future.

This chapter explores one possible response in the form of an economy based around bioregions. In the rest of the chapter I will consider how using bioregions as provisioning units might offer an alternative, more ethical and more sustainable way of meeting human economic needs. In the next section, I explore what bioregionalism might have to offer in terms of reconceptualising the economy to achieve sustainability. I then proceed to explore existing contributions to this discussion, the major issues currently arising in this field, and outline the key issues facing a bioregional economy.

Why bioregionalism?

The idea of bioregionalism originated on the American West Coast, and was developed by environmentalists in the 1960s and 1970s (Berg and Dasmann, 1977; Sale, 2000) who were seeking renewed relationships with the natural world as the basis for strengthening protection of precious environments and the species who depended upon them. The deepening of their knowledge of local climate, ecology, species and culture drew heavily on their understanding of the Native American tradition. This autochthonous connection to the land may be able to be relearned and this has a correspondence in Aldo Leopold's "land ethic" (Leopold, 1966 [1949]).

Interestingly, the other part of the world where the concept of 'bioregion' has had significant intellectual purchase is the Antipodes, which has its own indigenous community whose land ethic has persisted and may have influenced the thinking of intellectuals and policy-makers.

Bioregions are used to support the development of environmental policy, with considerable investment of energy by policy-makers into mapping their territories in terms of bioregions. The Australian Government (2012) has produced a map of the country's 89 bioregions, "each of which is a large geographically distinct area of similar climate, geology, landform, vegetation and animal communities".

A bioregional worldview requires an understanding of ourselves as part of a global community of species; within that multitude we seek to establish our place in space. It is for this reason Gary Snyder (1990: 44) has argued that, "Bioregionalism is the entry of place into the dialectic of history". This is a reaction against the impulse of the process of globalisation to consider ourselves—especially if we are wealthy consumers living in the energy-intensive societies of the West—to be somehow floating in a weightless off-world paradise while the heavy-lifting that is still required to feed our fantasies takes place beyond our comprehension and field of vision.

The globalised capitalist economy demands massive and increasing flows of resources extracted and processed using fossil fuels with which the finished products are then transported across the globe [Chapters 4 and 11]. The international division of labour has increased the energy intensity of this economy, as components and products were moved between low-wage economies in the South to the wealthy consumer markets in the West. This process is now being reversed to some extent, as consumers in the countries of the majority world, and especially in China, are demanding the same unrooted consumer lifestyles and the hedonist pleasure they are purported to endow. However, this only makes the challenge of achieving sustainability harder, as, every year, millions more join the high-energy consumption club.

The awareness of the unsustainability of such lifestyles is ever more apparent due to the increasing range of environmental crises from habitat and species loss, through climate change to disruption to the nitrogen cycle and soil loss. Yet, as my experience of agreeing on a text on climate change with Latin America parliamentarians in the run-up to the Conference of the Parties (COP) to the United Nations Framework Convention on Climate Change (UNFCCC) talks in Paris demonstrated to me (Eurolat, 2015), the suggestion that a high-energy lifestyle should become the exclusive preserve of Western citizens is deeply resented. So how are we to establish what is an appropriate level of resource and energy use? Here I think the bioregion can play a useful role both in limiting our consumption and pointing the way to a more satisfying ethic of consumption [see also Chapter 20]. A bioregion represents a clear consumption boundary and a natural limit to our acquisitiveness while also offering a new and more satisfying way of meeting our needs for sustenance and community.

Theorising the bioregional economy

A bioregion is literally and etymologically a 'life-place'—a unique region definable by natural (rather than political) boundaries with a geographic, climatic, hydrological and ecological character capable of supporting unique human and non-human living communities. Bioregions can be variously defined by the geography of watersheds, similar plant and animal ecosystems, and related identifiable landforms and by the unique human cultures that grow from natural limits and potentials of the region (Thayer, 2003: 3).

Unlike political boundaries, bioregional boundaries are flexible and ambiguous. According to Sale (2000), a bioregion is:

> any part of the Earth's surface whose rough boundaries are determined by natural characteristics rather than human dictates, distinguishable from other areas by particular

attributes or flora, fauna, water, climate, soils, and landform, and by the human settlements and cultures those attributes have given rise to.

(Sale, 2000: 55)

Bioregionalism has attracted philosophers and poets as much as biological and Earth scientists. As a worldview it includes a sense of deepening our relationship with the natural world: not neglecting or ignoring the knowledge that science has brought us but challenging us to recognise that the getting of wisdom requires a different attitude towards the natural world. The difference between statistical knowledge and wisdom has become increasingly evident due to practice in the field of economics, and perhaps most strikingly on the issue of economic growth. Neoclassical economists have defended the idea that the economy can continue to grow exponentially, blithely ignoring biophysical limits, because the statistics show there has been growth in the past. While scientific evidence has led to the realisation of the need for change, we will need deeper human wisdom to construct an alternative model for a provisioning system.

As the ecological economist Kallis and his colleagues note:

> The rise of the market economy in everyday life, with exchange occurring over ever greater distance, can be thought of as a wedge between our contact with nature and with the moral consequences of the decisions we make."
>
> *(Kallis et al., 2009: 19)*

We have become disembedded from our local places and disconnected from the consequences of our consumption behaviour, the impact of which may be felt on the pacific islands of Vanuatu or the melting tundra of the Arctic. Elsewhere (Cato, 2012), I have linked this need to reconnect with the local with the idea of economic history as being a process of dialectic between embedding and disembedding as described by Polanyi 2011 [1944]. Economic forces have a tendency to outstrip moral or social restraint, at which point a movement emerges to re-embed the economy in the human community more widely defined. The environmental movement is the current manifestation of this re-embedding force characterised by the will to develop a sustainable approach to provisioning and consumption. For Polanyi, part of the thinness of modern society resulted from narrowing down the nature of 'man' to being an individual economic agent operating without the guidance of social norms or the benefit of community. Polanyi claimed that the acquisition of goods was actually more important in terms of the social status it conferred rather than the material satisfaction it provided (a point we will come to in more detail in the following section):

> He [the consumer] does not act so as to safeguard his individual interest in the possession of material goods; he acts so as to safeguard his social standing, his social claims, his social assets. He values material goods only so far as they serve this end.
>
> *(Polanyi, 2011 [1944]: 48)*

A little over 100 years ago the idea of buying an identity was sufficiently novel for it to form the subject of study by institutional economist Thorstein Veblen. In *The Theory of the Leisure Class* Veblen writes that:

> The end of acquisition and accumulation is conventionally held to be the consumption of the goods accumulated [...] But it is only when taken in a sense far removed from its naïve meaning that consumption of goods can be said to afford the incentive from

which accumulation invariably proceeds. The motive that lies at the root of ownership is emulation.

(Veblen, 1994 [1899]: 17)

In other words we buy things in order to establish who we are and advertise that to others, the things we buy are, in the words of Hirsch (1976), 'positional goods'. As Veblen identified, part of the purpose of frantic consumerism is to establish our place in a pecking-order, where the majority will never have the financial resources to reach the top of the pyramid.

The next stage in the process of 'shopping for an identity' was achieved by two techniques invented during the twentieth century: fashion and built-in obsolescence. German sociologist Werner Sombart (1863–1941) called fashion "capitalism's favourite child" (Haug, 2006) precisely because of the way it drove the wealthy of his time to reject goods that were still serviceable if their design or styling could make them seem outmoded. The technique of reducing the lifespan of products to encourage further purchases was even more effective, whether by building death-dates into electronic goods or reducing the durability of light-bulbs. (The process was parodied in the post-war Ealing comedy *The Man in the White Suit* (1951), where an industrial chemist becomes a target of generalised hatred when he invents an indestructible fabric.) Both techniques seemed not only rational but humane during an era when the Great Depression meant that thousands were out of work since they stimulated aggregate demand, but in an era when the greatest crises facing us are environmental, they seem pernicious and threatening. Prior to this era our ancestors tended to undertake what can be called 'self-provisioning'; in other words they used their own skills and labour to meet their needs, whether through growing their own food or making (or at least mending) their own shoes and clothes [see also Chapter 46]. As the need to stimulate economic growth has become more frenetic, more and more aspects of our lives have become marketised. Even simple tasks, such as cooking and childcare, are often provided via a market relationship rather than for oneself. These high-pressured, energy-intensive consumption behaviours are powerful in creating our identity and sense of meaning as modern, global citizens. So in the context of a discussion about relocalising the economy, what might we be able to offer as a substitute?

Fleshing out the idea of the local economy

When developing my fuller vision of the bioregional economy (Cato, 2012), I set myself the task of designing the most rewarding and satisfying economy we could create for the global human community while keeping within biophysical limits. As shorthand, we could think of this as achieving maximum human well-being with minimum throughput of energy and resources (I am not ignoring other species here, since I think our well-being and theirs are mutually dependent) (Cato, 2011).

While the benefits of our hyper-mobile high-tech culture may seem immediately apparent for most people, the insights and wisdom gained from a bioregional approach are more subtle and harder-won. The sort of relationship we can develop with the natural world through a direct relationship with our local places and the species we share with them can challenge what Schiller called "the disenchantment of the world" (Angus, 1983: 141). Weber (1905/2002) picked up this theme in his *Protestant Ethic and the Spirit of Capitalism*, where he explored the relationship between the development of capitalism and the religion of Puritanism with its rejection of earlier ideas of the natural world as infused with an immanent divine spirit. In the wake of the Enlightenment members of Western society developed a sense of self that was independent from the natural world and increasingly independent from human communities. While accepting the practical knowledge that we have acquired, bioregionalism seeks to reconnect us at a deep, spiritual level with the natural world and a bioregional approach to economics has the reversal of this process of objectification, disconnection and disenchantment as central to its project.

This offers us a way of conceiving of the world that is quite distinct from the lines on maps resulting from conflict resolution and political negotiation that characterise our world of nation-states and political boundaries. Across these political units, though, some pre-existing geographical, climatic and cultural areas persist, such as The Cotswolds in the UK or the region of France known as Quercy. Such areas have survived because they have cultural resonance.

So how might we produce a vision for sourcing our goods and services in a much more localised system of production and consumption that reflects these human-scale boundaries? Herbie Girardet (2011) has begun this task with his idea of the movement from the Agropolis through Petropolis to Ecopolis. In his understanding, the original agrarian societies were naturally limited by the human- and horse-power they had available and so provisioning units were small, with the larger city-states and market towns being closely connected to a rural and productive hinterland. His vision of the current provisioning model is one dominated by the cheap and plentiful supplies of petroleum, hence its label of petropolis. In this world, distance is no object with energy-intensive systems bringing multifarious goods, water and energy to the urban dwellers and removing their waste products. The urban space then expands beyond its sustainable limits.

The bioregional approach to economics would result in something more like Girardet's vision of Ecopolis, as illustrated in Figure 47.1. Here the city is located in the centre of a series of concentric circles that provide for the majority of needs. Land is set aside for the production of vegetables, meat and dairy crops, biofuels, and textile crops. Other land is left wild for recreation and for the production of energy from wind and sun. Trade now plays a much more

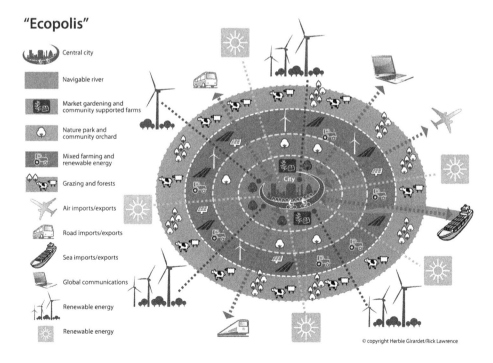

Figure 47.1 Herbie Girardet's vision of 'Ecopolis'.
Source: Girardet (2011).

limited role, for the import of sophisticated goods that cannot be produced locally; urban transport is largely public transport, together with a greatly increased role for walking and cycling.

The global trade system enables corporate arbitrage and profiteering at huge energy cost, yet any attempt to challenge this massive global exchange of goods and services is immediately criticised as threatening consumer choice, an argument challenged by Fellner and Spash (2015). The most obvious limitation of the bioregion as a provisioning unit is precisely its definition in terms of unique identifying flora and fauna, meaning that it is specialised in terms of the raw materials it can produce whether in terms of food or materials for the production of goods. Compared to the overwhelming variety offered by the global economy to wealthy consumers, a bioregional economy would offer less choice but a more locally rooted identity.

It should also be noted that the bioregion is not proposed as the sole source of provisioning, but rather the primary source. Clarifying the difference between a self-reliant bioregional economy and an autarkic self-sufficiency (e.g. the model of North Korea) may prove informative here. The former suggests a desire to provide for all of one's own needs and to deny those needs that cannot be met from local resources or by the effort of the local community. By contrast, 'self-reliance' implies a provisioning strategy that adapts needs to local availability and prioritises local production, but does not entirely abjure the need for imports and exports. For a bioregional economy, the first response to a need would be to look to the local to provide, and only where such provisioning is impossible—even after a re-evaluation of the difference between a 'need' and a 'want' (see Cato, 2012; [also Chapters 8 and 24])—would use of energy resources to import the good in question be considered.

The decision about when trade might be appropriate can be informed by the concept of trade subsidiarity, as illustrated in the grid reproduced in Figure 47.2. The conceptualisation of provisioning turns our existing paradigm on its head. The global supply-chain model facing wealthy consumers in the West is that a corporate megastore will match their every desire, whether this be for asparagus in November or manchego cheese in Manchester. Locality, provenance and seasonality are swept aside and the consumer's preference is assumed to dominate. Trade subsidiarity suggests just the reverse; namely, that a society would begin the quest for provisioning by favouring what is locally available and in season, and would seek to meet the needs of its people from what is locally available before going further afield. In this way, trade would be put back in its place of supplying what cannot be found locally, providing the icing on the cake rather than the cake itself.

Figure 47.2 presents a simplified visual representation of how we might make choices about where to source our goods. For example, a government committed to a bioregional approach could follow-up with supportive policies, such as taxes relating to the distance a good had travelled, and this might primarily be a tax relating to the embodied carbon content of a commodity (James and Cato, 2014). The first question is whether the raw materials or raw products are available locally, a decision based on climate and other favourable conditions for production. If so, consumers could seek to buy goods from local markets or local suppliers of services such as construction or furniture manufacture. In the case of goods that cannot be produced locally, consumers will need to seek a trade route to obtain them, but taking into account the need for trade to be on a fair and ethical basis.

Modernity encourages individuals to define themselves in terms of material objects, but because these change rapidly, due to fashion and technology, they have to be replaced. This means, consumers need a steady stream of products to fulfil the feeling of being satisfied with life. Most of the goods supplied in the market trade model of provisioning arise from the labour of others and often those in far-distant communities [Chapters 4 and 15]. Prior to the era of consumerism, human identity as members of a community was historically based on productive

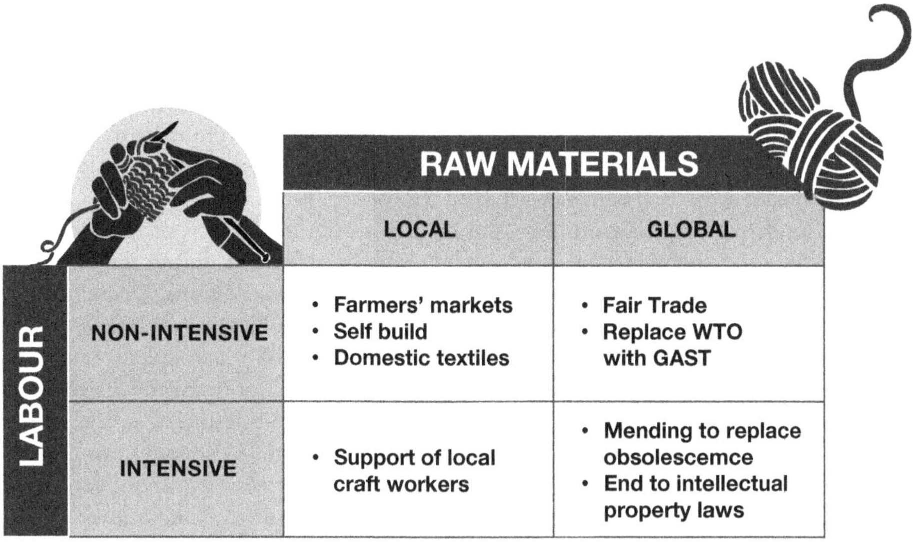

RAW MATERIALS		
	LOCAL	**GLOBAL**
NON-INTENSIVE	• **Farmers' markets** • **Self build** • **Domestic textiles**	• **Fair Trade** • **Replace WTO** **with GAST**

INTENSIVE	• **Support of local**
	  craft workers
		• **Mending to replace**
		  obsolescemce
		• **End to intellectual**
		  property laws

(row label: **LABOUR**)

Figure 47.2   Trade subsidiarity: simplified schema.

Note: WTO refers to World Trade Organisation; GAST refers to General Agreement on Sustainable Trade.

work rather than shopping habits. In a bioregional economy people's labour would once again become central to their identity so that people would come to be known as a baker, brewer, gardener or electronic engineer.

The variety of local provisioning can also offer great abundance. My home town of Stroud has its own apple, the Lodgemore Non Pareil, and the nearby village of Taynton is the proud possessor of varieties of apple, pear and walnut. These local varieties are available for sale in our farmers' market together with their cider and perry. The Gloucestershire love of apples is an example of what the French would call an attachment to *terroir*, the sense of pride in your local place and its specialities that could be taken as constitutive of a bioregional approach to provisioning. The contrast with a globalised market approach to provisioning is instructive. While the market economy needs global uniformity and standardisation, the bioregional economy revels in difference and local distinctiveness. Although it is easier to imagine local provisioning in a rural context the revisioning of cities [Chapter 48] is also well-advanced, as in the example of the think-tank Bioregion Birmingham.

At a deeper level, the acquisition of goods and services from the local environment can help individuals to embed more closely within their local places. That sense of connectedness could offer more psychological satisfaction. There is much to gain from understanding what Abram terms "the spell of the sensuous" where "The world and I reciprocate one another. The landscape as I directly experience it is hardly a determinate object; it is an ambiguous realm that responds to my emotions and calls forth feelings from me in turn" (1996: 29).

Abram describes the way that the patterns of nature are infinitely varied such that objects made from them continue to hold our attention rather than offering merely novelty value. So a chair skilfully made by hand can continue to delight for years and perhaps more so once it has been mended or re-seated several times. Knowledge of the person who made and mended the chair adds to a sense of personal connection within a local community. This might lead us to develop a new ethic of consumption based on sustainability, locality and ethical work. Craig (2006: 293) notes that this was the ideal held up by John Ruskin in his lectures to working men to whom he recommended "good consumption" based on "learning to read the 'powers' of natural resources and the 'virtues' of workers and consumers". The bioregional economy offers us the opportunity to find our place in a distinct and more satisfying way: through meaningful skilled work as part of a strong and closely related local community whose members can live comfortably in the knowledge that they are not demanding too much of the Earth. We would also have the satisfaction of knowing our local place through the consumption of local foods and products made with local materials.

Such an understanding of work has resonances with the idealisation of craft work that emerged in England following the rapid process of industrialisation during the nineteenth century and especially in the works of John Ruskin and William Morris. Their 'Arts and Crafts' movement reacted against the loss of beauty when objects were made without individual care, as well as the loss of quality in production. Ruskin particularly decried the loss of the spiritual value of goods whose making denigrated the labour invested in them. He valued 'manufacture' in its original sense of hand-wrought goods, rather than the artificial value of mercantile trade (May, 2010: 192). What the bioregional economy can offer is a strongly embedded local identity to replace the global consumer identity; a stronger sense of connection between people and between people and their local land; and a great sense of sufficiency and security. In the words of the Transition Stroud pioneers, it would offer us a 'low-carbon high life'.

Future directions

Many of the crises facing humanity could be conceptualised as trans-boundary issues. International problems range from the massive movements of humanity that constitute modern migration to the battle to reduce carbon dioxide emissions that are produced in one country but whose consequences are global. The concept of the global village should become more than a buzzword and that village needs some elders and some communitarian social norms. This requires that individuals recognise their global responsibilities while becoming locally rooted and accountable for the protection of their piece of the globe. While a bioregional approach enables the latter process it should in no way neglect consideration of the former.

The global economy, characterised by a consumption monoculture and hypermobility has a shallow allure that nonetheless leaves us feeling disconnected and disorientated. This explains the appeal to many of a bioregionalist vision as a response to the discomfort we experience when we live without boundaries. The corporations, that dominate global production and consumption, have benefited from becoming transnational organisations, while the citizens of Western democracies have been left with political power (i.e., a vote) that only extends as far as the nation-state whose power has been transcended (Della Porta, 2005). The challenge of bioregionalism is in finding the boundaries within which humans can feel secure. McGinnis suggests that this requires each person should re-inhabit their local patch of Earth:

> We should recognise that these senses and memories we share with other animals in a community are rapidly fading. Modern institutions make a series of sombre choices: to foster the development of formal economies and bureaucracies, to devalue informal economies and diverse communities, to control a 'static' nature as a resource, to develop technological and scientific instruments for making exploitation of the environmental machine more effective and efficient.
>
> *(McGinnis, 1999a: 62)*

From a bioregionalist perspective, establishing a different system of boundaries might enable a greater sense of security and a stronger identity based in a culture widely defined, and involving other species as well as other people.

As well as political and trade subsidiarity, a system of subsidiarity with regard to personal identities is implied, and that aspect and its implication must be developed. While becoming rooted in a local place may enable greater accountability for personal and local community consumption and waste production, the duty to act as global citizens remains and some issues can only be resolved at that level e.g., resource conflict, migration, and climate change. How these negotiations might take places is illustrated in Figure 47.3, based on a similar graphic and theorisation by McGinnis (1999b). He suggests the need for an engaged and participatory process of economic negotiation. The bioregional discussion takes us straight to the heart of the first boundary definition: How can local places be defined? Should this be done in terms of natural systems and process or in terms of bureaucratically enforced legal boundaries? At a deeper level he questions the process and procedures required to resolve conflicts.

One answer may lie in more participatory processes [Chapter 33] of economic negotiation, rather than in mechanical systems of legality and bureaucracy. McGinnis (1999b: 69) acknowledges what he calls this "fundamental border redefinition conflict", which he conceptualises as shown in Figure 47.3. For McGinnis the need for redefinition has three aspects.

1   The spatial, raising the question of whether to consider local places in terms of real geographical areas or in terms of politically designated boundaries.
2   The functional, concerning whether issues of sharing and relating are resolved through bureaucratic means (the discourse of laws and rights) or through learning to be ecological citizens.
3   The temporal, relating to the extent to which an area claimed for resource use is justified historically and considers the needs of generations stretching forward indefinitely into the future.

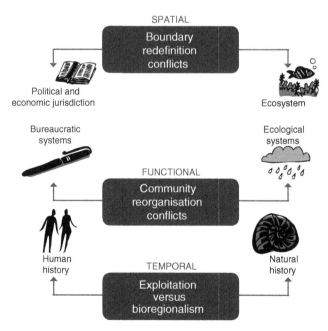

Figure 47.3   Boundary redefinition problems following McGinnis (1999b).

Concluding remarks

A bioregional approach to the economy extends and expands the call for a more local system of provisioning that has been central to the platform of green economics since its inception. It challenges the notion of the globalised consumer economy as offering satisfaction and criticises the extent of consumption of resources and energy that design of economy demands. In its place is proposed an economy re-embedded in the natural world and based on close relationships within human communities. It is a substitute that offers a different and deeper satisfaction and that sets the principles of sustainability and equity at its heart.

Key further readings cited

Cato, M.S. (2012). *The Bioregional Economy: Land, Liberty and the Pursuit of Happiness*. London: Earthscan.
James, R.F. and Cato, M.S. (2014). A bioregional economy: A green and post-capitalist alternative to an economy of accumulation, *Local Economy* 29(3), 173–180.
McGinnis, M.V. (1999a) (ed.), *Bioregionalism*. London: Routledge.
Thayer, R.L. (2003). *Life-Place: Bioregional Thought and Practice*. Berkeley, Calif.: University of California Press.

Other literature cited

Abram, D. (1996). *The Spell of the Sensuous*. New York, NY: Vintage.
Angus, I. (1983), Disenchantment and modernity: The mirror of technique. *Human Studies* 6(2), 141–66.
Australian Government (2012) Interim Biogeographic Regionalisation for Australia, Version 7. Commonwealth of Australia, Canberra. http://www.environment.gov.au/land/nrs/science/ibra/australias-bioregions-maps. Accessed 21 December 2016.
Berg, P. and Dasmann, R. (1977). Reinhabiting California. *The Ecologist* 7(10): 399.
Cato, M.S. (2011). Home economics: Planting the seeds of a research agenda for the bioregional economy, *Environmental Values* 20(4), 481–501.
Craig, D. M. (2006). *John Ruskin and the Ethics of Consumption*. Charlottesville, VA: University of Virginia Press
Della Porta, D. (2005). Globalizations and democracy. *Democratization* 12/5, 668–685.
Eurolat (2015), Euro-Latin America Parliamentary Assembly, Urgent Resolution on the Europe-Latin America position on issues related to climate and climate change in the context of the Summit of 2015 in Paris (COP 21).
Fellner W. and Spash, C.L. (2015). The role of consumer sovereignty in sustaining the market economy. In L. A. Reisch and J. Thørgersen (eds.) *Handbook of Research on Sustainable Consumption* (pp. 394–409). Cheltenham: Edward Elgar.
Girardet, H. (2011). *Creating Regenerative Cities*. Berlin: Heinrich Böll Foundation.
Haug, A. (2006), Gatekpeepers and knowledge diffusion in the fashion industry, paper presented at DRUID-DIME Academy, Winter.
Hirsch, F. (1976). *The Social Limits to Growth*. Cambridge: Harvard
Kallis, G., Martinez-Alier, J. and Norgaard, R.B. (2009). Paper assets, real debts: An ecological-economic exploration of the global economic crisis, *Critical Perspectives on International Business* 5(1–2), 14–25.
Leopold, Aldo (1949/1966). *A Sand County Almanac*. New York: Ballantine Books.
May, C. (2010). John Ruskin's political economy: 'There is no wealth but life', *British Journal of Politics and International Relations* 12, 189–204.
McGinnis, M.V. (1999b). Boundary creatures and bounded spaces. In McGinnis, M.V. (ed.) *Bioregionalism*. London: Routledge, 61–80.
Polanyi, K. (1944). *The Great Transformation: The Political and Economic Origins of our Time*, 2011 edn. Boston, MA.: Beacon Press.
Sale, K. (1991). *Dwellers in the Land: The Bioregional Vision*, rev. edn. 2000. Athens, GA: University of Georgia Press.
Snyder, G. (1990). *The Practice of the Wild*. Berkeley, CA: Counterpoint.
Veblen, T. (1899/1994). *The Theory of the Leisure Class*. Mineola, NY: Dover.
Weber, M. (2002). *The Protestant Ethic and the 'Spirit' of Capitalism and Other Writings*, P.R. Baehr and G.C. Wells (eds.). Harmondsworth: Penguin.

48

THE COMING SUSTAINABLE CITY

Laura Frye-Levine and Richard S. Levine

Introduction

Urbanisation is proceeding at a rate unprecedented in human history, with a projected growth of two billion city-dwellers over the next 20 years (UN Habitat, 2004). Throughout history, proto-sustainability has been negotiated at the scale of the city-region. Buffeted by complex competing factors, city-regions underwent many iterations of design over time. The great majority of modern urban development is, by contrast, informal and ecologically disconnected. Local balance-seeking processes have given way to the rapid growth of globalisation. Where contemporary policy conventions of city planning are in effect, they have not kept pace with nascent ecological standards in building and infrastructure design. Though recognition of the importance of cities to ecological economics continues to grow, the discipline has found it very difficult to wrest an operationally urban meaning of sustainability from within its boundaries. Current approaches do not provide instructions or a path forward for measurement, accounting or otherwise operationalising that knowledge (Boyd and Banzhaf, 2007; Wallace, 2007). In other words, no system has yet succeeded in analytically inverting familiar metrics and indicators to provide a means to operationalise a coherent sustainable whole at the city scale.

Diversity, proximity and complexity are distinctive features of urban life. These complexities undergird a social ecological system whose multiple interacting metabolisms are crucial dimensions of its strength (Moffatt and Kohler, 2008). Urban form is itself an influence of the cognitive aspects of relating to—and by extension creating—environmental social values (Miller, 2005; Tidball and Krasny, 2014). These qualities render the city an underexplored frontier for work in ecological economics. This chapter investigates some reasons for this conundrum and presents an operational definition of sustainability in *place*. We will argue that this is an essential innovation which bypasses the impediments created when sustainability is pursued with economic tools alone.

The discipline of ecological economics has been a latecomer to the conversation on sustainability and cities, a scale of analysis that has thus far come under the disciplinary purview of designers and policymakers. Neither neoclassical nor heterodox economics has historically had much to contribute beyond analytic optimisation of isolated systems. The journal *Ecological Economics* published its first article on the topic of urban ecology in 1996. Urban themes continue to account for only 3.8 per cent of articles, most of which are authored from the perspective of so-called 'developed nations'. Theoretical approaches within the discipline are likewise constrained. Ecological economists have, however, adapted the ecosystem services [Chapter 43] framework to the urban landscape. Bolund and Hunhammar (1999) identified at least six direct services—both cultural and social, as well as ecological—provided by ecosystems located within urban environments and called for their incorporation in urban planning decisions. Subsequent work in the field continues to classify and quantify a number of key biophysical and social benefits derived from experiences of ecological place and space within the urban scale of analysis.

A sustainable urban future

Scholars of urban sustainability stress that future research must engage at the scale of whole places and integrated systems (Jordan and Fortin, 2002). Multiple tools are available for assessing dimensions of sustainability and a growing body of research is engaged in optimising and operationalising those tools with the aim of characterising individual value streams. However, notably absent from the ecological economics literature are self-critical and reflexive studies. For example, what are the emergent consequences of the optimisation of individual 'ecosystem services' at the expense of macro-scale interactions within the city-system? The urban stage is inextricably linked to the goals exalted by ecological economics at large: equity, justice and power. Crucially, no metric or approach has thus far succeeded in linking the scale-consumption relationship of urban metabolism with social equity. The available metrics come up dangerously short in addressing these interactions. Consequently, the tools and the associated assessments currently in use by policymakers neglect key requirements for the transformation to sustainable urban futures. The sustainable cities of the future must, therefore, transcend efficiency-oriented calculation and managerialist intervention in isolated silos across the city system. We assert that sustainable cities can be operationalised within the disciplinary agenda of ecological economics and that sustainability must be pursued at the scale of the city-region.

Heeding to both the normative commitments of ecological economics and the primacy of place in urban life is therefore a qualitatively distinctive undertaking. We argue that this approach will require inverting the primacy given to reactive analytical metrics and instead honour the city-system as an indivisible unit of both analysis and synthesis. These advances are both possible and necessary. They can occur by building on the foundational contribution of ecological economics as a revolutionary scientific discipline with a unique potential to both inspire interest and promote integration. By nurturing the interests of equity and ecology in a coherent and grounded way, the city-region provides the crucial *place for sustainability to happen*. This requires a truly *ecological economics*, or 'science of sustainability', that provides key tools and theoretical commitments to reach this desired destination.

Past research

The methodological milieu of the past decade is characterised by a rise to prominence of the quest to measure baselines and evaluate progress. This imperative has led to a catalogue of various 'indicators of sustainability', e.g., air and water quality, vehicle miles travelled, ratio of waste recycled. Indicator approaches hope to operationalise measurement to achieve strong sustainability by tracking particular aspects of factors contributing towards (un)sustainability and promoting associated policy instruments [see Chapter 37 on sustainability indicators]. In a brazen effort to improve aggregate calculations of urban sustainability in closer approximation to ecological reality, ecological economics has deployed many of these tools. Three state-of-the-art indices of regional sustainability have risen to the foreground of the discipline (Siche et al., 2008), namely: the ecological footprint, the Environmental Sustainability Index and energy ratios.

The ecological footprint (EF) is land-area based and is most often implemented for the purpose of measuring the unsustainability of the aggregated but non-interactive actions of groups of individuals (Rees, 1992). A consumption based indicator, the EF is widely used by many researchers as well as several governments. It is meant as a starting point for evaluating the metabolism and scale of consumption; that is, the rate of throughput, a key concept in ecological economics [see Chapters 9–11]. The Environmental Sustainability Index (ESI) uses the nation-state as its unit of analysis and attempts to assess the maintained environmental assets of large regions (Esty and Porter, 2005). The ESI evaluates separately five 'dimensions of sustainability' and commensurates them to a final rating from 1 to 100 for country scale comparison. Inspired by the biophysical wing of ecological economics, 'emergy ratios' (Brown and Ulgiati, 1997) assess energy embodied in economic transactions. Their unit of analysis is the solar energy joule. In theory, energy ratios can be calculated at a variety of aggregate community scales, with the goal of implementing common standards of comparison for cities all over the world.

The academic and policy literature is rife with proposals to operationalise methods for a 'science of sustainability', yet these technically-focused debates have functionally narrowed the scope of sustainability discourse. Superordinate implementation of metrics restrict research to a particular analytical approach—the simple aggregation of individuals as metabolisers. To what extent do any of the commonly used indices—and their attendant units of analysis—have the ability to shepherd policy into a sustainability of practice? Of course, no single metric can account for the multivalent complexities of sustainability assessment. Critiques of a metrics-based approach to sustainability nevertheless point to the aggregating and compounding power imbalances [Chapter 14] and lack of meaningful engagement with social inequality embodied by indicator approaches. The commensurations entailed by the creation of sustainability metrics collapse concerns into a single unit of analysis. By definition, they evade engagement with incommensurability [Chapter 22], another key concept in ecological economics. Incommensur-ability of economic and natural capital—and between natural capital of different types—is a foundational tenet of the discipline's approach to 'strong sustainability' (e.g. Gowdy, 2005; Martinez-Alier et al., 1998). Yet, indicators are premised on numerous compromises of this principle. The commensurations entailed in indicator aggregation throw a cumbersome wrench in their compatibility with the ontological commitments of the discipline (Spash, 2012; see also [Chapter 2]).

Metrics-based analysis spatially depoliticises some of the most harmful ecological consequences through displacement of externalised effects, or more appropriately cost-shifting (Kapp, 1978), mainly to the global periphery [Chapters 4 and 15]. That is, each of these methods draws the critique that they inconsistently account for the driving forces of international trade, insufficiently differentiating between intermediate and final benefits (Wallace, 2007). For example, though the ecological footprint may at first appear to be a place-based measure, it is actually highly spatially ambiguous. Results obtained are significantly influenced by the statistical units deployed and per-capita data are aggregated without regard to interaction effects (Kocsis, 2014). Due to the complexity of calculation, a very limited production chain is typically employed (Weinzettel et al., 2014). Appropriately-scaled data are therefore difficult to amass, because of both the complexities inherent in defining regional boundaries, and the difficulties in the collecting of reliable and comparable data between them.

Ecosystem service valuation is nevertheless one of the fastest growing fields in both environmental and ecological economics (Jansson, 2013; see also [Chapter 43]). A consequence has been not only the flattening of entire ecological ways of knowledge (Spash and Aslaksen,

2015), but in addition the altering of the structure of ecological science by drawing research funding to models that focus on stock-flow stasis over complexity and change (Norgaard, 2010). Most importantly for cities, ecosystem services have the appearance of science but, like economics, originate from a profoundly placeless theoretical ideal. Their quantification invites a scripted set of technical interventions, conceived and inscribed in placeless space (Swyngedouw, 2011). The *de facto* state of governance endorsed by ecosystem services, and any ecological economics which applies it, is market fundamentalism geared towards efficient allocation (Boezeman et al., 2010; Weaver, 2013). Yet, as a matter of principle, ecological economics opposes key aspects of the technocratic governance implicitly enabled by neoclassically optimised policies that prioritise efficient allocation. Such optimisation violates a third foundational principle of ecological economics: that the economy is subordinate to biophysical systems as a basic matter of ontology (Spash, 2012). Economic efficiencies borne by consumptive choices generate both material and social rebound—magnified negative externalities that arise at larger scales and create social problems in distribution and ecological problems of scale. To achieve the tripartite ideals of ecological economics—justice in allocation, distribution and scale—a more comprehensive and dynamic process must be leveraged.

Current work

Gómez-Baggethun and Barton (2013) have synthesised the state of the art of methods and knowledge for evaluation and planning in urban ecosystems. All studies stress that the analytical reach of urban ecosystem services is not yet comprehensive, reiterating Bolund and Hunhmmar's (1999) foundational call to the discipline to investigate all aspects of value dimensions in the urban landscape. Crucially, these values are not just ecological and economic, but social and cultural as well. Most studies in the field continue to focus on a single 'ecosystem service' or a singular strand in the chain of production. These urban ecosystem services include social benefits such as: noise reduction, cooling, run-off mitigation, recreation, mental and physical health, social identity and cohesion and a sense of place (Gómez-Baggethun and Barton, 2013). Yet little integrative work on the relationship between services—particularly across social and ecological realms—has been attempted.

An ecological economic approach to urban sustainability must begin with the preanalytic understanding that valuation is always already a political act (Ernstson and Sorlin, 2013). That is, because values are constructed by humans in the social world, no act of evaluation or class of values is neutral or objective. However, social values are constructed in contexts whose social and ecological dynamics matter. Researchers emphasise the need for progress in integrating non-economic values into urban sustainability analysis, stressing the social, symbolic and cultural dimensions of social and urban life. These non-monetary benefits, considered, either as analytically distinct categories, or, perhaps more significantly, in global assessments of their synergistic benefits, are conspicuously absent from the literature on urban sustainability (Chan et al., 2012). It is the emergent nature of these dimensions of sustainability that comprises critical components of ecological economics' claim to the status of a post-normal science [Chapter 28]. Urban ecosystem assessments currently rely on behavioural assessments, including travel cost, avoided cost, replacement cost and other stated preferences (Gómez-Baggethun and Barton, 2013). Contingent valuation methods are particularly vulnerable to knowledge asymmetries and the construction of values (Spash, 2012). These methods are also highly sensitive to values that privilege existing social disparity. The cumulative consequences of approaches that privileges discrete categories may be an exclusion and undervaluing of consequential determinants of social welfare. In reviewing the literature on urban ecology for this chapter we uncovered very few attempts at addressing and integrating non-economic values into urban ecology.

The high heterogeneity and fragmentation on multiple scales that characterises urban space – coupled with the virtual impossibility of commensurating economic, social and ecological values – makes for an uphill battle in planning for ecological sustainability. Avoidance of the inherent analytic difficulty of this task has had repercussions of almost tragic proportions. Gómez-Baggethun and Barton (2013) join a chorus of voices calling for better methods to capture and articulate non-economic and incommensurable values in urban ecology. The current state of the art in urban ecological economics is a 'multi regional input-output model' (MRIO) put forward by Weinzettel et al. (2014), which combines aspects of the footprint and embodied energy approaches to sustainability assessment. MRIO allocates biomass products to their first users, creating the potential to bring accountability to the first-world drivers of consumption – that is, away from producing regions and into consuming regions. Currently this is the preferred method in use in the literature. Its great strength is that it offers the potential to directly link consuming and producing regions in the global hinterland. As such, it has the potential to unite an 'ecology *of* cities' with an 'ecology *in* cities' (Jansson, 2013).

Scholars engaged with socio-metabolic transition do not mince words about the complexity of operational tools that will be required. Weak sustainability means are a temptation akin to 'low hanging fruit'; unless the rebound of their cost and energy savings is re-invested and amplified by further intervention, their use impedes the ability to reach larger goals. The additive complexities of rebound and backfire have been shown to lead to unintended, unsustainable consequences across place, scale or time. Consensus is building among those working both in biophysical as well as social aspects of ecological economics that, because of social and material rebound effects, the necessary regime change cannot be achieved through the technical fixes of energy or material efficiency (e.g. Polimeni et al., 2009; Saunders, 1992).

Sustainability oriented means are, however, useful and vital components in larger sustainability-oriented processes, which imbed their effects within a succession of larger contexts. We are fortunate to have access to a vast and growing catalogue of weak sustainability means from which to build robust and resilient sustainable city-regions. These tools range from technologies to cultural practices; e.g. tree planting, soil and water conservation, low-energy light bulbs, but also integrative design processes and participatory methods. These means and methods are merely components of larger processes. They are not 'sustainable' in and of themselves, because, even though they may deliver major benefits in a particular place at a particular scale and time, they are placeless technologies. A system thus optimised for efficiency is doomed to accelerated throughput and growth; in contrast, a sustainable urban ecological system would not fall victim to its own success.

Future directions

The need for an analytical inversion

The crucial question posed in the Rio+20 deliberations remains unanswered: how can the special qualities of cities be leveraged to create a sustainable future? Though the tools it currently employs have not yet risen to the immense challenge of urban sustainability, ecological economics is marked by a robust history of envisioning radical reformulations of economic doctrine. We see the full acceptance of pluralist value criteria as a precondition for practicing ecological economics as post-normal science. Yet, no matter how sophisticated its applications, economic tools cannot in and of themselves provide whole solutions. Like neoclassical economics, the discipline's shortcomings cannot be rectified in a placeless space. Sustainability needs a place to happen.

All urban areas are composed of contiguous tracts of land inextricable from the plurality of their multiple connections to one another. Those studying the dynamics of urban consumption have long acknowledged the dependence of cities on an ecological hinterland. By actively validating that sustainability requires *a place to happen*, the sustainable city both provides a place and facilitates the means to arrive at that destination. Here we refer back to the work of Jordan and Fortin (2002) who argued that the emphasis of the discipline on sustainable scale should include topological concerns, that illuminating co-evolutionary dynamics has long been a revolutionary goal of the discipline [see Chapter 13] and that the spatial nature intrinsic to these dynamics is an inescapable aspect of their complexity. The challenge of urban sustainability is to rise to that revolutionary goal by recognising that these dynamics are made possible by relationships of proximity and place (e.g. Stewen, 1998). Rather than staring down a set of abstracted and depoliticised targets to be algorithmically shaved down by degree, urban sustainability will begin with the *city as place*.

As such, new linkages to foundational insights will propel this area of research forward. Daly and Cobb's (1994) early critique of traditional comparative advantage theory has already opened up the space in economic rationality for the promotion of local production on the basis of local sufficiency [see also Chapters 46 and 47]. As the marginalisation and precariousness of the global rural population continue to escalate, Grazi et al. (2007) calls for a renewed urban–rural compact. Rural populations face increasing socioeconomic marginalisation, even as they also ecologically subsidise urban places. Citing the crucial importance of considering the interaction effects among different urban spatial configurations and the dynamics of interregional trade, Grazi et al. (2007) advocate a spatial approach to sustainability. We see an urgent need to go a step further, countervailing the marginalisation of 'place-ness' that characterises the neoliberal condition. The mechanisms through which economic tools accomplish this—disconnection and disembodiment—are also the source of their operational vulnerability. Successful programmes for urban sustainability will emerge from leveraging and nurturing the very desirability of social and ecological connection.

Cities are hubs of linkage and innovation. Urban space positions people and places in proximity, rendering possible the negotiation of relationships at multiple scales. Cities are also nexuses of ecological exchange, pervaded by local ecosystems and living spatial commons, within which each species is continually interacting in a web of mutual influence. Historically 'proto-sustainable cities' drew from limited regional hinterlands, their diversity and resilience continually shifting around dynamic balance points, but always constrained by the limits of local ecology. Historical cities either progressed to greater diversity and stewardship or suffered the consequences: collapse through neglect or exploitation of their social and ecological commons. The placefulness of the city provides a strong field upon which to pursue and apprehend the goal of sustainability.

Ecological economics is now poised to challenge long held neoclassical assumptions about *how* sustainable urban ecologies might exist spatially in a heterogeneous and globalised world— moving beyond the externality-based approach of environmental economics and towards a renewed ecological foundational logic. Rather than seeing harmful consequences as 'externalities' to be compensated for, an ecological logic transcends a utility ranking focused on individual processes. Urban ecology is composed of a web of balance-seeking feedback effects negotiated within a healthy ecosystem. Thus, interdependence prevails over externality, moderating the growth and rebound tendencies of individual systems against overshoot and eventual collapse. Tackling the complexity of urban social and ecological dynamics necessarily requires attention to feedbacks and systemic interactions, pro-social behaviour and material rebound effects. These complex system dynamics are pivotal to an economics of urban sustainability. Crucially, the gravity and extent of interrelated social and ecological problems requires insights from beyond the economic social sciences. This exigence has become an invitation to invert the reductionist analytical priorities around sustainability.

A space for sustainability to happen

Urban communities are special. They contain and magnify the energy and power generated from competing interests, values and opinions negotiating for common identity. Indeed, the diversity of perspective and multiplicity of values that characterise social life in cities should not be seen as problems to be commensurated. Instead, their characteristic dynamism is the very source of creativity that will drive the resilient metabolism of the future sustainable town. Sustainability that is operationalised in a place will be the countervailing force against the unintended consequences of rebound and backfire. When primacy is not granted to economic analysis to rationalise the connections between ecological and social values, a citizen-driven scenario-building process becomes a safe and productive space within which to negotiate these relationships. The inhabitants of a city share a sense of common destiny.

We put forward the city-region as a conceptually strong and functionally operational unit of analysis within which to realise the core values of a truly ecological economics. The future sustainable city-region will not operate on the optimisation of any single criterion. Instead, it will draw on the synthetic power of inverting the analytical primacy of individual weak sustainability means. The sustainable city-region acknowledges the importance of interaction effects—cost-shifting, rebounds and backfire—and harnesses these interactions in the deliberate pursuit of common goals. The complexity of the dynamics occurring at all scales up to and including the city-region render these dynamic synergies possible. The socially and ecologically sustainable city is a safe place for conflict.

Here is an example of how the future sustainable city might operationalise a sustainability problematic. The 'Sustainable Area Budget' (SAB) is a design oriented inversion of the analytical ecological footprint metric that provides the starting point (Yanarella and Levine, 2011). The SAB is the area-based budget within which the sustainable community gains its sustenance, balances out its ecological impacts and on a net basis, and provides for all its major material and energy needs. From within the limits of the SAB, citizen-stakeholders are free to negotiate how they will choose to live within the limits of Nature. As such, the SAB is the master criterion for a process of creative negotiation and deliberative design. Within the SAB, citizens collaborate through an informed, multiple scenario-building process to propose and test potential scenarios for the design, implementation and operation of infrastructure and institutions.

Citizens operationalise the process of a locally contingent and discursively plural sustainability in context through a competitive and collaborative process we call the Sustainable City Game. The Game uses an Informed, Participatory, Balance-Seeking Process, in a particular, local place, bounded by its land resource budget (SAB) that is equity determined in proportion to its population. Diversity is the very source of the game's richness, creativity and complexity as the multiple alternative scenario-building process unfolds. The game facilitates negotiation by providing feedback as to the quantitative and systemic consequences of successive "what-if" trial and error iterations of proposed scenarios. The game process is guided by a Sustainability Engine™, a software library that stores an expansive catalogue of weak sustainability means, as well as aggregated data on an array of ecologically oriented large-scale projects (e.g., Eco-Cities, Transition towns, sustainable city-regions). The Sustainability Engine™ is an intelligent, interactive interface that facilitates the generation of detailed, information-rich models by plugging them into emerging scenarios. The Engine allows for the negotiation of contradictions, feedbacks, synergies, interactions and rebound effects within a catalogue of desired actions (Yanarella and Levine, 2011).

Each iteration of play allows participants to test how the effects of each scenario reverberate through the many other aspects of the physical and social terrain of the city-region. Because sustainability is not a matter of simple optimisation, these scenarios are not technocratically driven. Solutions are generated instead through the interaction of stakeholders and experts as they brainstorm, design and negotiate their emerging proposals. The Sustainable City Game affords researchers, policymakers and other change agents the means for understanding sustainability in a manner that goes beyond individual metrics. In principle, everything is negotiable—except equity and ecology. Proposed scenarios are viable as long as, on a net basis, they export no harmful imbalances beyond their territory or into the future. Through the playing of the game, the sustainable city becomes an attractor, eliciting viewers' ideas and critiques, as well as the interests of governments, agencies, industries, investors and trust funds.

The Sustainable City Game re-envisions the sustainable city as an ongoing design process, where the influences of small local changes can be projected through competing scenarios. The resulting sustainable city is amenable to immediate and meaningful feedback as a participatory democratic planning process. Each successive round of play brings forward the best models and sub-models, which in turn persist and are folded into competing scenarios. As the weakest models fall away, the surviving scenarios each get better, more complex, more inclusive and more balanced and will come closer to working within the boundaries of the Sustainable Area Budget (see chapter 6 in Yanarella and Levine, 2011).

Concluding remarks

The Sustainable City Game is a socially mediated technology of optimisation. It is an analytical inversion that privileges equity, social and ecological values. In providing a systems framework for the negotiation of sustainability oriented actions, power is given to communities to negotiate decisions without having to make unacceptable compromises. As such, the process of negotiating sustainability at the scale of the city-region is a process of implementing the values of social ecological economics. Rather than working from the 'old' economics of allocative efficiency and attempting to reintegrate social and ecological concerns by selling short-term 'win-wins', the Sustainability Game and Sustainable Area Budget offer a programme and process for urban design that achieves sustainability in allocation, distribution and scale. This comprehensive plan for urban sustainability hinges on citizens taking ownership of place. Because social and cultural needs are not essentially quantities or even quantifiable, they are privileged as the principal drivers of the entire process.

The sustainable city-region is effective as an alternative vehicle for the realisation of sustainability. In providing the operational space and base from which to synthesise a programme that works from first principles, the sustainable city-region is completely in line with the normative commitments of ecological economics. It is the smallest appropriate scale within which it is possible to adequately account for major material and social interactions, ecological impacts and dependencies of a human community and its ecologically dedicated hinterland— the core problem of urban sustainability.

Key further readings cited

Ernstson, H. and Sörlin, S. (2013). Ecosystem services as technology of globalization: On articulating values in urban nature. *Ecological Economics* 86(February), 274–284.

Gómez-Baggethun, E. and Barton, D.N. (2013). Classifying and valuing ecosystem services for urban planning. *Ecological Economics* 86(February), 235–245.

Grazi, F., van den Bergh, J.C.J.M. and Rietveld, P. (2007). Spatial welfare economics versus ecological footprint: Modeling agglomeration, externalities and trade. *Environmental and Resource Economics* 38(1), 135–153.

Jordan, G. J. and Fortin, M.-J. (2002). Scale and topology in the ecological economics sustainability paradigm. *Ecological Economics* 41(2), 361–366.

Yanarella, E J. and Levine, R.S. (2011). *The City as Fulcrum of Global Sustainability*. London: New York: Anthem Press.

Other literature cited

Boezeman, D., Leroy, P., Maas, R. and Kruitwagen, S. (2010). The (limited) political influence of ecological economics: A case study on Dutch environmental policies. *Ecological Economics* 69(9), 1756–1764.

Bolund, P. and Hunhammar, S. (1999). Ecosystem services in urban areas. *Ecological Economics* 29(2), 293–301.

Boyd, J. and Banzhaf, S. (2007). What are ecosystem services? The need for standardized environmental accounting units. *Ecological Economics* 63(2–3), 616–626.

Brown, M. and Ulgiati, S. (1997). Emergy-based indices and ratios to evaluate sustainability: monitoring economies and technology toward environmentally sound innovation. *Ecological Engineering* 9(1–2), 51–69.

Chan, K. M. A., Satterfield, T. and Goldstein, J. (2012). Rethinking ecosystem services to better address and navigate cultural values. *Ecological Economics* 74, 8–18.

Daly, H.E., Cobb, J.B. and Cobb, C.W. (1994). *For the Common Good: Redirecting the Economy Toward Community, the Environment and a Sustainable Future* (2nd ed.). Boston: Beacon Press.

Esty, D.C. and Porter, M.E. (2005). National environmental performance: an empirical analysis of policy results and determinants. *Environment and Development Economics* 10(4), 381–389.

Gowdy, J. (2005). Toward a new welfare economics for sustainability. *Ecological Economics* 53(2), 211–222.

Jansson, Å. (2013). Reaching for a sustainable, resilient urban future using the lens of ecosystem services. *Ecological Economics* 86, 285–291.

Kapp, K.W. (1978). 'The Nature and Significance of Social Costs'. In: Kapp, K.W. (ed). *The Social Costs of Business Enterprise, 3rd edition*. Nottingham: Spokesman, 13-27.

Kocsis, T. (2014). Is the Netherlands sustainable as a global-scale inner-city? Intenscoping spatial sustainability. *Ecological Economics* 101(May), 103–114.

Martinez-Alier, J., Munda, G. and O'Neill, J. (1998). Weak comparability of values as a foundation for ecological economics. *Ecological Economics* 26(3), 277–286.

Miller, J.R. (2005). Biodiversity conservation and the extinction of experience. *Trends in Ecology and Evolution* 20(8), 430–434.

Moffatt, S. and Kohler, N. (2008). Conceptualizing the built environment as a social–ecological system. *Building Research and Information* 36(3), 248–268.

Norgaard, R.B. (2010). Ecosystem services: From eye-opening metaphor to complexity blinder. *Ecological Economics* 69(6), 1219–1227.

Polimeni, J., Mayumi, K., Giampietro, M. and Alcott, B. (2009). *The Myth of Resource Efficiency : The Jevons Paradox*. London: Earthscan.

Rees, W.E. (1992). Ecological footprints and appropriated carrying capacity: what urban economics leaves out. *Environment and Urbanization* 4(2), 121–130.

Saunders, H.D. (1992). The Khazzoom-Brookes Postulate and Neoclassical Growth. *Energy Journal* 13(4), 131–148.

Siche, J.R., Agostinho, F., Ortega, E. and Romeiro, A. (2008). Sustainability of nations by indices: Comparative study between environmental sustainability index, ecological footprint and the emergy performance indices. *Ecological Economics* 66(4), 628–637.

Spash, C.L. (2012). New foundations for ecological economics. *Ecological Economics* 77(May), 36–47.

Spash, C.L. and Aslaksen, I. (2015). Re-establishing an ecological discourse in the policy debate over how to value ecosystems and biodiversity. *Journal of Environmental Management* 159 (August), 245–253.

Stewen, M. (1998). Discussion. *Ecological Economics* 27(2), 119–130.

Swyngedouw, E. (2011). Depoliticized environments: The end of nature, climate change and the post-political condition. *Royal Institute of Philosophy Supplement* 69(October), 253–274.

Tidball, K.G. and Krasny, M.E. (eds.). (2014). *Greening in the Red Zone: Disaster, Resilience and Community Greening* (1. ed). Dordrecht: Springer.

UN Habitat, 2004. *Urban Indicators Guidelines: Monitoring the Habitat Agenda and the Millennium Development Goals.* Nairobi, Kenya: United Nations Human Settlement Programme.

Wallace, K.J. (2007). Classification of ecosystem services: Problems and solutions. *Biological Conservation* 139(3–4), 235–246.

Weaver, R.C. (2013). Re-framing the urban blight problem with trans-disciplinary insights from ecological economics. *Ecological Economics* 90(June), 168–176.

Weinzettel, J., Steen-Olsen, K., Hertwich, E.G., Borucke, M. and Galli, A. (2014). Ecological footprint of nations: Comparison of process analysis and standard and hybrid multiregional input–output analysis. *Ecological Economics* 101(May), 115–126.

49

ECO-SOCIAL ENTERPRISES

Nadia Johanisova and Eva Fraňková

Introduction

A transition to an equitable and sustainable degrowth society (D'Alisa et al., 2015) calls for a re-thinking of conceptualisations of the economy and of the enterprise as well as for practical changes on the ground. While some—such as Fotopoulos [see Chapter 44]—have advocated abolishing private property, markets and money altogether, we take a more practical view. We envision seeds of the future by looking at enterprises and forms of provisioning in the here-and-now that do not comply with the mainstream model of the firm [Chapter 19], nor do they mesh easily within the capitalist growth paradigm.

The chapter opens with a discussion of mainstream and alternative conceptualisations of the enterprise and of the economy. Next, we turn to an overview of existing forms of eco-social enterprises and of their framings within different discourses and schools of thought. After giving some examples, we discuss five dimensions of a broad definition of eco-social enterprise, based on the literature and our own empirical research.

The economy and the enterprise in orthodox and alternative economics

A central part of the narrative of orthodox economic theory is the enterprise as a capitalist firm operating in a generalised and abstract market and producing goods and services to be consumed by utility maximising consumers and measured in money terms. Firms are assumed to be guided by self-interest and their success is measured by the scale of annual profits flowing to owners. They are also expected to grow in terms of output and assets and to aim for efficiency, seen as maximising outputs and minimising inputs. The economy, in this discourse, is the world where such firms operate and create wealth. In this chapter, we will refer to such an ontological perspective as 'market logic'. The theory of the firm, and the wider perspective of which it is a part, have been criticised for decades [see Chapter 19]. Orthodox economists can be found offering critiques (e.g., Ackerman and Nadal, 2004; Hill and Myatt, 2010: 46–168). Others, writing from more heterodox positions, have emphasised the role of unexamined assumptions in shaping the orthodox economic narrative of the firm.

Most notably, Karl Polanyi (2001 [1944]) criticised the narrative of a beneficial, self-regulating and naturally emerging global market, divorced from local culture, geography, tradition, environmental constraints and power relations [Chapter 14]. His analysis drew upon critical institutionalism [Chapter 3], history and cultural anthropology to discredit the assertion that humans are inherently prone to profit-led exchange, an assumption colouring orthodox economics since Adam Smith. Polanyi (2001 [1944]: 46, 48, 60) showed that, on the contrary, historically markets were localised and embedded in wider economies that were in their turn embedded in social systems constrained by social norms and a community ethos. Such social norms were antithetic to a market logic of profit maximisation and included a belief in a just economy, or as economic historian E.P. Thompson (2013 [1963]: 72) called it, "a moral economy". To give just one illustration of its manifestations, during uprisings in Ireland and England in the late eighteenth century, often led by women, over-priced bread, grain or butter was taken from sellers and sold at what was deemed a fair price to consumers. The proceeds were then returned by the rebels to the original sellers (Thompson, 2013 [1963]: 67–75).

The belief in a moral or social economy, immersed in social relationships and constrained by moral considerations, has never really gone away (Beer, 1953: 203; Clark and Johansson, 2016). The negative impacts of enterprises driven by the market logic on Nature and society have been recognised for some time (Kapp, 1975), and as they become clearer new critiques have been emerging. Ecofeminist political economist Mary Mellor (2006: 141) has critiqued "the economy, as it has become known in the west" as "carved out of the complexity of the whole of human and non-human existence" and as leaving aside the workings of natural systems, domestic work and non-market economies [see also Chapter 5]. Social geographers Gibson-Graham et al. (2013: 54) have argued that wealth is created by enterprises at the expense of Nature, workers, their families and wider communities, whose survival needs are implicated. Accepting this position, the argument is then that the proceeds of this wealth be re-invested in the ecosystems and communities whose wealth (often described as capitals) enabled the production in the first place.

To exit the orthodox reductionist conceptualisation of the economy, an ontological reframing has been underway for some time in heterodox economic literature. Summarising these new conceptualisations, Dash (2014: 11) describes the economy as "the ways people organise themselves collectively to make a living, and the ways a society organises itself to (re) produce its material life and well-being". Such a reframing of the concept of the economy does not aim to subsume new realms to the market logic. On the contrary, it highlights the limitations of such an approach in the face of a complex reality and questions its ontology and epistemology (Dash, 2014). Importantly, it broadens the economy to include, on the one hand, provisioning and caring activities outside the monetised sphere—such as subsistence, do-it-yourself, care for children and elders, work in the household and neighbourhood reciprocity (Bennholdt-Thomsen and Mies, 1999; Gibson-Graham et al., 2013: 7–15)—and, on the other hand, alternative economic entities in the liminal zones between market, State, community and commons, between profit and non-profit and between the monetised and non-monetised spheres of human provisioning (Johanisova et al., 2013: 10–11). These entities are the eco-social enterprises to which we turn next.

Eco-social enterprise: both old and new

Although often hailed as innovative and alternative, eco-social enterprises are not a new phenomenon. As part of the moral economy, they are as old as the hills. Medieval craft guilds and nineteenth-century co-operatives are historical examples (with many of the latter still operating in the twenty-first century), while traditional commons [see Chapter 38] are still very much with us. City gardens and allotments, communal burial societies, rotating credit and savings associations, informal Islamic money transfer systems, or solidarity networks enabling the livelihoods of slum dwellers in African cities (Latouche, 2007, chapter 6); these are only the tip of the iceberg of 'another economy' that remains invisible from the vantage point of the mainstream economics. As demonstrated in a case study from the Philippines, once the economy is reframed to include non-market and other alternative provisioning pathways and livelihoods, such existing diverse and non-capitalist economies can sometimes be rescued from oblivion (Gibson et al., 2010).

At the same time, there has been a burgeoning of new eco-social enterprises (often with a co-operative organisational structure). These can include: village transport systems; local food markets and community supported agriculture schemes; local currency systems and barter networks; communal organic farms and ecosystem regeneration initiatives; community radios, schools, gardens and cafés; work-integration social enterprises; producer, consumer, credit and renewable energy co-operatives; trading branches of non-profits; community land trusts; left-wing political squatters' communities; social banks, and many others. Although at times conceptualised as part of a third or fourth sector (Ridley-Duff and Bull, 2016: 38, 43), eco-social enterprises blur distinctions between sectors and can form hybrids, mutual linkages and umbrella groups.

Since the pioneering work mapping the alternative economy (e.g. Douthwaite, 1996), research interest has increased dramatically. Regional and national overviews have been emerging, e.g. Conill et al. (2012) for Catalonia or Welzer et al. (2014) for Germany. International research networks have also sprung up, such as the EMES International Research Network (http://emes.net) and the Community Economies Collective (CEC) and Community Economies Research Network (CERN) (www.communityeconomies.org).

What is an eco-social enterprise?

The concept itself, like much else in the field, is contested. The institutions of the alternative economy have been variously described, including designations such as: community enterprise (Douthwaite, 1996: 341), community economy (Gibson-Graham et al., 2013), (social) solidarity economy (D'Alisa et al., 2015: 154–155; Lewis and Conaty, 2012: 30–32), alternative economic spaces (Leysholn et al., 2003), social enterprise (Borzaga and Defourny, 2001), and eco-social enterprise (Johanisova and Fraňková, 2013). Of these, the discourse of social enterprise (with social economy sometimes used as a synonym) has been the most academically prolific and influential. Espoused by the EMES network and growing mainly from European intellectual roots, the concepts have entered the European Union (EU) political discourse, and organisations seen as social enterprises have garnered public funding at EU and national levels (European Commission, 2014). While defining social enterprise is an ongoing process (Ridley-Duff and Bull, 2016, chapter 2), most definitions focus on three aspects: (i) democratic governance structures and stakeholder governance involvement, (ii) an explicit public benefit aim, and (iii) some restrictions on profit/surplus distribution (Borzaga and Defourny, 2001; European Commission, 2014).

A weakness of the social enterprise discourse is its lack of a deeper critical approach to the mainstream economic ontology. Many texts on social enterprise accept the capitalist growth paradigm and its theoretical underpinnings and see social enterprises merely as a vehicle for generating employment and providing services to socially excluded groups. In their analysis of paths to sustainable welfare in a future degrowth society in Europe, Clark and Johansson (2016) caution against such reductionism, and against using the social enterprise concept as an instrument to legitimise neoliberal policies of privatising and out-sourcing welfare services. Rather, deeper reforms, as well as investment, is required on the part of governments to support a social economy, in the Polanyian sense, within all sectors of the economy (Clark and Johansson, 2016; Ridley-Duff and Bull, 2016: 39–42).

Others, coming from social geography and post-development perspectives, often drawing on Marxian analysis, have been explicitly critical of the mainstream economic paradigm. They seek to dismantle the hegemonic status of neoliberal discourse and to "take back the economy" (Gibson-Graham et al., 2013) by researching and actively promoting non-capitalist modes of economic reproduction and alternative economic spaces (Leysholn et al., 2003: 9). The CEC and CERN website, focusing on community economies, has emerged from this stream of thought. Topics vary from analyses of community supported agriculture (Cameron, 2015) to household work practices and traditional reciprocal and subsistence forms of provisioning (Leysholn et al., 2003, chapter 7; Gibson et al., 2010). Compared with the social enterprise model, an initiative does not have to operate in a monetised economy, be incorporated, produce and sell goods and services, or aim towards paid employment, in order qualify as an alternative economic space or a community economy (see Johanisova and Fraňková, 2013: 117 for a fuller discussion of this).

A weakness of some of this literature is a lack of critical engagement with mainstream economic concepts, with structure, finance and governance and with environmental concerns and limits. Although this is slowly changing, the literature linking the environmental crisis with eco-social enterprise remains sparse. Kothari (2009) has repeatedly argued that an ecologically centred vision calls for multifaceted support of surviving nonindustrial livelihoods, rather than for enhancing industrialised production modes, and has been active in documenting existing alternative economic spaces in India (http://kalpavriksh.org/index.php/alternatives). Lewis and Conaty (2012) have linked eco-social enterprise with combating climate change and progressing to a steady-state economy [Chapter 45]. Johanisova and Fraňková (2013) discuss the possible environmental dimensions of eco-social enterprises, including their financial and organisational governance structure, which arguably makes them less vulnerable to the growth imperative. Jackson and Victor (2013, chapter 4) look at community enterprises. By and large, however, in view of the rapid expansion of the movement (see e.g. the website of the RIPESS, The Intercontinental Network for the Promotion of Social Solidarity Economy, http://www.ripess.org), we may agree with Dash (2014: 6) that what we have here is a "practice in search of a theory". Especially a theory linking eco-social enterprises with the wider social ecological economics discourse.

Five examples of eco-social enterprise

The following five examples of eco-social enterprises, taken from the literature and our own research, are a small illustration of the myriad forms such enterprises can take.

Hostětín apple-juice plant (Czech Republic)

This is an enterprise established in 2000 in a village by the Slovakian border with the aim of creating a market for locally grown rare old apple varieties. Its foundation was aided by several grants and a loan from an ethical bank. It has since been producing high quality apple juice for local and national markets. The land and building of the plant are leased from a foundation that uses the income for grant funding. The plant itself is a business enterprise owned by a local association of non-profit organisations, and retained profits are earmarked for investment into the cultural and natural biodiversity in the region (Johanisova, 2005).

Appin community co-operative (Scotland)

This is a co-operative established in 1984 by people in a rural area in Western Scotland who took over the management of the local village shop threatened by closure. It has a membership of 250 (about half the local population) each of whom pays a one-time share of £50, and is entitled to one vote at meetings. The co-operative has a charitable arm, the Appin Community Trust, which receives funds primarily from profits from the village shop. This money has been used for many local projects over the years, such as rebuilding the shop and a local bridge and reflooring the village hall. Parts of the profits also go to a medical fund managed by the Trust that supplies residents with medical equipment and care not covered by the UK National Health Service (Johanisova, 2005; McNicol, 2015).

WyeCycle (England)

This enterprise, based in Wye, started out in 1989 as a Friends of the Earth group, and ran until 2013. It gradually became financially self-sufficient, with income from local authorities and from its own trading (e.g. selling glass, paper and compost). Its focus was on waste minimisation and it organised not only a kerbside recycling service in the area, but also local food projects and a community farm (all seen as paths to waste prevention). In addition, it ran a composting scheme, a furniture reuse centre and monthly swap-days of unwanted objects. It also employed several locals, with employment and social concerns gradually becoming an explicit goal of its operation. Its legal form was "company limited by guarantee", a non-profit business model (Johanisova, 2005). WyeCycle ended operations after the borough council signed a contract with a large commercial recycling firm.

Nayakrishi Andolon (Bangladesh)

This is an organic farmers' movement, which originated near Tangail in central Bangladesh in 1988 and now has over 300,000 members. Its members have been giving up industrial farming to improve their communities' health as well as soil fertility and biodiversity and to escape debt spirals that had forced many to sell their land. They have shifted from outside inputs and monoculture to composting, nitrogen-fixing plants, local varieties of crops and animal breeds and mixed cropping. An important part of the project is a seed saving network. Seeds are saved in households, with a shared seed centre in villages and several regional seed banks, storing thousands of local varieties of crop. Care for seeds requires sophisticated knowledge traditionally kept by women, and a renewal of this tradition has increased their status. From the beginning, the movement has been supported by the local non-profit organisation Policy Research for Development Alternative (UBINIG) that has facilitated knowledge sharing between the communities (http://ubinig.org/index.php/network/userNayakrishi/english).

Soninké blacksmiths (Mauretania)

The trade of traditional blacksmiths of the Soninké people in West Africa was largely destroyed in the early twentieth century by cheap imports from Europe. However, a small community of Soninké blacksmiths have continued to produce high-quality, low-priced axes, hoes, rakes and other tools as well as kitchen utensils for the local agricultural community in Kaedi, a town near the Senegal border. The community comprised 25 workshops with 60 master blacksmiths and 160 helpers, as of 1991 (Latouche, 2007: 142). They use cheap inputs such as scrap metal and make most of their own tools themselves. The workshops are in their own homes and wares are sold (sometimes for payment in-kind) at the local market, in the workshop or directly (i.e., made to order). Families grow their own food and supplement incomes by sales of crops, woodworking and dyeing of fabrics. Though incorporated as a co-operative since 1984, elders of wider families remain the key decision-makers (Latouche, 2007, chapter 4).

Dimensions defining an eco-social enterprise

Reflection upon and analysis of a broader range of eco-social enterprises, as exemplified above, allows key characteristics to be defined. We identify five dimensions of eco-social enterprises, drawing on existing definitions and on our own research, namely: (i) other-than-profit goals, (ii) using profits to replenish Nature and community, (iii) democratic and localised ownership and governance patterns, (iv) rootedness in place and time, and (v) non-market production, exchange or provisioning patterns.

Other-than-profit goals

As opposed to the capitalist firm, the founding documents of many eco-social enterprises contain explicit social, cultural and/or environmental aims, often interlinked. A primary non-financial motive is evident in the operations of the Hostětín, Appin and WyeCycle projects.

Similarly, the Nayakrishi communities have blended the goal of securing local livelihoods with the goal of systemic support for their natural environment, which directly provides for their sustenance in terms of food, fuel, building materials and medicine. The extractive relationship between resource (land) and producer (farmer) as assumed by the market logic gives way to another ontology: farming as a reciprocal nurturing relationship between human and natural communities. Within such a subsistence perspective (Bennholt-Thomsen and Mies, 1999) profit loses its importance or disappears altogether.

Compared with the Nayakrishi farmers, who have explicit ideological principles and are in conscious opposition to the mainstream economy, the Soninké blacksmiths are what Smith and Jehlička (2013) designate as "quiet sustainability"; there is no conscious effort to be different from or go counter to the mainstream. They do what they have always done (as members of a traditional blacksmith caste), while adapting to the present in order to sustain their livelihoods. As in many traditional commons regimes, the primary goals are sustainable and equitable livelihoods for the community, rather than profit for individual members or growth of their production.

Using profit/surplus to replenish Nature and community

As we have seen, critics have been calling for profit (or surplus) to be at least partly returned to the communities, both natural and human, that enabled its creation. Such an approach, aside from its obviously positive environmental and social implications, can also be seen as a brake on capital accumulation and the growth imperative. So what happens when an eco-social enterprise creates a financial surplus at the end of the year? This depends on its organisational structure and often also on the ethical commitment and decisions of its members. In the case of non-profit organisational structures, no profit can be distributed to members by virtue of the inner rules and institutional structure. In the case of a trading branch of a non-profit organisation, like the Hostětín apple juice plant, profits are used for public benefit as defined by the rules of the non-profit organisation.

The situation can be more ambivalent under other organisational structures, such as co-operatives. Co-operatives, and some other types of eco-social enterprise, are often able to distribute profits to members. However, if grant funding is a priority, they might decide to opt for 'asset-lock' status. This means that only a stipulated part of their profits can be re-distributed. In the event of the organisation closing down operations, its assets are transferred to another organisation with non-profit or asset-lock status. In the case of the Appin co-operative, its members decided to waive all dividends and use their surplus for mutually agreed local projects, beneficial to the whole community, via their Community Trust Fund. Other eco-social enterprises may discuss and negotiate the issue of surplus distribution, sometimes using it (or part of it) to support the start-up of other eco-social enterprises, or to cross-subsidise their own activities that would otherwise be financially unviable (Johanisova, 2005; Cameron, 2015).

Democratic and localised ownership and governance patterns

An important dimension of eco-social enterprises is an emphasis on democratic governance structures. This can take the form of a board of directors elected by members on a one-member-one-vote principle (e.g. the Appin co-operative), or of a self-perpetuating board of trustees, not elected directly by members, but rather chosen to represent different stakeholders (e.g. the Hostětín project).

In some cases the two modes (elected and appointed board members) may be combined, as with community land trusts. This is a type of American and British eco-social enterprise that takes land out of the market and puts it into community ownership in order to provide affordable housing, services, or land for local farming. A community land trust will typically have one-third of its board formed by representatives of tenants, one-third by representatives of the wider community, and the last third appointed to represent the public interest (Lewis and Conaty, 2012: 90). In some eco-social enterprises, such as the Argentinian worker-occupied factory Zanón, economic democracy takes the shape of all workers taking part in decisions directly, rotating positions of responsibility and receiving the same salary (Gibson-Graham et al., 2013: 51–53).

Governance is closely linked to ownership and indeed many eco-social enterprises are owned by their members. As opposed to mainstream firms with distant shareholders, these are often local people committed to the enterprise on a long-term basis. A democratic governance structure combined with a lack of obligation to maximise shareholder value may enable eco-social enterprises to step out of the market logic and aspire to serve the common good.

Rootedness in place and time

All the eco-social enterprises in the case studies have a strong and long-term commitment to their local area. For example, the Soninké blacksmiths use agricultural land on a commons basis and "depending on the importance of their rights, calculated according to the land they used before" (Latouche, 2007: 145). A strong link to land is a feature of many ecosystem regeneration projects and of traditional commons regimes [Chapter 38]. Here, as with community land trusts, we often find a rootedness in time as well as in place, with land seen not as a commodity (Polanyi, 2001 [1944], chapter 15), but rather as heritage involving the obligation of stewardship on behalf of future generations.

An aspect of the localised character of many eco-social enterprises with a strong environmental dimension is economic localisation. Douthwaite (1996: 42) has termed this "short-circuiting", while the degrowth movement speaks of "re-localisation" (see also Frankova and Johanisova,

2012; and [Chapter 47]). The idea of shortening links between producers and consumers in order to tread more lightly upon the Earth, and to rebuild local communities, lies behind many eco-social enterprise projects, especially those focused on food, e.g. the Hostětín and WyeCycle projects. It is especially evident in the Nayakrishi movement, where previously unsustainable open loops of fertiliser, seeds and pesticides have either been eliminated (pesticides) or closed (fertiliser, seeds).

Non-market production, exchange or provisioning patterns

Eco-social enterprises step out of the market logic through their commitment to other-than-profit goals and limits on profit distribution. However, many go further and operate in the non-market and even non-monetised economy. Examples of the latter are the Nayakrishi farmers and the Soninké blacksmiths growing their own food, while the blacksmiths also make their own tools. Traditional commons regimes are another vast sphere where provisioning often takes the form of subsistence.

Co-operatives, whose remit is to serve their members, rather than maximise profits, are well-placed to defy market logic. Some, like the Cooperativa Integral Catalana (CIC) operating in the Spanish province of Catalonia, straddle the non-market and non-monetised economies, with members' shares paid in Euros, in local community currencies or by a specified number of work-hours. Konzum, a Czech consumer co-operative, sources dairy, bakery and other products from small local producers, despite the fact that they would be cheaper from a wholesaler. The reasons given are support for local enterprises and employment in the area where its 4,000 members live. Other examples of non-market approaches might be emphasis on a fair price for producers as well as consumers, as in community supported agriculture projects, and investment focusing on socially and environmentally useful projects rather than on financial gain (Clark and Johansson, 2016), as practiced by ethical finance institutions.

Future directions

The activities, approaches and principles of eco-social enterprises appear to chime with the operational goals of social ecological economics, as suggested by Spash (2011: 360): "achieving sustained human well-being on the basis of the maintained health and functioning of Earth's ecosystems". However, surrounded as they are by a global economy, operating on principles that are quite different, they remain fragile and vulnerable. Therefore it is important to understand the power differentials involved [Chapter 14], and the dimension of resistance [Chapter 17], implicitly present within many eco-social enterprises. Promoting policies supportive of a social economy and economic localisation at international, national and local levels is crucial (Jackson and Victor, 2013; Clark and Johansson, 2016). So is support for an eco-social enterprise infrastructure (e.g., enabling organisations such as UBINIG, ethical finance institutions) and for their linkages and mutual support (Johanisova et al., 2013). Academically, an opportunity arises here to name and discuss the hidden assumptions behind different conceptualisations of eco-social enterprise and the epistemological and ontological implications of such assumptions (Dash, 2014). This could provide an impetus towards achieving an integrating interdisciplinary heterodox economic approach within the discipline of ecological economics (Spash, 2011).

Concluding remarks

We have discussed alternative conceptualisations of the enterprise and the economy to give an overview of existing eco-social enterprises and summary of current thinking on the topic. As existing economic entities that deviate in their goals, structure and operations from the mainstream firm discussed in economic textbooks, eco-social enterprises can be seen as important constituent parts of a future more equitable and sustainable post-growth/degrowth society. In concluding let us make three points. First, one thing that emerges from this analysis is that the term 'eco-social enterprise' is contested and many other concepts can be and are used to designate such projects. However, these institutions are united by the five common characteristics that we identified: other-than-profit goals, limits on surplus distribution, democratic ownership, rootedness in place and time, and non-market practices. Second, while movements explicitly espousing such principles have been to some extent registered on research radars and analysed from various perspectives, there remains a silent, other economy of non-industrialised, traditional eco-social enterprises that can equally be seen as harbingers of the future, yet can be passed over because they have strong roots in the past. Third, eco-social enterprises have been under-theorised within ecological economics, despite their strong economic and environmental dimensions. More attention to this topic would be rewarding both intellectually and in terms of expanding the imaginary regarding other enterprises and economies, more in tune with a social ecological future economy.

Key further readings cited

Dash, A. (2014). *Towards an Epistemological Foundation for Social and Solidarity Economy*. Occasional Paper 3. United Nations Research Institute for Social Development.

Douthwaite, R. (1996). *Short Circuit: Strengthening Local Economies for Security in an Unstable World*. Dublin: Lilliput Press.

Gibson-Graham, J.K., Cameron, J., Healy, S. (2013). *Take Back the Economy: An Ethical Guide for Transforming our Communities*. Minneapolis: University of Minnesota Press.

Johanisova, N. and Franková, E. (2013). Eco-Social Enterprises in Practice and Theory. In M. Anastasiadis (ed.). *ECO-WISE Social Enterprises as Sustainable Actors: Concepts, Performances, Impacts* (pp. 110–129). Bremen: Europäischer Hochschulverlag GmbHandCo.

Lewis, M. and Conaty, P. (2012). *The Resilience Imperative: Cooperative Transitions to a Steady-State Economy*. Gabriola Island, Canada: New Society Publishers.

Other literature cited

Ackerman, F. and Nadal, A. (2004). *The Flawed Foundations of General Equilibrium*. Abingdon, UK: Routledge.

Beer, M. (1953). *A History of British Socialism*. London: Allen and Unwin.

Bennholdt-Thomsen, V. and Mies, M. (1999). *The Subsistence Perspective: Beyond the Globalised Economy*. London: Zed Books.

Borzaga, C. and Defourny, J. (2001). *The Emergence of Social Enterprise*. Abingdon: Routledge.

Cameron, J. (2015). Enterprise Innovation and Economic Diversity in Community Supported Agriculture: Sustaining the Agricultural Commons. In Roelvink, G., K. St. Martin and J. K. Gibson-Graham (eds.). *Making Other Worlds Possible: Performing Diverse Economies* (pp. 53–71). Minneapolis: Minnesota University Press.

Clark, E. and Johansson, H. (2016). Social Economy and Green Social Enterprises: Production for Sustainable Welfare. In M. Koch and O. Mont (eds.). *Sustainability and the Political Economy of Welfare* (pp. 158–170). London: Routledge.

Conill, J, Cardenas, A., Castells, M., Hlebik, S., Servon, L. (2012). *Otra Vida es Posible: Prácticas Económicas Alternativas Durante la Crisis*. Barcelona: Editorial UOC.

D'Alisa, G., Demaria, F., Kallis, G. (2015). *Degrowth: A Vocabulary for a New Era*. Abingdon: Routledge.

European Commission (2014). *A Map of Social Enterprises and their Eco-Systems in Europe*. Brussels: European Commission.

Frankova, E., Johanisova, N. (2012). Economic localization revisited. *Environmental Policy and Governance* (22), 307–321.

Gibson, K., Cahill, A., McKay, D. (2010). Rethinking the dynamics of rural transformation: Performing different development pathways in a Philippine municipality. *Transactions of the Institute of British Geographers* 35(2), 235–255.

Hill, R. and Myatt, T. (2010). *The Economics Anti-Textbook: A Critical Thinker's Guide to Micro-Economics*. Halifax: Fernwood.

Jackson, T. and Victor, P. (2013). *Green Economy at Community Scale*. Report for Metcalf Foundation, Canada.

Johanisova, N. (2005). *Living in the Cracks: A Look at Rural Social Enterprises in Britain and the Czech Republic*. Dublin: Feasta.

Johanisova, N., Crabtree, T., Fraňková, E. (2013). Social enterprises and non-market capitals: a path to degrowth? *Journal of Cleaner Production* 38(1), 7–16.

Kapp, K.W. (1975). *The Social Costs of Private Enterprise*. New York: Schocken Books.

Kothari, A. (2009). A sympathetic critique of the Badhuri-Patkar model. *Economic and Political Weekly* 19 (12), 77–78.

Latouche, S. (2007). *La Otra África: Autogestión y Apaño Frente al Mercado Global*. Barcelona: Oozebap.

Leysholn, A., Lee, R., Williams, C.C. (2003). *Alternative Economic Spaces*. London: Sage.

McNicol, I. (2015). Founder and long-term chairman, Appin Community Co-operative, e-mail communication with N.J., 2.8.2015 and 3.8.2015.

Mellor, M. (2006). Ecofeminist political economy. *International Journal of Green Economics* 1(1/2), 139–150.

Polanyi, K. (2001 [1944]). *The Great Transformation: The Political and Economic Origins of Our Time*. Boston: Beacon Press.

Ridley-Duff, R. and Bull, M. (2016). *Understanding Social Enterprise: Theory and Practice*. Los Angeles: Sage.

Smith, J. and Jehlička, P. (2013). Quiet sustainability: Fertile lessons from Europe's productive gardeners. *Journal of Rural Studies* 32(4), 148–157.

Spash, C. (2011). Social ecological economics: Understanding the past to see the future. *American Journal of Economics and Sociology* 70(2), 340–375.

Thompson, E.P. (2013 [1963]). *The Making of the English Working Class*. London: Penguin.

Welzer, H., Giesecke, D., Tremel, L. (2014). *Futurzwei Zukunftsalmanach 2015/16: Geschichten vom guten Umgang mit der Welt*. Frankfurt: Fischer Verlag.

50

DEMOCRACY, PARTICIPATION AND SOCIAL PLANNING

Fikret Adaman and Pat Devine

Introduction

This chapter discusses how, in a future post-growth eco-socialist society, democratic and participatory social planning can address the social, ecological, economic and political challenges facing the world. The capitalist system produces both social injustice and ecological degradation, which together and separately give rise to social economic struggles and ecological conflicts. Since the political economy of capitalist structures depends on capital accumulation and economic growth, continuing resource depletion and environmental degradation without limit are inevitable. Attempts to make the capitalist system 'Greener' are futile when it comes to dealing with ecological pressures, given that the development of Green technology itself provides a new domain for further capital accumulation. Furthermore, the capitalist system necessarily creates inequalities and social conflict, which interact with ecological conflicts among different groups within and/or among nation States. Fortunately, another world is possible, a post-growth eco-socialist world, based on social ownership and participatory planning. The rest of this chapter sets out the institutional architecture and social processes on which such a society might be based.

The socialist concept of common ownership of the means of production and the ecological concept of stewardship of the commons converge in the need to transform private property into social property. However, while this is a necessary condition for achieving social control over economic activity and a sustainable relationship between human activity and non-human Nature, it is not a sufficient condition. It goes a long way in overcoming direct exploitation and it makes a start in enabling people to participate in exercising control over their immediate provisioning and productive activities, but it does not in itself overcome the anarchy of production, the result of atomistic decision-making that gives rise to outcomes that no one wished. Atomistic decision-making is bound to be hostile to ecological stewardship. It underlies the erroneous concept of the inevitability of "the tragedy of the commons" [see Chapter 38], with atomised decision makers pursuing their narrow self-interest without regard to the degrading effect of their combined decisions on the commons as a whole. Social ownership needs to be combined with participatory planning in order to coordinate interdependent decisions and consciously shape them in accordance with society's values and priorities.

Reliance on the market mechanism for decisions pertaining to investment and disinvestment, even if based on some form of social property as in most contemporary models of 'market socialism', cannot overcome the anarchy of production and does not provide a framework for conscious social decision-making in relation to human flourishing and ecological sustainability. Participatory planning should be distinguished from top-down, hierarchical technocratic planning and from computer-based iterative models seeking to aggregate the preferences of individuals or workplaces and communities. It is based on procedural rationality and conceived as a deliberative democratic process. In order to reflect the participatory and deliberative aspects of planning, we use the term 'social planning' and argue that in a post-growth eco-socialist society it will create a fertile milieu that fosters solidarity, cooperation, social justice and ecological stewardship.

The challenge is to envisage an institutional architecture and a set of social processes that promote the principles of deliberation and participation, and simultaneously address social, economic and ecological problems. The next section sets out the basic principles of a politically and economically self-governing society, in which participatory decision-making procedures are the norm, based on the principles of subsidiarity and the equal distribution of resources and power according to need. The section also assesses the ways in which participation and the distribution of power are discussed in the ecological economics literature. In the following section we look at the different scales or levels at which decision-making should take place and develop the principle of subsidiarity—that decisions should be made at the most decentralised level that enables all those affected by a decision to be involved in making and carrying out the decision, directly or indirectly. The section also assesses the ecological economics literature in terms of the different scales or levels of decision-making that predominate. In the core of the chapter, we outline the framework of a participatory democratic, post-capitalist, steady-state eco-socialist system based on decision-making through negotiated coordination by the social owners. As a reflection on future directions, we then illustrate how this might operate in relation to the pressing ecological question of human induced climate change [see also Chapter 42].

Participation and the distribution of power in the ecological economics literature

A key defining principle of ecological economics is that decisions should be taken not by scientific experts alone but also by those affected by the decisions. Ecological issues are typically subject to uncertainty [Chapters 12, 26–28], and yet require urgent action before the uncertainty can be resolved by further research. Decisions typically have different effects on different groups, which means that decisions necessarily involve judgement (Özkaynak et al., 2002; Ravetz, 2011). This is why ecological economics advocates decision-making through participatory deliberative structures to ensure the effective engagement of all relevant parties [Chapter 33]. Since those likely to be affected by the decision made may be differently affected and have different values and criteria for evaluating possible outcomes, there are both moral and economic efficiency arguments for them all to be included in deliberation over the various factors that have to be taken into account and together reach a decision with which all can live. Deliberative structures generally adopt a consensus building strategy, relying on procedural rationality and the quality of the decision-making process, rather than concentrating solely on the final outcome (Barry, 1999).

However, the ecological economics literature that aims at engaging with the current state of the world through procedural rationality and deliberative democracy for the most part fails to address the prevailing unequal distribution of power that is ubiquitous [see Chapter 14], to a greater or lesser extent, in all varieties of capitalism (Özkaynak et al., 2012). Exercises in promoting participation through consultation with those groups identified as legitimate stakeholders, while eliciting useful information about a community's preferences, nevertheless run the risk of creating disillusionment when the decision ultimately made by those with power ignores the outcome of the consultation process. There is therefore a danger of participatory consultation becoming a form of 'participation-wash'. The existence of participatory democratic deliberative institutions and procedural rationality is certainly a necessary condition for moral and efficient decision-making, but it is not a sufficient condition. In addition, what is needed is equalised power across the extended peer community, including all groups interested in and affected by the particular social, ecological or economic problems in question (O'Connor et al., 1996). The main cause of power inequalities is to be found in the inherent structure of the capitalist system, through the institution of private ownership of the means of production by capitalist corporations, legitimised and reinforced by the power of the State. These corporations, in the rivalrous process of the war of all against all, make the decisions that create the anarchy of production, with its sudden closures of workplaces throwing workers onto the scrap heap and destroying communities. They also pollute the environment, and contribute to climate change and the degradation of non-human nature by reckless exploration for new sources of fossil fuel and minerals and intensified chemically fuelled industrial agriculture.

However, there also exist variegated agency-based dimensions of power inequalities, such as the social division of labour, gender and ethnicity, which have a distinct and separate reality, although they always interact with the fundamental structural class divisions. One of the most important affordances of participatory processes, if they are real and not just formal, is that they provide the active experience that is transformatory in enabling people to move beyond being passive objects manipulated by others to becoming active subjects, subjective agents, collectively shaping their future together with their peers. People in general, and in their different roles as stakeholders in particular, need the subjective capabilities to be able to participate effectively in decision-making processes and engage in consensus building. The extension and deepening of democratic decision-making in all aspects of social, political and economic life, through various forms of participatory processes, requires active, as well as capable, agents and at the same time contributes to the further development of their capabilities. Participatory engagement is a learning process, building on the experience of past attempts, defeats and failures as well as successes. This, of course, is part of the experience within capitalism of participation in movements of resistance and movements prefiguring a post-capitalist world, but the full flowering of the developmental potential of participation requires the structural transformation of private ownership of the productive resources of society into social ownership.

The problem of scale

The mainstream neoclassical approach to the area of environmental policy that addresses the dual crises of environmental pollution and natural resource overuse is that of cost-benefit analysis. This approach is based on individual valuation of environmental goods and services, as revealed through actual or quasi markets using various valuation techniques, and has been forcefully criticised by social ecological economists. The core of the critique is that cost-benefit analysis formulates environmental problems as economic problems, stemming from externalities that arise due to the absence of a complete set of markets and property rights—in effect, it attempts to overcome 'market failure' by commodifying the whole of non-human nature (Adaman et al., 2003; Özkaynak et al., 2004).

Ecological economics starts from the recognition that environmental goods and services are intrinsically incommensurable [Chapter 22], and thus cannot be reduced to a single monetary indicator (Martinez-Alier et al., 1998). Instead of seeking to aggregate individuals' preferences as expressed in monetary values, it relies on deliberative decision-making institutions and processes. Consequently, it makes use of multi-criteria techniques [Chapters 30 and 31], which enable those affected by the decision to deliberate on the trade-offs between different objectives and concerns by considering a variety of indicators measured in their own units (Munda, 2008). These techniques support deliberative decision-making procedures by providing insights into the nature of environmental conflicts, as a basis for negotiations that increase the likelihood of arriving at compromises in a context of the divergent starting positions of different stakeholders [Chapter 33].

The principle of subsidiarity is that a society's decision-making structure should be multi-layered so that those affected, from the local to the global, are involved in the process. Yet, within the ecological economics literature the overwhelming focus is on local projects. Local projects, aiming at democratising decision-making and enhancing self-government, in the polity and the economy, are of course essential. Resistance to the ecologically and socially damaging demands of transnational corporations is primarily grounded in local struggles, and they embed a progressive and solidaristic agenda in people's daily lives. However, there is also the necessity of constructing a democratic governance structure up to and including the global level, as an alternative to the destructive form of globalisation increasingly imposed on our communities and cultures, our livelihoods and ourselves, by the global market mechanism. Without this there is a danger of localities becoming parochial enclaves, sometimes even competing against each other and creating an anarchic and chaotic environment. The local and the global should be envisaged as interdependent processes; global processes always involve some degree of localisation, and local processes are part of a larger globalised web of networks [see also the concept of 'glocal' in Chapter 40].

Ecological economics in general falls short of discussing the political and social economic framework within which the deliberative processes and multi-criteria techniques it advocates are implemented. More often than not, the context within which ecological problems are addressed and solutions are proposed remains essentially that of global corporate capitalism (Boulding, 1991). Reference is usually made to the importance of equity, social justice and well-being, but this vision is largely wishful thinking. It is *naïve* in the sense that a deliberative methodology based on the quest for societal consensus is incompatible with a capitalist market economy, however regulated, where power inequalities are endemic. Participatory decision-making, as opposed to consultation, can only be successfully realised by those who are social equals, with equal power and resources. Social planning, built on the principles of social ownership and participatory procedures involving equal participants, requires a global decision-making structure based on subsidiarity. An outline of the institutional architecture and social processes of such a society is set out in the next section.

Participatory democratic social planning

Participatory social planning on a global scale involves layered decision-making, with those affected at each level being involved in making the decisions and carrying them out. At each level the self-governing institutions of civil society, through the appropriate combination of direct and indirect democracy, decide on priorities and policies to implement them, drawing on their values, the current state of scientific and technical knowledge, and their own tacit social knowledge. In this way civil society controls the polity and the economy and mediates its relationship with non-human nature. At each level, from the local to the global, action takes place within a framework of universal human and ecological rights arrived at through a process of deliberation and negotiation. Participatory social planning is a transformatory learning process through which people are able to develop their full potential as social human beings (Adaman and Devine, 1997; Devine, 2010 [1988], 2002).

A steady-state economy [Chapter 45] is one in which the structure of production and provisioning changes, as technology and what contributes to human flourishing evolve, but the overall level of output and use of non-renewable natural resources does not increase. In an eco-socialist society much provisioning and caring activity is likely to be undertaken in the household and local community. However, some production will need to be undertaken on a larger scale by enterprises whose activities are interdependent and have to be coordinated. In modern economies the output of most enterprises consists of inputs into the activities of other enterprises—materials, machines and technical services—not of consumer goods and services. In addition, the amount of each good and service supplied needs to be enough to meet the demand for it. A post-growth society, like any modern society, will still be based on a division of labour and has to have a means of coordinating the interdependent activities of different enterprises and of considering the social and ecological implications of their activities [Chapter 44]. This is the challenge facing any attempt to develop a system of social planning.

Social planning starts with the social ownership of the enterprise which should be placed in the hands of its stakeholders, which means those affected by the activities of the enterprise. Typically the social owners will be those who work in the enterprise, supply its inputs and use its output, together with the communities in which it is located and other enterprises in the same industry. In an eco-socialist society, enterprises would be eco-social enterprises [Chapter 49], with the social owners including ecological groups committed to ensuring that the enterprise acts in an ecologically responsible way in relation to the technology used, the sourcing of inputs and the disposal of waste. The social owners, directly in small enterprises, through their representatives in larger enterprises, would deliberate and negotiate over policy in relation to the use of the enterprise's existing productive capacity, taking into account any differences of interest among the different groups and seeking to arrive at a mutually agreed outcome that all are prepared to accept.

At the level of the individual enterprise, ownership is social, neither private nor State. Enterprises engage in market exchange, selling their output to other enterprises, public bodies or consumers. However, the objective of social enterprises is not production for profit but production for the common good, as defined by those affected by their activities. A system of social planning that extends beyond the individual enterprise is needed when the structure of economic activity (productive capacity) needs to change in response to changes in technology or in what contributes to human flourishing. Enterprises may need to become smaller or to close; new enterprises may need to be established. Under social planning these changes will not be the outcome of the market mechanism, so it is important to distinguish between market exchange and the operation of market forces (Devine, 2010 [1988]).

Market exchange involves the use of existing capacity. The operation of market forces is how changes in the structure of capacity are brought about in capitalist (and market socialist) economies. Changes occur as a result of the separately made investment and disinvestment decisions of privately owned individual enterprises in pursuit of profit, without regard for the human, social or ecological cost. Enterprises and industries with falling levels of profitability, or sustained losses, decline or disappear; those with rising levels of profitability expand; and new enterprises and industries are created in new areas with high levels of expected profitability. However, these changes are not planned. Each decision-maker acts independently of the other decision-makers, even though the outcome of each individual decision depends on the aggregate outcome of all the separately made decisions. If too much capacity is installed in the aggregate, profit expectations are not met and disinvestment occurs; if too little capacity is installed, profit expectations are exceeded and new investment occurs. Coordination takes place *ex post*, after the earlier investment or disinvestment has taken place, after resources have been committed or withdrawn.

In a system of social planning, changes in capacity are planned by industry or sectoral development councils consisting of representatives of all the groups that will be affected by the decisions made, the social owners at the relevant level. Depending on the type of activity involved, these councils may be at the city, regional, national, international or global level, informed by the principle of subsidiarity that decisions should be made at the most local level consistent with all groups affected by a decision being involved in making the decision. The relevant level will be determined by the importance of economies of scale in production, the need to minimise transport costs, the desirability of having balanced economies wherever possible, the ecological and topographical characteristics of different locations and activities, and so on. The social owners at each level, through their representatives on the development councils, arrive through negotiation at a set of interdependent decisions, taking account of their differing interests and again seeking to arrive at a mutually agreed outcome considered by all to be acceptable. The interdependent decisions are coordinated *ex ante*, in contrast to the market mechanism where coordination occurs only *ex post*, after resources have been committed or withdrawn.

Based on these considerations it seems likely that at one end of the spectrum, in an eco-socialist society, global industrial agriculture will be replaced by organic food produced locally or regionally, while at the other end of the spectrum policies to mitigate climate change and preserve biodiversity will be agreed on globally. However, even when decisions have to be made on issues that affect the entire globe, the implementation of those decisions will obviously be disaggregated to the most local level possible. We propose that the only morally acceptable principle when thinking at the global level is a convergence on equal per capita access to natural resource use and waste disposal as the starting point, with negotiated variations agreed to take account of different climatic, ecological and topographic conditions, and also historic differences in levels of infrastructure development and ecological degradation.

In summary, social planning is a participatory multi-layered political and economic process through which civil society controls both the polity and the economy at each level of decision-making, as determined by the principle of subsidiarity. At each level civil society decides the priorities and direction of development of society, the allocation of resources, the character of technological change it seeks to promote, and so on, by relying on multi-criteria evaluation techniques. This process occurs within a framework set by more general levels of decision-making while also respecting the autonomy of less general levels. The institutional structure through which the process operates will be developed on the basis of experience, starting perhaps from the existing institutions of municipalities, regions, countries, international and global organisations, elected on the basis of universal suffrage or consisting of representatives of countries and international organisations. Alongside these bodies there are likely to be advocacy institutions representing different interests and expertise feeding into the decisions of the authoritative institutions. In conceptualising this future we are assuming the existence of an eco-socialist global society informed by the values of ecological sustainability and social justice, solidarity and mutual respect, and committed to the flourishing of all humanity and non-human nature, rather than a societal structure in which governments and international institutions are dominated by global corporations and their richly endowed lobbyists interested only in profits and stock market values.

Future directions

In considering the way forward we will briefly reflect upon how human induced climate change is being addressed. Neoclassical environmental economics approaches the problem through a cost-benefit framework (as meticulously conducted in the Stern Report on the Economics of Climate Change). Essentially the argument is that the use of fossil fuels and emission of greenhouse gases is under-priced, with the result that they are overused and overproduced, a situation of market failure. The solution is then seen as developing various schemes that correct for this market failure by increasing the price, such as carbon pricing, or a carbon tax or a market for permits to pollute in a cap-and-trade system. Social ecological economics rejects this approach, arguing that it effectively ignores uncertainty, incommensurability, ecological rights, and distributional inequity and poverty, and that its policy recommendations, particularly that of carbon markets, are *naïve*, failing to take account of social, ecological and economic reality (Anderson and M'Gonigle, 2012; Spash, 2007, 2010). That Pope Francis has recently come to recognise this is encouraging; in his recent encyclical (*Laudato Si'*, 2015) he states that:

> The strategy of buying and selling 'carbon credits' can lead to a new form of speculation which would not help reduce the emission of polluting gases worldwide. [...] Rather, it may simply become a ploy which permits maintaining the excessive consumption of some countries and sectors.

The Pope recognises that far from containing climate change such schemes are a way of avoiding radical change and legitimising business as usual and continued growth, which goes against all the scientific evidence on what is needed.

Eco-social planning, on the other hand, would start from the overwhelming scientific consensus that in order to keep the average global temperature increase within 2°C of the pre-Industrial Revolution level, or preferably 1.5°C, fossil fuel use needs to be phased out by 2050. Given the social moral imperative of convergence on equal per capita access to resources and waste creation, this means that there has to be a massive redistribution from the more developed to the less developed countries and from the rich to the poor in all countries. Within the richer countries there will have to be a radical change in lifestyles, moving away from excessive consumption to a focus on needs [Chapter 24] and human flourishing, that will make possible a fundamental shift from the expectation of endless growth to a steady-state or even degrowth economy (Spash, 2014). Within the poorer countries material and energy throughput increases may be needed, not to emulate the excessive consumption life styles of the rich countries, but to enable basic needs to be met for everyone. However, such development must be sensitive to ecological concerns—above all be based on clean energy systems rather than the fossil fuel dependent path of development historically taken by the developed capitalist countries—and it must also be careful to pay due consideration to the multifaceted interaction between the social sphere and ecological life.

Social planning in relation to climate change would involve all those affected by the decisions to be made, the entire global population. Through the multi-layered structure outlined above there would be negotiations between the social owners of the climate commons over how the necessary scientifically recommended reductions in fossil fuel use and greenhouse gas emissions should be allocated, taking account of the different circumstances of the participants in the light of the agreed set of common values. The allocations for each country would then be disaggregated and implemented through the layered decision-making structure, with all those affected at each level participating. Since major changes in lifestyles, urban design, the relationship between town and country, technology, food provisioning, and so on, would be involved, the changes would take time and priorities would need to be agreed. Only by participating in the discussions and decision-making processes through which these issues are addressed can people, in their multiple roles as citizens and stakeholders, come to understand the issues involved, recognise the interests of others, and become aware of the need to reach agreement on the far-reaching changes that will be necessary.

Of course, imagining how such a process could work is difficult if we start from where we are now. At the global level, negotiations have been ongoing for decades under the United Nations Framework Convention on Climate Change (UNFCCC). However, reaching a meaningful agreement has consistently proven problematic because the countries taking part are very unequally placed in terms of their contribution to greenhouse gas emissions and their political and economic power, and have primarily pursued their own national interest often dominated by corporate interests. Furthermore, there is no agreement on a common set of values and principles to inform the negotiations, such as convergence on equal per capita entitlements, and the major powers are in thrall to the dominant petrochemical and coal corporations. It is therefore no surprise that the Conference of the Parties to the UNFCCC ended their Paris summit with an agreement that has no major enforcement other than the promotion of an extended carbon emission trading scheme as the principal mechanism for reducing greenhouse gases. At the other end of the spectrum, the local level, there are contradictory forces in civil society: movements against fracking, but also against inland wind farms.

Capitalism is clearly incompatible with ecological sustainability and global justice, and there is a long way to go before eco-social planning based on participatory deliberation and negotiated decision-making might become possible. An important part of the political process through which that possibility might be realised will be the development of public debate about the issues involved and public understanding of the radical changes that are necessary. Social ecological economics has much to contribute to this as it recognises that the fundamental obstacle to progress is the capitalist system itself.

Concluding remarks

In this chapter we have set out the basic principles of a politically and economically self-governing society, in which participatory decision-making procedures are the norm, based on the principles of subsidiarity and the equal distribution of resources and power. The proposed system will be based on decision-making through negotiated coordination by the social owners in a multi-layered political and economic process, in which civil society will control both the polity and the economy at each level of decision-making. We believe that in addition to making transparent the degrading effects of the self-regulating market mechanism, vital work is required at local and macro levels on the concrete ways in which the institutional re-embedding of the economy in society and ecology can be realised. We think that the model of a self-governing society based on participatory planning as outlined above is a contribution to this, but further work is needed to fully incorporate ecological concerns in an explicit manner.

Although in capitalist democracies the prospects for ecological policies are severely limited by corporate dominance, we believe that civil society will continue to assume an important role in slowing down environmental degradation and in playing a transformatory role in creating economic and social prefigurative relations of a more solidaristic and ecologically sustainable structure. Encouragement can be taken from observing a rich and rapidly growing experience of ecological and social protest movements, at both local and global levels. These movements not only emphasise participatory decision-making procedures but also call for the democratisation of power and movement towards ecological sustainability and social justice. This experience can throw important light on the causal mechanisms for the development of such movements, the reasons behind their relative success or failure, and their transformative potential, or lack of potential, towards the self-governing society that we have outlined.

Key further readings cited

Adaman, F. and Devine, P. (1997). On the economic theory of socialism. *New Left Review*, 221 (January–February), 54–80.

Devine, P. (2010 [1988]). *Democracy and Economic Planning: The Political Economy of a Self-governing Society*. Cambridge: Polity Press.

Özkaynak, B., Adaman, F. and Devine, P. (2012). The identity of ecological economics: retrospects and prospects. *Cambridge Journal of Economics* 36(5), 1123–1142.

Ravetz, J.R. (2011). Postnormal science and the maturing of the structural contradictions of modern European science. *Futures 43*(2), 142–148.

Other literature cited

Adaman, F., Devine, P. and Özkaynak, B. (2003). Reinstituting the economic process: (re)embedding the economy in society and nature. *International Review of Sociology* 13(2), 357–72.

Anderson, B. and M'Gonigle, M. (2012). Does ecological economics have a future? Contradiction and reinvention in the age of climate change. *Ecological Economics* 84(December), 37–48.

Barry, J. (1999). *Rethinking Green Politics*. London: Sage Publications.

Boulding, K.E. (1991). What Do You Want to Sustain? Environmentalism and Human Evaluations. In R. Costanza (ed.), *Ecological Economics: The Science and Management of Sustainability* (pp. 22–31). New York: New York University Press.

Devine, P. (2002). Participatory planning through negotiated coordination. *Science and Society* 66(1), 72–85.

Martinez-Alier, J., Munda, G. and O'Neill, J. (1998). Weak comparability of values as a foundation for ecological economics. *Ecological Economics* 26(3), 277–286.

Munda, G. (2008). *Social Multi-criteria Evaluation for a Sustainable Economy*. Heidelberg: Springer.

O'Connor, M., Faucheux, S., Froger, G., Funtowicz, S. and Munda, G. (1996). Emergent Complexity and Procedural Rationality: Post-normal Science for Sustainability. In R. Costanza, O. Segura & J. Martinez-Alier (eds.), *Getting Down to Earth: Practical Applications of Ecological Economics* (pp. 224–247). Washington: Island Press.

Özkaynak, B., Devine, P. and Rigby, D. (2002). Whither ecological economics? *International Journal of Environment and Pollution 18*(4), 317–335.

Özkaynak, B., Devine, P. and Rigby, D. (2004). Operationalising strong sustainability: definitions, methodologies and outcomes. *Environmental Values* 13(3), 279–303.

Spash, C.L. (2007). The economics of climate change impacts à la Stern: novel and nuanced or rhetorically restricted? *Ecological Economics* 63(4), 706–713.

Spash, C.L. (2010). The brave new world of carbon trading. *New Political Economy* 15(2), 169–195.

Spash, C.L. (2014). *Better Growth, Helping the Paris COP-out?: Fallacies and Omissions of the New Climate Economy Report*. Discussion paper. Vienna: Institute for Environment and Regional Development, Wirtshafts Universität.

INDEX

Note: page numbers in *italic* type refer to Figures; those in **bold** type refer to Tables. Page numbers followed by 'n' and another number refer to Notes.

Subject headings in the index refer to significant information relating to the topic, rather than including every occurrence of the term. Cited authors are indexed where their work is discussed in some detail, or where the context is significant; simple citations are not included in the index.

Since the main topic of this title is ecological economics, entries for this term have been kept to a minimum; readers are advised to seek more specific topics.

Conga, Peru 419
Conill, J. 509
consequentialism 228
conservation 258, 260, 261, 263, 283; Africa 404,
    405; biodiversity 63, 363, 366; conflicts 51,
    165, 177, 283, 368, 415; conservation ethic
    256, 257,258; neoliberal 4, 63, 445; payments
    449, 450; policy 122, 279, 280, 281, 282, 448,
    471; problems 123, 124, 281, 285–6; and SMS
    278–9, 280, 281, 282, 283
Consoli, A. 80
conspicuous consumption 209
constitutive incommensurability 231
constructivism 18–19, 21, 22
consumer behaviour theory 80–1; and
    evolutionary economics 82; *see also* individual
    behaviour
consumer choice theory, neoclassical economics
    93–4
consumer sovereignty 210, 215, 218
consumerism 488, 492–3
consumption 203–4, 211; and climate change
    442–3; conceptual models 204–10; future
    directions 210; and happiness 478, *478,* 481–2,
    482–3; and work 217–19
consumption based material flow analysis 115
contextual values 352, 354–5
contingent valuation method (CVM) 244n1, 351
contributive justice 218
Convention on Biological Diversity (CBD) 448
'convivial tools' 458
Cooke, B. 342
Cooperativa Integral Catalana (CIC) 514
copper mining, 408, 415
Corn Laws, UK 44
corporate accountability **166,** 170
corporate culture 106
corporate nudging 208
corporate sector, and participation 347, 348
corporate social responsibility 170
CorpWatch 168
Corral Quintana, S.A. 309
corruption: South Africa 409–10
cost shifting 33, 36, 163, 387, 418, 451, 499
cost-benefit analysis (CBA) 35, 227, 228, 239,
    269, 311, 321, 351, 353, 355, 519, 523;
    deconstruction of 24; and the precautionary
    principle 70; and Safe Minimum Standards
    (SMS) 282–3
cost-effective analysis, and Safe Minimum
    Standards (SMS) 282, 283
Costa Rica 51, 420, 439, 450

Costanza, R. 53, 94, 254n2, 256, 448
costs, and Safe Minimum Standards (SMS)
    280–1
cotton industry 42
Council for the Development of Social Science
    Research in Africa 404
counter hegemony, resistance as 176–7
counter movement, resistance as 176–7
counter-conduct 179
counter-space 179
Courvisanos, J.A. 73
craft guilds 508
craft work 494
Craig, D.M. 494
creation needs 248, **249**
critical institutional economics 215–16, 219, 508
'critical mass', cyclists' rights **166,** 170
critical realism 13, 17–18, 19, 24–5, 34, 126,
    127n1, 148, 204; core positions 20–2; future
    directions 24; methodology 22–4; and power
    142, 147
critical welfare economics 220
critical zones 278, 279, 280, *280,* 284
Crown Lands, Canada 263n2
cultural analysis 49
cultural ecology, and political ecology 39–41
cultural growth 482–3
cultural turn 142, 174
CVM (contingent valuation method) 244n1, 351
Cyert, R.M. 195
Czech Republic: eco-social enterprises 510, 512,
    513, 514
Czech, Brian 467–76

D'Alisa, G. 53
Dahl, Robert 141, 144, *148,* **149**
Daily, Gretchen 122–3
Dale, G. 441
Daly, H.E. 134, 260, 279, 372, 377, 379, 383,
    385, 441, 442, 460, 469, 177, 502
dams: ecological distribution conflicts 163, 168–9
dangerous levels 284
Darwin, Charles 130
Dash, A. 508, 510
data analysis: multicriteria mapping (MCM)
    323–5, *324;* Q methodology 336–7, **337**
Davidson, Paul 67, 68, 69
Davidson, S. 342
Davies, B.B. 338, 343
Davies, Ben 331–40
Davies, G. 329
Davis, K.E. 389

Taylor & Francis eBooks

Helping you to choose the right eBooks for your Library

Add Routledge titles to your library's digital collection today. Taylor and Francis ebooks contains over 50,000 titles in the Humanities, Social Sciences, Behavioural Sciences, Built Environment and Law.

Choose from a range of subject packages or create your own!

Benefits for you

» Free MARC records
» COUNTER-compliant usage statistics
» Flexible purchase and pricing options
» All titles DRM-free.

REQUEST YOUR **FREE** INSTITUTIONAL TRIAL TODAY

Free Trials Available
We offer free trials to qualifying academic, corporate and government customers.

Benefits for your user

» Off-site, anytime access via Athens or referring URL
» Print or copy pages or chapters
» Full content search
» Bookmark, highlight and annotate text
» Access to thousands of pages of quality research at the click of a button.

eCollections – Choose from over 30 subject eCollections, including:

Archaeology	Language Learning
Architecture	Law
Asian Studies	Literature
Business & Management	Media & Communication
Classical Studies	Middle East Studies
Construction	Music
Creative & Media Arts	Philosophy
Criminology & Criminal Justice	Planning
Economics	Politics
Education	Psychology & Mental Health
Energy	Religion
Engineering	Security
English Language & Linguistics	Social Work
Environment & Sustainability	Sociology
Geography	Sport
Health Studies	Theatre & Performance
History	Tourism, Hospitality & Events

For more information, pricing enquiries or to order a free trial, please contact your local sales team: www.tandfebooks.com/page/sales

Routledge
Taylor & Francis Group

The home of
Routledge books

www.tandfebooks.com

Printed in the United States
by Baker & Taylor Publisher Services